THE MAKING OF MODERN SOUTH-EAST ASIA

VOLUME TWO
The Western Impact

D1482090

THE MAKING OF
MODERN SOUTH-EAST ASIA

VOLUME TWO

The Western Impact
Economic and Social Change

D. J. M. TATE

KUALA LUMPUR
OXFORD UNIVERSITY PRESS
OXFORD NEW YORK MELBOURNE
1979

Oxford University Press
OXFORD LONDON GLASGOW
NEW YORK TORONTO MELBOURNE WELLINGTON
KUALA LUMPUR SINGAPORE JAKARTA HONG KONG TOKYO
DELHI BOMBAY CALCUTTA MADRAS KARACHI
NAIROBI DAR ES SALAAM CAPE TOWN
● *Oxford University Press 1979*

ISBN 0 19 580332 9 *(cloth)*
ISBN 0 19 580333 7 *(limp)*

*Printed in Malaysia by The Art Printing Works Sdn. Bhd., Kuala Lumpur
Published by Oxford University Press, 3, Jalan 13/3,
Petaling Jaya, Selangor, Malaysia*

Preface

THIS is the second of a series of three volumes designed to serve as an introduction to the history of modern South-East Asia for students at pre-University level and beyond, as well as for the general reader. The series itself is presented not as a history of South-East Asia as a whole, but as a study of the modernization of South-East Asia as a result of the impact of the Western world. Within this context, this volume deals with various aspects of the economic and social impact of the spread of Western political power and modern trade and technology on the region. The emphasis here is on the economic effects and some of the immediate social consequences. At the same time, other social aspects, in particular that concerning education, are not dealt with here but appear in the third volume which primarily treats of the South-East Asian reaction to the West, or in other words the rise and development of nationalism throughout the region and its ultimate triumph.

The volumes of this series cannot, of course, lay claim to be free from bias, but it has been consciously written with the intention of avoiding the rival camps of Asian and Euro-centrism. The aim has been to try and present developments as they happened, bearing in mind the varying outlooks and interests of all parties involved. However the series does have a Malaysian bent, having been written in that country and with an eye for what would appear to have more immediate bearing and interest for Malaysians. The footnotes are designed hopefully as a useful supplement to the main text, with suggestions where further material on topics touched upon may be found.

This series can lay no claim to originality. It is almost wholly derived from secondary sources and in fact represents the cullings of many scholars of different backgrounds and differing outlooks. I gratefully acknowledge the great debt I owe to the researches and writings on South-East Asian history by a whole host of distinguished men and women, some of whose works are to be found quoted in the lists and articles at the end of each section.

Bukit Lela, Gombak   D. J. M. TATE
Kuala Lumpur
1979

Acknowledgements

IN the writing of this series, I must acknowledge my indebtedness to those who have given me encouragement and advice in its preparation. I am particularly grateful to my former teachers at the School of Oriental and African Studies of the University of London; to Professor C.D. Cowan who went far out of his way to offer suggestions and advice on points of detail and on general structure for the first volume, as well as to Professor D.G.E. Hall and to Professor Hugh Tinker, both of whom were kind enough to read and comment on portions of the manuscript. I also am particularly in debt to Professor Khoo Kay Kim of the University of Malaya for his observations and advice on the general structure of the second volume. I am also grateful to Encik Abdul Aziz bin Ismail, to Almarhum Engku Muda Orang Kaya-kaya Mahakurnia Raja Razman bin Raja Abdul Hamid, to Mr. Kenneth Whitbread and to a number of others for sundry encouragement and advice. I owe a very real debt of gratitude to the publishers who have displayed tact, patience and restraint during the somewhat prolonged production of this book. Last but not least I wish to thank a generation of Malaysian students who have provided the real inspiration for this work.

Contents

Maps

Tables and Diagrams

Appendix

DIAGRAMS of production export of selected raw materials from South-East Asia.

1. General Map of South-East Asia, 1939

LUZON

Manila

PACIFIC OCEAN

N

MINDORO

SAMAR

PANAY

Cebu

THE

NEGROS

PHILIPPINES

Zamboanga Davao MINDANAO

Menado

HALMAHERA

CELEBES

MOLUCCAS

CERAM

BURU

Ambon

WEST NEW
GUINEA

Makassar

Banda Sea

FLORES

SUMBA

TIMOR (Portuguese) *Arafura Sea*

I N D I E S

0 100 200 300 400 500 miles

I Introduction:
AGENTS OF CHANGE

SOUTH-EAST Asia today bears the unmistakable imprint of the West. Within the last 150 years there have been tremendous changes in the economic and social framework of the region, and even if much of the old way of life still survives cheek-by-jowl with the new world of machine production, mass markets and modern technology, the future is being fashioned by the forces of the industrialized world. An area once basically self-sufficient and self-contained has been converted into the world's principal source for half-a-dozen primary commodities and has been brought into almost total dependence on the vagaries of the world market. The spread of modern communications has ended the isolation of countless remote agrarian communities and has swollen the veins of a pedlar luxury trade into arteries for the conveyance of cheap, mass-produced, manufactured goods. While the peoples of the region remain predominantly rural, one-fifth of them now live in towns, many of which did not exist a hundred years ago. A population always low in relation to area has since the middle of the nineteenth century shown one of the fastest growth rates in the whole world. Rapid expansion in numbers has been accompanied by marked shifts in distribution. The once largely empty swamps and deltas of the mainland have been filled with settlers while into the region as a whole has come a massive influx of outsiders—mainly from the shores of southern China and southern India—creating in the process new patterns of society. The pace of change continues at an ever-increasing rate, but in a manner which is unevenly felt and leaves wide differences of economic and social development between the various countries of the region.

External influences
Behind this great transformation lies the phenomenon of the Industrial Revolution,[1] first apparent in eighteenth-century England and later becoming the dominant feature in the evolution of the maritime powers of north-western Europe and of north America. The industrialization of the West, to which a whole series of scientific discoveries and technological advances were closely linked, led to the irruption of a totally new economic system, based on factory machine production, into the traditional one based on agriculture. The new industrial societies which emerged in the West were no longer the self-sufficient entities of yore, but specialist communities dependent on raw materials from overseas as well as markets for their survival. The process was ultimately to be repeated in variant form within South-East Asia itself.

From the outset the region was inextricably involved in the industrialization of the West, not only as a natural source of raw materials and as a potential market but also as an agent in the genesis of the Industrial Revolution itself. The sixteenth- and seventeenth-century settlements of the Portuguese, Spaniards and Dutch represented the first outposts of Western commercial expansion. By the nineteenth century the great East-West trade route which the region bestrode had already become a Western highway. The foundation of the British settlements on the islands of Penang (1786) and Singapore (1819) presaged the entry of the Industrial Age.

Although industrialization did not start to take place within the region until towards the end of the nineteenth century, the whole course of South-East Asia's economic and social development after 1800 was increasingly determined by external factors emanating from industrial Europe. First and foremost amongst these was the extension of modern communications into the region, which was accompanied by an intensification of Western economic enterprise and investment, and by a whole gamut of inventions and scientific discoveries that helped to revolutionize agriculture and to promote new forms of production. The local economies of South-East Asia now became ever more subject to the world market and to the fluctuations of world trade. Large numbers of immigrants moved into the region in response to the new opportunities being created and far-reaching changes in population growth, distribution and occupation patterns took place. This is the background against which the activities of the various colonial powers and the economic and social development of the indigenous peoples of the region have to be considered.

The revolution in sea communications

The first elements of change from the West to affect South-East Asia were connected with the sea. Sea-power has always been one of the prime determinants in South-East Asian history, its possession a basic factor in the precocious upsurge of Iberian power in the region in the sixteenth century and in the more solid Dutch commercial hegemony which followed in the seventeenth. The nineteenth century saw two major innovations in the manner of sea communications, both by-products of the Industrial Revolution. The first was the entry of the steamship onto the avenues of world trade, and the second the opening of the Suez Canal.

The world's first steamships were born at the end of the eighteenth century, and put in their first appearance in South-East Asian waters in the 1820s. However, despite their obvious potential, for decades steamships laboured under serious handicaps in their struggle with sailing craft for supremacy on the trade routes. The first regular steamship service to pass through South-East Asian waters was established in 1845, but it was not until the second half of the century that steamers came into their own. Their final triumph was the result of improvements in the 1850s in the design and performance of the marine engine, which rendered them safer, faster and more commodious than their rivals. These improvements made themselves felt in the following decade and after the 1860s steamships reigned supreme on the world's shipping routes.

It was at this juncture (in 1869) that the opening of the Suez Canal took place, an event which was in large measure due to the existence of steamships themselves since the new Red Sea route now made available to international trade was quite unsuitable for sailing vessels. From the start the traffic using the Canal was predominantly steam. The number of steamships calling at South-East Asian ports increased spectacularly and the eclipse, within a decade of 1869, of the famous China tea clippers symbolized the defeat of sail. The new waterway cut down the distance between Western Europe and the Far East by one-third, shortened the voyage time by some ten weeks and produced a savings of $2\frac{1}{2}$ per cent in capital costs. There was great expansion of trade within the region since the local merchant now had more capital available to finance his own affairs. For the first time it became practicable to export perishable South-East Asian commodities to European markets and an economic proposition to import Western machinery into South-East Asia.[2]

The practical consequences of all this were reflected in various ways throughout the region. The new canal route helped to promote the conversion of Lower Burma, the Menam Chao Phaya basin and the Mekong Delta into one of the world's rice bowls and boosted the emergence of Rangoon, Bangkok and Saigon as leading ports of the region. Singapore was suddenly lifted out of the trade doldrums of the 1860s to go through a period of unprecedented expansion which set the seal on her role as the region's leading financial centre. The opening of the Canal was equally as timely for the rapidly expanding tin industry of the Malay Peninsula and for the new tobacco fields of Deli on the Sumatran shore opposite, while it also coincided with the phasing out of the Culture System and the inauguration of a new era of private enterprise in the Netherlands Indies. The opening of the Canal was also felt in the distant Philippines, tightening the bonds between the Spanish colonists in Manila and their homeland and contributing to the quickened pace of economic development in the islands. In all, the opening of the Suez Canal proved a powerful adjunct to the spread of Western economic imperialism in South-East Asia.

But the great stimulus to trade and economic development afforded by the Canal also served to exacerbate inter-colonial rivalries within the region. It facilitated the general forward movement of the colonial powers which characterized South-East Asian affairs in the last quarter of the century and intensified the contest for markets and raw materials between them. The era of unrestricted 'free trade' which had given Britain, as the pioneer industrial power, almost undisputed access to the markets of the region made way for the 'nationalization' of regional trade. The Dutch and the French in particular now found it possible to consolidate their own economic spheres of interest and the consequent decline in Britain's free trade role was reflected in the changing role of Singapore as the region's premier entrepôt port. While the volume and value of Singapore's own trade continued to expand, the area it served became more confined and increasingly centred on its Malayan hinterland. In the struggle between conflicting colonial interests, the new shipping companies of the powers involved became the principal instruments, for they could provide access to desirable areas, promote imperial interests and in general serve to channel trade within the bounds of clearly defined spheres of interest.

Steamship politics and the Conference System
The rise of powerful steamship companies was the natural corollary of the advent of steam. Capital outlay and overheads were high, so that newly-formed firms needed heavy backing and had much at stake. At first the British virtually had the field to themselves. The pioneer of regular steamship services eastwards was the P & O, but it was the Ocean Steamship Company (Blue Funnel Line) established in 1865 which secured an easy domination over all its rivals for nearly a generation by virtue of the superiority of its ships' design. British shipping interests held the ring up to the 1860s and the bulk of the international sea-borne trade in South-East Asia was handled by British firms, leaving the local carrying trade with a host of individual shippers drawn from the countries of the region and the ports of South China. The first shipping line of a rival European power to challenge the British monopoly on a competitive basis was the French Compagnie des Services Messageries Maritimes (founded 1851), which started to develop trade with Saigon. However it was only with the establishment of the German firm of Norddeutscher Lloyd twenty years later (in 1884) that competition between the lines of the colonial powers really became intense. The new German line, based on Singapore, built up regional services in all directions. Four years later, the Dutch in an all-out bid to break the British stranglehold over the shipping of the Netherlands Indies and also to check the German advance established the Koninglijke Paketvaart Mij (K.P.M.). The K.P.M. also initially made Singapore the centre of its operations but this was a temporary measure, and its main function was to by-pass the port, which it soon very largely achieved. The British response was to launch two new shipping firms, the first in 1891 designed to counter the Dutch on their own ground, and the second the next year aimed as a riposte to rival lines based on Singapore. Neither line was particularly successful, and within the same decade the second line had succumbed to its German competitors.[3]

In the meantime the K.P.M.'s development provided a classic example of the role that steamship companies could play in extending and consolidating empire. By creating new services with specialized vessels to the areas concerned, with the introduction of bills of lading in 1891 and by the granting to the company of the government contract for the conveyance of official mail and passengers, traffic was diverted from Singapore to Batavia, Surabaya and other Javanese ports and Java restored as the focal point for the sea-borne commerce of the Indies. The coming into existence of regular services to remote places helped to enhance Batavia's influence. Dutch business was encouraged by the possibilities of direct contact and the opening up of new credit facilities by government agencies made possible by faster and easier communications favoured Western enterprise in general at the expense of the traditional local Chinese monopoly. The K.P.M.'s ports of call grew into new centres of population and the company itself actively promoted trade and markets by advancing capital on easy terms. New industries were also stimulated. Many of these activities were in fact uneconomical and in the early years the K.P.M. ran at a steady loss despite its contract for government business. But after 1915 when the company's relations with the government were placed on a fairer basis, the K.P.M. came near to establishing a monopoly over the sea-borne commerce of the archipelago. On occasion it had to give ground to Chinese and local traders, but the K.P.M. was able to deal effectively with its European rivals, particularly when Dutch interests were too seriously threatened.[4]

In general, as the story of the K.P.M. shows, the role of the great shipping lines as agents of Western imperialism in South-East Asia was very important and accounts for the intensity of the rivalry between them. But the capital costs involved were so high that cut-throat competition threatened to be ruinous to all concerned. Apart from their high overheads the shipping firms had to cope with the fluctuations of an unsteady world market, while frequent changes in the types of cargo to be handled necessitated constant modification and refitting of vessels used. Ultimately the only solution lay in agreements between the various parties concerned to eliminate unfair and injurious competition and to protect themselves against the vicissitudes of the world market; agreements which equalized freight rates and the allocation of cargoes or which brought about mergers or amalgams between rival firms. From such agreements emerged what became known as the Conference System. The first of them, drawn up to end the extravagant competition between British lines on the India run, was signed at Calcutta in 1875 and laid down the pattern for the many other 'conferences' on the world's major shipping routes which followed. The Far Eastern Conference of 1879 introduced successfully for the first time a system of deferred rebates. In 1892 an agreement giving both parties fair opportunities in the Java trade ended the fierce rivalry between the K.P.M. and its British competitors. The Outward Bound Conference signed a year later halted the suicidal competition between another group of British firms. An agreement to regulate the rivalries involved amongst firms based in Singapore was not so easily arrived at, largely on account of the conflict of interest between the shipping firms and the long established local export agencies, and it was not until 1902 that the Straits Homeward Conference was firmly established. A series of other agreements reached between various interested parties between 1900 and 1914 ensured that the intense rivalry and cut-throat competition of the 1880s gave way to an integrated system of mutual concessions and price-fixing. Collusion was substituted for competition. This gave the shipping interests of the Western world an almost irreversible say in the conditions governing international transportation and trade and made the Conference System as it developed into an extremely powerful weapon for modern economic imperialism.

The spread of other modern means of communication
Steamships played a basic role in South-East Asian development if only because prior to the air age the only effective access to the region from the

West was by sea. But during the course of the nineteenth century steam triumphed on land as well though the railway, and communications were also revolutionized by the introduction of the telegraph. After 1900 the telegraph cable gave way before wireless and telecommunications and railway trains had to face the competition of motor-cars and aeroplanes. But by this time railways had come to form an essential part of the internal network of new states in the making, and were no longer mere extensions of sea routes. The telegraph remained more cosmopolitan, although it too became a vital internal link. Roads and modern motor transport followed the pattern of the railway and their role was primarily internal. Wireless telegraphy, telecommunications and aviation served both as sources of external influence and of internal control.

The spread of these new forms of communication played a vital part in the consolidation of Western imperialism. Each colonial power used the telegraph and its successors, for example, as an instrument with which to protect its own interests and to exploit its own resources as soon as it had mastered the technology to be able to do so. Britain on account of her far-flung interests and advanced technology played the leading role in laying down international cable links, which other powers subsequently extended. South-East Asia was first directly linked to the West in 1871. By the end of the century Singapore was connected to all the colonial capitals in the region, while the Dutch, French, Spaniards and Americans added on their own systems to the trunk routes, bringing their ports into touch with the interiors. The net result of all this was to quicken the pace of commerce and trade. Western investors were enabled for the first time to take a direct part in local stock market transactions and to manipulate the world market in South-East Asian commodities from their own capitals. It also made possible speedier political intervention.

However the development in the realm of communications up to 1941 with the greatest potential for change was the spread of aviation. The first flights in the region took place before 1914 but it was not until after the Great War that regular air services became established. Aircraft companies, like the shipping firms of the previous century, required large capital and their operations were full of political as well as of economic significance, with the result that from the outset they were national enterprises receiving the full backing and frequent participation of the home governments concerned. Yet it was the Thais who were amongst the quickest to grasp the potential significance of air communications and in 1922 they became the first to inaugurate a regular domestic air service in South-East Asia. The first international airline to serve the region was the Dutch Koninglijke Nederlandse-Indie Luchtvaart Mij (K.N.I.L.M.) in 1920, which was soon followed by similar enterprises of the French, British, Australians and Americans. By 1941 all the main centres of the region were interconnected with one another and to other continents by these various airline services. Significantly enough, both the Dutch and British air enterprises in the region were closely linked to their local shipping interests.

With the elaboration of these modern means of communication, South-

East Asia was brought still more effectively within the orbit of the new world-wide industrial order and came even more completely under the domination of the interests of Western capital and trade.

The revolution in technology: new inventions, markets and products
Before the Industrial Age Western merchants had come to South-East Asia for commodities which had a scarcity value, and in as much as they interfered with local production, this was primarily done with a view to restricting rather than increasing the supply. The prime example of this was the trade in spices. Other exotic products from South-East Asian forests brought handsome returns while the Dutch in Java made coffee and sugar the chief luxury articles of the region's trade in the seventeenth and eighteenth centuries. The emergence of the industrialized societies of the West after 1800 shifted the centre of attention away from rarity towards abundance, eclipsing some traditional products in the process, promoting others and creating new needs of their own. Spices had already ceased to be important by the start of the nineteenth century as the Dutch had lost their monopoly control over their cultivation. Coffee in the long run also declined as far as the region was concerned before the changed circumstances. The commodity enjoyed half a century's respite under the artificial conditions created by the Dutch Culture System, itself essentially a pre-industrial device, but from 1875 onwards suffered increasingly from the fluctuations in the world market to which it was now exposed, as well as from the onslaught of crop disease. Although the new techniques of agricultural science found ways around these difficulties, planters now turned to safer and more profitable crops such as tobacco, tea and ultimately rubber. In 1941 coffee was still widely grown throughout the region, particularly in the Netherlands Indies, but its value as an export cash crop was greatly reduced.

Some traditional crops, on the other hand, obtained new leases of life. Sugar was one of them. As a food sugar was more important than coffee and in wider demand on the steadily expanding consumer market. As a cash crop in the mid-nineteenth century, it flourished in Java and Thailand and rose to become the mainstay of the Philippines economy. For a couple of decades at the end of the century it seemed set fair to become the major industry of the Malay Peninsula as well. In Java sugar—like coffee—owed much of its nineteenth century predominance to the Culture System, but—unlike coffee—immediately benefited from the System's decline, which permitted an inflow of private capital into the Indies and facilitated the swift mechanization of the industry. In fact because of the mechanization of sugar milling in the 1850s, as far as the sugar industry was concerned the Culture System had already started to become obsolescent. With the ushering in of the Liberal Era in 1870 new capital poured in, new factories were built and Java's sugar production more than doubled. The private banks which now replaced government as the source for capital loans insisted on increased efficiency and research into new and better sugar strains. The introduction of railways onto the island cheapened costs and facilitated expansion, and the industry as a whole went from strength to strength (despite two severe trade depressions in the 1870s and 1880s) and reached its apogée in the 1920s. Liberalization of trade and mechanization played similar roles in the rise and development of the sugar industry of the Philippines, although its survival and expansion after 1900 owed much to American tariff policy which gave the Philippines crop an assured market in the United States. The short-lived successes of the Thai and Malayan sugar industries during the nineteenth century, on the other hand, were due to their more limited resources and their inability to withstand the competition of other world producers. Overseas competition, fluctuating prices and plant disease also raised mounting problems for producers in Java in the first decades of the twentieth century. These problems were met by increasing recourse to co-operation within the industry and by the application of technology and research. The formation of representative bodies for the whole industry, the continued introduction of new and better machinery, the application of modern fertilizers on a large scale and the fruits of research all played their part.[5] Without such measures and advances, it is doubtful whether sugar could have survived as one of the region's major cash crops.

Coconuts, fibres, hardwoods and minerals—above all tin—were chief amongst other traditional products of the region which acquired a new role and value as a result of the forces generated by the Industrial Revolution in the West. Amongst the fibres, the most spectacular rise was that of abaca or Manila hemp. Its emergence began in the 1790s with the invention of a machine for cleaning the hemp. The opening of the Philippines to world trade in the 1830s and the growth of the connexion with the United States, stimulated after 1850 by the establishment of regular steamship services across the Pacific, provided the abaca producers with a guaranteed market with the rope manufacturers of New England. Under the administration of the United States itself a protected market ensured continued expansion. But of far more consequence to the region as a whole were the developments which promoted the rise of the modern coconut industry at the end of the nineteenth century. Coconuts, with their all-purpose utility, have always had an important part in the subsistence economy of the region, while copra and coconut oil started to become an important item in the inter-island trade of the Great East and of the southern Philippines as early as the seventeenth century. However, it was due to certain advances in the technology of processing of vegetable oils made in the West in the 1880s and 1890s which assured the coconut of its future. There was now a sudden increase in the world demand for vegetable fats and oils for use in the manufacture of soaps, candles and cooking fuels. Production was further stimulated by the extension of steamship services throughout the region and by the role of Chinese middlemen who served as the first mediums of contact between the local growers and the outside world. As Macassar and Manila, Penang and Singapore rose up as entrepôt ports and processing centres, Chinese firms played the leading role as dealers. Since the copra industry, on the other hand, with its dependence on simple, natural processes, did not require expensive machinery or expertise in its preparation for export, it became one of the few new industries of South-East Asia where Western technology could not be brought to bear. For these reasons the actual production and processing of the crop remained largely in the hands of South-East Asians themselves, and copra production grew into an extensive smallholders' industry, bringing unaccustomed touches of prosperity to remote corners of the region for several decades. The Philippines after 1900 emerged as the world's single largest producer of copra, followed by Netherlands India which by 1941 provided one-third of the world's supply. If the contribution of other South-East Asian countries to world supply were marginal, the expansion of the coconut industry in their domestic economies was significant.

Although hardwoods remained to a large extent an under-exploited source of wealth in the region, the introduction of modern saw-milling techniques, mechanized equipment and improved communications led to a great increase in lumbering. Teak in particular came to play a major part in the export economies of Burma and Thailand. In other countries, however, lumbering continued to be a much more marginal form of economic activity.

The rise of tin

Above all the Industrial Revolution created a new demand for minerals, and in the case of South-East Asia the mineral in greatest abundance was tin. More than any other commodity apart from rubber, this mineral has played a revolutionary role in the development of those areas where its main deposits lie. The chief beneficiary has been the Malay Peninsula, situated on the thickest, richest part of the great tin belt which stretches from the mountains of Yunnan to the extremities of the Sunda Shelf. The discovery of how to fuse tin with copper to produce bronze at the dawn of history ushered in a new age of technical advance and brought tin itself into high demand. Tin was one of the principal attractions for the first Hindu traders to come to South-East Asia and within the region itself bronze found multiple uses. Nevertheless prior to 1800 the demand for tin remained limited, although its value as an article of trade was sufficient to prompt persistent attempts to monopolize it by various parties, in particular the Dutch who from Malacca made prolonged and determined efforts to control the entire tin trade of the Straits. The bulk of the tin mined in the region prior to the nineteenth century went to China.

As a result of the Industrial Revolution a whole new range of uses for tin as an alloy came into existence, particularly in connexion with the rise of the electrical and automobile industries. But the revolutionary increase in the demand for tin after 1800 sprang from the rapid expansion of the tin-plate industry. After 1800 the tin-plate manufacturers were easily the largest single consumers of tin. In 1805 they were already buying up one-third of total world production, by mid-century they were consuming at least half. The industry, which had its origins in fourteenth-century Germany, was now virtually an English monopoly, meeting 'practically all the world's requirements'. The expansion of the tin-plate industry was itself the consequence of the rise of the tin-canning industry. The tin-can, a hermetically-sealed, non-corrosive container for food or drink, was actually invented during the Napoleonic Wars at the beginning of the century, but did not come into its own for another generation. However by the 1850s large urban centres of population in Western Europe had been created by the process of industrialization, whose inhabitants required the food surpluses being produced in Australia and elsewhere. The tin-plate industry received further stimuli from North America because of the Civil War (1861-5) there, the rise of commercial oil production and the increasing use of corrugated tin roofing. Improved communications facilitated demand, and after the 1840s in particular there was a tremendous upsurge in world tin consumption. Demand reached its peak in the last quarter of the century and doubled again between 1900 and 1930.

Up till the 1820s hardly any tin from South-East Asia found its way onto the European market, the needs of which were met almost entirely by the production from the mines of Cornwall in England. However after 1820 Cornish tin production could no longer cope with the growing demand from European consumers, and for the first time South-East Asian tin could be sold in Europe at much lower rates. By 1850 Europe was importing three times as much tin from South-East Asia as from Cornwall and Cornish tin-miners only held their own in Britain itself because of high discriminatory tariffs against foreign competition. In 1853 these tariffs were lifted and South-East Asian tin started to flow into the British Isles as well until the point was reached some twenty years later when consumption of tin imports exceeded that of the Cornish mines. The successful entry of South-East Asian tin onto the European market was the signal for the rise of the modern tin-mining industry of the region itself. Until the 1860s the bulk of the regional tin came from Bangka. Bangka tin enjoyed a high reputation because of the efficiency of its smelting techniques and the honesty of its dealers; but when the far richer and more accessible deposits of the west coast states of the Malay Peninsula were opened up in response to the increasing world demand, Straits tin secured a natural supremacy.[6] During this period tin-mining was virtually a Chinese monopoly throughout the region, but at the end of the century the Chinese position became undermined as Western technology started to play a decisive role. As early as the 1860s Europeans had introduced new drilling methods and improved furnaces for smelting. The next decade saw the introduction of the steam pump, followed shortly afterwards by the introduction of gravel pumps and monitors and the first application of Australian technology to South-East Asian mining. These innovations formed the thin end of the Western wedge, important because they reduced the industry's dependence on cheap labour which was where Chinese enterprise held the advantage. The decisive blow against the traditional Chinese monopoly over tin-mining came with the invention of the chain-bucket dredge, which was operated for the first time in the region (at Phuket) in 1907. The tremendous capacity of the tin dredge outclassed anything a Chinese miner could do and gave the Westerners from this time onwards a dominant share in the industry. By 1930 two-thirds of the total tin output of the Netherlands Indies, nearly one-third of Malaya's (now the world's greatest producer) and three-fifths of Thai production came from this form of mining.

The end of Chinese domination in the region's tin industry was also hast-

ened by the penetration of Western interests, armed with huge capital resources and superior techniques, into the field of tin-smelting, control over
which held the key to the whole industry. The breach was made by an
Anglo-German firm based on Singapore which successfully established itself
in the richest tin-mining areas of the Malay Peninsula in the late 1880s. By
the end of the century this firm was smelting the great bulk of Malayan tin
as well as that of neighbouring producers. Tin-smelting remained a Western
monopoly up to 1941. In all, because of this and other developments, Western, and in particular British, interests in the twentieth century secured a
stranglehold over the tin-mining industry in South-East Asia, even though
the Chinese still retained a substantial share. Throughout this period world
supply failed to keep up with demand, placing South-East Asian tin at a
premium on the market and enabling the Malay Peninsula to keep its position as the world's leading tin exporter.

New products: oil, rubber and palm-oil
Amongst the entirely new products and industries in the region which arose
out of the process of Western industrialization, the first was oil. The oil
industry was the offspring of the internal combustion engine and the subsequent rise of the automobile and aircraft industries. From the outset the
industry was the tool of the West, requiring large outlays of capital. Jungles
had to be cleared, roads and bridges built and rivers dredged before drilling
operations could begin. Elaborate machinery was necessary to drill shafts
that might go down to depths of over 4,500 feet. Refineries had to be constructed to deal with the crude product and fleets of tankers had to be made
available to carry the fuel to its destinations. A large labour force was essential
and the facilities for this had to be created in regions hitherto uninhabited
and inaccessible. All these things meant the mobilization of great resources
and the application of scientific techniques to overcome the great problems
involved. In such circumstances the oil industry came inevitably to be dominated by mammoth corporations, which were almost wholly Western-
owned. In the event the exploitation of the oil resources of the region turned
out to be largely an Anglo-Dutch affair, with the United States and Japan
securing a foothold in the area. Royal Dutch Shell, the Anglo-Dutch concern
which acquired the largest stake in the industry, was in many respects a pre-
cursor of the great international firms of the second half of the twentieth
century. It represented an alliance of British and Dutch capital, transcending
national boundaries.[7]

The birth of the rubber industry was another outcome of Western enterprise, but in this case it had a far more widespread impact and significance
for South-East Asians themselves. The genesis of the industry took place in
the Malay Peninsula whose development was radically accelerated as a result,
but the Netherlands Indies and French Indo-China also became great rubber
producers while rubber became an important contributor to the economies
of Burma, Thailand and British Borneo.

The immediate cause for the 'rubber revolution' which erupted with unexpected suddenness in the 1900s lay in the great leap in world rubber market

prices at the end of the nineteenth century. A series of technical advances during the course of the century had steadily stimulated demand,[8] but the decisive event was Dunlop's invention of the pneumatic tyre in 1888. Within ten years the first pneumatic tyre was fitted to a motor vehicle and from this moment onwards the future of the rubber industry was wedded to the motor industry. The rise of the motor industry was enhanced further by the equally swift rise of aircraft manufacture and the demand for rubber soared between 1900 and 1914. Brazil, the traditional supplier, could not cope with this vast new demand and in 1911 for the first time Malayan estate rubber took the lead on the world market. The success of Henry Ford's experiment at mass production in the motor industry of the United States converted that country into the world's best customer for natural rubber.

The fact that British planters in Malaya were able to take advantage of the situation and found a new industry so rapidly reflects the potency of scientific research and the new technology of the industrialized world. For a generation British officials in London had been conducting a constant search for new crops or products to serve as fresh sources of enrichment in the empire. As early as the 1860s as part of this endeavour some rubber seedlings had been sent to Calcutta from Peru. This little experiment failed but in the 1870s more rubber seedlings were obtained, this time from Brazil, and finally planted with success in Singapore and other centres in the region. The new plants had to wait another twenty years before the right moment for their exploitation came, but when the coffee industry struck disaster at the end of the century and rubber prices soared at the same time, rubber moved into the twentieth century irresistibly triumphant. Rubber's survival as a successful commercial crop during the twentieth century was only ensured through the fruits of further research, but in contrast to oil—and oil palm cultivation—rubber was simple to cultivate and so rapidly spread as a smallholder's crop. In this way it added a new dimension to the subsistence economy of the region and helped alleviate the penury of many thousands of peasants in the western half of South-East Asia as coconut cultivation relieved those in the eastern half.

The third major new product to appear on the scene as the result of advances in industrial technology and science was palm-oil. The oil palm had been introduced to South-East Asia some time before rubber, but it became established as a commercial crop in the wake of rubber's success. Until the beginning of the twentieth century, the oil palm flourished functionlessly since the technical problems involved in extracting and processing the oil had not yet been solved nor did the world market offer any inducements. With the new openings for vegetable oils at the turn of the century and with the invention of a new crusher for the palm in West Africa, the situation changed. The lead in converting oil palm into a commercial crop in South-East Asia was now played by Adrian Hallet, a Belgian entrepreneur with large interests in the Belgian Congo. Armed with the necessary technical information about oil palm cultivation and taking advantage of the infrastructure of communications and services available for the rubber industry in the Culture Zone, in 1911 Hallet opened up his first oil palm estate in that area. His gamble paid off. By 1920 the superiority of the Sumatran product over its West African rivals was already established, a consequence of the application of scientific techniques and the most up-to-date machinery for planting and cropping. Not long afterwards oil palm cultivation became firmly established across the Straits in Malaya, and the industry as a whole became largely dominated by the great Franco-Belgian concern of Socfin.[9] In the 1930s the Netherlands Indies and Malaya between them were producing nearly one-third of the total world supply.

The expansion of rice production

One consequence of improved communications, growing populations, new cities and greater specialization of occupations was the tremendous increase in demand for South-East Asia's most basic and traditional crop—rice. While island South-East Asia was being groomed by the new industrial imperialism to concentrate on the cultivation of profitable cash crops and on the exploitation of its mineral resources, the great rice-producing regions of the mainland were being schooled into rice granaries. The economies of Burma, Thailand and Cochin-China came by and large to centre on their new role as rice exporters. To bring this about Western engineers employed their skills and ingenuity to drain the swamps of the Irrawaddy and Mekong Deltas and to convert them into vast padi-prairies. The greatest achievement was that of the French in Cochin-China who overcame the complicated problems of water-control in that region by the construction of a network of canals which served the double purpose of draining the land in the flood season and of conserving the waters during the dry season. The building of this complicated irrigation network has been described as being 'among the great works in technical history'. Equally impressive was their work in Tonkin where another elaborate network of canals, sluices, barrages and dams strove to overcome the acute problems of land shortage and overpopulation. By 1941 modern irrigation works extended over one-third of the Tonkin Delta and a quarter of a million acres had been reclaimed. Comparable achievements were wrought by the Dutch in Java and by the British on a smaller scale in Burma.

The impact of Western medicine

Closely associated with the penetration and progress of Western enterprise throughout the region and indeed forming an indispensable part of it was the spread of Western medical and health techniques. South-East Asia in the nineteenth century was probably one of the unhealthiest areas in the world, as Western soldiers, missionaries, explorers, miners and engineers discovered to their cost. Malaria in particular was the scourge of the whole region. This 'and fevers unspecified' stalked the jungle, hills and creeks of South-East Asian lands, while tuberculosis, pneumonia, dysentery and enteric fever, typhus and hookworm lurked in the fetid and overcrowded tenements and alleyways of the port cities, fed by the huge annual turnovers of immigrants. When the Americans took over power in the Philippines they found 50,000 people a year dying of cholera, which also made periodical and devastating sweeps across mainland South-East Asia. Beri-beri was the king of the deficiency diseases, of which yaws and trachoma were other common examples. Apart from the great sum of human misery which the prevalence of such diseases indicates, their existence posed a serious threat to Western enterprise in the region. The very survival of the tin and rubber industries of the Malay Peninsula was jeopardized by the widespread virulence of beri-beri and malaria respectively. The cost of constructing railway lines, roads and telegraph communications was rendered excessively high in terms of human life, while the opening up of new lands was hindered, and on occasion had to be abandoned.

It therefore became a matter of enlightened self-interest for colonial regimes to enforce rigorous health measures, and if the sums of money involved were immense, the returns in the form of enhanced economic development and increased productivity provided handsome compensation. Slowly at first but after 1900 with ever greater efficiency the Dutch, British, French and American colonial administrations in the region made full use of the latest advances in medical science in order to combat disease and to extend health services in the territories under their control. Medical research centres were established which made important contributions to the solution of local problems.[10] The results were highly impressive. By the 1920s death-rates throughout the region had dropped significantly while the birth-rate soared; epidemic outbreaks had been curbed or completely eradicated, endemic diseases contained and a start made in changing public attitudes towards health and hygiene.

The battle against malaria affords a striking illustration of how the impact of Western medicine made itself felt in the region and of the sort of problem that had to be faced. The great discovery in 1897 by a British Indian Army doctor called Ross that the anopheles mosquito was the carrier of the malaria virus was the outcome of a generation of shared research by scientists in the Western world. The process had begun thirty years previously (i.e. in 1877) when the hitherto unsuspected relationship between insects and certain tropical diseases was established by Manson, another British doctor. Three years after this, Alphonse Laveran, a young French medical officer serving in Algeria, found the malarial parasite in human corpuscles for the first time, a discovery soon confirmed by a group of Italian scientists conducting similar investigations. These developments convinced Manson, now medical adviser to the British Colonial Office, that some sucking insect must complete the life cycle of the parasite, an idea he communicated to Ross whilst the latter was on leave from India. Ross's discovery on his return was therefore the direct consequence. However, the discovery of the cause of malaria was not the end of the problem. It took another three years for Ross's discovery to be put to use; this was done by Watson, the district surgeon of Port Swettenham in the Malay States, who was looking for means to check the disease which was threatening the survival of the new port. Watson's anti-malarial measures had dramatic results—within two years of the area around the town being drained and so made uninhabitable for mosquitoes, malaria 'had ceased to be of any practical consequence', Port Swettenham was saved and it had been conclusively shown that the disease could be contained. But not long after it was also discovered that there were many different species of anopheles mosquito, each with its own characteristics and habits. What would work against the *anopheles umbrosus* which haunted the stagnant creeks around Port Swettenham proved totally ineffective against the *anopheles maculatus* that frequented the fast-running streams of the hinterland hills where most of the new rubber estates were being planted. In this way the elimination of malaria from the region as a whole turned out to be a prolonged and exhausting affair, requiring the painstaking study of the local variety of anopheles in each particular area. The French took a whole decade to discover that the most dangerous carrier in the mountains of Annam and Tonkin was quite different from the killers of the Malay Peninsula, while it was not until 1928 that the offending anopheles carrier was successfully identified in British North Borneo.

All the same, malaria ceased to be the threat to health and progress that it formerly had been and its containment demonstrated the efficacy of modern scientific research. Western medicine repeated such triumphs in a hundred different fields, bringing about a great alleviation of human suffering and causing social changes of the deepest consequence. For the first time since human settlement in the region the endless struggle between man and his environment started to turn in favour of man, and for the first time in South-East Asian history over-population rather than underpopulation emerged as a barrier to material progress.

The forces of change: political and economic pressures
A major consequence of South-East Asia being converted by the impact of Western industrialization into a major source for primary raw materials was to make the region extremely sensitive to the fluctuations of a world market over which it exerted no control, since its inhabitants themselves were vassals of Western consumers. As world trade ebbed and flowed in consonance with the movements of Western politics, South-East Asia was as much affected as if the region had been situated next door to Europe itself. World politics in this age of industrial imperialism were in effect Western politics writ large. At first only those parts of the region already within the orbit of world trade were affected, but as Western colonialism expanded so did the measure of the region's total involvement, until by the opening of the twentieth century there remained few areas in South-East Asia which were not in one way or the other touched by international events.

The Revolutionary and Napoleonic Wars represented the first major world event of the nineteenth century to have its impact on South-East Asia. Its repercussions were reflected in the resurgence of British power in the region, the foundation of the British settlement of Singapore in 1819 and in the destruction of Dutch mercantilism. In the second half of the century industrialism was sufficiently developed in north-western Europe and in the United States of America to bring about a crisis caused by the effects of overproduction, cheaper manufacturing techniques, saturated domestic markets and intensified competition for overseas ones. The crisis thus spawned and known as the 'Great Depression' started in the early 1870s and continued with intermittent bouts of recovery until the mid-1890s. It was characterized by steadily falling market prices and a descending cost of living, which hit expanding enterprise in South-East Asia and had far-reaching consequences for the pattern of economic development in the region. Tin, coffee and sugar were three commodities particularly affected. The onset of the depression nearly ruined the tin entrepreneurs of the Malay States, despite the great boost that they had received from the British forward movement into that area, while it proved nearly fatal for the coffee planters of the Netherlands Indies and ended coffee's primacy amongst Indies' exports. The sugar industry survived and in the end actually emerged stronger than before, but its character had been changed. The typical sugar magnate of the Indies now gave way to the sugar corporation. Individual planters, forced to turn to banks or to established firms for help, ended up by being absorbed into newly-created limited companies controlled by these bodies. At the same time these regional banks and agencies themselves fell under the closer supervision of their backers in Holland, so that from the 1880s onwards policy was decided in Amsterdam, Rotterdam or The Hague rather than in Batavia as had been the case before. By the 1920s the sugar industry of the Indies was firmly in the hands of the merchants of those cities, who exercised their control through the medium of mammoth business corporations. This trend towards corporate business enterprise and monopoly was the most general result of the Great Depression of the nineteenth century. Not only the sugar industry but all the major economic activities of the Indies came under the aegis of powerful, inter-locking financial interests based on Amsterdam, London or Antwerp. A similar process could be observed in the trade and commerce of the Straits Settlements and the Malay States, which by the end of the nineteenth century was dominated by a handful of business houses with interests in every field. The tin industry in particular (i.e. the Western part of it) evolved within the next two decades into a vast network of inter-locking companies with their headquarters and master-control in London. Protectionism, always the hall-mark of French colonial policy, resulted in a small group of concerns owning all the major French investments in Indo-China. Half-a-dozen Western firms manipulated the rice, teak and rubber trades of Burma and Thailand. The copra industry of the Philippines was in the hands of two major American companies. Yet despite the growth of monopoly and the increasing particularism of rival colonial powers, the roots of Western enterprise remained surprisingly cosmopolitan. Anglo-Dutch interests predominated in oil. British enterprises overshadowed the rubber plantations of the Netherlands Indies and Franco-Belgian capital financed the bulk of the oil palm estates in Sumatra, Malaya and Cochin-China.

Between 1900 and 1941 two major events brought about further modifications in the structure of industrial capitalism and redirected the course of economic development within South-East Asia. The first was the Great War (1914-18) which together with the Little Depression following in its wake eliminated Germany, one of the most thrusting of the colonial powers, ended the era of unimpeded capitalist expansion in the region and led to the first coherent attempts at an international scheme of restriction of production. Restriction was first tried with the rubber industry whose major producers were badly affected by the world-wide drop in rubber prices. After an abortive effort to start a scheme of voluntary restriction, the British producers acted alone and launched the Stevenson Plan, which embraced all the major (British) rubber producers in the world and imposed mandatory limitations on rubber exports. The Stevenson Plan failed since the Netherlands Indies and other smaller rubber producing countries refused to join in, thereby undercutting the whole project. But the British had no sooner abandoned the Stevenson Plan themselves when the Great Depression occurred, the second major event of the century. The effects of the Great Depression were so profound that this time no one could escape its effects, and the outcome was the signing of the first International Rubber Restriction Agreement by all the major rubber producers of the world in 1934. Similar international agreements restricting or controlling production were completed in the 1930s for nearly all the major products of the region, the most important of which were those regarding tin and sugar. Some commodities, on the other hand, were unprotectable. The copra industry of the Netherlands Indies, for instance, could not be shielded from the drastic fall in prices, since Indies' oil accounted for only 3 per cent of the total on the world market and was locked in deadly competition with other vegetable oils. The prosperity of the inhabitants of the Great East vanished overnight and once again they returned to a subsistence way of life.

The Great Depression of 1929 forms a watershed in the history of the region. Apart from promoting still greater collusion between international capital, it destroyed for ever the unchallenged hegemony of the Western colonial powers over the trade and commerce of South-East Asia and eliminated the last vestiges of free trade. It also caused basic changes of policy regarding immigration into the countries of the region which had in turn far-reaching social and economic consequences internally.

The first and most obvious result of the Depression was the emergence of Japan as a serious competitor in the heart of the spheres of interest of the Western colonial powers. This was the prime factor in the spate of new duties and tariffs erected throughout the region in the 1930s, which involved not only the protectionist regimes of the French or the Dutch but also the Straits Settlements, for so long the bastion of British free trade.[11] At the same time, a nationalistic regime in Thailand, having rid itself of the shackles of the unequal treaties imposed in the previous century by the Western powers, started to develop protectionist measures of its own so as to build up some degree of Thai participation in the national economy. Indeed the impact of the Great Depression brought home to the indigenous peoples of South-East Asia as never before the realities of their situation. Widespread unemployment and the conflict of interest with the small but economically powerful alien minorities in their midst made South-East Asians question the nature and efficacy of colonial rule. The colonial powers were forced to reconsider the whole basis of their social and economic policies. Unrestricted immigration was brought to an end and the encouragement of local industry was no longer regarded as a sentimental ideal but as a practical necessity.

The instruments of Western enterprise

Alongside the impact on South-East Asia of economic and political forces from outside, Western economic institutions set up inside the region itself soon became important instruments of change in their own right. The key role was played by Western business houses established in the heart of the region, for they fostered trade and channelled it, thereby forming a crucial element in determining patterns of development. The prototypes of such concerns were naturally to be found in the Straits Settlements and Java, the earliest South-East Asian centres for the new industrial imperialism, while British interests predominated as the pace-setters of the industrialization process. In fact, until the era of intense colonial rivalries which started in the 1870s, Singapore was the fulcrum of Western commercial enterprise in South-East Asia. It transacted a large part of the region's modern business and was the nucleus from which the forces of change radiated. The Philippines were opened from Singapore, so was Bangkok and many parts of the Indies as well.

The typical instruments of Western enterprise to be found at Singapore were the European import-export firms, which by serving as managing agencies for Western manufacturers towards the end of the nineteenth century dominated the port's entrepôt trade with America, Europe and India. Originally started by individual merchant adventurers, they developed into huge business concerns which, besides their basic commercial activities, had become finance and credit houses, investors in real estate and promoters of new enterprises of all kinds.[12]

The operations of these Singapore firms were marked by their close relationship with local Chinese traders, a feature typical of trade and commerce throughout the region by the 1900s. Bulk imports and exports were mainly handled by European firms, while the machinery of collection and distribution was mostly in Chinese hands. The Chinese were the middlemen *par excellence*, linking the European merchant importer with the South-East Asian peasant consumer. They served as the medium for the disposal of the manufactured wares of the former to the latter, and provided the means whereby the South-East Asian producer could dispose of his produce on the world market. With their long experience of trading in the region, their knowledge of local languages and conditions and their Western contacts, the Chinese proved most adept in this role and many enterprising individuals who chanced their luck overseas made their fortunes.

After the 1860s financial houses rose to play a much more prominent role as heightening colonial rivalries forced the promotion of Western enterprise along much narrower, nationalistic lines. This was especially true of protectionist regimes such as that of the French in Indo-China, where the Banque de l'Indochine founded in 1875 a little later assumed the functions of a state bank, although still remaining a private concern, and was successful in stifling the encroachments of rival colonial concerns into this French preserve.

The culture banks in the Netherlands Indies, originally formed in the dying days of the Culture System to promote agriculture, performed a similar role for Dutch interests. In the Philippines a succession of Spanish banks founded in the nineteenth century to further Spanish investments were superseded after 1900 by American banks formed for the benefit of American investors. Only in the truly *laissez-faire* environment of Thailand and of the British possessions in the region did banks and firms rise and fall according to fortune and their own merit—those surviving into the twentieth century reaping a huge reward.

Even after the Second World War these various instruments of Western enterprise and innovation were still well-anchored in the region, their assets worth millions of dollars, their interests interlocked and their position seemingly immune to depression, war or revolution.

Catalysts of change: the role of Chinese and Indian immigrants
Closely associated with the Western impact was the large-scale immigration of Chinese and Indians into South-East Asia. Both races, of course, had each been making its own substantial contribution in the region since the dawn of history, leaving a characteristic imprint upon indigenous ways and culture, but in the nineteenth century they appeared in new guise. Now subject to the same over-riding pressures from the West as South-East Asians themselves, their new role was as catalysts of change, acquiring in the process a position in their own right. They were not all, or always, subordinate to the Western pace-setters; on occasion they served as partners and thereby became joint beneficiaries. In any case, in sharp contrast to earlier times, the new Chinese and Indian immigrants into the region did not assimilate with the South-East Asians themselves; they remained apart, a foreign element in the body politic of the region, and while expediting change helped to give rise to new multiracial polities with all their attendant problems.

Since 1800 by far the greater role has been played by the Chinese, if only by virtue of sheer weight of numbers. Although they formed a mere 5 per cent of the total population of the region in 1947, this presence was made significant by the manner of its distribution. Chinese settlement was concentrated in key economic areas, that is in those areas which were the most highly developed and most closely integrated with the mainstream of world trade. Singapore was virtually a Chinese island, and throughout the region the Chinese were to be found mainly concentrated in the towns or in the mining areas. In short, the Chinese minority, small and unevenly distributed, represented a factor that could not be ignored, particularly since to a remarkable degree the economic life of the region lay in their hands.

Basically the Chinese did not form an economic entity of their own, however much they remained self-contained as a community. In the economic sense they formed part and parcel of the new world of trade, commerce and industry promoted by the West. They did also initiate enterprise—they were the pioneer tin-miners and planters of modern Malaya—but these initiatives in the long run depended on the infra-structure of modern communications, financial facilities and new technology proffered by the West, and in opening

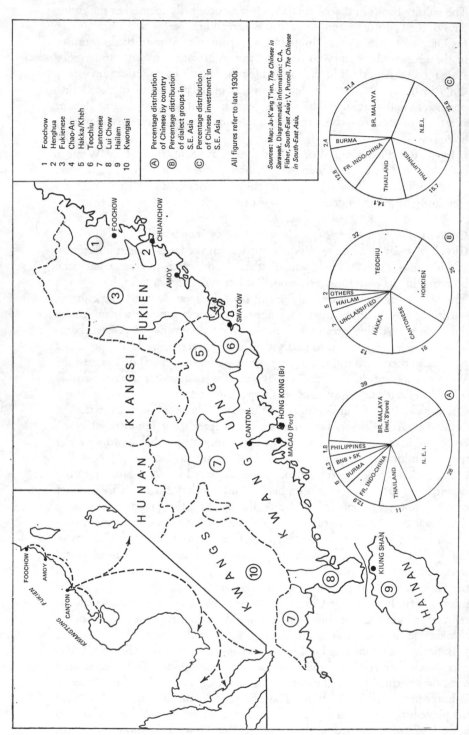

Sources: Map: Ju-K'ang T'ien, *The Chinese in Sarawak*. Diagrammatic information: C.A. Fisher, *South-East Asia*; V. Purcell, *The Chinese in South-East Asia*.

All figures refer to late 1930s

1 Foochow
2 Henghua
3 Fukienese
4 Chao-An
5 Hakka/Kheh
6 Teochiu
7 Cantonese
8 Lui Chow
9 Hailam
10 Kwongsai

Ⓐ Percentage distribution of Chinese by country
Ⓑ Percentage distribution of dialect groups in S.E. Asia
Ⓒ Percentage distribution of Chinese investment in S.E. Asia

Ⓒ BR. MALAYA 31.4 · N.E.I. 23.6 · PHILIPPINES 15.7 · THAILAND 14.1 · FR. INDO-CHINA 12.8 · BURMA 2.4

Ⓑ TEOCHIU 32 · HOKKIEN 25 · CANTONESE 16 · HAKKA 13 · UNCLASSIFIED 7 · HAILAM 5 · OTHERS 2

Ⓐ BR. MALAYA (incl. S'pore) 39 · N.E.I. 28 · THAILAND 11 · FR. INDO-CHINA 12.9 · BURMA 5 · BNB + SK 4.3 · PHILIPPINES 1.8

2. Southern China: Main Centres of Emigrants and Places of Origin of Main Dialect Groups

up new fields of their own inevitably helped to extend Western penetration. Nevertheless, the Chinese role grew increasingly important in its own right, as middlemen in the field of commerce, as labourers in the new mines, estates and factories. From their midst sprang the individuals who built up their fortunes and rose up to form an extremely wealthy and influential élite in local society. From the immensely rich to the immensely poor, Chinese immigrants in the lands of South-East Asia came to reflect the full spectrum of society.

The origins of the Chinese presence in South-East Asia were not, of course, related in any way to the West, but were linked to the expansion of Chinese civilization in China itself. The repercussions of the conquest of South China by the emperor Ch'in Shih Huang Ti made themselves first felt under the ensuing Han dynasty on the Vietnamese of the Tonkin Delta, who subsequently came to be the only South-East Asian people to adopt Chinese culture. Two hundred years later Chinese merchants and adventurers had arrived on the shores of the Gulf of Siam and beyond, and from this time onwards periodical accounts, growing more detailed, accurate and frequent with the passage of time, speak of Chinese contacts with the region. Archaeological finds provide further evidence of mounting Chinese activities. However up till the nineteenth century, such contacts tended to be spasmodic and Chinese migration into the region was neither substantial nor sustained.

Although the great increase in Chinese immigration after 1800 was induced by Western activities, internal developments within China still played a major part. The basic factor was the mounting impoverishment of the south of China. Two centuries of peace under firm Manchu rule permitted substantial population growth without a corresponding rise in food production. In the first half of the nineteenth century natural disaster and political unrest aggravated conditions, while the intrusion of the West, symbolized by the opium trade and the First Anglo-Chinese Wars, worsened matters still further. The final expression of these accumulated evils was the great Taiping Rebellion which ravaged the heart of the country and claimed over 20 million lives before it was finally crushed half a generation after it had begun. Such circumstances created the pressure to migrate, which was facilitated by the opening up of new opportunities by Western enterprise in South-East Asia and by the provision of the means to get there cheaply. The coming of the steamship cheapened and quickened the passage still further, and the consequences were soon seen in the huge numbers of Chinese who flocked to the ports, plantations and mines of South-East Asia in quest of their fortunes. The migrants travelled under appalling conditions and their treatment on arrival became an international scandal, but the few who made good were sufficient to induce others to follow. Towards the end of the century conditions gradually improved, partly as a result of measures taken by the colonial authorities most closely involved, partly because of the organizations developed by the various overseas Chinese communities themselves to protect their kind.

The great traffic in migrants between China and South-East Asia continued at an ever-increasing pace and without, on the whole, any restriction until the third decade of the present century. Up till the Great Depression of 1929 the nature of the Chinese exodus remained basically transitory, although the size of the Chinese colonies in the region inevitably increased. After 1929 Chinese immigration into the region in general became subject to stricter controls, including Malaya, the area which had most readily absorbed the largest number. As the flow from China was checked, those left behind in the region started to think for the first time in terms of permanent settlement and so amongst the reduced numbers now allowed into South-East Asia there was a far higher proportion of women. These trends gave the Chinese established in the region a new and far greater political significance.

The overwhelming bulk of the Chinese who arrived in the region in the nineteenth century were, as they always had been, from the south of China, in particular from the three southern coastal provinces of Fukien, Kwangtung and Kwangsi. Of the nine major speech groups involved, the Cantonese, Hokkien, Hakka and Teochew were the most prominent. The manner of their distribution in South-East Asia itself was determined by a variety of factors, such as the chronology of the opening of the 'treaty' ports and of new steamship services, established connexions within the region and incidental events such as the periodical natural disasters which afflicted the provinces of South China. The long experience of the Southern Chinese in trade and commerce, which they had monopolized from their home ports for so long, was another important element in their emergence in South-East Asia.

The value of the Chinese presence in the region after 1800 was, from the Western point of view, irrefutable. However, while they became essential agents of Western enterprise, they were also its most wily rivals and constituted the potential enemy from within. In the pre-industrial era the Spaniards and the Dutch lived in constant fear of the far more numerous Chinese settled in their midst, but massacre and expulsion only drove home the point of Chinese indispensability. After 1800 colonial policy rarely went beyond legislative discrimination. The French, the Dutch and the Americans tended to keep a close surveillance over their Chinese populations, but in British territories (until the 1930s) neither the British masters nor their Chinese 'subjects' regarded each other as more than birds of passage bent on the same purposes, for which co-operation was of mutual benefit. The attitudes of South-East Asians themselves towards the Chinese were more complex. Generations of Chinese lived in peace and harmony throughout the region, closely linked with their indigenous neighbours in their everyday affairs; yet they were the ready targets of nationalist resentments because of their domination of the local economy. Be that as it may, the Chinese minority represented a vital element in the new emergent world of South-East Asia and the material progress achieved within the region since the 1800s would have been impossible without them.

On the other hand, the Indian presence in the region after 1800 was of a totally different calibre. Far less widespread, being mainly confined to the British territories, they were also far fewer in number and in terms of economic power far behind the Chinese. Like their Chinese counterparts, most of the Indian immigrants during this period arrived as labourers, but socially

Indian communities remained far less variegated. Although Indian contacts with South-East Asia were undoubtedly more ancient than those of the Chinese and their impress on South-East Asian civilization and culture became indelible, this had little connexion with the hordes of labourers who crossed to and fro over the Bay of Bengal at the behest of British planters with evergrowing momentum after 1880. Probably the only vestige of India's historical bonds with the region was preserved in this period by Indian Muslims who had traded in South-East Asian waters for generations and who were the first to take advantage of the great influx of their countrymen into the area to ply their wares.

Four-fifths of the Indian immigrants in Malaya in 1941 were Tamils from Madras, while the great majority in Burma came from the same source. The bulk of this great Tamil group in both countries were manual labourers; their failure to rise above their origins lay largely in the circumstances of their employment. Unlike his Chinese counterpart, the average Indian labourer did not come at the behest of his fellow-countrymen but as a recruit to work on the estate of a European owner who favoured him because of his 'docility' and 'amenability to discipline'. From the 1880s onwards his recruitment was subjected to a growing amount of official supervision, designed more in the interest of the employer than the employee, and worked under a regime at its worst severely repressive and at its best heavily paternalistic. Social mobility was also impeded by the restrictive mould of his own society. Strict discipline and regimentation were the main features of an Indian immigrant's life, and the short-term contract he was offered prevented his establishing a foothold in the region. Nevertheless the Indian communities of the region were leavened by a small but highly significant group of immigrants of a totally different order, for which the Chinese had no parallel. The exigencies of British colonial rule created a demand for western-educated clerks, hospital dispensers, court-pleaders and teachers, while a pool of such people existed in India and Ceylon around such centres as Madras and the Tamil belt of Jaffna where Western education had already taken root. These, together with the still smaller traditional merchant class, encouraged by the new openings for them in Burma and the Straits Settlements, started to settle there and to form a small professional middle-class, whose influence by the 1930s was out of all proportion to their numbers.

The pattern of Indian immigration was quite uneven. In Burma there lived a substantial minority which in 1930 numbered 1 million, and whose role could be equated with that of the Chinese elsewhere; after the British they held the largest investments, held over half the cultivated land in fee and dominated in commerce and trade. In the Straits Settlements and the Malay States, on the other hand, the Indians formed much smaller minorities, completely overshadowed by the Chinese. In the 1930s, apart from the small pool of business and professional men, the mass of the Indians in the Peninsula were the descendants of the indentured labourers of the early part of the century, still occupying the same strata of society as rubber-tappers, road and railway workers, and municipal or port labourers.

In general, the role of the Indian immigrant in South-East Asia since 1800 has tended to be one almost wholly subordinate to the circumstances created by the colonial powers themselves. Unlike the Chinese in the region, they were rarely in a position to instigate initiatives of their own.

*   *   *   *   *

For the best part of one hundred years, in some cases for longer, in a few others for less, the inhabitants of South-East Asia became the powerless participants in developments over which they had little influence and less control. During that period, the various pressures outlined above were brought to bear, pressures generated by the process of industrialization which in fact guided the actions of the Western colonial powers themselves as much as it did the destiny of the region as a whole. Modern communications and the new technology, inventions and scientific discoveries, the forces of markets and investment, trade cycles and depressions, conflicting economic interests and outright war, together with the unpredictable interaction of human energies that these things released helped shape the modern world of South-East Asia today.

Column headers (repeated across the chart): **BR. MALAYA & BORNEO | BURMA | FRENCH INDO-CHINA | NETHERLANDS EAST INDIES | PHILIPPINES | THAILAND**

ABACA (B)

	Br. Malaya & Borneo	Burma	French Indo-China	Netherlands East Indies	Philippines	Thailand
AREA	.35				292	
PRODUCTION	1.2				183	
EXPORT — Volume	1.2				166	
EXPORT — Value	4				12.2	
DOMESTIC CONSUMPTION	—				6	
WORLD PRODUCTION	.6				95	

MAIZE (J)

	Br. Malaya & Borneo	Burma	French Indo-China	Netherlands East Indies	Philippines	Thailand
AREA		(45)87	(38)500	2045	(38)913	8
PRODUCTION		—	565	2037	427	7
EXPORT — Volume		—	508	215	—	—
EXPORT — Value			(38)18	.7	—	—
DOMESTIC CONSUMPTION		—	10	—	100	100
WORLD PRODUCTION		—	—	80	—	—

RUBBER (M)

	Br. Malaya & Borneo	Burma	French Indo-China	Netherlands East Indies	Philippines	Thailand
AREA	1331	45	126	1300	5	140
PRODUCTION	501	8	61	432	—	34
EXPORT — Volume	468	9	(38)60	439	—	38
EXPORT — Value	54	12	(38)22	31	—	12.9
DOMESTIC CONSUMPTION	—	—	—	—	100	—
WORLD PRODUCTION	(40)38.7	(40).45	(40)4.5	(40)38.4	—	(40)3.1

TIN (M)

	Br. Malaya & Borneo	Burma	French Indo-China	Netherlands East Indies	Philippines	Thailand
AREA	—	..	—	—		—
PRODUCTION	77	2	1.6	40		13.4
EXPORT — Volume	63	2	1.6	38		14
EXPORT — Value	26.3	1	2.6	8.8		18.6
DOMESTIC CONSUMPTION	—					—
WORLD PRODUCTION	37.3	.4	1.16	18.4		7.7

CINCHONA (M)

	Br. Malaya & Borneo	Burma	French Indo-China	Netherlands East Indies	Philippines	Thailand
AREA				(E)17		
PRODUCTION				10.4		
EXPORT — Volume				6.5		
EXPORT — Value				1.4		
DOMESTIC CONSUMPTION				—		
WORLD PRODUCTION				80		

PALM-OIL (M)

	Br. Malaya & Borneo	Burma	French Indo-China	Netherlands East Indies	Philippines	Thailand
AREA	(E)28			(E)82		
PRODUCTION	46			238		
EXPORT — Volume	43			238		
EXPORT — Value	—			3		
DOMESTIC CONSUMPTION	—			—		
WORLD PRODUCTION	8.6			(40)39		

SUGAR

	Br. Malaya & Borneo	Burma	French Indo-China	Netherlands East Indies	Philippines	Thailand
AREA		(40)31	43	85	230	2.5
PRODUCTION		(40)39	43	547	1076	19
EXPORT — Volume		—	—	1110	893	—
EXPORT — Value		—	—	5.3	40.3	—
DOMESTIC CONSUMPTION		100	100	—	—	100
WORLD PRODUCTION		—	—	5 (P) / 12 EX	11 (P) / 9 EX	—

TOBACCO

	Br. Malaya & Borneo	Burma	French Indo-China	Netherlands East Indies	Philippines	Thailand
AREA	(40)2.3	(40)54	—	170	(38)58	9
PRODUCTION	—	45	—	(E)47.5	35	4
EXPORT — Volume	—	—	—	50	—	—
EXPORT — Value	—	—	—	4.3	—	—
DOMESTIC CONSUMPTION	100	100	100	70	90	100
WORLD PRODUCTION	—	—	—	5.7	—	—

COFFEE (M)

	Br. Malaya & Borneo	Burma	French Indo-China	Netherlands East Indies	Philippines	Thailand
AREA	7	13		(E)107	—	
PRODUCTION	—	1.5		62.4	3	
EXPORT — Volume	—	.5		97	—	
EXPORT — Value	—	.1		2.8	—	
DOMESTIC CONSUMPTION	95	—		—		
WORLD PRODUCTION	EX	—		7	—	

PEPPER (SK)

	Br. Malaya & Borneo	Burma	French Indo-China	Netherlands East Indies	Philippines	Thailand
AREA				(E)2.6		
PRODUCTION				20		
EXPORT — Volume	3		4	31		
EXPORT — Value			.6	.7		
DOMESTIC CONSUMPTION			—	—		
WORLD PRODUCTION			—	70		

TAPIOCA PRODUCTS (J)

	Br. Malaya & Borneo	Burma	French Indo-China	Netherlands East Indies	Philippines	Thailand
AREA				(J)950		
PRODUCTION				7759		
EXPORT — Volume				447		
EXPORT — Value				1.9		
DOMESTIC CONSUMPTION				80		
WORLD PRODUCTION				80		

COPRA / COCONUT PRODUCTS (M)

	Br. Malaya & Borneo	Burma	French Indo-China	Netherlands East Indies	Philippines	Thailand
AREA	247	(40)4	—	(E)42.1	1051	(38)50
PRODUCTION	CA.76 CO.40	—		CA(E)33	583	—
EXPORT — Volume	CA.76 CO.40	—	(38)10 CA506	CA330 CP210		
EXPORT — Value	3.4	—	CA.6	CA6.6	CA10 15.3	.2
DOMESTIC CONSUMPTION	—	—	—	—	90	
WORLD PRODUCTION	CA4.5 CO.10	—	—	CAEX 32	CA40	—

PETROLEUM (B)

	Br. Malaya & Borneo	Burma	French Indo-China	Netherlands East Indies	Philippines	Thailand
AREA	—	—				
PRODUCTION	(40)1000	(38)1000		(38)7400		
EXPORT — Volume	921	1000		5878		
EXPORT — Value	39	31		17.5		
DOMESTIC CONSUMPTION	—	—		—		
WORLD PRODUCTION	.5	.5		3.5		

TEA (M)

	Br. Malaya & Borneo	Burma	French Indo-China	Netherlands East Indies	Philippines	Thailand
AREA	3	(40)1	3	(E)139		
PRODUCTION			.8	74.5		
EXPORT — Volume			.7	67		
EXPORT — Value	.08		.8	5.1		
DOMESTIC CONSUMPTION	100	95	—	—		
WORLD PRODUCTION				EX 17		

KAPOK

	Br. Malaya & Borneo	Burma	French Indo-China	Netherlands East Indies	Philippines	Thailand
AREA			—	(E)24.4		
PRODUCTION			—	20		
EXPORT — Volume			3	19		
EXPORT — Value			.8	.7		
DOMESTIC CONSUMPTION			—	—		
WORLD PRODUCTION			—	EX 70		

RICE (M)

	Br. Malaya & Borneo	Burma	French Indo-China	Netherlands East Indies	Philippines	Thailand
AREA	261	5054	5000	(J)3824	(38)2080	3392
PRODUCTION	324	4940	3945	4007	2179	2711
EXPORT — Volume	—	2842	1605	..—	.—	1558
EXPORT — Value	—	38	(38)36	.3	—	53.5
DOMESTIC CONSUMPTION	100	43	60	96	100	43
WORLD PRODUCTION	.—	EX 44	EX 25	—	.—	EX 24

TEAK

	Br. Malaya & Borneo	Burma	French Indo-China	Netherlands East Indies	Philippines	Thailand
AREA		7511		829		2655
PRODUCTION		475		400		189
EXPORT — Volume		319		—		85
EXPORT — Value		7		—		4.2
DOMESTIC CONSUMPTION		—		90		(30)45
WORLD PRODUCTION		75		—		20

KEY

● Area = hectares (000)
● Production/export volume = metric tons (000) except for teak = cu. metres (000)
● Export value/domestic consumption/world reduction = percentages
● All figures for 1937 except where indicated (years in parentheses).
☐ Areas shaded—not applicable
● BRITISH MALAYA & BORNEO
  M = Malaya only   B = Borneo only;   Sk = Sarawak only.
● NETHERLANDS EAST INDIES
  J = Java only.
● AREA/PRODUCTION
  E = Estates only.
● WORLD PRODUCTION
  = production only unless otherwise indicated: i.e.
  EX = exports
  P = production
● COPRA/COCONUT PRODUCTS
  Copra only unless otherwise indicated: i.e. CA = copra
  CO = coconut oil
  CP = coconut products

1. Production/Export Figures for Main Raw Materials from South-East Asia, 1937–1940

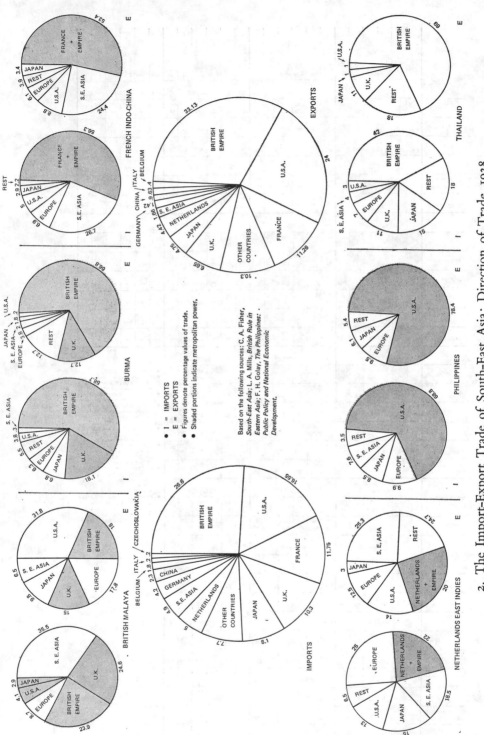

2. The Import-Export Trade of South-East Asia: Direction of Trade, 1938

A RAILWAYS

	1	2	3	4	5	6	7	8	9	
BR. MALAYA & N. BORNEO										1,894 km
BRITISH BURMA										3,296 km
FRENCH INDO-CHINA										2,908 km
NETHERLANDS EAST INDIES										7,339 km
U.S. PHILIPPINES										1,352 km
THAILAND										3,418 km

B POSTS, TELECOMMUNICATIONS AND RADIO

	Br M & B	Br Burma	FIC	NEI	Ph	Th
POST OFFICES		372	338	657	1,062	832
TELEGRAPH (line in '000 km)		13.4	20	14.3	13.6	
PHONES ('000 subscribers)		4	7.3	28.7		
RADIOS ('000 licensed)		6.3	9	54	30	
POPULATION (millions)	5	16.8	23	62	15.9	14.5

C ROADS

		('000 reg'd vehicles)
BR. MALAYA & BORNEO	47,000 vehicles	10,373 km
BRITISH BURMA	20,000 vehicles	27,304 km
FRENCH INDO-CHINA	20,000 vehicles	35,656 km
NETHERLANDS EAST INDIES	82,352 vehicles	51,000 km
U.S. PHILIPPINES	56,000 vehicles	24,477 km
THAILAND	4,500 vehicles	3,587 km

3. Communications in South-East Asia in the late 1930s (A) Railways (B) Posts, Telecommunications and Radio (C) Roads

Sources: Admiralty Handbook: Indochina; Admiralty Handbook: Netherlands East Indies; H. M. Baker, Sabah, The First Ten Years as a Colony; C. A. Fisher, South-East Asia; Lim Chong-Yah, Economic Development of Modern Malaya; L. A. Mills, British Rule in Eastern Asia; C. Robequain, Malaya, Indonesia, Borneo and the Philippines; S. Runciman, The White Rajahs; V. Thompson, Thailand, The New Siam; G. F. Zaide, Philippine Political and Cultural History.

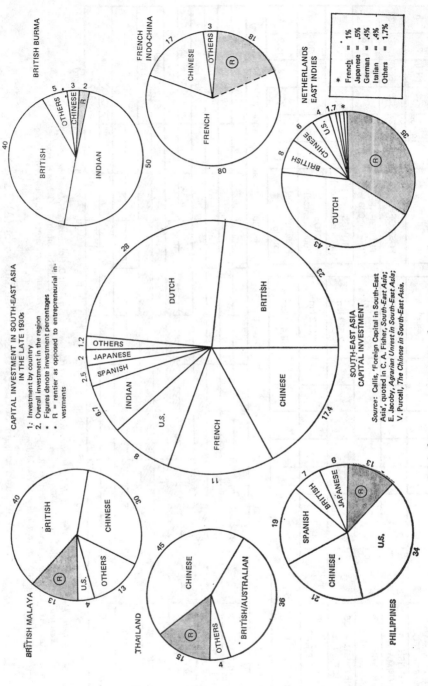

CAPITAL INVESTMENT IN SOUTH-EAST ASIA IN THE LATE 1930s

1: Investment by country
2: Overall investment in the region
* Figures denote investment percentages
R = rentier as opposed to entrepreneurial investments

BRITISH BURMA

BRITISH 40
INDIAN 50
OTHERS 5
CHINESE 3
R 2

FRENCH INDO-CHINA

FRENCH 80
CHINESE 17
OTHERS 3
R 18

NETHERLANDS EAST INDIES

DUTCH 43
BRITISH 8
CHINESE 6
U.S. 4
* 1.7
R 35

French _ = 1%
Japanese = .5%
German = .4%
Italian = .4%
Others = 1.7%

SOUTH-EAST ASIA CAPITAL INVESTMENT

BRITISH 23
DUTCH 28
OTHERS 1.2
JAPANESE 2
SPANISH 2.5
INDIAN 6.7
U.S. 8
FRENCH 11
CHINESE 17.4

Source: Callis, 'Foreign Capital in South-East Asia', quoted in C. A. Fisher, *South-East Asia*; E. Jacoby, *Agrarian Unrest in South-East Asia*; V. Purcell, *The Chinese in South-East Asia.*

BRITISH MALAYA

BRITISH 40
CHINESE 30
OTHERS 13
U.S. 4
R 13

THAILAND

CHINESE 45
BRITISH/AUSTRALIAN 36
OTHERS 4
R 15

PHILIPPINES

U.S. 34
CHINESE 21
SPANISH 19
BRITISH 7
JAPANESE 9
R 13

4. Capital Investment in South-East Asia in the late 1930s

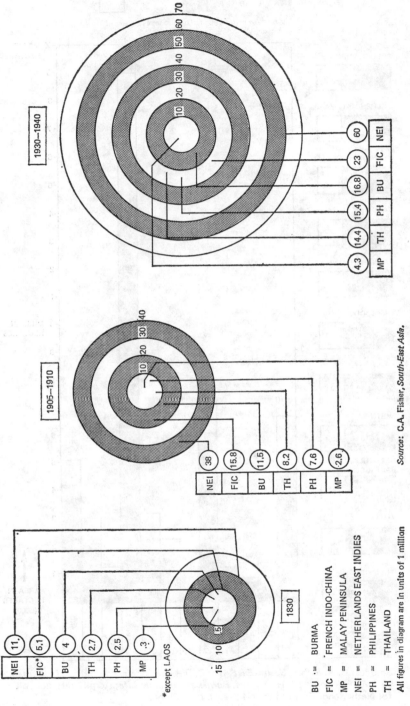

BU	=	BURMA
FIC	=	FRENCH INDO-CHINA
MP	=	MALAY PENINSULA
NEI	=	NETHERLANDS EAST INDIES
PH	=	PHILIPPINES
TH	=	THAILAND

*except LAOS

All figures in diagram are in units of 1 million

Source: C.A. Fisher, *South-East Asia.*

5. Population Growth in South-East Asia, 1830–1940

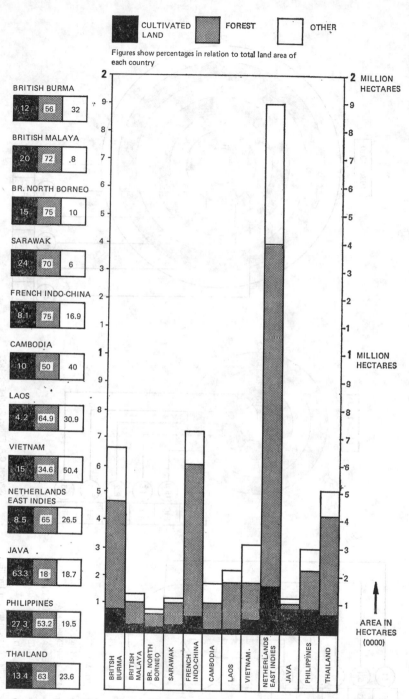

CULTIVATED LAND **FOREST** **OTHER**

Figures show percentages in relation to total land area of each country

BRITISH BURMA	12	56	32
BRITISH MALAYA	20	72	.8
BR. NORTH BORNEO	15	75	10
SARAWAK	24	70	6
FRENCH INDO-CHINA	8.1	75	16.9
CAMBODIA	10	50	40
LAOS	4.2	64.9	30.9
VIETNAM	15	34.6	50.4
NETHERLANDS EAST INDIES	8.5	65	26.5
JAVA	63.3	18	18.7
PHILIPPINES	27.3	53.2	19.5
THAILAND	13.4	63	23.6

2 MILLION HECTARES

1 MILLION HECTARES

AREA IN HECTARES (0000)

BRITISH BURMA — BRITISH MALAYA — BR. NORTH BORNEO — SARAWAK — FRENCH INDO-CHINA — CAMBODIA — LAOS — VIETNAM — NETHERLANDS EAST INDIES — JAVA — PHILIPPINES — THAILAND

Sources: C. A. Fisher, *South-East Asia*; C. Robequain, *Malaya, Indonesia, Borneo and the Philippines*; J. R. Andrus, *Burmese Economic Life*; Admirien Handbook for Netherlands East Indies and French Indo-China.

6. Land Utilization in South-East Asia in the late 1930s

[1]The Industrial Revolution has been succinctly described as 'the rise of modern in dustry', J.R. Hicks, *A Theory of Economic History*, Oxford University Press, London, 1969, p. 141, while Arnold Toynbee identifies the rise of modern industry with the 'four great inventions' (Arkwright's water-frame, 1769; Hargreaves' spinning jenny, 1776; Crompton's mule, 1779; and Kelly's self-acting mule) which together with the application of steam power to these and other mechanical inventions revolutionized manufacturing. Hence 'revolution' here is applied in the sense in which one speaks of the Neolithic Revolution, that is of a process of economic, social and cultural change caused by the introduction of new modes of production. The chief characteristic of the Industrial Revolution has been the substitution of the individual techniques of production typical of mediaeval craftsmen by team production carried out in factories governed by the laws of machines. Since such a process has evolved in different industries at different rates and in different places at different times, the Industrial Revolution as a whole cannot be pinpointed with exactitude to one particular area or to one particular development. This has given scope for varied interpretations as to the meaning and application of the term, but the mainstream of historical opinion accepts that the Industrial Revolution or the rise of modern industry as such emerged and acquired its salient characteristics in the century which followed the cotton-machine inventions in eighteenth-century England. The term 'Industrial Revolution' itself is often associated with the German political thinker, Friedrich Engels, who used it in his writings in the 1840s, but there is evidence that the term was current amongst French writers at least two decades earlier.

[2]For a full discussion of the impact of the opening of the Suez Canal on the trade of Singapore and the Straits, see G.E. Bogaars, 'The Effect of the Opening of the Suez Canal on the Trade and Development of Singapore', *JMBRAS*, XXVIII, 2 and XXXXII, 1, 1969.

[3]For the background to shipping rivalries and politics, refer to G.C. Allen and Audrey G. Donnithorne, *Western Enterprise in Indonesia and Malaya*, George Allen & Unwin, London, 1954 and C.D. Cowan (ed.), *The Economic Development of South-East Asia*, George Allen & Unwin, London, 1964.

[4]The German firm of Norddeutscher Lloyd, for instance, was forced to withdraw its services with the ports of North Sumatra in the 1900s.

[5]One of the greatest achievements in sugar research came in 1925 with the development of a revolutionary new strain of sugar-cane (PJ 2878), which enabled production per acre to rise by 60 per cent.

[6]For the background to the rise of the tin industry, see Wong Lin-ken, *The Malayan Tin Industry to 1914*, University of Arizona Press, 1965, pp. 3–17.

[7]For the general background to oil mining in the Indies, see Allen & Donnithorne, op. cit.

[8]i.e. in particular, the discovery of the process of vulcanization, brought about by heating rubber in combination with sulphur, which provided the basis on which the modern rubber industry could be built. Vulcanization altered the physical properties of rubber, making it far stronger and durable without losing its pliability or elasticity. It also removed rubber's offensive odour and surface adhesiveness. See T.R. McHale, *Rubber and the Malaysian Economy*, M.P.H. Publications, Singapore, 1967, p. 14.

[9]For further details about Socfin and the palm-oil industry in general, see J.S.D. Rawlins, 'French Enterprise in Malaya', *JMBRAS*, XXXIX, 2, 1966.

[10]The oldest such centre in the region was at Weltevreden, just outside Batavia, where Eijkman was the first man to prove scientifically the connexion between beri-beri and polished rice. Other centres included the two Pasteur Institutes in French Indo-China, the Institute of Medical Research in Malaya, the Harcourt-Butler Institute of Public Health in Burma and the Bureau of Science in the Philippines.

[11]The Straits Settlements were obliged to adhere to the decisions of the Ottawa Conference of 1932, by which the new system of 'Imperial Preference' was imposed on the British colonial empire.

[12]Amongst the most celebrated of such business houses today are Guthries, Bousteads and Mansfields. For background, see Allen & Donnithorne, op. cit.

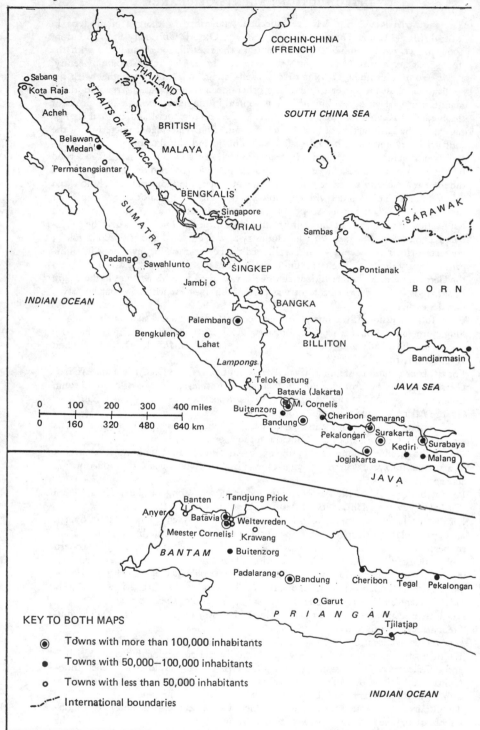

COCHIN-CHINA
(FRENCH)

THAILAND

SOUTH CHINA SEA

Sabang
Kota Raja

Acheh

STRAITS OF MALACCA

BRITISH

MALAYA

Belawan
Medan

Permatangsiantar

BENGKALIS

Singapore

RIAU

SUMATRA

SARAWAK

Sambas

Pontianak

Padang
Sawahlunto

SINGKEP

Jambi

BORN[EO]

INDIAN OCEAN

BANGKA

Palembang

Bengkulen
Lahat

BILLITON

Lampongs

Bandjarmasin

Telok Betung
Batavia (Jakarta)

JAVA SEA

0   100   200   300   400 miles
0   160   320   480   640 km

Buitenzorg M. Cornelis
Bandung   Cheribon Semarang
Pekalongan Surakarta
Kediri Surabaya
Jogjakarta   Malang

JAVA

Banten Tandjung Priok
Anyer   Batavia Weltevreden
Meester Cornelis Krawang

BANTAM Buitenzorg

Padalarang Bandung   Cheribon Tegal Pekalongan

Garut

PRIANGAN

Tjilatjap

KEY TO BOTH MAPS

◉ Towns with more than 100,000 inhabitants

● Towns with 50,000–100,000 inhabitants

○ Towns with less than 50,000 inhabitants

–·–·– International boundaries

INDIAN OCEAN

3. General Map of the Netherlands East Indies, 1940 (with Java in inset below)

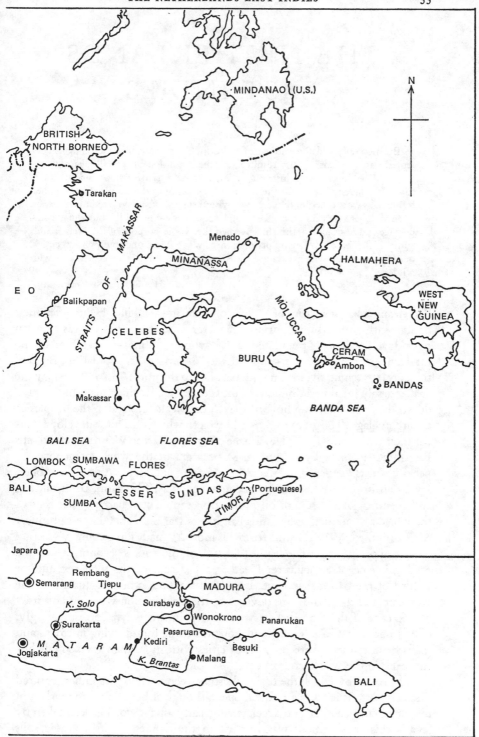

THE NETHERLANDS
EAST INDIES

'But not only did the pattern of Government succeed in establishing a contented state of affairs, it also resulted ... in the expansion of a well-balanced economy. The Government introduced Western industrial methods and manufactures and thereby promoted the material well-being of the people. Distinguished technicians were called in to plan and advise; usury was banned; credit banks were opened. There was no room for complacency—there never is—but quiet competence and restrained optimism governed the whole purpose of the Netherlands authorities. There were many peoples; there was but one omnibus political entity, one Government which exercised its powers clemently, beneficently and with wisdom.'

Professor P.S. Gerbrandy.[1]

THREE and a half centuries of Dutch colonialism called into being a far-flung nation with almost schizophrenic characteristics. In the centre was Java, an over-developed, over-populated island whose confines—9 per cent of the total land area of the Indies—supported two-thirds of its population. Beyond this core, stretching over thousands of miles to the north, east and west lay the vast, sparsely inhabited domains of the Outer Islands which nevertheless produced the overwhelming bulk of the export wealth sustaining the peoples of the archipelago. The great resources of wealth which the Dutch developed under their rule cannot be denied. On the eve of the Pacific War the Netherlands East Indies produced or exported 82 per cent of the world's cinchona, 79 per cent of its pepper, 70 per cent of its kapok and 38 per cent of its rubber. It was an important source for coconut products, fibres, tin, palm-oil, tea, coffee and sugar. Although oil production represented barely 3 per cent of the world's total, the Netherlands East Indies was the second largest producer east of Iran, while the revenue from this industry made it the country's second most important export. Another feature of the Indies' economy was the predominance of agriculture. Nearly 70 per cent of the total revenue, or a third of the national income, came from export crops. A quarter of the whole area of the islands was devoted to their cultivation while on Java itself 70 per cent of the land surface was utilized in this way. Correspondingly, only 5 per cent of the total population was to be found living in towns and (before 1941) there were only seven cities with more than 100,000 inhabitants each in the whole country.

The process by which the basic subsistence economy of the Indies acquired these characteristics was a gradual one, although it became more marked in the nineteenth century and accelerated greatly after 1870. The lead taken by Java in this development was implicit in the richness of its volcanic soils which came to support the only genuine agrarian power centre in the archipelago and made the island the focal point of its culture. Although the Europeans came first and foremost for the spices of the Moluccas, Java's importance was not lost for long on the Dutch who within a decade of their arrival had earmarked it as the local headquarters of their power. By the eighteenth century Javanese sugar and coffee had displaced nutmeg, mace and cloves as the mainstays of Dutch enterprise in the region. The exploitation of Java was intensified in the nineteenth century under a restored Dutch regime which introduced the so-called Culture System, virtually converting the island into a vast market garden for Western Europe. Under the Culture System the development of Java reached its climax and the mould of twentieth century Javanese society was cast. Sugar and coffee retained their prime positions, although important new crops, notably tea and cinchona, were added. But by the time that the Suez Canal was opened in 1869, a new era was dawning. The system of government monopoly yielded before a new order of private capital and free enterprise. With this, great changes in the pattern of development followed. Up to this point tin and pepper had been the only important commodities to be produced outside Java. Under the new impetus of private capital, new crops were tried and new industries arose, all of which were centred in the Outer Islands. Amongst these were tobacco and oil, and later on rubber and palm-oil. During the first decade of the twentieth century the traditional exports of the Indies had been surpassed by these newcomers and Java had been displaced by Sumatra as the chief source of income and wealth.

The development of Java
Nevertheless the outstanding feature of the economic development of the Indies under Dutch rule was the intensive exploitation of Java. By the start of the twentieth century the island had reached saturation point as far as its productivity was concerned. By 1930 Java and Madura were carrying a population of forty-one and three-quarter millions and the intensity of population pressure on the land is indicated by the size of the average landholding which was a mere $1\frac{1}{2}$ acres per head in 1941. The basic reasons for Java's over-development lay, as Fisher points out,[2] in its intrinsic productiveness, in the evolution of a sophisticated agrarian culture based on the principal rice-bearing regions and finally in the market-garden techniques and hydraulic expertise which the Dutch applied to the production of export crops. But the characteristics of Java's economic development today were determined above all by the application of the Culture System in the nineteenth century.

Generations before, however, Java had superseded the Moluccas as the chief object of Dutch interest. 'The island of Banda and the Moluccas are the chief mark at which we shoot',[3] declared the Directors in the early days of the Dutch East India Company (VOC), but although the Company's motto was 'therefore plough the sea', it was soon clear that it could not operate effectively without a base on land. The VOC ruthlessly imposed its monopoly over the Moluccas, as indeed it had to in order to survive,[4] but it was evident that those islands would not provide a firm base. Java offered an appropriate alternative, situated at a focal centre for archipelago trade and the source of abundant food supplies. The subsequent founding of the Dutch headquarters in the Indies at Jakarta in 1619 led inevitably to the Company's involvement in Javanese politics. The need for security led to the long drawn out struggle with Mataram. The first weapons in this contest were economic blockade, the Sunan's attempt to deprive Batavia of its rice teaching the Dutch to grow their own. The Company's concern to dominate all local trade both to strike at Mataram and to complete its own monopoly led to its interest in the produce of Java. In the second half of the seventeenth century the Company took the first step in its transition from merchant to land-lord, from seeking trade to seeking tribute. The imminent collapse of the Mataram dynasty before Trunojoyo led in 1677 to the first of those treaties by which its rulers traded their heritage for their security. The treaty of 1677 was a turning point in the evolution of the Company and of Dutch colonial power in the archipelago. For not only did the Dutch acquire valuable terri-tory (West Priangan and Semarang) but important commercial concessions as well, amongst which was the undertaking of the Sunan to supply them with a large fixed quantity of rice each year at market price. Bantam's ruler found himself making a similar agreement regarding pepper in the following decade, and so began the system which in the eighteenth century was to provide the main source of the Company's profits—the system of 'forced deliveries' or, as Furnivall puts it,[5] 'tribute disguised as trade', and of 'con-tingencies', which was tribute undisguised. The forced deliveries, extended as Mataram's kings made fresh concessions to secure Dutch backing for their authority in the successive internal upheavals they faced, were ostensibly trading contracts by which rice or cash crops were supplied to the Dutch in Batavia on terms highly favourable to the Company; since they were im-posed in lieu of payment for services rendered, the Javanese princes were compelled to abide by their terms. The contingencies were the cash crops grown at the behest of the Company on lands which the Company had acquired and directly ruled. Here the local Javanese aristocrat was required to enter into a contract to provide certain quantities of a specified cash crop in place of the tribute he formerly paid to the court of Mataram or Bantam. The main crops involved were rice, pepper, sugar, coffee and indigo, thereby giving the Dutch a direct stake in agricultural production on the island. Sugar and coffee soon displaced spices and pepper in importance in the Company's ledgers and the Javanese ruling classes became inextricably in-volved with the Company's officials as their principal agents. For the Dutch, by demanding tribute in kind, were in fact exploiting the feudal-type bonds which linked the Javanese peasant to his overlord. The payments which the Company made for its forced deliveries from Mataram, on the other hand, rarely went into the hands of the cultivators themselves, but were held by the landlord or by the Chinese lessee to whom many estates were farmed out.[6] For as long as the Company survived this system was allowed to devel-op and become consolidated, turning Java into the richest and most prof-itable of its domains.

The overthrow of mercantilism: the debate on colonial policy
At the end of the eighteenth century, however, this monopolistic system of exploitation was challenged. The free trade, utilitarian school of thought led

by Adam Smith and his contemporaries[7] in Europe questioned the efficacy and productivity of forced cultivation and state monopolies and recommended the virtues of free enterprise and individual ownership, which, they argued, acted as far greater stimuli to economic progress. These liberal ideas found their exponents in Holland as much as elsewhere and in the disturbed circumstances which came at the close of the century, they found an outlet. The first circumstance which permitted a challenge to the old way of doing things was the impending collapse of the Company itself. Its final downfall was precipitated by the outbreak of the French Revolutionary Wars in 1792, leading three years later to revolution in Holland itself, followed by a French occupation and domination which lasted until the overthrow of Napoleon Bonaparte in 1814. Against the background of this period, during which Holland underwent five major changes in its form of government, the whole field of colonial policy was re-examined and debated, while Java was made the scene of important experiments which shaped Dutch colonial policy in the nineteenth century and influenced the development of the island as a whole.[8]

The debate on colonial policy which now took place basically turned on the merits of free as opposed to state enterprise. The case for free enterprise was first formally presented by Dirk van Hogendorp, the son of a well-placed Company official, who in 1800 published a 'Report on Conditions in the Batavian Possessions in East India'. Based on the utilitarian theory of self-interest, which Hogendorp, unlike many of his European contemporaries, held to be as applicable in the East as in the West, he argued for the five basic principles of a liberal political economy—private ownership of land, freedom of the person, freedom of trade, the abolition of forced labour and personal services, and the provision of good, impartial and inexpensive justice.[9] The counter-premise of the protagonists of mercantilism was well summed up in the report of the second Nederburgh Committee of 1802 which maintained that 'in a sense excluding all injustice, the colonies exist for the mother country, and not the mother country for the colonies'. This argument then went on to show that the mother country's interests were not to be served by the establishment of private ownership of the land in Java or by the liberating of the Javanese peasant from his enforced burdens. Nederburgh and his supporters, having the weight of the Dutch establishment behind them, won the day. But events overwhelmed them when in 1806 Napoleon Bonaparte set up his Kingdom of Holland giving the country a new constitution and bringing it much more closely under French supervision. The new regime saw a revival of Hogendorp's influence and of his plans for Java, and the appointment of Marshal Daendels in 1807 as governor of the island with instructions to 'cure the abuses which had crept in under the Company' and to 'improve the lot of the common man and protect him from arbitrary treatment' marked the first attempt to secure their practical application in the Indies.

The first Liberal experiment
Nevertheless the days of free enterprise were not yet at hand. For the next

twenty-five years attempts were made at its establishment, but all of its various authors were beaten by circumstance. Daendels, whose own arrival in Java was delayed by the necessity to evade British naval patrols, quickly found his whole position undermined by the British blockade which robbed Java of its natural overseas markets. So although he set out to replace compulsory cultivation with a system of regular land rent, to abolish forced labour and to prevent the alienation of village lands to Chinese merchants, the new governor ended up by doing the very opposite. At the same time, he had to cope with corruption and incompetence on the part of his officials, with the indifference of the Javanese cultivators and with a severe shortage of private entrepreneurs or private capital. When he was recalled by Napoleon in 1811, Daendels had completely failed in his economic aims.

The Daendels' regime, after a brief interlude, was followed by a British interregnum of four years under the hand of Stamford Raffles. Raffles, as steward for Britain, went all out to secure the retention of Java for the British Crown, and was therefore committed to the idea of a free economy based on self-supporting peasants who paid land rent. For British interests, as opposed to those of the Dutch, required a market in which to sell, not merely a source of cheap cash crops, which in turn presupposed a prosperous peasantry able to purchase the manufactured goods the British had to offer. Raffles was able to introduce his land rent system, although his tenure of power was too short to see its consequences. But financial stringencies compelled him too to follow Daendels and sell large estates to private owners and to continue with compulsory coffee cultivation and the use of forced labour.

When Dutch rule was finally restored in 1816, the new administrators were also committed to Liberal principles. The Commissioners-general came with instructions to improve 'the lot of the common Javanese', to encourage free cultivation, to introduce a land rent system, and to implement a decree throwing all commerce in the Indies to open competition. On arrival, they found of course that Raffles had already taken important steps along the same path, and after consulting local opinion, Elout, their leader, decided to adopt the British system in its essentials. This meant accepting Raffles' land revenue system and encouraging free peasant cultivation, supplemented by capitalist enterprise and state intervention as and where necessary, policies which were confirmed with the publication of the Regerings-Reglementen (RR) of 1818.[10] However, the Commissioners-general soon found themselves in grave difficulties, inherent in a policy which went against the true interests of Holland at that time, since open competition laid Java bare to the activities of British (and American) firms against whom, without protection, the Dutch themselves could not compete. Other problems arose. Van der Capellen, left behind in sole charge after 1818, became concerned over the problem of state revenues since the land rent system was not yet operating effectively and private capitalists were in fact in competition with government enterprise. With their cash advances to Javanese cultivators and their large-scale land leases in the semi-autonomous principalities of Surakarta and Jogjakarta, they were threatening to undermine the independence and prosperity of the very groups on whom the new Liberal policy was to be based.

Developments in the early 1820s settled the fate of the liberal experiment once for all. Coffee, one of Java's staple exports, suffered a disastrous slump on the world market in 1822, which completely destroyed the financial equilibrium of the Indies administration, while the competition from British and American interests continued unchecked. Finally in 1825 the Java War broke out, which made the problem of Java's finances a basic political issue in the Netherlands themselves.

The foundation of the Nederlandse Handlesmattschappij (N.H.M.) in 1824 by the king himself was in reality the first step towards the bringing of the Liberal experiment to an end. The specific purpose of the new company was to combat British competition, which, so the king had been informed by Muntinghe the previous year, dominated Java's trade. The Articles of Association stated explicitly that the N.H.M. was intended to serve as an import and export agency for the Dutch throughout the whole world and that it would even take the place of a regular consular service in providing Dutch merchants and businessmen with the commercial information which they required. With its capital of ƒ37 million, the N.H.M. felt sufficiently well backed to meet the British challenge. However, the Count du Bus de Gisignies, a liberal 'poorer for the loss of some illusions',[11] who replaced van der Capellen in 1825 as governor of Java, made one last effort to run things on liberal lines. Stating in his report of May 1827, that while with Raffles the aim was to 'increase the welfare of the peasant and we can sell him more', he aimed to 'increase production and the peasant will be able to buy more',[12] du Bus sought to boost output through the supply of Western capital, technology and supervision. Advantage was to be taken of the availability of cheap labour in thickly populated districts to grant concessions to Western capitalists on easy terms while Javanese aristocrats would be encouraged to go in for farming on a large scale by granting them land in place of allowances. The legal basis for du Bus's scheme was provided by the RR of 1827, but it was still-born, strangled by the exigencies and high costs of the Java War.

The Culture System
The way, therefore, was open for the abandonment of the Liberal experiment entirely and its substitution by the old principles of forced cultivation and compulsory services in new guise as the Culture System. Under the Culture System, which created a planned economy on an 'imperial scale', the stage was set for the period of the most intense exploitation in the island's history, as a result of which the Javanese economy acquired the features that it has today. However, the Liberal experiment also left its mark, for the remodelling and centralization of the administration of Java created the institutional framework which made the implementation of the new System possible.

The Culture System was introduced simply to make Java pay, that is to make Java show a profit and to enable this to happen on the resources of Java alone. Since the end of the previous century, when the VOC finally collapsed, the Dutch administration of Java had been run at a loss. Despite an apparent climb to recovery after 1816 the situation became aggravated again after 1822 with the collapse of the world coffee market, which struck at the island's principal export crop. Following this van der Capellen found himself obliged to raise a huge loan in British India, which was one of the chief reasons for his recall in 1825; then came the disaster of the Java War which left the Indies government with debts of over ƒ30 million. In the meantime the economy of the homeland had not yet recovered from the national catastrophe which accompanied the revolutionary and Napoleonic epoch in Europe, and despite the efforts of their new and energetic ruler, William I, the Dutch middle classes were not showing any sign of reasserting their former initiative and enterprise. It was at this juncture that Johannes van den Bosch, a confidante of the king with a considerable and varied experience of administration and social reform both in Holland and overseas, came forward with his scheme. Van den Bosch saw, in short, that the only solution which could bring in quick returns was to revert to a monopoly system of trade. He rejected the liberal solution of Raffles based on the independent peasant cultivator as being suitable neither to Dutch needs nor to the Javanese background; he rejected du Bus's plans for private capital on the sound grounds that in fact there was none such forthcoming. Moreover monopoly was essential to overcome the crushing competition of British and American traders. So van den Bosch proposed the re-establishment of a system based on compulsory cultivation. In this way cash crops would be supplied at the most economical rate and shipped for disposal on the European market. Amsterdam and Rotterdam would be restored as the chief centres for tropical produce in Europe, and a guaranteed market would be created in Java itself for the disposal of the goods from Holland's own newly-developing industries. The plan implied of course a government monopoly over the shipment and disposal of the produce as well as over their cultivation and delivery. But the instrument for this was already at hand in the shape of the N.H.M., founded by the king himself but so far not living up to the high hopes it had engendered. So the N.H.M. was made the backbone of the complementary Consignment System, whereby all the cash crops delivered under the Culture System were to be transported in the company's bottoms back to Holland for their disposal on the European market.

Although the prime object of the System was to convert the Java deficits into credits, van den Bosch argued that this would work out to the benefit of government and cultivator alike, since the rewards would be shared by both. In the detailed schedule for the System laid down in the RR of 1830, there were many checks and safeguards designed to ensure that the System should not be abused or weigh unduly heavily on the cultivator. In place of the established land rent which was reckoned in terms of two-fifths of the value in cash of the landholder's crop, the government would take one-fifth of its value in kind. In other words the landholder or village was to devote one-fifth of the land for the cultivation of an export or cash crop stipulated by the government, working it without pay in place of paying for the land rent. The cultivator was not to be required to give more of his labour than the cultivation of an equal amount of rice would have required, and should the value of the crop so produced exceed in value the original land rent, the balance would be credited to him by the government. In the case of sugar-cultivation, where more elaborate arrangements were necessary to prepare the commodity for the market, van den Bosch laid down that the cultivators in a particular village should be divided into four groups—one for planting, one for reaping, one for transporting the crop to the factory and one for the factory itself. In any case the same general conditions applied, while any extra services were to be paid for. The System, which was started on a voluntary basis, was inspired by the existing arrangements between the Dutch authorities and the coffee-growers of the Priangan, who paid no land rent at all but remitted their dues in coffee to the government. As in the Priangan the new system was to be administered by the traditional Javanese regent who in this way reassumed considerable authority as a sort of plantation overseer, while a European official was appointed as his supervisor. Van den Bosch made it his first aim to raise the production of export crops in general in the island to the level of the Priangan where the average yield was estimated at ƒ5 per household.

The implementation of the Culture System

Van den Bosch was appointed governor-general of the Indies in 1828 and arrived to take up his appointment at Batavia at the beginning of 1830. His first steps to implement the system were made during his first tour of the island soon afterwards, when he entered into agreements with certain village headmen for the supply of sugar-cane and indigo in place of money for land rent. At the same time, he encouraged European contractors to take over the produce and prepare it for export on behalf of the government. In August the same year van den Bosch made his first contracts with the N.H.M. for shipments of indigo and sugar. The shipments were to be made in Dutch vessels and to be paid for by bills of exchange at eight months after the date for the quantity delivered. In April 1831, to encourage their interest, officials—European and Javanese—were granted commissions based on the percentages of the cash crops delivered from their districts.

The early results were very successful. At the end of the first year, van den Bosch was able to balance the Indies accounts for the first time in the century and he anticipated remitting ƒ5—ƒ6 million within the next five years for the payment of debts long outstanding. But this promise was not necessary to secure the official confirmation of the system, for in the same year the outbreak of the Belgian War of Secession[13] made its implementation indispensable. The Belgian War was the last of the great tribulations which had afflicted the Dutch people since 1792. The loss of the Belgian provinces was a serious blow to van den Bosch's plans to stimulate the development of home industries because they contained the principal manufacturing centres in the kingdom. Of more immediate concern, however, were the expenses of the war which had to be met, together with the lamentable fact that hitherto William I had raised the extra money he needed for his pet schemes from Belgium itself, a source now denied him. It now became clear that the Culture System would have to serve not merely as a scheme to make Java pay out of its own resources but also as an instrument for saving Holland itself. As Baud, van den Bosch's successor in Java and a staunch supporter of the System aptly declared, under it Java became 'the lifebelt on which the Netherlands kept afloat'.[14] The System was made compulsory in 1831, in particular for sugar and indigo. By the instructions of the following February, officials were required to deliver cash crops at the rate of ƒ2 per head from their respective districts. At the beginning of 1833 the System was extended to coffee and to other crops.

The results of the Culture System

In terms of its aims, the Culture System must be adjudged a great success. 'Java poured forth riches upon riches on the homeland as if by a magician's wand', wrote the Dutch historian, de Waal.[15] The batig slot, or surplus balance on accounts being closed, which was remitted from the Batavian treasury to Holland annually mounted from an average ƒ9.3 million a year between 1831 and 1840 to an average of ƒ14.1 million in the next decade, and reached its peak in 1851 with ƒ15 million. Between 1840 and 1874 an estimated ƒ781 million were remitted to Holland as the batig slot, four-fifths of which was accounted for by the profits on coffee. With these huge sums, Holland was able to effect a complete economic recovery; the national debt was settled, the foundations of the national railway system laid and Amsterdam was restored as one of the great financial capitals of the West. The N.H.M., which had had such a shaky start, was transformed. In 1831 it was reorganized to enable it to cope with the role van den Bosch had assigned it as a commercial agent for the government and the firm moved from its headquarters at The Hague to Amsterdam. In 1833 the company advanced money to the government for the first time against sales of produce, and also undertook to import goods and bullion into Java at its own expense against the proceeds of government cultures on the island. In 1835 the N.H.M. was extending its operations to the private sector, as more speculators became involved, and played an important role in securing a market for Dutch cottons. By 1840 two-thirds of Java's exports passed through the company's hands.

In Java itself the System promoted a tremendous expansion in staples like sugar, coffee and indigo which in fact were and remained its mainstays, and it also brought about considerable diversification of the island's economy by stimulating the cultivation of other products such as tea, tobacco, cinnamon, cochineal, pepper, silk and cotton. It must be admitted that most of these, for various reasons, did not prove a great success at the time, although some, particularly tea and tobacco, became important later. The Culture System also led to the introduction of scientific methods of agriculture, especially after 1833 when a salaried Director of Cultures was appointed to take the place of the unpaid Agricultural Committee.

A great improvement in communications also took place. In 1830 Daendels' trunk east-west road was still the only major highway on Java, but twenty years later an English observer was comparing the state and extent of Javanese roads and bridges favourably with those of British India. These new roads were built by the conscript labour which the Culture System made so available, as were also the first modern irrigation works in the island. The construction of a 'huge' irrigation canal to support the indigo culture in Bagelen, west of Jogjakarta, and to supply the new administrative centre of the Purworejo region, the draining of the basin of the Lukolo river and the commencement of the modern irrigation system in the Brantas Delta were all carried out in this period. A number of factories were also built, particularly for the indigo industry. Other evidence of the general material progress in Java in the first ten years after 1830 was to be seen in the steady rise of population, in the increased revenues from salt and bazaar dues, as also from the land, and in the rise and spread of rice production. All this, coupled with the simultaneous rise in cotton imports, which even more significantly fell within the next decade when things were not going so well, shows that there was without doubt considerable economic development in Java under the Culture System.

The region where the Culture System worked at its best was in the sugar-growing districts of East Java. Here the evolution of a system of shared risks between European entrepreneurs and Javanese planters favoured careful supervision of planting and cropping so as to ensure a proper balance between sugar and rice production. In consequence the government got its deliveries and the peasant also prospered since he had a new source of income in addition to his rice. Division of labour gave rise to a new class of people who earned their living as carriers, not cultivators, and became in fact the customers of the latter. In general, all partook in the new prosperity, albeit the Javanese to a modest degree.

However, the System operated unevenly, and while it worked well in some areas these were limited and happened to be suitable for the crops in question. On the other hand there is plenty of evidence of mistakes, carelessness and abuse, all of which bore down on the cultivator. Although, for example, coffee is a hill crop, determined and disastrous attempts were made to grow it in the plains. Attempts to plant tea in the Japara residency also proved a burdensome failure, while soon after the System's introduction Baud himself was complaining bitterly of ill-chosen factory sites, poor labour organization and incompetent management. More serious still was the basic failure to ensure a proper balance between cash and food crop production. Van den Bosch laid great stress on the need to secure adequate rice cultivation and a stream of ordinances (1837, 1844, 1847) from Batavia repeated his warnings. But they too often fell on deaf ears. The limitations on land and labour were all too frequently ignored. One-third or even one-half of the cultivators' or village land was taken up in many cases, and there were some even more extreme instances.[16]

Together with this went gross carelessness, deliberate or otherwise, in administration. Land used for sugar was not de-rooted before being handed back to the cultivator for padi-planting; rice-bunds were broken down for sugar or indigo and not replaced; services beyond those required by the System were very poorly paid, if at all, while—in the case of sugar—the cultivator was usually paid for his crop not by the cane he delivered but according to the final output from the factory. Another severe burden on the cultivator was the stipulation that he should bear the costs of transporting his crop to the government store or factory. Had such centres been numerous this would not have mattered much, but a parsimonious administration intent on extracting every ounce of profit (which indeed was what made the great contributions to the home-land possible), sited its stores sparsely to serve wide areas. Journeys of thirty miles from the fields to the delivery station were common, distances of up to eighty miles not unknown, the costs of which were entirely borne by the cultivator.

Behind all these abuses and injustices lay the iniquitous commission system which gave officials their incentive to ensure the maximum deliveries from their districts. Fixed at 10 per cent of their value in 1831, handsome deliveries could pay handsome dividends, and it was not unusual for Dutch and Javanese supervisors to be able to double and more than double their ordinary salaries by these means. The annual bill for the payment of these commissions stood at around ƒ1 million, based on three cash crops alone. Apart from the inducement of the commission, government officials were made to feel that their careers depended on good results—as the Dutch Resident of Pekalongan discovered in 1835 when he was put on half pay because of the failure of the local indigo culture—while those who protested too much against the System soon found it advisable to leave. In the case of the Javanese officials, the abuse was probably worse for the regent was 'a Javanese prince... The question for him is not that of getting his living; he must live according to his rank.' The answer lay in making the fullest use of his traditional rights, now confirmed to him by the Batavian administration, so as at least to make ends meet.[17] The net result was to increase the cultivators' burdens manifold.

The final folly came in the early 1840s in the Residency of Cheribon which, when the System was begun, had been predominantly a rice-growing area. However, within the first ten years, the residency came to be planted with coffee, sugar, tea, indigo and cinnamon. Then the decision was taken to add rice itself to the list of cash crops, and in 1843 a firm was granted the contract to collect the dues in rice and mill the produce for export. The immediate consequence was a famine in which hundreds died and thousands fled to other districts. From this point right into the 1860s famine was endemic in certain parts of Java. In the epic famine of 1849–50 in Central Java, over one-third of a million persons are reckoned to have died whilst in some of the worst-affected regencies starvation and flight reduced their populations to one-third of the original number.[18] Accompanying the famines were other signs of decline. Rice exports understandably fell off, but so did cotton piece-good imports—although other imported articles, mostly for European settlers, retained their normal level. There was also a decline in exports, though this was partly due to changed conditions on the world market outside. It was evident as the Culture System entered its second decade in the 1840s that it had reached its limits and that it had become an agent for increasing poverty rather than one which brought—at least in some areas— growing prosperity.

The effects of the Culture System

The Culture System has had a bad press. As Furnivall points out, it was followed by a liberal reaction, and liberals painted it in the darkest colours. The modern age of nationalist feeling also finds one of its scapegoats in the Culture System, so that to arrive at a balanced appraisal of the System becomes a difficult matter, 'rather like trying to ascertain the truth about a heresy which survives only in the works of the orthodox'.[19] As Furnivall also indicates, it can be doubted whether the Javanese peasant would in fact have come off any better had he been subjected to the Raffles-Muntinghe experiment of petty smallholdings and free enterprise which would probably have landed him in the arms of the moneylender, or to du Bus's scheme of capitalist exploitation where the profits would have gone to the European planters.

What does matter about the System is its effect on the development of the Javanese economy, and ultimately on that of the Indies as a whole. In the first place there was the sheer concentration of Dutch effort on Java. Although the System was also applied in the late 1830s to parts of West Sumatra and North Celebes, it was really only of significance on the island of Java itself. Even so, at its height, that is between 1840 and 1850, government cultures occupied a mere $5\frac{1}{2}$ per cent of cleared land (1845), a figure that had dropped by over 2 per cent ten years later, and it never involved more than a quarter of the island's population in any one given year. But this was enough to accentuate still further the differences between Java and the other islands of the archipelago in terms of development and population. It also marked the growth of a basic dichotomy in the colonial economy of the Indies, between the sphere of export crop production dominated by Western capital, management and techniques on the one hand, and that of production for native consumption on the other. The first sphere where the Javanese played a purely passive role and received a diminutive share of the profits which accrued, was capital-intensive and prosperous; the second was labour-intensive and one in which the Javanese was the central figure as he sank into deeper poverty.

Yet another by-product of the System was the benefits it bestowed on the Europeans and even more so on the Chinese in the country. They filled the role of the middlemen—the contractors, millers, agents, distributors, and the like. The Chinese in particular gained a position of influence and power in trade and commerce out of all proportion to their numbers, a fact which was amongst the first things to arouse the attention of Indonesia's future nationalists.

The Liberal revival

Despite the excesses and the impoverishing effects of the Culture System, there was no serious movement against its application either in Java or in the other islands. There was some unrest in Pasaruan when the System was extended to sugar in 1833 and isolated and spasmodic outbreaks elsewhere, but the more general Javanese reaction took the form of low yields and indifferent labour.[20] In fact, the movement to end the Culture System had its roots in Holland and was fundamentally the fruit of the seeds of prosperity sown by the System itself in that country.

The Culture System was brought to an end by those who wished to abolish the government monopoly over the produce and trade of the Indies and to open up the colonial field to free enterprise. The new exponents of free enterprise revived the old controversies over colonial policy which had dominated the opening years of the century, and now repeated the Liberal arguments to support their views. Private enterprise had in fact never disappeared from Java even when the Culture System was at its height. Free cultivation had been permitted to continue under the System[21] and although its expansion was ultimately frustrated, private enterprise was on occasion actually encouraged. However, since according to the 1815 constitution granted to the newly-restored kingdom the colonies were the private domain of the king himself and their administration beyond the scrutiny or control of the States-general, colonial affairs remained a closed book for most Dutchmen, while in the depressed state of the country in the years which immediately followed the restoration there was little interest in public matters. Furthermore, the outbreak of the Belgian War in 1830 made it unpatriotic for the ensuing decade to question what was going on. But Liberalism revived in measure as prosperity was restored and the benefits of the Culture System made themselves felt in Holland's economic and commercial life. The first attention of the new generation of liberals was directed to the issue of the royal prerogatives over colonial affairs.

Their first opportunity to act came with the crisis of 1839, precipitated by King William I's request to the States-general for a loan of ƒ56 million to meet state debts to the N.H.M. and elsewhere. Already perturbed by the N.H.M.'s refusal to honour a draft for ƒ2½ million forced upon it by van den Bosch earlier in the year and by the news from the Indies tha thet Java Bank was refusing to cash its notes for silver, Holland's assemblymen declined to grant the loan, rejected the estimates for 1840 and demanded a strict accounting of the Indies finances. Heavily defeated, van den Bosch retired from office and the king, faced with a public repudiation of his policies, abdicated in favour of his son. The king died in 1843 and van den Bosch followed him to the grave six months later.

The downfall of van den Bosch marked the first step towards a Liberal victory over the Dutch Crown for control of the colonies. Under parliamentary pressure later the same year, the new Colonial Minister, Baud, who was determined to defend the batig slot at all costs, passed an amendment to the Fundamental Law purportedly giving the States-general a say in the colonial finances, but which in fact yielded no real power to the Assembly at all. However, Liberals now had something to bite their teeth into, and under the leadership of a Leyden professor called Thorbecke, they formed for the first time a coherent political group in the struggle with the Crown. Sudden victory came with the Year of Revolutions in 1848, the repercussions of which in Holland turned King William II 'from diehard to radical in a single night'.[22] Baud was dismissed and under Thorbecke's influence the country received a new constitution which definitively established the supremacy of parliament in all spheres. The new constitution provided for the drafting of fresh fundamental laws regarding the colonies and empowered the legislature to pass new laws concerning currency, financial administration and other matters as the need arose.

The rise of the Liberals: the parliamentary struggle

Although the Liberals had cleared the first hurdle and the way was open to control the direction of colonial policy, they still had to win the States-general over to their ideas. The Liberal Party in the Assembly was now led by the doctrinaire Thorbecke and the humanitarian Baron van Hoevell. Its ranks were swollen by the rising lobby of planters from the Indies who sought an outlet for their enterprise in Java, and of the manufacturers canvassing for new markets for their goods. Towards the end of the 1850s the exposure of the abuses of the Culture System enlisted the sympathies of the general public for the Liberal cause.

The Liberal struggle to control the States-general occupied the energies of half a generation. Under the first Liberal ministry of Thorbecke (1849–52), little progress was made towards the drafting of the fundamental laws regulating colonial affairs, for the Ministry of the Colonies was in the hands of Pahud, who was conservative. After an abortive attempt in 1851, the colonial RR was eventually passed in 1854, framed by Baud who was once again in office. Despite its conservative antecedents, the RR of 1854 was an important step forward. Although vague out of political necessity, it replaced arbitrary administration of the Indies with the rule of law, and made it possible for later and more progressive administrations to bring about effective control over colonial policy. It came into force in 1856. The Liberals themselves, who opposed the 1854 law for not being liberal enough, remained in parliamentary opposition for the rest of the decade, but grew in influence and crystallized their ideas. Under van Hoevell they concentrated their attention on the iniquitous sugar contracts.

In 1860 the tide turned decisively in the Liberal favour. A conservative member of the States-general secured a resolution in favour of the legal regulation of sugar contracts. In the same year public opinion was roused by two publications, one a book and the other a pamphlet, both of which exposed the abuses of the Culture System in round and unequivocable terms. The book, 'Max Havelaar', was written by Edward Douwes Dekker, a retired Indies official, under the pseudonym of 'Multatuli'. Dekker put with maximum force the humanitarian case against the Culture System. The pamphlet, which was entitled 'Sugar Contracts', embodied on the other hand the more practical criticisms by van der Putte, a retired sugar contractor from Java, of the whole system with cogent explanations as to why it was not only inhumane but also unprofitable. In arguing for the abandonment of government monopoly in favour of a system of granting free access to land and labour, van der Putte was sounding a new and much more pragmatic note in the Liberal chorus. His call was heard and well received by the directors of the N.H.M. and of the big banks. The Liberals had arrived.

The Liberal policy

In 1862 the new wave of public support for the Liberal Party placed Thor-becke back in power for the second time, with van der Putte as his Colonial Minister. A Liberal economic policy for the Indies was at once launched. In the same year the pepper culture was abandoned with the government interest being sold to private entrepreneurs. In 1863 cloves and nutmeg followed suit. In 1864 the important Accounts Law was passed by the States-general, which made it mandatory for the Indies Budget to be passed annually by the Assembly, securing at last effective scrutiny of colonial policy and finances. The cultures in indigo, tea, cinnamon and cochineal were given up in 1865 and that in tobacco the following year. For the cultures which remained the commission system was ended in the same year. In 1870 the Sugar Law, framed by the conservative minister, de Waal, was passed, providing for the progressive abandonment of the sugar culture in twelve annual stages, starting in 1878. Coffee, the most profitable of all, however, was retained until 1917. In 1870 de Waal also passed the Agrarian Law which laid down the basis for Dutch land policy in the Indies from that time onwards.

The thirty years from 1870 until the end of the century marked the hey-day of Dutch Liberalism. During this period more or less free rein was given to private capital to invest, speculate and exploit in the Indies while the Dutch home and colonial administrations withdrew more and more into the role of ring-masters. While, as we have seen, developments within the home country itself largely accounted for the Liberal triumph, its upsurge was also brought about by other attendant factors such as technological advance and improved communications which created a demand for more capital and made it at the same time more readily available. In this respect the opening of the Suez Canal in 1869 was an event of supreme importance for the Indies for it 'changed the whole economic environment'[23] and brought about much more intimate contacts in all spheres between the region and Europe.

De Waal's Agrarian Law was important because it created the conditions under which private enterprise might flourish in the Indies without upsetting the traditional structure of local society. The law itself was a statement of general principles regarding land policy, the details of which were worked out in subsequent ordinances and decrees. With the passing of van der Putte's tariff law of 1872 and the steps taken to abolish or reduce compulsory labour the apparatus for a Liberal economic colonial policy was completed.

Developments during the Liberal Era

The immediate results of the Liberal Policy were to be seen in a new spurt in production, particularly in sugar which was the industry which stood to gain most from the new course. The growth of private participation in this industry rose from 9 per cent in 1870 to 97 per cent two decades later; there was a similar increase in production and private enterprise in tea, coffee and even rice on Java, besides the development of new crops on the Outer Islands. There was also an extension of irrigation works on Java, a great improvement in communications and a general rise in revenue.

At first the lead in developing private enterprise was taken by individuals and small firms, mostly those having long connexions with the country. However the financial and harvest failures of the early 1880s destroyed the small individual entrepreneur and made possible the entry of the large corporate limited companies which through their links and combinations with powerful financial concerns came to dominate the colonial economy. At the same time there is little evidence that the Javanese benefited much by the new policy, or even felt its effects at all. For the era of Liberalism, despite all the brave prognostications of its standard-bearers, did nothing more than to accentuate the basic dichotomy of the island's economy that had appeared under the Culture System.

It was also during the Liberal period that the tremendous divergency between the development of Java and that of the Outer Islands was thrown into sharp relief. While between 1870 and 1900 the exploitation of Java reached its saturation point, the same period witnessed the 'take-off' in terms of economic development of the Outer Islands, particularly Sumatra and Borneo.

The rise of the Outer Islands
The failure of the Dutch to pay much attention to the Outer Islands prior to the last quarter of the nineteenth century was primarily brought about by the limitations of their own resources. The Culture System itself was nothing less than a device to raise the Javanese economy by its bootstraps, and was in reality based on the availability and exploitation of cheap labour which the underpopulated spaces of the rest of the archipelago could not provide. Van den Bosch perforce concentrated his efforts on Java, because 'except for Banda, Bangka, and—before long, I flatter myself—Sumatra, the rest are all unprofitable burdens.'[24] Consequently up till the second half of the century Dutch sovereignty outside Java was represented merely by officials 'planted out as animated coats of arms to warn off trespassers.' But in the 1860s and 1870s a new set of circumstances started to operate. In 1863 Nienhuys demonstrated the great potential of the soils of East Sumatra with his new tobacco venture and within the same decade the discovery of oil deposits on the island enhanced interest still further. This time there was capital available, created by the Culture System, and the means of exploitation facilitated by the concurrent improvements in communications.

The process of economic development in the Outer Islands, however, was confined to certain comparatively small areas. First and foremost came the Culture Zone of East Sumatra, centred on Deli, Asahan and Langkat, whose prolific, volcanic soils produced first tobacco, then rubber and oil palm, and where capital investment, a large percentage of which was not Dutch, was heaviest. The Padang Highlands formed a secondary region to the west, where pepper and rubber became of great importance and some coal was worked.[25] The discovery of oil deposits in Sumatra, near Pangkalan Brandan in the north and the Jambi-Palembang area further south, opened up these regions, as did its discovery near Balikpapan, Kutai in east Borneo.

The new exports corresponded with the needs of the industrializing West,

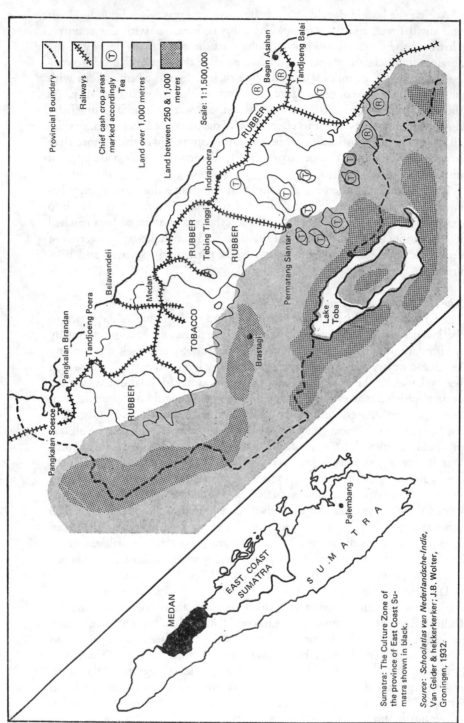

Legend:
- Provincial Boundary
- Railways
- Chief cash crop areas marked accordingly (T = Tea, R = Rubber)
- Land over 1,000 metres
- Land between 250 & 1,000 metres

Scale: 1:1,500,000

Place names and labels:
Pangkalan Soesoe, Pangkalan Brandan, Tandjoeng Poera, Belawandeli, Medan, Bagan Asahan, Tandjoeng Balai, Indrapoera, Tebing Tinggi, Permatang Siantar, Brastagi, Lake Toba

RUBBER, TOBACCO, RUBBER

SUMATRA, MEDAN, EAST COAST SUMATRA, Palembang

Sumatra: The Culture Zone of the province of East Coast Sumatra shown in black.

Source: Schoolatlas van Nederlandsche-Indie, Van Gelder & hekkerkerker; J.B. Wolter, Groningen, 1932.

4.   The Culture Zone of the Province of East Coast Sumatra

offering raw materials in demand by Western industry instead of the traditional cash crops which were grown in Java. Because of this, the new exports from the Outer Islands soon exceeded in value those of Java so that while in 1870 they only accounted for 13 per cent of the total value of Indies exports, by 1900 they contributed 30 per cent of the total and thirty years later still accounted for over half. With the collapse of the sugar and coffee markets which followed the Great Depression of 1929 the exports from the Outer Islands played a preponderant role in the export economy of the Indies.

The export crops of the Indies: spices
By the twentieth century spices, which were amongst the oldest elements in the trade of the archipelago had completely lost their significance. The Indies were famous as their source in the days of Rome in the West and of Han China to the North, and were the main goal of Arab and Indian traders, and later on of the Portuguese and Spaniards, Dutch and Englishmen who sailed to South-East Asia. Peppers were to be found growing over a wide area stretching from India to Java; the other spices—cloves, nutmeg and mace—were confined to the Moluccas. The Moluccan spices now grow elsewhere as well and are of no consequence; only pepper has retained something of its former importance, accounting for 79 per cent of the world's exports and ranking fourteenth in 1941 amongst those of the Indies themselves.

Seemingly a blessing, the possession by the Moluccan islanders of the source of the primary spices could well be considered a curse. The story of their exploitation is marked by violence and bloodshed from the time of the rise of the original Malay sultanates that controlled them till the final establishment of the Dutch monopoly two centuries later. The imposition of this monopoly, which took fifty years to be made fully effective, brought ruin, impoverishment and in certain cases extinction to the islanders. The policy of the VOC was simply to restrict production in order to maintain high prices. This meant securing complete political control over the region, which was swiftly done, and then using this power to restrict planting. This policy destroyed the prosperity of the Moluccas for ever and reduced not only their productivity but also their population.

However, none of this could ensure the continued profits of the trade on the world market, and although production was controlled by the Dutch government till 1864, the monopoly had already been lost a century before. In 1770 the French introduced the clove tree to their island of Mauritius. From there it spread to the Americas—the West Indies, the Guianas and Brazil—and to East Africa where Zanzibar became the main producer. By 1939 only 2 per cent of the world's supply of cloves came from the Moluccas themselves and even Java imported its supply from Zanzibar for the flavouring of local cigarettes. For nutmegs, on the other hand, the Moluccas remained the chief source of supply, although they came to be planted more widely within the region itself—in the Celebes, and on Java, Sumatra and Penang—as well as in Bengal, on the French island of Reunion, Brazil, French Guiana and the West Indies. When the spice trade was thrown open to free enterprise in 1864, it became centred on Singapore and fell largely into the hands of Chinese middlemen until the rise of Macassar as an ocean-going port in the first decades of the twentieth century restored its position as a spice mart.

Pepper, however, did not undergo the decline of the other spice crops. Sumatra remained the main centre of production where it was grown under government compulsion until the middle of the nineteenth century. It was the mainstay of Achinese and Bantenese power in the sixteenth and seventeenth centuries and accounted for the early presence of the Dutch and the English on the Sumatran west coast. When pepper was opened to free enterprise after 1862 it developed into an important smallholders' crop. In 1930 99 per cent of Indies production was in Indonesian hands. Exports rose sharply in the decades prior to the Pacific War, the quantity doubling between 1930 and 1939; unfortunately, however, this increased productivity was more than offset by the fall in world market prices. In this period 85 per cent of total production came from the Lampongs district of South Sumatra.

The Dutch themselves introduced one new spice crop, cinnamon. First started under Daendels without much success, it was taken up by van den Bosch under the Culture System with better results, and finally by private enterprise in 1865. By the 1930s it was an entirely Indonesian crop.

Sugar
By the beginning of the eighteenth century the spice trade had already been replaced by sugar and coffee as the main staples of the colonial economy of the Indies. Of the two, sugar has the longer history. It apparently came to Java in the days of Majapahit and by the time the Dutch arrived on the scene some two hundred years later, it was being grown along the coastline from Jakarta to Japara, although not in sufficient quantities to meet demand so that some was still being imported from Siam and China. Under Dutch guidance sugar production expanded till it became the most important crop of the islands, a position it maintained up to the 1920s when it was overtaken by rubber. After that the industry encountered increasing difficulties and fell to fifth position amongst the Indies exports by which time it accounted for only 5 per cent of world production. In its hey-day the Indies sugar contribution was double that amount and it occupied a pre-eminent position in the Javanese economy. Just before the Great Depression of 1929-33, the industry represented a Dutch investment of ƒ 794 million, 180 factories were in operation and the industry provided employment for 60,000 people on a permanent basis, a figure which swelled to one million during the harvesting season. Sugar cultivation took up nearly half a million acres a year or one-fifth of the padi-lands of Java. Seventy per cent of this cultivation was concentrated in the richest rice-growing regions in the east of the island, in particular the districts around Surabaya, Tegal, Pekalongan and in the principalities of Surakarta and Jogjakarta.

In the early days of its expansion, direct Dutch participation was limited, the Dutch East India Company concerning itself only with the marketing of the produce, dealing with the Chinese who were the millers, the middlemen and ultimately the principal growers. With active Dutch encouragement

Chinese immigrants planted the lands around Batavia with the crop so that production rose from 196 piculs in 1637 to over 100,000 piculs a year a hundred years later. A large amount of this was absorbed locally, especially for the making of arrack, but by this time sugar was also established as the leading export of the Dutch Company. Towards the end of the eighteenth century the Dutch promoted sugar cultivation beyond the Batavian lands to Cheribon and along the north coast. Production still lay predominantly in Chinese hands. The Chinese supplied the Company, obtaining the cane which they did not grow themselves from Javanese territorial chiefs who extracted it as feudal dues from the peasantry. Chinese merchants also acquired these feudal rights and their excesses in the use of forced peasant labour led ultimately to Dutch legislation being passed to restrain them.[26] At the beginning of the nineteenth century, in the disturbed conditions which marked the administrations of Daendels and Raffles, sugar production slumped disastrously, primarily because government was unable to advance credit to the Chinese millers. The industry did not recover fully until the introduction of the Culture System.

Sugar under the Culture System
The Culture System transformed the industry, placed it firmly in Dutch hands at the expense of the Chinese, and laid the foundations of the golden age which was to follow. It was under the System also that evolved the close integration between Western enterprise and capital on the one hand and the Javanese cultivator on the other. As a crop the conditions required by sugar are almost identical with those required for wet-rice cultivation—an ample water supply during the growing season and dry weather for the harvest. Such ideal conditions existed in the monsoon regions of east and east-central Java. Furthermore, the harvesting and the milling require a large labour force such as available in a rice-rich region, while the land just harvested could not be used for sugar for another three years. So a system based on a simple rotation of two crops—sugar and usually rice—naturally developed with an adequate supply of labour ensured. A sugar factory built with Western capital and managed by Europeans served a rice district and developed contractual ties with the Javanese villagers in it. The form that these took varied according to locality but the basic pattern was the same.[27] The social consequences are described later. From the production point of view this system eventually proved a spectacular success.

At first, however, van den Bosch found himself confronted with the problem of how to recruit the contractors to build the factories, to mill the sugar and to act as the link between the cultivators and the government who collected and marketed their crop. In the early 1830s capitalists who were prepared to sink their money in such a venture were hard to come by, particularly Dutch ones 'who could not be beaten out of their homes with sticks'.[28] They were deterred by the high initial costs and by the risks of engaging under a new and untried system, leaving the field to Englishmen, Frenchmen, Chinese and even Indians which was not the idea at all. To induce his fellow-countrymen to become contractors, van den Bosch offered generous terms such as liberal building advances to cover capital costs till the profits started to come in, no duties on imported machinery and free or cost-price supplies of timber and other materials. The contractors had to bear the actual costs of planting, harvesting and delivery, but the government helped again by laying down fixed rates for the area of land cultivated, the coolies hired, the transport used and the fuel necessary. In theory all peasant labour, apart from that involved in the actual growing of the crop, was voluntary, but compulsion was permitted on the understanding that the labour so employed would receive wages. Furthermore, though the contractor had to supply the government with the produce at a fixed rate which was below the market level, it was high enough to ensure a profit, and after 1842 he was able to sell off the sugar which exceeded the official quota on the free market. Finally, the contractor was virtually guaranteed against any substantial loss by being allowed to surrender his contract at any time after the third year if things were not going well. Even despite these measures the response was slow at first. Van den Bosch was obliged to set up state factories under British managers and use 'gentle persuasion' on reluctant capitalists to 'compel them to become millionaires'.[29]

But with pioneer contractors soon earning under the new system between ƒ2,000 to ƒ5,000 a year, the message at last got through and the sugar industry entered upon a new epoch of expansion. Even van den Bosch's sanguine hopes of raising 400,000 piculs a year by 1840 were exceeded more than twofold by that date, and sugar—together with coffee—rose to carry the Culture System. Amsterdam was restored to its previous position as the leading European mart for sugar and coffee and the Chinese millers were now virtually eclipsed by the influx of Dutch contractors who availed themselves of van den Bosch's opportunities. The area under cultivation increased by 18 per cent between 1833 and 1861, and productivity by a spectacular 300 per cent during the same period. This progress was clearly not wholly due to van den Bosch's inducements. Improved techniques, the increasing use of modern machinery, the introduction of intensive planting methods and the setting up of model factories also played their part. The first steam machines to take the place of handpressing were introduced by a British firm in the 1820s; figures for machinery imports which steadily mounted in the decades following 1830 are further evidence of the modernization of the industry, for most of the equipment imported was for sugar. Improvements in technique became even more marked after 1850.[30]

Although under the Culture System sugar was a government concern, van den Bosch's need for the services of private contractors provided private capital with an opening, and the subsequent success of those under contract to the government stimulated more. By 1839 production from private as opposed to government crops accounted for three-eighths of the whole, a fact which so alarmed van den Bosch that by a new law of that year he prohibited the lease of fresh lands for sugar cultivation to private entrepreneurs. This measure proved singularly effective, for on the eve of the government retreat from sugar in 1870 only four of the one hundred sugar factories in operation on the island were privately-owned.

Sugar after 1870: the golden years

The passage of de Waal's Sugar Law in 1870 marked the surrender of official monopoly to private enterprise and the step by step dismantling of the Culture System. The problem of harnessing labour which van den Bosch had set out to solve was now replaced by that of harnessing capital, ushering in the Liberal Era of unprecedented expansion and profit for the sugar lords. This process continued, with its ups and downs right into the twentieth century, reaching its peak in the 1920s. In 1920 itself sugar earned for the Netherlands Indies over ƒ1 million in export revenues, a sum greater in value than that of all the colony's other exports put together.

In the meantime government participation shrank from 91 per cent in 1870 to 3 per cent and subsequent extinction by 1890. The organization and system of production on the other hand were little affected by this change-over to private enterprise. The European contractors and their factories remained, but now as free agents no longer tied to government. Wages replaced forced labour and rents replaced rates on the land used, but the arrangements between factory and village based on the eighteen-month rotation of crops, the subsistence economy of the rice-field and the supply of adequate labour were continued and became consolidated.[31] The introduction of more modern methods of irrigation bound the system still more closely together, while the role of the cultivator remained unchanged, although his lot probably worsened.

The years of unfettered free enterprise fall into two parts. During the first phase—from 1870 to the crisis of the 1880s—the ring was held by individual private capitalists and speculators. It was the golden age of the sugar magnates. Wealthy and influential men, many of whom had lived in the Indies for years in and out of government service and had played their part in agitating for the end of the Culture System, they were the first to avail themselves of the fresh opportunities opened up by the abandonment of government cultures. The Rent Ordinance of 1871 drew them to sugar since its conditions made investment in any other field risky.[32] Then came two serious crises, the first in 1877-8 and the second in 1883-4, which cut sugar prices on the world market by half and shattered their prosperity. The first of the two crises broke as a result of falling prices caused by the emergence of the sugar-beet industry in Europe. The decline in world sugar prices continued for two decades, reaching its nadir in 1897-8. In the meantime the industry had been struck another blow by the outbreak of a blight in 1882 which attacked sugar-cane in Java, leading to crop failures and the financial crisis of the following year. Apart from eliminating the individual planter and concentrating control in the hands of financial groups in Holland, these crises also paved the way for greater co-operation within the industry itself.[33] The first experimental stations, maintained jointly by the sugar producers, were founded in the 1880s to research into agricultural and mechanical problems. In 1889 the first congress of sugar manufacturers was held and in 1895, in response to a new crisis caused by the outbreak of a root disease, a representative body for the whole industry, the Algemeen Syndikaat van Suikerfabrikanten (ASSF), was founded. In 1902 a convention of sugar

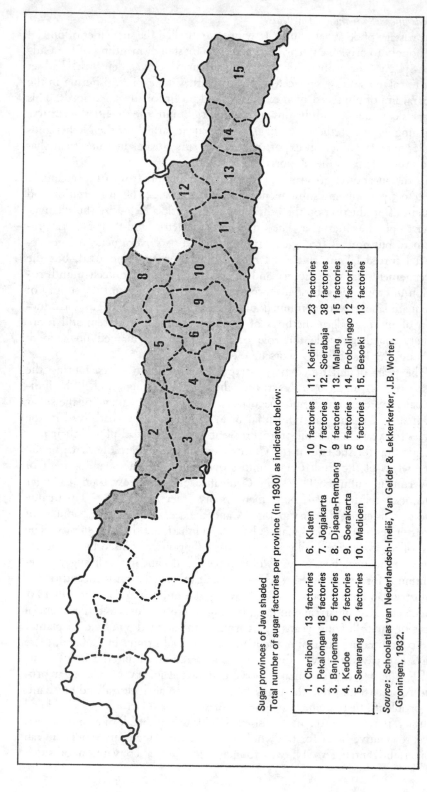

Sugar provinces of Java shaded
Total number of sugar factories per province (in 1930) as indicated below:

1. Cheribon	13 factories	6. Klaten	10 factories	11. Kediri	23 factories
2. Pekalongan	18 factories	7. Jogjakarta	17 factories	12. Soerabaja	38 factories
3. Banjoemas	5 factories	8. Djapara-Rembang	9 factories	13. Malang	15 factories
4. Kedoe	2 factories	9. Soerakarta	5 factories	14. Probolinggo	12 factories
5. Semarang	3 factories	10. Madioen	6 factories	15. Besoeki	13 factories

Source: Schoolatlas van Nederlandsch-Indië, Van Gelder & Lekkerkerker, J.B. Wolter, Groningen, 1932.

5. Sugar Production in Java, 1830–1940

manufacturers at Brussels 'gave new life to sugar' by reducing duties and cutting subsidies thereby putting cane-sugar on a newly-competitive basis with beet-sugar. In 1907 the various experimental stations for sugar were brought under the control of one administration and this was placed in the hands of the ASSF in 1912. In 1918 the Vereeniging van Javaanse Suiker Produktoren (Union of Javanese Sugar Producers) was formed to deal with the problem of surplus stocks which had accumulated during the course of the Great War.

The effectiveness of these moves towards collaboration and co-operation between sugar producers in the Indies is demonstrated not only by the survival of the industry through the various crises by which it was confronted in the last quarter of the nineteenth century, but also by its continued expansion and establishment as the country's prime export. The most telling illustration of the progress achieved is the fact that while the value of sugar exported in 1937 was roughly equivalent to that for the year 1875, the quantity was six times as great.

The decline of sugar

Nevertheless the sugar industry was unable to escape the crippling effects of the Great Depression of 1929. It was too heavily capitalized to miss the shock of plummeting world market prices, particularly at a time when its own overseas markets were contracting. The industry which had given place to rubber as the leading export of the Indies in 1925 now sank to fifth place; its production was halved, the area under cultivation reduced drastically and over two-thirds of its factories were closed down. All the same, confident of the ability of the VJSP to manipulate stocks and maintain prices, the Batavian administration at first ignored international attempts to meet the situation. But such a policy soon proved impracticable and in 1931 the Indies became an adherent of the Chadbourne Plan, designed to shore up world market prices by reducing production and imposing quotas. This did not solve the problem, however, as many sugar producers in the Indies did not agree with the scheme. Finally, at the end of 1932, Batavia set up a new central selling organization, membership of which was made compulsory, called the Nederlandse-Indie Vereeniging voor de Afzet van Zuiker (NIVAS). This body imposed strict controls over the transportation and sale of sugar within Java, and with strong government backing its measures proved effective. The number of factories operating was reduced again, measures were taken to increase local demand and output was cut down from nearly 3 million to ½ million tons a year. In 1934 NIVAS went so far as to propose that no sugar should be planted at all in that year, but the protests of producers who faced extinction ensured that a restricted area was planted.

In 1937 more effective international action was taken to control production and prices and to adjust supply to demand. An International Sugar Council was set up in London by the Conference of Sugar Producers which represented most of the countries concerned, to overcome the deficiencies of the Chadbourne Plan, the effectiveness of which had been severely reduced by the defection of the four major world producers.[34] After this till the outbreak of the Pacific War, sugar in the Indies experienced a mild recovery, largely induced by the spate of fresh stockpiling caused by the suspected imminence of the War itself. However, one of the chief weaknesses of the sugar industry of the Indies, by comparison with its rivals, was that it lacked a protected market for its exports.

Coffee

Alongside sugar, coffee was the mainstay of the Dutch colonial economy for three centuries, but after the 1880s it was overtaken by other crops in importance. By 1937 coffee had sunk to ninth place in terms of export value and contributed only 7 per cent towards total world exports. It nevertheless remained an important crop in the economy of the Indies, and one in which the Indonesian share was considerable.

Unlike sugar, coffee was a contribution of the Dutch. In 1616 a Dutch trader at the Arab port of Mocha had observed that the people grew a bean 'used to make black water which they drink warm',[35] but it was another fifty years before the commodity was brought to Holland (i.e. 1661) and another generation before the first attempts were made to grow it in Java. In 1713 the first consignment (2,000 lbs) of Java coffee was dispatched to Europe and from that year onwards the coffee industry did not look back. High prices stimulated Javanese participation and soon coffee was vying with sugar and pepper for supremacy as an export crop. By 1750 coffee had won. In that year it became the Dutch Company's largest single source of revenue, and it kept its primacy for over a hundred years. However right from the very beginning coffee revealed its extreme sensitivity to market prices, and was subject to constant fluctuations in price, demand and policy. In 1721 overhasty planters were already cutting down their coffee trees, confronted with a dramatic fall of 75 per cent in world prices, and were replanting with pepper, whose price was rising. In 1733 the Dutch Company found it expedient to force Mataram to suppress coffee-planting in its domains because of overproduction in the Priangan. Violent fluctuations continued in the ensuing decades and the spread of coffee-planting in Central and East Java beyond Dutch control only worsened matters. Eventually the Dutch found their solution through the development of the system of 'contingencies' and 'forced deliveries'[36] which enabled them to exercise an absolute control of production throughout Java through the medium of the Javanese ruling class.

Coffee in the nineteenth century

The nineteenth century was the boom century for coffee; it expanded rapidly, reaching its climax in the 1870s. But the century began badly enough for the industry as it did for all economic development in the Indies. With overseas markets cut off by British seapower, warehouses full of rotting stocks, plantations deserted for want of purchasers, the industry did not recover until the Wars were over. However, immediately after 1816 coffee underwent instant recovery, both production and prices rising by roughly 300 per cent within three years. Then in 1823 the bottom dropped out of

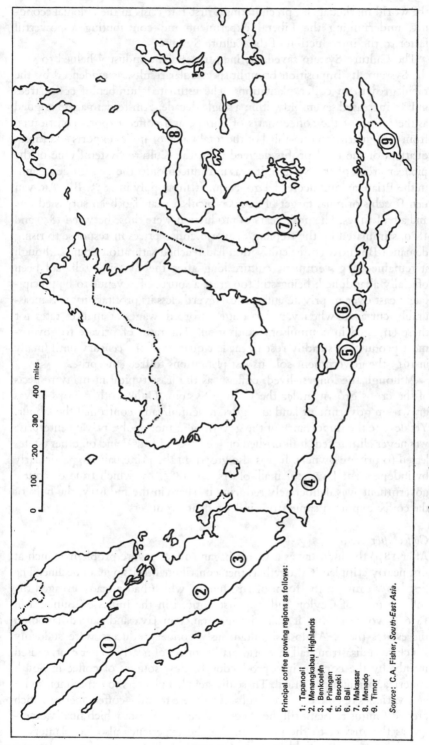

Principal coffee growing regions as follows:

1: Tapanoeli
2. Menangkabau Highlands
3. Benkoelén
4. Priangan
5. Besoeki
6. Bali
7. Makassar
8. Menado
9. Timor

Source: C.A. Fisher, South-East Asia.

6. Coffee Production in the Netherlands East Indies, 1830–1940.

the world market again, precipitating a first-rate crisis in the colonial economy, undermining the Liberal experiment and contributing a powerful factor to the introduction of the Culture System.

The Culture System saved the industry and the industry helped to save the System. Its imposition brought spectacular results, as evidenced by the rapid growth of coffee plantations. The estimated number of coffee trees in Java increased sevenfold within a single decade, Amsterdam again reigned as the queen of the coffee marts of Europe and coffee exports contributed from one-quarter to one-third of the total value of Indies exports and three-quarters of the total profits derived from the Culture System. One of the pioneer crops of the System, it was introduced onto the government lands in the Priangan and decreed a government monopoly in 1833. By 1840 van den Bosch's original target of 400,000 piculs a year had been surpassed one and a half times. The peak years of production were those between 1849 and 1880, stimulated by the trebling of world coffee prices in response to rising demand. But now coffee cultivation had reached saturation point, although it remained a government culture long after the System itself had been officially abandoned, being still too great a source of revenue to be precipitately cast over to private enterprise. Nevertheless its profitability was measurably curtailed when van der Putte enforced wages at market rates for those engaged in compulsory cultivation. The ratio of private to government production steadily rose in the last quarter of the century until finally in 1915 the government sold its last plantations to free enterprise.

Although the longest-lived, coffee was the least typical in many respects of the crops grown under the Culture System. Unlike other crops it was grown on government land and government already controlled the labour. Yet despite the importance of the government monopoly, private enterprise was never eliminated. It flourished on the P & T Lands[37] and on other estates leased to private owners. It was also grown in the principalities, particularly by independent Javanese smallholders. By 1885, by which time of course government was deliberately reducing its share in the industry, the bulk of the coffee exported came from independent producers.

Coffee after 1870

After 1870 the industry as a whole began to face severe problems which at first nearly crippled it altogether, then contributed to its overall decline. The first blow came in the form of rust fungus which had already ravaged the coffee estates of Ceylon and was first noticed in the Indies on Sumatra in 1876. Two years later it made its appearance in Java and caused havoc on the estates there. Almost simultaneously coffee producers were suddenly struck by a disastrous fall in world market prices of nearly 50 per cent, caused mainly by the coming into production of new sources of coffee in South America, particularly Brazil. These disasters led planters to experiment with new varieties of coffee seed and substitutes were found—coffee liberica which proved fungus resistant till the 1890s, and coffee robusta which finally emerged as the answer to the problem. But the experience also led planters to experiment in other fields as well. On the P & T Lands and other leading

Javanese estates they experimented with tea, and later on rubber; other private enterprises in Sumatra and the Molukse Handels-Vereniging in Minahassa carried out similar experiments. So while the industry as a whole rose to the occasion, it suffered a decline as a result of diversification.

The wild fluctuations on the world coffee market in the fifty years which followed 1879, coffee's peak year in the nineteenth century, brought about the steady decline of the industry from its former pre-eminent position. In 1885 coffee was overtaken by its old rival, sugar, as the principal export of the Indies. At the end of the century it was superseded by oil, then tin, then rubber, until by 1937, despite its great productivity, it had sunk to ninth place amongst the main exports of the Indies. But as coffee lost its former importance, the Indonesian share in it grew. This was particularly evident outside Java—in Sumatra, Celebes, Bali and Timor where cultivation of the crop had spread during the latter half of the nineteenth century. In Sumatra coffee was first introduced after the Padri Wars to the Menangkabau Highlands above Padang, but later the Indonesian coffee-growers were to be found concentrated in the Palembang uplands. Coffee-growing in the Celebes was introduced by the Molukse Handles-Vereniging and was centred on Minahassa. By 1929 50 per cent of the total output and 75 per cent of export production came from Indonesian growers. In this process the Outer Islands ousted Java as the chief centre for coffee production in 1920 and a decade later their output was twice as great.

The rise of the Indonesian smallholder was a natural development since coffee had always had a strong appeal for him. It was a crop which was easy to farm, involved no high overhead costs and required no elaborate machinery for its processing. For the independent growers in Sumatra and the other Outer Islands, the crop became a welcome secondary source of income, giving them a place and a share in the profits of the Indies export trade and acting as an important medium for the introduction of a money economy and its associated values.[38] Even the Javanese planter who fell under the mercantilist system of the VOC in the eighteenth century to be converted into a permanent landless agricultural labourer under the Culture System and after in the nineteenth century was better off than most of his countrymen who were similarly placed.[39]

Against this background, European-owned estate coffee changed its character. The estates or the firms which managed them became more and more involved with Indonesian smallholders, assuming the role of their agents and exporters. In certain cases European firms actually engaged themselves in organizing the Indonesian planters, as was the case in North Celebes where the Molukse Handles-Vereniging specialized local production for the North European market. The Dutch retained their predominant position in the estate industry, although the Germans were also strongly represented. European coffee planters followed the trend of the late nineteenth century towards monopoly and organized themselves into the Algemeen Landbouw Syndikaat (General Agricultural Syndicate), largely as a result of the financial crisis of the 1880s in order to protect and promote their interests.

The final disaster which struck the coffee industry prior to the Pacific War was the Great Depression of 1929. However this affected world market prices and local incomes but not production, since the industry was already largely a smallholders' affair run by the Indonesians themselves, so that the question of cutting back did not arise. In fact the problem of the coffee industry now was the problem of chronic overproduction. Even in 1937, when the effects of the Depression had practically worn off, world production exceeded consumption by 50 per cent and in the Indies the warehouses were stacked full with a year's supply of stock. As in other fields of production heavy government intervention was necessary to save the situation. A Coffee Fund was set up from the revenues obtained by imposing a levy on all coffee imports to Holland, which were then earmarked for meeting export premiums on Indies coffee and for assisting research into growers' problems, especially those of the smallholder. These measures served to uphold the industry, but the outbreak of war in Europe in 1939 caused another sharp depression as it closed substantial European markets to the Dutch and exports fell drastically.

Tin

Apart from spices and peppers, sugar and coffee, up till the nineteenth century the Dutch derived profit from only one other major export, namely tin. In 1937 tin was the third most valuable export of the Indies, making her the world's third largest producer with a contribution of one-fifth of total world production. Tin was the only major commodity to be found entirely outside Java, its deposits being restricted to the off-shore islands of Bangka, Belitung (Billiton) and Singkep which form the tail end of the great tin belt stretching southwards from Yunnan.

Tin lay undiscovered in the Indies, at least as far as the Europeans and international trade were concerned until around 1710 when deposits were found on Bangka. Bangka at that time was part of the sultanate of Palembang, but the Dutch, who had established some shadowy influence over that state for the sake of its pepper, soon showed interest. In 1722 they were able to exploit the difficulties of the sultan, who was facing a rebellion, to secure a monopoly over the trade. This tin monopoly was confirmed by another treaty in 1755 but proved virtually ineffective since Dutch power generally was on the decline. However, at this stage the Dutch were only interested in controlling the commerce in tin, not its mining, so that the rulers of Palembang overcame the problem of digging it out of the ground by recruiting Chinese miners, particularly from Yunnan where mining methods and experience were well established. As a result from the beginning the Chinese dominated the industry and it was not until the last decade of the nineteenth century that their methods were replaced by those of the West.

Closer European supervision of the industry was heralded by Raffles who in 1812 caused his client Sultan Najmuddin of Palembang to sign away his rights over Bangka and Billiton. But when the Dutch returned in 1816, no further step to control the industry was taken till 1850 when Chinese secret society riots on Bangka led Batavia to establish its own administration there and on neighbouring Belitung. The subsequent discovery of tin on Belitung

Tin Exports in volume (metric tons) and value (guilders: £)

Volume (000)		Value (000)	Volume (000)		Value (000)
1870		7,000	1925	30	94,000
1880		9,500	1930	35	58,000
1890	12	9,000	1932	18	18,000
1900	16	24,000	1937	38	84,000
1913	21	37,000	1940		82,000
1920	22	65,000			

7. Tin Production in the Netherlands East Indies, 1870–1940

prompted the formation of the first Western mining company in the Indies. Known as the Billiton Tin Company, it was brought into existence as a private concern largely at the instance of the enterprising Prins Hendrik, a brother of the Dutch king. In 1861 this firm was converted into a public company in order to raise more capital, and despite initial difficulties it was soon paying extremely handsome profits. Inspired by this example and by the expanding world tin market, other Dutch capitalists decided to try their hand, and in 1887, having secured the concession from the Sultan of Riau-Lingga, the Singkep Tin Company was also formed. However the Singkep concern failed to show a profit until 1907.

The Chinese remained in control of the actual mining operations until the 1890s, since the Dutch companies operated on a contract basis with the Chinese miners. At the end of the century, however, the Chinese position was undermined as Western technology came into play. The first steam engine in the islands was used in 1890. The chain bucket dredge appeared for the first time in 1920. By this time Bangka tin had long been overtaken by Straits tin in quality and quantity but the tin production of the Indies sur-passed sugar and coffee in terms of export value at the end of the century and almost doubled between 1913 and 1929.[40]

One of the main features of the Indies tin industry was the large part played by the government in it. This was due partly to the reluctance of private capitalists to invest in the industry and partly to the Dutch desire to restrict foreign competition. The Mining Decree of 1850 and the amend-ments of 1873 were designed to attract private capital but apart from the Billiton Tin Company there was no response until the revelation of the huge profits being made on Belitung caused by the s'Jacob affair of 1882[41] inspired the formation of the Singkep venture. The Billiton and Singkep Tin Com-panies were the only two private concerns in the whole industry, while the Bangka mines remained under government control. The Mining Law of 1899 was also framed on the assumption that mining would be carried out by private enterprise but subsequent amendments were made to provide for state participation, primarily to preserve Dutch interests and to inhibit foreign investors. When the Billiton company's lease expired in 1924, it was taken over by a new firm, the Gemeenschappelijke Mijnbouw Maatschappij (Joint Mining Company, Billiton, or GMB) in which the government had a con-trolling interest. In 1933 this new company bought over the Singkep mines but ran them separately. Four years later moves were afoot to bring all the tin enterprises under central control by amalgamating the Bangka and Belitung concerns. The necessary legislation was never put into effect because of the Pacific War. In the 1920s there were two attempts to launch other private ventures—the Stannum Company founded in 1925, to operate at Bangkinang on the eastern slopes of the Padang Highlands in West Sumatra, which was wound up in 1930, and the N.I. Tin Exploitation Company, started in 1926 and closed in 1931.

The impact of the Great Depression of 1929 was less severe on the Indies tin industry as the Dutch were low cost producers and the large measure of government control facilitated adjustments in production and supply. Nevertheless the effects were bad enough, the value of tin exports dropping by two-thirds between 1930 and 1932. At the same time the absence of substantial private interests in tin made it easier for the Batavian administration to participate in international restriction schemes. In 1931 the Dutch joined with Britain and Bolivia in a scheme to restrict production, becoming a member of the International Tin Committee set up to control it and of the International Tin Pool designed to buy and store surpluses. In 1934 a new International Tin Agreement was signed and renewed again, although not without difficulty, by all the countries concerned in 1936 for another five years. These measures proved very effective. As early as 1934 the International Tin Pool was able to sell off surplus stocks at a profit and the following year it was clear that the general trade depression was lifting. As for the Indies the value of tin exports rose from their 1932 nadir to record levels in 1940.

The Indonesian share in the tin industry was negligible. Labour was provided by the Chinese and in later years capital by the Westerners. In striking contrast to the Malay Peninsula, the tin mines of Bangka, Belitung and Singkep were remote from the normal centres of population and trade, which meant that widespread ancillary services had to be developed to support the industry—power stations, charcoal plants, engineering workshops, timber-yards, waterworks, printing works, hospitals and hotels. In most of these Chinese found employment while the local Indonesian population fished and built boats. Only near Bangkinang were small deposits worked by the Indonesians themselves, but their output was not significant.

Tea

The staples of the Netherlands Indies economy—sugar, coffee, pepper and tin—were joined by new commodities during the course of the nineteenth century, among the first of which was tea.

The cultivation of tea was introduced into the Indies in 1824 under government auspices, but the industry did not really start to flourish until the end of the nineteenth century by which time it had come under the control of private enterprise. This was due to a series of technical factors which had to be overcome and could not easily be so until new circumstances at the start of the new century made faster progress possible. After 1900 the tea industry expanded rapidly until it was checked by the Great Depression of 1929. On the eve of the Pacific War, the Indies produced 17 per cent of the world's tea exports and tea ranked sixth amongst the exports of the Indies.

Tea was first brought to Java in 1824 by von Siebold, a German botanist commissioned by the Batavian government to acquire certain plants and shrubs from Japan for its experimental plantations at Buitenzorg (Bogor) and Garut. This led two years later to Jacobson, a tea expert in the employ of the newly-formed N.H.M., being sent to South China, this time specifically for tea. Jacobson brought back with him not only fresh seeds but some Chinese tea-growers and processors to boot. Now Inspector of Government Tea Plantations, he proceeded forthwith to launch tea-growing experiments in various parts of Java. The fledgling industry was quickly incorporated into the Culture System, and the government built tea-processing factories near its tea gardens. But the new crop would show no profit. So van den Bosch, adopting the same methods as with sugar and coffee, leased out the tea gardens to private contractors who in return for advances to cover their initial expenses planted on government land and sold the crop at fixed rates to government. However tea still failed to pay, and so became one of the first cultures to be lifted (1865). All the same during the ensuing twenty years even private enterprise failed to do much better. Javanese tea had a poor reputation; it was of inferior quality, prey to rust fungus and the best lands for its cultivation had been pre-empted by the far more successful crops of coffee and cinchona.

The crisis in the coffee industry and the drop in world market prices for cinchona in the last decades of the century provided tea-growers with their first real break. Both coffee and cinchona planters turned their attention to tea for the first time and better lands became available. More basic, however, were changes within the industry itself. The first of these was the introduction of Indian strains, largely through the efforts of John Peet, an Englishman who had planted tea in both Ceylon and India and came to Java as adviser to local tea-growers. Another factor was the great improvement in the techniques of tea planting and processing. In the late 1870s came the mechanical methods already employed in India and Ceylon, followed in the 1900s by wet-leaf shifters, stalk-eliminators, tea-sorters and other specialist machines invented by various individuals and firms in the industry. This work of research and experimentation was encouraged by the formation of the Soekaboemische Landbouw Vereeniging in 1881. This organization co-operated with the government gardens at Buitenzorg, leading in the end to the setting up in 1902 of a Tea Experimental Station, which was maintained by funds from the industry and was provided technical assistance by government. Other contributions included the Institute of Plant Diseases' valuable work on tea diseases and pests and the opening of a government tea seed nursery which freed planters from their dependence on India. In 1905 a Dutch firm pioneered in the establishment of a tea-testing bureau. As a result of all this the quality of Javanese tea was so improved that by the early 1900s it was being regularly quoted on the London market and found new openings in the United States of America and in Australia. By 1910 the industry was firmly established in the Indies, particularly in the Priangan which became one of the leading tea districts in the country and one of the most important in the world.

Since the further extension of tea planting on Java was no longer practicable for want of land, the industry now spread to Sumatra, particularly to the Culture Zone around Permatang Siantar in the East Coast Residency. The first Sumatran estate was opened in 1911 by the British firm of Harrison Crosfield; several Dutch companies with tea interests in Java followed suit while Batavia set out to encourage tea planting on the island by opening up an experimental station in the south, and later some estates of its own. In 1928 the Kayu Ara Estate in West Central Sumatra was laid out and opened, to become one of the largest in the world.

The impact of the Great Depression in 1929 brought this expansion to a sudden halt. Prices fell disastrously on the world market and with them the value of tea exports dropped by over half. Large-scale retrenchment of labour and the closing of factories followed. Matters threatened to become worse when the extension of the system of Imperial Preferences was announced after the Ottawa Conference of 1932. The solution lay, as elsewhere, in international co-operation to restrict production and internal efforts to encourage local consumption and to lower costs. This called for closer government supervision and intervention in the industry, which became increasingly apparent in the years which followed. These measures had a moderate success and were partly responsible for the survival and recovery of the industry. On the eve of the Pacific War, while the value of tea exports still remained at nearly half the figure for the 1920s, its volume had declined by only 20 per cent.

The Indonesian share in tea was necessarily limited by lack of capital and technical knowledge, both of which were essential to the industry. Nevertheless there was a steady increase in the production from Javanese and Sumatran smallholders from the $1\frac{1}{2}$ per cent of the 1880s to the 30 per cent of overall production estimated for 1940, a growth stimulated in particular by the boom conditions of 1910 and 1911. Smallholder processing was done by growing the crop and selling it as wet-leaf to the Western estates. This gave rise to the 'opkoop' factories started by enterprising European and Chinees entrepreneurs, which specialized in processing the leaf. A few of these were run by the Indonesians themselves.

Cinchona

Another crop which developed as a result of Dutch official enterprise was cinchona. This took place in the 1850s, although cinchona had been known and grown in the region for generations, having been first introduced by the Portuguese and Spaniards in the sixteenth century. In terms of value, cinchona was far from the forefront amongst the exports of the Indies, but all the same in 1937 the Indies was the source of 82 per cent of total world production.

The acute shortage of quinine in the mid-nineteenth century caused the Botanical Gardens at Buitenzorg (Bogor) in 1852 to send one of its men to South America to collect fresh seedlings and to plant the first cinchona estates near Bandung in 1854. When the crop of 1854 matured fifteen years later, Java at once became the world's major producer, contributing two-thirds of the available supply.

Despite this spectacular beginning, the industry was to be dogged by a series of crises, each of which nearly crippled its future. The first came with the low quinine content of the bark of the original trees, which threatened financial failure. Cinchona was saved on this occasion by a new strain, *cinchona ledgeriana*, introduced from Peru, which had a demonstrably high quinine content. Planted in Java, it proved so successful that private enterprise was attracted for the first time. With the ending of the Culture System, more land was turned over to private investors. The second crisis broke in the 1880s with the discovery that *cinchona ledgeriana* would not grow twice on the same ground; once again cinchona planters faced ruin. This time they were saved by a Dutch nurseryman visiting Java who suggested that the *cinchona ledgeriana* be grafted onto one of the older, lower-yielding strains. 'This suggestion saved the industry.'[42] The grafting took and the new Priangan bark eclipsed all its rivals. The third crisis which began in the 1890s stemmed basically from overproduction. The cinchona planters and government, however, worked together and by various means managed to keep in production and even expand their activities, even though their counterparts in India were forced out of existence by the same circumstances. Constant research at the government experimental station, greater protection for the producers and the opening of a quinine factory at Bandoeng in 1898 all played their part. The cinchona planters also formed an association of their own to meet the challenge of a group of German and Dutch manufacturers who tried to corner the market. After tedious manoeuvrings a *modus vivendi* was reached between the two parties in 1913 which survived until 1939. An organization called the Kima Bureau was set up in Amsterdam to handle transactions between them.

In the twentieth century the area under cultivation steadily grew but production catered for a constantly fluctuating market which in 1926 led to areas of cinchona plantation being turned over to tea. In 1932 government intervened to keep the experimental research station from closing as a result of the Great Depression. It also introduced restrictions to protect the market for estate producers. Indonesian smallholders on the other hand had little opportunity to establish a foothold in the industry and their share of production remained small—only 1½ per cent of the whole in 1937—because of the capital outlay and specialization involved. Nevertheless they were provided with some opportunities in the 1920s and 1930s by Japanese investors who advanced credit to them on easy terms, bought up their crop and then undersold the Dutch estates, a serious matter for the latter since their output was already 100 per cent in excess of world needs. The official controls over cultivation and exports after 1932 were in fact directed as much to deal with this situation as to deal with general conditions on the world market outside.

Oil

In 1937 the Indies produced a meagre 2.8 per cent of total world output of oil, yet this industry came second in importance in export value. Serious commercial production started only in 1893.

The presence of oil had been observed in various seepages in the main oil regions of the Indies for generations but the first steps to do something about them were only taken after von Baumhauer, a German scientist, reported favourably on the presence of oil deposits near Cheribon in 1860. The first licences for prospecting were issued soon afterwards and by 1863 the Mines Service knew where the principal resources on the island were located. But the first drillings on Java in the 1860s and 1870s yielded insufficient amounts to be profitable and it was not until the discovery of much richer deposits in Sumatra and Borneo that the oil industry really got under way-

The development of the Sumatran deposits originated with the investi.

Refineries		Capacity
1. Pangkalanbrandan	(B.P.M.)	19,000
2. Plaju	(B.P.M.)	45,000
3. Plaju/S. Gorong	(N.K.P.M.)	45,000
4. Chepu	(B.P.M.)	15,000
5. Wonokromo	(B.P.M.)	2,500
6. Blora (Kapuan)	(N.K.P.M.)	500
7. Balikpapan	(B.P.M.)	42,000
8. Tarakan	(B.P.M.)	*

Capacity = barrels per day
* Dehydrating plant only

Oil production in volume (metric tons) and value: 1900–1940		
	('000)	£ (millions)
1900		5
1913	960	113
1920	1,784	310
1925		173
1929		164
1930	4,021	190
1932	3,885	97
1937	5,878	165
1940	3,850	170

Source: Admiralty Handbook.

THE MAIN OIL-FIELDS OF THE INDIES

I North Sumatran Field

First successful boring by Zijlker made around Aru Bay, 1884.

In 1930s main fields were Rantau, Serangjaya, Perlak and Palu Tabuhan; the bulk from Rantau, opened in 1929; older fields of Telaga Said and Darat exhausted by 1940. All worked by B.P.M. N.I.A.M. worked small field on Pulau Panjang, north of Pangkalan Susu.

II Palembang-Jambi Field

Richest field in the Indies, yielding 38 per cent of all crude oil in 1937; oil mined in area since 1898; in the 1930s mainly worked by B.P.M. and N.K.P.M., bulk of production from fields newly found in 1937.

Area between Sungai Kampar and Sungai Rokan prospected with positive results by the N.K.P.M. and N.P.P.M./N.K.P.M. discovered a new field at Lirik in Indragiri.

III Central and East Java Fields

Oldest known fields in the Indies and first to be prospected; centred in Rembang and Surabaya; worked since 1889. In 1930s chief concessionaires were B.P.M. and N.K.P.M. The N.P.M. also had a concession but not yet in production.

IV West Borneo Fields

(a) Mahakam Basin-Balikpapan: first discovered in the 1880s; chief concessionaires in the 1930s were B.P.M. and N.K.P.M.

(b) Sangkulirang Bay: operations started in 1931; concessionaires were Japanese; production still limited (i.e. in 1940).

(c) Tarakan and Bunju: Tarakan field in operation since 1907; in the 1930s concessionaires were B.P.M. and N.K.P.M.; oil on P. Bunju discovered in 1923 but not exploited prior to 1941.

V The Great East Fields

(a) Ceram; field at Bula worked by B.P.M. since 1914; produced 5 per cent of Indies total in 1937.

(b) New Guinea (West Irian): the Vogelkop intensively prospected by the N.N.G.P.M. since 1935 and wells sunk at Klamono, Wasian and Mogoi.

B.O.M. Borneo Olie Maatschappij (Japanese)
B.P.M. N.V. de Bataafse Petroleum Maatschappij (Royal Dutch Shell)
N.I.A.M. N.V. Nederlandse Indische Aardolie Mij. (Netherlands Indies Government + B.P.M.)
N.K.P.M. N.V. Nederlandse Koloniale Petroleum Mij. (Esso/Stanvac)
N.N.G.P.M. N.V. Nederlandse Nieuw-Guinee Petroleum Mij. (combined)
N.P.P.N. N.V. Nederlandse Pacific Petroleum Mij. (Caltex)

8. Oil in the Netherlands East Indies: Areas and Production, 1900–1940

gations of A.J.S. Zijlker, the manager of a local tobacco firm, into oil seepages near Langkat in the Culture Zone. Finding the oil excellent, he obtained a concession from the Raja of Langkat and in 1883 started drilling.
But he immediately found that he could not cope with the technical problems
involved and that the development of his wells in fact lay well beyond his
own resources. So in 1890 he sold his concession to a group of financiers who
floated the Royal Dutch Company. Under its dynamic general manager,
J.B. Kessler, the new company now turned to deal with the formidable problems with which it was faced, which included oil fields located in deep and
hitherto inaccessible jungle, an almost total absence of communications and
no labour force immediately available. More crucial still the long time between the production of the oil and its sale to the consumer meant an initially
slow return on capital invested. Although by 1896 Kessler had made considerable progress, the finances of the Company remained shaky. At this
juncture the fortunes of Royal Dutch were rescued by Henry Deterding, at
that time sub-agent of the N.H.M. in Penang. Having advanced N.H.M.
capital for the new industry on the security of the oil itself, Deterding joined
Royal Dutch and became the man responsible for the sales of the product.
Deterding's intervention in 1896 resulted in the formation of a new policy of
selling direct to consumers as much as possible and of enlarging the Company's market outside the Indies. But although he did much in both directions two years later Royal Dutch was confronted with even more serious
difficulties arising from the sudden drop in supply from a number of the
Sumatran wells and from the Company's conflict with the powerful Standard Oil Company of New Jersey (Esso). In the cut-throat competition for
markets between the two concerns which now ensued, Standard Oil tried
first to acquire a controlling interest in Royal Dutch itself and then become
a producer in the Indies as well; blocked both ways, the American firm then
followed a policy of underselling Royal Dutch wherever they had a common
market. By 1900 the position of Royal Dutch had become very precarious
indeed. To deal with this situation Deterding kept up his policy of selling
direct to consumers and sought to reduce costs, lower prices and raise efficiency by employing scientific methods of prospecting and production and
by reaching agreements with regional competitors. He also acquired the
timely backing of the great European banking house of Rothschild. Consequently, in 1902 Royal Dutch came to an understanding with the Dordtsche Petroleum Mij[43] and two years later bought out the French-owned
company with its fifty wells near Palembang. In 1907 Deterding brought
about the merger between Royal Dutch and the Shell Trading and Transport
Company of London.

The Shell Trading and Transport Company was the creation of a Dutch
prospector called J.M. Menten and a London sundries merchant called Mar-
cus Samuel.[44] Samuel had become involved in the oil industry as an exporter
of Russian oil to the Far East. The success of this enterprise and backing from
Rothschild's led him to float the Shell Trading and Transport Company in
1897. Soon running foul of Royal Dutch in his search for markets, Samuel
listened sympathetically to the appeals of Menten for backing for his oil

discoveries in Borneo and agreed to take up the Bornean concession. But investment proved costlier than expected, the British government was not to be moved by appeals for support on strategic grounds, and although the wells of Balikpapan soon started paying handsome dividends, a *modus vivendi* with Deterding was clearly desirable. Hence drawn from opposite poles, as it were, by mutual self-interest both parties entered into an association which has endured.

Although private enterprise clearly played a key role in the development of the oil industry in the Netherlands Indies, the Dutch colonial administration also took an active part, both in promoting the new industry and in ensuring that Dutch interests were properly safeguarded. Accordingly in 1910 and again in 1921 amendments were made to the basic Mining Law of 1899 to provide for oil mining under state control, direct or indirect, and for the creation of mixed companies operated jointly by private interests and the government. In the latter year, under a special ordinance enacted to ensure the Dutch exploitation of the newly-opened Jambi oil field, the Colonial Minister empowered Royal Dutch to work the field on behalf of the government.

On the eve of the Pacific War the principal oil fields in the Indies were in Sumatra, Borneo and Java with some lesser fields in Ceram and Irian Barat. In Sumatra the chief deposits were in the north around Pangkalan Brandan and in the south at Pleju and Sungai Gerong near Palembang. The oil from Java came mainly from Chepu near Rembang and Wonokromo near Surabaya. The fields of Balikpapan and Tarakan were the main ones in Dutch Borneo.

Oil was 'perhaps the most important single objective of the Japanese in the campaigns of 1941-2'.[45]

Tobacco

Tobacco, which had been a crop in the Indies for over two hundred years, suddenly rose to prominence contemporaneously with oil at the end of the nineteenth century and in the course of the next fifty years established itself as the country's seventh export in terms of value and with its Deli leaf offered blends which were unsurpassable. On the eve of the Pacific War there were three main centres of production in the archipelago—the most famous and most profitable in the rich Culture Zone of North-east Sumatra and two older regions in Central and East Java.

Tobacco was first introduced to South-East Asia from the Americas by the Spaniards and the Portuguese in the sixteenth century and was quickly taken up by Javanese farmers. But the quality was poor and the crop never assumed any importance amongst the exports of the VOC throughout the whole of its course. It was prevalent enough to attract the attention of Muntinghe during Raffles' regime, however, and it did not pass unnoticed by van der Capellen. But during the administration of van den Bosch, probably as a consequence of the Java War, production and exports declined markedly. Tobacco was made part of the Culture System along with other doubtful runners and was organized along the lines of the sugar industry—by government contractors; but not having the same importance as sugar, tobacco growing was not subjected to such close supervision or control and private enterprise was able to develop an important share in the industry in the middle years of the nineteenth century. In 1866 the tobacco culture was abolished, along with several other cultures which had not shown a good profit.

Up to this point tobacco was still a slow runner, confined to the island of Java where it was grown on the sawah lands of the principalities by the Javanese themselves and in East Java where European capitalist and Javanese planter shared the risks. The East Java industry developed considerably after 1860, particularly in the region of Besoeki where a five-year contract system evolved by which the Western entrepreneur provided the seedlings, paid the land rent and then bought the produce for sorting, processing and export. The development of this arrangement in East Java promoted the industry and gave the area the predominance in tobacco growing in the 1880s.[46] However the golden age of the tobacco industry was not brought about in East Java but in Sumatra.

The pioneer of the industry in Sumatra was Jacobus Nienhuys, the son of an Amsterdam tobacco broker, who arriving in Java in early 1863 with a mind to plant tobacco in Besoeki decided to try in Sumatra instead. Obtaining a concession from the local ruler, he was soon planting tobacco on the banks of the Deli River. Nienhuys' instinct proved right. The first shipments of his tobacco to arrive at Amsterdam got a very good reception and he now had no difficulty in finding backers. Finally in 1869 the Deli Maatschappij was formed, half of the capital being put up by the N.H.M. and the rest by Nienhuys himself and two associates.[47] The great success and expansion of the Company which followed was mainly due to Jacobus Cremer, its manager, whose methods formed the model adopted by other tobacco concerns. The formation of the Deli Mij. marked the opening of this part of Sumatra to Western enterprise and to the development of the Culture Zone which became the richest source of exports in the whole archipelago. The Company's success quickly attracted capital—mostly British, German and Swiss. A boom followed, at the height of which a hundred firms were dabbling in tobacco. The Deli leaf acquired a magic reputation and outbidding the best from Havana was enabling certain tobacco firms to pay out dividends of over 110 per cent in the 1900s.[48]

But not all those who ventured into tobacco were so successful as the Deli Mij. Tobacco planting is an intricate and delicate affair, requiring—in order to obtain the quality demanded on the world market—a large outlay of capital, much labour and much land. Being grown in a totally undeveloped region with a scanty and subsistence level population, huge sums were also needed to provide other essential services such as transportation, water supplies, health facilities and administration.[49] Many speculators misread the signs and went in too rashly. They did not survive the first serious crisis caused by a substantial fall in prices in 1891 which ended tobacco's reign as the region's sole export crop. By 1918 out of the 100 firms, only four survived and even they had to diversify their interests. The Deli Mij. threw open some of its land to rubber and oil palm and branched out into coffee, sisal and tea estates. It also secured an interest in the Nederlandse Rubber Unie (N.R.U.) which bought and processed smallholders' rubber. These four companies also combined their interests into the powerful Union of Tobacco Planters, which had its headquarters at Medan.

The most important changes that took place after 1918 were brought about by the penetration of the cigarette manufacturers into the industry. Large cigarette factories were erected in the country, resulting in a new injection of capital into the industry and in considerable improvement in the quality of the tobacco grown. At first the tobacco manufacturers depended upon imported leaf but started taking from local producers as well, following the system prevalent in East Java, making contracts with peasant cultivators and also with estates. They also raised the supervision of cultivation to a new pitch of efficiency by setting up 'leaf stations' in the heart of the tobacco-growing areas, complete with sheds for buying, curing, grading and packing. By the 1930s the average station had an annual turnover of half a million pounds of tobacco and was manned by a European manager with Chinese assistants and Indonesian labour. As the European pioneers in East Java had done, the manufacturers provided seed and fertilizers to their farmer-contractors, and occasionally cash advances as well. They also provided detailed instructions on how to tend the crop.

Meanwhile Indonesian smallholder as opposed to Western or Western-controlled production also flourished and expanded in the second half of the nineteenth century, and still more so in the first decades of the twentieth. In 1924 smallholder production reached its peak, covering an area twice as great as it had been at the turn of the century. In 1931 it accounted for 79 per cent of all the tobacco grown in the Indies. Most of this tobacco was grown on Java, emphasizing the divorce between the Western-dominated export industry with its large capital investment and labour force in Sumatra and the Javanese smallholders' production which was directed to an expanding home market.

Rubber

One of the last of the new export crops to be introduced to the Indies, rubber was soon to become the first in importance. In 1937 the rubber industry was leader amongst the exports of the Indies and contributed 38 per cent to the world total.

Rubber only started to assume any significance in the Indies economy in the first years of the twentieth century, and substantial production was not achieved till 1914. Prior to the Pacific War, Indies rubber owed much to Malaya, being able to benefit directly from the earlier experience and mistakes of the Malayan industry and, when rubber as a whole was faced with the problem of overproduction, was sheltered by its more developed neighbour.

Experiments with rubber in the Indies predate those in the Peninsula. The first, conducted with the native *ficus elastica* in 1864 and similar attempts with another strain a few years later were unsuccessful, and in 1876 or 1877 some of Wickham's seeds were planted at Buitenzorg. But attempts by

Buitenzorg to popularize them amongst Western planters proved as futile as Ridley's efforts across the Straits of Malacca. In 1898 barely 2,500 acres were under rubber in the whole of Java. Serious attention to rubber was shown only at the turn of the century. In 1900 the Forest Department laid down the first (state-owned) rubber plantation in the Indies. Three years later private enterprise took the plunge when the P & T Lands investigated the progress of the industry in the Malay Peninsula and Ceylon and started planting on its own domains. One or two others followed suit. The new industry was entirely in European hands, for no Indonesian had the necessary capital while the Chinese were barred from holding land.

From 1906 to 1914 the rubber industry underwent rapid expansion as planters and speculators rode on the crest of its first big boom. Encouraged by a deliberate official policy of light taxation, Western capital—Dutch, French, British, Belgian and American—was attracted from all sides. The first area of expansion was the Culture Zone of East Sumatra where the tobacco planters had already cleared the land, created the infra-structure of communications and administrative services, acquired the labour which the new industry needed and also provided the expertise for they were considered the most experienced in the Indies. Harrisons Crosfield opened the first estate in Sumatra in 1906, which they sold three years later to the United Serdang (Sumatra) Rubber Plantation Limited, one of the first rubber companies in the Indies to be floated on the London market. In the same year (1909) *hevea brasiliensis* was officially adopted by the Forestry Department. The famous P & T Lands were bought up by the new rubber firm of Java United Plantations Limited in 1910, subsequently reconstituted as Anglo-Dutch Plantations Limited. This year (1910) also saw the advent of powerful Franco-Belgian interests with Adrian Hallet who founded the Société Financière des Caoutchoucs (Socfin) which was to become the main channel for Franco-Belgian investment in South-East Asia and acquired extensive holdings in the Netherlands Indies. Now the rubber manufacturers stepped onto the scene, led by the monolithic United States Rubber Company which by 1912 had established a firm foothold in Sumatra through its subsidiary, the Holland-America Plantage Mij. Two years later both the Goodyear Tyre Company (in Sumatra) and the Italian firm of Pirelli (Java) had set themselves up in the Indies as well. Nineteen thirteen was the first year of substantive exports. By 1925 rubber had become the leading export of the country, surpassing sugar. A large proportion of the capital invested in the industry was non-Dutch.[50]

However rubber in the Indies was soon enough confronted with problems identical to those which faced its sister industry in Malaya, in particular overproduction, compounded by the two great trade depressions of 1920 and 1929. The attempt by the major producers of both countries to meet the crisis caused by the first of these depressions by restricting their output and exports on a voluntary basis did not work, undermined by the private estates who had under the same circumstances either to increase their production or perish and by the growing army of smallholders on whom no proper check could be imposed at all. The Stevenson Plan which the British then put forward in its place found a welcome amongst the large estate owners in the Indies but was rejected by the Batavian administration on the grounds that the more efficient estates could weather the crisis and that restriction would strike at the prosperity of the smallholders which the government was anxious to encourage. So when the Plan went into operation the Netherlands Indies stayed out, thereby causing its failure for the same reasons that the attempts at voluntary restriction had failed previously. In any case, shortly after the introduction of the Plan, the rubber market started to recover, stimulating Indies producers, especially smallholders, so that while the Malayan industry remained pegged down to its self-imposed restrictions, planters in the Indies could take full advantage of the new boom. Production soared and the Indies moved ahead from providing one-third of the total world supply in 1925 to producing half of it in 1927.

The Indies, with its increased production, could not escape the repercussions of the far more acute and prolonged Depression of 1929. The problem posed by the very large role of the smallholders again deterred Batavia from committing itself to renewed schemes for international restriction, but after the failure of a second 'tapping holiday' in 1930 and under the mounting pressure from an influential minority of large estate producers who feared smallholder competition, in 1932 rubber exports were subjected to control for the first time and a system of licensing was introduced, the proceeds of which were used for research.[51] In 1934 the Netherlands Indies subscribed to the International Rubber Restriction Agreement which was to be in force for four years. This Agreement which was extended for another four years in 1938, proved to be quite advantageous to the Indies rubber industry, in particular as a result of the adjustable quota system which enabled the Indies' quota to be placed on par with that of Malaya by the end of the decade.

From the earliest days the importance of rubber research was realized and carried out in the Indies. The main research centres were the Algemeene Landbouw Syndikaat at Buitenzorg, founded in 1913 by various associations of rubber, tea, cinchona, coffee and cocoa producers in Java, and the Algemeene Vereeniging van Rubberplanters ter Oostkust van Sumatra (AVROS) with its headquarters at Medan. The Indies took the lead in research into bud-grafting and the production of more productive clones. Experiments in bud-grafting were first introduced in Java in 1913 and put into practice there four years later. By 1920 the ordinary yield per acre had been more than doubled. During the 1920s further great strides forward were made and by 1928 newly-developed budstock and selected seeds were being exported to Singapore and Kuala Lumpur. Successful research in bud-grafting finally produced in the early 1930s such clones as AVROS 49 and the fabulous TJ 1 which raised the productivity of the rubber tree up to 4,400 pounds per acre. Another significant development in the rubber industry was the growth of ancillary rubber manufactures.

Rubber was the one new crop which proved a boon not only to the foreign planter but to Indonesians as well, particularly in the Western half of the archipelago. By 1942 there were nearly ¾ million registered smallholders, occupying more than half the area under rubber and accounting for at least half of total production. Prior to 1941 an estimated five to six million people derived their cash incomes from rubber. The majority of the small-holders were to be found in Sumatra, especially in Palembang (25 per cent), Jambi and the East Coast Residency which together with areas in South-East and West Borneo made up four-fifths of their number.

The earliest reports of smallholdings came from Jambi in 1904, and the first cargo of smallholder rubber sailed in 1911. An important part in the spread of rubber smallholdings was played by Muslim pilgrims who learned of the great success of rubber as they called at Malayan and Ceylonese ports on their way to the Holy Land and through them developed a lively trade in seedlings. Smallholder production became significant after 1915 and spread rapidly. While smallholders benefited as a result of the Little Depression of the early 1920s, since they were less vulnerable and did not have large over-heads, they were seriously affected by the restrictions imposed on production after the Great Depression of 1929. Under the system imposed by the author-ities in order to comply with the IRRC's quota, estate production was con-trolled by export licences, while the smallholders, of whose extent and where-abouts the Dutch administration was often only dimly aware, were made to pay a special export duty on their produce. This duty, which was constantly being raised in attempts to control their rising production, created serious discontent. In 1937 therefore changes were made. Smallholders were regis-tered and then licensed in the same manner as the estates and a special quota allocated for them. A second registration carried out in 1938 made it clear to what extent the amount of smallholder territory had been underestimated.[52]

Nevertheless the smallholder survived, and rubber played the same role in the peasant subsistence economy in the western half of the archipelago as copra in the eastern part.[53]

Oil palm

The latest arrival onto the scene as an export product was palm-oil. Although the oil palm was introduced into the Indies some time before rubber, it only became established in the twentieth century. By 1937 it had risen to eighth place in importance amongst Indies exports and accounted for 19 per cent of total world exports and for nearly 50 per cent of world production. The oil palm took root mostly in Sumatra—in Acheh and the Culture Zone—although some were also planted in Java.

The first oil palms, the *eloeis guieensis* from West Africa, were imported and planted on an experimental basis in both Java and Sumatra by the Buiten-zorg Botanical Gardens in 1848, with the encouragement of the Dutch home government. But oil palms languished in the Indies until the end of the cen-tury when the new worldwide demand for vegetable oils and the initiative of Adrian Hallet transformed the situation. By 1915 he had planted over 6,600 acres in Sumatra with the new crop. Amongst a number of important concerns which became interested in oil palm at this time were Harrisons Crosfield, the RCMA and H.V.A., and in the 1920s the industry expanded rapidly.[54] In 1922 28,000 acres were under oil palm, in 1930 150,000 acres with forty-eight estates.

The Great Depression of 1929 naturally affected the industry but nothing to the same extent as its contemporaries in other fields, primarily because palm-oil was cheaply produced and served an expanding market. Although arrangements were made between local companies concerning marketing, no official attempt at restriction—impossible in view of the ever-present competition of other vegetable oils—was ever made. During the 1930s the area under oil palm actually increased, especially as failing rubber planters and others turned to it as a way out of their difficulties. By 1940 270,000 acres stood under the crop, and there were sixty-four estates in production, of which fifty-six were in Sumatra. Typically enough the bulk of Sumatra's production went overseas, particularly to the United States while Java's produce, on the other hand, was largely absorbed by the local soap manufacturers.

The oil palm industry was manifestly unsuitable for the smallholder or independent producer. Even the harvesting of the fruit demands much time and attention, as it becomes quickly bruised and the quality of the oil is easily impaired. The processing can only be done with expensive machinery. It was therefore an estate crop *par excellence*, from which the Indonesian was completely excluded.

Coconuts, copra and coconut-oil

One product native to the region which remained substantially an Indonesian affair was the coconut. In the twentieth century it assumed major importance amongst the exports of the Indies. By 1941 nearly one-third of the world's copra exports came from the archipelago, particularly from the Outer Islands. Copra was also fourth in value amongst Indies exports.

The rise of the coconut industry on the world market is associated with the technical advances in processing which stimulated the demand for vegetable oils at the end of the nineteenth century, with the spread of modern steamship services in the islands during the same period, mainly with the expansion of the K.P.M., and with the role of Chinese traders who acted as the agents for the Indonesian growers. The Chinese invariably owned primitive kilns; they bought the crop from the Indonesians and advanced cash on easy terms; in this way they were soon tapping the profits of the trade and bringing it under their control. As Macassar and other ports (particularly Penang and Singapore) rose up as entrepôts for the copra trade, Chinese firms played the leading role as dealers.

Western participation on the other hand was limited by the effective competition of low cost producers. Although government established a couple of experimental stations and model plantations to stimulate the industry, Western enterprise was on the whole restricted to exporting the crop. Certain firms went into the opening up of plantations themselves, the most prominent of which was the Molukse Handels-Vereeniging, founded by a group of Amsterdam merchants in 1866. The M.H.V. opened some coconut plantations in North Celebes, but also bought from local producers. A Danish company (the Aarhus Oil Mills) maintained an important establishment in Macassar.

While the Chinese were the principal millers and shared the export trade with the Westerners, 95 per cent of actual production was in Indonesian hands. For the Indonesian subsistence farmer of the eastern half of the archipelago, copra had the same significance as rubber had for smallholders in the western half. Eighty per cent of the volume and 60 per cent of the value of the trade of the Great East came from the copra industry. Its expansion after 1900 introduced the use of cash to the islanders and lifted them out of their subsistence economy; they abandoned their diet of sago and the coconut itself and imported rice from as far afield as Thailand, French Indo-China and Burma. The industry increased threefold between 1900 and 1913 and demand continued to soar in the 1920s. Although Chinese middlemen siphoned off a substantial portion of the profits, there is no doubt that the Indonesian grower shared in the general prosperity.

The Great Depression of 1929 was a serious blow to the industry. There was little the government could do to protect the grower or the exporter from the drastic fall in prices and the consequent drop in living standards. Only in 1940 with the severe shipping shortage caused by the outbreak of war in Europe was Batavia able to step in and exercise some control. It established Coprafonds, an export agency which created a monopoly over all exports, bought cheaply when the market was good and used the profits to bolster prices when the market was weak. But the private field had greatly contracted.

Lesser products: indigo and fibres
Indigo—the deep blue dye so characteristic of Javanese cloth—today has been almost completely eliminated by synthetic competitors, yet it was for three centuries one of the principal products of Java and a mainstay of Dutch revenues. Included in the VOC's system of deliveries and contingencies since the end of the seventeenth century, indigo production suffered its first set-back under Raffles who encouraged the consumption of imported English cotton-piece goods at the expense of the Javanese cloth industry, but it recovered again under du Bus de Gisignies who was out to restore Dutch trade. Under the Culture System indigo came third in importance although it was described as 'the most obnoxious' and 'one of the most laborious' of the cultures from the Javanese producers' point of view. In 1840 the industry reached the peak of its production but twenty-five years later was sold out to private enterprise, alongside several other cultures. The shadows of indigo's decline were first cast by the invention of synthetic dyes in 1875. By 1896 the synthetic product was on the commercial market and by 1913 large quantities of synthetic dyes were being imported into the Indies.

Amongst the various fibres grown in the Indies sisal and cantala between them held eleventh place in 1937 in terms of export value, while kapok came thirteenth. In fact kapok was the most important fibre product of the Indies before the Pacific War, accounting for 70 per cent to 80 per cent of world production. It was mainly grown in Central and East Java, on Madura, in South Sumatra and on Bali, Lombok and Celebes. Although the first kapok factories were started by Indonesians, they were soon taken over by Chinese;

91 per cent of production (in 1931), on the other hand, remained in Indonesian hands. In 1935 the world economic situation led the Dutch to place the crop under government supervision so as to improve its quality and to control but not to restrict its export. As for sisal and cantala, the Indies was the world's second largest producer in 1937. Their main market was the U.S.A. and the chief regions of cultivation were in Java and Sumatra.

Cotton was important as a domestic crop in the twentieth century but once had been an important export, and was one of the original products demanded by the VOC under its system of contingencies and forced deliveries. Cotton cultivation was extended under Daendels but with the Culture System came Dutch-manufactured piece-goods. In 1848 two-thirds of clothing in the Indies still came from homespun cotton but tariff manipulation in favour of the textiles of Twante led to Dutch domination of the market. Indies cotton production received no more encouragement until 1919 when the Government Textile Institute of Bandoeng was set up, followed in 1926 by the first cotton-wool factory. After 1929 however, under the pressures of the Great Depression together with the penetration of the Indies market by Japanese goods and the repercussions amongst Indonesian nationalists of Gandhi's *swadeshi* movement, the colonial government was stimulated into further action. Greater participation by Western enterprise was encouraged, which resulted amongst other things in a co-operative weaving-shed venture at Tegal in 1937. The cotton textile industry of the Indies faced fair prospects on the eve of the Pacific War.

The role of rice
Although in 1941 the Indies was the largest rice producer in the region, and rice was one of its basic products, it could no longer be considered an export crop.[55] Of the 13 million tons harvested in 1940, the greatest proportion by far—over three-fifths—came from Java. Rice had been the traditional export of the island in the past; it had formed the basis of Mataram's power in the seventeenth century, and that of Majapahit and earlier agrarian empires, and it had been the fulcrum of Javanese influence throughout the archipelago prior to the arrival of the Dutch. Javanese rice had sustained the Malacca Sultanate at the height of its power, the pepper ports of Sumatra, the spice islanders of the Moluccas and the latter-day entrepôt of Macassar. It had been and remained the staple diet of the people and was grown everywhere, but only in surplus in the fertile, volcanic plains of Central and East Java. With the Dutch ascendancy rice cultivation continued to flourish and expand but came to play a different role. It was still an important export for the region in the eighteenth century, but during the course of the nineteenth the main rice-growing districts of the island became enmeshed in the fast-rising sugar industry for reasons already described. In Central and East Java the rice farmer became a part-time sugar planter as well. Production increased but gradually fell behind the pace of population growth. In mid-century rice production was expanding at least as rapidly as the population on the island, but after 1875 it started to lag behind. By the 1900s rice imports to Java exceeded rice exports, and to all intents and purposes it was not only a wholly Javanese

dominated industry but also almost completely a crop destined for domestic consumption alone. At the same time, the actual consumption per head of population had declined from an average of 251 lbs. a year in the third quarter of the nineteenth century to 218 lbs. in 1927, a reflection of both reduced circumstances as well as a more varied diet. However the impact of the Great Depression and the subsequently drastic decline in the sugar industry served to boost the cultivation of rice. By 1940 Java was producing sufficient to cover her own needs with a little bit to spare for export to the Outer Islands.

The rise in Javanese rice production also owed much to Dutch support. Confronted with the problems of overpopulation and food scarcity, the Dutch launched as part of their Ethical Policy a vast scheme of irrigation works which increased the area cultivable by 25 per cent. They also founded at the same time (i.e. in 1905) the Experimental Station for Rice and Secondary Crops at Buitenzorg (Bogor), which later succeeded in producing strains with a yield 25 per cent as great as the normal unselected varieties grown. Valuable work was also done in combating crop diseases and pests. But the Dutch did not make much headway in changing methods or techniques of cultivation, largely because the circumstances of economic development had made the farmer a prisoner on his own land.

Teak and other forest products

Although half of the Indies is covered by forest, prior to 1941 this resource was comparatively little exploited. This was partly due to the fact that over 68 per cent of the forested area lay in the Outer Islands, particularly in Borneo and West Irian, which were still very undeveloped before the Pacific War, while on Java and Madura the forest acreage had been greatly reduced by the intensive cultivation on those islands. Of the various products of the forest by far the most important for the national revenue as an export was teak, invaluable for its strength and durability and in high demand for shipbuilding.[56] The principal teak forests were in East and Central Java, with smaller reserves in the Lesser Sundas and Celebes. Up till the nineteenth century the VOC ruthlessly exploited these resources to meet the needs of its ships, godowns and wharves. By 1750 the northern coastal districts of Java had been stripped of their teak reserves and the timber had to be brought from inland. Under the system of contingencies and forced deliveries certain villages were charged with teak deliveries in lieu of all other services, but these people were savagely exploited. Daendels abolished the teak quotas but was soon forced to restore them because of the financial difficulties he faced. The production of teak continued on a compulsory basis up till 1865 when the industry was thrown open to private enterprise.

The first efforts at using scientific methods for the teak forests date from 1849 when a group of German forestry experts were employed in the jungles of Rembang, followed in 1857 by trained foresters sent from Holland. In 1858 the first Inspector of Forests was appointed, marking the start of a great improvement in forest administration and of teak forest control. In 1865 in consonance with the opening of forests to private enterprise a new Forest Ordinance classified forest areas and established forest reserves. Under the

Forest Ordinance of 1897 which established a regular Forest Service and laid down the system of forest administration which prevailed till the last days of Dutch rule, the exploitation of the forests was regulated with provision for both private and state enterprise. The valuable teak forests were the subject of special regulations, and by 1941 nearly all the teak reserves on Java had been brought under direct government control and were served by a system of narrow-gauge railways. Systematic reafforestation was started on Java and Sumatra in 1910.

Indonesian participation in the production of the 'jungle forests' was far greater than that of the teak forests where they served merely in a labouring capacity. One-eighth of total Indonesian production before 1941 came from forest sources, although this figure includes rubber and copra. While the exploitation of large areas of jungle forest was conducted under lease (forest concessions) Indonesians also participated on 'a fairly large scale', especially in South Borneo and around Palembang. On Bengkalis and in the Riau archipelago, Chinese 'panglong' timber cutters, with a ready market in Singapore, had an important share.

The development of communications

A necessary concomitant of colonial economic development was the growth and spread of communications. The development of communications provoked a revolution in itself, eliminating time barriers, opening up previously inaccessible regions to commerce, stimulating local trade and facilitating the movement of people. Modern communications started to proliferate in the nineteenth century, beginning with Daendels, the first great modernizer, in Java, accelerating under the Culture System and reaching its peak with the triumph of Liberalism and the new pressures released by the opening of the Suez Canal.

That Java was the scene of the first significant development in communications was the natural outcome of the concentration of Dutch enterprise on that island together with the availability of a large and pliable labour force and the accessibility of funds. The first modern road on Java, linking Anyer on the Straits of Sunda with Panarukan in East Java, was built by Daendels for both strategic and economic purposes between 1808 and 1811 at a frightful cost in human life. This trunk road, running through the most thickly populated regions along the northern coastline, forms the backbone of the present road network on the island. During the course of the nineteenth century this network grew as branch roads were built—particularly between 1830 and 1870 under the pressure of the Culture System—to connect the chief plantation areas and to facilitate the transportation and exporting of crops. But the evolution of a comprehensive road system for the whole island had to wait for the twentieth century when the invention of the motor-car made it imperative. Plans were laid within the first decade of the new century and work started in 1912. By 1938 the system was more-or-less complete, with two basic routes running east-west and serving the northern and southern halves of Java.

In the rest of the Indies, road development started much later and was

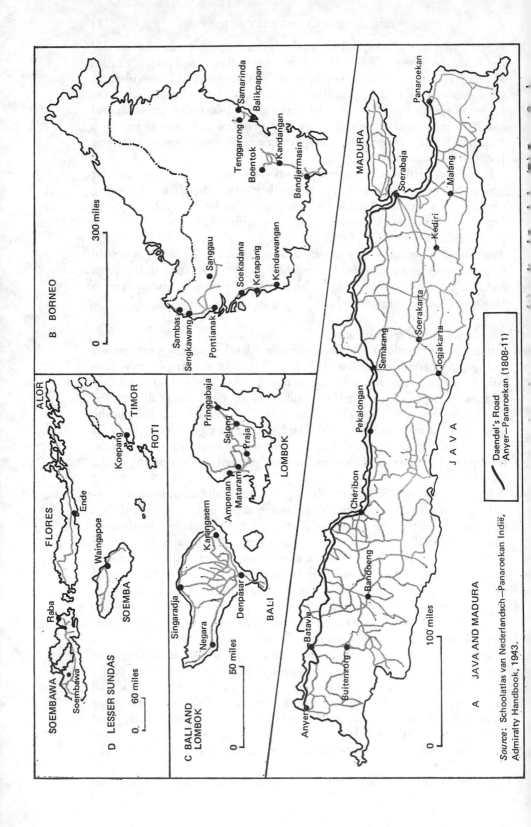

B BORNEO

300 miles

0

Samarinda
Tenggarong
Balikpapan
Boentok
Kandangan
Bandjermasin

Sanggau
Soekadana
Ketapang
Kendawangan

Sambas
Sengkawang
Pontianak

ALOR

FLORES

TIMOR

Koepang

ROTI

Ende

Waingapoe

SOEMBA

SOEMBAWA

Raba

Soembawa

D LESSER SUNDAS

60 miles

0

Pringgabaja

Selong

Praja

Ampenan

Mataram

Karangasem

LOMBOK

Singaradja

Negara

Denpasar

BALI

C BALI AND LOMBOK

50 miles

0

MADURA

Panaroekan

Soerabaja

Malang

Kediri

Semarang

Soerakarta

Jogjakarta

Pekalongan

Chéribon

Bandoeng

Batavia

Buitenzorg

Anyer

J A V A

Daendel's Road
Anyer—Panaroekan (1808-11)

A JAVA AND MADURA

100 miles

0

Source: Schoolatlas van Nederlandsch—Panaroekan Indië,
Admiralty Handbook, 1943.

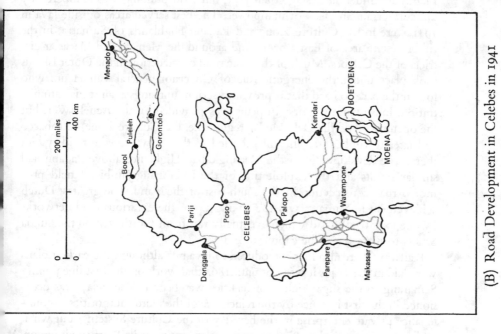

(B) Road Development in Celebes in 1941

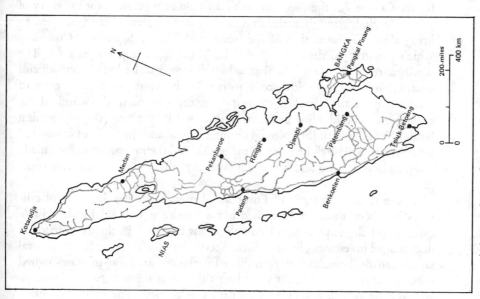

10. (A) Road Development in Sumatra in 1941

much more limited. Not only did the Dutch turn their attention to the Outer Islands at a much later stage than Java, but road building was hampered by difficult terrain and lack of manpower. The best served areas outside Java in 1941 were in the Culture Zone and Padang Highlands of Sumatra, in the rubber estate area of East Borneo and around the Menado and Macassar districts of the Celebes. Much of the basic road construction in the Outer Islands took place under the energetic rule of Governor-general van Heutz who forced the pace so hard that it provoked serious uprisings against his administration. In Sumatra the first impetus was provided by the Acheh War, but the opening up of the Deli-Medan region (i.e. the Culture Zone) to tobacco and later to rubber, tea and oil palm led to the growth of the road system there. The development of the Menangkabau Highlands above Padang had similar results and the exploitation of the Palembang-Jambi oil field promoted road construction in the south-east of the island. The greatest Dutch achievement in Sumatra was the linking up of these various road networks by one long trunk road which eventually ran from Oosthaven on the Sunda Straits to Kota Raja, the capital of Acheh.

Railways were also first introduced to Java but although the earliest plans were laid in the 1840s it was not until 1864 that work on the first line joining Semarang to the sugar-rich principalities was begun. The delay was occasioned in the first instance by the reluctance of the Dutch authorities to countenance private enterprise in the hey-day of the Culture System[57] but when under van Twist in the 1850s more liberal views prevailed, private investors proved chary of the risks involved. Finally, with van der Putte as Minister for the Colonies in the 1860s and with the field being cleared for the entry of private capital, enough enthusiasm and encouragement were generated to bring about the formation of the Nederlandse Indise Spoorweg Company which was granted the concession to build the Semarang line in 1862. The significance of this line was that although it had to be built over difficult country, it would provide access to one of the most profitable centres of production on the island. Two years later the Company also acquired the concession to build a line between Batavia and Buitenzorg (Bogor), joining Java's chief port with the colonial summer capital and the focus of coffee and tea cultivation. The difficulties of the terrain and the ravages of disease made progress heavy going and it was not until 1873 that the two lines were completed.

By this time the interest of European planters in the development of railways had been thoroughly roused but a prudence induced by the visible evidence of the expenses and complications involved in their construction discouraged investment in new lines. Accordingly in 1875 the States-general sanctioned the spending of ƒ1 million for the construction of state-owned railway lines in Java and four years later the first of them, between Surabaya and Malang with a branch to Pasaruan, was opened. The 1880s saw great advances in railway building with both government and private enterprise playing their part. A natural division of labour developed: government concentrated on strategic lines which opened up remote parts of the islands without the possibility of any immediate return, while private enterprise

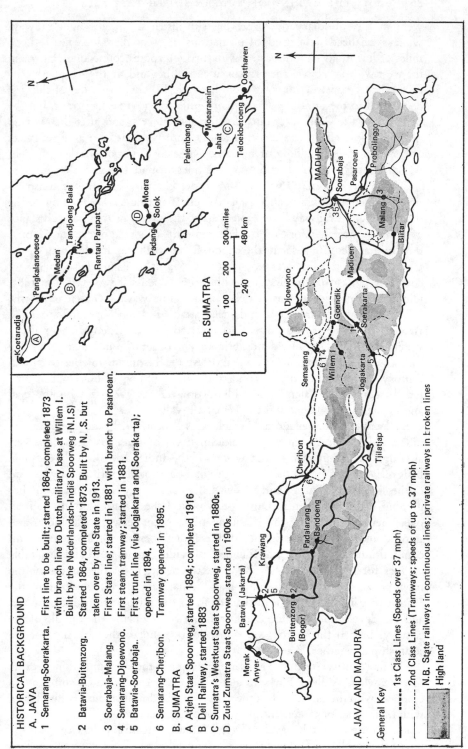

HISTORICAL BACKGROUND

A. JAVA

1 Semarang-Soerakarta. First line to be built; started 1864, completed 1873 with branch line to Dutch military base at Willem I. Built by the Nederlandsch-Indië Spoorweg (N.I.S)

2 Batavia-Buitenzorg. Started 1864, completed 1873. Built by N. .S. but taken over by the State in 1913.

3 Soerabaja-Malang. First State line; started in 1881 with branch to Pasaroean.

4 Semarang-Djoewono. First steam tramway; started in 1881.

5 Batavia-Soerabaja. First trunk line (via Jogjakarta and Soerakarta); opened in 1894.

6 Semarang-Cheribon. Tramway opened in 1895.

B. SUMATRA

A Atjeh Staat Spoorweg, started 1894; completed 1916

B Deli Railway, started 1883

C Sumatra's Westkust Staat Spoorweg, started in 1880s.

D Zuid Zumatra Staat Spoorweg, started in 1900s.

A. JAVA AND MADURA

General Key

----- 1st Class Lines (Speeds over 37 mph)

—— 2nd Class Lines (Tramways; speeds of up to 37 mph)

N.B. State railways in continuous lines; private railways in broken lines

▨ High land

B. SUMATRA

0   100   200   300 miles
0   240   480 km

II. Railway Development in (A) Java and Madura (B) Sumatra in 1941 went in for subsidiary tracks serving sub-districts, and for light railways which specialized in the needs of plantations. By 1900 there were nearly 2,000 miles of line in Java and Madura, with through routes connecting Batavia in the west with Surabaya, the principalities and beyond. In the twentieth century railway construction was more limited. The boom period of the first decade led to the building of 310 more miles of government track, but the outbreak of the Great War curtailed further projects, and after the War up till 1941 most effort was directed to the improvement of existing services rather than to the building of new ones. The most important development was the electrification of sections of the lines around Batavia.

Outside Java, Sumatra was the only other island where railway construction assumed any significance. The Acheh War caused the building of the first line, a light railway from Kota Raja to the shores of Aru Bay, a distance of some 300 miles. Work on the line was started in 1894 under van Heutsz, then military commander in the region. Later, with the development of the Culture Zone, this line was extended southwards to Pangkalan Susu, being completed in 1916. The first line within the Zone itself was started in 1883, joining Medan with its port at Belawan. This line was then extended northwards, southwards and inland and finally attained a length of some 330 miles. Around the same period government started the construction of a railway system in the Padang Highlands, primarily in order to join Padang with the state-owned coalmines at Sawahlunto. At the beginning of the twentieth century the government also undertook the building of lines which ultimately connected Palembang with Oosthaven, as well as with the coal and oil fields near Lahat and the Lematang valley.

As far as the archipelago as a whole was concerned, by far the most significant development in communications was in those by sea. However, although predominance in the waters of the Indies had been the original basis of Dutch power in the region, this had deteriorated seriously by the end of the eighteenth century and was virtually eclipsed by the events at the beginning of the nineteenth. During this period the British came to gain an overwhelming share of the maritime trade both between the Indies and Europe and between the islands of the Indies themselves. To counter this competition the N.H.M. was founded, providing guaranteed and profitable cargoes for Dutch bottoms for the next generation; at the same time the monopoly made the Dutch sluggish and lethargic and led them to allow the British to gain a decisive lead over them in the introduction of steamships and the development of the Mediterranean route during the middle of the century. Indeed the Dutch were slow to respond to the challenge of the steamship altogether.

The first Dutch attempt to reassert their stake in the shipping business came in 1842 when Willem Ruys founded the first private Dutch company to compete with the N.H.M. But the scene was still dominated by British firms, with their superior vessels and more economical services. In the late 1840s de Vries, a retired Dutch naval officer, founded a steamship service with the intent to establish a Dutch monopoly over all inter-island communications but failed when in 1863 his firm lost the contract for the conveyance of government mails and passengers to the British-owned Netherlands Indies Steam Navigation Company. The N.I.S.N. Co. held the government contract for the next thirty years, giving British interests a virtual monopoly of the marine services of the archipelago. In fact not until the dismantling of the Culture System which ended the protective Consignment System as well, and the opening of the Suez Canal in 1869 were Dutch shipowners forced to face up to the competition offered by foreign steamships. Ruys reacted by changing from sail to steam in 1870, while in the same year the first of the modern Dutch steamship companies, the Nederlandse Stoomvaart Mij., was formed to trade specifically with the East. But the continuing stranglehold of British competition hampered progress and compelled rival Dutch concerns to work more closely together. In 1875 the Rotterdam-Lloyd Steamship Association came into being, formed by a combination of small shipowners under the leadership of Ruys. In 1883 the Association was converted into the Rotterdamse-Lloyd Mij. In 1888 Rotterdam-Lloyd and the N.S.M. pooled their resources and with capital provided by the Dutch government and N.H.M. formed the Koninglijke Paketvaart Mij. (K.P.M.) and in 1892 they reached agreement to co-operate and divide the shipping trade of the Indies between them. In 1902 they combined again to form the Java-China-Japan Lijn with services to the Philippines, French Indo-China, China and Japan, and in 1906 and 1908 opened up other services between Java and Bengal and Java and the west coast of the United States.

The establishment of the K.P.M. was the masterstroke in the reassertion of Dutch maritime interests in the Indies, conceived primarily to break the back of British competition in the Indies themselves. The first aim was to wean the dependence of certain areas of the archipelago, in particular the Great East, from their dependence on Singapore as the focal point for their export trade. This had been achieved within its first twenty years. On the eve of the Pacific War the K.P.M. was indisputably supreme in the trade of the archipelago. Five-sevenths of the traffic at Indies ports in the 1930s consisted of K.P.M. vessels. The Company was also a substantial employer of Indonesian labour and maintained a nautical school at Batavia (from 1898), besides a nautical institute at Tanjong Priok for surveying and charting purposes.[58]

The development of air transport in the twentieth century was closely related to the shipping companies. In 1928 on the initiative of the K.P.M., the Deli Mij., and the N.H.M., and with the active co-operation of the Dutch government, the K.N.I.L.M. came into existence. The first services were from Batavia to Bandung and from Batavia to Semarang. A decade later its services had been extended to Saigon and Australia. Apart from the routine duties of transporting passengers, mail and freight, the K.N.I.L.M. performed valuable services in conducting aerial surveys, particularly over the Vogelkopf area of West Irian. There were seven main international airports in the Indies in 1941.

Posts, telegraphs and radio proved very important elements in the weaving together of the emerging entity of the Indies. Postal services were first introduced into Java by Daendels who made every village along his great trunk road contribute to the maintenance of the system by providing men, horses

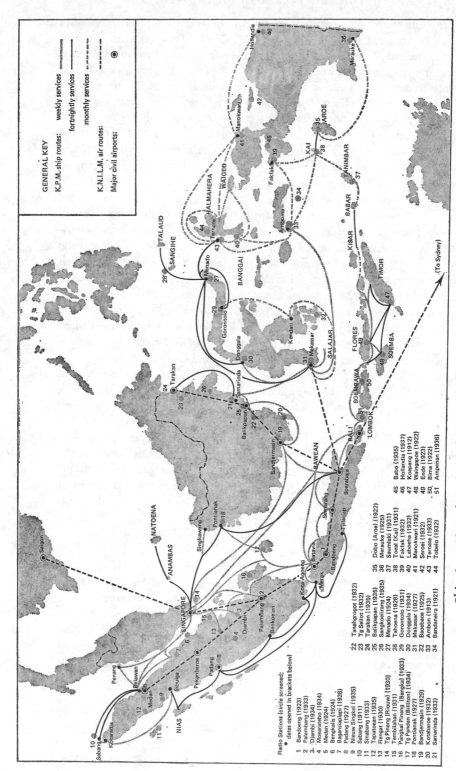

GENERAL KEY

K.P.M. ship routes:
weekly services ════════
fortnightly services ────────
monthly services ─ ─ ─ ─

K.N.I.L.M. air routes: ▪ ▪ ▪ ▪ ▪
Major civil airports: ◉

Radio Stations (circle screened;
● dates opened in brackets below)

1	Bandoeng (1923)	22	Tanahgrogot (1932)	35	Dobo (Aroe) (1922)	45	Babo (1935)
2	Palembang (1933)	23	Tg Seltot (1932)	36	Merauke (1925)	46	Hollandia (1937)
3	Djambi (1934)	24	Tarakan (1935)	37	Saumlaki (1931)	47	Koepang (1912)
4	Moearatebo (1934)	25	Balikpapan (1935)	38	Toeal (Kai) (1931)	48	Waingapoe (1922)
5	Medan (1924)	26	Sangkoelirang (1935)	39	Faktak (1932)	49	Ende (1923)
6	Bengkalis (1924)	27	Rengat (1930)	40	Laboeha (1932)	50	Seroei (1932)
7	Bagansiapiapi (1928)	14	Tg Pinang (Riouw) (1930)	41	Manokwari (1921)	51	Ampenan (1936)
8	Padang (1927)	15	Tembilahan (1931)	42	Manokwari (1921)		
9	Nieuw Singkel (1935)	16	Pangkal Pinang (Bangka) (1933)	43	Ternate (1933)		
10	Sabang (1911)	17	Tg Pandan (Billiton) (1934)	44	Bandaneira (1921)		
11	Sinabang (1933)	18	Pontianak (1927)				
12	Tapatoean (1935)	19	Bandjermasin (1929)				
13	Rengat (1930)	20	Kotabaroe (1932)				
		21	Samarinda (1933)	28	Menado (1924)		
				29	Gorontolo (1931)		
				30	Dongala (1934)		
				31	Makassar (1927)		
				32	Baoebaoe (1925)		
				33	Ambon (1913)		
				34	Samarinda (1933)		

12. Shipping, Air and Radio Communications in the Netherlands East Indies in 1941

and a small sum to meet expenses. In 1862 the government instituted a regular postal service for most areas under Dutch control, laying down conditions for the conveyance of all mail and establishing a uniform postal rate. After this there was steady and uninterrupted development and improvement up till the outbreak of the Pacific War in 1941. The first telegraph line in the Indies ran between Batavia and Buitenzorg (Bogor), opened for official use only in 1856. The following year the line was extended to Surabaya with a branch to Ambawara from Semarang and was opened to the general public. The early days of the telegraph were full of difficulties and hazards caused by long distances over jungle, swamp and mountain, with frequent break-downs resulting from forest fires or packs of wild animals, although where possible railway lines pioneered the routes. Attempts to lay down the first submarine cables linking Java to the outside world proved even more diffi-cult. The first such link between Batavia and Singapore via Muntok, laid in 1859, had to be abandoned three years later because of repeated breaks. Another line, between Anyer and Teluk Betung in South Sumatra laid in 1871, was completely destroyed by the eruption of Krakatoa in 1883. Finally in 1884 a new cable between Sumatra and Java was laid which fared better and was extended year by year till 1925 when radio-telegraphy began to take its place.

Radio-telegraphy started in the 1900s as a means of communication be-tween ships at sea and shore installations. In 1909 the important wireless sta-tion at Sabang was erected and other government stations opened on Java, Timor and Ambon a few years later. By 1937, as a result of a government report recommending the spread of radio stations to facilitate inter-island communications, there were over 50 transmitting stations in the Indies.

Private enterprise was responsible for the installation of the first telephone system in the Indies, in the 1890s. In 1906 the thirty-five separate private networks were united together in one organization under government con-trol. Radio-telephone links on an experimental basis were established be-tween the Indies and Holland in 1927 and opened to the public in 1929. Public broadcasting began around 1928. On the eve of the Japanese invasion there were twenty-four broadcasting stations, all of which were on Java except for the one at Medan.

With the accelerated spread of modern communications in the twentieth century, for the first time the general economic development of the Indies began to acquire a unity. In all this Java stood out as the focal point, the pivot of all communications, the powerhouse for industrial development, the ad-ministrative and managerial nucleus of the archipelago as a whole.

Population growth and distribution

The most immediate fact of the economic life of the Indies is the huge size of its population and the uneven manner of its distribution. The great num-bers of people are indeed commensurate with the equally vast dimensions of the country but the way in which this population is distributed is not so. Java stands head and shoulders over the other islands as we have seen already in terms of development, and likewise in terms of the number of its inhabitants.

With two-thirds of the entire population of the Indies concentrated in Java and Madura in 1930, they had by far the highest densities of population in the archipelago. In 1930 the average density in Java and Madura was 817 persons per square mile, although in Java itself these figures ranged from a minimum of 632 per square mile to over 1,000 per square mile. The only other island in the Indies to approach this figure was Bali with a density of 503 persons per square mile. The Outer Islands, on the other hand, had very low averages—Sumatra with forty-four per square mile, the Celebes with fifty-six per square mile, the Moluccas with eighteen per square mile, Borneo with twelve per square mile and West Irian with only two persons per square mile.

The natural fertility of its rich volcanic soils together with the development of efficient and advanced agricultural techniques account for the comparative density of Java's population prior to the coming of the Dutch but not for the spectacular rise in population which took place during the course of the nineteenth century and after. This growth, as we have seen, was the direct consequence of the fact that Java was the main object of Dutch efforts at exploitation, particularly after the introduction of the Culture System in 1830. The intensification of Dutch rule brought about great economic advances, and resulted in much fresh land being brought under cultivation and new means of livelihood being created. The peculiar conditions created by the sugar industry in particular formed an important stimulus for an ever-rising population. Java, too, was probably the only colonial territory in South-East Asia where Western measures and concepts of hygiene were successfully applied during the nineteenth century.

Meanwhile the Outer Islands were held back by lack of manpower. Probably before the introduction of cash crops to particular parts of Sumatra and Borneo, the natural balance between Man and his environment went against him in his struggle for survival. The resources of the Outer Islands were too scattered to prompt development as in Java, and the local population which could maintain itself only by subsistence farming because of paucity of numbers was continually limited by disease and war. In fact, with the Dutch Forward Movement in the archipelago only those regions which were associated with the production of export crops saw any increase in their populations. Such was the case with the Menangkabau Highlands of West Sumatra where rubber followed pepper as an important export crop. An even clearer example is provided by the Culture Zone on the Sumatran east coast which because of its excellent soils and accessibility to the international trade route became the centre for the production of four major crops, besides developing as a major centre for oil production on account of the deposits there. The same holds true for the major population centres in the Great East, such as Minahassa in North Celebes and Macassar in the south, both closely connected with the copra industry, and the islands of Ambon, Ceram and Banda in the Moluccas with their fertile lands and specialist crops. The only exception to the general rule that population growth marched hand in hand with colonial economic development is offered by the island of Bali, which was thickly populated before the Dutch take-over at the beginning of the twentieth century. This is attributable to the rich volcanic soils of the island, sophisti-

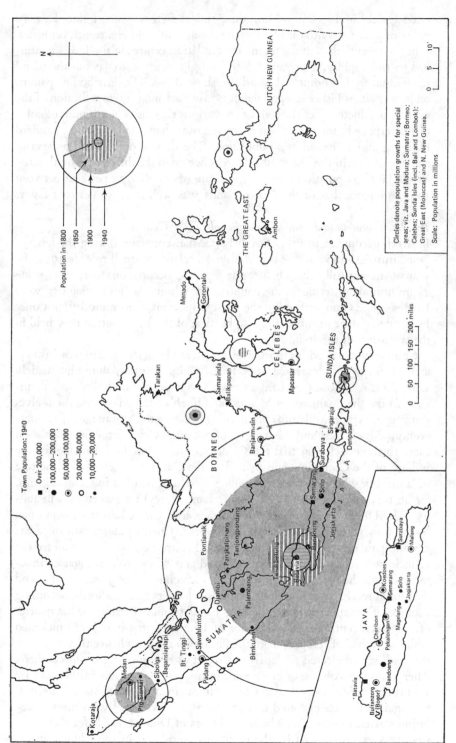

13. The Netherlands East Indies: Population Growth and Distribution, 1800–1940

Town Population: 1940

■ Over 200,000
◼ 100,000–200,000
◉ 50,000–100,000
◎ 20,000–50,000
○ 10,000–20,000
•

Population in 1800
1850
1900
1940

Circles denote population growths for special areas; viz. Java and Madura; Sumatra; Borneo; Celebes; Sunda Isles (incl. Bali and Lombok); Great East (Moluccas) and N. New Guinea.

Scale: Population in millions

DUTCH NEW GUINEA

THE GREAT EAST

Ambon

Menado
Gorontalo

CELEBES

Macassar

Tarakan
Samarinda
Balikpapan

BORNEO

Banjarmasin

Pontianak
Pangkalpinang
Tanjongpandang

Djambi
Palembang

SUMATRA

Bengkulen

Kotaraja
Medan
Ptg. Siantar
Sibolga
Bagansiapiapi
Bt. Tinggi
Sawahlunto
Padang

Tjilatjap
Batavia
Bandoeng
Semarang
Solo
Surabaya
Madioeng
Jogjakarta

JAVA

Singaraja
Denpasar

SUNDA ISLES

0 50 100 150 200 miles

Batavia
Buitenzorg (Bogor)
Cheribon
Pekalongan
Bandoeng
Magelang
Koedoes
Semarang
Solo
Jogjakarta
Surabaya
Malang

JAVA

0 5 10°

cated agricultural techniques and the political factors which induced a mass influx of Javanese onto the island in the seventeenth and eighteenth centuries.

In the twentieth century the main population centres in the Indies continued to rise rapidly, a process which brought nemesis to Java as the island reached saturation point and could absorb no more. The distribution pattern on Java itself, as Fisher has pointed out,[59] formed an accurate reflection of the relative productivity of the soils of the various regions. The stimulus of colonial enterprise in the Outer Islands, on the other hand, led to a rising standard of living and an expanding population. The decline of Javanese prosperity and rise of that in the Outer Islands are reflected in the different growth rates. While Java's population increased at a rate of roughly 20 per cent between 1920 and 1930, that of the Outer Islands was well over 50 per cent faster.

Population growth and immigration; the role of the Chinese
In striking contrast to other South-East Asian countries during the last 150 years, immigration into the Indies played a relatively small role. In 1930, the year of the last full census before the Japanese occupation, there were some $1\frac{1}{2}$ million aliens living in the country, of whom the great majority were Chinese. The Chinese formed the most important alien minority, not only by virtue of their numbers but also because of the key position they held in the economy of the Indies.

Chinese contacts with the archipelago stretch back to the dawn of history, and when the Dutch arrived, they found Chinese settlers thinly but widely scattered throughout the islands, already in far greater numbers than themselves. Like the Spaniards in Manila, the Dutch of Batavia found themselves confronted with the dilemma of choosing between the advantages of Chinese economic usefulness and the dangers of potential Chinese revolt. Coen soon came to the conclusion that the Chinese were in fact indispensable for the welfare of the Company, and that while the Company itself played the role of 'a mighty wholesale trader', retailing would be best left in Chinese hands, for 'in this connexion, and even as merchants, (they) far exceed ours in ability'. The Dutch also valued the direct trade link with China itself kept open by the flow of Chinese junks from the north. Coen's pragmatism ruled the day and paid off handsome dividends for all concerned, not least of all for the Chinese whose numbers steadily increased and whose role as sugar contractors enabled them to penetrate the domestic economy of Java, well beyond the Dutch reach. They multiplied as moneylenders and landlords, becoming a source of vexation to Dutchmen and Javanese alike. During the last quarter of the seventeenth century the pace of Chinese entry into Java quickened with the arrival of refugees from the Philippines from whence they had been expelled or had elected to depart as a result of deteriorating prospects there. After 1700 the volume of clandestine immigration rose still further and by 1733 there were already 80,000 Chinese living in and around Batavia itself. It was against this background that an atmosphere charged with mutual suspicion started to generate. The natural fears of Dutch officials for their own security were intensified by the mounting unruliness of the Chinese in the countryside, many of whom were unemployed as a result of fluctuations in the sugar and coffee markets. Chinese suspicions on the other hand were fomented by rumours of impending moves by the Dutch authorities against them, and the decision in 1740 to deport all those Chinamen who could not prove that they were making an honest living was the main trigger that set off the uprising which followed. With the Chinese in the districts around Batavia in arms against them, the Dutch response was to expel all the Chinese resident within the city walls, giving rise to the 'Batavian Fury' which cost the lives of some 10,000 Chinamen. However a small but useful minority survived and as in the Spanish Philippines, when things had quietened down the Chinese community once more demonstrated its economic usefulness and waxed prosperous in the process. The government policy of farming out revenues to the Chinese which became a marked feature of the failing days of Company rule, became a powerful source of Chinese prosperity. By the end of the eighteenth century, the Chinese were the middlemen *par excellence* of the Indies.

Up till 1800 the great bulk of Chinese immigration and settlement was confined to Java and Madura, although there were isolated pockets elsewhere, including the tin-rich islands of Bangka and Belitung where Chinese miners had been first introduced by the sultan of Palembang in the early eighteenth century, and also West Borneo where the Malay ruler of Sambas had brought them in the 1760s in order to mine for gold. In the nineteenth century Chinese labour was specifically recruited for newly developing areas in the Outer Islands, especially the Culture Zone where the scarcity of local inhabitants caused an acute labour shortage. Between 1885 and 1931 an estimated quarter of a million Chinese labourers passed through the new port of Belawan, recruited either direct from Swatow or via Penang and Singapore to work on the new estates in the area. This 'coolie' traffic which was operated at great profit to its agents and procurers and at great cost to the labourers themselves gave rise to a scandal at the turn of the century and a subsequent falling off in numbers, particularly after 1910 when Chinese labour was steadily replaced by Javanese. In the twentieth century in general Chinese immigration met with increasing obstacles, for although disturbed political conditions in China itself stimulated the arrival of fresh waves of immigrants, the demand in the Indies for Chinese labour fell off in the face of spreading mechanization and rising nationalist sentiment. Nevertheless the numbers arriving were still considerable. Between 1900 and 1930 they averaged 28,000 a year and between 1920 and 1930 in particular the rate was around 40,000 a year. Although the Great Depression of 1929 and the restrictive measures which followed had their effect, in 1937 alone 31,000 Chinese immigrants entered the country.

The Chinese in the Indies fall into two main groups—those born in the country (known as *peranakan*) and those who have migrated straight from China. In 1930 the census figures revealed that in Java and Madura, 70 per cent of the Chinese population were local-born but that in the Outer Islands the majority of Chinese settlers were recent immigrants. The largest speech-group in the country were Hokkien (over half a million) who were traditionally the earliest arrivals in the islands. The Hokkien were to be found concentrated in consequence mostly in Java and Madura, but also in the Great East where they formed over half the local Chinese population. The Hakka came next, originally settlers in west Borneo in the eighteenth century but now found in considerable numbers in Java, on Bangka and Belitung and in east Sumatra. Third in terms of numbers came the Cantonese, who were more evenly distributed throughout the archipelago, and lastly the Teochew who were located in the Riau-Lingga archipelago, in north-west Borneo, Bangka, Belitung, Jambi, Indragiri and the Culture Zone further north where they were particularly associated with the tobacco plantation industry.

As much to shield their own interests as those of the Indonesians, the Dutch forbade the Chinese to own land or to be employed in government service. Apart from this the Chinese were free to operate as they willed and to move to any part of the Indies.[60] In keeping with the general pattern of Chinese settlement in South-East Asia, most Chinese were to be found concentrated in the towns, the chief exception being the belt of planters, miners and agricultural labourers who lived in an arc sweeping from the west coast of Borneo to the east coast of Sumatra across the islands of the Riau-Lingga archipelago. Equally typical the largest single group of Chinese (36 per cent) comprised traders, shopkeepers, and petty pedlars; in general the Chinese dominated the retail trade as much as the Europeans did the wholesale trade, and they formed the essential link between import agency and peasant consumer, fulfilling a host of functions in the process. Another substantial group—nearly one-third—were engaged in the production of raw materials, namely tin, oil and the crops of the Culture Zone. The remainder formed the bulk of those engaged in various industrial enterprises from the multitude of small family concerns to the new factories opened in the 1920s and 1930s by various capitalist entrepreneurs. Finally at the top existed a small, very influential and very rich group of Chinese tycoons with widespread interests in shipping, finance and the cash crops of the Indies and elsewhere in the region besides.

The Indonesians: the poverty of Java

In great contrast to the aliens in their midst the majority of the Indonesians themselves remained in poverty and squalor and had a minimal share in the development and productivity of their homeland. According to the 1930 census 90 per cent of the Indonesian population lived in the rural areas and of those 'gainfully employed' 70 per cent were confined to agriculture and the low returns obtained from it. Two-thirds of these were smallholders, living at best little above subsistence level, while the bulk of the remainder formed a landless agrarian proletariat. Only some 15 per cent were in industry and another 5 per cent in commerce. Of those in industry by far the greater number were involved in handicrafts. Only some 120,000 Indonesians were employed in the large Western factories and a bare 40,000 in the mining industry. The contrast between the living standards of the Indonesians, taken as a whole, and those of the Chinese and Europeans in the country, may be exemplified by other figures taken at random. Seventy per cent of the European inhabitants of the Indies in the late 1930s lived in brick houses as compared to 30 per cent of the Chinese and 4½ per cent of the Indonesians; 74

per cent of the Europeans in the country paid car tax as opposed to 17 per cent of the Chinese and 9 per cent of the Indonesians; out of 54,000 licensed radios in the Indies in 1937 33,000 were paid for by Europeans and 12,000 by Indonesians. All this clearly shows the Indonesian predicament in their own country. They formed by and large the labouring class and their employers were foreigners; furthermore their standard of living was uniformly low while that of their masters was high.

However, the distribution of poverty was uneven amongst the Indonesians themselves. The problem was far more acute on Java than on the Outer Islands. Most of the scattered populations of the archipelago lived in blissful ignorance of the economic progress brought by the West, their subsistence economies undisturbed and their calm not stirred into discontent by rising expectations. Even in those regions where the modern world of commerce and trade had penetrated, the abundance of land and scarcity of labour had caused a generally shared and growing prosperity. The coconut cultivators of the Great East had had a taste of affluence, while rubber with its simple requirements for cultivation fitted easily into the shifting culture economy of Borneo and Sumatra, freeing the cultivator from dependence on his subsistence crops. In the Menangkabau Highlands and in wide areas of the Great East, a new virile smallholder class appeared who came to contribute an important part to the export of rubber or copra, as the case might be, and easily adapted to the intrusion of a money economy. So while Javanese society 'advanced towards vagueness'[61] and became more faceless, in the specific regions of the Outer Islands local society was transformed and developed a new individuality of its own.

In Java the problem of poverty had become sufficiently acute by the end of the nineteenth century to provoke official concern. The prime factor in the steady impoverishment of the Javanese lay doubtless in the over-exploitation and over-population of the island. The manner of economic development itself helped to promote the spread of poverty in a process which is clearly exemplified by the evolution of the sugar industry. Although sugar was one of the mainstays of the Dutch colonial economy for the greater part of their rule, and in addition had much in common with rice cultivation, it never developed into an important industry for the Javanese smallholder. The costs of milling the harvest and of transportation required a considerable outlay of capital well beyond the reach of the subsistence farmer, and placed him in the hands first of the Chinese and then of the Europeans. Equally important was the attitude of the Dutch administration throughout the various metamorphoses its economic policy underwent. Under the monopoly system, whether of the East India Company or of the Dutch Crown after 1830, competition from independent Javanese producers was clearly undesirable. It would undermine the whole scheme of forced cultivation, not only by creating a permanent threat of underbidding but by placing labour and land at a premium. Both the Company and the Crown could exercise sufficient political pressure through the existing feudal structure to prevent such things from happening and by the time that free enterprise came into its own, the European monopoly of milling, the legal restrictions imposed on land use by the Agrarian Law and related legislation, and the fact that there was no longer any land available for free development tied the Javanese peasant down to his role as subsistence producer. In the 1920s only 3 per cent of the total sugar intake to the factories came from independent Javanese planters.[62]

Meanwhile most Javanese sugar cultivators formed part of the system controlled by the Dutch, and their lot had in no way improved after a century of expanding production, exports and profits. The way in which the industry developed as a kind of partnership between Western capital and management on the one hand, and Javanese labour on the other, resulted in the Javanese cultivator becoming enmeshed in a vice-like cycle from which he had no means of escape. The peasant became a prisoner of the system of feudal dues and services which had developed under the rule of Javanese princes, and which were reinforced later by the Dutch East India Company's 'contingencies' and 'forced deliveries'. The demise of the Company at the end of the eighteenth century brought little change. For the first decades of the new century all economic production in Java was paralysed by the situation created by the Revolutionary and Napoleonic Wars, and although the Culture System which revived the economy became a powerful agent for the spread of money, it merely tended to keep the Javanese cultivator imprisoned in his poverty. In parts of East Java the System was scrupulously implemented as laid down, and in such cases the cultivator benefited. But more often than not, officials proved to be more concerned about sugar production and the commissions they could earn rather than with the fate of the rice crop, while the manner in which the System itself was administered served merely to bolster the feudal authority of the Javanese aristocrats and to hinder the rise of an independent class of peasant proprietors. It was easier for the administration to deal with the village as a unit rather than with individual cultivators, thereby encouraging communal as opposed to private ownership.

It was under the Culture System that the industry acquired the characteristics which it carried forward with it into the twentieth century—rice and sugar as complementary crops, rising productivity and a rising population. The main sugar-producing areas of Java contained the richest rice-lands, bearing the highest yields and having the densest populations.[63] A clear cycle had come into existence. Sugar cultivation required improved irrigation, which under nineteenth century conditions could only be brought about by the application of many hands—available in a rice-rich area which already supported a considerable population. Improved irrigation increased rice production which enabled a further rise of population, creating in turn the need for greater rice production, more irrigation and so on. In other words, sugar needed labour; labour needed rice; improved rice yields stimulated further population growth which in turn depended increasingly on labour-intensive techniques to raise production in order to prevent a decline in the existing standard of living. Under the Culture System the political control and supervision were too tight to make escape feasible. Both European officials and the Javanese hierarchy had a vested interest in making it work.

What evidence there is suggests that with the change-over to the Liberal

Policy after 1870, while the industry flourished as never before, the Javanese cultivator sank into ever-deeper penury. The Liberal Policy in fact represented a change of management, not of system, and under the new management the pressures increased. European sugar contractors still preferred to deal with the village as one unit. Although technically speaking under the liberal dispensation the cultivator was now a free agent, he was hemmed in by the new land laws which though guaranteeing him against the alienation of his own land placed virgin soil beyond his reach. He could not opt to leave his land and work on the coffee estates since the estates subsisted on a permanent labour force and provided no openings for others. There were no outlets in industry, for the profits made from the Indies were used to prevent, in the words of Furnivall, the Netherlands from becoming another Portugal, and not for the development of Java.[64] Some Javanese peasants from the sugar provinces found a solution in migrating as contract labourers to the newly-opening tobacco and rubber plantations of the Culture Zone and a smaller number managed to make their way to Johore and other parts of the Malay Peninsula where freer opportunities awaited them. For the great majority, however, it was a case of staying put, working ever harder to produce more rice to feed more mouths and maintain the same level of living—a water-treading process described by Boeke as 'static expansion'.[65] Even at the start of the nineteenth century there was evidence of local over-population. By the end of the century the area under sugar cultivation had increased by barely one-sixth but the population had quadrupled. In terms of economic exploitation Java in general, and the sugar-lands in particular, had reached saturation point.

From what has been said it is clear that Javanese impoverishment was also very closely linked to the evolution of colonial land policy. The Javanese smallholder received his first official recognition from Raffles who purposed to make him the basis of his land-rent system, but the ending of the Liberal experiment and the imposition of the Culture System a decade and a half later discouraged individual land ownership. The smallholder now stood out as a target for the demands of government in the person of the local aristocrat. Greater security lay in land fragmentation and communal ownership and, as we have just noted, this was more suitable to the needs of government officials and private contractors. In this way the development of an independent class of smallholders was stultified, social distinctions became blurred, and the Javanese cultivator became a labourer on his own land, isolated from the market and the world of commerce. The Liberal Period, inaugurated by the Agrarian Law of 1870, did not improve matters from the Javanese cultivator's point of view, despite the much vaunted purpose to protect Indonesian land rights. The Agrarian Law was fundamentally designed to facilitate the opening up of virgin land to private capitalists in consonance with Liberal ideas, on conditions which ensured ultimate government control and protected Indonesian-occupied land from alienation to foreigners. Notwithstanding this, in the 1870s even the safeguards against alienation were nearly swept away by the tides of Liberalism, as under the leadership of van der Putte the Dutch Liberal Party attempted to secure conversion rights over Indonesian-held lands. These attempts were ultimately defeated and in 1875 a conservative ministry laid down in legal form the tradition of Dutch colonial policy that Indonesian land was inalienable.[66]

The two most important decrees which implemented in detail the general principles of policy contained in the Agrarian Law were the Agrarian Decree of the same year and the Rent Ordinance of 1871. The Agrarian Decree divided land into two broad categories—private and state, the latter comprising both free (or 'waste' i.e. uncultivated) land and unfree land which meant land held in tenure by Indonesians. The Decree laid down the conditions by which Dutch subjects (from Holland or the Indies) or Dutch firms or foreign firms registered in Dutch territory could lease portions of the free or waste lands. The Rent Ordinance of 1871 laid down the terms on which shorter-term leases could be made of 'unfree' or Indonesian-held lands and provided for government intervention to safeguard Indonesian interests. All contracts involving Indonesian land were to be registered.[67]

But as we have seen all this legislation did not save the Javanese peasant from further impoverishment. The Javanese planter, 'hemmed in on all sides by a crystallised pattern'[68] created within the framework of these laws and the system that grew up with them remained little affected by the progress taking place around him. The population continued to rise steadily, the area under Javanese tenure remained the same and the amount of land actually available for cultivation steadily shrank. By the end of the century it had become clear that after a generation of Liberalism, Javanese welfare was not rising but sinking. The coffee industry was in marked decline, conditions in the sugar industry had become oppressive and the only new sources of wealth and production were to be found outside in Sumatra and Borneo. By 1900 Java was ceasing to pay dividends. From that time onwards the main Dutch preoccupation was no longer one of trying to increase production for profit but to increase it in order to lift Javanese living standards or at least to prevent their continued decline.

The problem of Javanese poverty: the Ethical Policy

Official recognition of the problem was heard for the first time in 1901 when Queen Wilhemina spoke of 'the diminished welfare of the population of Java' and of 'the moral duty' which Holland owed to the Indonesians. The same speech marked the announcement of a new course in Dutch colonial policy in the Indies which was to be marked by a revival of government participation in economic development and was to be directed specifically at improving the lot of the Indonesians themselves. The new course which came to be known as 'the Ethical Policy', reflected changing conditions both in the Indies and in Holland. In the Indies the Liberal creed was outworn largely because individual enterprise and initiative, so prominent in the 1870s, had given way under the pressures of the following decade to the domination of a handful of interlocked corporations, linked in their turn to great international financial houses. Collusion and combination had replaced the hurly-burly of free competition.

The changes in the Indies were mirrored in the politics of Holland itself.

The old quarrel between the exponents of private versus state enterprise died away in the 1880s, creating a political vacuum into which new political combinations and groupings arose, in particular as a consequence of the emergence of socialism as a new force on the scene. In colonial affairs the socialists stood for a combination of the economic progress which liberal capitalism offered and the conservative concept of state intervention to guard against its excesses. At the same time the traditional attitudes of the older parties were considerably modified by the introduction of a wider franchise and proportional representation in 1896, so that both right and left reflected a broader cross-section of public opinion.[69]

The results of these new trends soon made themselves apparent in policy statements and political speeches. The conservative leader, de Kuyper, was the first to formulate the idea of moral responsibility in his electoral manifesto of 1880, entitled 'Ons Program' (Our Programme). In 1899 van Deventer in an article in 'De Gids', a political review, refurbished Liberal policies with his concept of 'a debt of honour' and with his programme for measures to protect Indonesian rights and to promote their moral and material development. Van Kol, for the socialists, was shaping a constructive socialist policy along similar lines so that it could be seen that by the turn of the century the main political currents in Holland itself were in favour of a colonial policy which would restrict unbridled free enterprise and which would take more positive steps to improve living conditions for Indonesians.

A premature attempt to implement these new ideas was made in 1891, but it was only at the end of the century that circumstances combined to bring about a change. Against a background of economic crisis and the expensive Acheh War, the parties of the right succeeded in setting up a coalition in 1901 and in forming a new ministry under the veteran de Kuyper. Attention had already been directed to the Indies by the outbreak in 1899 of a severe famine in the Semarang residency which lasted for two years and which was generally interpreted as evidence of the Liberal failure to promote prosperity. Under the new Colonial Minister, Idenburg, a Welfare Investigation Commission was appointed to look into the Semarang question in particular and the whole problem of Javanese poverty in general.[70]

Nevertheless, the aura of idealism which surrounded the new 'Ethical Policy' was thoroughly impregnated with self-interest. The official calls for government in the interests of the (Indonesian) governed also met the practical needs of the various private enterprises promoted during the Liberal Era. There was the ever-growing army of businessmen, planters and speculators who looked to the colonial government to open up the Outer Islands and who, as they settled in increasing numbers in the Indies, also sought the provision of social services which would make their lives more tolerable. The extension of such services to Indonesians would also enhance their concerns by creating a pool of locally-trained clerks and technicians to work in their offices and factories and on their estates, while improved medical facilities would mean a healthier, sturdier labour force. There was also present on the scene for the first time as an effective force the new Dutch industrialists, particularly those in textiles, while even Dutch workmen, not wishing their own jobs to be jeopardized by the competition of cheap colonial labour, had a vested interest in promoting Indonesian welfare. For the first time Dutch prosperity was seen not to depend on low wages, but on the growing welfare of the Javanese masses.

Another factor was the need to meet the challenge of British competition which was biting deep into the Dutch colonial economy. All these considerations pointed to the same conclusion; that the *laissez-faire* economics of Liberalism no longer worked. Government had to intervene actively and promote economic progress amongst its Indonesian subjects, not only because this was the right thing to do but because it was also the best way to protect and extend Dutch interests.

The implementation of the Ethical Policy during the course of the next few decades resulted in important shifts in administrative as well as in social and economic policies, a very prominent item of which was the policy of decentralization or of devolution of authority from Holland to that of Dutch officials in the Indies themselves. As far as the problem of falling living standards and over-population in Java is concerned, the new course emphasized the promotion of irrigation, emigration and education, to which were added measures to improve health conditions, provide new credit facilities, encourage economic development in general and protect the Indonesians against the excesses of capitalist enterprise.[71]

The campaign against poverty: irrigation and rural credit

Irrigation, and through irrigation, agriculture was one of the main targets in the programme for Javanese welfare after 1901. In fact, the needs of sugar estates had already promoted irrigation works in Java prior to the launching of the Ethical Policy. An Irrigation Brigade was instituted as a section of the Corps of Engineers in 1885 and four years later the first Irrigation Division was created to deal with the Serayu River. This pioneer scheme was so successful that it was applied more generally and by 1912 there were seven irrication schemes in operation. After that date the amount of irrigated area in gava and Madura steadily increased so that in the present century (up to 1941) nearly 3 million acres were brought under water, nearly equalling all the irrigation work carried out in the archipelago previously. The work of the Dutch in extending irrigation to Java has been described as their 'greatest achievement' and as 'the greatest factor in maintaining a proper balance between food crops and produce for export'. It was a very difficult and costly undertaking, carried out principally in areas which were thickly populated and heavily farmed and where no interference with food production could be tolerated. But although the area under wet-rice cultivation increased by 24 per cent between 1900 and 1940, this was not sufficient to keep pace with the rise in population.

Another way to rescue the Javanese peasant from his all-pervasive poverty was to provide him with sources of easy credit for his basic needs without letting him sink into greater indebtedness. Rural poverty in Java bore all the characteristics typical of South-East Asia as a whole, but intensified by the density of population. The spread of a money economy, government taxa-

tion and the new needs created by the growing availability of Western manufactured goods plunged the Javanese villager, with his limited sources of
income, into hopeless debt. The medium for credit was usually the Chinese
shopkeeper who advanced his seasonal loans or ran the local pawnshop.[72]

As was the case with irrigation, the problems of the sugar industry led to
the first attempts to set up credit institutions. But the major role in their
development was played by de Wolff van Westerrode, an assistant resident
whose plan published in a professional journal in 1898 for a network of
savings banks and village co-operatives caught the eye of Cremer, now
Minister for the Colonies. In consequence de Wolff was made the head of a
commission charged with working out a plan for state pawnshops and agricultural credit banks. The commission brought into being a series of banks
ranging from subdistrict to village level and providing for savings and credit
in cash and in kind. However when in 1905 the first instructions were given
out regarding the extension of such facilities, contrary to de Wolff's own
ideas they placed the administration of the new banks in the hands of the civil
service. The directive of 1905 determined the character of the social credit
movement in the Netherlands Indies. All the credit institutions set up by the
Dutch were virtually government agencies financed from government funds
and run by government officials.[74]

By 1912 every regency in Java (but not Madura) possessed a bank at sub-
divisional level and over 13,000 other banks. In the Outer Islands, however,
the number of these banks was minimal. The various credit banks were
never formally linked, once again contrary to de Wolff's wishes, but the
danger of local bankruptcy prompted a policy of centralization in the 1920s.
Finally in 1933 a General Popular Credit Bank (Algemeen Volkscrediet
Bank) was set up with authority over the local banks. The banks at village
level which were designed to play the main role in the official campaign
against rural indebtedness did not eliminate the moneylender but they reduced the Javanese peasant's dependence upon him by providing an alternative and cheaper source of credit. However, as has been pointed out, the ultimate result was of doubtful value, for if the peasant's poverty was alleviated,
it was not banished and these facilities had little or no impact on his basic
attitudes or outlook, without a change in which little progress was feasible.

State pawnshops, started in 1900, were also initiated by de Wolff and
developed into a very widespread service which became a source of substantial revenue and profit to the colonial administration. They also gave the
Javanese poor better terms and more security than could ever have been
obtained from private concerns.[75] Co-operative credit societies, on the other
hand, played a comparatively minor role, and as a whole catered mainly for
government servants. As such they made little contribution towards overcoming Javanese poverty, conceived more as a means of avoiding insolvency
than of promoting co-operation. Most of the credit obtained was used not to
further agricultural enterprise but to promote private trade.

Transmigration

At the heart of the problem of Java's poverty was its over-population. An

obvious solution lay in emigration, or transmigration as the Dutch preferred
to call it, to the vast, thinly-peopled spaces of the Outer Islands. Van Deventer placed such measures in the forefront of his welfare programme. The
first practical proposals to resettle Javanese in other parts of the archipelago
were put forward by Idenburg and Fock in 1903 and put into practice in
1905, when a batch of colonists from Kedu were settled in the Lampongs of
South Sumatra. In 1908 the experiment was extended to Benkulen (Bangkulu) and a third batch went there in 1911. Between 1918 and 1928 a number
of smaller groups of Javanese were sent to the Culture Zone.[76]

However, these early efforts at resettlement were not a success. Good sites
for settlement were hard to find, since obviously the most promising areas
were already occupied; the sites actually selected were often poorly chosen
as a result of inadequate surveys, so that the new settlements produced poor
returns. They were subject to epidemics and the prejudices of the settlers
themselves did not make matters easier. By comparison with the recruitment
and transportation of Javanese labour by private enterprise to work on the
estates of Deli, the official transmigration scheme was both costlier and on a
far more limited scale. Consequently the scheme languished and virtually
stopped altogether in the decade which followed the Great War.

But in the early 1930s, as a result of natural disaster and the impact of the
Great Depression which created thousands of unemployed in Java itself and
brought back thousands more from overseas, the transmigration scheme was
re-examined and revived. Wiser for its experiences, Batavia set up a special
body, the Agricultural and Colonisation Bank, which devised a new system
of settlement built up around a nucleus of pioneers who prepared the way
for later arrivals. The first settlers under the new scheme were the victims of
the eruption of Gunong Merapi in Central Java in 1930. After 1936 the pace
of transmigration was accelerated and in 1937 a Central Commission for
Emigration and Colonisation was formed. Between 1936 and 1939 the number of Javanese settlers in the Outer Islands rose from 63,000 to 206,000 and by
1941 the Dutch were within sight of their goal of moving 100,000 people a
year from the island.

Of those who went, the great majority were destined for Sumatra, some
were settled in the Celebes and a few went to South or East Borneo. Freed
from their debts and over-crowded conditions, the settlers were obviously
better off and were soon able to improve their standard of living, and if their
arrival often aroused local resentment, their presence in the long run tended
to exert a beneficial influence since their better farming techniques became
known and frequently adopted by their indigenous neighbours. The usual
practice was for the settlers to be granted 2½ acres of land per head, although
this was little more than the average holding in Java itself and they were
limited to growing subsistence crops.

By 1941 transmigration had achieved much, but as usual it was still not
enough to meet the demands of the situation. Even the target of exporting
100,000 people a year was insufficient when viewed against the annual increase of population in Java which was six times as great. The Dutch envisaged eventually reaching a rate of a quarter of a million or over annually,

but there was also the problem of where to settle them all. For all the vastness
of the Outer Islands, the places suitable for colonization were in fact restricted, and there were already signs of congestion in such areas.[77]

Industrialization
The crying need in order to raise Indonesian standards of living was to raise
Indonesian productivity; if this were true for the Indies as a whole, it was
especially true for Java, which with its great labour reserves could be converted into the workshop of the archipelago. A thorough-going industrialization of at least the Javanese economy indeed became the subject of 'intermittent discussion' from the turn of the century. Idenburg recognized the need
clearly in a great speech of 1902 when, having ascribed Java's poverty to its
surplus population, declared that the thing was 'first of all to promote industry for the benefit of the native population' and 'to call into existence native
industry with native capital'. Other leaders of the new course were in agreement. Van Deventer's survey of 1904 contained an appendix by Rouffaer
on native crafts, and Fock had schemes in mind for the promotion of both
European and Indonesian industry in the island. These good intentions led to
a flurry of activity, but it all petered out into nothing. Western investors
were not impressed by the prospects offered by local enterprise; Chinese and
Arab businesses were self-contained affairs and the Indonesians themselves
had no capital to offer. But basically any serious industrialization undertaken
by the colonial government of Batavia could only be carried out at the expense of Western interests in the Indies themselves, which politically was not
feasible. Furthermore, allied to the problem of lack of capital there was the
equally difficult problem of lack of demand.

A second opportunity for Javanese industrialization came in 1914 with the
outbreak of the Great War which cut off the Indies from Western manufacturers and also from markets for its own exports. Industrialization was
discussed again, and Idenburg, now governor-general in Batavia, headed a
new committee to investigate the possibilities. The government also sent van
Kol to study industrialization in Japan and to consider its relevance to Java.
In 1916 an industrial consultant was appointed and in 1918 an industrial section of the department of Agriculture, Industry and Commerce was set up.
Attempts were made to produce food products for European settlers in Java
and to manufacture soap, paper and textiles for a wider market. To make
good the shortage of skilled technicians a technical institute was founded at
Bandung in 1919.

But with the end of the war in Europe and the resumption of the 'normal'
pattern of trade, local industries languished once more, and some of the new
concerns had to close down altogether. Naturally enough Dutch manufacturers in Holland deplored the creation of competitors within their own market and exerted pressure to prevent this from continuing to take place. As a
result prior to 1930 the industrialization of Java had proceeded little further
than the initial stages of processing raw materials such as sugar, oil and
rubber, and the provision of maintenance facilities for various modes of
transportation. On the other hand, the colonial government did manage to

assist to some extent the Indonesian movement to revive traditional handicrafts. Cottage industry was resuscitated and developed through the formation of 'industrial centrals', small factories of some ten to fifty persons, which put the finishing touches to goods made in the house.[78]

The advent of the Great Depression and the economic devastation that it left in its wake completely changed the picture. Faced with unemployment on an unprecedented scale, there was need for fresh government thinking and action on the question, and the faltering, limited steps of the previous two decades proved that they had some worth after all, as they provided something to build on. The 'industrial centrals' were now made the nuclei for a much more active promotion of handicraft industries with government aid. There was also considerable expansion in the Indonesian (as opposed to the Western) cigarette industry as well as in the manufacture of pottery, furniture and hats. By 1939 some 2½ million people—all save 100,000 being Indonesians—were engaged in these minor or light industries. However, there was also a corresponding increase in Chinese take-overs and management, and all attempts by Indonesian members of the Volksraad to secure legislation prohibiting such alien participation in industry were defeated.

During the same period (1930–41) there was also a significant expansion in Western industrial enterprise brought about largely as a result of Dutch concern over the potential political repercussions of Javanese economic distress and over the deepening incursions of Japanese manufactures into the colonial market. To a certain extent these developments were also a natural outcome of the growth of the maintenance industries already established. By 1941, primarily because of deliberate government policy, 70 per cent of the large-scale factories were concentrated in Java but sited in different regions; Batavia had its soap and margarine plants, Semarang produced textiles and motor-tyres, Surabaya was a centre for rubber tyres and shipbuilding, Bandung for textiles and quinine and Garut and Tegal had their spinning mills.

Conditions of labour

The existence of a reservoir of cheap, exploitable labour in the Indies was an important factor in the rise and success of Dutch capitalism. In the seventeenth and eighteenth centuries it had been the mainstay of the VOC, which had coerced the Javanese aristocracy into extending their feudal privileges in its interests. The Culture System of the nineteenth century had been unabashedly founded on the principle of forced labour. Under the Liberal Era which followed, labour was freed but it remained cheap.

Nevertheless, as the Western world raised its own standards of humanity and concern for the less fortunate, the effects percolated to the Indies. Forced labour was traditional in Indonesian society throughout the archipelago. Slavery was an established institution. Compulsory labour existed in a variety of forms, dictated by local conditions and custom. Slavery which was officially abolished in Java in 1860 had already been in decline for some time as changed conditions made it less economical. However it did not disappear so readily from the other islands in the archipelago and persisted in certain areas right up to the outbreak of the Pacific War.[79]

The first steps towards the ending of forced labour or compulsory services were also taken in the nineteenth century, stimulated by the growing recognition that they were more often than not inefficient and uneconomic. Paradoxically the Culture System itself did much to confirm this realization, particularly on the sugar fields where extra services were paid for. In 1849 paid labour was made use of for the first time on public works at Surabaya, and with such success that after this all public works were required to be built with hired workmen instead of forced labour. In 1882 the government introduced a capitation tax payable in place of compulsory service and then used the proceeds both to commute such service and to pay for labour on projects not suitable for it. Village services were made commutable eight years later and in 1902 an order was issued remitting all compulsory services in Java and Madura without any further payments.[80]

Predictably the pace of reform was much slower in the Outer Islands and in 1930 it was reckoned that some two million men were still liable to give twenty days a year of their labour on public works and that only a third of this number were in a position to commute their services. However the Great Depression greatly hastened their end by creating great pools of surplus labour which were employed on road building and the like.

In Java compulsory labour at village level, as well as on private lands, persisted up till the eve of the Pacific War, despite official attempts to bring it to an end. In 1912 Batavia decided that compulsory services on private estates should be ended by re-purchasing them, but the cost of doing so was formidable and by 1941 the situation remained much as it had been at the start of the century. In the principalities compulsory services still carried on, but forced labour was officially abolished in them before the outbreak of the Pacific War.

Another aspect of forced labour was that of recruitment for employment overseas. The VOC had played a large part in this traffic, exporting Javanese for service in the Antilles and elsewhere, and in the nineteenth century Batavia still recruited Javanese coolies for Surinam. However in 1863 state participation in such activities came to an end and in 1887 the recruitment of Javanese labour for overseas was prohibited altogether except with express official sanction. Under the 1887 regulation a few thousand Javanese each year were allowed to be recruited for employment in British Malaya and British North Borneo, in New Caledonia and French Indo-China.

The decline or abolition of forced labour meant the rise of either contract or free labour to take its place. Contract labour held the field in Java in the wake of slavery's decline and as in turn it gave way to free labour with the ending of the Culture System, it found a new lease of life in the plantations of East Sumatra. The chief drawback of the contract system from the employer's view-point was the ease with which his labourers could break their contract and abscond. To meet this problem, a penal sanction was passed for contracts in the sugar residency of Surabaya in 1829. Soon this penal sanction was legalized throughout Java and Madura. When the police regulations of

1872 were promulgated the penal sanction was also included, but the mounting liberalism of the age would not permit its retention when the regulations were revised seven years later. Employers in Java by this time were not much concerned because most had already switched over to free labour; however its abolition in 1879 was not taken so lightly in the Culture Zone where a skeleton administration, primitive conditions and an immigrant labour force of Chinese coolies raised the old problem of desertion and breach of contract in an acute form. The result was the Coolie Ordinance of 1880, first confined to East Sumatra but later extended more generally throughout the Outer Islands, granting sweeping powers to employers over their own labour.

In practice in the kind of frontier society developing in the swamps of the Culture Zone where an uprooted and mixed labour force was ruled over by a fiercely competitive and all-male European society, abuse of the Ordinance was likely to and did take place. The extent to which it had done so was ultimately revealed by the great Deli scandal at the end of the century which provoked the first attempts to curb employers' powers. Questions about labour in the Culture Zone had been raised in the Dutch Parliament in the 1890s, but the true exposure of the whole system came with the publication of an article in 1902 entitled 'The Millions from Deli' (De Millioenen uit Deli), which revealed in detail the fate of those labourers who had broken their contracts and other abuses. A wave of indignation swept Holland. The promoters of the Ethical Policy were now in power, and Idenburg, as Colonial Minister, was delighted to get this justification for reform. The commission which he immediately appointed to investigate the charges upheld them as substantially true in its report.

This marked the beginning of a long struggle to remove the penal sanctions from the statute book. For two decades conservative elements in the Batavian administration and in the upper chamber of the Dutch Parliament were successful in preventing any such step from being taken, but by the new labour ordinance of 1924, penal sanctions were made subject to review every five years. In 1929 the United States Blaine amendment further discouraged the use of contract labour and stimulated new legislation restricting still more the application of penal sanctions.[81] Meanwhile the emergence of a new generation, the children of the original contract labourers, as a resident force, together with the impact of the Great Depression caused more and more firms to abandon contract labour altogether, so that when the penal sanction was finally abolished in 1941 it and the system of labour associated with it was already virtually a thing of the past.

Apart from this, other steps were taken to ameliorate labour conditions in the Culture Zone. In an effort directed against the professional recruiter of labour who was in many respects the worst villain of the piece, regulations were passed in 1908 and in 1911 which aimed at encouraging local planters to appoint their own recruiting agents. This official initiative met a response from the Deli Planters' Association which in 1915 set up its own labour agency at Semarang. In 1930 professional recruiting was forbidden entirely while an Immigration Chamber was established at Medan to prevent labourers from being filched from their original employers by rival companies.

The general trend in the twentieth century was for contract labour to give way to hired or free labour, a process well under way much earlier in Java under the pressures of the Liberal Era. But the substitution of contract by free labour was by no means an unmixed blessing, for the hired workman was usually brought into the employ of the Western planter through the medium of his hereditary territorial chief.[82] The average Javanese farmer was still a slave to the traditions of his society, for unlettered and ignorant, he had no awareness of his new rights and so naturally failed to exercise them. At the same time he usually became soon embogged in debt. He was offered the hire for his labour in advance, which he invariably accepted. He then spent the money before the harvest and was therefore obliged to work the next season, whether he liked it or not, in order to redeem his debts. It was like a more sophisticated form of debt-slavery. The only way out was to run away, burn the crop, murder the mandor or steal the produce in the vain hope of being able to dispose of it without getting caught.

Towards the end of the nineteenth century the combined pressures of Dutch politics, growing unrest and misery amongst the labouring masses and the rise of new managerial techniques and values led to attempts to improve the lot of the working man, which paralleled the struggle to humanize the system of contract labour. In Java in the 1890s the government passed regulations to check the abuses brought about by planters advancing credit to their labourers, particularly on the sugar plantations where the first practical steps were also taken at the same period to establish minimum wage rates. These norms were subsequently arranged to apply to all labour including that under contract. Under the impetus of the newly proclaimed Ethical Policy and the impact of the Deli scandal in the 1900s, a systematic programme of legislative action aimed at defining more precisely the rights and obligations of employers, inspecting and supervising labour conditions and encouraging the replacement of contract by free labour was launched. The first step came in 1904 when a labour inspector was appointed to check and supervise conditions in the Culture Zone. The duties of labour inspectors were broadened in 1908 and in 1921 a labour inspectorate was established. Meanwhile in 1905 the first Factories Act applicable to Java was passed and in 1911 the Free Labour Ordinance guaranteeing regular wages, proper accommodation and sufficient food was promulgated. A string of subsequent ordinances enlarged and improved upon these conditions, so that on paper at least the Netherlands Indies could boast the most comprehensive and advanced labour legislation of any European colony. Yet, despite all these efforts in the mid-1930s many ordinary workmen still preferred the security of contract labour to hired.[83]

Nevertheless, as the twentieth century rolled on, the trend towards free labour and even to the emergence of a clearly-defined working class, particularly in Java and East Sumatra, was accentuated. The extension of labour legislation destroyed the old collusion between employer and hereditary territorial chief, the traditional authority of the latter over the villager was loosened, while in Java in particular the mounting pressure of population bore down heavily on the traditional social structure. Such pressures multiplied after 1929 so that in Java, at least, labour problems began to assume characteristics similar to those in other industrialized societies.

Health and medicine

The Dutch as colonists were pioneers in the development of health measures in the tropics, but prior to the twentieth century these were carried out primarily for the benefit of the European community. Vaccination, introduced by Raffles, was extended by the Dutch and formed the basis for the nucleus of an Indonesian medical service in 1851. The earliest public sanitary regulations were promulgated in 1829 for Surabaya and during the course of the nineteenth century extended over the interior of the island. But in 1900 there were only 308 'medical practitioners' in the whole of the Indies, seventy-six of whom were European, mostly to be found in Java. In that year the budget allocation for health services was little more than f2 million, and a decade later this sum had risen by only 50 per cent.

However, the outbreak of bubonic plague in 1911 for the first time under colonial rule produced a change of attitude and large sums were at once allocated for its prevention. From this date the progress made was impressive. The bubonic plague itself was curtailed and its victims reduced from over 14,000 in 1911 to barely fifty by 1937. Cholera was virtually eliminated from Jakarta, malaria and smallpox strikingly reduced. These results were achieved by building hospitals and dispensaries, carrying out mass inoculations, improving housing conditions, and disseminating health propaganda. By 1935 the death rate had been brought down to a figure below twenty per 1,000 which was good even by European standards. An important part was played by medical research institutes and Christian missions. The work of Eijkman at the Weltevreden laboratories in the early 1890s exposed the cause of beri-beri and saved hundreds of lives. Swellengrebel and Rodenwalt made major contributions to the conquest of malaria. The Rhenane Lutheran Mission ran one of the first successful leper colonies at Huta Salam in Batak country in Central Sumatra. Nevertheless, as in most other aspects of colonial effort, much was left to be desired and it cannot be said that Western hygiene and medicine were accepted widely enough to have become permanently effective. Outside the big towns of Java or the well-administered estates of the Outer Islands, health standards remained primitive or were non-existent. The size of the problem and the area involved were overwhelmingly great. Legislation to enforce health measures was good but its implementation imperfect for want of staff and funds. More profoundly still, behind this comparative failure lay the question of deeply-rooted traditions, superstitions and ignorance.

The Ethical Policy and the Dutch contribution

In general the Ethical Policy affords a classical example of well-intentioned efforts being applied too sparingly too late. Despite the undoubted progress made in terms of Indonesian economic development and welfare in the twentieth century, the new course adopted after 1901 was fundamentally a failure in all its aspects. Although the Dutch understood the problem, they could not or would not apply the right solution. They tried to solve everything within the framework of the old colonial economy. Heavy foreign investment in the Indies determined the pattern of development, but foreign capital was not interested in stimulating local productivity which would also mean raising wages, because its main profits were derived from the cheapness of the Javanese labour market. The bulk of colonial capital was invested in large-scale agricultural and mining concerns and the bulk of the profits flowed back to Europe or to the United States.[84] There was virtually no investment in Indonesian enterprises as such and scarcely any mechanization so that productivity and the general standard of living remained depressed. In this light the measures undertaken in the name of the Ethical Policy appear as they truly were, measures to deal with symptoms not causes, mere palliatives to restore but not to cure, attempts to patch up the holes caused by the wear and tear of exploitation.

But if the Ethical Policy failed in its attempt to deal with Javanese poverty, it was successful in accommodating the Indies to the needs of the Western imperialism of the twentieth century, for the irrigation works, new credit facilities, health clinics and schools apart from alleviating Indonesian problems also served Western needs at the same time. The chief beneficiaries of the marked extension of irrigation were the great sugar millers and planters, while the promotion of public health benefited European employers who required a sturdy labour force in place of the coolies who died by the hundreds from beri-beri, malaria and other such diseases in the nineteenth century. The Ethical Policy met the immediate problem of staving-off a disastrous plunge in living standards on the island which would have ruined the entire colonial economy, although it did not succeed in laying the foundations upon which a more prosperous Indonesian society could be built for the future.

For most Indonesians were still confined in 1941 to agriculture and the low returns that obtained with it. The remarkable expansion and diversification in Javanese food production, for example,[85] which took place did not imply any alteration in the existing and established pattern of labour-intensive farming and poverty; it simply indicated that the land had been put to even more intensive use. The average Javanese holding remained at around 1½ acres, too small for efficient cultivation, and current pressures did not encourage the growth of larger units. Likewise, whatever progress may have been made in terms of securing basic minima of decency in wages and working conditions, the living standards of Indonesian labour remained depressed, usually at little more than subsistence level. As far as the ordinary free or hired worker was concerned, his lot was hard and insecure. While his overseers were permanent and comparatively well rewarded, he was usually employed seasonally or part-time for paltry wages. Mechanization was neither common nor generally encouraged, for labour was cheap and abundant; where mechanization did exist it usually brought more hardship by taking away the livelihood of a good many workers. And yet without mechanization there was not much hope of higher productivity upon which any rise in living standards must depend. Those who were employed by European concerns were probably better off, although in East Sumatra the traditions of contract labour and the penal sanction died hard. Modern working conditions were mostly to be found in such Western mining and industrial concerns and also in transport where the environment was more Westernized and traditional paternalism had given way to individualism and the attitude of fighting for one's own rights, as the existence of trade unionism, however emasculated, shows. But most Indonesians still lived out their lives within the shell of their traditional society, working on the land, living in their kampongs or working in small family concerns where, if the truth be known, under the guise of intimate bonds of obligation exploitation was as intense as anywhere outside. It is true, however, that in the 1920s and 1930s the money economy was spreading rapidly, that great inroads were being made into this subsistence kind of society and culture, and that traditional ties were yielding perceptibly as payment in cash replaced that in kind.

The Great Depression of 1929, salutary though some of its consequences may have been, was on the whole a great disaster for the Indonesian people, more particularly for the Javanese who bore its brunt and were the most vulnerable to outside pressures. In the Outer Islands hundreds of thousands of copra and rubber smallholders had to revert to subsistence levels after decades of comparative affluence and prosperity but the severe problem of unemployment which arose in East Sumatra was easily passed over by sending the immigrant labour back home to Java. On Java there were no escape routes and no retreats. Huge numbers were thrown into unemployment and although many were apparently absorbed back into the rural economy, what this meant in practice was that a heavier burden was placed upon an already impoverished and underemployed peasantry. The decline of sugar planting, the closing down of sugar factories and plantations and the lowering of wages deprived thousands in the central and eastern parts of the island of their supplementary incomes. A depressing but presumably accurate picture of living conditions on the island was revealed by the report on 'Living Conditions of Plantation Workers and Peasants on Java in 1938-40'.[86] After two centuries of colonial rule which had brought great changes to the face of the islands, bared their potential and caused men to amass great fortunes, the Indonesians themselves were to be numbered *en masse* as amongst the most poverty-stricken people on earth. They worked hard for long hours and low wages, prisoners in their own land, for 'workers who have to accept such wages are not really free men'. Indeed it is difficult to disagree with Lasker when he says that 'Colonialism, even under the most favourable circumstances, condemns the masses to live in poverty'.[87]

¹Professor Gerbrandy was the prime minister of the Dutch government-in-exile (in England) during the German occupation of Holland between 1941 and 1945.

²Charles A. Fisher, *South-East Asia: A Social, Economic and Political Geography*, Methuen, London, 1966, p. 237.

³Quoted by the Dutch historian, Colenbrander, in his Geschiedenis, ii, 97, and cited by J.S. Furnivall, *Netherlands India: A Study of a Plural Economy*, Cambridge University Press, Cambridge, England, 1967, p. 25.

⁴See Furnivall, op. cit., p. 22.

⁵Ibid., p. 37.

⁶The practice of farming out lands to the Chinese became commonplace in the second half of the eighteenth century, and by the 1790s according to the Dutch historian Bergsma, more than one-eighth of the villages (negorijen) belonging to the Company were leased to the Chinese.

⁷Utilitarianism as a school of thought is identified with the premises that men are the best judges of their own interests, that their goal is happiness and that the proper object of legislation is to bring about the greatest good for the greatest number. These ideas are particularly associated with the English philosopher and economist, Jeremy Bentham (1743–1832), whose belief that men are guided solely by self-interest found expression in his *Introduction to the Principles of Morals and Legislation* published in 1789. The utilitarian philosophy was further developed by men like John Stuart Mill and Henry Sidgwick and formed the core of English nineteenth-century liberalism. However, the classic case for a free trade economy as opposed to mercantilism was made by Adam Smith (1723–90), the Scottish political economist and philosopher, in his *magnum opus*, *The Wealth of Nations*, published over a decade earlier in 1776.

⁸For the general background to the collapse of the United East India Company and to the Revolutionary and Napoleonic Wars, refer to Volume I, p. 62 and p. 91, note 30.

⁹Translated into practical proposals, van Hogendorp recommended the abolition of all forced labour and the substitution of a land tax in kind. The cultivator was to become the owner of his own plot. Rice lands were to be left entirely to the Javanese, who should also be encouraged to grow cash crops for sale at fair market prices in other lands. The cost of public works was to be met by a capitation tax in cash or kind, and trade, if not entirely decontrolled, was to be liberalized. Government activities were to be confined to administration and its officials paid regular salaries. Van Hogendorp also advocated a land survey and registration, the abolition of monopoly farms, the establishment of a forestry service, regular postal service and a standing army.

¹⁰Regerings-reglement (hereafter referred to by the abbreviation RR) means 'constitutional regulation'. The RR of 1818 defined the organization of the colonial government, administrative divisions and the judicial establishment. In so doing the principles of (i) land rent as the basis of state revenues, and (ii) a civil service of salaried officials, were confirmed. The 1818 RR also settled the manner of the administration of state monopolies, and laid the foundations of the modern public works department, a public health service, and of a schools system. For a full discussion of these RR and the principles on which they were based, see Furnivall, op. cit., pp. 89–112.

¹¹See de Waal, *Nederlands-Indië in de Staten-general*, quoted by Furnivall, op. cit., p. 100.

¹²See Dr. R.W. Baron van Hoëvell, *Reis over Java*, quoted by Furnivall, op. cit., p. 101.

¹³The Austrian (formerly Spanish) Netherlands which constituted what today is Belgium had been overrun and annexed by France during the early days of the Revolutionary Wars. By the peace settlement of Vienna (1815) these territories were not restored to the Austrian Hapsburgs, but were joined to the former United Provinces of the Netherlands (Holland) to form the new kingdom of the Netherlands under the royal house of Orange. This union was never popular with the Belgians who are distinguished by religion (Roman Catholic as opposed to Protestant) from their Dutch cousins. The war lasted for eight years and ended in the establishment of Belgium as a separate kingdom under the guarantee of the major European powers.

¹⁴See Baud, quoted by Furnivall, op. cit., p. 119.

¹⁵See de Waal, op. cit., p. 127.

[16]For further details, see Clive Day, *The Policy and Administration of the Dutch in Java*, Macmillan, London, 1904; Oxford University Press reprint, Kuala Lumpur, 1966, pp. 259–64.

[17]For a detailed description of the role of a Javanese regent, see E.D. Dekker, 'Multatuli', *Max Havelaar or the Coffee Auctions of the Dutch Trading Company*, Edmonston & Douglas, Edinburgh, 1868, pp. 65–7. The quotation above comes from this source.

[18]See Day, op. cit., p. 315 and Furnivall, op. cit., p. 133.

[19]See Furnivall, op. cit., p. 135.

[20]For evidence of this, see Day, op. cit., pp. 273–4.

[21]There were in fact four types of European-held land during the period of the Culture System, namely private lands—concessions made mostly under Raffles and which lay quite beyond government jurisdiction; lands on 20-year leases from the government—mostly associated with du Bus de Gisignies; land concessions known as 'enterprises', based on voluntary agreements with Javanese landowners; concessions in the principalities of Jogjakarta and Surakarta.

[22]Quoted by Furnivall, op. cit., p. 152. Eighteen forty-eight was 'the year of revolutions' in Europe; virtually every European state, with the notable exceptions of Britain and Russia, underwent constitutional change at the instance of revolutionary mobs.

[23]See Furnivall, op. cit., p. 174.

[24]Quoted by Furnivall, op. cit., p. 177.

[25]Although the Indies are rich in mineral deposits only tin and oil had real economic significance prior to 1941, with coal a poor third. The main coal fields were in west Sumatra and south-east Borneo, coal deposits being discovered at Sawahlonto in Sumatra in 1868—which from 1891 in the absence of private enterprise were worked by government. Other government coal mines were at Pulau Laut (off the Bornean coast) from 1905 till 1931, and at Bukit Asem, near Muara Enim (East Sumatra) from 1918. The only private coal mines were in Banjarmasin. Valuable bauxite deposits in the Riau archipelago were worked from 1935 by a private concern. Gold (and with it silver) is found widely over all the islands, especially in west Sumatra, Menado and also in Borneo, but nowhere on sufficient scale to warrant large operations. The commercial extraction of manganese started in Central Java and the Preanger in the 1890s. Large iron deposits were suspected but remained inaccessible. Phosphorus and sulphur were mined and exported, and there was some diamond mining from Borneo riverbeds.

[26]The feudal rights were over the people who lived on the land, not over the land itself, which meant that the villagers involved were placed completely at the mercy of their Chinese landlords. Not only was there gross abuse of their position by the Chinese, but a severe loss of revenue to the Company as well since the Javanese regents were unable to make good their dues on the lands left to them. This experience was an important factor in the formulation of the basic principle of later Dutch colonial administration that Indonesian lands should be inalienable to outsiders.

[27]Sugar cultivation takes 18 months—3 months for planting, 12 for growing, and 3 for harvesting, after which the land must be given over to other crops for 3 years. So after each period of 18 months, a different portion of village land was allocated for the crop, while the rest was used for rice. The villagers were required to set aside a certain proportion of their land for the cultivation of the sugar under the supervision of a headman; the cultivation was paid for in terms of the quality of the land by the contractor, as also were the reaping, transportation and milling. In Jogjakarta and Surakarta where the Culture System did not apply, similar arrangements were developed through the leasing of feudal rights, while in the sparsely-populated Brantas Delta the land was rented and the labour hired, with government often advancing the money for this on condition that the yield was sold back to it at its own price.

[28]Mansvelt, *Geschiedenis van de Nederlandse Handelsmattschappij*, quoted by Furnivall, op. cit., p. 141.

[29]See Furnivall, op. cit., p. 143.

[30]For details of annual imports of machinery, see Clifford Geertz, *Agricultural Involution*,

University of California Press, 1966, p. 68. Production costs were considerably lowered by the introduction of light tramways. In general, between 1833 and 1861 while the area planted increased by some 18 per cent, productivity tripled.

[31]The private concerns developed a formal contract system whose duration was usually 21 years. This allowed the completion of seven cycles, during each of which thirds of the village land were devoted in turn to sugar, rice and a dry crop; it took three years for all the village land to have been used for sugar, thus completing the cycle. The 21-year period enabled the contractor to recoup his considerable capital outlay in the setting up of a factory, its maintenance and other overheads. For more details of the system, see Geertz, op. cit., pp. 87–9.

[32]The Ordinance restricted leases to a maximum period of 5 years for Indonesian lands under customary tenure and to 20 years for such lands held in private ownership (later extended to $21\frac{1}{2}$ years). As these time limits were not sufficient to justify capital outlay on buildings or on slow-maturing crops, private investment was channelled towards sugar.

[33]This gave rise to the so-called 'culture banks', of which the N.H.M. was the pioneer. After the 1880s the directors of the N.H.M. prudently decided to widen their interests and reduce their dangerous dependence on agricultural produce. This enabled it to weather the sugar and coffee crises of the 1880s and 1890s, and by 1915 it was half-banker and half-planter. Two other large financial concerns which came to dominate the sugar industry were the Handels Vereeniging Amsterdam (H.V.A.) founded in 1878, and the Cultuur Maatschappij der Vorstenlanden, formed from the enterprises of independent planters in the Javanese principalities during the crises of the 1880s. All three organizations were backed by and interlinked with well-established banks. In general, the culture banks supported 103 sugar factories and financed two-thirds of total Indies production in 1912.

[34]Namely the British Empire, the United States of America, Japan and the Soviet Union.

[35]See Furnivall, op. cit., p. 39.

[36]Under 'contingencies', the cultivator was obliged to supply about twice the amount of the produce that was acknowledged and paid for, the balance being absorbed by the perquisites of officials, etc. Likewise the regents tied by the system of 'forced deliveries' demanded of their cultivators twice the amount they officially surrendered to the Company.

[37]P & T Lands (Panumakan and Tjiasen Lands), a large freehold estate of half a million acres west of Batavia, sold to private (British) interests during the administration of Raffles in order to raise revenues.

[38]For the impact of coffee cultivation on Menangkabau society in the Padang Highlands, see Bernard Schrieke, Indonesian Sociological Studies, Vol. I, Van Hoeve, The Hague, 1953, esp. pp. 99–104. For details of comparative figures of living standards of workers in different industries/occupations see W.F. Wertheim, Indonesian Society in Transition, Van Hoeve, The Hague, 1964, pp. 283–4.

[39]The fact that in Java coffee is a hill crop divorced from the rice-fields and grown on hillsides cleared of the jungle, helped to create a new class of 'fully proletarianised' workers living and toiling exclusively on coffee estates. In the early days of the Culture System, labour for the European plantations was still drawn from the lower-lying, rice-growing villages, but after a few years most estates had fully-fledged coolie settlements established on them.

[40]This rise was greatly assisted by new inventions such as the Vlanderen furnace, a new 'ingenious drill' developed on Bangka used to ascertain the metal content of casserite, and the gravel pump, used for the first time on Belitung in 1910. The greatest impact was made by the tin dredge which allegedly 'can remove more casserite in a day than would accumulate in a generation' (Admiralty Handbook, London, 1943, p. 261).

[41]In 1882 Governor-general Frederik s'Jacob renewed the Billiton concession on his own authority on the most favourable terms, even though to do so was to flout the 1873 amendment, and although the original concession had another 10 years to run. In the ensuing uproar in the Dutch parliament, the concession was revoked and s'Jacob forced to resign.

[42]Allen and Donnithorne, op. cit., p. 93.

[43]The Dordtsche Petroleum Mij was first started in 1887 and was reconstituted in 1890 in order to work deposits near Surabaya for the local market.

[44]The name 'Shell' originated with Samuel's first business in London, which *inter alia* dealt in painted shells imported from the East.

[45]See Fisher, op. cit., p. 236. The two most important non-Dutch oil firms engaged in drilling in the Netherlands East Indies were Esso (Standard Oil of New Jersey, now Standard Vaccum Petroleum/Stanvac), and Caltex Standard Oil Company of California and Texas.

[46]See Allen and Donnithorne, op. cit., pp. 96-7 for further details, especially regarding the activities of George Birnie, a pioneer British tobacco planter in this region.

[47]Ibid., p. 97. The delay in setting up the Deli Mij was caused by differences over policy between Nienhuys and his backers. Nienhuys wanted to contract out the planting to Chinese while the others wanted direct participation. The backers prevailed.

[48]In 1938 the Deli leaf was still fetching prices on the world market four to five times higher than any other cigar tobacco, including Havana.

[49]The greatest single expenditure was on the construction of an ocean-going port at Belawan, started in 1890.

[50]For further details, see Allen and Donnithorne, op. cit., pp. 117-20.

[51]The new policy was also influenced by Batavia's desire to keep in the good books of the United States whose market was of prime importance to the Indies, and by the need to be co-operative over rubber restriction so as to ensure reciprocal co-operation over the restriction of other commodities.

[52]In fact, several authorities regard the underassessment of the smallholder as deliberate. See Lim Chong-yah, *Economic Development of Modern Malaya*, Oxford University Press, Kuala Lumpur, 1967, pp. 61-2.

[53]Rubber gave the Indonesian peasant a rare opportunity to take part in his country's export trade. He was introduced to the use and power of money and neglecting food production became a richer man. Within two decades in the Padang highlands of Sumatra, the Menangkabau for example 'became what the Java sawah peasant, struggling to keep head above water for more than a century, never did; an acquisitive businessman fully enmeshed in the pecuniary nexus', Geertz, op. cit., p. 122 et seq.

[54]R.C.M.A. (Rubber Cultuur Mij. 'Amsterdam'); H.V.A. (Handelsvereniging, Amsterdam), one of the original 'culture' banks.

[55]After the Malay Peninsula, the Indies had the highest yield per acre in the region and the most extensive area under the crop. Two-thirds of the 15½ million acres under the crop in 1938-9 were in Java.

[56]In Java and Madura forests covered 15 per cent of the total land area, while in the Outer Provinces 68 per cent of the land was under forest. Amongst the more valuable forest products are hardwoods such as *meranti* and ironwood (Borneo), ebony (Macassar), softwoods such as Sumatran pine (*tusam*—important for its resin), sandalwood (Timor), bamboo and nibong palm.

[57]Notably under Governor-general Rochussen who as late as 1848 was still refusing to spend government funds on railway construction or to grant licences to private railway construction companies.

[58]The renascence of Dutch shipping promoted the development of harbour facilities. Batavia's port of Tanjong Priok was constructed between 1872 and 1893; other ports developed by 1900 included Chilachap (Tjilatjap), Emmahaven (for Padang) and Belawan.

[59]See Fisher, op. cit., p. 289.

[60]Up till 1910, however, all Chinese resident in the Indies were required to have passes before travelling anywhere in the interior.

[61]Geertz, op. cit., pp. 102-3. What Geertz implies is that the complete subordination of the average Javanese village to the economic circumstances which dominated it and over which it could exercise no control—the intrusion of a money economy, the demands of the world market, the stratified social system, etc.—effectively took away any

chance of individualism or the need for individualism. Survival lay in merging with the group.

[62]However a significant change seemed to be in process as a result of the impact of the Great Depression and of the subsequent inroads made by the Japanese into the industry. The Japanese courted the Indonesian smallholder in order to underbid established Dutch concerns. By 1939 the contribution of independent smallholders to sugar production had gone up to 5 per cent.

[63]One of the principal themes of Geertz's book, *Agricultural Involution*, is its demonstration of the close relationship between rice-growing, sugar cultivation and population density. See in particular his tables on pp. 71-2 and accompanying arguments, op. cit.

[64]See Furnivall, op. cit., p. 151. In fact Furnivall in this context was referring to the batig slot or the annual contribution of the Indies to the home treasury under the Culture System, but the same was equally true of the profits and remittances under the system of free enterprise.

[65]Boeke's comment quoted by Geertz is taken from his *Economics and Economic Policy of Dual Societies*', The Hague, 1963. Geertz himself coined the phrase 'agricultural involution' which became the title for his study of the economic development of Java. For Geertz's own definition of 'agricultural involution' see op. cit., pp. 80-1.

[66]The Liberal Party's principle of conversion was that all Indonesian lands should be transferred from traditional (i.e. communal) ownership to private (i.e. individual) ownership on the European pattern. This was advocated on the grounds that communal ownership was an obstacle to good cultivation; it also meant in practice that with individual rights established, Europeans would be free to acquire Indonesian land since absolute property rights included the rights over transfer and disposal. This issue which separated the pragmatic liberals from the humanitarian ones remained in balance for the first half of the 1870s.

[67]For full details of the Agrarian Law, see Furnivall, op. cit., p. 178 et seq.

[68]See Geertz, op. cit., p. 90.

[69]In 1887 the Dutch parliament (States-general) had its first socialist deputy and the following year the Conservatives suffered a crushing defeat at the hands of the electorate whilst the Liberals became hopelessly divided amongst themselves. The emergence of the socialists as a new secular party on the left prompted the formation of an alliance of political groupings on the right which took shape with the formation of the Clerical Party.

[70]The Commission which was finally dissolved in 1914 did not detect evidence of a general decline in Javanese welfare but it contributed a series of valuable articles and monographs on various aspects of Javanese economic life, and was the first of a number of similar investigations carried out subsequently.

[71]Amongst the various measures taken in the name of the Ethical Policy between 1900 and 1941 only two direct financial contributions were made, the first in 1905 for the improvement of economic conditions in Java and Madura, and the second in 1936 to help tide over the impact of the Great Depression. In terms of the allocation of funds, the revenues devoted to welfare increased by three times in this period from what they had been at the start of the century.

[72]Charles Robequain, *Malaya, Indonesia, Borneo and the Philippines*, Longman, London, 1958, p. 199.

[73]For more details, see G. McT. Kahin, *Nationalism and Revolution in Indonesia*, Cornell University Press, New York, 1952, p. 21.

[74]See Furnivall, op. cit., p. 358.

[75]But see Kahin, op. cit., p. 22.

[76]These Javanese were more of a labour reserve than agricultural colonists.

[77]For criticism of transmigration, see Fisher, op. cit., p. 294.

[78]The Indonesian movement referred to here means the emerging nationalist movement. The Javanese handicraft industry fitted in well with the tradition of *gotong-royong* and with the seasonal patterns of unemployment associated with the growing of crops.

[79]The increasing supply of free labour in Java made it profitable to recruit workers on the open market. See Wertheim, op. cit., p. 241.

[80]In practice, such services continued to be enforced for the upkeep of roads, bridges and aqueducts for another 15 years (i.e. till 1917) when they were finally replaced by the capitation tax.

[81]The Blaine Amendment prohibited the importation of goods into the United States produced by workers anywhere in the world subject to the penal sanction. For further comment on this, see Wertheim, op. cit., p. 256.

[82]See Wertheim, op. cit., p. 244.

[83]Another reason why in the Javanese principalities at least the contract system seemed preferable was that the free labourer was liable to local taxation whereas the man under contract was not.

[84]For the nature and size of Western investment in Indonesia, see H.G. Callis, *Foreign Capital in South-East Asia*, New York, 1942, and also Erich H. Jacoby, *Agrarian Unrest in South-East Asia*, Asia Publishing House, Bombay, 1961, pp. 59–63 for a general discussion.

[85]Maize, tapioca, sweet potato, groundnut, soya beans, potatoes, and chillies had all undergone substantial expansion in production since 1870, particularly tapioca which in 1937 covered one-tenth of the cultivated area of Java and Madura, and contributed nearly 75 per cent of the total world supply.

[86]For a detailed discussion of the findings of this report, see Wertheim, op. cit., pp. 259–68.

[87]Bruno Lasker, *Human Bondage in South-East Asia*, Chapel Hill, 1950, quoted by Wertheim, op. cit., p. 255.

Books and articles for further reading

Allen, G.C. and Donnithorne, A.G., *Western Enterprise in Indonesia and Malaya*, George Allen & Unwin, London, 1962, 2nd. imp.

Bastin, J., *Essays on Indonesian and Malayan History*, Donald Moore, Singapore, 1961.

Cowan, C.D. (ed.), *The Economic Development of South-East Asia*, George Allen & Unwin, London, 1964.

Day, C., *The Policy and Administration of the Dutch in Java*, reprinted, Oxford University Press, Kuala Lumpur, 1966.

Dekker, E.D. ('Multatuli'), *Max Havelaar or the Coffee Auctions of the Dutch Trading Company*, Edmonston & Douglas, Edinburgh, 1868.

Fisher, C.A., *South-East Asia: A Social, Economic and Political Geography*, Methuen, London, 1964.

Furnivall, J.S., *Colonial Policy and Practice: A Comparative Study of Burma and Netherlands India*, reprinted, New York University Press, New York, 1956.

————, *Netherlands India: A Study of Plural Economy*, reprinted, Cambridge University Press, Cambridge, 1967.

Geertz, C., *Agricultural Involution: The Process of Ecological Change in Indonesia*, University of California Press, Berkeley, 1966.

Jacoby, E.H., *Agrarian Unrest in Southeast Asia*, Asia Publishing House, Bombay, 1961.

Kahin, G. McT., *Nationalism and Revolution in Indonesia*, Cornell University Press, New York, 1952.

Lasker, B., *Human Bondage in South-East Asia*, Chapel Hill, 1950.

Legge, J.D., *Indonesia*, Prentice-Hall Inc., New Jersey, 1964.

Purcell, V., *The Chinese in South-East Asia*, Oxford University Press, London, 1965, 2nd. ed.

Robequain, C., *Malaya, Indonesia, Borneo and the Philippines*, Longman, London, 1958, 2nd. ed.

Schrieke, B., *Indonesian Sociological Studies* (2 Vols.), Van Hoeve, The Hague, 1955.

Steinberg, D.J. (ed.), *In Search of South-East Asia: A Modern History*, Oxford University Press, Kuala Lumpur, 1971.

Vandenbosch, A., *The Dutch East Indies: Its Government, Problems and Politics*, University of California Press, Berkeley, 1944, 3rd. ed.

Wertheim, W.F., *Indonesian Society in Transition: A Study of Social Change*, Van Hoeve, The Hague, 1964, 2nd. ed.

———— (ed.), *Indonesian Economics: The Concept of Dualism in Theory and Policy*, Van Hoeve, The Hague, 1961.

II BRITISH
SOUTH-EAST ASIA

COVERING an area about half that of the Netherlands East Indies but spread out over even greater distances and disparately administered, it is impossible to treat the various territories which made up the British Empire in South-East Asia as an entity. Apart from the fact that they all owed their allegiance to the British Crown, there was nothing politically, socially or economically to bind together Burma, the states of the Malay Peninsula, the trading colonies of the Straits Settlements, or the undeveloped expanses of Sarawak and British North Borneo. All had their own characteristics and peculiar problems, and contrasted with one another unevenly in terms of development and progress. While Singapore developed into one of the great cosmopolitan trading centres of the world, the neighbouring states of Malaya could boast no town of more than 120,000 inhabitants. Burma became one of the great rice producers of South-East Asia and acquired a sizeable Indian immigrant population. The Malay Peninsula flourished on its twin assets of tin and rubber and became the largest area of Chinese settlement in the region. On the other hand, the North Borneo territories remained backwaters of economic progress, with small populations and no prominence in the world of international trade. In any case, historical, political and geographical circumstances determined that these scattered domains could never become part of a more integrated whole, so that in dealing with them each is taken in its turn.

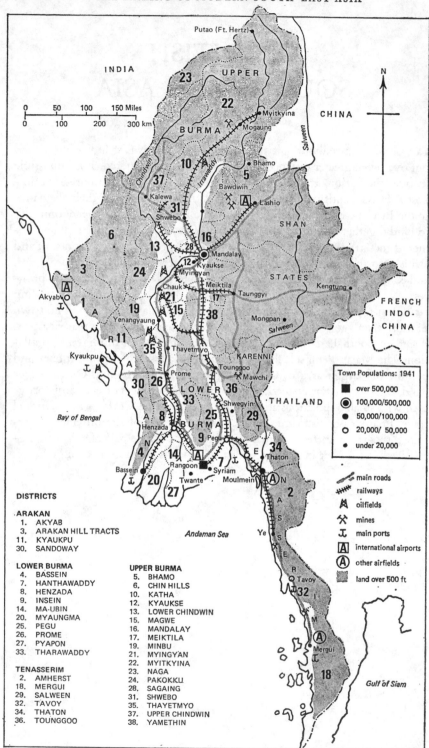

14. General Map of Burma, 1941

A. British Burma

'The province is already one of the brightest jewels in the Imperial diadem of India; and its lustre will increase in proportion as inducements are offered for the influx of the capital and the labour necessary for more rapid development in the immediate future.'

John Nisbett, *Burma under British Rule—and Before*, London, 1901.

THE 120 years of British rule wrought fundamental changes in the economic and social structure of Burma. In 1824 the total population of the country was reckoned at 4 million; on the eve of the Japanese invasion in 1942 it was four times as great. Traditionally a self-contained nation catering for her own needs, Burmese life was based on a simple, agricultural village economy which provided its own rice or millet, vegetable oils, fish and salt, its own silk and cotton, its own pottery, tools and weapons. The rulers of Burma were not interested in foreign trade, and for reasons of policy actively discouraged it. What surplus rice there was, was carried from Lower to Upper Burma, while to maintain these supplies in cheap abundance, the exporting of rice overseas was expressly forbidden. The only item that did attract overseas commerce was teak, valuable for ship-building. Communications were sparse and principally by water. In the dry areas the ox-cart was most general.

In 1941 Burma presented a wholly different picture. The country was now engaged to the world trading system and the world market. It was the world's largest exporter of rice—providing two-fifths of world supplies—, which with oil accounted for two-thirds to three-quarters of the country's exports. Other export commodities included timber (especially teak), lead, wolfram, tin, vegetables, raw rubber, raw cotton, cattle hides, matches, zinc and copper. At the same time, Burma imported most of her material needs, including finished material goods, 15 to 20 per cent of which comprised cotton yarn, thread and piece goods.

Rice

The most spectacular economic development under British rule was the tremendous growth in rice production. The rice trade changed the face of Lower Burma, bringing with it great achievements and greater problems.

Although Burma had been exporting rice as early as the days of the Malacca Sultanate, and the Dutch reported supplies from Arakan in the seventeenth century, under the Tounggoo and Konbaung kings hardly any rice was exported at all.[1] However, with the lifting of all restrictions on trade which was the first consequence of British rule in Arakan and Tenasserim, rice production expanded in these two provinces within the first decade. In Tenasserim it went up by 50 per cent between 1845 and 1852, while in Arakan, favoured with cheaper labour and food supplies, the growth rate was faster still. By

1852 Akyab was the most important rice exporting centre in the world of its day, while the area under rice cultivation increased fourfold after 1830. But the real rice revolution took place in Lower Burma a couple of decades later. Before 1852 the most important commercial products of Lower Burma were salt and fish and no rice was exported at all. This was not only because of Ava's prohibitions on rice exports and its absorption of any surplus but also was a consequence of the wars and political upheavals of the late eighteenth and early nineteenth centuries, all of which served to depopulate and impoverish the region.[2] Yet Lower Burma was potentially ideal for rice-growing. The land was suitable and the water supply abundant. British rule added to these natural advantages by bringing security to the farmers, an outside market for their produce, conditions where easy credit and seasonal labour became readily available, and the means by which the produce could be conveyed swiftly and in bulk by the development of modern means of communication and transport.

After 1852 therefore there was a general rise in rice production. To a large extent this was stimulated by the ever growing demand for rice on the European market whose traditional sources of supply had either become inadequate or had been interrupted by political disturbances.[3] Other markets opened out too, particularly in the fast developing regions under Dutch and British rule in island South-East Asia with their new plantation industries, mining operations and growing populations. The opening of the Suez Canal in 1869 helped to accelerate the trade still further, and promoted the expansion of Rangoon, Akyab, Moulmein and Bassein as the leading ports of the country. More significant for the rice traffic itself were changes in the type of rice exported, made possible by the introduction of fast steamships along shortened trade routes. Cargo rice replaced husked rice and helped give rise to the rice-milling industry. Further improvements later in the century, principally in the speed of steamship services, enabled cargo rice in its turn to be substituted by white milled rice, and in 1915 new milling techniques made possible the export of parboiled rice.[4]

The rise of Burma's rice mills was also stimulated by other nineteenth-century technical advances. The first power-driven rice mill was erected in Rangoon in 1861 and by 1940 there were some 700 such mills all over the country. In the beginning the milling industry was European dominated but towards the end of the century the European share fell by a sharp 20 per cent.[5] Its place was taken by a multitude of smaller concerns, many employing less than ten men apiece with outputs ranging from 10 to 75 tons a day. The smaller millers had several advantages such as much lower overheads and the availability of a cheap labour supply. They were able to set themselves up nearer the source of the padi, at railway junctions, along canals and at key river jetties. They also benefited from the introduction in the 1900s of small, cheap and efficient German-made machine units which reduced transport costs. Nevertheless, the sheer size and capacity of the big European mills situated at the main rice ports ensured that they still retained a lion's share of the trade, and prior to the Pacific War they still produced one-third of the rice milled in Burma.

As a result of these developments, Burma became one of the world's great rice granaries, exporting by 1941 4 million tons a year. 'The growth of the rice industry is, in essence, the story of modern Burma.'[6] The growth of population, the changing standard of living, Indian immigration, the development of communications, social change and political problems were all closely related to the enormous growth and expansion of the country's rice trade. Rice led to the repopulation of Lower Burma but prevented the growth of large towns, for two-thirds of the total population depended on agriculture for their livelihood and 70 per cent of the cultivated land was devoted to padi. Rangoon, the capital and the country's chief business centre through which nine-tenths of its trade passed, still had a population of only half a million. Next came Mandalay with little more than 150,000 inhabitants in 1941.

Oil

Up till 1930 rice accounted for from one-half to three-quarters of the total value of Burma's exports, but after that date oil became the country's principal foreign exchange earner. Oil was mined under the Burman kings. The oil-wells were centred at Yenangyaung which for centuries had supplied Burmese homes with fuel for their lamps and the means by which wood, mats and palm-leaf manuscripts were preserved. But methods of production were primitive—the wells were dug by hand—and slow, so much so that by the 1880s American-imported kerosene was successfully competing with local oil, even in the Yenangyaung district itself. In 1886, however, the Burmah Oil Company was formed by a British firm in Rangoon which dealt in local oil, and the new company had soon bought up the government leases and several private wells. Within five years the Burmah Oil Company had driven the American-imported kerosene off the market and was exporting the first barrels of Burmese oil to India and by 1896 to Penang as well. Ten years later the company opened its pipeline from the oil fields to its new refinery at Syriam. In 1923 Burmese oil production stood at 273 million tons, but this still represented a small percentage of total world production, a mere 5 per cent of world output in 1941. In that year the Burmah Oil Company which in 1908 had become the parent of the great Anglo-Iranian Oil Company monopolized three-quarters of Burma's oil production. The remainder was produced by three other concerns—the Indo-Burma Petroleum Company which was linked with the Rangoon firm of Steel Brothers & Co. Ltd., and had a refinery at Seikkyi; the British Burmah Petroleum Company with its refinery at Thilawa; and the Nath Singh Oil Company. There were three other centres of production apart from Yenangyaung which passed its peak in 1921. Oil was the only Burmese industry before the Pacific War in which Burman labour predominated.

Timber

The next most important export of the country, holding second place in value till superseded by oil in the first decade of the twentieth century, was timber, in particular teak. Burma's teak has the longest history of all her exports. It was used by Arab traders in the sixth century A.D. It was the basis of Burma's flourishing ship-building industry during the seventeenth century and was a principal object of Anglo-French rivalry during the eighteenth. In 1752 Alaungpaya declared teak to be a 'royal tree', while about a hundred years later, soon after the British annexation of Lower Burma, Lord Dalhousie made teak the property of the Crown. The following year (1856) a Forestry Department under a Chief Conservator of Forests was set up to make sure that the resources of the forests were properly worked. This measure came about largely as a result of British experience in Tenasserim during the previous twenty years. The timber industry there had developed in the 1830s, after a slow start, to become Tenasserim's most important source of wealth, stimulating in the process a revival of the ship-building industry which was further enhanced after 1847 when the British Admiralty began to take an active interest. But methods of control were ineffective with the result that by 1850 the teak forests of the Amherst district had been destroyed. With that experience in mind, the new Forest Department developed very careful controls over the cutting and extraction of timber. Under its management, the more valuable and easily accessible forests were declared forest reserves for lease to private contractors under special conditions or for preservation by the Department.[7]

By 1941 Burma was the source for three-quarters of the world's teak supply and had a production of 400,000 tons. The timber industry came to be dominated by a small number of large firms. Six of these enjoyed 'long leases', five of them being European and one Indo-Burman. The largest of them was the Bombay-Burmah Trading Corporation which had been the main instrument for precipitating the Third Anglo-Burmese War. In 1924 when 'The Six' had their long leases renewed, their combined capital investment totalled Rs 100 million and they employed a labour force of 55,000. The fact that a few large companies should monopolize the timber industry was to a large extent inevitable, since a considerable amount of capital was required to cover the expenses of extracting the timber.

Other products
After oil, lead, wolfram and tin were the principal mineral exports of the country, although their export value was only a fraction of that of the former. The lead came exclusively from the Bawdwin mines some forty miles northeast of Lashio, and those near Namtu, both of which were owned by the Burma Corporation. For many years a scene of Chinese mining activity, these mines were individually probably amongst the richest for both lead and silver in the world, and were the sole source of copper, nickel, speiss and cobalt in Burma. As for tin, Burma ranked as South-East Asia's fourth largest producer before the Pacific War, but her production lagged far behind that of the other three. Although Burma stands at the head of the long chain of tin deposits stretching southwards to the Sumatran islands of Bangka and Belitung tin-mining, which was a Chinese affair, produced an insignificant 100 tons a year before 1910, when a British firm, attracted by the discovery of wolfram at Mawchi near Toungoo, started operations there. The Mawchi mines proved to have the richest individual tungsten and the third richest individual tin de-

posits in the world and by 1941 were producing half the tin and tungsten in Burma. The rest came mainly from small mines, mostly British-owned, and worked by sluice and dredge, in the Tavoy district of Tenasserim. Small quantities of rubies and sapphires, for which Burma has been famous since ancient times, were mined at Mogok, north of Mandalay, and some coal, salt and jade at other centres.

Burma's other exports made only a fractional contribution to the country's earnings. The Burmese rubber industry was an off-shoot of the industry in the Malay Peninsula, but production was confined to Tenasserim where the first estates were opened at the start of the twentieth century, since the country as a whole lay too far to the north for successful cultivation. The large estates were almost entirely controlled by big European enterprises like the ubiquitous Steel Brothers while most of the 3,693 smallholdings in the country were in the hands of Burmans. The labour on the estates, on the other hand, was predominantly Indian.

The development of communications

The export trade which in general fashioned Burma's economic evolution under British rule laid its imprint on the development of the country's communications, and as Rangoon—whose role had been earmarked by Dalhousie as Singapore's had by Raffles—swiftly grew into the country's principal port and city after 1852, so all routes led to Rangoon.

However, the waterways never lost their importance as the chief arteries of communication. Most important of all, of course, was the Irrawaddy, navigable the 850 miles up to Bhamo. By 1900 inland water transport had become the virtual monopoly, as far as long distance passenger services and heavy traffic were concerned, of the Irrawaddy Flotilla Company, while Arakan's coastal trade was largely in the hands of the Arracan Flotilla Company. The Irrawaddy Flotilla Company, established in 1863, started operations in a big way in 1875, and ten years later provided the vessels which carried the invading British troops to Mandalay and bore back King Thibaw and Queen Supayalet to captivity. Although in 1940-1 the volume of freight carried by the Company amounted to only one-quarter of that borne by Burma Railways, taking into account the innumerable smaller Burmese craft that also operated, the waterborne total was probably the same as that of the railways. Important additions to the water-way system were the Twante Canal and the Pegu-Sittang Canal.

Railway construction in Burma, which was initially dictated more by strategic than commercial considerations, owed its impetus to the development of railway policy in India. The first line, completed in 1877, joined Rangoon to Prome, some 161 miles away on the then frontier with the independent realm of Ava (Upper Burma). This line had been proposed in 1868 but as no private firm was willing to take up the contract and as Calcutta had already decided that lines should be built by the state, construction was finally started by the Indian government in 1874.[8]

After this, railway construction in Burma was rapid. The Rangoon-Toungoo line was opened in 1885, just in time for the Third War, and extended to

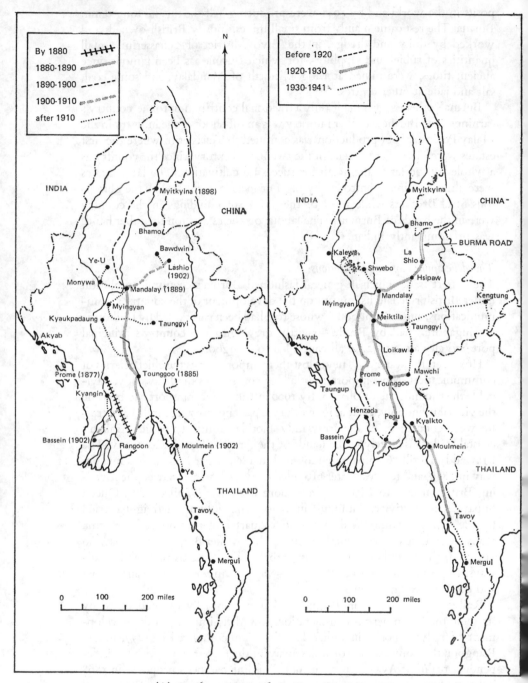

15. (A) Railway Growth in Burma, 1877–1941
     (B) Road Development in Burma, 1860–1941

Mandalay by 1889, to become the main highway for immigrants from the north. By 1898 the line stretched to Myitkina. Although the Burma State Railway easily paid its way after 1882, in 1896 it was leased to the privately-owned Burma Railway Company, a change-over from state to private enterprise made by Calcutta without any reference to local Burmese conditions. Under this new management Burma's railways continued to expand and prosper, aided by the favourable conditions created by the country's political stability and economic development. The track was extended by another 1,970 miles and the volume of passenger and freight traffic increased substantially.[9]

Nevertheless in 1929, the state once again took over control, but although this change received the support of nationalist politicians it was once again dictated by political and economic considerations in India which had little or no bearing on the Burmese scene. The new state enterprise, now known as Burma Railways, quickly ran into difficulties and within one year of operations was running at a loss. Road and water communications were developing and offering more serious competition, but the impact of the Great Depression was harder still, drastically reducing passenger and freight traffic and so substantially cutting down receipts. The opening of the Burma Road in 1939 gave the railways a new source of business and enabled them to start balancing accounts but by this time the state system had become a new burden for the nation as a whole, for with the formal separation of Burma from India, the original loans with which the Indian government had financed their construction in the nineteenth century now had to be paid back.

Until 1920 when motor traffic became established in Burma, there were hardly any surfaced roads in the country. River and rail transport handled all Burma's needs, while the delta region did not lend itself to the construction of overland routes. After 1920 a considerable number of roads were built so that by 1941 there were 6,800 miles of surfaced roads in the country, with another 5,600 miles of roads motorable in the dry season. But in proportion to Burma's size and population these are not very large figures, and in 1941 there were less than 20,000 registered motor vehicles in the land—most of them in Rangoon.

However in 1939 the first international road link was completed, the celebrated 'Burma Road', which linked Lashio in the north with Kunming in China.[10] The outbreak of the Pacific War and Burma's involvement in it led to the building of two more international routes—the Stilwell Road from Ledo and the Shwebo-Kalewa Road to Imphal in India. But these routes were built for specific military and strategic needs, and after the war, Burma's new rulers appeared to revert to the pattern of pre-war administrations where fears of uncontrollable immigration, the high costs involved for small returns and the vested interests of the shipping companies in the *status quo* won the day.

Air services in Burma were also very limited prior to the Pacific War. Rangoon's airport at Mingaladon served four international airlines of which Imperial Airways (now BAC) had certain exclusive rights. Only two other airfields, those at Lashio and Akyab, were of commercial importance. There were no facilities for Burmese to acquire flying knowledge and experience within the country before a Civil Aviation Centre was established in 1941.

Postal and telegraphic communications in Burma were reasonably adequate for the needs of the country by 1941, but broadcasting and the telephone services were very undeveloped. Since the development of the latter was dependent to a large degree on educational standards and urban development, both of which were very restricted in British Burma, their limited growth is understandable.

Population: patterns of growth

Since under British rule Burma evolved primarily into a rice-bowl, its population, as it expanded, remained predominantly attached to the land. Apart from the great rate of population growth—it quadrupled within a century—there were two main changes in the population pattern of the country under British rule. First was the re-peopling of Lower Burma with the consequent shift of economic and political power away from the traditional centres in the Dry Zone of the north; secondly was the introduction of a sizeable immigrant population into the country, in particular, Indians.

The growth of population in Lower Burma during the second half of the nineteenth century was mainly the result of a large-scale migration from the north and forms part of 'the most spectacular development of her economic history',[11] the conversion of the jungles and swamps of the delta into a plain of padi. This movement of people reversed the population ratios between Upper and Lower Burma. In the mid-nineteenth century there were over 3½ million people in Upper Burma compared to under 1½ million in the south. Just over thirty years later the population in the south was greater than that of the north by 25 per cent. In 1931 the population of Lower Burma still exceeded that of the north by nearly 1 million. The growth rate in Lower Burma is even more strikingly conveyed in terms of population densities. Between 1872 and 1900 the density of people per square mile in Lower Burma rose from 31 to over 90 and by 1931 had increased again by another 50 per cent. A density of 31 per square mile is very low and since the success of rice production had made itself apparent in both Tenasserim and Arakan, it became British policy to fill the empty spaces of the Irrawaddy Delta so that the costs of acquiring and administering the newly-acquired province could be met and justified. With its natural advantages, rice cultivation was the answer and immigration became essential.

There were two possible sources for migrants—Upper Burma and India. Upper Burma was nearer and more convenient, and British efforts were soon directed to ensuring a flow from that direction. The treaty of 1862, the first effective commercial agreement between the British administration in Lower Burma and the kingdom of Ava, contained two clauses providing for freedom of movement between the two territories. Apart from this the British in Lower Burma encouraged immigration into the south by imposing no restrictions on entry or on migrants acquiring land. New settlers were exempted from the payment of taxes for several years and the colonial administration went out of its way to promote the immigration of Shans, 'well

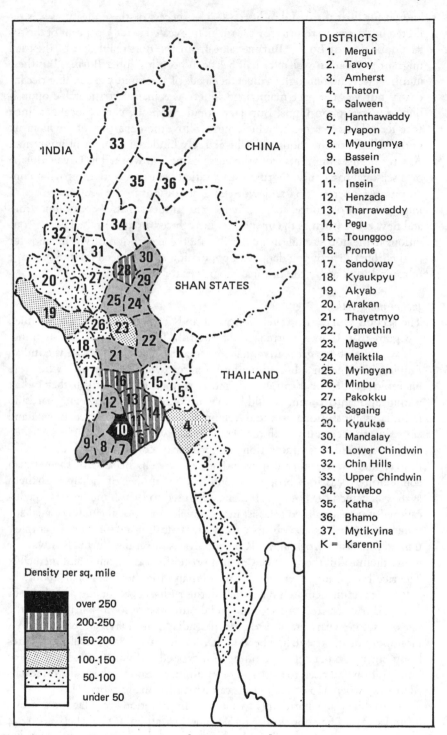

DISTRICTS
1. Mergui
2. Tavoy
3. Amherst
4. Thaton
5. Salween
6. Hanthawaddy
7. Pyapon
8. Myaungmya
9. Bassein
10. Maubin
11. Insein
12. Henzada
13. Tharrawaddy
14. Pegu
15. Toungoo
16. Prome
17. Sandoway
18. Kyaukpyu
19. Akyab
20. Arakan
21. Thayetmyo
22. Yamethin
23. Magwe
24. Meiktila
25. Myingyan
26. Minbu
27. Pakokku
28. Sagaing
29. Kyaukse
30. Mandalay
31. Lower Chindwin
32. Chin Hills
33. Upper Chindwin
34. Shwebo
35. Katha
36. Bhamo
37. Mytikyina
K = Karenni

Density per sq. mile

over 250
200-250
150-200
100-150
50-100
under 50

16.   Burma: Population Density by District, 1941

known for their thrift and industry'.[12] The success of these measures was reflected in the census returns for 1881 which revealed that 8½ per cent of the total population of Lower Burma came from the north and that of the total
migrant population well over half had been born in Upper Burma. But these
numbers were not enough to meet the needs of the rapidly expanding rice industry nor was the pace maintained. There was in fact considerable opposition to migration in Upper Burma, particularly on the part of local headmen
who feared loss of revenue which must follow the departure of the menfolk
of the village for the south and who actively hindered permanent migration.
As a result most migrants from the north came and worked in Lower Burma
on a seasonal basis only. During the twentieth century, with improving conditions in Upper Burma and worsening conditions in the south, the pace of
migration fell off more steeply. Stable government, better communications
and new crops (such as the groundnut introduced in 1906) raised living conditions in the north, while in Lower Burma the absorption of virgin lands for
cultivation, the growing density of population and the need for and shortage
of capital took away the original incentives for migration.

Indian immigration

The second source, however, remained and immigration from India filled
the gaps that Upper Burma could not fill. To the official British mind,
this was one of the great advantages of treating Burma as part of the Indian
Empire. The Indian sub-continent was overcrowded with people who were
unemployed or under-employed, and it seemed to the British that Indian
immigration into Burma would be to everyone's benefit—relieving hardship
in India whilst stimulating the development of under-populated Burma and
enriching the economy with new crops and new techniques.

Although Indian immigration was primarily connected with the rice industry, there were other important factors as well. Because of their Indian
connexions, the British brought a considerable number of Indians with them
as they occupied the country. Indians were used to British methods, and edu-
cationally were qualified to assist in the development of the new colonial administration. It was also cheaper from the British point of view to employ
trained Indians to work in the Rangoon docks or on the Burma Railway, or
to use them to fill the vacancies in such professions as teaching and medicine.
The rice boom, however, created the demand for cheap seasonal labour.

Private recruitment in India to help in the rush to open up the padi-fields of
Lower Burma started in 1870. Indian labourers were soon pouring in at the
rate of 15,000 a year, and after the British India Steam Navigation Company's
monopoly of the traffic had been broken in the early 1880s, resulting in fares
being cut by 50 per cent, the numbers increased sixfold. By 1900 the rate of
immigration had risen to a quarter of a million a year and the peak was reached in 1927 when 430,000 labourers came into Burma to work. [13]

Meanwhile official attempts to sponsor immigration were far less successful and also on a far more limited scale. The first attempt, made between 1874
and 1876 as a measure to relieve the distress caused by the great Bengal famine
of that period, was not from the British point of view a success. The Madras

Emigration Scheme tried a year later was even more short-lived than its predecessor, and destroyed the notion that a switch from Bengal to the presidency from which most of the private immigrants came would prove successful. The last official effort came in 1883 when a plan to get cultivators from North Bihar to settle on uninhabited tracts in Pegu and Shwegyin was a total failure. Thereafter government left matters to private enterprise. In fact, government-recruited labour had never enjoyed much popularity with private employers, all the more so after 1876 when labour legislation designed to protect the immigrant from undue exploitation laid down too many unprofitable conditions.[14]

Despite the great and increasing volume of Indian immigration, only a small proportion of the migrants came to stay. Contrary to the misplaced optimism of government officials, few Indians were in a position as a result of their poverty or sufficiently enticed by the prospects to want to do so. Furthermore caste restrictions made it difficult for them to bring their wives and families. Instead, migration was largely seasonal. To the great benefit of the steamship companies, the average labourer arrived for the harvesting season, then went from the padi-field to the rice mill and finally returned to his village in India to await the next season.

Nevertheless in 1931 there were over a million Indians resident in the country. Until the period of the Great War (1914-18), the presence of this large racial minority presented few problems, since the Burmese were almost wholly agriculturalists while the shortage of labour in commerce and industry was conveniently met by the immigrants. But after 1920 circumstances began to change, and as each community encroached on the other's preserves, competition between them developed. In this competition the Indians tended to come out better. As labourers they were more readily employed because they were used to a lower standard of living and were therefore prepared to work for lower wages. With the spread of Indian landownership, Indian landowners tended to prefer Indian tenants who were more docile and of their kind. The maistry system of recruitment gave Indians a virtual monopoly of employment in certain occupations, and Europeans with an Indian background preferred to employ Indians. Mounting friction was brought to a head by the impact of the Great Depression in 1929 which brought about large-scale foreclosures on land by the Indian chettyar community and created widespread unemployment. As a consequence the 1930s saw several ugly communal clashes centred on Rangoon. The basis of all these disturbances was primarily economic and their net result was to reduce immigration considerably, as well as to lead to a decline in the number of Indian settlers in the country.[15] The separation of Burma from India in 1937 and the signing of the Indo-Burman Immigration Agreement of 1941 accelerated the process, and with the great exodus which took place before the advancing Japanese armies in 1942, the total Indian population in Burma was more than halved.

The Chinese in Burma

The other great minority race of South-East Asia, the Chinese, on the other hand, were poorly represented in Burma. According to the 1931 census

there were under 200,000 Chinese in the country out of a population of over
9½ million, and on the eve of the Pacific War the number still stood below a
quarter of a million. Throughout its history Burma has had political and
commercial connexions with China, but the difficulties of the mountainous
overland route between the two countries prevented Chinese influence from
becoming either substantial or sustained. In between bouts of war, invasion
and upheaval,[16] a slender but significant trade developed up the Irrawaddy
through Bhamo to Yunnan and beyond, and grossly over-estimating its value
the British made repeated attempts to participate in it during the nineteenth
century. But when finally in 1894 Britain and China signed a treaty regarding Burmese trade,[17] its results proved most disappointing. It was this trade
route and the settlement of various polyglot tribes on Burma's Chinese
frontiers which account for the earliest Chinese presence inside Burma, and
in 1931 approximately one-third of the Chinese population of the country
consisted of 'mountain Chinese' from Yunnan. The immigration of Chinese
by sea into Tenasserim and the delta region only took place after the establishment of British rule. By the 1930s over two-thirds of the Chinese in Burma were immigrants by sea and were to be found concentrated in the delta—
more than half, in fact, within a 100-mile radius of Rangoon itself, with the
rest fanned out along the railway line and steamer routes. Sixty-eight per
cent of the Chinese who came by sea were to be found in the delta area. In
contrast to their compatriots in other South-East Asian lands, the Chinese in
Burma managed to assimilate themselves to a remarkable degree, and although they were also an object for attack during the anti-foreign riots of
1931 they were not regarded as a serious problem by most Burmese prior
to the outbreak of the Pacific War. The great bulk of them were involved in
commerce and industry, and completely dominated mining. However the
events which followed the Japanese invasion of China in 1937 and Burma's
subsequent involvement in the world war which followed, completely changed the picture, and whereas after 1945 the Indian minority rapidly dwindled
in size and importance, the Chinese, with a rapidly increasing birth-rate, were
growing in number and assuming an important political problem for the future.

The Burmese and the agrarian problem
However, as far as the Burmese themselves were concerned, within three
generations of British rule they appeared to have become beggars within
their own homeland. The wealth of the country which had undoubtedly
been greatly developed lay in immigrant and alien hands. Apart from the
lion's share held by the British who besides dominating banking, monopolized the ownership of the plantations and mines, controlled the oil industry
and played the leading role in timber, cement and cotton, 70 per cent of Burma's foreign trade was with India and was largely controlled by Indians,
while the public utilities were either British-owned or run by the state. This
left the Burmese mainly as farmers and even here nearly half the land was
held in fee by Indian moneylenders. The rice trade commanded the Burmese

economy and the poverty of the rice farmer became the most outstanding and urgent problem that Burma had to face under British rule.

This agrarian problem naturally centred on Lower Burma where by 1941 10 million acres of land were under rice cultivation. Two-thirds of all arable land throughout the country were devoted to rice-growing—most of it in Lower Burma. By 1936 over one-fifth of this rice land was owned by the chettyars, while by 1939 in some districts of Lower Burma as much as 70 per cent or more of the agricultural land was in the hands of absentee landlords. Since apart from the land known to be under the ownership of chettyar and other moneylenders, probably another 10 to 20 per cent was mortgaged, in the country as a whole barely half the Burmese peasantry actually owned the land they worked on, while in the rice-growing districts of the delta the proportion was considerably less.

The existence of large estates and rich landowners is not an evil in itself, but in the case of Burma the alienation of land to foreign moneylenders was closely linked to rural poverty and indebtedness. While landlords became richer, their tenants became poorer. It has been reckoned that between 1870 and 1931 the value of agricultural wages dropped by as much as 20 per cent. The chettyars added to their estates because their tenants could not pay their rents. The tenants could not pay because they were already in debt, and the conditions of their tenure left them with too small a margin of profit to free themselves from indebtedness. Furthermore both landlord and tenant were dependent on the price of rice on the world market, and within Burma itself the price was effectively controlled by the small group of (mainly British) rice exporters who held the trade. Hence the agrarian problem and the plight of the Burmese peasantry revolved around indebtedness, land alienation to foreign landlords and the conditions of tenancy.

British rule liberated the Burmese from the social and economic restrictions and abuses of traditional Burmese society and this alone made possible the conversion of Lower Burma into a rice granary. At the same time the British also introduced novel factors into Burmese life which contributed considerably to the problem of rural poverty. The most basic of these new factors was the spread of a money economy, to which were closely bound new systems of land tenure, making land itself a commodity which could be bought and sold in a country where it was regarded as hereditary and inalienable. As a result the padi planter soon found himself at the mercy of circumstances which were either beyond his control or his comprehension, and his attempts to cope with his new situation were more often than not rendered useless both by his own conservatism and by mismanaged official attempts to help him out of his troubles.

The intrusion of money into the self-sufficient economy of the Burmese village has been described as a 'shattering national experience that no people anywhere could have passed through unscathed'.[18] Padi could no longer be bartered as more and more land was turned to rice production and large surpluses accrued. Fishing, the other staple of the traditional economy, became a specialized occupation. So both the farmer and the fisherman needed money to meet their needs, while the penetration of cheap Western manufactures into the countryside created new demands which only the possession of money could gratify. Apart from this, although the British created the conditions by which rice production could flourish, money was still necessary to open up the land. Seed had to be bought, implements, carts and cattle acquired, labourers for the harvest hired and ordinary living expenses met. Since the pioneers were smallholders, they had no choice but to borrow, and although some of them managed to make their way, clear their debts and retain their independence, the great majority were obliged to mortgage the land they had cleared in order to survive.

Land policy and credit

The very act of clearing land of course involved questions of ownership. Under Burmese government there were four main types of land tenure, all of which implied hereditary and permanent occupation by the cultivator.[19] Under the British, land acquired a marketable value and land ownership was regarded as a form of capital, subject to the laws of an economic system based on the concept of free enterprise and free trade. British policy was to try and integrate the new settlers into this system by bringing into being a class of small peasant proprietors who would create stability owning the land they worked, and who would help defray the expenses of administration by paying their dues direct to the state. In the event, despite experiments with five different systems of land tenure, this general aim was never achieved.

The earliest and simplest form of tenure was the lease system, the purpose of which was to simplify land assessment by settling the land rent at a fixed rate for a specific term, and to encourage occupiers to keep the land they had already cleared as well as to extend its area. This aim was achieved with such success that government itself had to bear conside rable loss in revenue, especially after 1870 when rice cultivation became so profitable that no further inducements were needed. So after 1876 no new leases were issued, and in its place government based its system on squatters' rights. The 'squatter' system was regularized by the Burma Land and Revenue Act of 1876 but although this found great favour in districts already settled where extensions were being made to existing holdings, it was subject to abuse.[20] In order to prevent squatters from disposing of or losing the land they had cleared and to induce them to take permanent title to it, the British applied, side-by-side with the squatter system, the *patta* system derived from India, by which the cultivator was exempted from the payment of land revenue until his plot granted by government should become profitable.[21] The problem here was to select suitable applicants who were bona fide cultivators and who were in fact in a position to clear and cultivate their land without havin grecourse to moneylenders. Moneylenders themselves covered up against the danger of the lands of their debtors being confiscated by imposing higher interest rates, while because of the various conditions attached, *patta* land could command less credit than squatter land. Although the latter problem was catered for by legislation in 1906, the *patta* system was abandoned altogether soon afterwards. It had given rise to certain administrative difficulties, and in any case had failed to check the spread of land alienation and moneylending.

Another direction which the government tried with a view to speeding up development in the earlier days was to offer capitalists large blocks of land on a variant of the *patta* system, in the expectation that they would import more labourers to work on their estates. But, as was the case in Cochin-China, capitalists proved just as speculative as smallholders, and the various government officials, lawyers, clerks and others who took advantage of this opportunity contented themselves in most cases with subletting or renting their land to their neighbours, or even merely with selling them firewood. Most of such concessions were eventually reacquired by government by voluntary surrender or by forfeiture for breach of contract. Under another system introduced and applied after 1910 with greater success, tracts of waste land were allocated to specially picked groups of peasant cultivators who were then set to work on reclaiming and cultivating the land. Within the limitations imposed by restricted government funds and inadequate supervision, this 'colonization' system proved in many respects the most successful.

However, in general, the various systems of land tenure devised by Rangoon did not, as we have seen, produce the desired results; even the colonization scheme was handicapped from the start by a lack of suitable waste tracts for opening to cultivation.

The Burmese cultivator thus found himself at the mercy of the forces of the commercial market with its ever fluctuating prices and of natural hazards such as floods or drought, murrain, pests and disease. Any of these factors, alone or in conjunction with others, could destroy his precarious solvency. He also tended to be bound to poverty as a result of the social environment and the attitudes it engendered which determined his values and his behaviour.[22] Not only did the cultivator fail to perceive the burden that his social obligations imposed upon him, but he usually completely lacked the bourgeois sense of the value of money. In a world which he regarded as governed by an inexorable fate, money was a thing of chance—good to use if it was available but not to be held as more permanent than anything else or of greater value. In such circumstances the hope of developing an independent class of peasant smallholders, such as might be found in Western Europe, holding its own in an evolving money economy was wishful thinking indeed.[23]

Nevertheless every cultivator understood the need for money and was fully disposed to take advantage of the various forms of credit which were extended to him. Private sources were always the most important; in the early years of the opening of Lower Burma they were the only ones. Indian moneylenders, used to British law and finance and with a long commercial tradition of their own, were to be found at the principal seaports willing to advance credit. Moneylending became the particular preserve of the chettyars, who first appeared in numbers in Burma during the 1850s. By the end of the century 'there was a chettyar within a day's journey of every cultivator' in the well-populated parts of Lower Burma. It was estimated that in the 1930s two-thirds of the loans issued in Lower Burma were provided by the chettyar community. In Upper Burma, on the other hand, the leading role was taken by Burmese moneylenders.

The chettyars were reluctant to foreclose on land unless forced by circumstances to do so. But foreclosing happened on a large scale in 1907, due to the collapse of the United States money market, and again, more disastrously still, during the Great Depression. Prior to 1929 the chettyar's stake in agriculture had been enormous in terms of credit advanced. However, after the Depression and as a result of the increasing nationalist agitation in the country in the 1930s, the chettyars greatly restricted their moneylending activities, so much so that on the eve of the Japanese invasion (1942) the volume of their stake had been reduced by four-fifths. Even so, chettyar investment totalled one-third of all foreign investments in Burma before the Pacific War, and taken collectively they formed the largest single block of investors in the country. Moneylenders are rarely popular amongst those to whom they lend their money, and as nationalist temper mounted in Burma, the chettyars became singled out as the scapegoats of the agrarian crisis; but it must be admitted that by providing capital when and where it was wanted, they also fulfilled a need.[24]

Nevertheless, by any yardstick, the alienation of land from peasant producer to moneylender was a development to be avoided, and the British did make efforts to provide credit facilities for the benefit of the former. The Land Improvements Loan Act of 1883, the first official measure, quickly proved ineffective, partly because of the long delay between application and award and of the difficulty of repayment since loans were usually made to large groups of joint borrowers. The Agriculturalists' Loan Act of 1884 therefore was passed to make good these defects by enabling the cultivator to borrow on easier terms, but although this measure proved more successful it tended to be made use of only in those districts where the market value of land was low and therefore private sources of credit not so readily available. In general, the advantage of a comparatively low rate of interest (only 10 per cent) was more than offset by official red tape and delay, while private moneylenders offered more lenient terms on the same security. The advantages of the government loan system in fact seemed to be so doubtful, although they doubtless served in cases of extreme hardship, that the Banking Enquiry Commission of 1929 recommended that in those areas where credit could be better obtained from other sources such as banks, co-operatives or even chettyars, government loans should not be offered.

More promising was the introduction of the co-operative movement which took place in the 1900s at the instigation of the British Indian government. Founded in 1905 under the terms of the Indian Co-operatives Societies Act of the previous year, it was placed under a Registrar of Co-operative Societies and in 1910 a Burma Provincial Co-operative Bank was set up to help its activities. The co-operative movement was to become an almost entirely government-sponsored affair, and with the relative failure of the government's loan programme already an established fact, it concentrated on the rural areas and on the granting of loans. However, the first co-operative movement expanded too rapidly, lacked sufficient properly trained personnel and placed too much reliance on local rural credit society unions which had neither proper supervision nor knowledge of co-operative techniques. The result was that within its second decade the movement faced a nearly complete break-

down, symbolized by the difficulties faced by the Burma Provincial Co-
operative Bank in 1928. A Commission of Enquiry was set up which showed
clearly that the Bank was insolvent and the whole movement on the verge of
collapse. The Calvert Commission liquidated the Bank in 1932, and also recommended the liquidation of many of the weaker co-operatives, and advocated the reconstruction of the movement along sounder lines. The process
of liquidation brought hardship to many since it involved all forms of property being seized and expropriated, but in December 1935 a new start was
made to build up the movement once more under a Burmese registrar. Even
when the co-operative movement was at its greatest extent it covered a bare
100,000 of the entire population. Only 2 per cent of the crop loans were provided by the co-operatives in Pegu which was one of the districts where the
movement was most successful, and in general, except for Mandalay, the percentage was even smaller. Therefore the co-operative movement made little
or no impression on the basic problem of rural poverty and the land alienation which was its symptom.[25]

Land alienation and attempts at reform
By the late 1930s land alienation had reached the extent that more than
one-third of the cultivated land in the country was in the hands of non-agri-
culturalists, and more than one-quarter of that was owned by absentee landlords. The process of land alienation was more marked in Lower Burma, the
main reason being that the factors contributing to peasant impoverishment
were more pervasive in the south, as well as the fact that Lower Burma had
experienced a longer period of British rule. In Upper Burma land had less
commercial value and so offered poorer security for the moneylender. Landlords were mostly Burmese, less virgin land was available and in any case under
the Upper Burma Land and Revenue Regulation of 1889, occupiers of state
land were forbidden to mortgage the land they occupied. For all these more
favourable circumstances, however, even in Upper Burma there was a steady
trend towards land alienation.

Between 1890 and 1940 a whole series of efforts were made to pass measures to check the spread of land alienation, which were all ultimately thwarted by interested parties, affording a classic example of how foreign interests
established under the lee of a colonial administration could prevent measures
which were in the best interests of the country as a whole. The first attempt
came in 1891 with the Burma Agricultural Relief Bill, which aimed to protect the Burmese peasant from expropriation. But although the Bill had the
support of the Government of India, in Rangoon it was maintained that land
alienation had not yet assumed sufficient proportions to justify it. This argument won the day, despite the efforts of Smeaton, the Financial Commissioner, and certain other government officials to raise the matter again.[26]

In 1906 the issue was revived by the able governor, Thirkell-White, who
championed the Land Alienation Bill of that year, a law which would have
prohibited the permanent alienation of land and provided the creditor with
more limited forms of compensation. Although once again the measure had
the support of the Government of India, the pressure of a united front of local

interests succeeded in getting it eventually withdrawn under Thirkell-White's successor, Adamson, in 1911.[27] In the meantime a number of official enquiries all confirmed the growth of the problem and the plight of the peasant cultivator.[28] The Couper Report of 1924, in particular, spotlighted conditions of tenants and labourers in thirteen selected districts of Lower Burma, but the subsequent attempt to introduce fresh land alienation legislation raised (in the words of the official annual report for the year) 'such a storm of protest from landowners that government decided not to proceed with it'. Agrarian conditions were investigated by several special committees appointed for the purpose in the 1930s. The recommendations of the 1931 and 1934 committees were officially rejected as 'impracticable', while the 1932-3 committee could not get round to agreeing, perhaps understandably in the circumstances, to the practicability of making any report at all.

Interwoven with the problem of land alienation was that of tenancy. In 1939 some six million acres or 60 per cent of the cultivated land in thirteen selected districts of Lower Burma were leased to tenants on full fixed rents. Although not so pronounced in other areas, the pattern was typical of the country as a whole with full fixed rents predominating, rents rising at a faster rate than padi prices and a marked instability in tenure. The principal evils which the average tenant faced were unduly high rents, no security of tenure, unfair clauses in his agreement and little remission on his rent in lean years.[29] Another aspect of the problem was subtenancy. But while large estates tended to grow, the size of individual plots remained from between 15 to 30 acres, for the landlord had no interest in reducing the number of his tenants who formed a steady source of income for him.[30] High rents and short leases meant that few tenants stayed long in one place, so that there was a constantly shifting population of landless or evicted tenant-farmers moving from village to village.

Official note of the tenancy problem dated back to the 1860s but as was the case with land alienation, seventy years of effort to impose remedial measures were always blocked by the influence of entrenched interests in the country. In 1869 a scheme was devised by which village tracts were to be divided into lots, the number of which that could be owned by any one individual being restricted in order to discourage speculation by non-cultivators. But this scheme and an amended version of 1871 were abandoned in the face of heavy criticism. In the 1880s the Government of India, on the basis of its experience elsewhere, urged Rangoon to be on the watch-out for the spread of tenancy. This ultimately led to the Tenancy Bill of 1892 which wanted to enable tenants to buy the land they were cultivating on the basis of two or three years' rents. Rejected locally as being too radical, Calcutta in 1896 introduced a far more comprehensive scheme against the personal judgement of the Chief Commissioner in Rangoon, Sir Frederic Fryer. This marked the start of a battle which raged for the next three decades between the Government of India and certain enlightened officials in Burma on the one hand, and the army of government servants, landlords, European businessmen and Indian moneylenders who ganged up together to oppose all reforms, on the other.

The 1896 Bill which intended granting heritable but non-transferable rights of occupation to tenants was opposed on the grounds that the tenant stood to gain too much at the expense of the landlord. Whether this was true or not at the time, the force of this argument was being swiftly eroded by the twin pressures of increasing land shortage and mounting population. Nevertheless, faced with a formidable barrage of opposition from those under him and not really believing in the measure himself, Fryer in 1897 advised Calcutta to shelve the matter, which was done, though with some reluctance.[31]

In 1900 Fryer presented a revised Burma Tenancy Bill which dropped the provisions for occupancy rights but retained those for fair rents in a modified form. However, this time Calcutta, feeling the Bill to be inadequate, referred it back to Rangoon where it was reconsidered 'in a leisurely way' over the next few years. The outcome was the Burma Tenancy Bill of 1906 which created a new category called 'protected tenants', who, occupying land normally used by its landlords for purposes of rent, would be inalienable. When placed before the Burmese Legislative Council in 1908 the measure ran into the opposition of the by now familiar coalition of senior government officials and private interests who managed to bog the Bill down in 'intermittent and half-hearted' discussions up till 1914 when the issue was finally laid to one side entirely.[32] But the Couper Report of 1924 produced plenty of evidence of the harm being done to the Burmese tenant-farmer and of the increasing gravity of the problem. Yet even the Burma Agrarian Bill of 1927, a very watered-down version of earlier efforts, was abandoned in the face of vigorous protests, mainly from the landlord community.[33]

In all, despite the patent evidence of mounting agrarian distress and unrest which appeared on all sides in the late 1920s and early 1930s, the strength of the opposition by the vested interests involved blocked the path to reform. A leading role in this was taken by the European rice millers who since the 1870s had attempted to work together so as to force down the price of the rice they bought. In the 1920s a particularly powerful combination known as the 'Bullinger Pool' came into existence, but attracted so much unfavourable attention that government was obliged to set up a commission of inquiry into their affairs.[34] British interests naturally enjoyed the strongest position in the country and were well placed to protect their own. Apart from their privileged social position, British businessmen in Burma possessed a powerful voice in the Burmese Chamber of Commerce and dominated the Legislative Council.

However, the coming into force of the new constitution in 1937 destroyed or at least seriously weakened the entrenched security of the foreign business community in the country, and for the first time serious steps could be taken to deal with the agrarian problem. In 1938 the new government of Dr. Ba Maw set up a Land and Agriculture Committee with the task of going into the whole question of rural poverty in all its aspects. The fruit of the Committee's work was the Tenancy Act of 1939 which entitled tenants to renew leases, set up machinery to fix fair rents and contained several other provisions to protect the tenant as well as the landlord. But the Act proved unworkable, since it placed an impossible burden of work on the district officers who were supposed to put it into practice. An amended Act was passed in 1941 but did not reach the Senate because of the outbreak of the Pacific War.

The Committee was also responsible for the Land Alienation Act of 1941 and the Land Purchase Act, both of which could not come into effect on account of the war. The last contribution of the Committee was the production of a draft Bill on moneylending, which would, if passed, have compelled the registration of all moneylenders and would have made their accounts subject to audit.

So, although in 1941 more realistic attempts were being made to deal with it, the agrarian problem remained one of the most burdensome that the country had to face.

The evolution of British colonial policy

The agrarian problem was the outcome of a colonial policy dictated by *laissez-faire* economics and the incorporation of Burma as a province of British India. The first determined the manner of Burma's economic development under colonial rule and the second the British approach in dealing with the problems that arose.

British rule over Burma began just as the mercantilism of the English East India Company was in its death throes. The free trade theories of Adam Smith and the interests which promoted them in Britain itself had already destroyed the Company's monopoly over the Indian trade a decade before the annexation of Arakan and Tenasserim, and took away its last monopoly, that over the China trade, a decade later.[35] In its place, liberalism reigned supreme. The Second Anglo-Burmese War took place in the age of Cobden who decried the war but exalted free trade. Liberalism was a convenient creed for the British who as pioneers of industrialization could proclaim the virtues of free trade without fear of being worsted in the fray. It implied finding a market for British goods and stimulating prosperity so that Britain should have good customers, ideas which lay behind the plans to create an independent class of peasant smallholders in the rice plains of Lower Burma. Closely linked to the concept of individual, as opposed to state, enterprise was the idea of self-sufficiency. A hall-mark of British colonial policy, particularly in the nineteenth century, was that colonies should pay their own way, or in other words, live within their own resources.

As in the Netherlands Indies, the British expected Liberal policies to engender general progress all round, amongst Western entrepreneur and native producer alike. But although *laissez-faire* economics undoubtedly promoted great economic development in Burma, it was nevertheless plain by the end of the nineteenth century that this goal was not being achieved. As Burma's rice exports soared, her peasantry was becoming steadily more impoverished, while conditions of immigrant labour were degradingly low. At the same time the virtues of *laissez-faire* liberalism were also being challenged in Britain both by a new breed of capitalist who realized that a depressed working class made for poor and inefficient labour as well as an unpromising market, and by the mounting pressures of organized labour itself. There was in general a greater concern for more effective management. Joseph Chamberlain talked in terms of running the British Empire as one would a piece of real estate or a business enterprise, implying that it was the duty of government to promote efficiency and welfare as necessary adjuncts to good management.[36]

The new philosophy of empire, so reminiscent of the Dutch Ethical Policy in its origins and aims, found its leading exponent in India at the turn of the century in the viceroy, Curzon, and as a province of India Burma was duly affected, although not in a way necessarily relevant to her own conditions. Social welfare as such still remained subordinate to the claims of economic progress, the real change being that after 1900 government increasingly took the place of individual enterprise in promoting economic advance. This process reached its culmination with the setting up of a Colonial Development Fund in 1929, the main object of which was to stimulate agriculture and industry in the colonies, but in such a way that British economic interests would directly benefit. At the same time, in deference to the time-honoured principle of self-sufficiency, grants were limited to development that could be maintained out of local resources. This rather narrow approach was modified considerably by the Colonial Development and Welfare Act of 1940 which gave more latitude for investment in projects of indirect rather than immediate benefit or in those beyond local resources. However, as far as Burma was concerned, the provisions of this Act came too late.

Industrialization

As part of the official policy of economic development in Burma after 1900, industrialization played only a minor part. But if the British themselves made no serious attempt to promote industrialization, this was due more to local conditions and circumstances rather than to the opposition of vested interests. Burma lacked essential raw materials such as coal and iron which would have made an industrialization programme feasible. There was an absence of skilled technicians and suitable labour and a lack of capital for enterprises which would give less rapid returns than those associated with the processing of raw materials. In addition there was not sufficient demand within the country itself to justify the setting up of local factories for the production of bicycles, electrical goods and so on which were cheaply and easily imported from abroad. Above all, under British rule the Burmese economy had become too closely integrated with those of India and Europe, so that the country specialized in the output of raw materials and semi-finished products in exchange for manufactured goods. Laissez-faire policies and the Indian connexion prevented Burmese industry from getting any substantial protection from Indian competition while after 1932 Imperial Preference ensured that goods from other parts of the British Empire paid low tariffs. Even foreign imports were lightly taxed.

Consequently prior to 1942 Burma's industrial development was very limited. According to the census figures of 1931, a bare 11 per cent of the working population was engaged in trade and industry, nearly half of whom were concentrated in and around Rangoon. Rice-milling accounted for two-thirds of the factories and half of this labour, while sawmills, cotton gins and oil refineries processed these other raw materials for export. European, mainly British, firms, led by Steel Brothers, controlled a large proportion of these industries, although Indian capitalists also had a considerable stake. An Indian concern owned the largest sugar refinery in the country, opened in 1930 at Zeyawaddy, and an Indian Muslim firm dominated the knitted underwear trade.

Four-fifths of those listed in the 1931 census as being engaged in manufactures were in fact involved in the rural cottage industry, producing handicrafts. Amongst these cotton spinning, sizing and weaving were the largest and the most important, engaging just over a quarter of a million people. Next came lacquer, followed by other handicrafts such as tailoring, carpentry, jewellery and pottery.

Social welfare: health and labour

In terms of the implementation of social welfare there was a marked contrast between the British approach in Burma and that of the Dutch in the Indies. The British were far more pragmatic and far less concerned about specifics. No British 'ethical policy' was proclaimed or spelt out, even though it was often implied, and superficially at least the British did much less than the Dutch in promoting social welfare amongst their colonial subjects. In the case of Burma, social and economic measures were usually a reaction to Indian rather than local conditions (although in the 1920s and 1930s there was a tempered response to the pressures of Burmese nationalism), while local commercial and business interests were able to deflect programmes injurious to their interests for extended periods of time. In general, therefore, the direct promotion of social welfare in Burma was restricted in scope, basically limited —apart from the various attempts to alleviate agrarian distress—to the fields of education and health and to certain elementary measures to protect labour.

In the field of public health, the main impulse came from India, particularly at the turn of the century under the viceroyalty of the modernizing Lord Curzon. Up till this point, medical and public health services in Burma had remained primitive. In 1864 the post of Sanitary Commissioner was created but in conjunction with responsibility for jails and hospitals as well. It was not till 1908 that a separate Public Health Department was established.[37] One of the chief characteristics of the public health and medical services in Burma under British rule was their signal failure to become popular amongst the people of the country. It was reckoned at the beginning of the century that barely $\frac{1}{2}$ per cent of the indigenous population patronized the public hospitals, and forty years later the situation was not much improved. The Burmese attitude to Western medicine was coloured by frank disbelief, while Buddhist strictures against the taking of life hindered the implementation of such basic health measures as getting rid of vermin. Another factor which prevented government from winning the confidence of the people was that since the earliest days the medical services had been virtually an Indian monopoly. At the beginning 'everything was done to minimise expense', which meant in practice that hospitals were staffed down to menial level by Indians. Furthermore Burmese found entry into the medical services difficult, even after the opportunities for doing so were widened with the setting up of a medical college in 1907, because the profession was Indian dominated, and it was this factor, as government was prepared to admit, that dissuaded many Burmese from trying out Western medicine. Government efforts to combat the major diseases which ravaged the country were not very successful. Only in the case of smallpox was notable progress made, although the Malaria Board (set up in 1927) had some effect in certain localities. By and large public health measures were rarely effective beyond urban centres in a predominantly rural country, and even in the towns their efficacy depended directly on the competence of the local authority. As with everything else, all was concentrated in Rangoon. One-third of all the medical practitioners registered in Burma practised there.

By 1941 Burma had 315 government hospitals, handling an average of three million patients a year. There were also some mission hospitals, the most important and useful of which catered for the frontier peoples. In 1926 the Harcourt Butler Institute of Public Health was founded as a centre for training and medical research. The majority of those employed in the medical service remained non-Burmese.

Being the child of Liberalism, the British colonial administration in Burma was slow to intervene to protect labour or to restrain capital. Apart from this, prior to 1942, in a country with a handful of industries the amount of organized labour was very small, so that little government intervention was in fact called for. It was not until 1926 that trade union activity was officially permitted, and another eight years after that before effective steps were taken to ensure minimum wage levels and to prevent child labour in factories.[38] Indeed Rangoon subscribed to the theory, which also held sway for so long in Batavia, that cheap labour was indispensable for the promotion of economic development. One of the principal reasons for the encouragement of Indian immigration was to procure such labour just as the official subsidies of immigrants' passages in the 1880s were designed to keep the wage rate down. Later on, as evidence of the miserable conditions under which these labourers lived multiplied, remedial action was opposed on the grounds that any improvements, including in wages, would render Burmese exports uncompetitive on the world market.[39] Nevertheless official reports and surveys spoke regularly and repetitiously of worsening labour conditions. Living and working conditions were at their worst amongst the Indian immigrants, partly because they formed the bulk of the urban labour, partly because of the maistry system by which most of them were recruited, and partly because they were simply looked upon and employed as cheap labour. Their own standards of living were considerably lower than that of the Burmese, and they were prepared to work under conditions that no Burmese would ever have done. Their plight remained unchanged right up to the last days of British rule. 'I have been shocked and saddened', wrote Baxter in his report as chairman of the Committee on Indian Immigration in 1941, 'to see under what grievous disabilities a large part of the labouring population of Rangoon works and lives. Housing conditions are often very squalid in the extreme; wages are low, and in many cases settlement is made only at long and irregular intervals.'[40]

During the nineteenth century the labour market was dominated by the

Indians, but after 1900 a marked change took place on the scene. By 1931, although Indian labour was apparently still preferred in the docks and the rice mills and continued to predominate in transport and domestic service, Burmese provided the greater part of the labour force in the country as a whole, not only in agriculture, but also in industry. This trend carried on into the fourth decade. Indeed, as conditions on the land grew worse, the Burmese peasant started to look for his future elsewhere. The communal tensions between Burman and Indian labourer which inevitably resulted burst into the open with the dock riots of 1930 and 1931, and were reflected in the growing militancy of Burman worker organizations in the years which followed.[41]

After 120 years of British rule Burma was undeniably a more developed country. It had made considerable material progress and its inhabitants enjoyed a higher standard of living than did most of their neighbours. But the Burmese themselves were far from contented with their lot. The price of material progress had been a high one: cultural and social disorganization and a disproportionately small share in their country's new prosperity. As Collis has put it: 'The Burmese found themselves, instead of being a poor people in a poor country, a poor people in a rich one, which is a very different thing.'[42]

[1] Political instability and a subsistence economy were the main reasons for this. The main rice-growing areas of the Kyaukse region and of the Delta could easily be cut off from the royal capital by an uprising. See G.E. Harvey, *History of Burma*, Longman Green, London, 1924, p. 350.

[2] There are also other factors to be considered; for discussion on this point, refer to Michael Adas, 'Imperialist Rhetoric and Modern Historiography: The Case of Lower Burma before and after the Conquest', *JSEAS*, III, 2, 1972.

[3] Europe's traditional sources of supply were Italy—scene of the Franco–Austrian War of 1860 and the subsequent campaigns to unify that country—India which was disturbed by the 'Mutiny' of 1857, and the United States which was torn by the Civil War of 1861–5.

[4] The impact of the opening of the Canal on the Burmese rice industry can be over-emphasized. The first rice steamer did not pass through the Canal till 1872 and it was not until the 1880s that it became cheaper to send rice by steamer via the Canal route instead of by sail round the Cape of Good Hope to Europe. However, one effect of the opening of the Canal was the accelerated development of the Netherlands East Indies and of the Malay Peninsula, which created new markets for Burmese rice within the region itself. The advantage cargo rice had over husked rice was that the latter deteriorated fast in overheated, ill-ventilated and often damp holds. Cargo rice was also less bulky.

[5] An important contribution to the rise of the Burmese rice-milling industry was the invention in 1880 of a husk furnace in place of coal for running the mills by C.R. Cowie, the owner of a rice-milling firm. This cheapened costs and eliminated waste.

[6] Hugh Tinker, *The Union of Burma: A Study of the First Years of Independence*, Oxford University Press, London, 1957.

[7] In 1941, 58 per cent of the total surface area was covered by forest. For details of forest production and control, see J. Russell Andrus, *Burmese Economic Life*, Stanford University Press, California, 1948, p. 96 et seq.

[8] The fact that railway policy in Burma was decided in Calcutta was one of the consequences of the incorporation of Burma as a province of the British Indian Empire in 1886. For the politics of railway development in Burma and its Indian ramifications, see Josef Silverstein, 'Railroads in Burma and India', *JSEAH*, V, 1, 1964.

[9]For more details, especially regarding the promotion of the Burma Railway Company, see Silverstein, op. cit., p. 20 et seq.

[10]The 'Burma Road', built over extremely difficult country, was constructed at the urgent instance of Generalissimo Chiang Kai-shek's government in Chungking in its life and death struggle with Japan. With the Japanese already in control of all the major ports and sea approaches to China, the overland route from Burma represented the only way by which the Chinese could get the supplies they needed to carry on their struggle. The existence of this road was a major factor in the Japanese decision to occupy Burma in 1941.

[11]D.G.E. Hall, *A History of South-East Asia*, Macmillan & Co., London, 1955.

[12]Cheng Siok-hwa, *The Rice Industry of Burma: 1852–1940*, University of Malaya Press, Kuala Lumpur, 1968, p. 115.

[13]Most of the immigrants came by three main routes—along the coast from Chittagong to Akyab; direct by sea from Calcutta to Rangoon; and across the Bay of Bengal from the Coromandel Coast to Rangoon and other Delta ports.

[14]i.e. such as the clauses in the Labour Act of 1876 which stipulated limited working hours, free medical aid and basic provisions to be supplied at fixed prices. However the basic factor for the failure of the government schemes was the easy availability of jobs in rice and saw mills, in the dockyards and on public works which gave quick returns.

[15]The major outbreaks were those of May and June 1930, disturbances in the Delta in the wake of the Saya San Rebellion of 1930–1, and the anti-Muslim riots of July 1938, also in Rangoon. The May riots of 1930 were by far the most serious.

[16]The first major Chinese intervention in Burma was with the Mongol conquest and domination (1281–98) which destroyed the Burman kingdom of Pagan. The rise of Manchu power and the downfall of the Ming dynasty led to a period of Chinese incursions between 1644 and 1662, most of which were successfully repulsed. The last occasion for Chinese interference was between 1765 and 1769 when the Emperor Ch'ien Lung took up the cause of the Chinese residents of Bhamo against local Burmese officials. The ensuing attacks were also repulsed.

[17]The Treaty of 1894 provided for free trade between China and British Burma for the ensuing six years, after which the prevailing tariff of the (British controlled) Chinese maritime customs was to be imposed. Chinese vessels were granted the freedom of the Irrawaddy and Chinese travellers the right of entry into the country, with a Chinese consul to protect their interests at Rangoon.

[18]Report of the Burma Provincial Banking Enquiry Committee, 1929–30, Vol. I, p. 57, quoted by Cheng, op. cit., p. 178.

[19]However, the basic concept behind land ownership was that all lands not specifically granted out were the property of the king; loss of land occurred for political reasons, not economic ones.

[20]See Cheng, op. cit., p. 139.

[21]'Patta' is an Indian term for 'grant of land'.

[22]i.e. the traditional ceremonies regarding birth, marriage and death had to be observed, and involved considerable sums of money. Every Burmese had to pay towards the upkeep of Buddhist institutions and towards other village affairs. See the example quoted in Cheng, op. cit., p. 180.

[23]Ibid., p. 180; quotation from E.G. Pattle, 'Some Factors Affecting the Economic Position of Agriculturalists', *Agriculture in Burma*, iii, 118.

[24]In the words of the Report of the Burma Provincial Banking Enquiry Committee, 1929–30, 'the Chettyars have been well remunerated for the service they have rendered Burma; but that does not alter the fact that the service has been rendered'. Quoted in Cheng, op. cit., p. 190.

[25]For more details about the co-operative movement in Burma, see Andrus, op. cit., J.S. Furnivall, *Colonial Policy and Practice*, New York University Press, 1956, pp. 113–14 and Cheng, op. cit., p. 193 et seq.

[26]See Smeaton's analysis of the situation and his arguments for measures to arrest the process of land alienation; quoted in Cheng, op. cit., p. 151.

[27]Those opposed to land reform included senior civil servants, European businessmen and the chettyar community. The commonest grounds for objection were that the Bill would reduce the peasant's credit-worthiness because of the new restrictions on the creditor, and would slow down the rate of expansion as the peasant himself would no longer borrow. The sacred rights of property were also invoked, while Adamson himself justified his decision to put aside the reform on the grounds that the term 'agriculturalist' was not properly defined, that the credit system of the country (meaning the chettyar community) would be seriously disturbed, that local officials would have too much power, and that the whole thing would be administratively too costly. For Calcutta's comments on Adamson's decision, see Cheng, op. cit., p. 150.

[28]Apart from the Couper Report of 1924, the most noteworthy was that of Clayton into the condition of the agricultural population in 1908–9 which paid special attention to the Delta area.

[29]The problem of excessive rents became accentuated after 1920, by which time the major part of the Delta had been brought under cultivation and the competition for land correspondingly heightened.

[30]Land fragmentation did not take place despite the existence of Buddhist laws of inheritance requiring the division of property amongst all the heirs of the deceased. This was circumvented by a rotational system of cultivation by members of the family, or by one buying out the rest.

[31]For the terms of the 1896 Bill and Calcutta's comments on its rejection, see Cheng, op. cit., pp. 167–8.

[32]Ibid., p. 169.

[33]Ibid., p. 169.

[34]The country's four leading rice firms were involved, following a common buying and selling policy and controlling in effect directly and indirectly two-thirds of Burma's rice exports. The government's interim report of 1931 absolved the Pool of the accusation that it was responsible for low market prices, but many remained unconvinced by the official argument. See Furnivall, op. cit., pp. 197–9 and Cheng, op. cit., pp. 67–8.

[35]i.e. by the Charter Act of 1833 which was passed by the British Parliament to extend the English East India Company's life for a further 20 years but which removed the Company's last trading monopoly—over all British trade with China.

[36]Joseph Chamberlain, one of the most influential British conservative statesmen at the end of the century, imbued British imperialism with a new mercantile spirit, foreshadowing the end of the long reign of liberal principles in colonial policies. He was Colonial Secretary from 1895 till 1905.

[37]The new department was placed under the Sanitary Commissioner whose influence, according to Furnivall, 'was limited by his ignorance of the country and the people'.

[38]i.e. under the terms of the Factories Act and the Payment of Wages Act, both passed in 1934.

[39]See Furnivall, op. cit., p. 150.

[40]Regarding labour conditions, in 1872 it was reported that there were in Rangoon barracks 'capable of accommodating 500 coolies'; in 1881 the density of population in the heart of Rangoon was stated to be double that of Liverpool, Britain's most overcrowded city. The Census Report of 1891 commented on the high mortality rate among Indian immigrants who, being 'crowded together in insanitary lodging houses, (they) swell the death rate of our chief towns', while 'thousands lived in the veriest hovels in the suburban swamps (of Rangoon) with the most disgusting filth piled up in heaps or fermenting in pools at their very doors'. The Royal Commission on Labour in India, in its report of 1931, described 'overcrowded tenements with more than 40 persons to a room, and streets choked with a permanently resident outdoor population'. The Commission was also struck 'by the contrast between the thought and foresight devoted to technical and commercial aspects of industry and the comparative neglect of the labour aspects'. All quotations from Furnivall, op. cit., pp. 150–9.

[41]At the beginning of the century, according to the Census Report of 1901, 'the Burman, as we know him', was 'essentially a non-migratory, unbusinesslike, irresponsible crea-

ture, perfectly incapable of sustained effort, content with what can be gained by a minimum of toil'. Quoted by Andrus, op. cit., pp. 20–1. The basic fallacy of this judgement only became apparent with the new circumstances prevailing in the 1930s.
[42]Maurice Collis, *Trials in Burma*, Faber & Faber, London.

Books and articles for further reading

BOOKS

Andrus, J.R., *Burmese Economic Life*, Stanford University Press, California, 1948.

Cady, J.F., *A History of Modern Burma*, Ithaca, New York, 1958.

Cheng Siok-hwa, *The Rice Industry of Burma: 1852–1940*, University of Malaya Press, Kuala Lumpur, 1968.

Christian, J.L., *Modern Burma*, University of California Press, 1942.

Furnivall, J.S., *Colonial Policy and Practice*, New York University Press, 1956.

Hall, D.G.E., *Burma*, Macmillan & Co., London, 1950.

Harvey, G.E., *History of Burma*, Longman Green, London, 1924.

Jacoby, E.H., *Agrarian Unrest in Southeast Asia*, Asia Publishing House, Bombay, 1961.

Purcell, V., *The Chinese in Southeast Asia*, Oxford University Press, London, 1965.

Steinberg, D.J. (ed.), *In Search of South-East Asia: A Modern History*, Oxford University Press, Kuala Lumpur, 1971.

Tinker, H., *The Union of Burma: A Study of the First Years of Independence*, Oxford University Press, London, 1957.

Trager, F.N., *Burma: From Kingdom to Independence*, Pall Mall Press, London, 1966.

ARTICLES

Adas, M., 'Imperialist Rhetoric and Modern Historiography: The Case of Lower Burma before and after Conquest', *JSEAS*, III, 2, 1972.

Cheng Siok-hwa, 'Burmese Rice Industry in the Nineteenth Century', *JSEAH*, VI, 1, 1965.

Silverstein, J., 'Railroads in Burma and India', *JSEAH*, V, 1, 1964.

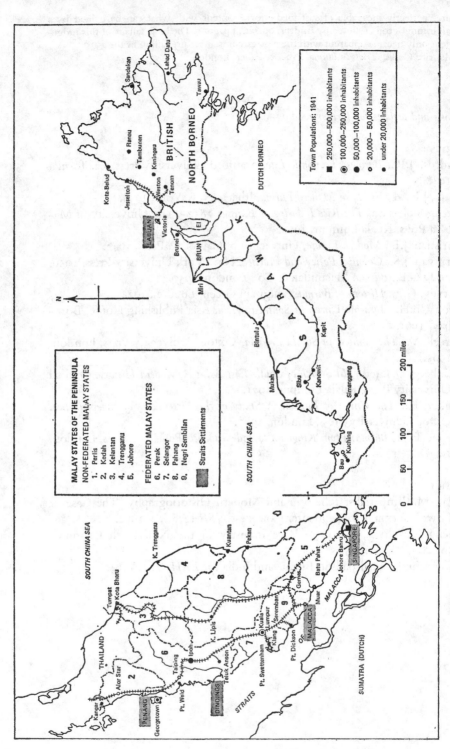

MALAY STATES OF THE PENINSULA

NON-FEDERATED MALAY STATES

1. Perlis
2. Kedah
3. Kelantan
4. Trengganu
5. Johore

FEDERATED MALAY STATES

6. Perak
7. Selangor
8. Pahang
9. Negri Sembilan

Straits Settlements

Town Populations; 1941

■ 250,000–500,000 inhabitants
◉ 100,000–250,000 inhabitants
● 50,000–100,000 inhabitants
○ 20,000–50,000 inhabitants
• under 20,000 inhabitants

0   50   100   150   200 miles

17. General Map of British South-East Asia, 1941 (Malay Peninsula and North Borneo)

B. British Malaya

(i) THE STRAITS SETTLEMENTS

'You may take my word for it, this is by far the most important station in the East, and as far as naval superiority and commercial interests are concerned, of much more value than whole continents of territory.... If no untimely fate awaits it, it promises to become the emporium and pride of the East.... It would be difficult to name a place on the face of the globe with brighter prospects. This may be considered as the simple, almost magical, result of that freedom of trade which it has been my very good fortune to establish.'

Sir Thomas Stamford Raffles, Correspondence, 1819.

THE real nucleus of British power in South-East Asia did not rest at Rangoon but some 1,300 miles to the south at Singapore, the capital of the Straits Settlements. In 1941 Singapore was the hub of British financial and commercial interests in the region, and the fulcrum of British military power. Sited at a natural cross-roads of international trade, it rose from a barely inhabited tropical island in 1819 to become by the middle of the twentieth century, the world's fifth largest port. With the finest harbour facilities of the region, it provided one of the choicest, most varied markets on earth, and was equipped with some of the world's greatest financial and commercial expertise.

Singapore's rapid rise and success have tended to eclipse the stories of the other settlements, namely Penang, Malacca, Labuan and the Dindings. Penang's growth was also impressive, another virtually uninhabited island which after 1786 quickly rose to become the natural entrepôt for the adjacent lands. Malacca, on the other hand, which had a long trading background of its own long before the coming of the British, found its decline accelerated with the rise of Singapore. Labuan, a British possession since 1846, never materialized into the formidable rival of Singapore popularly conjectured, and when it became part of the Straits Settlements in 1907 was no more than a stagnant backwater. The Dindings proved even less significant and was retroceded to Perak in 1935 after sixty years as part of the Straits Settlements.

Apart from becoming a thriving centre of international trade, the Straits Settlements also served as a conduit for the percolation of British influence into the Peninsular Malay States, and from Labuan across to the shores of northern Borneo. In this way, they acted as the powerhouse for economic and social change as well as the leading centres for foreign, especially Chinese, immigration into the region.

The rise of Singapore

All that Raffles predicted for Singapore was swiftly justified by events. By 1820 it was directly linked with all the most important ports of the region eastwards and was meeting the costs of its own administration. By the end of its first decade Singapore was firmly established as the centre of all British trade with the archipelago and as headquarters of British trade with China, and despite occasional setbacks this trade continued to expand steadily in the decades which followed.

Singapore's sudden upsurge as an entrepôt port was in the tradition of Sri Vijaya, Malacca, Acheh, Bantam, Macassar and other ports in the region which had risen and flowered in response to the circumstances of their time. The patterns of island South-East Asia's trade were determined by the region's location astride a major artery of world commerce and by the nature of the distribution of its own natural resources. As a result the trade of the archipelago fell naturally into two sections, international and regional, separate but closely integrated. The region's location on the great East-West trade route, the land barrier presented by the mainland and the regime of the alternate monsoons made the islands a natural half-way house and transhipment centre for traders from China and from the West. At the same time the archipelago had its own valuable products to offer—known collectively in the nineteenth century as Straits Produce[1]—which, distributed over the whole wide canvas of the islands, individually produced by little, isolated, self-contained communities, had to be collected and brought to a convenient place for assembling in bulk and for selling to the outside world. So the needs of both international and regional trade demanded an entrepôt which could serve both as a port of call for the traders from outside and as a collecting centre for the products of the region.

The time-honoured solution to the problem of how the port-empires of yore should maintain their grip over the trade of the region was monopoly, but at the best of times this solution was only partially successful, for the archipelago was too vast, particularly in the days of a limited technology, for any one power to dominate the whole. The very existence of a strong monopoly exercised by any one particular power would invite the establishment of a 'free' port, to which those who sought to evade the monopoly would flock to do their business. In many respects Singapore was an heir to this tradition, but Raffles' concept of a 'free' port was a novelty.[2] In his eyes and in those of generations of merchants who followed, the free port–free trade principle was the basis of Singapore's rise and prosperity.

However, apart from the attractions of Singapore as a free port, circumstances in general at the beginning of the nineteenth century favoured the emergence of a new emporium in the region. In the field of international trade new pressures were beginning to make themselves felt, emanating from private British traders seeking new outlets for their activities, their interest in the archipelago stimulated by the Industrial Revolution in Britain and the development of the China trade in the East. One group of these traders, based on India and usually referred to as 'country traders',[3] had become increasingly drawn towards the China trade since the middle of the eighteenth century, as its importance grew with opium from Bengal and tea from China itself. The value of this trade was enhanced still further by the great leap forward in the tea trade which, following Pitt's Commutation Act of 1784,[4] became one of the most important sources of the English East India Company's profits. A second group of private traders, based in Britain itself, reflected the growing power of British (Lancashire) cotton manufacturers who since the 1770s had been anxiously on the look-out for new markets for their cheap, mass-produced factory wares. The traditional markets in North America, Europe and Africa had been lost and the growing British trade with China seemed to offer the most promising prospects for the future. The key to the China trade lay in South-East Asia. Straits produce found a ready market at Canton, while the unpredictable attitudes of China's rulers towards Western trade made the establishment of a trading base in the adjacent area of the archipelago appear the most practicable alternative. In the meantime the opportunities for British trade within island South-East Asia visibly increased with the decline of Dutch power in the region. When in 1813, under the pressure of private interests, the English East India Company was deprived of its monopoly over the India trade and the commerce of the Far East was opened to unrestricted competition, a new era had dawned in the history of British commercial imperialism.[5]

Raffles was fully aware of these circumstances when he acquired Singapore. With its acquisition placed beyond any doubt by the settlement's instant commercial success, private British trade now had the outlets it desired. Singapore's ideal location, stable government, the *laissez-faire* trade policy and such incidental factors as the settlement's status as an 'Indian port'[6] and misguided Dutch attempts to raise tariffs at their own ports in the archipelago to protect their own trade all served to confirm the port's spectacular rise. In other words, Singapore's rapid success was not a result of the free trade formula alone. It worked because it fitted in with the needs of the times, for the formula was not always successful, as the fate of other free ports opened within the region later in the century demonstrates. Singapore succeeded because it was, *inter alia*, first in the field; once established, it became unchallengeable.

The role of Singapore and patterns of trade

The character and organization of Singapore's trade as it developed faithfully reflected its circumstances. Singapore rose as and remained essentially an entrepôt port, for although pepper and gambier were successfully grown for a couple of decades, the island on the whole produced nothing. As an entrepôt port, Singapore on the other hand handled bulk goods in transit, served as a centre for distributing goods from the international traffic throughout the area, and acted as a collecting centre for regional products, which were then processed for re-export. After its first fifty years, 90 per cent of the European and Indian manufactures landed at Singapore were re-shipped for destinations further east, while the overwhelming bulk of Singapore's exports westwards (i.e. 95 per cent) were not in local produce. This pattern continued a prominent feature of the island's trade, even after the 1870s when new circumstances brought important changes in local economic and social conditions.

Manufactured goods, of which cotton textiles were by far the most important, came from the West in general and from India. Most of the cotton goods were re-shipped for ports throughout the archipelago, but they were also important in the commerce with China, Siam and Cochin-China. Opium was important for the trade of the archipelago, Siam and Indo-China, but from one-third to half of it was re-exported to the China market. Westwards in exchange went traditional Straits produce to which in the twentieth century were added rubber, palm and coconut oil, copra, pineapple and petroleum. Spices, rattans and gambier had lost much of their former importance by 1800, but gutta percha was introduced via Singapore onto the world market for the first time. Sago (tapioca) was another significant new Straits product of the period, and peppers formed an important minor export.[7] The centuries-old trade in areca and betel-nut still held its Indian market into the twentieth century, but after 1900 new products rose to prominence and thereafter held the centre of the stage. The three major new items of Straits produce in terms of volume and value were tin, rubber and oil. Tin itself was also one of the oldest products of the region but until the rise of Straits tin after 1840 it was a virtually unknown element in Western trade. By mid-century the ports of the Straits Settlements had cornered the market in tin exports from the region, serving as an outlet not only for the tin fields of the Malay Peninsula but for those of Dutch-controlled Bangka and Belitung as well. The cutting off of the Indonesian supply of tin for Singapore in 1932 had a drastic effect on the value of the island's tin re-exports, which was compensated for to some extent by the growing trade with Siam. Overshadowing tin was the trade in rubber, which after its spectacularly swift rise during the 1900s completely dominated all other exports, converting Singapore, set in the heart of the world's richest rubber-producing area, into the world's leading rubber mart. The discovery of oil within the region after 1860 added another element to Singapore's westward trade and by 1900 had become a large part of it. Canned pineapples emerged as one of the most recent of the new exports, an industry which developed into a Chinese monopoly based in Malaya.

Singapore's trade with China came a good second in importance to that with the West, especially during the first fifty years. During this period, the island's connexions with China were based on its position as the main headquarters and transhipment centre for all British trade with Canton. Above all, Singapore served as the means by which private British traders could evade the East India Company's monopoly of the trade (until this was abolished in 1833). The main commodities in this trade were Straits produce, opium, Indian and European textiles, and on occasion (when the harvest failed in South China itself) rice. Although after 1823 the traffic in opium overshadowed all else, as far as Singapore was concerned its value declined with the appearance in the 1830s of the new opium clippers which sailed direct between Bengal and China. However Singapore still remained the main distribution centre for opium in the archipelago. At the same time the trade in piece-goods, particularly in those from Europe, steadily mounted and by the 1830s formed a major part of the China trade. However, with the ending of the Company's China trade monopoly in 1833, Singapore's usefulness to private traders as a transhipment centre was also ended, and although in fact the general volume of its trade with China continued to rise, this lagged far behind the amount of direct trade which now grew up between China and the West. Silk, tea and cassia constituted the leading articles exported from China to the West via the Straits Settlements.

The signing of the Treaty of Nanking in 1842 marked the beginning of a more general modification of the Colony's pattern of trade with China. One major change was the decline in the junk trade which since the 1830s had carried half the Colony's commerce with Canton. However with the opening of the China trade to all British merchants in 1833 and more so with the acquisition of Hong Kong in 1842, the junks lost much of their usefulness for Singapore and Western merchants, who turned more and more to the European windjammers which, their sails crammed for speed, offered far greater security against pirates and provided the added inducement of maritime insurance which no traditional junk master could think of catering for. As the trade of the junks with Singapore declined in volume, so their cargoes changed from merchandise to human beings. By the 1860s the junks were the chief bearers of crowds of immigrants answering the call of the new tin mines of the Peninsula, where their labour was in greatest demand. Another major change was Singapore's decline as a transhipment centre, since Hong Kong now filled this need, but the general expansion of Western trade with China more than made up for this, so that the total volume of the island's commerce with China continued to expand. After 1863, however, the trade began to fluctuate, largely a result of the great upsurge in direct trade between China and the West caused by improved steamship services, a trend accentuated still further by the opening of the Suez Canal in 1869. Another modification in the China trade took place in the 1870s when manufactured goods arrived in Singapore from China for the first time. Nevertheless the China trade never lost its importance, mainly because importers to Singapore had at their disposal such a wide variety of markets to choose from to suit the circumstances of the moment. In the twentieth century up to the 1940s Singapore provided the main outlet for China goods destined for both the American and European markets, and the China trade as a whole was a major factor in averting serious economic disaster for the Colony at the time of the Great Depression of 1929-33.

Singapore's entrepôt trade within the region was also very considerable, even if overshadowed by that between China and the West until the rise of tin, oil and rubber as the main regional exports. This regional trade was subject to much more fluctuation, and while during the first decades the island was undoubtedly the prime emporium of the archipelago, many of its regional markets disappeared during the course of the century. But this was made good by the expanding volume of trade within the areas which remained. In the meanwhile Singapore had been the headquarters for British trade with the archipelago since 1825 and goods from the Colony continued to form a large share of regional imports right up till 1941. Singapore (with Penang) also provided the largest market for Indies exports until 1932 when Holland itself took the lead. The Colony's trade with the archipelago, however, was bound by the terms of the Anglo-Dutch Treaty of 1824, and much of the energy of both merchants and officials in the Straits Settlements in the middle

decades of the nineteenth century was devoted to protesting against alleged
Dutch discrimination against British trade in violation of the treaty terms.
Yet in fact the ratio of British to Dutch trade with Java was almost fifty to
fifty.[8] From Java to the Colony came European piece-goods (for the Batavian market was frequently overstocked), rice, destined largely for local consumption or China, and a variety of spices and exotica, while in the opposite
direction flowed Indian, Chinese and European piece-goods, opium, silks,
china and iron-ware, cordage, gunnies and saltpetre. If the 1824 Treaty
tended to impede the Colony's commerce with Java, the spread of Dutch
control to the Outer Islands proved a stimulant, despite the threat of discriminatory tariffs which this extension implied. In the case of Sumatra, Singapore
had a smaller share in the trade than did Penang, but she absorbed all of Jambi's
exports and a good part of Siak's as well. The spread of Dutch power over
the island from the 1840s onwards[9] drew the alarmed cries of the Straits merchants, but in the event the subsequent increased volume of trade belied their
fears. Dutch interference on Bali, Lombok and the Lesser Sundas, on the
other hand, did curb Singapore's trade with those islands.[10]

The increase in private British merchants in the region after 1813 stimulated
a revived interest in the commercial prospects of Thailand, which since its
traumatic seventeenth-century experience with the French had severely
restricted Western trade. In 1818, with apparent official encouragement, some
British and American merchants reopened trade at Bangkok, but despite this
Western trade continued to languish under unfavourable conditions for the
first half of the century. On the other hand Thai trade with the Straits Settlements grew, Penang developing a valuable trade with South Thailand and the
Gulf both by sea and overland and Singapore, after Burney's mission of 1826,
becoming the main port of call in South-East Asia for Thai junks. The most
valuable Thai exports were sugar and pepper, with markets in the West via
Singapore, teak and rice—used in the Straits Settlements—and salt which was
distributed throughout the archipelago. In return the Thai junks bore home
the inevitable British and Indian piece-goods, British woollens, opium, Straits
produce and some glassware. This junk trade flowed smoothly until the 1830s
when in an attempt to tighten the royal monopoly of Thailand's export trade,
Western-style square-riggers were built at Bangkok, the commerce in sugar
and rice became a royal preserve and the few Western enterprises in the Thai
capital were placed under heavy pressure (1842). The Colony's trade with
Thailand dropped sharply and with sugar a royal monopoly future prospects
looked dim. The Singapore Chamber of Commerce, representing the views of
the majority of the Colony's mercantile community, considered the Thai trade
not worth the trouble of putting pressure on Bangkok, but a small group of
European merchants with a stake in the sugar trade succeeded in bringing
about Brooke's mission there in 1850. The mission was a complete failure, but
the accession of King Mongkut in 1851 led to the epoch-making Bowring
Treaty of 1855, which brought about a rapid liberalization of Thailand's trade
structure and policies. The old restrictions on Western traders disappeared,
extra-territorial privileges were granted, and for the first time the European
trade was placed on an equal footing with the traditional junk trade. Singa-

pore's trade with Bangkok soared rapidly just as the junk trade equally as rapidly declined, no match (as was the case with the China junk trade ten years before) in open competition for the security, regularity and reliability of Western vessels. The fresh competition between Westerners and Chinese for the Thai trade had detrimental consequences for Singapore, since European traders soon took to exporting directly to Europe as their only way out of the Chinese stranglehold. But Thailand remained an important customer for the Colony's British cottons and in general Singapore continued as an important centre for Thai trade.

Singapore's trade with the countries of Indo-China never acquired the volume or importance of the Thai trade. In the case of Cambodia, ignorance about the country and the threat of piracy deterred significant trade till the 1850s. The trade was virtually a Chinese monopoly, although the King sent his own junks annually to Singapore. The extension of French control brought any further commercial development to an end. While the prospects of trade with Vietnam (Annam) appeared much brighter and Vietnamese rulers took more positive steps than any of their neighbours to nurture a trade with the Colony, the trade itself languished, mainly because the bulk of Annam's commerce was oriented towards China. Western involvement in Annam in the mid-1840s over the missionary question interrupted the slow expansion in Vietnamese trade with the Colony, and in 1850 the royal trade stopped altogether, although the Chinese junk trade actually grew larger during the ensuing decade. The French conquest of Cochin-China and the opening up of Saigon as an international port in the early 1860s at first served as a new stimulus, Saigon's rice forming an important element in the Colony's trade for the rest of the century, but exports to Cochin-China and to the rest of Annam declined as the French grip became more firmly established. The Vietnamese trade remained primarily a monopoly of the Chinese merchants, many of whom had their own steamships or used square-riggers, and whose intimate knowledge of the market and lower overheads gave them a decisive advantage over their European rivals.

Changes in the entrepôt trade
Singapore's greatest days as an entrepôt port were during the first century of her existence, a period during which she held the widest markets and served the widest area, was the collecting and distributing centre for the whole archipelago and much of mainland South-East Asia besides, and an important appendix to the trade of China. After 1869, however, as the pace and volume of the trade of the region increased, it also acquired a 'nationalistic' bias. Singapore's overseas markets shrank and her custom contracted to the areas more immediately adjacent. Fortunately for the Colony, the expanding wealth and volume of this local trade more than compensated for the losses suffered elsewhere.

The modifications in the profitable China trade in the 1830s were the forerunners of p rofounder changes to come. The establishment of other free ports in the regtion, particularly those under Dutch auspices, seemed to pose an even more serious threat. In the event, however, the effect was to stimulate regional trade which was ultimately to the benefit of the Colony itself. Penang and Malacca developed to a lesser or greater degree as feeder ports of Singapore, Kuching emerged primarily as an outport, while Labuan failed to flower at all. The Dutch free ports grew into nothing more than local collecting centres, the only one which presented a potential threat as a rival entrepôt being Macassar.[11] However, although Macassar's establishment as a free port in 1847 caused a sharp drop in the number of Bugis vessels calling at Singapore, this decline did not mark a falling off of the trade of the Great East with the Colony but merely a change in the way it was conducted. The products of the area were now collected at Macassar and from there transhipped more and more in square-rigged vessels with their advantages of speed and reliability. Since at the same time the Dutch failed to give their 'free' ports the absolute freedom of trade for which Singapore was renowned, there was little danger of Macassar eclipsing the Colony, as Butterworth confidently predicted in 1846.[12] So it proved to be.

Of far greater significance for the future of the Colony were the rise of the steamship in place of sail and the opening of the Suez Canal in 1869. The rise of direct services between the West and regional ports had, at first, unfavourable repercussions for the Colony, which was naturally excluded, as did the new practice of using direct bills of lading between regional ports and European manufacturers, which obviated the necessity to do more than make transhipment at Singapore.[13] The Colony's trade with China, Vietnam and Thailand was increasingly affected by these developments after the 1860s, and had not the British still dominated the shipping of the archipelago up till the 1890s Singapore would have experienced heavier losses in her regional trade. The opening of the Suez Canal, on the other hand, brought about a remarkable expansion in the volume of trade through the region, reflected by the growth of European firms doing their business in the Colony, especially German ones. The Colony reaped the advantages of cheaper and shorter communications with Europe, and benefited in full from her location which made the island the natural centre for a regional network of communications. By 1870 Singapore was virtually the General Post Office for the entire region. The advent of the telegraph enhanced still further her commercial facilities and the volume of her trade.

Nevertheless the very factors which enlarged Singapore's trade also facilitated the rise of her rivals, in particular the French and the Dutch whose abilities to extend and consolidate their own colonial empires had been immeasurably increased. As the rival colonial powers staked and exploited their claims, the trade of the region became more compartmentalized, and many of Singapore's former markets in South-East Asia slipped beyond her grasp. The establishment of the K.P.M. in the 1890s was another great blow, resulting in the trade of the Great East being diverted from the Colony. At the turn of the century the development of new ocean ports in the region facilitated more direct trade between the areas they served and their European and North American markets.[14] The first result of the Great War on trading patterns was to undermine Singapore's traditional role as the rice mart of South-East Asia. During the acute rice shortage in the aftermath of the War in 1919, the rice merchants of Rangoon, Saigon and Bangkok found it more profitable to trade directly with their customers in the archipelago, and as the rice links disappeared so did the channels along which other articles of trade had run.[15] The impact of the Great Depression of 1929 improved the position of the Japanese, already formidable competitors in the region with their cheap manufactured goods, and forced the various colonial powers to take steps to protect their own immediate interests. The Dutch abandoned their open door policy in the Indies and imposed tariffs to protect their Javanese industries, with immediate effects on Singapore's trade. In 1932, in response to these new pressures and to the world economic situation as a whole, the British introduced their own system of protective tariffs for British and Empire goods, known as Imperial Preference.[16]

However, alongside the disappearance of the Colony's regional markets, the overall volume of trade increased. The trade was now increasingly with the hinterland and immediately adjacent areas. The rise of the tin and rubber industries brought prosperity to the Peninsula and enabled Singapore to change from the region's leading entrepôt port into Malaya's principal outlet. The six-fold increase in the coastal traffic between the Malay States and Singapore in the 1870s was the first sign of this expansion, a direct reflection of the rise of tin and of the impact of the British Forward Movement into the Peninsula. Rubber in the 1900s boosted Malayan trade much further. By 1935 almost one-third of the Colony's imports and one-sixth of her exports were in Malayan goods and 95 per cent of the Peninsula's trade was passing through the Straits Settlements, a great contrast to the maximum of 4 per cent prior to 1865.

The organization of Singapore's trade

Apart from the obvious role of situation and circumstance, Singapore also owed much of its success to the organization of its trade and to the facilities it could offer. The system was founded on the principles of free trade, and trade flourished through the initiatives of individual merchants and entrepreneurs. Government neither promoted nor interfered in trading activity beyond providing the basic requisites of competent administration and a sound currency. Under such conditions individual merchants were free to thrive, and different groups and communities went each their own way, specializing in those aspects of commerce for which they were best adapted. By the end of the first decade, Singapore had evolved a system where the basic functions of collection and distribution neatly dovetailed into one another, and wholesalers, retailers and petty traders had worked out the means for dealing with each other and handling their own affairs to their common benefit.

The chief beneficiaries of the Colony's free trade system were the Europeans and the Chinese, although later in the century Indians also acquired some share and after 1900 the field opened still wider. As far as the port's entrepôt trade with Europe, America and India was concerned, European enterprise virtually monopolized the field throughout the nineteenth century and continued to predominate in the importation of overseas manufactures up till 1941. By 1900 this trade was firmly in the hands of great merchant houses which served as managing agencies for Western manufacturers, handling their goods on a commission basis on the market. Until the 1860s these merchant houses were mostly British, several of them founded by men who had settled in Singapore in its earliest days; but by the end of the century they were overshadowed by other non-British concerns, amongst which the Germans took the lead. At the end of the Great War there was another period of expansion in European mercantile enterprise. The British share remained relatively reduced, with the Germans and the Japanese making most headway at Britain's expense. In general the Germans made the most progress between 1919 and 1939, although they were checked by Japan's spectacular thrust during the years of the Great Depression.

Despite the European predominance, Asians started to establish a foothold for themselves, especially after 1900. By this time several Straits Chinese had founded successful links with Britain and Europe, but their number greatly increased after 1919 when there was a much better understanding of Western markets and techniques and more financial resources available. Indian competition, facilitated by direct connexions with the Straits Settlements, also intensified and grew in range after 1900, and much of the ground lost to European, especially British, competition over the previous hundred years was made good.[17] The Ceylonese won a special corner for themselves in the jewellery trade. Yet for all the inroads into their once almost exclusive control over the international channels of trade, the merchants of Europe still more than held their own in Singapore on the eve of the Pacific War, largely by virtue of their close links with manufacturers and firms in Europe itself as well as to their unwillingness to grant extended credit, without which for most Asian traders no business could be done. At the other end of the scale stood the Indonesians and Malaysians themselves, who had no part at all in that part of the Colony's entrepôt trade which went beyond the waters of the region.

In the business of wholesale distribution, participation was much more general. While Chinese firms predominated in the Straits Settlements (and in the Peninsula), they were heavily dependent for credit on Western importers who were thereby able to penetrate the local market deeply without being directly involved in it. In fact, as outlined above, bulk imports and exports were handled very largely by European firms, but the machinery of collection and distribution was mainly, although by no means entirely, in Chinese hands.[18] The distribution system as it evolved in the nineteenth century has survived up till the present time, although the development of modern communications has led to direct ordering and importing on the indent system.[19] The collection system, exemplified by the traditional chinchew[20] and largely a consequence of Chinese predominance in the local carrying trade, evolved in a similar manner.

By the twentieth century Indonesians and Malaysians had ceased to have a significant share in the distributing or carrying trade based on the Colony, but until the triumph of steam they had formed an important element in the general system of commerce. This was especially true of the Bugis who settled at

strategic points from the Celebes and Borneo's east coast to the Sundas and
Singapore and displaced the Malays and the Arabs as the carriers of the
trade of the Great East in the first half of the nineteenth century. Nevertheless
by the 1870s the days of the traditional Malaysian trader were numbered
and his share in the Colony's entrepôt trade already in marked decline. It was
undermined first by the rise of the square-rigged vessels which followed the
spread of British influence to North Borneo, then by the opening up of Macassar as a free port (which of course diverted much of the Bugis trade
from Singapore) and finally with the advent of steam itself.[21]

Singapore's development as a centre of commerce and finance
The great expansion in trade and shipping which followed the opening of
the Suez Canal in 1869 made the improvement of Singapore's port facilities an
urgent matter. The facilities which did exist had been developed by the Tanjong Pagar Dock Company, which, founded a few years previously, had
barely managed to survive. The opening of the Canal in fact saved the company and enabled it to finance the rapid programme of expansion which now
followed. By the end of the century the company, having eliminated its chief
rival by amalgamation, had brought the various shipyards, docks and wharves
which made up Keppel Harbour into one unit connected to the town centre,
and this together with the Outer Roads, now protected by a long break-
water, made Singapore the largest port in South-East Asia. But the company
was slow to reinvest or carry out further improvements, so that in 1905 it
was expropriated by the government which set up in its place an autonomous
body known as the Singapore Harbour Board.[22] The new board immediately launched a far-reaching programme of renovation and expansion
which was completed by 1914. After the Great War more improvements
were necessary, but the Great Depression intervened and it was not until
1941 that these were finished. By this time Singapore could boast of being
the most extensive and best equipped port in the whole of East Asia, if not
the world. This was a major factor in the Colony's continued success and
prosperity as the major entrepôt port of the region.

Another factor for Singapore's success was the unrivalled financial facilities which the port could offer. At first, as a result of the acute shortage of
specie, Singapore's trade was carried out almost entirely on borrowed capital
and it developed essentially on a barter basis up till 1835 when the European
mercantile community, who were in fact the sole source of credit, made their
first attempts to place the trade on cash credit lines. After 1835 cash sales replaced barter with settlement theoretically fixed for three months, but in
practice for longer and often by instalments; in fact, since all European pur-
chases from the Chinese were on a strictly cash terms basis, Chinese merchants
were in reality still trading on European capital. The cash credit system also
encouraged hasty and at times injudicious speculation on the part of the
Chinese merchants who were dependent on the sales of the goods they had
acquired on credit in order to settle their accounts. Failure invariably hit the
European firm involved as well, the Chinese merchant concerned frequently
absconding before his European creditors could catch up with him. The ex-

tension of the Insolvent Law of India to the Colony in 1846 in an attempt to deal with this problem proved useless, as its terms could so easily be evaded. The Colony's first major trade recession which started in the 1850s and lasted till 1861, causing the failure of several Chinese firms, led the European community to call for tighter measures of control, even to the extent of discontinuing credit sales altogether. However, it was soon realized that the Chinese stake in the general nexus of trade, with their wide ramifications and widespread regional investments, made them far too strong to be dealt with in this way.

So the credit system survived and indeed its flexibility was one of the Colony's great sources of strength, making it the ideal centre from which much of the region's trade could be financed and sustained. However, the need for more regular and stable institutions of finance had long been felt, and soon after the decision to substitute barter for cash credit in 1835 the first steps were taken to establish banks in the Colony. There were four banks and eleven agencies in Singapore in 1865 when the first banking crisis broke. The banks rode out the crisis but narrow profit margins imposed by fierce competition, although beneficial for Singapore's traders, made banking itself a hazardous enterprise. Before the end of the century more financial crises, usually engendered by external factors, had forced the dissolution or withdrawal of five major banking firms from the Colony. Those that survived were joined by Chinese and Indian banks for the first time in the 1900s to maintain Singapore's position as one of the leading financial centres in the Far East.

Singapore and the shipping lines

The evolution of the great shipping interests in the region also played a vital role in the growth of the Colony's trade. For the first few decades the question of shipping lines was immaterial to the Colony's welfare, as the bulk of the international trade was handled either by the British 'country' traders based on India or by the East India Company itself, while the local carrying trade of the archipelago rested in the hands of countless individual traders, Malaysian or Chinese. The picture changed, however, in the 1850s with the rise of powerful steamship companies, and still more so after 1869 with the opening of the Suez Canal. The intense and bitter rivalry between colonial shipping interests which ensued ultimately gave way to collaboration between them and to the rise of the Conference System. The first of the conferences to affect the Colony—the Far Eastern Conference (Hong Kong and Japan) of 1879—was a success, but the first moves to apply the Conference System to Straits trade failed. The problem was how to accommodate the interests of the well-established, powerful merchant houses of the Colony with those of the shipping lines. Between 1885 and 1895 three attempts were made, the third one only becoming effective in 1897 as a result of a special agreement between the shippers and three of the largest export-agencies in the Colony. The key to this agreement which bound the signatories to co-operate closely and to exclude all outsiders lay in a secret rebate, strictly confined to their own number. This ensured the support of the most important shippers and by 1902 the Straits Homeward Conference had the support of seven of the Colony's export firms, handling between them two-thirds of Singapore's trade with the West.[23]

This great shipowners' monopoly was by no means welcome in all quarters. Between 1897 and 1907 a number of firms outside the System tried to challenge it but were either bought over or thwarted by their own inability to combine forces. Nevertheless in 1902, their numbers having trebled with the general expansion of Singapore's trade at this period, they did succeed in bringing about the establishment of a Commission of Enquiry into the effects of the Conference on the Colony's trade. The Commission's report was ambivalent and unsatisfactory to the opponents of the Conference who continued their agitation against it, but in the meanwhile in 1906, in response to the widespread criticism of the Shipping Conference System as a whole, the British home government set up a royal commission on shipping rings. Its report of 1909 also prevaricated, but it at least condemned the secret rebate of the Straits Homeward Conference as an 'undesirable expedient' and prompted moves in Singapore which culminated in a compromise settlement in 1911, abolishing the secret rebate and placing the deferred rebate on a triennial basis.[24] The 1911 agreement left the Conference System intact and scarcely impaired, but the agitation against it died away until the 1930s when it was revived again by the pressures of the Great Depression. In consequence another commission of enquiry was appointed by the colonial administration, but its terms of reference were wider than the issue of the Conference System, and its report of 1934 left the system again unscathed.

If the Conference System preserved the interests of the shipowners, it did not guarantee the maintenance of Singapore's position as the leading entrepôt of the region. To ensure that some local control over shipping was necessary, a fact recognized early on by the Chinese for whom the natural corollary to the extension of their business interests in the region was the development of shipping lines by which to serve them. Prior to the establishment of the Straits Steamship Company in 1890, the Chinese had the preponderant share of the local shipping business, but all were small family concerns consisting of a few vessels and limited capital resources. The opportunities opened up in the 1870s for establishing a new local line with sufficient capital to exploit the fast expanding avenues of trade were grasped by Bogaardt, the new manager of Mansfield, who saw that a business based on the local carrying trade in tobacco from Deli, rice from Bangkok and spices and sugar from Borneo and Java to the godowns of the colony for their transhipment elsewhere would rest on sound foundations. He raised the capital by persuading the Holt brothers (of the Blue Funnel Line) that a feeder service of this nature, in which their own company had an interest, would enhance their international operations. Bogaardt then forged close links with the newly-formed tin-smelting company of Straits Trading and by 1890 had succeeded in bringing together three of the Colony's leading Chinese capitalists to combine with his firm (Mansfield) in setting up the Straits Steamship Company.[25]

Up till 1914 the company's operations were mainly limited to the Straits Settlements and the west coast of the Peninsula, monopolizing all the first class traffic of the Straits, besides the tin for Straits Trading and a good share of the new trade in rubber as well. The sudden collapse of the German firm of Nord-deutscher Lloyd as an immediate consequence of the outbreak of the Great War in 1914 was an unexpected windfall for the company and marked a new stage in its development. The post-war period proved a golden age for the company, as indeed it was for all coastal shipping in South-East Asia. The company cashed in on the upsurge in sea-borne trade against which inadequate land communications could not compete and on the boost given by the expansion of the rubber industry, and grew rapidly, building new ships and taking over rival concerns. However its expansion was delimited (as well as safeguarded) by two important agreements with other lines, the first in 1924 with the K.P.M. which restricted the Straits Steamship vessels in the Netherlands Indies to Sumatra and Pontianak, the second being the much more important Victoria Point Agreement of 1925 which defined the spheres of operation of the five major shipping lines involved.[26] In the 1930s the Straits Steamship Company was the largest of the nine coastal lines based on Singapore, but its profits never surpassed those of the peak year of 1928.

In the 1930s all the coastal steamship lines faced growing road and rail competition, the Straits Steamship Company being particularly affected in its freight trade after the completion of the Johore Causeway in 1922. Despite this, the coastal lines continued to be intimately linked with the economic development of the Straits Settlements, as indeed they had been from the middle of the previous century, and they played an important role in Singapore's transformation from being an entrepôt for the whole archipelago to an entrepôt for the waters immediately adjacent to the Peninsula and North Borneo.

Despite the natural advantages of its position, Singapore was slow to develop its air communications. The first of its airports was not completed till 1930,[27] the year in which weekly air services were started by K.L.M. between the Colony, Palembang and Batavia. Imperial Airways extended its London to Karachi service to Singapore via Alor Star in 1933 and made Mansfield its agents in the Colony. In 1938 Singapore became the junction for the two legs of the imperial airmail service opened between London and Sydney. By this time the Colony had also been linked by air to the Peninsula.[28] Singapore also developed into a natural centre for wireless communications, and from 1935 was the headquarters of the British Malaya Broadcasting Corporation, sited at Paya Lebar.

The development of Penang

Penang, the oldest of the Straits Settlements, was the most significant after Singapore. Penang dominated the trade of her own area, which ranged from the Mergui archipelago to the north across to the shores of northern Sumatra and down to the west coast of the Malay Peninsula. In fact, the trading spheres of Penang and Singapore represented a natural division between the south-eastern and north-western sectors of the region.

Before Singapore's rise, Penang had strained to capture the eastward trade as well, but was not well situated to do so. Although the most attractive market in the region prior to 1819, traders from the east had to brave the pirates and the contrary winds as they made the long haul up the Straits of Malacca.[29] The effects of Singapore's opening were soon felt on the entrepôt trade of Penang. The eastward trade vanished overnight; within three years the value of the trade at Singapore had surpassed that of Penang, and by the end of the decade Penang's trade stood at less than half the value of the trade of the southern settlement.

For the greater part of the nineteenth century Penang's commerce fluctuated, the port being as sensitive as Singapore to changes in the region but being less favourably placed to cope. For the first two and a half decades, however, Penang prospered, boosted by the eclipse of Dutch power and by the opening up of the whole region to unchallenged British commerce. But a combination of circumstances brought about recession soon after 1810; the British occupation of Java restored that island to its natural position as the centre of trade for the archipelago; Penang's valuable China trade (in tin, pepper and cotton) became paralysed for want of shipping space; the Achinese market shrank as a result of endemic civil strife, and the British war with the United States cut off another valuable source of commerce. Coupled with these setbacks was Penang's failure to develop into a great naval base. Calcutta had raised the status of the settlement to that of a presidency in 1805[30] in anticipation of the growth that was expected to follow. But by 1810 it was already clear that the naval project would never materialize. As the island dropped from view as a naval centre, leaving as a legacy a top-heavy administration, official efforts were made at retrenchment. However, little was achieved in practice and by 1818 Penang was facing what was probably 'the most critical period in its history',[31] a crisis aggravated by the prolongation of the Achinese troubles, the renewed pressure of Thailand on the Malay mainland and above all by the restoration of the Dutch presence in the archipelago.

Bannerman, the island's new governor, cast around for solutions. Having made ineffectual efforts at economies and having failed to find some locally grown staple such as coffee, cotton or hemp to serve as a new cash crop, Bannerman devised a comprehensive scheme to corner the market in Malayan tin, thereby shutting out the Dutch and safeguarding Penang's own future. Bannerman's tin scheme[32] marked the English East India Company's only attempt to engage directly in the local trade of the Peninsula. The scheme centred on the west coast states of Malaya, which at this time were in a disturbed condition caused by Thai interference. But all Bannerman's efforts to secure agreements with the Malay rulers of Kedah, Perak and Selangor came to nought and by 1820 he had come to the conclusion that the cause was a lost one and the scheme was abandoned. In the meantime the governor's other plans elsewhere in the archipelago to promote British trade had also borne little fruit. In fact, at the beginning of the 1820s, after a decade of recession and stagnation, Penang's commercial prospects looked extremely bleak.

Five years later things looked much more hopeful, but Penang's trade was still subject to fluctuations and actually dropped a third in value between 1825 and 1830. This new decline reflected the repercussions of the Anglo-Dutch Treaty of 1824, the disturbances in Kedah, Perak and Siak, the loss of the gambier trade to Singapore and a general change in the pattern of commerce with India and China. By 1829 it had become clear to Calcutta, if not to the Company's officials on the island itself, that Penang's establishment was excessive for its requirements. The costs of the recent Anglo-Burmese War also had to be taken into account. Accordingly Fullerton, in charge of the newly created Straits Settlements, was told that Penang would lose its status as the fourth presidency, with the corresponding reduction in officials that this implied, and that the capital of the Straits Settlements would be trans-ferred to Singapore. These changes took place in 1830, the latter despite the exertions of Fullerton who pleaded for Malacca as the seat of British power in preference to Singapore.

After 1830 Penang's trade started to recover and in fact never underwent such sharp decline again. This was partly due to the revived China trade, but the settlement was also developing more and more into an outport for Singa-pore itself, particularly as far as the Western trade was concerned.[33] Penang shared in the general expansion of trade which affected the whole region after 1870 and benefited in particular from the opening up of the Culture Zone in North Sumatra and from the spread of British control over the west coast Maaly states. In general between 1875 and 1900 Penang's growth rate and commercial expansion doubled Singapore's, but in the twentieth century the pace evened out as the island became affected by the same factors which touched Singapore itself. After 1900 Penang's interests were increasingly centred on the development of the Malay lands of the Peninsula immediately adjacent. Her port facilities also expanded and in 1913 placed under a Harbour Board, similar in character to the one in Singapore.

The development of Malacca

Malacca, which at the time of the establishment of the British presence on Penang and Singapore was still a Dutch possession, had been in a process of slow decline for over a century, a result of 'strenuous' Dutch efforts to divert its trade to Batavia and of a steadily silting harbour. The rise of Penang after 1786 gtreatly reduced Malacca's entrepôt trade; Singapore brought it to an end alogether. Malacca's commerce continued to decline thereafter, reaching its nadir in 1829 and remaining moribund until the 1840s. By this time the town had become another of Singapore's outports, serving as a collecting centre for its own hinterland and for the Sumatran shore opposite, an area which marked the confines of Malacca's commercial influence. Of the pro-ducts sent down to Singapore for transhipment elsewhere, tin was 'by far the most important'. Malacca's growth mid-century was hampered by the erratic politics of the Menangkabau tin states of the hinterland as well as by the settlement's own unsatisfactory land laws, but it nevertheless found a new prosperity with the rise of the tapioca industry at this time. Malacca also shared in the general expansion of commerce and trade in the last quarter of the century, although this share was relatively small since the new ocean steamships did not find it worth their while to call there on the short voyage between Penang and Singapore. Of greater significance to Malacca was the birth of the rubber industry at the turn of the century, all the more so as one of the pioneer estates was located in Malacca Territory, and its trade received considerable boost in consequence. But the settlement remained a commercial dependency of its great southern neighbour and even its stake in the growing trade of the Malay States remained very small. In short, Malacca never came near to re-establishing her classical pre-eminence under British rule, although the town itself expanded enough to be the fourth largest in the Peninsula prior to 1941.

Labuan and the Dindings

The fourth of the Straits Settlements was Labuan. Its position and coal deposits inspired hopes of another Singapore rising to hold the trade of Borneo and the Great East in fee, but such dreams proved extravagant and unjustified. Within a few years of the new settlement's foundation, it was clear that it was destined to be another of Singapore's outports, a role it fulfilled for the rest of its days as a British possession. The free trade formula was applied but did not work. There was a limited trade in Borneo produce; Borneo people could not afford to take much in return. The traders from China, the Philippines and the Great East still preferred to sail past the island en route to Singapore, discouraged by the prevalence of local piracy and by the negative attitudes of Brunei and Kuching. The climate of Labuan was unhealthy in the extreme and there was no rush of merchants in the early years to settle there and make it their base. Only in 1850 did Chinese and Indian traders from Brunei itself, weary of the whims and extortions of the sultanate, arrive to lay the foundations of a resident mercantile community. In the meantime the first European company to get a mining concession found the coal hard to mine and bungled its management. Its successors did better but Labuan coal proved inferior and belied the great expectations entertained of it. The island's trade showed signs of development during the 1860s, aided by the general growth of commerce between Singapore and Borneo, but by 1890 had stagnated. Labuan was transferred to the administration of the British North Borneo Company in that year, without bringing about any change in its economic fortune, and fifteen years later reverted back to the Straits Settlements. During the twentieth century (up to 1941) Labuan's growth was minimal.

The last territory to form part of the Straits Settlements was the Dindings, a coastal district of Perak which though ceded to Britain in 1826 was never formally occupied until 1874. The main purpose of this acquisition was to contain local piracy, and although the Dindings possessed in Lumut the finest natural harbour on the Peninsula's west coast, plans to develop it never bore fruit prior to 1941. In 1935 the Dindings was handed back to Perak as part of the process of rationalization of boundaries; as a commercial area it never had any significance.

The free trade question

As far as those who resided in the Straits Settlements were concerned, their prosperity was inextricably tied to the liberal doctrines of free trade. Yet this credo was questioned from the very beginning by the distant authority of Calcutta, more concerned with balanced budgets and the public purse than with the risks of commerce and private profit. The first challenge came in 1821 with Calcutta's order that the duties on opium, already enforced at Penang, should be applied to Singapore. This directive was ignored and by the time the issue reached London in 1827, the free trade principle had already been extended to Penang and Malacca. The East India Company's attempt in 1826 to levy a 2½ per cent duty on goods in transit in Singapore was also vetoed by London after protests from the Colony. This did not deter Fullerton from proposing new taxes and duties on a variety of things in his quest to justify the preservation of the fourth presidency, proposals made void by his failure in 1830.[34]

In the 1830s Calcutta made fresh attempts against the Colony's free trade status in order to meet costs. In 1836, so as to meet the alarming growth of piracy in the waters of the Straits, the Company sent out a steam gunboat, extended Admiralty Jurisdiction to Singapore, then arguing that protection must be paid for, started drafting a new tariff.[35] News of this leaked out and the subsequent outcry was sufficient to cause Calcutta to back down. Matters came to a head in the 1850s when Calcutta imposed light dues on merchant vessels using Singapore so as to pay for the construction of the Horsburgh lighthouse. After two years of intensive agitation the offending legislation was withdrawn, but in 1855 in an atmosphere already embittered by the case, Calcutta passed the Indian Currency Act, making the Indian rupee legal tender in the Straits, and at the end of the same year another measure levying port dues to meet the costs of harbour facilities. The Currency Act provoked a massive protest meeting which not only condemned the new law but led for the first time to the demand that control of the Straits Settlements be transferred from Calcutta to London. In the meanwhile the port dues issue had been settled satisfactorily by the intervention of the influential Old Singaporeans, a body of former residents of the Straits, in London in 1856, and Calcutta was rebuked for its renewed attempts to interfere with the free trade status of the settlements. In 1862 Calcutta found a new pretext for imposing harbour dues in the Straits which, as soon as it became known, was met with a howl of opposition in the settlements. The transfer of the administration from Calcutta to London in 1867 brought this particular matter to an end.[36]

But the transfer did not guarantee the merchants of the Straits Settlements the better hearing that they expected. Ord, the first colonial governor under the new dispensation, intimated that he would impose duties if necessary to balance the budget. In the event, however, the rapid expansion of trade during the 1870s and 1880s eased the financial situation of the Settlements and their free port status was not challenged for another fifty years. When the question was raised again in the early 1930s, circumstances had already changed radically. The area that the Settlements now served had become narrowed down to the lands immediately adjacent, and they were well on the way to becoming primarily the main channels for the trade and industry of the Malayan hinterland. Against this background came Clementi's proposal in 1931 for a Malayan Customs Union, embracing both the Malay States of the Peninsula and the three peninsular Straits Settlements. His proposals, however, were not only rejected outright by commercial circles in the Colony, but also by the Malay States themselves. Rebuffed, Clementi now called for a customs union confined either to the Malay States or comprising the Malay States, Malacca, Province Wellesley and the Dindings. These proposals were also rejected, and their main outcome turned out to be the retrocession of the Dindings to Perak in 1935, since the discussions had highlighted the anomalies of this district's position.

At the same time the repercussions of the Great Depression which stimulated a great upsurge in Japanese competition on regional markets at the expense of Singapore's traditional customers brought a challenge to the free trade principle from another direction. More specifically, the Japanese challenge to British textiles encouraged the concept of Imperial Preference, which when finally introduced into the Straits Settlements in early 1932 affected the Malay States more than the Colony.[37] In 1935 the London government administered another blow to the free trade principle with its decision to impose a quota system on the importation of foreign textiles throughout the British Empire. Although this had a direct impact on the Colony's trade and instantaneously aroused strident opposition, more remarkable was the fact that in some quarters this protectionist measure was welcome. For the first time in the Colony's history, opinions were divided over the issue of the port's free trade status. Those who supported the textiles quota were themselves importers of Lancashire textiles, in obvious need of some protection for their wares. Significantly enough, there were other voices of support, coming principally from the small but growing body of local manufacturers who also needed protection against outside competition.

The rise of local industry
In the 1930s the voice of these manufacturers was still too small to make itself heard effectively, but their presence was recognized. Amongst the Settlements, Singapore had the most advantages for the growth of a manufacturing industry. As a natural distributing centre for the region, it was unrivalled; it possessed abundant labour and a resourceful, industrious population, the sons of self-made pioneers; it was a thriving hub of commerce with capital available for investment in any form of business enterprise, and boasted adequate and cheap supplies of power, moderate taxation, sound currency and a stable administration. However prior to 1941 these built-in advantages were more than offset by the competition for its labour and capital offered by the rubber and tin industries of the Peninsula, by a comparatively high wage structure for its workers and the fact that its capital resources were dominated by foreign interests which were unlikely to encourage the building up of local secondary industry. There was also a dearth of locally-trained technicians. Economic nationalism and protective tariffs were cutting off the best potential markets in the region as well as that of China, while Imperial Preference had its limitations as well.[38] Such were the factors that led to the dismissal of the local manufacturers' arguments for a Malayan Customs Union and for protective duties in the 1930s. Their economic importance did not yet outweigh the objections to their case.

So up till 1941 the manufacturers of the Straits Settlements were left to fend for themselves. In practice local industry developed as an ancillary for the products of the Peninsula's mines, estates and forests, as maintenance and repair services and as producers of the local consumer goods which could easily undercut the imported variety.[39] Of all the industries in the Straits Settlements, tin-smelting stood head and shoulders above the rest, and indeed had world stature. This industry, which was dominated by Straits Trading and Eastern Smelting, virtually monopolized the smelting of all the tin mined in South-East Asia up till 1933, and received shipments of tin for smelting from as far afield as Alaska and Uganda. The Straits Trading Company originated in 1887 out of the partnership between a German and an Englishman (Muhling-haus and Sword), who teamed up with a plan to break the Chinese monopoly over tin-smelting in the Malay States. The Eastern Smelting Company established itself in Penang in 1911 by taking over an older smelting concern. Both firms were basically British-owned and Straits Trading in particular enjoyed a great deal of government support from the very beginning. Both companies also received substantial official help early in the twentieth century in thwarting an American attempt to get a foothold in the Malayan tin industry. As a result the tin-smelting industry remained a British preserve and, of more immediate importance for the Colony, its future there was assured. The two companies continued to dominate the industry, and despite the almost total loss of Indies tin after 1932, Straits Trading managed to survive by increasing ore imports from other countries in the region.

The two other most substantial Straits industries before 1941 were light engineering and pineapple canning. The Colony possessed in United Engineers the largest engineering firm in South-East Asia. The Singapore Harbour Board also maintained a large engineering establishment and the foundation of the Naval Base in the 1920s added to the Colony's shipyard facilities. The pineapple canning industry, reportedly started through the initiative of a French settler in Singapore who made his living by selling canned pineapples to vessels calling at the port, came to be developed largely by the Chinese. Despite the fact that the industry proved to be a highly speculative affair and its organization remained primitive, production trebled between 1904 and 1929. The Great Depression did not have the same devastating effect that it did on some other industries.

Prior to 1919 there were very few other manufacturing concerns of consequence in the Straits Settlements. The first significant expansion was stimulated by the Great War which created shortages of consumer goods imported from overseas. Nevertheless when the Singapore Manufacturers' Association held its first exhibition in the Colony in 1932, only two large concerns from this period of expansion still survived. The Depression and the accompanying stagnation of international trade, however, created favourable conditions for the continued growth and expansion of the Colony's fledgling manufacturing enterprises and between 1930 and 1941 several more important undertakings took root. By 1941 Singapore possessed important manufacturers of beer and aerated waters, matches, soap and cold storage goods. In this development the initiative came nearly all from the Chinese.

As in everything else, Singapore was the real hub of manufacturing development. Penang had its tin smelters and a sprinkling of small, family concerns; Malacca virtually nothing. Labuan, as much in industry as in all else, turned out a great disappointment.

The role of agriculture

Making a greater contribution than industry, but likewise completely over-shadowed by the magnitude of the entrepôt trade, was agriculture. As far as Singapore was concerned, agriculture became progressively less important as the land became occupied by more people, houses and factories, but it was important in Penang and the mainstay of Malacca. Furthermore, the various experiments in planting which took place in these settlements in the nineteenth century provided invaluable experience to both European and Chinese entrepreneurs and gave them a basis for their subsequent expansion into the Malayan hinterland. All three settlements were the scene of abortive experiments in the growing of spices and also of coffee; with far greater success for a number of years pepper, gambier and tapioca were planted, while in the north sugar at one stage developed into a major industry. Then at the beginning of the twentieth century came rubber, which virtually swept all other crops to one side. One of the first rubber estates was opened in Malacca, and on the eve of the Pacific War this crop was making a substantial contribution to the economy of the three settlements.

Of the total acreage under rubber in the Settlements before 1941 most was to be found in Malacca Territory. The greater part was estate rubber, of which over half the acreage was European. Singapore itself had been the scene of the first successful experiments with rubber, but the pioneering of large-scale planting was carried out by Tan Chay-yan, a Chinese tapioca planter in Malacca in the mid-1890s. In 1905 Malacca was still the only one of the three settlements where rubber was planted on a large scale, having become accepted by the Chinese as a welcome alternative to their failing tapioca crops. But in Province Wellesley and Penang, sugar planters—Chinese and Europeans alike—were also turning in relief to rubber which underwent rapid expansion in the north after 1905. Similar developments took place in Singapore.

Next to rubber as a profitable twentieth-century cash crop came the coconut. Coconut plantations were mostly owned by Malay smallholders and their gain was small for copra prices were low and middlemen soaked up whatever profit was available. Planting on a large scale had been going on for almost a century. Considerable expansion took place in Province Wellesley, Penang and Malacca between 1900 and 1920 with the development of new processing techniques for the oil and of new uses for copra.

In terms of area, in 1941, after coconut came rice. Rice cultivation was exclusively a Malay concern. Its main centre was Province Wellesley. Malacca was also important, which was why Fullerton aimed to make Malacca Town the capital of the Straits Settlements, but production failed to expand there, largely on account of the complexities of the land tenure system. After 1905 rice was pushed aside by rubber, though it still retained some importance.

However, in the early days of the Straits Settlements, the main hopes for the future of Singapore and Penang, if not Malacca, were seen to lie in their conversion into new spice islands, producing pepper, cloves, nutmeg and mace. This faith in the future of spices was to lead planters, European and Asian, on to a series of experiments which despite initial promise resulted in almost total failure.

The first of the spice crops to show promise was pepper, and Penang became the scene of the earliest experiments in its cultivation. From this point of view, Penang was particularly well placed to be a testing ground, situated as it was adjacent to the traditional pepper-growing areas of north-west Sumatra. The Chinese were the first planters but the Europeans were swift to follow, with Francis Light and other senior Company officials setting the example by planting pepper on their own estates. Indeed, a hall-mark of the new industry was the participation of both Chinese and Europeans and the close association which grew up between them. Only the Chinese could provide the labour that the European planters needed, so Western capital financed Chinese cultivation. The costs of planting in Penang proved much higher than in Sumatra, but the Penang vines also proved seven times as productive, a factor which explains the persistence of planters on the island, even after 1825 by which time pepper's prospects in general seemed quite hopeless. For despite its high quality and prolificity, the Penang vine was foredoomed by circumstances beyond its control. The sudden closure of the European market after 1805 forced Penang's planters to turn despairingly to the Chinese market, only to find access increasingly difficult. Then came the depredations by insects which attacked the vines, the continued depression in world market prices and the rise of other more successful crops on the island. By 1835 total annual production amounted to less than 2,000 piculs and 'the jungle usurped the extensive tracts formerly under pepper'.

Pepper cultivation in Singapore, in contrast to Penang, developed together with gambier, a natural ally, which was being grown by Malays and Chinese when the British first occupied the island.[40] Gambier and pepper flourished together for the best part of the century as a Chinese smallholder industry, spreading locust-like across the island and reaching across the Straits of Johore. However, after 1850 both crops started to go into a slow decline. Soil erosion, lower prices and new land legislation in the Colony which interfered with the independence of the squatters on whom the industry was based, making the opportunities which beckoned in Johore all the more attractive, were the contributory factors. The secret society disturbances of the 1850s also played their part. The final decline in the 1900s was brought about by other causes, principally by the swift advance of rubber. After 1905 most planters lost all interest in what had once been the mainstay of Singapore's agriculture. Although Europeans showed some interest, gambier and pepper farming remained predominantly a Chinese industry in the hands of smallholder-squatters, financed by the shopkeepers and merchants of the town.

Gambier and pepper were also grown in Malacca in the course of the nineteenth century, but never acquired the significance that they had in Singapore. Large plantations were established only after 1850, planting before this having been either limited to domestic consumption or ended in failure, and achieved importance in the 1870s and 1880s. Increased demand for gambier from local tanners and dyers and improved market prices for pepper overseas coincided with the decline of the once predominant tapioca industry and with the adoption of a more liberal land policy by the Straits authorities. The result was rapid expansion, reaching its peak in the 1890s. The sudden decline and eclipse which followed in the 1900s was brought about by the same factors cutting down tapioca and sugar cultivation elsewhere in the Settlements. First and foremost was the rise of rubber. Government, with its decision to discourage the depredations of gambier and tapioca on the soil, also played an important part. Gambier was reduced to the status of a catch crop, while pepper suffered a disastrous drop in prices and the vines were attacked by caterpillars. As in Singapore, pepper and gambier planting in Malacca remained a Chinese affair and, in general, followed very closely the lines of the southern settlement. Indeed, Chinese activities in this field represented basically an extension of their industry in the Colony and Johore.

Malacca was the chief centre for tapioca production in the Straits Settlements throughout the nineteenth century and the 'cornerstone of Chinese enterprise for over fifty years'.[41] At first, however, deterred by the intractable land problem, the Chinese merchants of Malacca preferred to concern themselves with commerce or with the local tin mines than venture into any agricultural enterprise. But the overwhelming competition of Singapore and the rise of tin-mining centres elsewhere forced them to resort in the end to some other field. Early in the 1850s tapioca became Malacca's first export crop and during the ensuing two decades its cultivation expanded rapidly, fanning out in a crescent across the centre of the Territory. In the 1870s it spread from its original centres along newly-constructed roads to the borders of Negri Sembilan and beyond, and south-eastwards along the coast. In the wake of this planting came tapioca factories and pig-farms. In the 1870s and 1880s tapioca production in the Straits was almost wholly confined to Malacca Territory. Its swift growth was suddenly checked in 1881 by a disastrous fall in prices, which continued for the next five years, and also by a new official policy aimed at restricting the industry because of its 'devastating' effects on the soil. However as the effects of the trade depression made themselves felt, British officials had second thoughts. For tapioca, wasteful or not, had become the mainstay of Malacca's economy, accounting for four-fifths of government receipts, and with the industry's near collapse, trade and commerce as a whole were seriously affected. Consequently the new policy against tapioca planting, coinciding with a recovery in market prices, was reviewed and relaxed. After 1887 tapioca was again on the march, making handsome profits and more than doubling its acreage. The only apparent bar to even greater expansion was a growing labour shortage, but the new boom turned out to be a temporary one. In 1889 prices started to slip once more and by 1895 had dropped below economic levels. Although planted for another ten years, conditions became less and less favourable and planters took up other crops, especially rubber. Tapioca assumed increasingly the role of a catch crop on the new rubber estates and between 1894 and 1911 the land under its cultivation shrank by over one-third. The industry underwent minor revivals in 1913 and again in 1917 and 1920, but it had been replaced by rubber as the major cash crop of Malacca.

The organization of the tapioca industry appears to have followed closely the pattern of other Chinese agricultural enterprises in the Straits. Labour was provided by fresh immigrants recruited by contractors who received advances from wealthy Chinese merchants against delivery of the crop at a fixed rate. A small group of Chinese based in Malacca Town financed the industry, controlled its ancillaries and reaped the main benefits. They owned most of the tapioca concessions and plantations. They also apparently dominated the carrying trade associated with the industry and were behind the extension of tapioca planting into neighbouring districts of Negri Sembilan. Tapioca cultivation in Singapore and Penang never reached the proportions that it did in Malacca, nor did it acquire the same significance.

The attempts by planters in the Straits to promote the cultivation of other spices took up a good part of the nineteenth century, proving in the words of Cameron 'a most disastrous deception to all who have engaged in the culture'.[42] In Malacca the 'deception' was comparatively brief, for from the outset local conditions were not favourable. The basic problem was the land question with the resulting insecurity of tenure which discouraged would-be investors. Apart from this, capital itself was hard to come by. So production was confined to a few small plantations. In the 1840s some nutmeg and cloves were still being produced but after 1850 were of little note.

Penang on the other hand was the scene, from its earliest days, of optimistic and earnest attempts to make it the Moluccas of the Straits. Light's administration regarded spices as a likely source of revenue for defraying the costs of government, and Light himself took a leading part in procuring plants for cultivation. Nevertheless all concerned were due for disappointment. Costs were high and returns were slow. As this became apparent, official enthusiasm and support evaporated like the morning dew, leaving private cultivators to flounder on in their ignorance of the correct techniques of planting, so that they too became apathetic in the face of continually low yields. Yet a small group of European planters in Penang persevered despite the lack of official support, and eventually their faith was to win its temporary reward. There were already signs in 1813 of an approaching nutmeg millenium. The return of the Moluccas to their Dutch owners in 1816 prompted the anticipated rise in prices and promoted fresh speculation and planting in spice crops. However, the London market quickly dropped again and although the nutmegs weathered the low prices and glutted warehouses of the early 1820s, clove production collapsed entirely. Meanwhile the nutmeg continued to move steadily towards its golden age, and by 1830 market prices were riding high, bringing in large profits for the first time. The patience of the pioneers won its reward and others were quickly stimulated to plant, leading to an expansion which spread to the mainland opposite.

The spectacular success of the nutmeg planters of Penang had immediate repercussions in Singapore, inducing a 'nutmeg mania' amongst both Europeans and Chinese. Just as in Penang, from the beginning of British settlement on the island efforts, both official and unofficial, had been made to propagate spice production, with results similarly disappointing though for different reasons. Frenetic speculation by Europeans in nutmeg cultivation began with the foundation of the Agricultural Society in 1836. The introduction of easier conditions for obtaining land contributed to the doubling of the nutmeg acreage between 1840 and 1848. The European example was followed after some hesitation by the Chinese after 1845. European planting reached its peak in 1850, but the Chinese being late starters did not reach theirs until the middle of the decade, by which time ominous portents had begun to appear. The eclipse of nutmeg cultivation in both Penang and Singapore was sudden and simultaneous. In many respects the planters, particularly those in Singapore, had little but themselves to blame. They had gambled recklessly on the inflated prices of the hour without heed of the high operating costs, the inherent instability of the market, or of the factors determining land values in the Straits at that period. They themselves blamed their mounting difficulties on an allegedly unsympathetic government. However, the final blow was administered not by human hand, but by a small beetle which started to attack the plants in the 1840s. The attacks spread, but their cause remained undivined. By 1855 a large proportion of the nutmeg grown in Penang and Singapore had been affected, and by 1860 there was not one plantation which had escaped. Ignorance of proper methods of cultivation and failure to diagnose the real cause contributed largely to the nutmeg disaster.[43]

The organization of spice cultivation was similar to that of other forms of agriculture at the time, the actual cultivation being done by the Chinese while plantations themselves were divided between large European estates worked by Chinese contract labour and squatter smallholdings sustained by advances from merchants and shopkeepers.[44]

Sugar: its rise and fall

The most successful cash crop in the Straits prior to the introduction of rubber was sugar-cane. The main centre of production was Province Wellesley. Some was also grown on Penang Island and sporadic attempts were also made in Singapore and Malacca.

The pioneers of the sugar industry were the Chinese who reportedly started planting in Province Wellesley shortly before 1800, although most of the pioneer plantations appear to have been opened between 1810 and 1820. The rise of the Chinese population in the province between 1820 and 1833 was probably a direct consequence of the expanding sugar industry. By 1840 several planters had made their fortunes, but after this date the Chinese side of the industry failed to expand any more, inhibited by the establishment of European estates. The first European attempts at sugar planting soon after the British occupation of Penang proved a failure, and it was not until the 1830s that European enterprise essayed a comeback. The first Western estate on the mainland was opened in 1840, and this was followed by twenty years of rapid expansion of large-scale Western planting. By the 1850s the industry was a completely European-dominated affair. A major factor for this development was the extension to Penang of the colonial preference[45] on sugar imported to Britain in 1845, but the main reasons lay in a happy combination of ideal climate, suitable soils and easy accessibility. Fuel from the broad stretches of mangrove swamp was plentiful, and labour readily available. The success of the Europeans and the survival of the Chinese in the industry after the 1840s reflected the strengths and weaknesses of the crude, labour-intensive methods of the latter. The poor quality of Chinese-processed sugar gave the Europeans their opening on the market, but low overheads enabled the Chinese producers to withstand Western competition as well as falling prices during a depression. The Chinese plantations were organized and financed on very similar lines to other Chinese agricultural enterprise. The bulk of the planting on the mainland was financed and controlled by Chinese merchants in Penang. The European estates, on the other hand, fell into two categories—those owned and managed by local European residents, and those in the hands of absentee landlords. In either case professional management ensured the introduction of the modern techniques on which the European rise depended. As a result of the Western penetration into the industry, by the 1860s, it fell into two distinct sections. The processing side was completely European dominated with its expensive machinery and superior techniques. The planting side remained Chinese and traditional. The one was modern and progressive, with implications for social change; the other conservative, leaving the social organization which it used largely intact.

The sugar industry of the north continued its progress from 1860 up till the end of the century, crossing over the frontier into Perak with the trends already established becoming ever more pronounced. The highly capitalized processing side of the industry with its huge factories and costly equipment led to an increasing desire for more complete control over the planting side in order to ensure a smooth flow of the raw material. But this the Chinese contract system would not permit, and despite its growth the European sector began to face mounting difficulties, including the outbreak of cane disease and more serious labour shortages. The labour problem became particularly acute after the Transfer of 1867, by which time European planters were relying extensively on Indian indentured labour both in the factory and in the fields. Closer official supervision of recruitment, a high death-rate and desertions, and the rising competition on the labour market of the Culture Zone of north-east Sumatra and of the tin industry in Perak bore down heavily on the industry, on top of which during the 1880s came the general world trade depression and the rise of the European sugar-beet industry. However, the last decade of the century witnessed a remarkable recovery and both acreage and production reached record heights, an advance which was mainly attributed to 'economical management and improved machinery'.[46] It was also partly due to an easing in the flow of Indian labour. But it proved to be the Indian summer of sugar in the north, for within the next fifteen years planting was almost completely discontinued. Penang could not compete with Cuba or Java on the world market and cope with the old problems at home as well. Indian workers, despite the new arrangements, were still hard to get and wages doubled and trebled upon what they had been ten years before. The abolition of indentured labour in 1910 robbed planters of their most reliable source of supply, while fuel had now become so scarce and costly that by 1903 rising prices forced the smaller estates which did not use modern machinery to turn to other crops. Most Chinese plantations had abandoned sugar by 1905; the European-owned estates were not long in following suit. By 1913, the year in which the last sugar factory closed down, there were only 31 acres of land still under sugar in Penang and Province Wellesley.

As for Singapore and Malacca sugar never flourished as it did in the north. The attempt to start large-scale planting in Singapore took place at about the same time as in Penang, led by the same group of ardent agriculturalists who put their faith in spices. Convinced by the local Chinese example, by the high prices of sugar following the emancipation of slaves in the British Empire, and by the apparent suitability of Singapore Island in terms of climate, soil and labour, they believed it could be made into a profitable affair. Singapore's exclusion from the preferential duties extended in 1846 to Penang and Malacca was a major reason why this did not happen. The island's sugar industry therefore laboured under a handicap from the start, and by the end of the 1840s it had become obvious that it could not succeed. In Malacca, where some Chinese had been planting sugar for some time, efforts to introduce the industry on a large scale took place in the mid-1840s as a consequence of the preferential duties. But the two large concerns and several smaller ones formed failed to evolve, thwarted by the complexities of the land problem, and after this no further attempts were made in the Territory.

Of the various moves to promote other crops during the course of the nineteenth century none made any headway. There were attempts at coffee planting in Penang and Singapore, especially in the latter prior to 1850, but despite the subsequent success of coffee in the Malay States, the crop failed to take in the settlements. Efforts to plant cotton were a complete failure. Some indigo was grown on a small scale by Chinese planters in Penang.

In general, although many of the bright hopes held out for the production of cash crops in the Straits ended in disappointment, the experience gained helped to lay the foundations on which the rubber industry was later able to build. However, the Straits Settlements thrived first and foremost on their trade, into which most of the available capital was reinvested until the rise of the tin industry in the Malay States after 1850. Capital investment in agriculture was also discouraged by the confused conditions of land tenure in the Straits, of which the prime example was afforded by the case of Malacca.

The Malacca land problem

Malacca's complex and perverse land problem had its origins in the British take-over of 1824 when the new administration's policies ran against the conflicting claims of Malay farmers and European landowners, the latter known collectively as 'the Dutch Proprietors'.[47] The crux of the matter lay in the Dutch Proprietors' claims to absolute ownership of the lands they held, most of which they had farmed out to Chinese, as opposed to the traditional Malay land tenure system—untouched since the days of the Malacca Sultanate—by which the land was inalienable and the occupant-tenants' rights indefeasible. For Fullerton in Penang, intent on restoring Malacca as the focal point of the

Straits based on its agriculture, the need to overcome this problem so as to encourage planters and foster estate production was imperative. In order to do so, in 1825 he set up a commission of investigation to clarify the true position with regards to land tenure. With the commission's report two years later the way was open to impose a solution, but from the outset the actual steps taken, in particular the decision to expropriate the Dutch Proprietors in 1828, prolonged the muddle for another fifty years. To buy out the European landowners was reasonable but the compensation offered was far too generous and imposed a heavy burden on the Territory's administration. More serious still were the problems raised by the new land code of 1830 which, in an attempt to make the best of both worlds, combined Malay and English land practice and created 'incessant confusion'.[48] The new land settlement was made totally dependent on the implementation of a comprehensive survey, but since no such survey was begun until 1858 it was inoperable. The situation was rendered still more impossible in 1835 when the Recorder of the Straits Settlements declared the Malacca Land Code invalid in any case on the grounds that it exceeded the legislative powers of the Straits authorities. Deprived of legal sanction, the lease-titles issued under the Code since 1830 had now to be rescinded and the local government was powerless to pass new legislation to take its place. A ruling of the previous year (1834) that the laws of England were applicable to the Straits Settlements meant that as far as the land question was concerned, all litigation would have to be determined by English legal precedent, even where only Malay precedents were involved.[49]

With the government of the Straits Settlements powerless to pass land laws and the Malay peasantry of Malacca refusing to conform to English usage, in 1837 Calcutta decided to appoint a Commissioner for the Far Eastern Settlements, W.R. Young, in order to investigate the state of affairs. Unfortunately, 'far from improving conditions at Malacca, his intervention seems if anything to have made them worse'.[50] Young declined to introduce new legislation, relying on persuasion to set things right. He conceded to the Malays the right to permanent occupancy of their lands provided they paid their traditional dues, but insisted that these should be paid in cash as soon as possible. This solved nothing since cash the Malays were not prepared to pay and continued to resist all official attempts to make them do so. Malacca's land revenue still failed to meet the cost of compensating the Dutch Proprietors and agricultural development remained seriously impaired. The stalemate continued till the 1860s when Calcutta passed a new land act and implemented a partial land survey. The Land Act of 1861 finally disposed of the problem of the Dutch Proprietors by allowing them to commute their annuities into a lump sum compensation, an offer which most of them accepted. All cultivators other than the Malays were to be regarded as squatters, liable to whatever terms the administration chose to impose upon them. The Act also authorized the disposal of state land, subject to a quit rent negotiated with the purchaser. The land survey was made part of the Act and the presence of an official surveyor (since 1853) meant that the systematic surveying of the Territory was at last begun. But since the Act still insisted on an annual cash quit rent instead of payment in kind, Malay resistance to the land policy continued; they refused to sign leases, evaded paying dues and opened new lands in defiance of the law. After 1861, on the other hand, the granting of new leases and titles to unoccupied land could be handled satisfactorily, so that planters were now encouraged to invest and expand for the first time. A final settlement of the problem of Malay land dues, however, remained unsettled until the reforms of W.E. Maxwell twenty years later.

Land administration in Penang and Singapore
Vague and vacillating policies marked the land administration of the other two settlements for many years, but the problem at issue was not Malay hereditary rights since both islands, prior to British occupation, had been barely inhabited, but the terms on which land could be acquired. Francis Light, without any experience in this field and lacking official instructions, eventually issued 'measuring papers', which for want of anything better became the equivalent of land titles. Instructions received from Calcutta in 1794 and again in 1796 proved to be so impracticable as to be totally inoperable, so that the Penang authorities were obliged to continue with their own *ad hoc* arrangements. Light and his successors also suffered from an almost complete lack of suitable staff which hampered the implementation of the very rudimentary land measures they laid down and, as in Malacca, no satisfactory solution was possible without a proper survey of the island's land holdings. When Penang became the Fourth Presidency in 1805 no land survey had yet been carried out, and the administrative changes which followed did not bring relief, since Dundas, the new governor, failed to grasp the situation properly and issued new measures which virtually paralysed agricultural enterprise. To put matters right, in 1809, Calcutta issued another directive on land, which became the basis of the settlement's land administration until the arrival of Fullerton as governor in 1824.

Armed with instructions to settle the land problem once and for all, Fullerton submitted his recommendations to Calcutta in 1826, and these were accepted in their entirety the following year. However, from the outset Fullerton's land scheme was a failure. It engendered local opposition because the length of his proposed leases suited nobody, and the scheme also quickly ran into the same legal troubles that dogged the governor's efforts to resolve the Malacca land problem. The validity of the scheme was successfully challenged in the courts in 1829, and when the legal discrepancy was put right by Calcutta two years later, Sir Benjamin Malkin, the Penang Recorder, undid everything by declaring the regulations *ultra vires* on the same grounds that the Singapore and Malacca land laws were to be declared invalid three years later. As a result of Malkin's ruling, the Penang Land Regulation Act of 1831, designed by Calcutta as the finishing touch to Fullerton's work, was never implemented.[51]

In the meantime a similar confusion over land matters had arisen in Singapore, where the earliest titles had also been granted in virtual perpetuity. Land administration remained unsatisfactory up till the late 1820s, Fullerton's land-lease scheme of 1827 proving as unpopular in the south as it was in the north and for the same reasons. Young in 1837 introduced some ameliorative measures and proposed some far more radical changes, including the saleability of Crown lands by public auction. In 1840, in response to protests from both settlements, the length of leases for agricultural lands was confirmed at twenty years, and under further pressure Calcutta abandoned the leasing system altogether, and sanctioned the straightforward alienation of Crown lands in fee simple for the purposes of agriculture. With the passing of this measure in 1843 the land tenure problems of cash crop planters were broadly speaking brought to an end, but the far more complex issue of Malay land tenure rights remained and did not find a final solution until the appointment of Weld as governor in 1880.

Weld's experience of land problems in New Zealand and Australia led to Maxwell, his nominee to the newly created post of Commissioner of Land Titles in Singapore, being sent to Australia to study land administration there. Maxwell was instructed to pay particular attention to the Torrens system of land conveyancing,[52] and on his return he brought about the enactment of the Crown Lands Ordinance of 1886, which provided for grants in perpetuity subject to a quit rent and a statutory form of Crown Title on the Australian system. In the same year Maxwell also secured the promulgation of the Malacca Land Ordinance, by which Malay land holdings under ten years continuous occupation were confirmed as permanent, heritable and transferable. Holdings were now to be determined by demarcation carried out by 'a native agency'—usually the *penghulu*—and registered in a *mukim* register, which became 'in effect though not in intent' a record of title. This disposed of the expensive problem of conducting a thoroughgoing land survey of all property, which for so long had clearly lain beyond the government's ability to carry out, and also got rid of the necessity to use formal English instruments of title for Malay smallholdings. With this the Malacca land problem found a definitive solution.

Land in Labuan

Labuan, the Cinderella of the Straits Settlements, was the first territory in the British Empire to make registration of land transfers a condition for their validity. But any excellence of land administration on that island was wasted, as agriculturally it proved as disappointing as it had proved commercially and in all other aspects. Labuan's chief product was tapioca, while some rubber, fruit and coconuts also came to be grown.

---

[1]'Straits produce' was the trade term used to include 'all agricultural or mineral products grown or produced in the Malayan archipelago and brought to British Malayan ports for the purpose of grading, bulking or otherwise preparing for shipment to consuming countries'. Lennox A. Mills, *British Rule in Eastern Asia*, Oxford University Press, London, 1942, pp. 111–12.

[2]i.e. merchants were free from any dues on their goods in transit, whereas at the traditional centres of 'free' trade (ports which defied the Dutch monopoly, for example) local rulers still exacted their fee through the system of 'presents', commissions and shares in the trade.

[3]The term 'private British traders' is used here to distinguish British merchants who did

business on their own account, as opposed to the merchants of the English East India Company who (up till 1833) held the monopoly rights over all British trade with China. The 'country traders' were permitted to trade eastwards from India under licence granted by the Company.

⁴Pitt's Commutation Act reduced the duty on tea imports into Britain from 100 per cent to 12½ per cent. Apart from the rise in the trade in opium and tea, the country traders found that they needed a new market for Indian piece-goods as well which, as a result of industrialization in England, could no longer find a place in Europe.

⁵The loss of the Company's monopoly over all British trade with India was the price its directors had to pay for getting the British parliament to renew its charter and to extend its privileges for another 20 years. This left only one trade monopoly, that with China, which was abolished in 1833.

⁶The significance of Singapore's legal definition as an 'Indian port' (as it came under the ultimate jurisdiction of the British Indian government in Calcutta) was that as such it could be used by country traders to have dealings with the Chinese without actually infringing the Company's monopoly.

⁷Sago owed its emergence as an export crop to the development of a new technique for producing the flour by some Malacca Chinese.

⁸For full details of the acrid and involved controversy over alleged Dutch infringements in tariff policy, see Wong Lin-ken, 'The Trade of Singapore, 1819–69', *JMBRAS*, XXXIII, 4, 1960, p. 45 et seq.

⁹For details of the diplomacy and politics involved, see Anthony Reid, *The Contest for North Sumatra*, Oxford University Press, Kuala Lumpur, 1969, esp. Chapter 1.

¹⁰A small but flourishing trade in Balinese rice, and also coffee and rice smuggled mostly from East Java, grew up after 1824 between the Balinese principalities and Singapore in exchange for British piece-goods, opium, and Chinese copper cash. Singapore had trading connexions with Lombok, in particular with Ampenan which was on the China/India–New South Wales route and was also visited by American whalers. It was reported in the 1830s that there were more British ships there than at any other port in the archipelago apart from Singapore itself. Between 1830 and 1844 the settlement's trade with Bali, Lombok and Sumbawa increased five-fold, but dried up as the result of effective Dutch action against smuggling in Java in the 1840s.

¹¹Macassar's position made it an ideal collecting centre for the Moluccas, the Sundas, Java, East Borneo and Celebes itself. The existence of the British colonies in Australia and their burgeoning links with the ports of India and China also touched Macassar.

¹²See Wong Lin-ken, op. cit., p. 103.

¹³Bills of lading enabled the large-scale merchant to obtain his imports from the region and the outport producer to sell his produce outside by mere transhipment at Singapore, instead of as formerly ordering manufactures from a Singapore importer and selling produce to the same source.

¹⁴i.e. Port Swettenham, opened in 1901; Macassar which acquired oceanport facilities in 1918, and Belawan (for Medan) in 1921. Belawan absorbed the bulk of Penang's trade with Sumatra and ended Penang's role as a transhipment centre for Burmese rice.

¹⁵For example, the direct links between Singapore and Celebes were broken as a result of the ending of the transhipment of Thai rice for Macassar via the Colony.

¹⁶Although designed to help British interests and to protect Singapore's trade, imperial preference was not well received in the Colony as it conflicted with the basic principle of free trade. In practice its imposition had only mild effects on the Colony's commerce and failed to overcome the Japanese challenge. The passing of the Importation of Textiles (Quota) Ordinance of 1934, aimed at protecting the Colony's fledgling textile industry, converted the Riau archipelago into the main centre for transhipping and smuggling textiles into the Colony for the first time.

¹⁷Indian merchants were able to increase the scope of their activities by acting as agents for Japanese textiles.

¹⁸For examples of successful Chinese merchants, see Song Ong-siang, *One Hundred Years' History of the Chinese in Singapore*, University of Malaya Press, Singapore, 1967;

also C.B. Buckley, *An Anecdotal History of Old Times in Singapore, 1819–1867*, University of Malaya Press, Kuala Lumpur, 1965. Important non-Chinese merchants of the Straits included great Arab families such as the Alkofs and Alsagoffs, and in later years a number of Japanese and Indian concerns.

[19]i.e. orders made in duplicate, one copy each held by purchaser and supplier, thus enabling direct transactions—bills of lading provide one example of this.

[20]The chinchew or supercargo voyaged on the ships travelling from Singapore to the outports it served in the region. On arrival he bought up local produce from his Chinese contacts there who had already acquired it from local producers; on return to Singapore he then sold his merchandise to Western exporters, through the medium of brokers. As the area served by Singapore's entrepôt shrank, so did this system, although it survived into the twentieth century, particularly in the peninsular (east coast) trade and with the K.P.M. ships based in the Colony. In general, the chinchew gave way to the dealer in Singapore itself, who rose up as a result of the growth of his local knowledge and experience, which enabled him to conduct his transactions directly. At the same time many of the smaller Chinese broker concerns became absorbed by European companies.

[21]For descriptions of the Malaysian carrying trade of the area, see Wong Lin-ken, op. cit., p. 76, and also C.A. Gibson-Hill, 'The Indonesian Trading Boats at Singapore', *JMBRAS*, XXIII, 1, 1950.

[22]For further details regarding the Board, its organization and achievements, see Lennox A. Mills, *British Rule in Eastern Asia*, Oxford University Press, London, 1942, pp. 113–15.

[23]For background, see Chiang Hai-ding, 'The Early Shipping Conference System of Singapore, 1897–1911', *JSEAH*, X, 1, 1969.

[24]On the strength of the Royal Commission's recommendation, a petition signed by over 700 persons was made to the Straits Legislative Council, calling for the appropriate legislation. This resulted in the Freight and Steamship Bill of 1910, passed with only a single vote against, which would have imposed a 20 per cent duty on Conference ships. However, the following year (1911) the compromise referred to was reached between Sir John Anderson, the governor of the Straits Settlements, and the leaders of the Conference System whilst the former was on leave in London.

[25]For the background to the rise and growth of the Straits Steamship Company, see K.G. Tregonning, *Home Port Singapore: A History of the Straits Steamship Company Limited, 1890–1965*, Oxford University Press, Singapore, 1967.

[26]i.e. P & O, British India, Alfred Holt & Co. (Blue Funnel), the China Navigation Company and the Straits Steamship Company. As far as Straits Steamship was concerned, the Agreement confined its services to the Straits sphere encompassing the area enclosed between Victoria Point and Bangkok to the north, East Sumatra, Borneo and South Philippines, with rights of access to the China sphere. The Straits sphere was also open to Holts and the China Navigation Company.

[27]i.e. the R.A.F. base at Seletar, started in 1927 as part of the work on the new naval base complex. The Kallang field which became the main civil airport was not opened till 1937.

[28]The air links with the Malay Peninsula were started in 1937 by the Australian motor firm of Wearne Brothers.

[29]This problem was particularly acute for the Bugis sailors who came with the south-west monsoons which blew from early April till October. They had to arrive early if they were not to be caught by the contrary north-east monsoon which began in September or even sooner, and so be stranded for a season in Malacca.

[30]The Settlements formed part of British India which at this period was divided into the three presidencies of Bengal, Bombay and Madras, each under a governor.

[31]For the background to Penang's early years, see C.D. Cowan, 'Early Penang and the Rise of Singapore', *JMBRAS*, XXXIII, 2, 1950. Quote is taken from p. 8.

[32]For full details of Bannerman's tin scheme, see C.D. Cowan, 'Governor Bannerman and the Penang Tin Scheme', *JMBRAS*, XXIII, 1, 1950.

[33]However, according to Cameron (*Our Tropical Possessions in Malayan India*) by the 1860s Penang's pepper imports from Sumatra and rice from Thailand exceeded those of Singapore. Also in contrast to Singapore, Penang's export trade (largely in locally produced goods) exceeded the value of her import trade by more than half. Prior to the 1870s Penang had already established 'a valuable trade' with the west coast states of the Peninsula.

[34]If the principle of free trade seemed axiomatic for Singapore, this was certainly not the case with Penang, 45 per cent of whose revenues were derived from tariffs.

[35]The extension of Admiralty jurisdiction to Singapore meant that the legal authorities in the Straits acquired the power to try cases of piracy on the spot; previously all such cases had to be sent to Calcutta for hearing, meaning in effect that because of the delays and difficulties involved justice was not done.

[36]For the background to the controversial question of Calcutta and the merchants of the Straits Settlements, see Lennox A. Mills, 'British Malaya, 1824–67', *JMBRAS*, XXXIII, 3, 1960, esp. Chapter 14; also C.M. Turnbull, 'The European Mercantile Community in Singapore, 1819–1867; *JSEAH*, X, 1, 1969, p. 24 et seq.

[37]For a full discussion of the complicated politics surrounding the customs union proposals, see R. Emerson, *Malaysia: A Study in Direct and Indirect Rule*, Macmillan, New York, 1937; see also L.A. Mills, *British Rule in Eastern Asia*, op. cit.

[38]e.g. Imperial preference was not operative in India, Australia or South Africa; the Canadians were prepared to give favoured treatment only in exchange for a dumping duty and in the limited Malayan market the system favoured British manufactures.

[39]Locally manufactured consumer goods in 1941 included soap, matches, cigars and cigarettes, bricks and tiles, cement, fertilizers, metal boxes, pewter, sauces, beers and beverages, minerals, electric batteries, wire fencing, aluminium ware, pottery, clothing and biscuits.

[40]Gambier was an ideal crop for the subsistence farmer, requiring little labour or attention and maturing in little over a year. It served as a useful catch crop for pepper, its usefulness heightened by the fact that its refuse (from boiling) could be used as a manure for the pepper vines.

[41]James C. Jackson, *Planters and Speculators: Chinese and European Agricultural Enterprise in Malaya, 1786–1921*, University of Malaya Press, Kuala Lumpur, 1968, p. 53.

[42]John Cameron, *Our Tropical Possessions in Malayan India*, Elder Smith, London, 1865, p. 161.

[43]See Jackson, op. cit., pp. 125–7.

[44]During the first 6 or 7 years, whilst the nutmeg was maturing, the squatter sufficed on a small advance to clear the land and to grow enough bananas, nilam, vegetables or indigo to support himself on. When the spice crop started to mature, he would then acquire a larger advance at higher rates of interest, since the risks involved were still great.

[45]By the Sugar Act of 1836 sugar and rum imported into Great Britain from parts of the Empire were granted preferential duties, but the Straits Settlements were not included. As a result of agitation by Penang planters, the duties were extended to Penang and Malacca (but not Singapore) in 1846, thereby opening a new market in the United Kingdom.

[46]Quoted by Jackson, op. cit., p. 153, from the Penang Annual Report for 1891.

[47]For further details regarding the Malacca Land Problem, see Mills, *British Malaya*, op. cit., Chapter VI. Maxwell described the matter as 'one long history of want of knowledge on one side, and fraud and evasion on the other'. Quoted by Mills, p. 118.

[48]The Regulations laid down in effect that existing titles would be held according to Malay rights but future titles and jurisdiction would follow English practice. This meant that in future all land dues would have to be paid in cash rather than in kind, and that all landowners would have to hold an English title-deed for their land.

[49]The Recorder's ruling of 1834 was based on the Charter of Justice Act of 1826 which extended the law of England to the Straits Settlements and abrogated all previously existing laws there. His decision of 1835 was based on the grounds that the Land Regu-

lations of Singapore passed in 1830 were invalid because they went further than impos-
ing taxes, which was the only type of legislative power delegated by the Supreme
Government in Calcutta to the Straits Settlements authorities; by this token the
Malacca Land Regulations were also null and void.

[50]Mills, ibid., p. 130.

[51]The Land Regulations of 1831 provided for the re-establishment of the post of Collector of Land Revenues, abolished with the Presidency in 1830, and for the replacement
of all existing land grants with new ones which would form the only legal title to land
after 1 January 1832.

[52]By this system, all instruments relating to land titles are registered with the government
land office, so that the title, whatever its form, will be clearly indicated in one original
document rather than in a multiplicity of deeds.

Books and articles for further reading

BOOKS

Allen, G.C. & Donnithorne, A.G., *Western Enterprise in Indonesia and Malaya*,
George Allen & Unwin, London, 1954.

Buckley, C.B., *An Anecdotal History of Old Times in Singapore, 1819–1867*,
University of Malaya Press, Kuala Lumpur, 1965 (reprint).

Chick, Sir Louis (ed.), *The Economic Development of Malaya*, Report by the
World Bank, Government Printer, Singapore, 1955.

Clodd, H.P., *Malaya's First British Pioneer. The Life of Francis Light*, Luzac &
Co., London, 1948.

Collis, M., *Raffles*, Faber & Faber, London, 1966.

Cowan, C.D. (ed.), *The Economic Development of South-East Asia*, George
Allen & Unwin, London, 1964.

Davies, D., *Old Singapore*, Donald Moore, Singapore, 1954.

Emerson, R., *Malaysia: A Study in Direct and Indirect Rule*, University of
Malaya Press, Kuala Lumpur, 1964 (reprint).

Fisher, C.A., *South-East Asia: A Social, Economic and Political Geography*, Methuen & Co. Ltd., London, 1964.

Hahn, E., *Raffles of Singapore: A Biography*, University of Malaya Press,
Kuala Lumpur, 1968.

Jackson, J.C., *Planters and Speculators: Chinese and European Agricultural Enterprise in Malaya, 1786–1921*, University of Malaya Press, Kuala Lumpur,
1968.

Lim Chong-yah, *Economic Development of Modern Malaya*, Oxford University
Press, Kuala Lumpur, 1967.

MacKenzie, K.E., *Malaya: Economic and Commercial Conditions in the Federation of Malaya and Singapore*, Her Majesty's Stationery Office, London,
1952.

Mills, L.A., *British Rule in Eastern Asia*, Oxford University Press, London,
1942.

Pearson, H.F., *People of Early Singapore*, University of London Press, London,
1955.

————, *Stories of Early Singapore*, University of London Press, London,
1955.

Purcell, V., *The Chinese in South-East Asia*, Oxford University Press, London, 1965.

Robequain, C., *Malaya, Indonesia, Borneo and the Philippines*, Longman Green, London, 1958.

Simkin, C.G.F., *The Traditional Trade of Asia*, Oxford University Press, London, 1968.

Song Ong-siang, *One Hundred Years' History of the Chinese in Singapore*, University of Malaya Press, Singapore, 1967 (reprint).

Steinberg, D.J. (ed.), *In Search of South-East Asia: A Modern History*, Oxford University Press, Kuala Lumpur, 1971.

Swettenham, Sir Frank, *British Malaya*, George Allen & Unwin, London, 1906.

Tregonning, K.G., *Home Port, Singapore: A History of the Straits Steamship Company, 1890–1965*, Oxford University Press, Singapore, 1967.

ARTICLES

Bogaars, G.,' The Effect of the Opening of the Suez Canal on the Trade and Development of Singapore', *JMBRAS*, XXVIII, 1, 1955.

Bonney, R., 'Francis Light and Penang', *JMBRAS*, XXXVIII, 1, 1965.

Cowan, C.D., 'Early Penang and the Rise of Singapore', *JMBRAS*, XXIII, 2, 1950.

————, 'Governor Bannerman and the Penang Tin Scheme', *JMBRAS*, XXIII, 1, 1950.

Gibson-Hill, C.A., 'The Indonesian Trading Boats reaching Singapore', *JMBRAS*, XXIII, 1, 1950.

Jackson, J.C., 'Chinese Agricultural Pioneering in Singapore and Johore', *JMBRAS*, XXXVIII, 1, 1965.

Khoo Kay Kim, 'Biographical Sketches of Certain Straits Chinese', *Peninjau Sejarah*, II, 2, 1967.

Mills, L.A., 'British Malaya, 1824–67', *JMBRAS*, XXXIII, 3, 1960.

Rawlins, J.Sig.D., 'French Enterprise in Malaya', *JMBRAS*, XXXIX, 2, 1966.

Sharom Ahmat, 'American Trade with Singapore, 1819–65', *JMBRAS*, XXXVIII, 2, 1965.

————, 'J.B. Balestier, First United States Consul in Singapore', *JMBRAS*, XXXIX, 2, 1966.

Tarling, N., 'British South-East Asian Interests in the Nineteenth Century', *JSEAH*, VIII, 1, 1966.

Tregonning, K.G., 'The Early Land Administration and Agricultural Development of Penang', *JMBRAS*, XXXIX, 2, 1966.

————, 'The Origins of the Straits Steamship Company in 1890', *JMBRAS*, XXXVIII, 2, 1965.

Wong Lin-ken, 'The Trade of Singapore, 1819–69', *JMBRAS*, XXXIII, 4, 1960.

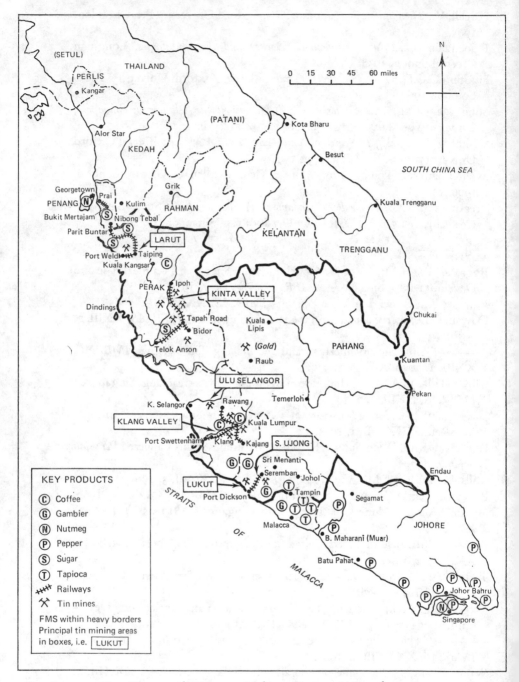

18.   Nineteenth Century Malaya: Economic Development

(ii) THE PENINSULAR MALAY STATES

'I do not pretend that in our dealings with the native states of the Malay Peninsula, we have been actuated by a spirit of pure disinterestedness. I do claim that our actions will bear a close scrutiny, and that it has resulted in an almost unmixed good to all the States themselves, while a new and rich field has been opened to the commerce of all nations.'

Sir Andrew Clarke,
India, Ceylon, S.S., British North Borneo & Hong Kong, 1899.

In 1850 the hinterland of the thriving Straits Settlements, in which were placed the Malay States of the Peninsula, was, as far as the rest of the world was concerned, a little-known and thinly-peopled tract of mountain, forest and swamp, which produced little. The transformation of this area within two generations into one of the world's leading producers of tin and rubber was as dramatic in its way as Singapore's rise into a great international port. Along with the economic came social change, equally as striking, reflected in the emergence of a new multi-racial society where the immigrants tended to outnumber the indigenes. The new Malaya's overseas trade was almost on par with that of the Netherlands East Indies, although her population was but a fraction of her neighbour's, while Malayan income per capita became the highest in the region. On the other hand the economic development of the Peninsula was irregular and unbalanced. Rubber and tin overshadowed the economy, putting the country's prosperity at the mercy of a volatile world market. A population, with a favourable ratio to resources, living in a country nearly three-quarters covered by virgin forest had to import two-thirds of its rice and most of its timber. While development was rapid in the tin-rich west coast states, the rest remained very little changed from what they had been before. The social imbalance stood out still more clearly. In Malaya's multi-racial society the bulk of the wealth was in the hands of the immigrants who mainly lived and worked in the towns on the western side of the Peninsula, while most of the indigenous Malays continued their subsistence level existence within the cocoon of their traditional agrarian communities.

Tin in the nineteenth century
The evolution of modern Malaya is rooted in the rise and growth of its two basic industries, rubber and tin. Rubber came to occupy by far the most important place in the economy, but the tin industry is much older and has played a major part in the historical development of the Malay States. However, the transformation of the tin industry from a primitive and limited affair into the highly capitalized and mechanized operations of today began in the nineteenth century in response to the new demands created by the progress of the Industrial Revolution in Europe. The Malay tin states were soon affected, and by the mid-1860s Straits Tin was superseding both Bangka and Cornish tin and had regained its natural position as the premier tin export of South-East Asia and indeed the world.[1]

The growing demand for tin and the rising prices which accompanied it stimulated the search for new deposits, leading to the discovery of several rich new fields between 1820 and 1870. By the beginning of the 1870s the main centres of mining in the Peninsula were in Larut, already established as the leading source for Straits Tin, Ulu Selangor and the Klang Valley, and Sungai Ujong where mining had been carried out since the 1830s. All these mines were worked by Chinese, and their influx and the improved methods they brought with them was an important factor in the riumph of Straits Tin after 1870.[2] But in the last analysis the quality of tin depends on the quality of the smelting, and here again Chinese techniques proved decisive in placing Straits Tin in the fore.

The quick success of Straits Tin excited the interest of European merchants and speculators. As early as 1800 a group of British merchants in Penang were reportedly doing a flourishing business in Phuket tin, but the first serious attempt by a Western firm to go in for tin-mining on a big scale came half a century later when the Singapore firm of Patterson Simons acquired a large concession in Pahang. But the project became entangled in the politics of the Pahang Civil War and the firm ended up with its mines confiscated, an episode which caused Western investors to fight shy of further forays into the tin business for some time. The high prices of the 1870s precipitated a bout of new attempts, particularly in Sungai Ujong and Selangor, but once again these ventures became ensnared in local politics and had to be abandoned. In fact the primary reason for the failure of Western enterprise to make headway in the tin industry prior to 1874 lay in the anarchy prevalent in the Malay tin states themselves. This anarchy retarded all mining enterprise in the Peninsula and prevented the full flowering of the industry until the spread of British control created more favourable conditions.

The British Forward Movement of 1874 marked the start of a 24-year period of unparalleled expansion and prosperity for the Malayan tin industry. Despite two major depressions caused by sudden drops in tin prices, world tin output trebled within this period without ever fully catching up with world demand. In this general expansion Straits Tin took the major share. Between 1874 and 1883 the Peninsula progressed from fourth to first amongst the world's producers and by 1890 was producing more than all the other tin-producing areas combined. Apart from steadily rising demand, the main reason for this tremendous upsurge was the swift resumption and development of mining activities in Perak, Selangor and Negri Sembilan, from where the bulk of the Straits Tin came, following the restoration of peaceful conditions under British rule.

For ten years after 1874 the Larut district of Perak was the principal centre of tin-mining in the Peninsula. It was the first district to come under effective British control and was easily the most accessible district on the west coast for the mining and exporting of tin. At the beginning of 1874 Larut was still destitute, save for the presence of 4,000 Chinese fighting men, but as soon as it became clear that stable conditions had returned, the Chinese merchants of Penang, who were the principal investors, started to advance their capital in order to reopen the mines. In the next four years production quadrupled, despite the drop in world tin prices and the fierce competition on the world market of the rapidly expanding tin industry of Australia. The richness of Larut's deposits and the favourable discrepancy between Perak and Penang piculs provide the explanation.[3] Larut reached the peak of its prosperity in the 1880s during a boom caused by the recovery of the world tin market and aided by government incentives. However at about this time rich deposits around Taiping, upon which Larut's primacy was based, began to fail, foreshadowing the general exhaustion of the easily-worked surface tin in the district as a whole. During the following ten years (i.e. 1884-94) Larut's output steadily declined while that of Kinta, to the south, suddenly rose up. The first signs of increased activity in Kinta were to be seen in 1882. From 1884 onwards there was a great influx of Chinese miners and production rose correspondingly. In 1885 it had reached nearly half, the next year two-thirds, of the Larut figure, and in 1889 it surpassed it. By 1895 Kinta was producing three-quarters of all the tin mined in Perak and was by far the richest centre of production in the whole Peninsula.

The decisive factor in Kinta's rise was the exhaustion of the Larut fields as far as the Chinese methods of the day were concerned, coupled with a disastrous drop in the tin price in 1884 which forced the closing down of most of the mines around Taiping and caused a large number of Chinese miners to migrate in search of employment elsewhere. The subsequent recovery of the tin price, the very favourable position the Penang advancers found themselves in, and the fantastic richness of the Kinta deposits accelerated the movement into the district which by the 1890s had assumed the proportions of a 'tin rush', which lasted up till 1895. The mining population of the district leapt from 4,000 in 1882 to over 50,000 in 1895 and Ipoh was transformed from an obscure market village to the second town in the state. Tin production in the other mining districts of Perak never attained the proportions of either Larut or Kinta.

The introduction of British rule in Selangor, however, did not result in any immediate recovery. From 1874 till 1879 the tin industry stagnated, inhibited by high production costs and shortages of labour and capital. The chief tin mines were situated some distance inland and were further removed from any of the ports of the Straits Settlements than any other mining area on the west coast. Freight costs were high and capital was harder to raise, while Chinese miners were attracted to the quicker returns obtainable in Perak. Because of all this the recession of the 1870s was all the more keenly felt in Selangor. The state also suffered from the fiscal policies adopted by the new British administration.[4] Lack of capital and of production mean lack of revenue for the government which was, therefore, unable to spend so much on development as was possible in Perak.

With the recovery of the London tin market in and after 1879, however, production picked up rapidly and in the 1880s became the fastest in the whole Peninsula. Government encouragement, the introduction of the steam pump (especially after 1884), the growth of communications and the great richness of some of the deposits assisted in this rise. During the period of even more rapid expansion which followed in the 1890s, the Kuala Lumpur area still remained the main centre of production and up till his death in 1885 Yap Ahloy largely dominated the mining in the state.

The general progress of the tin industry in Negri Sembilan after 1874 was far more limited. The richest and most accessible deposits had already been worked out, so that although the tin duty was the lowest of all the three west coast states, Negri Sembilan was the worst hit by the depression of the 1870s. The tin sands of Sungai Ujong and Jelebu, the two main tin areas, were simply not workable at depression prices and by 1877 it was reckoned that 40 per cent of the Chinese labour force available two years earlier had taken itself off elsewhere. Heavy taxes on imports such as salt, pork and oil which were farmed out at monopolistic rates added to the burdens of the industry. The lack of readily available capital was another factor. The small businessmen of Malacca, who formed the chief investors in the state, were inevitably chary of risk, were unable to sustain setbacks easily and had less control over their labour. Nevertheless, despite all these drawbacks, during the 1880s some progress was made. Communications were improved and the annexation of Jelebu to Sungai Ujong was done largely with an eye to stimulating the development of mining enterprise in that state. On the other hand the very favourable concessions granted to two European companies in Jelebu greatly hindered the growth of Chinese mining there. The creation of a state council in Sungai Ujong in 1883 proved a useful medium for attracting bigger capitalists to invest from outside, aided by special legislation to induce them to do so. But after 1892, a peak year, tin production from Negri Sembilan as a whole started to decline.

Apart from the three west coast states, Pahang was the only other area in which attempts were made at tin-mining on a substantial scale in the nineteenth century. These centred mainly on the activities of the Pahang Corporation which after many vicissitudes succeeded in working the underground mines at Sungai Lembing to profit in the last decade of the century. The tin mined in the other states prior to 1909, notably in Kedah and Johore, was negligible.

In the general upsurge of Malayan tin production between 1874 and 1896 the great improvement in the techniques of production and the introduction of Western machinery were to prove of ever-increasing significance. By far the most important Western innovation in this period was the steam pump. Its eventual adoption by Chinese miners was a great boon to their enterprise, because by surmounting the perennial drainage problem the industry was able to maintain a fast rate of expansion. The adoption of more scientific and effective methods of prospecting was another important development, eclipsing the traditional Malay *pawang* who up till the 1880s virtually monopolized all such activities. By 1895 the *pawang* was discredited and by-passed in Perak and Western methods of prospecting were being widely followed in both Selangor and Sungai Ujong. However, Western methods were none too reliable at first, so that the Chinese methods of prospecting by pitting was frequently used up till 1914. During the 1890s the introduction of the Chinese *lanchut kechil*, a small portable, coffin-shaped washbox, proved of particular value to the small miner or group of miners who could now exploit poor surface ores and the abandoned workings of old mines, not profitable by other methods.

During this period, to all intents and purposes, tin-mining was a Chinese monopoly and Chinese techniques and methods of working, financing and organizing determined in large measure the lines along which the industry developed.[5] Mining operations appear to have been mainly financed from the Straits Settlements and the Chinese credit system enabled both big merchants and petty shop-keepers to participate in the industry. In general these mercantile interests controlled the industry, although in the late 1890s, as a result of the pressures tin was undergoing, the Indian moneylender sometimes played a role.[6]

The reasons for Chinese dominance in this period are not hard to find. Chinese methods did not require a large capital outlay. They depended on labour-intensive techniques, the working of easily accessible deposits which required hardly any mechanization. The labour force was manoeuvrable and mobile, and the miners 'could be turned into fighting men at short notice'.[7] The organization and success of Chinese mining in the last resort depended on the great secret societies which were controlled by the mineowners and used by them to dominate and exploit the labour force. In the anarchic conditions prevalent in the tin districts prior to British control, the societies provided the rudiments for self-government and self-protection. After 1874 they continued to play a vital part, from the mineowner's point of view, in recruiting and controlling the steady flow of labourers into the mines.

As a result of this Chinese predominance, the Malays as participants in the industry were almost completely ousted, while all attempts—with a couple of notable exceptions—by Western enterprise to gain a foothold in the industry met with failure up till the turn of the century.

The extent to which tin-mining was in Malay hands at the beginning of the nineteenth century is hard to determine.[8] The Malay ruling class as lords of the land sponsored mining activities or worked their mines with capital and labour obtained from Chinese advancers. On the other hand, from the beginning, the use of foreign labourers on the mines was seemingly inevitable, particularly as the demand for tin grew. The tin states were sparsely populated till mid-century by Malays for whom, at subsistence level, mining could only be a part-time occupation. The Malays had neither the capital nor the knowledge nor the means to develop mining operations on a large scale. As the need for such mining arose, it could only be answered by a full-time and mobile labour force such as only the Chinese merchants in the Straits Settlements could finance and the landless, hungry villagers of South China could supply. Prior to 1850 the Malays still managed to contribute a substantial proportion of the Peninsula's tin output, although their social organization and mining techniques were no match for the far more sophisticated methods of the Chinese. Malay mining methods and smelting techniques were primitive, their organization undeveloped and laborious. There was no division of labour, only one pit was worked at a time, drainage systems were inadequate and no effective way of disposing of the slag was ever devised. But what rendered Malay mining totally uneconomic were wasteful observances sanctioned by custom, so that production costs were determined not by market conditions but by tradition.[9]

To the overall failure of Westerners to get a foothold in the industry until the end of the nineteenth century there were three notable exceptions; a French company that started operations in Kinta in 1881, the Pahang Corporation, and two smaller concerns in Jelebu, Negri Sembilan. The French company survived three or four other Western companies operating in Perak probably because it compromised with reality and allowed Chinese miners to work its concessions on a tribute basis. In Selangor a rash of companies were floated between 1882 and 1884, but within 12 months only one was still in operation and existing by virtue of 'book-making' profits only. The two European companies in Jelebu, being granted exceptionally favourable terms, were able to show a working profit every year between 1889 and 1895. However the most successful Western venture was that of the Pahang Corporation which, due to the quite different conditions posed by lode as opposed to alluvial mining, was able to establish an undisputed position in the industry in Pahang itself. The Corporation, officially floated in 1887, had its origins in the huge concessions of 1883 over an area which covered nearly one-fifth of the whole state. The company survived a severe political crisis in its first years but for the best part of the following decade was beset by a whole host of other problems.[10] It was not until 1896 that the Corporation was able to realize its first genuine profits and declare its first real dividends. Despite a speculative boom in the early 1890s and the speculation which had taken place prior to British rule, only one other Western firm was successfully mining tin in Pahang in that year. Meanwhile the British Pahang administration was unable to do much because of its own limited resources, the financial consequences of To' Bahaman's uprising and official indecision as to the best way to develop communications.

In all, the period which witnessed the upsurge of Straits Tin to the leading position on the world market was one in which Western enterprise failed to make any appreciable headway at all in the mines of the Peninsula. Western firms could not escape high costs and overheads. Land itself was usually acquired secondhand and therefore at a higher rate. The employment of European staff was infinitely expensive. Mining equipment was costly to buy, install and maintain. Labour was a major difficulty: Malays would not work as wage labourers, Indians proved unable to take the strenuous type of labour needed for the mines, and on the whole Chinese workmen were unwilling to work for a non-Chinese employer. But Western miners had partly themselves to blame for their problems. Careless prospecting and bad management were rife and led to many failures. Those that survived did so in most cases by coming to terms with Chinese methods and organization.

The Chinese miners apparently had all the cards in their hands, and for three decades played them with skill and to their considerable profit. Nevertheless even the Chinese miners had their setbacks, including two severe and prolonged periods of recession on the world market. The first (1875-82) was in most cases only surmounted with the active support of the newly established British administration. The repercussions of the second (1889-93) completely modified the credit system on which Chinese mining was run and gave Western enterprise its first opening, in particular through the medium of the smelting industry. This depression also loosened the grip of the mineowners over their labourers, with profound effects on working conditions in the industry. These changing circumstances together with a number of other factors bespoke the end of Chinese supremacy in the Malayan tin industry and the rise of the Western element in the course of the ensuing three decades.

In fact, alongside the enterprise of Chinese merchant capitalists and the exertions of Chinese labourers, the tin industry in the nineteenth century also owed much to the encouragement and assistance of the various British state administrations. British Residents had a natural desire to stimulate European, and in particular British, enterprise and they nurtured long-term schemes for the development of plantation agriculture, but in the context of the 1870s tin was the one obvious immediate source of revenue. Therefore, from the outset, it was official policy to promote the restoration and progress of the tin industry as quickly and by all means possible. This implied ensuring adequate supplies of capital and labour, providing proper communications for access to the tin fields, and the laying down of land and labour policies that would nourish and protect the industry.

In 1874 the immediate problem was lack of capital, which was essential for the restoration of derelict and abandoned mines in the west coast states, soon to be hard to come by because of the recession which began in 1875. The British state administrations met this crisis by loans to individual miners, by reducing production costs through judicious taxation policies and by adopting the farming system for the collection of specific revenues already used in the Straits Settlements. The farms, in particular, not only provided substantial revenues at no cost to the administration, but also enabled it to shape the development of the state. Meanwhile the farmer stood to make a fortune and bidding was keen.[11] Equally as vital as capital was labour, and the labour supply was equally as unsteady. Malay chiefs had long discovered that they could not rely on the manpower of the *kampong* to work their mines, nor did the Malay peasant see the necessity to subject himself to the miserable conditions that Chinese mineowners inflicted on their coolies. Chinese know-how and capital dominated the industry so Chinese manpower followed in consequence. But the labour force was always transitory, dictated basically by the state of the tin market and the system and terms of employment. Later other factors came in, chief amongst them being the growing competition on the Chinese labour market from neighbouring territories, which, coupled with the uncooperative attitude of the imperial authorities in China itself, served to raise the price of labour in the Malay States and contributed to the recession of the 1890s.[12] Well aware of these problems, the British state administrations from the beginning did everything to encourage Chinese immigration and, without hesitation, extended the principle of unrestricted entry applied in the Straits Settlements to the Protected States, a policy adhered to up till 1930.[13] In response to the serious labour shortage of the late 1880s caused by outside competition, the Straits authorities set up (in 1890) a royal commission to go into the whole question. All attempts to establish a scheme of officially assisted Chinese immigration broke down, but government encouragement of

immigration was in fact enough. Chinese immigrants poured into the Protected States and with them the tin industry flourished and grew.

The development of communications

In terms of expenditure the greatest contribution made by the British to
the progress of tin-mining in the nineteenth century was in the field of communications. The allocations from the state budgets were very high, mounting
in the cases of Perak and Selangor to nearly 50 per cent of their total expendi-
tures from the 1880s onwards. In the Protected States over 1,700 miles of
roads were built between 1881 and 1910 at an average cost of $25,000 per
mile, but this was far cheaper than railway construction which cost about
twice as much. By the end of 1901 the governments of these states had invested $23 million in the construction of 360 miles of railway. By 1909 this
figure had doubled. The original stimulus for the building of the first roads
and railway lines sprang from the needs of tin and the almost total absence of
any means of communication except by river prior to 1874 meant that this
had to be one of the first tasks of the new administrations. In return, tin mining expanded, government revenues increased and more money was put
back into road and rail construction.

Since tin was the prime factor, the first object was to open up links between
the tin mines and the coast. This was initially done by building cart roads between the mining centres and the nearest navigable points on the local river-
way. But the roads before the age of motor vehicles were inadequate to cope
with the rapidly expanding needs of the tin miners. Railways were essential
and as soon as conditions and financial circumstances permitted, a start was
made on building them. Work on the first eight-mile stretch between the
mines at Taiping and the coast at the mouth of the Larut River was started in
1881. Within the next fifteen years all the principal tin-mining districts were
linked with their respective ports and the growth of an inland, longitudinal
connexion linking these centres to one another had already begun. In 1895 a
line stretched from Kuala Lumpur southwards to Sungai Besi and northwards
to Kuala Kubu, while in Perak a line from Ipoh ran towards Taiping and had
reached the Perak River at Enggor; Taiping was joined to Pondok Tanjong
on the way north and another line was advancing southwards beyond Bagan
Serai. In 1901 all these lines were amalgamated as the F.M.S. Railways and
by 1903 a continuous link by rail ran from Prai to Seremban.

Road construction was now turned to linking mines to railheads, since
bullock carts could not compete with railway wagons, while the railway
lines themselves called into existence a series of new ports. The first of these
was Port Weld, at the terminus of the line from Taiping, and for a brief seven
years was the third busiest port in Malaya. But after 1892 this short pre-eminence ended with the sudden decline in Larut's tin production and with the
opening of the Kinta Valley line two years later. By 1898 Port Weld had
already been displaced by Teluk Anson, the Kinta line's terminus, as Perak's
largest port and the opening of direct rail communications between Larut
and Penang in 1902 destroyed its value forever. The new railway line also
brought into being Port Dickson at the coastal end of the Sungai Ujong line,

KEY PRODUCTS

- Ⓒ Coconuts
- OP Oil Palm
- Ⓟ Pineapples
- ▨ Main rubber growing areas
- ⚒ Tin mines unless otherwise indicated.
- ✟✟✟ Railway in 1910
- ✶✶✶ Extensions 1910-1920
- -------- Extensions 1920-1941
- —— Main roads in 1941

Main rice growing areas named in boxes
States within the thick lines
represent the Federated Malay States

19.   Malaya, 1941: Economic Development

and in 1901 Port Swettenham, set amidst the malarial swamps of Kuala Klang. Despite some early teething problems Port Swettenham was destined to become the premier port of the peninsular mainland. By the middle of the 1880s these new ports were linked by frequent and regular steamship services with one or other of the Straits Settlements. In the development of these coastal sea communications, the formation in 1890 of the Straits Steamship Company based on Singapore marked a major step forward.

Just as the railways speeded up communications by sea, so the roads facilitated the spread of telegraphic communications.

Behind this remarkable growth in communications was Frank Swettenham who had an imperialist's understanding of their importance both for immediate needs and for the future. Wherever he was in authority, road and rail communications were pushed ahead to the limits of the states' capacity. His most significant contribution was in railway development. Swettenham played a major role in the promotion of the Klang Valley railway and was the author of a memorandum on railway building in the Malay Peninsula submitted to Chamberlain, British Colonial Secretary, in 1896. He proposed the development of a north-south line joining up all existing stretches and linking Penang to Singapore overland; he wanted a line from Kuala Lumpur to cross the Main Range to reach Kuala Lipis in Pahang and had wider visions of rail links which would reach from the Peninsula into Burma. Such plans required bold thinking for the capital outlay was enormous and the governor of the Straits Settlements (Sir Charles Mitchell), for one, thought it bad economics to base railway development on large, unsupported loans as Swettenham proposed to do. However, Chamberlain favoured Swettenham and as a result his plans to join together all the existing lines in the Peninsula were approved, a decision subsequently regarded as 'the most important step taken for the development of the country following the Federation proposals'.[14]

However the greatest problem in the development of communications in the Peninsula remained the question of finance. In the case of roads the start was necessarily slow and depended directly on the recovery of the tin industry. The policy of keeping within the limits of state revenues was followed in all of the Protected States until the 1880s when Swettenham, gambling on the returns new roads would bring in terms of trade and production, lavished funds up to and beyond the hilt. From the mid-1880s onwards, therefore, road construction was partly based on credit. In the case of the railways, credit was inevitable because of the large amount of capital involved in their construction. But usually the government preferred to exercise a direct responsibility in their building rather than hand over the business to private enterprise. In consequence all the lines in the Protected States, apart from the Sungai Ujong Railway, were built by the government, and in 1908 that line was also bought over by the F.M.S. administration. Fortunately for the states concerned, the new railway lines on the whole proved to be good revenue earners and not only promoted the welfare of the tin and other industries but also brought direct gains to the government.

The rapid growth of communications in the Protected States between

1874 and 1900 was an extremely important factor in the success and expansion of the tin industry and both fed from one another. The new communications at the same time had important modifying effects on the economy as a whole, although this remained dominated by tin. The penetration of the new roads and railway lines into virgin tracts of jungle opened up new land, led to the growth of new villages and townships and stimulated new enterprises.

The evolution of land policy

Equally important for the tin industry were the administrative measures taken after 1874 to create a framework of laws and institutions by means of which private enterprise could develop and flourish. The first task was to devise a land code which could form a proper basis for the establishment of mining rights. The lead was taken by Perak in 1877 with the setting down of conditions for the leasing of mining land and sanctions for the proper and regular working of concessions. In the same year Hugh Low laid down the principle that the actual owners of mining land be obliged to see that it was worked. Two years later came the comprehensive Perak Land Code which included all previous legislation passed piece-meal on the subject. By the time that similar legislation was passed in Selangor and Sungai Ujong in the 1880s, three basic principles formed the mining policy throughout the three Protected States: all rights in and over the land were vested in the state; the owners of mining land could only claim first option in exploiting it; and ancestral landowners could only claim royalty for tin-mining that they themselves facilitated. In 1895 mining legislation was carried to its ultimate conclusion with the passing of the Perak Mining Code and with the creation of the post of Wadenf of Mines armed with legal authority in mining cases. The Code, which ormed the substance of the Mining Enactment of 1899 operable throughout all of the newly created Federated Malay States, granted the British Resident far greater powers over land itself and made ancestral lands forfeitable if not worked for two consecutive years. In the meantime (in 1895) the governments of the four Protected States passed comprehensive labour legislation, defining the rights and responsibilities of mine labourers. The effect of all this government legislation was to give direction and shape to the tin industry, making mining land a marketable commodity and checking speculation. Miners gained security of tenure and the value of land became relatable to production costs. More fundamentally still, the state administrations gained the means to develop and guide the industry along the lines it desired.

The evolution of land policy inevitably raised the whole question of official attitudes towards the economic development of the Malay States. The dangerous dependence of the economy of the Protected States on tin was recognized and the state administrations strove to overcome this by encouraging agriculture, either through the promotion of a cash crop plantation industry based on Western capital or by fostering the growth of a settled farming population of Malaysian (or other) smallholders. In the event it became official policy to encourage both.

The policy-makers of the Protected States were fortunate in possessing a good example in the Straits Settlements of what not to do as far as land policy was concerned; at the same time conditions in the States themselves were nearly ideal for the evolution of a balanced land policy—virgin soil in abundance and a flourishing tin industry to finance development. Land could be alienated as and how required and both Western estate agriculture and smallholder farming could be encouraged without danger of a conflict of interests. The basic features of the land policy which evolved in the Protected States and eventually the whole Peninsula were established by W.E. Maxwell. In his Perak Land Code of 1879 two basic principles of Malay land tenure were embodied, namely, that ownership was vested in the ruler and that alienation could take place on condition that land rent was paid, the land worked and the fruits of it taxed. State land was divided into four categories, with a special inducement for investors of 999-year leases for all agricultural land, with permanent, transferable and heritable rights against the payment of a fixed premium, a survey fee and fixed land rent. The Perak Code formed the basis of all the land regulations subsequently passed in the other Protected States, and in 1897, a year after the creation of the Federated Malay States, a new land enactment was passed under the auspices of Swettenham to cover all the four states. With this the Protected Malay States now had the practical land policy necessary for their development. There was provision for the miner, the plantation owner and the smallholder, while government arrogated to itself disposal rights over timber and mineral resources and set aside certain tracts as forest reserves. The sheer abundance of land ensured that competition for land did not become a problem at least until the closing years of the nineteenth century.

The encouragement of commercial agriculture

The new land policy enabled the state administrations to pursue their primary objectives of encouraging large-scale plantation agriculture. Capitalists were also lured to invest their money in the opening of estates by the selective taxation of agricultural exports according to the nature of the crop and its importance to the local economy, by the granting of loans, by remissions of rent and the postponement of export duties.[15] European entrepreneurs in general received preferential treatment, with generous loans on easy terms—partly because of sentiment and political advantage but largely because it was from them that the greatest returns were expected. It was also the general trend to spend liberally on service roads to open up the areas acquired by European concessionaires, except for Pahang where circumstances conditioned official policy against the European entrepreneur. Yet despite these inducements, European attempts at establishing a foothold in the planting of commercial crops fared little better than their efforts to break into the tin-mining industry. The Chinese were the pioneer planters and settlers in the Protected States as far as cash crops were concerned, virtually monopolizing the planting of pepper, gambier and tapioca in Negri Sembilan and Selangor and holding a predominant share in the sugar industry of Perak. European enterprise prior to the rise of rubber was confined mainly to sugar, in which a substantial sum of Western capital was invested, and to coffee which was almost a Eu-

ropean monopoly. But the coffee plantation industry itself stood on the brink
of disaster in 1895 while sugar declined drastically shortly afterwards.

Pepper and gambier
The oldest form of commercial agriculture in the Protected States was the
cultivation of pepper and gambier which, pre-dating the British Forward
Movement, was an offshoot of the industry in Singapore and Malacca. However, there was a much more rapid expansion in the planting of these two
crops after the extension of British control had taken place, and in the 1880s
they entered upon a new phase as prices nearly doubled on the world market
and as the state administrations of Sungai Ujong, Perak and Selangor issued
special land regulations to promote their cultivation. The fever for gambier
and pepper planting displaced tapioca as the major commercial crop of Sungai
Ujong, penetrated hitherto untouched districts in Selangor and spread into
'Old Negri Sembilan'.[16] During the 1890s the industry in the west coast tin
states as a whole reached its climax.

After 1900 gambier and pepper planting in these states went into sharp
decline. It was now felt that these two crops, and tapioca too, were bringing
more loss than gain because of the wasteful, soil-exhausting characteristics of
their cultivation. Negri Sembilan started to control the spread of their cultivation by laying down new conditions for land leases; Selangor followed
suit. By 1903 there were signs that the new policy had been accepted by planters but the marked decline of area under pepper and gambier which followed
was not precipitated so much by government actions as by the spectacular
upsurge of rubber. By 1914 pepper and gambier had ceased to be the most
important cash crops of either Negri Sembilan or Selangor.

Gambier and pepper planting never acquired any significance elsewhere
in the Peninsula save for Johore, beyond the pale of British authority. In fact
Johore was their earliest centre in the Peninsula and the scene of their greatest
expansion, a direct consequence of being adjacent to Singapore where the
land available for planting diminished as the rate of immigration increased.
The movement of Chinese planters into Johore from the Island began in earnest in the late 1820s, attracted by the spacious tracts of rich virgin soil, by
the nearby convenience of Singapore's expanding facilities and ready market,
and by the encouraging attitude of Johore's rulers, the Temenggong family,
who saw in Chinese enterprise their most productive source of wealth. Immigration rose steadily in the 1830s and by the following decade there were substantial numbers of Chinese in the state, settled principally along the rivers
flowing into the Straits of Johore and easy of access from Singapore Island.
Stimulated by the growing demand from Britain and North America, cultivation continued to expand uninterrupted for the rest of the century; it
moved up the west coast and in the 1880s also up the east. During the same
decade Johore's pepper and gambier exports to Singapore mounted rapidly.
By 1890 there were over 200,000 Chinese in Johore, 'who were chiefly gambier and pepper planters', their settlements located on all the rivers flowing into the Straits of Johore and along either coast as far as Muar and Endau. Then,
for the same reasons as in Negri Sembilan and Selangor, the industry under-

went sudden decline. The two crops remained the state's principal exports up till 1910, but their volume had already declined by 40 per cent since 1890. In the next few years, as prices fell and labour left the plantations for the new rubber estates, the decline became faster still. Between 1912 and 1917 exports of the two crops fell in volume by another 60 per cent and the abolition in 1917 of the *kang-chu* system, on which the whole industry had been based, sounded its death knell.

The industry was a wholly Chinese affair in Johore as well as in Negri Sembilan and Selangor, and was almost entirely financed and controlled from Singapore. The closest links were naturally those between Chinese merchants in Singapore and planters in Johore. Close ties also bound Singapore to the planters in Negri Sembilan and Selangor but whereas in Johore the Chinese pepper and gambier planters played the part of colonists opening up virgin lands, in the other two states they were settling down in a region with an already established (Malay) population and where other crops were grown. In terms of actual organization the industry of Johore was characterized by the famous *kang-chu* system with its plantations, *kangkars* and *bangsal*.[17] From the Johore point of view, the system solved the problem of administering a foreign community without the means or personnel to do so directly whilst preserving the fiction of Malay sovereignty; from the point of view of the Chinese settlers, it enabled them to live and work according to their own customs and laws without interference, eased the process of immigration and in all left them to their own devices. The system also worked out most favourably for the *kang-chu* himself. Although initially dependent on the backing of some gambier and pepper merchant in Singapore, he was soon able to turn things to his own advantage. Many *kang-chu* became very rich men and by the 1870s were to be found in retirement in Singapore, having delegated their authority to lesser lights. By this time the system itself was becoming more and more institutionalized. The Johore Law of Kang-chus of 1873 spelt out in detail the rights and responsibilities of the *kang-chu* himself, while the establishment of a Gambier and Pepper Society (the *Kang-kek*) in 1867 in Singapore gave the advancers and planters in the industry complete control over the prices of the produce sold in the Colony. When this highly profitable and flourishing system, however, was brought to an end in 1917 pepper and gambier had been displaced by rubber in Johore as much as elsewhere.

The rise and fall of tapioca

The cultivation of tapioca ran parallel to that of gambier and pepper and shared much the same vicissitudes and ultimately the same fate. As we have already noted, the tapioca industry had its origins in Malacca where techniques for producing 'pearl sago' had first been evolved.[18] For organization and finance Malacca remained the centre of the industry in the Peninsula throughout the nineteenth century, and in consequence the main areas of tapioca planting in the Malay States were to be found concentrated along the borders of Malacca Territory, particularly in Negri Sembilan. Tapioca cultivation acquired considerable importance in the nineteenth century, its principal market being

Britain where the product was used in the preparation of foodstuffs and for industry.

The extension of tapioca planting by Chinese planters in Malacca Territory into the neighbouring principalities of Negri Sembilan began in the mid-1870s, springing from the extension of the Malacca plantations right up to the border, the attractive land terms available on the other side, and the increasing difficulties for planters within the settlement itself. This initial expansion also coincided with a period of booming prices on the general market and with the extension of British control over Sungai Ujong. Planting in Rembau and the states of 'Old Negri Sembilan' began in the early 1880s, in this case before the establishment of British control. The devastating fall in tapioca prices, which occurred in 1881 and lasted for five years, virtually killed the industry in Sungai Ujong where by the 1890s the crop had become relatively insignificant, but in Old Negri Sembilan the plantations survived, largely because of the more favourable land terms obtainable from the Malay administrations of the latter, where the tapioca planter was still welcome as a breaker of virgin soil and as a potentially permanent settler. Hence in these states tapioca planting continued to expand in the late 1880s, accompanied by an increase in tapioca factories and in Chinese immigration. The bulk of actual production was concentrated in Rembau which in 1888 contributed over half the tapioca exports and contained three-fifths of the factories and two-fifths of the Chinese population of Old Negri Sembilan. In the 1890s there was little increase in the area under tapioca or in the volume of production; what changed was merely the distribution of the crop. Outside the Menangkabau states, tapioca planting was confined to much more limited areas in Johore, Selangor, Perak and Kedah. For while Malacca's merchants could find few alternative forms of agricultural or industrial development, elsewhere the field was dominated either by tin or by different crops such as sugar or later coffee. In the rest of the Peninsula, where tapioca planting started at all it did so fitfully and failed to gain a firm foothold.

As with gambier and pepper, the decline of tapioca after 1900 was rapid. It vanished overnight from Selangor and after a last upsurge had disappeared as a significant crop from Perak also by 1914. The same thing happened on the much larger holdings in Negri Sembilan. Tapioca, like pepper and gambier, withered before the triple thrust of official policy, falling prices and the rise of rubber.[19] As a cash crop it never played so large a role as that of pepper and gambier in the opening up of new areas or in the introduction of new settlers, and its extreme wastefulness incurred official disapproval. But tapioca did contribute to the laying of the foundations upon which the modern rubber plantation industry was to be built.

Perak and the sugar industry

In Perak the earliest substantial growth in commercial planting appeared as an offshoot of the already well-established sugar industry in neighbouring Province Wellesley. The extension of sugar across the border into Perak was one major factor in the failure of other forms of agriculture to make much headway in the state prior to the 1890s. The sugar plantation industry was also different in character from the pepper, gambier and tapioca industries of the south in that it required a much greater capital outlay and for this reason also attracted European investment.

The beginnings of sugar planting in Perak took place in the flat, swampy plains of Krian, a direct consequence of the spread of British power over Perak and of the very favourable conditions that Krian itself offered. Lying adjacent to the drained fields of the Province, Krian provided the same conditions—an expanse of flat, low-lying coastal lands criss-crossed by numerous waterways bordered by mangrove swamps full of suitable timber for fuel. Furthermore the greater part of the land lay still untouched and was within easy reach of Penang. At the same time there was no more land available for expansion in Province Wellesley itself so that there was a ready response when under the new British dispensation sugar planters were encouraged to cross the border. By 1879 there were already five Chinese estates opened in the district, initiating a process of expansion which continued until the 1890s. By this time the amount of suitable land still available in Krian was rapidly decreasing so that Chinese planters started to move into the equally ideal Matang district of Perak. Meanwhile operations in Krian were intensified, steam machinery became more generally used and a number of canals were dug to improve irrigation and drainage. But although the area alienated for sugar increased, productivity did not, for most of the new extensions were to enable the opening up of more land for fallow periods.

Up till 1883 sugar planting was solely a Chinese affair, virtually monopolized by the merchants of Penang who financed and thereby controlled all the planting and the processing. Labour too was almost exclusively Chinese. However in 1884 the first European enterprise in the state was established and by the end of the century the European stake in the industry had become considerable, covering about one-third of the total acreage alienated. The European interest was completely dominated by two firms which held most of the land between them—the Perak Sugar Cultivation Company Limited and the Straits Sugar Estates Company. Both companies organized their concessions into groups of very large estates, employed a sizeable European managerial and technical staff, used Indian indentured labour and employed the most up-to-date machinery. During the 1890s Perak's sugar production rose phenomenally and as production figures soared expansion continued. In the face of this Western competition, based on heavy capital investment and the employment of cheap labour, the larger and wealthier Chinese estates tended to adopt the same methods, turning over to the use of modern machinery and even recruiting European engineers and overseers. By the end of the century nearly half the Chinese estates in Krian had switched over to steam and by this time a clear distinction had developed between the extensive, Western-type estate and the traditional smallholding.

In 1902 came sudden decline. By 1905 Chinese planting had shrivelled back to Krian and by 1914 Perak had to all intents and purposes ceased to export sugar. Symptomatic of the decline of all the major commercial cash crops of the time, sugar was in the first instance victim of government policy, in this case the adoption in the 1890s of a new scheme to promote rice production.

The Krian project in particular occasioned heavy government expenditure, leading officials to oppose further alienation of land for sugar planting. When the project was completed in 1906 the land still available was severely restricted and 'this played a major part in the decline of sugar planting in the area'.[20] In the meanwhile sugar lands not affected by the rise of padi fell before the sweep of coconuts and rubber.

Within the short span of thirty years the sugar industry of Perak became the most important agricultural enterprise in the state and second to tin in terms of export value. At the end of the century when the industry was at its peak, Perak's sugar exports were twice those of Jamaica and a third of those of British Guiana, the world's largest producer. It was undoubtedly the most successful of all the cash crops essayed in the Malay States in the nineteenth century.

Coffee

Next to sugar and promising to equal it in importance after 1880 came coffee, the only agricultural enterprise to be almost wholly European controlled. Unlike the other cash crops already discussed, coffee planting was unknown in the Malay States prior to 1874. Its rise and development took place within the last quarter of the century and attained boom proportions in the 1890s. Production reached its zenith in 1904-5 and then went into sudden decline along with sugar, pepper, gambier and tapioca. During the period of its growth and expansion coffee was planted from Johore up the west coast to Perak with the greatest concentration in Selangor, which in its hey-day produced three-quarters of the total exports of the F.M.S.

The first coffee estates in the Protected States, opened in 1877 in Perak by European coffee planters from Ceylon, were failures. The planters lacked experience and knowledge of local conditions, communications were poor and official land policy in the state at that time not encouraging. In the meantime other European pioneers had fared better in Selangor and Sungai Ujong where the first estates were begun in 1879. In the 1880s other estates were opened, but as in Perak the absence of effective communications, labour difficulties and a drop in world coffee prices brought most to the brink of failure. During this period the most promising progress appeared to be in Johore, whose ruler was swift to encourage the new industry. That factor and the state's proximity to Singapore made Johore especially attractive, but in the event coffee came to be confined almost exclusively to the small, accessible districts of Johore Bahru and Batu Pahat.

The genesis of the Malayan industry lay in coffee's decline in Ceylon, where the appearance of a deadly fungus in 1869 on the European estates of that island caused coffee planters to look towards the Malay Peninsula. The general depression of 1876-85 prevented any expansion in the industry until the late 1880s but with the recovery of the market and the first fruits of the pioneers being shown a second wave of planting took place. This time the main area of activity was Selangor, particularly around Kuala Lumpur, but the real coffee boom did not begin until the 1890s, precipitated by a new combination of factors. The first of these was the dislocation of the coffee industry of Brazil, the world's main producer, as a result of the abolition of slavery in that country in 1888, to which were added a new government drive to attract European planters to invest and open up land in the Malay States and a radical improvement in the availability of labour. In Perak between 1890 and 1895 new coffee estates sprouted up in all districts save for one. In Selangor the expansion of the late 1880s continued at an accelerated rate, the bulk of the estates being located in Klang as a result of the state government's policy of keeping areas of mining and agricultural enterprise apart. In fact the Selangor administration in its eagerness to cash in on the coffee boom overreached itself and in 1895 auctioned off large tracts of land in that district which proved to be peaty and largely unsuitable for coffee. This was the only example of land speculation by government in Selangor but, as Maxwell complained, speculation by private enterprise also took place and had to be catered for by special legislation. The coffee boom also affected Negri Sembilan after 1892.

Equally important for the industry was the great improvement in the labour supply. Towards the end of the 1880s the Straits authorities started to subsidize steamship services across the Bay of Bengal and the migrants' depot at Negapatnam was opened shortly after. The flow of Indian labour increased and the rising demand for their services raised wages and attracted better quality workers. The coffee planters tended to prefer 'free' as opposed to indentured labourers. There was a spectacular rise in the number of Tamils employed on coffee plantations in the 1890s.[21]

The decline in coffee planting after 1896 was as sudden and as absolute as that of the other commercial crops at the end of the nineteenth century. A sharp fall in prices occurred after the peak season of 1894-5, brought about by an overstocked market, and by the time they began to recover after 1903 the industry had suffered other heavy blows. *Haemelia vastatrix*, the fungus that had killed the Ceylonese industry, appeared in Selangor in 1894; a caterpillar onslaught followed in 1899. Planters themselves were careless about curing and marketing techniques so that the quality of Malayan coffee exported was poor and made little headway on a steadily more competitive market. By 1900 coffee planters, more especially outside Selangor, were losing their faith in the prospects and estate owners were looking around for alternatives, the most promising of which was rubber. After 1903 the decline in coffee in favour of rubber became general, including in Selangor where faith in coffee had burned brightest. After 1909 there was virtually no more coffee grown in Perak and Negri Sembilan and in the F.M.S. as a whole there were less than 6,000 acres under cultivation, most of which was to be found around Klang.

Coffee planting required considerable capital investment and technical knowledge, both of which were provided by the European planters of Ceylon who formed the core of the new industry in Malaya. The European domination of the industry was also a direct outcome of official encouragement, particularly so in Perak. Other races were not excluded but their lack of capital consigned them to minor roles. Both Chinese and Malay coffee planting was reported during the height of the boom, particularly in Negri Sembilan, but with very few exceptions these were all smallholdings. Despite the swift demise of coffee in the 1900s, this official endeavour was not entirely wasted, for the coffee plantations played a vital part in providing the foundations for the rubber industry that rose in its traces.[22]

The collapse of the emergent coffee estates was the last in a series of failures by European commercial enterprise to establish itself in the Peninsula in the nineteenth century. The reasons for this failure in tin-mining have already been discussed. The failure in agriculture emanated from similar causes. No European enterprise of the time could compete with a Chinese concern in terms of overheads. The labour supply was inadequate and unreliable while the market for the various cash crops essayed was unpredictable. Under such circumstances no amount of government support could be of much avail. It was only at the beginning of the new century when rubber hit the jackpot in terms of world demand that Western enterprise was able to come into its own.

The promotion of smallholder agriculture
Although the main efforts of the state administrations in the Protected States were aimed at promoting the development of tin-mining and estate crops, attention was also paid to the need to bring into being a settled population of peasant smallholders to occupy and till the land. Official measures to this end were limited but important enough to have made a significant contribution to the general pattern of development by the end of the century. The policy of unrestricted immigration, for instance, was not designed solely to provide an adequate labour force for the mines and the estates, but to encourage the entry into the Peninsula of prospective subsistence farmers as well.[23] The response from Malaysians in Sumatra and the archipelago was good, and several agricultural colonies were launched by district officers in Perak and Selangor, the largest and best known of which was the one at Sitiawan founded in 1886. Closely related to this movement were schemes of government assistance by means of rent remissions, the supplying of seed and the granting of small loans. In general official policy consciously sought to promote the cause of the smallholder and used a liberal fiscal policy as the principal means of doing so. This policy was generally justified on the grounds that land had no value unless it was productive, and that the drainage and irrigation of swamp and jungle by new settlers was ample recompense for rents forgone in the initial years. It was also argued that no agriculturalists would be obtained at all without government assistance, since they had no means of their own. However, there were also powerful voices which did not agree with this reasoning, and who, led by W.E. Maxwell, 'had no faith in colonization schemes which begin with bribing Malays with advances and loans to take up land and at the end of a few years leave a deficit which has to be written off...'.[24]

The issue as to the desirability of encouraging the immigration of Malaysian smallholders was also raised by problems of land administration. The implementation of Maxwell's admirable ground rules quickly ran into the practical difficulties of carrying out a comprehensive survey. In an era of rapid development with survey priority being given to the lines for roads and railways, the layouts of towns and the demarcation of large agricultural blocks and leases, the ideal of doing the same thing for every Malaysian smallholder was unattainable. With the solution of the intractable Malacca land problems to his credit, Maxwell now (in his capacity as British Resident there) applied the same principles to Selangor. In the process he introduced three new guidelines into land administration; the recognition of title to land by right of occupation, the replacement of survey by demarcation as the basis for its definition, and the rent settlement to be based on periodical reassessment. The first two of these together with the Torrens System by which the policy was to be implemented were unexceptional and generally accepted; the principle of periodic reassessment met with a barrage of opposition from most officials, headed by Swettenham who argued that such a practice was alien to Malay tradition. The real point was that Maxwell regarded the encouragement of a settled Malay peasant population as unproductive and a revenue liability which would impoverish the state. Swettenham and his allies, on the other hand, believed that the creation of a settled farming population, in good time, would yield its reward in the form of indirect revenue. The issue was finally settled, after five years of bitter controversy, by the Land Enactment of 1897. The new measure vindicated Maxwell's principles as far as title and right by demarcation were concerned. Superficially the new code also recognized his principle of reassessment, but in such a modified form as to render it nugatory.[25]

Rice in the nineteenth century

Any policy of encouraging Malay agriculture was tantamount to encouraging rice production, although at this stage it was not yet official policy to encourage Malaysians to plant padi to the exclusion of everything else. Rice cultivation was the oldest agricultural industry in the Peninsula, and Malay culture was deeply associated with it. In terms of land and labour used, rice rated next to rubber in importance in the twentieth century, but it was also the least remunerative form of agriculture, which was why, of course, it remained almost exclusively a Malay crop. In the hey-day of British rule abundant and cheap supplies of rice from Burma, Thailand and Cochin-China were usually available, while natural conditions in the Peninsula itself were far from ideal for the cultivation of large crops. There were few extended plains for such planting; Kedah was the main exception and the only area known to have produced rice surpluses as far back as the days of the Malacca Sultanate. Furthermore the state of Malay rice cultivation in the second half of the nineteenth century was deplorably inefficient. The greater part of the rice harvest came from dry padi, popular because it could be grown on hill-sides or partially cleared land and required no ploughing, irrigating or manuring. But this system was wasteful and soil-exhausting. Linked with shifting cultivation, a *ladang* of dry padi could only be worked for a couple of seasons before it had to be abandoned. Wet rice cultivation was also practised. Skills, methods and tools varied widely from one locality to another, although the men of Kedah and immigrants from Sumatra, Kelantan and Patani enjoyed the reputation of being more skilful than the rest. There were some attempts

at irrigation but this was not general outside Kedah; where irrigation was practised in the Protected States it was apparently done by outsiders. In general
nineteenth century rice cultivation especially in the Protected States was depressing, based mainly on shifting *ladang* culture and generally devised to provide merely sufficient for the needs of the district in which it was grown.
Synchronized planting under the direction of *penghulus*, once known, had
long been forgotten. Failure to clear and burn the land systematically encouraged vermin and pests to flourish. The reports of nineteenth century district officers were full of harvest failures and of meagre crops, usually the
consequence of poor methods or sheer mismanagement.

Government support for rice cultivation was urged by district officers who
saw in it the chief means of helping the Malays, although not all were sanguine
about the prospects for success. At higher levels increased rice production came
to be considered from a security point of view. In the 1890s dependence on
overseas food supplies seemed to be a very weak point in the armour of British Malaya.[26] However in fact only one major rice-growing scheme was
launched in the nineteenth century in the Protected States, although much
discussion took place about other projects. This was the Krian scheme, started
in 1896 and finally completed ten years later at a cost over three times the
original estimates. The British Resident of Selangor proposed, in 1896, the
draining of the Tanjong Karang area north of Kuala Selangor as well, but,
despite a survey carried out the following year, this plan was not implemented because it was considered too costly in relation to the anticipated
yields.

Outside the Protected States, Kedah was the only Malay state to make
some progress in rice production prior to 1900. Probably the original home
of rice cultivation in the Peninsula, Kedah's shifting *ladang* cultivation gave
way to a sedentary wet-rice culture in the seventh and eighth centuries, while
the Kedah Plain itself rose as the rice-bowl of the state with the establishment
of Alor Star as capital in the second half of the eighteenth century. Up till
1850 the main area under padi extended from the foothills of the Main Range
to the fringes of the coastal swamp which stretched from Gunong Jerai (Kedah Peak) to Perlis. In the second half of the nineteenth century under conditions of political stability rarely known before, the great task of irrigating
this swampy belt was begun. By 1900 three main canals had been built, opening up the coastal districts of Kota Star and Yen to rice.

The Malayan economy in 1900

By the end of the nineteenth century the salient features of the modern
Malayan economy had emerged. The bulk of the development had taken
place on the western side of the Peninsula, especially in the west coast tin
states, which by this time had been under direct British control for over a
quarter of a century. Perak and Selangor had or were about to become the
most populous states in the Peninsula, more than half their inhabitants being
immigrants, mainly Chinese. Their economies still rested basically on tin,
by far the most important export, but the foundations had also been laid for
a substantial plantation industry. New towns unheard of a generation be-

fore had sprung into being—Taiping, Ipoh, and Teluk Anson in Perak, Kuala Lumpur, Rawang, Kajang and Port Swettenham in Selangor, Seremban in Negri Sembilan—and were linked together by a trunk railway and an ever expanding network of roads. Kedah and Johore which also faced the Straits of Malacca, although not under direct British rule, had also developed as a result of their close proximity to the two hubs of Penang and Singapore. The development of the Kedah Plain into a rice granary was accelerated by the rise of a new and expanding market and in the south the state was touched by the extension of commercial agriculture. Johore had been opened up by settlers from Singapore and on its west coast was developing new townships like Muar (Bandar Maharani) and Batu Pahat (Bandar Penggaram). The eastern side of the Peninsula, on the other hand, had been barely touched either by economic change or by the influx of an immigrant population. Kelantan and Trengganu still remained the theoretical vassals of Bangkok and maintained a spasmodic trade with the emporium of Singapore. Pahang, despite the newly installed presence of a British Resident, was hardly more affected, while the east coast of Johore remained an unpopulated wilderness of jungle, swamp and mountain. Communications, except by sea, were non-existent on this coast. While on the western side of the Peninsula a new multi-racial society was growing up, with its economy tied to the great world markets of trade and with its roots tapping the sea-lanes of the Straits of Malacca, on the east coast the traditional economy and society of the Peninsular Malays lived on, in a self-sufficient way, at a level little beyond subsistence and as yet immune to the currents of change from outside.

From 1900 till 1941 there was little change in this basic pattern, merely an accentuation of the dichotomy between the western and eastern sides of the Peninsula. The rise of the rubber industry added a new element and the pattern of foreign penetration was modified further by the upsurge of European interests at the expense of those of the Chinese. With this the moulding of modern Malaya was complete.

The rubber revolution

The two most outstanding economic developments in the Peninsula between 1900 and 1941 were the dramatic rise of the rubber industry and the rapid assertion of Western predominance in that and in tin-mining.

At the beginning of the century the quest by a generation of British officials for a Western stake in commercial agriculture suddenly paid off and yielded huge dividends. The birth of the rubber industry was induced by a series of fortuitous circumstances in the 1890s which pushed up rubber prices to phenomenal heights on the world market and found the Malay States ideally placed to take advantage of the situation. What followed was the 'rubber revolution' in which virtually all contemporary cash crops were swept aside by the avalanche to plant rubber. By 1910 there were already half a million acres under the new crop and by 1914 the acreage had doubled again, the planted area being progressively extended over the next fifteen years at an average of 100,000 acres a year. By this time (i.e. 1930) rubber covered two-thirds of the cultivated area in the Peninsula and had established itself as Malaya's most important export crop. In the 1930s expansion was much slower, although the area under cultivation still increased by some 27,000 acres a year.

Rubber's sudden triumph had been preceded by a generation of frustration and failure. In the 1870s and 1880s sugar or coffee, with their apparent promise, firmly held the attention of European enterprise. The appointment of H.N. Ridley as Director of the Singapore Botanical Gardens probably saved the day for rubber. He took up his post in an atmosphere already strongly prejudiced against rubber but, convinced of its future, he persevered with single-minded determination to prove his point. With painstaking research he overcame the technical problems which stood in the way of profitable tapping and finally in 1891 developed his 'ibidem' system which made rubber cultivation an economic proposition for the first time. However up till 1895 he made no progress whatsoever in his self-appointed mission to convert Western planters in the Peninsula to rubber as a cash crop.[27] Much more persuasive than his reasonings were the sudden collapse of the coffee market and the rising demand for rubber itself. This and the blight which attacked many coffee estates almost simultaneously forced European coffee planters to consider 'some less expensive and more profitable form of cultivation'. At the same time Chinese and other planters, discouraged by government legislation against soil-exhausting crops such as tapioca, pepper and gambier, also began cautious experiments in planting rubber between their other crops. The Singapore firm of Guthrie's, destined to become the largest rubber estate holders in the Peninsula, laid down their experimental plantation in 1895; others followed suit. This was followed by intensified experimentation with different strains of rubber, tapping techniques and methods of planting. It was not until 1910 that *hevea brasiliensis* established undisputed primacy over all other strains. By 1908, however, the main problems associated with planting itself had been overcome.

Between 1897 and 1904 rubber planting established itself as a major industry with pioneer estates being opened up in various parts of the F.M.S. and elsewhere in the Peninsula. By 1902 virtually every coffee planter had committed himself to a greater or lesser degree, while in the north the sugar growers of Krian and Province Wellesley were beginning to take interest. During the next couple of years the tempo of expansion accelerated appreciably and by 1904 planting was also begun on a commercial scale in both Kedah and Johore.

After 1904 the period of hesitancy was over and rubber embarked on an era of rapid and virtually unchecked expansion which lasted until 1921. The truly boom years were those between 1905 and 1912, occasioned by the basic inelasticity of supply, for rubber takes time to mature and prices were bound to stay high until the crops planted in the Peninsula came to maturity and began to flood the market—which did not occur till 1910 and after. In the interim fantastic profits were to be made on the stock market, enormous dividends were paid and the dark groves of rubber spread into every state in the Peninsula. This was followed by a period of less frenetic growth and consolidation which was only brought to an end by the trade recession at the end of the Great War. The bases for expansion were the easily accessible districts on the west coast which had already been opened up for other crops, in particular coffee. So Matang in Perak, Klang in Selangor and the Seremban district of Negri Sembilan formed the earliest centres for the new industry and the crops spread along the arteries of communication into other areas.

Up till 1906 four-fifths of the land opened to rubber still lay in the west coast states of the F.M.S., although a start had been made in Pahang, Kedah, Kelantan and Johore. Poor communications was the chief factor preventing the extension of planting so rapidly in the other states, particularly on the east coast, although in Johore Sultan Ibrahim's keenness to speed up the development of his state helped to compensate for this, and speculation was prompted by the construction of the Johore section of the north-south trunk railway line. In Kelantan rubber planting would probably not have taken place for many years had it not been for the existence of the huge Duff concession. Duff himself cashed in on the rubber boom by advertising for concession hunters in 1906, and thus encouraged the state government to follow suit. By 1908 nearly a quarter of a million acres in the Peninsula had been taken up by rubber, the most extensive area to be covered by any one commercial crop in its history. During the next four years in the United States, under the stimulus of Henry Ford, the American car industry expanded fast and against a crescendo of rising prices and spiralling dividends on the London market, a rash of new rubber companies sprang into being, often on a purely speculative basis, and the number of estates and land under rubber increased rapidly. Chinese and Malay landholders were able to cash in handsomely on this land rush, some of the more enterprising amongst them planting rubber solely to attract a European buyer. The main activity was still centred on the west coast states of the F.M.S., especially in Perak and Selangor, but the effects of the boom were felt throughout the Peninsula except for Trengganu. Development as before hugged the existing lines of communication until no new land was available. In Negri Sembilan and Johore planting followed the newly opened trunk railway; Kedah, with its close links with Penang, saw considerable expansion of rubber in the southern part of the state. Elsewhere lack of communications continued to be the main factor retarding faster growth. In Trengganu where the first rubber estates appeared in 1911, the absence of a suitable land policy prevented any boom expansion from taking place.[28]

The great expansion spree came to an end in 1912, and although the industry continued to grow and develop for the next ten years, it was at a much more moderate pace. Many estates were now yielding, so that production figures went up, and as prices inevitably declined from the pinnacles they had touched in 1910, companies and estates rationalized and became fewer in number, and dividends steadied to more normal averages. The industry still expanded, paid well and attracted investors, but its very expansion now became a factor tempering its development. With Malayan rubber assuming the lead on the world market, the price of rubber and the Malayan economy became more vulnerable to market fluctuations. However, rubber was now sufficiently well developed for it to withstand setbacks, and despite generally falling prices and rising costs, investment in the industry was too great to be

abandoned precipitately. In this investment, companies held the lion's
share since, by virtue of their organization and resources, they could withstand price fluctuations to a reasonable degree. Furthermore, the answer to
rising costs was found to lie in planting more widely, since costs decreased in
proportion to the amount of rubber produced—a matter of some consequence
as the profit margin diminished.

The first check to expansion actually occurred in 1913. Prices fell, causing
an immediate reduction in the area planted with new rubber. The outbreak
of the Great War the following year brought about further problems at first;
however, planters received government aid which helped to tide things over
and by 1915 the war demand for rubber soon brought about a recovery. By
the end of 1917 over one million acres in the Peninsula had been alienated for
rubber, of which three-fifths were in the F.M.S., mostly on the west coast.
But the industry now received a new check as a result of this over-rapid expansion. Land officers had to close their books indefinitely, unable to cope
with the flood of applications. In 1918 prices dropped drastically and in the
same year both Britain and the United States imposed severe restrictions
on rubber imports. Malayan dependence on the American market was
already marked.[29] Profits fell, the number of companies dwindled, dividends
were not declared; the demand for new rubber land dropped off almost
to nothing and once again planters started thinking of alternatives. The rubber
price rose somewhat in 1919 but fell once more to crisis levels in 1920. By
1921, after two decades of unparalleled expansion and profit, the Malayan
rubber industry faced the stark realities of over-production, depression and
restriction.

Nevertheless by this time rubber was established on a far broader scale than
any other commercial crop in the country's history. Large amounts of capital
had been invested and the welfare of a large segment of the population had
already become dependent on it. The pattern of the industry was now clearly
stamped on the Peninsula. Most of it was concentrated in the west coast states
principally in Perak, Selangor, Johore and Negri Sembilan and to a lesser
degree in Kedah. The industry was largely in European hands, although
Asian smallholders were assuming an ever-increasing and significant share.
The supremacy of Western interests stemmed from, in the first instance, the
heavy capital outlay that starting a plantation involved, which lay well beyond
the means of most Asians at the time and was also beyond what an individual
European planter would be likely to raise. As a result, from the outset, the
number of estates under individual ownership were few, and soon became
fewer. Planters perforce had to turn to someone to finance them, and so there
sprang into existence numerous companies, some started as purely speculative concerns raising capital from expectant shareholders in Europe or America, others financed by merchant houses in Singapore or later still by rubber
manufacturers themselves.[30] However, initially company formation was slow,
for investors overseas had still to be convinced of the bonanzas that rubber
could bring, and it was not until 1908 that the movement began in earnest.
After that for the next few years the floating of rubber companies became a
speculative affair with London emerging as the focal point for investment. In-

vestment was further stimulated by the stabilization of the Straits dollar at a fixed rate to sterling at this period. By 1908 almost all European-owned rubber estates on the west coast were held by companies floated in London. After that year the small firms which were usually based on one estate, typical of companies floated before 1903, were mostly absorbed by larger undertakings.[31]

The planters themselves represented all types and conditions of men, mostly drawn from the British Isles, Australia and Ceylon. In later years they came to enjoy considerable political influence, especially in the F.M.S., through the Planters' Association of Malaya (P.A.M.), established in 1907. In that same year the Rubber Growers' Association was formed in London to represent the interests of investors in the United Kingdom.

Although rubber became primarily an estate industry, smallholders came to play an increasingly important part in its development. In the 1930s two-thirds of the total acreage under rubber belonged to estates which produced three-fifths of total peninsular production. The majority of the estates were in Western hands, although in 1921 Chinese held one-fifth of the total estate acreage in the Peninsula, their holdings being concentrated in Johore and Kedah. European estates were generally far larger than the Asian ones, a trend observable from the pioneer years. Alongside the Europeans, the Chinese also had an important share in the ancillary industries which grew up with the plantations, and the rubber entrepôt trade of Penang and Singapore was largely a Chinese affair. While by the 1920s the European estates were mostly run by public companies, the Asian estates were usually run by their owners or by private concerns. The Malay failure to have any share in the rubber industry except as smallholders was consonant with their general failure to participate in the expanding economic development of their own country. Most Malays lacked the capital, had no connexions with the world of commerce and industry and knew nothing of its techniques. However, the Malay share in the smallholding acreage was substantial, a result of the favourable climate and environment, the ease with which rubber could be cultivated and the relatively low costs involved. In fact, the smallholders of Malaya (and elsewhere) followed in the wake of the big estates, profiting from their experience and making use of the infra-structure created by the industry—the new network of communications, processing and marketing facilities, and later the fruits of research. The spectacular results of the first rubber boom provided the initial stimulus to Malay planters and also provoked an influx of Sumatrans and Javanese who took the lead amongst the Malayan small-holders. Less vulnerable to price fluctuations, the smallholders were able to hold their own or even expand in periods of recession. Although no exact figures are available by the end of 1917 in several districts of the west coast nearly half the total acreage was in their hands. In the difficult years of the 1920s and 1930s the area under smallholdings did not decrease, their distribution following closely the pattern of the great plantations.

From the beginning the rubber industry enjoyed the favour of the government; indeed official actions were largely responsible for its advent. The perennial problems were capital, land and labour, but by the end of the nine-

teenth century broad solutions to these had been found. With the upsurge of
rubber the existing policy of modifying land regulations to meet specific requirements and of advancing credit to pioneer planters was continued and
intensified. But when confronted with the dimensions of the movement in
1904 the F.M.S. government called for a special report on the state of agriculture in general and its prospects. The report, written by J.C. Willis,
Director of the Royal Botanical Gardens in Ceylon, recommended that agricultural policy be based on European planter, Asian smallholder and
immigrant alike, so that capital, a settled farming population and labour
would all be available, and proposed the formation of a special department
to improve and carry out research in the techniques of agriculture. In response to the report, in 1904 itself, a new programme of loans for planters
was launched and the following year a new department of agriculture set up
in Kuala Lumpur, while the main centre for agricultural research was also
transferred there from Singapore.

The Planters' Loan Scheme of 1904 met with immediate success. The initial $500,000 earmarked for the scheme was trebled in 1908 in the face of a mi-
nor recession, and increased by a further $1 million during the much sharper
crisis of 1913-14. Although the assistance which the planters received was
necessarily limited, it was invaluable in providing encouragement and in
persuading many individual planters to weather the first storms. As for labour, on the other hand, although by the end of the nineteenth century the
principle of unrestricted immigration into the Protected States was firmly
established, the flow from India was nowhere sufficient to meet the exigencies
of the new industry. The setting up of the Tamil (later Indian) Immigration
Committee and Fund at the instigation of the planters in 1906 did much to
alleviate this shortage. The volume of Indian immigration into Selangor
nearly trebled between 1908 and 1913 and for both Perak and Negri Sembilan there were marked 'increases'. In the first two states the rubber industry
became indelibly associated with Tamil labour, but in Negri Sembilan, Johore
and Kelantan the greater proportion of the labour force was Chinese.[32] A
rational land policy having already been secured by 1900, government now
merely confirmed existing trends and met specific problems as they rose.
The two main F.M.S. land enactments of 1903 and 1911 modified the basic
law of 1897 so as to better cater for planters' interests and to better ensure
that the maximum development of land took place. The government also
took steps to try and check harmful and excessive speculation in land, and
moved energetically against Malay speculators who were considered to be
hampering the development of the European estates. In those non-federated
states where the planting interest was strong, official favour was likewise extended. The Johore Land Enactment of 1910 was passed under the pressure of
growing rubber interests along the new railway line; Kedah adopted land
regulations more favourable to planting interests after the extension of British
control there in 1909 and the foundations of land tenure by registration were
slowly extended in Kelantan after 1910. In short, as the rubber revolution
gained momentum land policy developed along lines favourable to the new
planting interest. Perhaps the most extreme example of this came from Negri

Sembilan where in 1904 government offered its famous 'lallang' terms, making abandoned tapioca or pepper lands available to European planters for a song, which resulted in the state becoming a predominantly rubber producing area.

The government's role was equally as important with regard to the technical problems facing the pioneer, which at moments seemed serious enough to threaten the future of the industry as a whole. These problems centred on tapping methods, the correct use of soils and plant disease, and the solutions to them came from the newly established Agricultural Department at Kuala Lumpur and from such organizations as the Rubber Growers' Association. However after 1910 the government left the burden of research to private enterprise which itself was not generous in allocating funds. Only as a result of the new pressures after the Great War was more positive action taken, and somewhat belatedly in 1926 the Rubber Research Institute was established. In the same period private enterprise also made some important advances, following up lines of its own.

The most serious problem that faced rubber was that of over-production. Great fluctuations in world rubber market prices, which the industry is not sufficiently adapted to withstand, have characterized its brief history. The earliest recessions were those of 1907 and 1913, but as the industry was still not fully developed, it escaped the full impact of the falling market. The much more serious recession of 1918-21, however, was nemesis for the European planter whose woes were compounded by the arrival of the smallholder onto the scene, while the contemporaneous spread of rubber planting in Thailand, Burma and above all French Indo-China only made matters worse. The actual ending of the war itself brought about temporary relief in 1919 as rubber manufacturers, anticipating a new boom, hastily brought up surplus stocks at favourable rates. But their optimism was misplaced; the consumer market in the West had in fact shrunk, the cost of living was higher and labour scarce and expensive. Prices slumped once more and by 1921 the outlook for the European estates was described as 'dismal'. Chinese and other Asian smallholders were even harder hit, unable to dispose of their product to their local dealers who were unable to afford large stocks. A government commission set up early in 1921 to examine the overall economic situation reported back later the same year that in the case of rubber 'all roads lead to restriction'.[33] In fact the Rubber Growers' Association had already tried out a voluntary restriction scheme of its own based on an agreement between the major British and Dutch rubber concerns in the region, but this had to be abandoned at the end of 1921, failing on account of the exclusion of smaller private estates and smallholdings which simply increased their production. The industry now pressed for full-scale government intervention. The result was the formation in October 1921 of the Stevenson Committee which was dominated by the Rubber Growers' Association. Largely under the influence of the Association but also guided by the need for American dollars and the desirability of excluding American influence, in 1922 the Committee recommended restriction on the understanding that the leading estates in the Netherlands Indies would agree to join in. These recommendations were accepted and the Stevenson Plan came into operation at the end of the same year (1922). In making this decision, the Malayan authorities were also concerned about the serious social and political repercussions of spreading unemployment and of local financial instability.

The Stevenson Plan restricted production by means of punitive duties and a prohibition on the alienation of fresh lands for planting. After being enforced for six years, the Plan was abandoned in 1928 without having achieved its basic objective. The refusal of the Netherlands Indies as well as the rubber producers of Thailand or French Indo-China to take part was a major cause for this failure but, to a large extent, the Plan did not succeed owing to the sheer perversity of fortune. It started to operate just as the recession was lifting, stimulated by a fresh demand from the American market. In consequence the chief beneficiaries of the steep rise in prices which followed were those outside the scheme. For Malayan planters, the Plan brought few satisfactory results. The country's predominance as a rubber producer was weakened, and relations with the United States, Malaya's best customer, were soured.[34] The Plan had an adverse effect on the smallholders whose interests had barely been taken into account. They were particularly hard hit by the restrictions on the planting of new land, so that while their overall stake in the industry continued to increase, their expansion was curtailed and they became the last to receive the benefits of official advice and assistance.[35]

The Stevenson Plan was abandoned in 1928, after a fact-finding visit by Ormsby-Gore, the British Colonial Secretary, to the region, just in time to make way for a second and far more severe recession which wrought fundamental changes in the rubber industry throughout the world. The Great Depression of 1929 caused rubber prices to plummet to unimagined depths and it was five years before the industry, as a whole, began to recover. As prices fell, so did wages; huge numbers of estate labourers were thrown into unemployment and once again (the first time being between 1919 and 1923) the government was obliged to finance large-scale and costly repatriation schemes. Financial losses suffered by investors were also very heavy. However, at the same time the Great Depression acted as an effective spur towards reorganization and efficiency and had a healthy effect on the industry as a whole. A thorough if painful pruning of costs took place; better tapping systems were effected, higher yielding crops introduced, improved processing machinery installed, higher productivity per labourer achieved and many other long-needed economies brought about.[36]

The impact of the Depression soon convinced Malayan planters of the necessity for a new restriction plan, and this time producers in the Netherlands Indies were more favourably inclined. The resultant International Rubber Regulation Agreement signed in 1934 was undoubtedly of great benefit to the rubber industry as a whole but, in practice, proved again more advantageous to Malaya's rivals than to Malaya herself as a result of the peculiarities of the quota system. To implement it, the F.M.S. government created the post of Controller of Rubber to assess estate and smallholder production. The smallholders suffered most from the restrictive practices now adopted, an effect which might well have been deliberate. Whatever the case, the smallholder contribution to world production declined, and since the Agreement could be and was more rigorously enforced in Malaya than elsewhere, the Malayan smallholder presumably got the worst deal of all.[37]

The rise of the palm-oil industry

In the wake of rubber came the oil palm. Born in 1917 as rubber planters faltered under the growing pressure of their first real recession, fifty years later palm-oil ranked fourth in value amongst Malaya's exports. From the outset palm-oil was solely an estate product, the manner of processing being far too complex and the costs far too high for any smallholder.

Like rubber, the Malayan origins of the oil palm are to be traced to the Botanical Gardens of Singapore where in the 1860s some seeds of the plant were brought over from Ceylon. There they were sown, grew and languished for forty years, waiting for their Ridley and serving their time as ornamental shrubs. The new demand for vegetable oils at the end of the century gave the oil palm its first opening in the region. One year after the first exclusively oil palm estate was started in Sumatra (1911), the F.M.S. Department of Agriculture at Serdang started planting the crop and a number of rubber planters in Selangor also began experiments on their own estates. One of these, Henri Fauconnier, became the first man to open up in 1917 a plantation devoted wholly to oil palm in the Peninsula, 'spurred on' by his old friend Adrian Hallet, who was already meeting with success on his Sumatran holdings. In this way from its earliest days the Malayan industry was closely associated with the great Franco-Belgian firm of Socfin.[38]

The opening of Fauconnier's estate ushered in the first phase of the industry's evolution in the Peninsula, characterized by a rapid increase in the area under cultivation though a much slower growth in production. By 1926 there were 19 estates in the country, all within the borders of the F.M.S. and Johore, concentrated at the most favourable points along the main road or railway and deriving full advantage from the amenities which the rubber industry had served to create. In the late 1920s the rate of expansion accelerated markedly under the stimulus of fresh encouragement from the Department of Agriculture, so much so that between 1927 and 1932 the acreage under oil palm doubled.

The second phase of expansion between 1930 and 1941 saw a slowing down in the rate of planting and a rapid rise in output, as the trees planted earlier came to maturity. In 1934 palm-oil exports stood at five times their figure for 1930. Unfortunately this sudden cornucopia coincided with a drastic fall in prices, which, as an official commission of enquiry elicited, was brought about by an untimely series of factors little related to the Great Depression.[39] The obvious solution lay in reducing costs, the greatest single contributory factor to which was the expense of transportation. In 1931 Socfin pioneered a breakthrough by starting to ship its oil in bulk. In 1933, when the first direct shipment to Europe took place, work was commenced on oil storage installations at Port Swettenham (Port Klang). By 1936 most of the Malayan palm-oil was being exported in this fashion, bringing down costs and enabling the industry to weather the first effects of the oil recession. In the same year the recession itself came to an end as fortuitously as it had begun, so that the industry resumed its expansion both in planting and in capital investment. The industry's growth rate proved to be the fastest of all the major producers, and although Malaya continued to rank fourth, her contribution to the world market rose by 11 per cent between 1930 and 1940. Ownership was entirely in European hands and Socfin, whose acreage amounted to one-quarter of all the oil palm planted in the Peninsula, stood head and shoulders above the rest.

Compared to rubber, the oil palm industry occupied a far inferior place in the Malayan economy before 1941, but it intensified the European stake in the country and further accentuated the development of the western side of the Peninsula. The final consolidation of Western economic supremacy was completed by the rise of European predominance in tin.

Tin in the twentieth century

The creation of the Federated Malay States in 1896 appeared to usher in a new era for tin, for from that time until 1914 there was an ever-rising demand for the metal which the world's available resources were unable to meet. During this period Malayan tin output doubled. By far the greatest part of this spectacular increase came from Perak, in particular the Kinta Valley, which was now the world's most productive field. Selangor, on the other hand, reached the peak of its production in 1894 and Negri Sembilan ten years later. In Pahang, where mining was virtually synonymous with the progress of the Pahang Corporation, the two largest tin lodes in the world were being worked at Sungai Lembing. At the same time the industry itself underwent a number of important modifications. New techniques were introduced, old mining methods changed, and there was a growing involvement by the government in the running and management of the industry. These changes were partly the consequences of the depressed tin prices between 1896 and 1899 and they played an important part in the promotion of Western enterprise at the expense of that of the Chinese. In 1906 Western mines accounted for about 10 per cent of Malaya's total output; by 1920 the figure amounted to 30 per cent.

The great increase in government intervention in the industry, often directly in support of Western entrepreneurs, was undoubtedly a major factor in the Western rise and the Chinese decline in the industry. But the Chinese also suffered from built-in defects in their own organization, including a perennial shortage of capital and their inability to adapt sufficiently to meet changing circumstances.

Changing circumstances created the need for more capital. By 1900 most of the superficial, easily-worked tin deposits in the Peninsula had become exhausted while no new rich fields had been brought to light. The only alternative was to re-work abandoned mines, digging deeper to extract the ore. At first Chinese miners relied on their own ingenuity and improvizations, such as the *ta-lung* system of the 1890s, to meet their new problems but all their attempts to overcome the problem of getting the ores to the surface as the mines went deeper failed, making Western equipment and a greater capital outlay indispensable. The answer was found to lie with Western steam-powered winding gears and other mechanical devices. In a parallel development, the old water-wheel gave way steadily during the first decade of the twentieth century to the steam-engine. After 1907 the use of mechanical power spread rapidly amongst Chinese miners. Between 1900 and 1914 several other new techniques were introduced, including dredging which was to transform the industry. But largely for reasons of cost these did not interest the Chinese miners, who turned to hydraulicing almost wholesale. In fact the increased need for Western technology in tin-mining at the turn of the century was a decisive factor in the relative decline of the Chinese share in the industry.[40]

Dredging originated in Australia. In 1912 the newly formed Malayan Tin Dredging Company introduced the first bucket dredge into the country. The subsequent rise of bucket-dredging reshaped the industry and gave to Western enterprise the lion's share for the first time. For despite the high capital outlay and expert supervision necessary, which excluded Chinese participation from the very start, the new dredges could operate in swampy and virtually undrainable land, handling vast quantities of soil which made the mining of low grade tin land, uneconomic by Chinese methods, a paying proposition.

The Chinese suffered another severe setback with the loss of their monopoly over smelting which they had held unchallenged up till the formation of the Straits Trading Company in 1887. The smelting monopoly was crucial since in the last analysis it was the smelters who controlled the tin industry as a whole, being identified with the advancers of the capital which made it possible to open up and run the mines. The close links between Chinese smelters and advancers in the industry had made it extremely difficult for European competitors to establish a foothold. However, in the late 1870s Chinese smelting was shaken by rising fuel costs and by official action against certain of their practices.[41] It was in such circumstances that the Straits Trading Company, the first Western enterprise in the smelting industry, was able to make its way. Within twenty years the new firm was smelting 70 per cent of Malaya's total tin output (itself one-third of the whole of world production). This success wa partly due to the attractive terms the firm was able to offer for tin ore and to the advantages of being able to smelt on a large scale outside the Malay States themselves, but Straits Trading owed an even larger debt to the Bitish state administrations and the Colony for receiving the means with which to outride the considerable Chinese opposition. But although Straits Trading flourished and the Chinese monopoly over the smelting industry vanished forever, Chinese participation was by no means eliminated. In 1914 the Chinese share in smelting still amounted to 15 per cent, the rest being dominated by two British concerns.

Apart from rising costs, failing deposits and technological changes, Chinese tin miners found their problems multiplied by other factors towards the end of the nineteenth century. First and foremost was the problem of labour. The great fluctuations in tin prices in the 1890s not only raised technological costs but created growing difficulties over the recruitment of labour. The years of recession led to a falling off of recruitment from China, then after 1896 when the tin price rose and labour was once more in demand, it became hard to come by. With labour at a premium, it also became more difficult to control. The breaking of the influence of the old secret societies, especially after 1891, and changes in the structure of tin-mining itself, first evident in Kinta, altered the relationship between the mineowner and his labour force.[42] As a result, basic labour costs rose, adding greatly to the expenses of mining. On top of all this came increasing legislative interference by the various British authorities, some of which, such as the Perak Mining Code of 1895, was designed to protect developing Western interests and some inspired by more humanitarian considerations. While the Labour Code of 1895 was a great step forward towards preventing undue exploitation and guaranteeing certain minimum conditions of work, it inevitably raised mining costs still further. The abolition of the revenue farms (the farms for pawnbroking and spirits were abolished in 1909 and that for gambling in 1912) also adversely affected the Chinese miners and their whole credit system, for the farms had been of great value to them as a means of indirect profit which had made it possible for them to weather years of recession and to maintain otherwise uneconomic mines. The most serious blow, however, from the mineowners' point of view was the imposition of government control in 1910 over the importation, preparation and sale of opium. In fact, the year 1910 marked a turning point for the Chinese tin industry in the Peninsula. While it was a 'fairly successful year' for Western companies, Chinese miners were 'less active'. In the years that followed, many Chinese mines failed to pay their way despite good market prices. By 1929 over half the tin production of Malaya was in European hands. By 1936 the Chinese share of total production had dropped to 36 per cent, but 81 per cent of the total labour force in all mines (i.e. European and Asian owned) was still Chinese.

Up till 1914, the great bulk of all tin-mining was confined to the Federated Malay States.

After 1914 the Malayan tin industry became increasingly mechanized and its operations more and more efficiently run and controlled. The most significant development was in the growth of dredging which advanced so rapidly that by 1927 it accounted for nearly one-third and by 1937 for one-half of total output. Requiring large capital outlay and skilled techniques, dredging remained an exclusively European affair and was the chief cause for the European ascendancy in tin in the twentieth century. Mechanization was also carried out in other fields. The great open cast mines, once solely a Chinese preserve, were completely mechanized during the 1920s and 1930s, with Western companies opening up new mines for the first time. Although accounting for a relatively small percentage of total production, hydraulicing, dominated by the gravel pump, became virtually a Chinese monopoly. In a reverse of nineteenth-century roles, after the 1920s many Chinese took to leasing parts of European concessions and paying tribute on the proceeds, since gravel pumping was most profitably used on areas worked over by dredges. The main technical innovations during these years came from Cornwall, Australia and the United States.

As the easily accessible deposits in the Peninsula were exploited, the need to locate and demarcate new fields was met by the Geological Survey Department, while the Mines Department continued to supervise the industry in general, dealing with the apportionment of water supplies, the problem of silt and 'tailings' and seeing to the enforcement of safety regulations and like measures. The F.M.S. Mining Enactment of 1935 rationalized government policy and the principles upon which it was based.[43]

The continued pace of technological advance and the high capital costs involved in equipment and maintenance tended towards the inevitable consolidation of Western control over the industry and its concentration in the hands of inter-locking financial concerns. In this process, as was the case with the rubber industry, an important part was played by the managing agencies of the Straits Settlements, particularly in the 1930s. Chinese mining, however, lay completely outside these combines.

In 1929, a peak year for tin production, Malaya produced around 37 per cent of total world tin output. However dependence on the American market meant that the Great Depression came as a very great blow when it struck in 1929. Fluctuating prices and recessions were characteristic of the industry but during the 1920s pressures caused by over-production had been building up and after 1926 the tin price had been steadily slipping. The first attempts to deal with the Great Depression were made locally by closing all applications for mining land. This was followed by efforts to limit production on a voluntary basis but this proved to be impracticable. Finally in 1931 came the first International Tin Agreement, signed by the British government on behalf of Malayan tin producers. The Agreement and its implementation aroused much hostility in mining circles. The general complaint was that the country's capacity had been seriously, if not deliberately, under-assessed. Prospecting came almost to a standstill and the further growth of the industry was prevented.[44] On the other hand, the Malayan industry suffered far less than it would have done had there been no restriction at all. After 1933 the tin price started to pick up satisfactorily and as the shadows of the Second World War lengthened, world market prices were not far off their 1920 figures and the industry as a whole was in a healthy condition.

Communications in the twentieth century

The Peninsula's infrastructure of rail and road had been laid at the dictates of the tin industry and the network already woven was a major factor in determining the location of the new rubber plantations. As a result the bulk of the new communications continued to be concentrated on the western side of the country. The 1900s saw the completion of the west coast railway and the rapid multiplication of roads in the west coast states where the rubber boom was at its height. Between 1911 and 1929 this road network was extended to link up with Singapore in the south and with Alor Star and Kangar in the north. During the same period the east coast railway was opened (1931), an epic achievement carried out at high cost, and Singapore Island was joined to the mainland at Johore Bahru by a stone causeway which carried both road and rail (1925). The onset of the Depression terminated further schemes of expansion.

After 1931 road development was aimed at breaking the isolation of the east coast states and in serving areas not reached by rail. By 1941 Kelantan had been linked to Pahang by a coast road from Kota Bharu, while in Johore new roads ran up the state's two coastlines.

As had been the case in the nineteenth century, the financing of rail and road construction was basically met from the revenues of tin and now rubber. The railways were the property of the F.M.S. government which therefore bore the brunt of the cost. Fortunately the profitability which had characterized railway operations in the Peninsula from the beginning continued without a break up till 1929. The Depression brought about a rapid drop in receipts and in 1931 the F.M.S. Railways experienced their first deficit. It was not until 1934 that a new surplus was achieved and railway traffic never regained its previous heights. Increasing sums of money had to be spent on renovations and maintenance and the competition from the roads, already significant in the 1920s, had become a serious matter. On the west coast the road network was good enough to provide an excellent alternative to rail and enterprising Chinese entrepreneurs were providing the services of fleets of lorries, mosquito buses and taxis. This growth of road traffic also affected the coastal steamship business and hastened the decay of the Peninsula's newborn ports. The burden of road development, however, was borne by the individual states; this meant that the more undeveloped ones lagged behind.

In the 1930s eight civil aerodromes were built, all of them on the west coast. Wearne's Air Services pioneered the first internal passenger flights in 1936 and Alor Star became the first Malayan port of call on an international air route in 1933. By 1941 the Peninsula was served by trunk telephone lines which linked all the main centres on the west coast and radio broadcasting had been in operation for over a decade.

Rice in the twentieth century
The drive to expand rice cultivation at the end of the nineteenth century wilted in the heat of the rubber boom which followed. The newly established padi experimental station at Titi Serong in Krian was understaffed and its officers not conversant enough in Malay to be able to persuade 'a conservative and easy-going peasantry' to improve their methods, while the equally new research branch of the Agricultural Department at Serdang in Selangor, preoccupied with the problems of rubber planters, had no rice research specialists at all. In the general euphoria created by the rubber boom there were many officials who opined that rice production should be left to other lands. However, the impact of the region-wide rice shortage at the end of the Great War caused a change of attitude,[45] and the policy of promoting Malay padi agriculture was revived. In 1917 the F.M.S. Rice Lands Enactment empowered the British Resident to forbid the cultivation of any crop other than rice on Malay-held lands and the following year the general F.M.S. Land Enactment of 1911 was amended so as to prohibit the alienation of any state land suitable for rice cultivation (with or without irrigation) for any other purpose. The new policy was reaffirmed in 1919 by a report in its favour by Dr. Butler, the Director of the Imperial Agricultural Institute at Pusa, in India, on whose recommendations the scope of the Agricultural Department's

work on padi was increased. Research into various strains of padi commenced at Titi Serong in 1915 was now supplemented by the opening of a new padi experimental station in Malacca in 1921, while Butler's main proposal that a separate organization be established to deal with rubber so that the Department could concentrate on other crops, above all rice, eventually led to the creation of the Rubber Research Institute.

But although some progress was made, especially with regard to improved rice strains, the campaign to promote and extend rice cultivation was not very successful prior to 1930. Although the Krian and Malacca stations had established sixteen pedigree strains of rice by 1925 and yields had increased by over 30 per cent by the beginning of the 1930s, the Malayan rice industry as a whole had not taken off at all. In 1924 a committee was appointed to take up the British Resident of Selangor's suggestion of 1895 that the swamps of Tanjong Karang be converted into a new rice-bowl, but work on this project did not actually begin until 1940. The rival attractions of rubber and coconuts were still too strong in the 1920s. The drainage and irrigation of rice lands—apart from Krian—remained inadequate for want of money, and the admirable enactments passed in all the Malay States to ensure that rice was grown on the lands for which it was designated were rarely enforced during this period. The fact that the Department of Agriculture itself was headed by a civil servant instead of a specialist together with the frequency of promotions and transfers hindered the formation and implementation of a coherent policy. The most significant development of the decade was that the promotion of rice agriculture became irreversibly identified with the British administrations' 'pro-Malay' policy.

As a result of the Great Depression, in the 1930s, the British authorities became 'obsessed' with the idea of stepping up rice production and for the first time self-sufficiency in rice was proclaimed the official goal. The 1931 report of the Tempany Committee, appointed to go into the question, proposed strict controls over the growing of rubber on rice lands, the placing of water control under a separate department, an increase in research and field work on padi and steps to break the stranglehold of price-fixing mill owners. The committee's recommendations resulted in the creation of the Drainage and Irrigation Department in 1932. The new department quickly provided testimony to the accuracy of the Tempany Committee's observations on the importance of water control and within the next five years added over 40,000 acres to existing irrigation schemes in the F.M.S. and the Straits Settlements, cleared 17,000 acres of swamp and jungle in north-west Selangor and launched the important Sungai Manik project in Lower Perak. Other measures to promote rice cultivation after 1931 included the appointment of specialists to the Department of Agriculture, the establishment of government rice mills, the extension of co-operatives and rural credit, and the opening of more experimental stations and testing beds. In consequence rice production was raised sufficiently for imports for domestic consumption to drop by 10 per cent within the decade. In terms of people employed and acreage taken up, rice cultivation came next to rubber; but it was a poor second. At world level the Peninsula remained a most insignificant producer.

Coconut

After rubber, coconut products—mostly in the forms of coconut oil and copra—were Malaya's most important agricultural export. In 1937 coconut products rated third in value as exports—though only a fraction compared to the earnings from tin and rubber—ranked third in terms of acreage and fourth in terms of manpower. Around 1935 over one-third of the total area under coconut in the Peninsula was to be found in the coastal districts of the F.M.S. and Johore. Malaya was the world's fourth largest exporter of coconut products.

The coconut was primarily a smallholders' crop grown mostly by Malaysians. For this reason the industry received the early attention of the government. The control of coconut pests and diseases was begun in 1902 and the Coconut Inspection Staff of the Department of Agriculture was set up not long afterwards. In 1919 the Department acquired an estate for research purposes and in 1924 a Coconut Experiment Station at Klang was established. One-third of the total acreage in the Peninsula was the property of large estates. European interests emanated from Singapore towards the end of the nineteenth century, one of the first plantations being opened up near Port Dickson in 1896 by a German merchant resident in the Colony. After this date, coconut planting in the F.M.S. expanded quite rapidly. By 1910 there were a quarter of a million acres under the crop, which represented the maximum extent it was to acquire.

In the 1920s and 1930s coconut planters, along with all the producers of natural and vegetable oils, were confronted with severe difficulties caused by price fluctuation and decline. By 1926 the price of copra had sunk to a level that was uneconomic for estate and smallholder alike. The threat thus posed to the future of some 165 estates and the livelihood of over 300,000 smallholders caused the setting up of an official committee of enquiry in 1934 which, in its report, pointed to the inferior quality of Malayan copra and recommended that special efforts be made to improve it. As a result of the steps subsequently taken to raise the quality, by 1938 much of Malayan copra had achieved a higher quality than its rival product from the Netherlands Indies.

By this time a general recovery in world prices had taken place, although the golden days of the beginning of the century never returned. By 1937 the value of Malayan coconut exports had nearly reached the 1930 figures but the amount produced was twice as great. By 1939 coconut oil exports surpassed the 1930 level five times but this too was offset by much lower prices and by the fact that part of this figure included re-exports from the Indies.

Pineapple

Pineapple was the only other significant crop in the Peninsula prior to 1941. Entirely in Chinese hands, the industry ranked third in value amongst Malayan agricultural exports and although planted only in Perak, Selangor and Johore covered over 75,000 acres. Malaya was the second largest exporter of tinned pineapples in the world.[46]

The original stimulus for pineapple growing came from Singapore towards the end of the nineteenth century, led by Europeans who set up the first canning factories on the island in 1888. These were soon taken over by Chinese who had gained a whip hand by opening up plantations. The extension of pineapple growing to the mainland followed in the 1900s, closely linked to the rise of rubber. Pineapples served as an excellent catch crop in the rubber groves, were hardy, provided quick returns and were suited to all types of soil. Up till the end of the 1920s pineapples continued in this role and production expanded almost unchecked. The success of the industry lay in its cheapness. Completely dominated by the canners who monopolized the market, the growers received a pittance for their produce. The 'factories' where the fruit was canned were primitive sheds and all the work was done by hand. Freight costs were minimal since the plantation areas were all within easy reach of either Singapore or Port Swettenham (Port Klang).

However, these cheap methods eventually backfired. The ban on the further alienation of land for rubber spelt the end of the pineapple's career as a catch crop. Between 1929 and 1934 the area planted with pineapples as a sole crop rose from one-eighteenth to three-fifths of the whole, a transformation which implied that much more care had to be taken over cultivation as well as over canning and grading. A report by the Pineapple Conference, convened under government auspices in 1931, recommended official assistance in the form of research, the establishment of estates, laws to ensure better working conditions, better techniques, certain uniform standards and more publicity. As a result research into pineapple cultivation was started at Serdang and two new pineapple experimental stations were set up. In 1934 the registration of factories and their periodic inspection was introduced and the following year a Canning Research Officer was appointed. By 1937 two-thirds of the area under pineapple was planted as a sole crop. However, over-production and cut-throat competition brought about a drastic fall in prices the next year (1938) and in 1939 the industry entered into a new phase with the passing of an ordinance establishing a Central Control Board and limiting the building of new factories.

Other products
As for other crops, tea, tobacco, fruits and vegetables were also grown and had some local importance. Tea was grown with the most success, particularly in the Cameron Highlands of west Pahang. Tobacco growing was older established and more widespread and from the 1920s onwards smallholders planting this crop received the encouragement of the Department of Agriculture. The Department between 1919 and 1939 operated twenty-eight experimental stations throughout the Peninsula which *inter alia* conducted research, demonstrations and supplied materials for various crops, though not too much progress was made or was to be expected while rubber retained its predominance.

Amongst minerals, apart from tin, only iron had any economic importance before 1941. The principal deposits worked were in Trengganu and Johore, exploited by Japanese interests which shipped the ore direct back to Japan. Some coal was mined in Selangor and Perak. Small deposits of gold—most from the Raub district—tungsten (wolfram and scheelite) in Perak and

Trengganu, manganese, bauxite (from south-east Johore) and ilmenite were also mined for export.

Forest and timber products

Although three-quarters to four-fifths of the Peninsula is covered by forest or jungle, forest products and the timber industry played only a small part in the pre-1941 economy. The bulk of the forest lands in the east coast states were valueless because of their inaccessibility, while on the west coast the activities of the Chinese tin miners in their search for fuel for their smelting furnaces became so destructive in the second half of the nineteenth century that although government acted in time to preserve sufficient reserves in Perak and Negri Sembilan, in Selangor the reserved area soon proved inadequate for future needs. A small forestry department was set up in 1883, on the recommendation of Fred McNair, the Colonial Engineer and Surveyor-General, under the control of the Director of the Botanical Gardens, Singapore, its prime task being to establish forest reserves. In 1911 a separate Forestry Department for the F.M.S. and the Straits Settlements was created under a Chief Forestry Officer. Under the guidance of this new department, the area of declared forest reserves was gradually extended. In 1915 this amounted only to 6.6 per cent of the total forest area but after 1918 the area was increased despite the opposition of planting and mining interests so that by 1938 well over a quarter of the forest land in the F.M.S. consisted of reserves.

But exploitation was slow. In 1918, largely through the efforts of Cubitt, the Chief Forestry Officer, for the expansion and elaboration of the work of his department, a Forest Research Officer was appointed, followed three years later by the initiation of training courses. The Department's establishment was enlarged in 1925, a School of Forestry founded at Kepong in 1927 and timber research laboratories set up at Sentul in 1929 to test Malayan woods for commercial purposes. In the meanwhile activity in the non-F.M.S. was bolstered by the creation of the various state forestry departments between 1920 and 1935.

As for those unreserved lands still under state control by virtue of not having been alienated, the main problem was to prevent the wastage of valuable timber before alienation took place. At the same time only limited progress was being made in the direction of developing commercial enterprise out of the timber resources of the Peninsula. It was only in the 1930s that saw-milling became established, though it quickly rose up to become one of the country's most important secondary industries.

---

[1]The reasons for the re-emergence of Straits tin lay primarily in Bangka's inability to cope with the rising demand from European consumers. At the same period the British market was also opening for the first time. In 1842 the British Parliament reduced the tariffs on tin imports, a measure of direct benefit to miners in the Malay Peninsula since preference was given to tin importers through British territories; in 1853 duties on tin imports into the United Kingdom were repealed altogether.

[2]The key to all mining operations was water and the want or the excess of it raised great

problems for the miners. As such Chinese inventions like the deep drain, the chain-pump and the *lanchut kechil* in nineteenth-century mining operations were very important. See Wong Lin-ken, *The Malayan Tin Industry to 1914*, University of Arizona Press, Tucson, 1965, pp. 48–50.

[3]The Penang pikul was 8 per cent lighter than the Perak weight.

[4]Provisions and supplies for miners remained expensive because the government failed to reduce tin duties in conformity with falling market prices and because of the continued existence of many other miscellaneous duties such as on opium, rice, tobacco and oil. This matter was the subject of a petition to the government from Yap Ah-loy in 1879.

[5]For details regarding the *kongsi* and tribute systems of mining and the financing and organization of Chinese mining in the nineteenth century in general, see Wong, op. cit., pp. 60–4.

[6]Wong, ibid., p. 63.

[7]Wong, ibid., p. 40.

[8]Raffles and Newbold both declare that the Malays were the principal miners in the Peninsula at this period but Dutch sources suggest that even at this stage the Chinese were mainly responsible for the mining and exporting of tin from Perak and Selangor. That the mining activities carried out in Lukut, Sungai Ujong and later on in Larut were done with Chinese capital and labour raised by the local Malay territorial chief is well known; the Malay chiefs also as a rule monopolized food supplies and provisions for the labourers until the establishment of British administration enabled Chinese to hold land in their own right.

[9]For examples of this, see Wong, op. cit., p. 46 and see also Chai Hon-chan, *The Development of British Malaya, 1896–1909*, Oxford University Press, Kuala Lumpur, 1964, p. 178, note 62.

[10]For further details of this episode, see Wong, op. cit., p. 123 et seq.

[11]The principal farms were in pawnshops, gambling, spirits and opium. The periodic auctioning of the farms gave the authorities the opportunity to promote the development of specific districts by setting up farms in them in order to attract fresh capital. This technique was used in Perak in 1880 with the creation of a new opium farm to woo the capitalists of Penang; a few years later Selangor opened up the revenue farms of the Klang Valley to Penang financiers in order to attract new money into the capital-starved industry. Both moves achieved their aims.

[12]Competition on the labour market became acute in the 1880s, in particular as the planters of the Culture Zone of East Sumatra formed an association (1881) to recruit labourers directly from its source in South China and as, after 1883, the demand for Chinese labour from the Straits Settlements for the new domains of the British North Borneo Company made a decisive impact for the first time. In the 1890s the problem became more acute by the great extension of public works, particularly on road and rail construction, and by the growing needs of coffee and sugar agriculture.

[13]The need for and importance of Chinese labour had always been obvious to British administrators. For telling quotes, see Emily Sadka, *The Protected Malay States, 1874–95*, University of Malaya Press, Kuala Lumpur, 1968, p. 50 and Eunice Thio, *British Policy in the Malay Peninsula, 1880–1910*, Vol. I, University of Malaya Press, Singapore, 1969, p. 180.

[14]Chai Hon-chan, op. cit., p. 187.

[15]i.e. the network of Malay petty tolls and taxes on all forms of goods and products entering and leaving the country were swept away. As for the new cash crops, pepper and gambier were taxed in all the states, coffee in Sungai Ujong when it was first planted and later on in Perak and Selangor as well. Tapioca was only taxed in Sungai Ujong, in some of the other Menangkabau states and in Selangor. Sugar which acquired some importance in Perak in the 1880s and 1890s was apparently never taxed at all.

[16]'Old Negri Sembilan' consisted of the Menangkabau states of Rembau, Tampin, Jelebu and Sri Menanti which with British prompting formed a federation in 1889. Refer to Book I, pp. 164–5.

[17]By the *kang-chu* system, each settlement of Chinese planters held and worked its land by virtue of a 'surat sungai' granted to it by the Johore government in the name of the Temenggong. The headman, in whose name the land was held, was known as the *kang-chu* or 'lord of the river' and was in charge of all that went on in his settlement and for the construction and maintenance of paths and the clearing of the river in return for the payment of rent or taxes due from the settlement. By virtue of these responsibilities, the *kang-chu* held the key to a fortune—he was granted the opium and gambling farms, and held exclusive rights over pawnbroking, the sale of liquor, the slaughtering of pigs and sale of pork—perquisites which were as important and as lucrative to pioneer Chinese agriculturalists as they were to Chinese miners. The land covered by the grant was known as a *kangkar*, which actually referred to both the headquarters of the settlement and to the plantations worked on. The area of a *kangkar* ranged from 2,500 acres to 20,000 acres but any Malay villages or properties within its compass were not to be disturbed or even traded with. The term *bangsal* referred strictly to the ground actually planted with gambier and pepper, with its gambier cauldron and furnaces; such plots averaged between 10 and 50 acres in size. The term 'plantation' was more loosely applied to any patch of land where pepper or gambier was planted.

[18]Refer to p. 152.

[19]The death blow to widespread tapioca planting was probably the abolition of indentured Chinese labour in 1914 which took away the source of cheap labour on which the plantations depended.

[20]J.C. Jackson, *Planters and Speculators: Chinese and European Agricultural Enterprise in Malaya, 1786–1921*, University of Malaya Press, Kuala Lumpur, 1971, p. 172.

[21]Coffee cultivation was labour intensive. The plantations had to be clean-weeded and the plants pruned and handpicked during the two main seasons of the year, while smaller crops ripened the whole year round. On the pioneer estates in Selangor this was found to demand a labour force of 40 to 60 for each 100 acres but the workers were hard to come by. The Malays were not interested in that kind of labour, the Chinese were taken up by their tin-mines. Some Javanese labour was imported but European planters naturally preferred Tamils whom they were used to from their days in Ceylon.

[22]i.e. it led to the introduction of European planters into the country and familiarized them with local conditions: the opening up of virgin land, the evolution of a favourable land policy, the development of a subsidiary network of roads and cart-tracks, and the facilitation of labour immigration cleared the way for rubber planting when the time came. The high capital costs of coffee planting also stimulated the growth of the organization which was greatly to assist the expansion of rubber planting a few years later, since in most cases planters had to turn for financial support to business houses in Singapore, which subsequently developed into 'agency-houses' managing their affairs. Furthermore the presence of the European planters in the country led to the formation of the Planters' Association which was to play an important part in the years to come in shaping the course of the rubber industry.

[23]In theory this type of immigration was open to all races. In 1883 Swettenham was advocating the introduction of Chinese rice-farmers with government assistance if necessary; a few years later the district officer of Kuala Langat was contemplating the importation of Burmese and Thai farmers on a large scale to till the soil. But in practice the response from others besides Malaysians was very limited.

[24]For a full discussion of the controversy around this issue, see Sadka, op. cit., pp. 360–2.

[25]The most serious deviation from Maxwell's original intentions regarding land tenure was the sweeping aside of the provision that customary tenure was applicable to Muslims only.

[26]This was against a background of the mounting resentment amongst other Western powers at the colonial hegemony of Britain which found overt expression in the widespread support for the Boers against the British in the South African War at the end of the century. Another source of British concern was the rising might of imperial Germany and its new navy.

[27]This was despite the fact that various efforts to promote rubber had been made for over

half a generation in the Malay Peninsula. Ridley's efforts to promote rubber amongst the coffee planters of the day won him ridicule and on at least one occasion an official rebuke from the governor who told him to desist from growing 'exotics'.

[28]In the case of Trengganu, another important factor was the complete absence of any suitable land regulations prior to the 1920s.

[29]By this time the United States consumed 77 per cent of world production, while 63 per cent of estate production on the world market came from the Peninsula.

[30]A common process in the early days was for a planter by himself or with friends to acquire a concession, plant it with rubber and then sell it to either an existing company or to one floated specifically for the purpose. In either case he usually ended up with a share in the company and remained as manager on the actual estate.

[31]In the spawning of the rubber companies a key role was played by the established European merchant-houses of the Straits Settlements which in consequence came to hold a dominating position in the industry as a whole. The planter in search of capital and the investor (in Britain) in search of his manager found their brokers in these local firms, thus giving rise to the 'typically Malayan arrangement' of managing-agency concerns. Malayan estate owners entered into a kind of partnership with them. The merchant-houses, with their connexions and access to the London money-market, were able to float companies with capital provided by local estate owners and investors in Britain. The merchant-house was then usually made the managing agent and secretary of the new company. In this way groups of estates linked to parent companies with their headquarters in London were managed by these Singapore concerns which provided the managers and the technical advice for the estates while supervising their financial administration. Often the merchant-house itself acquired a number of estates.

[32]In the case of Negri Sembilan and Johore the predominance of Chinese labour is accounted for by the fact that Chinese agriculturalists had already been prominent on the scene for decades, while the rival pull of tin was either not so great or non-existent. In the case of Kelantan the labour supply had always come from indentured Chinese labourers and continued to do so.

[33]The idea of restricting rubber production was first mooted by the Rubber Growers' Association in 1913 but the swift recovery of the market under wartime conditions killed the proposal. The idea was resurrected by the much severer crisis of 1918, but when the Great War ended later the same year government lost interest and all plans were shelved. With the onset of the Little Depression which followed, it was left to private enterprise to make the initial attempts at a voluntary restriction scheme.

[34]United States rubber purchasers considered they were being held to ransom by Malayan producers and readily transferred their custom to cheaper producers elsewhere.

[35]No smallholder interests were represented on any of the bodies set up to discuss restriction. Their ability to survive was because of their far lower overheads; in the 1920s it was reckoned that an Asian smallholder bore a quarter of the expenses of the average European estate owner.

[36]In consequence high-cost producers in the Peninsula in 1932 could produce their rubber at a rate which was nearly half as low as that of a low-cost producer in 1929.

[37]Sir Neill Malcolm, the Chairman of the British North Borneo Company, reportedly declared in 1936 'that one of the primary objects of the Rubber Control Scheme was to protect European capital in plantation companies in Malaya, Borneo and the Netherlands East Indies from competition arising from the production of rubber by natives at a fraction of the cost involved on European estates'. (Quoted by Lim Chong-yah, *Economic Development of Modern Malaya*, Oxford University Press, Kuala Lumpur, 1967, p. 82.) Fear of rubber 'going native' was a very real one amongst the Europeans in the industry and the smallholders certainly did not stand to benefit from the Agreement which *inter alia* prohibited virtually all new planting and severely restricted re-planting —at first to 80 per cent of the planted area. There were of course strong arguments for the necessity of such restrictions, otherwise limiting production would surely fail as it had done under the Stevenson Plan because of increased output from newly planted

trees. Whatever the case, under the existing conditions of the International Rubber Regulation Agreement an estimate showed that the smallholders' contribution to total world production was on the decline and would continue to decline to half its original size within twenty years of 1939 if it continued.

[38]For the activities of Hallet, Fauconnier and the rise of Socfin in the Malay Peninsula, refer to J. Sig. D. Rawlins, 'French Enterprise in Malaya', *JMBRAS*, XXXIX, 2, 1966.

[39]Vegetable and animal oil production had been over-stimulated by exorbitant prices on the world market in the 1920s so that palm-oil and coconut-oil producers in Malaya, Sumatra and the Congo—not to mention whalers in the Antarctic and soya-bean farmers in Manchuria—had all rushed to produce more. When this new wave of production made itself felt, world consumption was already declining because of changes in eating habits and the rise of economic nationalism. The Commission also pointed out that restriction was no remedy because of the sheer impracticability of trying to control the production of such a wide range of natural oils.

[40]Chinese methods of raising capital were inadequate for meeting the new needs. See Wong, op. cit., p. 218 et seq. Hydraulicing underwent considerable technical improvement prior to 1914, with the introduction of the hydraulic elevator, the gravel pump and the pressure pump—all from Australia. Of these by far the most important was the gravel pump which became the most widely used method of mining in operation, right down to the present time.

[41]For a full discussion of the Chinese fuel problem and government steps, see Wong, op. cit., pp. 157-61.

[42]For details of this, see Wong, ibid., p. 179 et seq.

[43]The basic points laid down in the Enactment were (a) that minerals were the property of the state in which they were found; (b) that no prospecting could be carried out without licence; (c) that mining leases were for 21-year periods, with provisos for extension; (d) that the control of leases was vested in the individual states; (e) that federal revenues took the form of export duties.

[44]For a full discussion of the Agreement, its background and implications, see Lim, op. cit., p. 57 et seq.

[45]The shortage which affected the main rice producers in the region lasted from 1917 to 1921, affecting Malaya severely since it depended largely on rice imports. Prices shot up, estate and mine-owners had to subsidize their rice rations for their low-paid employees and rice rationing had to be introduced. Employers of labour were encouraged to plant their own foodstuffs and the government had to bear the costly burden of importing rice from Saigon and reselling it at reduced prices inside the country.

[46]However, Malaya lagged far behind Hawaii, the world's leading producer, whose output was twenty-eight times as great.

Books and articles for further reading

BOOKS

Allen, G.C., & Donnithorne, A.G., *Western Enterprise in Indonesia and Malaya*, George Allen & Unwin, London, 1954.

Chai Hon-chan, *The Development of British Malaya, 1896–1909*, Oxford University Press, Kuala Lumpur, 1964.

Chick, Sir Louis (ed.), *The Economic Development of Malaya*, Report by the World Bank, Government Printer, Singapore, 1955.

Cooke, E.M., *Rice Cultivation in Malaya*, Eastern Universities Press, Singapore, 1961.

Cowan, C.D. (ed.), *The Economic Development of South-East Asia*, George Allen & Unwin, London, 1964.

————, *Nineteenth Century Malaya: The Origins of British Political Control*,

Oxford University Press, London, 1961.

Emerson, R., *Malaysia: A Study in Direct and Indirect Rule*, University of Malaya Press, Kuala Lumpur, 1964 (reprint).

Fisher, C.A., *South-East Asia: A Social, Economic and Political Geography*, Methuen & Co. Ltd., London, 1964.

Gullick, J.M., *Indigenous Political Systems of Western Malaya*, The Athlone Press, London, 1958.

————, *Malaya*, London, Ernest Benn, 1963.

Jackson, J.C., *Planters and Speculators: Chinese and European Agricultural Enterprise in Malaya, 1786–1921*, University of Malaya Press, Kuala Lumpur, 1968.

Jackson, R.N., *Immigrant Labour and the Development of Malaya; 1786–1920*, Government Press, Kuala Lumpur, 1961.

Jacoby, E.H., *Agrarian Unrest in Southeast Asia*, Asia Publishing House, Bombay, 1961.

Khoo Kay Kim, *The Western Malay States; 1850–73: The Effects of Commercial Development on Malay Politics*, Oxford University Press, Kuala Lumpur, 1972.

Lim Chong-yah, *Economic Development of Modern Malaya*, Oxford University Press, Kuala Lumpur, 1967.

Loh Fook Seng, Philip, *The Malay States, 1877–1895: Political Change and Social Policy*, Oxford University Press, Singapore, 1969.

MacKenzie, L.E., *Malaya: Economic and Commercial Conditions in the Federation of Malaya and Singapore*, His Majesty's Stationery Office, London, 1952.

Mills, L.A., *British Rule in Eastern Asia*, Oxford University Press, London, 1942.

Purcell, V., *The Chinese in South-East Asia*, Oxford University Press, London, 1965.

Robequain, C., *Malaya, Indonesia, Borneo and the Philippines*, Longman Green, London, 1958.

Sadka, E., *The Protected Malay States; 1874–1895*, University of Malaya Press, Kuala Lumpur, 1968.

Sheppard, M., *A Short History of Negri Sembilan*, Eastern Universities Press, Singapore, 1965.

Silcock, T.H., & Fisk, E.K., *The Political Economy of Independent Malaya*, Eastern Universities Press, Singapore, 1963.

Steinberg, D.J. (ed.), *In Search of South-East Asia: A Modern History*, Oxford University Press, Kuala Lumpur, 1971.

Swettenham, Sir Frank, *British Malaya*, George Allen & Unwin, London, 1906.

Thio, E., *British Policy in the Malay Peninsula, 1880–1910: The Southern and Central States*, Vol. I, University of Malaya Press, Singapore, 1969.

Tregonning, K.G., *The British in Malaya: The first Forty Years, 1786–1826*, University of Arizona Press, Tucson, 1965.

Wong Lin-ken, *The Malayan Tin Industry to 1914*, University of Arizona Press, Tucson, 1965.

ARTICLES

Allen, J. de V., 'Two Imperialists', *JMBRAS*, XXXVII, 1, 1964.

Bonney, R., 'A Short History of Kuala Kubu Bahru', *JHSUM*, I, 1, 1960.

Cheng Siok-hwa, 'The Rice Industry of Malaya; A Historical Survey', *JMBRAS*, XXXXII, 2, 1969.

Chiang Hai-ding, 'The Origins of the Malayan Currency System', *JMBRAS*, XXXIX, 1, 1966.

Drabble, J.H., 'The Plantation Rubber Industry in Malaya', *JMBRAS*, XXXX, 1, 1967.

Griffiths, R.J., 'The Birth and Growth of Kluang in Johore', *MH*, 12.2.1969.

Gullick, J.M., 'Captain Speedy of Larut', *JMBRAS*, XXVI, 3, 1953.

Harrison, C.R., 'The First Forty Years of the Malayan Railway', *MH*, 4.1.1958.

————, 'The Last of the Creepers, I', *MH*, 7.1.1961.

————, 'The Last of the Creepers, II', *MH*, 7.2.1961.

Jackson, J.C., 'Batang Padang 90 Years Ago', *MH*, 10.1.1965.

————, 'Chinese Agricultural Pioneering in Singapore and Johore,' *JMBRAS*, XXXVIII, 1, 1965.

————, 'Kuala Lumpur in the 1880s', *JSEAH*, IV, 2, 1963.

————, 'Malay Mining Methods in Kinta', *MH*, 8.2.1964.

————, 'Malayan Tin Mining', *JSEAH*, IV, 2, 1963.

————, 'Rice Cultivation in West Malaysia', *JMBRAS*, XIV, 2, 1974.

————, 'Tapioca', *MH*, 10.2.1967.

Khoo, Gilbert, 'A History of Kuala Kota Muda', *JHSUM*, I, 1, 1960.

Laidin bin Alang Musa, 'The Background to the Ulu Langat Valley', *MHJ*, II, 1, 1955.

Loh, Philip, 'Social Policy in Perak', *PS*, 1.1.1966.

Middlebrook, S.M., 'Yap Ah-loy', *JMBRAS*, XXIV, 2, 1955.

Ramsay, A.B., 'Indonesians in Malaya', *JMBRAS*, XXIX, 1, 1956.

Ratnasingham, R.L., 'The Duff Syndicate in Kelantan; 1900–1902', *JMBRAS*, XXXXV, 1, 1973.

Rawlins, J. Sig. D., 'French Enterprise in Malaya', *JMBRAS*, XXXIX, 2, 1966.

Sharom Ahmat, 'The Structure of the Economy of Kedah: 1879–1905', *JMBRAS*, XXXXIII, 2, 1970.

Short, D.E., & Jackson, J.C., 'The Origins of an Irrigation Policy in Malaya: A Review of Development Prior to the Establishment of the Drainage and Irrigation Department', *JMBRAS*, XXXXIV, 1, 1971.

Sidhu, J.S., 'Railways in Selangor, 1882–1886', *JMBRAS*, XXXVIII, 1, 1965.

Turner, G.E., 'A Perak Coffee Planter's Report of 1902', *MH*, 2.1.1955.

Wayte, M.E., 'Port Weld, Larut', *JMBRAS*, XXXII, 1, 1959.

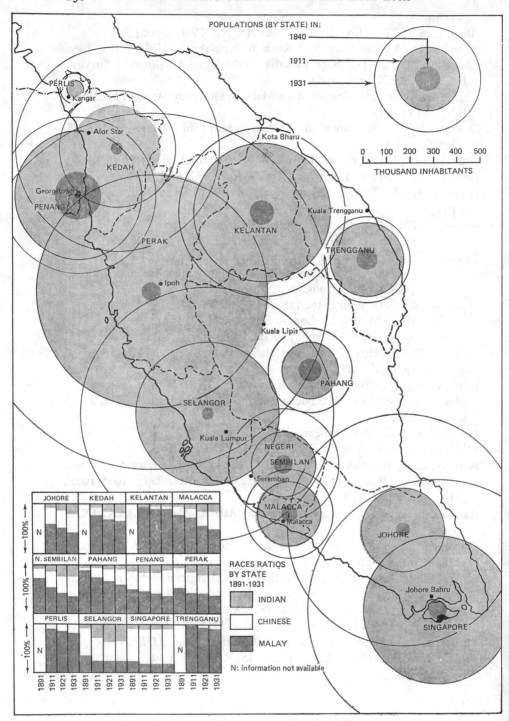

20.   British Malaya: Population Growth and Distribution, 1840–1941

(iii) THE STRAITS SETTLEMENTS AND THE PENINSULAR MALAY STATES

ALTHOUGH throughout the period of colonial rule the Straits Settlements and the Protected Malay States formed two distinct political entities and indeed economically fulfilled two distinctive roles, their close proximity resulted in the forging of inextricable bonds between them. This was particularly so in the realm of government administration and policy, especially with regard to immigration, labour, health and social welfare measures, and in the evolution of an education system.

Population growth and distribution

In terms of population the Straits Settlements served primarily as the funnel through which the new inhabitants of the Malay Peninsula poured. In the process both the Colony and the Malay States acquired polyglot communities which, created by the same general circumstances, became sharply differentiated by local conditions. In the Peninsula the mould of settlement and the phenomenal increase in numbers was largely determined by the tin and rubber industries. Malaya's population growth was at double the average rate for the region as a whole between 1830 and 1950 and reached its peak in the first decades of the twentieth century. The country absorbed the largest number of immigrants from outside of all the region, so much so that by 1931 the indigenous Malays no longer formed the majority amongst the total population of the Peninsula. The bulk of the new settlers and the great majority of the local inhabitants were to be found on the western side of the Peninsula where the tin-mines and rubber estates lay. The inhabitants of the Straits Settlements were equally as diverse but from the very beginning the Chinese occupied the dominant place amongst them. Two-thirds of the population of the Settlements were concentrated in Singapore whose startling growth rate was directly related to the rise of its trade.

The rapid rise in population in South-East Asia during the nineteenth and early twentieth centuries was brought about both by a great upsurge in natural increase and by massive immigration from outside—factors inherent in the spread of Western imperialism which, as Fisher points out,[1] established a new security for life and property and promoted new economic opportunities and development. In the case of the Straits Settlements and the Peninsular Malay States, immigration was by far the most important factor,[2] prompted by the liberal, *laissez-faire* policies of the British administration which made it possible for new-comers to pursue their interests and become rich without fear of arbitrary despoliation or expulsion. Tin made the Peninsula a land of opportunity, entry to which was already secured by the existence of the Colony whose inhabitants held in their hands the capital and machinery for development. The extension of British power after 1874 simply made conditions more favourable still. The rise of commercial agriculture, culminating in the birth of rubber, and general economic expansion necessitated the creation of an infrastructure of public works and of a communications network which created a 'voracious demand' for labour never fully satisfied until the 1930s for the tin states were the most sparsely populated of the whole Peninsula, and their Malay inhabitants eked out their lives at subsistence level. Their manpower was only available after the harvest season and their mobility was severely restricted by the almost total absence of communications. Even later in the century, as the country was being opened up, the Malays were not to be lured onto the tin-mines or into the rubber estates to work for foreign employers under the slave-like conditions that prevailed.

Since labour was not to be obtained locally, it was drawn from the 'inexhaustible reservoirs' of China, India and (to a much lesser degree) the islands of the archipelago. The first heavy immigration into the Peninsula was associated with the tin industry and became evident in the 1830s and the 1840s. After British intervention had taken place, the pace quickened immeasurably and the numbers, although fluctuating with demand and price, rose steadily. Commercial agriculture, a significant factor in the nineteenth century, played a major part in the twentieth. The peopling of Johore's interior was started by Chinese pepper and gambier planters but the main role was played by Indians, first in sugar and coffee and then in rubber. The peak period for Indian immigration was between 1900 and 1920, directly linked to the growth of the rubber industry, but Indians started coming on a large scale in the mid-1880s in response to the new programme of public works, especially road and rail construction, initiated by Swettenham and his contemporaries. As a result Perak and Selangor, which in 1800 were amongst the most poorly populated states of the Peninsula, had become the most heavily populated by the end of the century. After 1911, however, the most spectacular increases took place in Johore, spurred by the completion of the trunk railway (1909), the rapid spread of rubber planting which followed and by the later development of the palm-oil and pineapple industries. In general between 1911 and 1957 all the states of the Peninsula doubled or trebled their populations with the exceptions of Kelantan and Trengganu, which continued beyond the main stream of development prior to 1941.

Meanwhile in the Straits Settlements, growth rates varied from time to time according to changing circumstances. Penang led for the first half of the nineteenth century until Singapore caught up in the 1850s and finally won the lead between 1900 and 1910. Malacca's growth rate shot up after the 1870s and between 1900 and 1920 was faster than those of the other two as a consequence of the swift development in quick succession of the tapioca and rubber plantation industries.

The evolution of immigration policy

British policy towards immigration into the Straits Settlements and the Malay States was dictated primarily by economic considerations and was grounded in a pragmatic, *laissez-faire* outlook which went unaltered until 1928. Light and Raffles set the tone by welcoming and encouraging immigration as essential to the welfare and development of the Straits Settlements and for the first fifty years of their existence the matter was left entirely to private enterprise with no official intervention or control whatsoever. The

ever-increasing volume of immigration after 1850, however, led to the first
official measures of supervision, partly to check abuses in the recruitment and
treatment of labour but primarily to ensure an adequate flow of workers for
the tin fields (and later for the plantations) of the Malayan hinterland. British
intervention in the Malay States took place in the name of economic progress
because, in the last analysis, the Malays had failed to handle the problem of
Chinese immigration. Once in control, all British officials were agreed upon
the need for unrestricted immigration and most regarded the Chinese as indispensable. A generation of British Residents made the volume of Chinese
immigration into their states their barometer of progress, while the Malay
rulers of Johore went out of their way to foster Chinese immigration. Indian
immigration, on the other hand, was largely the outcome of pressure from
British officials and planters who had had connexions with India themselves.
The first attempts to improve the flow of labourers from South India in the
1880s came at the instance of European planters in Perak and Selangor and
enjoyed the support of Weld, who, as governor of the Straits Settlements, favoured Indian immigrants not only on economic but also on political grounds.
In general, the various British administrations in Malaya used all means to
facilitate both Chinese and Indian immigration with scant concern for the
possible social or political consequences.

   The outstanding characteristic of all immigration up till 1930 was its im-
permanence. Prior to that date Chinese and Indians were essentially birds of
passage, in their own estimation as much as in that of the indigenous inhabitants or of British officials—which in fact was what made a policy of unrestricted immigration either feasible or tolerable. In social terms this meant
that there was a great imbalance in sex ratios, with the males forming the
overwhelming majority.

Population patterns after 1930
The Great Depression of 1929 brought the era of unrestricted immigration
to an end forever, marking a watershed in the history of population growth
in the Straits and the Peninsula. As over half a million labourers were shipped
back to their homelands at government expense, measures were taken to
impose controls on the numbers coming into the country. The first of these
was the F.M.S. Immigration Restriction Ordinance of 1928 which empowered the authorities to restrict or prohibit immigration in times of emergency.
Put into practice for the first time in 1930, for both the Colony and the Malay States, it was followed three years later by the Aliens Ordinance which
placed restriction on a permanent basis. Under this legislation all immigration
was now subject to a quota system but up till 1938 restriction was only
applied to male immigrants. The Chinese community was the most affected
by the new controls and regarded them charged with political bias but in
fact their position as a permanent element in the country was consolidated.
The absence of any check on female immigration up to 1938 led to an unprecedented inrush of Chinese women into Malaya, stimulated still further by
the outbreak of the Sino-Japanese War in 1937. In consequence the sex ratio
for the Chinese normalized and the proportion of local-born Chinese amongst

the total resident Chinese population increased 'at a rate far more rapid than anyone could possibly have guessed thirty years ago'.[3] The Indian position, on the other hand, which was scarcely touched by the new immigration laws, was adversely affected by a ban on the emigration of unskilled Indian labourers to Malaya which was imposed by the Indian government itself in 1938. This measure, coupled with the effects of the Depression which had halted all private immigration for three years, crippled the growth of the Indian population in the Peninsula and virtually froze the Indian community into its present proportion. However, as was the case with the Chinese, in the long run the new circumstances after 1930 helped to promote a more stable Indian community in the country. The sex ratio likewise became more normal and the proportion of local-born Indians increased.

In general, the 1930s witnessed very important changes in the characteristics of the immigrant communities in the Straits Settlements and the Peninsula. Under the changed conditions imposed not only by immigration controls but also by effective international restriction of tin and rubber production and by the loss of overseas markets, these communities shrank a little but became at the same time more committed to the stake they had already acquired. Another significant development in this period was that for the first time under the British aegis, the proportionate decline in the Malay(sian) population was reversed.[4] As Silcock and Fisk have observed: 'In a sense the demographic foundations of modern Malaya were laid in the economic depression of the 1930s.'[5]

The role of the Chinese

According to the 1947 census almost one-half of the population of the Peninsula and over three-quarters of that of Singapore[6] consisted of Chinese. In terms of numbers and economic power the Chinese formed the most important of the immigrant communities. While the British provided the administrative framework, the Chinese furnished the manpower and energy without which the rapid development of the Straits and of the Peninsula could never have taken place.

Although the great influx of Chinese migrants occurred in the nineteenth and twentieth centuries, reaching its high water mark in the 1920s, Chinese contacts with the area go back to the dawn of history. There is clear evidence of Chinese settlement in fourteenth-century Tumasik and of substantial trading connexions during the Malacca Sultanate. Permanent Chinese settlement at Malacca itself, however, probably took place only after the Portuguese conquest. From that time onwards, the Chinese formed an important element in the population of the port. The foundation of the British settlements in Penang and Singapore led to a limited exodus of the Malacca Chinese to these two places and they have formed the nucleus of the populations there ever since. Up till the nineteenth century, however, there was little indication of Chinese settlement in the interior of the Peninsula, apart from Kelantan. In the nineteenth century itself, apart from the planters in Johore and the tin miners in the west coast states Chinese traders and miners were also active in Pahang.

As elsewhere in the region, the Chinese of the Straits and the Peninsula fall into various speech groups, amongst which the Hokkien and the Cantonese are by far the most numerous.[7] Most Chinese of all groups were of peasant stock but despite their origins possessed an independence and versatility which enabled many of them to branch out into various new activities. By 1941 the Chinese had penetrated every aspect of the economy. They formed the bulk of the business community and the majority of the labouring class. They provided professional men in law and in medicine, in education and in technical fields; they had cornered several fields of agriculture and assumed the lead in industrial development. Chinese dominated the retail trade and owned oil mills, iron foundries, shipping companies, motor agencies and banks. Socially they had come 'to fill positions on every rung of the economic and social ladder', headed by a relatively small group of very wealthy financiers, bankers and mineowners, followed by a considerable middle class of managers and executives, professional men, independent traders, skilled technicians and artisans, with, at the bottom, 'the huge array of coolies sweating out their lives in backbreaking labour of all varieties'.[8] A broad distinction could also be drawn between the minority who were local born, found concentrated in the ports and towns as businessmen, teachers, lawyers, shop-keepers and clerks, and the immigrant Chinese who formed the bulk of the labouring and artisan population.

As a community the Chinese of the British period were self-reliant and self-contained, a natural consequence of language and culture and of the manner of their immigration. For a variety of reasons, the British left the Chinese largely to run their own affairs, while the Malay regimes of the Peninsula prior to British control had perforce to do likewise. After 130 years of intensive immigration and settlement under the shadow of British power, the Chinese community had done very well for itself. The main Chinese investments in the country were in tin-mining; they also had a 10 per cent share in the rubber estate industry, a large stake in shipping, virtually monopolized the fledgling secondary industries of the country, dominated the trade in dried and cured fish and had a large slice of general trade and commerce. Rice cultivation was about the only occupation where, partly as a result of official policy, the Chinese did not gain a foothold.

The European stake
Nevertheless the Chinese share in the Malayan economy was dwarfed by that of the Westerners, of which the lion's share was British held. Two-thirds of Western investments were in rubber and one-sixth in tin dredging, with British interests overwhelmingly predominant. The gargantuan size of Western investment in general and of British holdings in particular stood out in stark contrast to the exiguous numbers of Westerners actually resident in the country, most of whom belonged to the highly-paid executive, managerial or professional classes, a small ruling élite which dominated the country's life and determined its policies. Many of the real owners and financiers of the Western investments, however, did not live in the country at all, and had never been there.

The Indians in Malaya

The Indian community in Malaya in 1941 was far smaller than that of the Chinese, mainly consisting of labourers, skilled and unskilled, from South India. In fact from the earliest days of British settlement in the Straits, the Indians had been associated with labour. Before 1800 Indian convicts were already being used on the construction of public works. They were liberally treated and some, on their eventual release, had become wealthy enough to acquire landed property. Convict labour came to an end after 1873 but the demand for Indian labourers remained.[9] Indentured Tamils from South India replaced the convicts as roadmakers, and later on in the Peninsula as the railway builders, and as the employees of the municipalities of the Settlements and the new townships in the Malay States. In the second half of the nineteenth century, however, most of the Indian labourers who came were brought in to work on the sugar and coffee estates opened by Europeans in Penang and Province Wellesley and subsequently in Perak and elsewhere in the Peninsula. More particularly they became the chief source of labour on the rapidly spreading Western rubber estates in the first decades of the twentieth century.

Apart from the great labouring majority there was also a highly significant, though small, segment of Indians, who were much better placed. Making up some 10 per cent of the total Indian community, many of them had connexions with the Straits which went back for centuries, as was the case with the South Indian Muslim traders who now furrowed their businesses in the tracks of the hosts of labourers and who dated their origins in the Straits to the first days of British settlement. There were also Indians from the North who had arrived as recruits in the police or the army, or as clerks, traders and middlemen. By the 1900s these formed an important element in the Colony's mercantile community, were prominent in the professions and possessed an important mouthpiece in the North Indian Chamber of Commerce.[10]

The social pattern of the Indian community in the Malay States was virtually identical with that in the Straits Settlements, and their distribution kept closely to those areas of the Peninsula most exposed to Western economic penetration. By the early twentieth century Indian labourers in the states were irrevocably identified with rubber plantations, the Public Works Department, hospitals and town boards. As in the Straits Settlements the nucleus of the Indian élite was formed around the Jaffna Tamils of North Ceylon who, at one period, almost monopolized teachers' posts in English-medium schools and government clerical posts. They had been the first to arrive amongst the English-educated and quickly found employment in the nineteenth century in clerical jobs both in government service and outside. Their families and relatives followed and they came to enjoy an influence out of all proportion to their numbers. English-educated Tamils from South India itself appeared on the scene early in the twentieth century, and like their Jaffna cousins found similar opportunities of employment. Their influence too far exceeded their numbers, particularly as amongst them were 'university men with high expectations' who make their way up in the professions as doctors, lawyers, journalists and teachers.

Another distinct group was made up by the chettyars who entered the Malay States from Singapore towards the end of the nineteenth century. By the 1930s they were well established in all the major towns of the Peninsula, owning extensive properties including valuable urban land.

Malaysian 'immigrants'

To trace the rate or extent of Malaysian 'immigration' into Malaya after the establishment of British rule is no easy task, primarily because most of the migrants came of their own accord and were not subject to official scrutiny or registration. They were easily absorbed into the Malay social background because of the basic similarities of culture, outlook and occupation and the attitude of the British authorities was to regard the new arrivals as merely reinforcements to the existing indigenous population of the country so that immigrants and indigenes tended to be lumped together under one general heading in official statistics. Indeed it is hard to see how it could have been otherwise. The very concept of 'immigration' into the Peninsula by Malaysian groups from the archipelago makes no sense if viewed against the historical and cultural background of the region and only acquires some kind of validity with the arbitrary separation of Malaya as a political entity from the rest of the Malaysian world during the course of the nineteenth century. However, the influx of Malaysians from over the water which took place after 1800 was the direct consequence of the new economic opportunities brought into being with the spread of British power.

In the Straits Settlements Malaysians increased in number but declined in proportion to the immigrant population and tended to retain their role as primary producers. The comparatively few Malays, for instance, who crossed over to Penang after its occupation by the British engaged in jungle felling and rice-growing. In Province Wellesley opposite, rice was also grown by Indians, Chinese, Burmese and Thais but they were completely outnumbered by Malay farmers. The Malays formed the bulk of the farming community in Malacca Territory and dominated the fishing industry of Penang and Singapore. In the nineteenth century, Malaysians had a considerable share of the local carrying trade of the archipelago, but this role steadily diminished, particularly after the coming of the steamship. In general, the Malaysians not only became outnumbered in their own territory but also failed to play a significant part in the new commercial economy in the Settlements.

As for the Malay hinterland of the Peninsula, no regular scheme for encouraging Malaysian immigration ever existed. As word of the new opportunities in the Peninsula spread throughout the archipelago, the influx began of its own accord, although it received official encouragement, particularly from the west coast states because of the desire to establish a settled peasant population in the country. Malaysian immigrants were also encouraged keenly by Johore, probably in order to redress the balance in what had become by the second half of the nineteenth century a preponderantly Chinese community. At any rate, the largest groups of Malaysian settlers were to be found in these states.

The most numerous amongst the Malaysian new-comers were the Javanese, who started coming to Malayan shores in large numbers after the 1870s. They acquired a reputation amongst foreigners for their industry, thriftiness and the simplicity of their ways. Although a number were recruited under contract, the great majority came on their own. The largest concentration was in Johore where they formed 'a broad belt' mostly as coconut planters along the west coast. There were also Javanese settlers spread along the length of that coast up to the boundaries of Krian in Perak. Settlers from various parts of Sumatra were to be found in patches over all the west coast states. Apart from the great Menangkabau enclave in Malacca and Negri Sembilan and parts of Selangor which had been there for centuries, most recent Menangkabau settlers had opened smallholdings further inland. Of all the Sumatran groups the Menangkabau were the most active and the most prominent, enjoying a great reputation as itinerant salesmen and virtually monopolizing Malay retail trade. As a whole, the Sumatrans were the closest to the indigenous Malays, often with actual blood ties. From Borneo, the Banjarese formed a well-defined group. Initially found in 'pretty solid' numbers in the Krian district when they played a leading role in making it into a rice-bowl, their experience caused them to be invited to settle in the new rice scheme areas of Sungai Manik in Lower Perak and of Tanjong Karang in Selangor. By the beginning of the twentieth century the Bugis settlers of yore had long dispersed, although many of their descendants still lived in Selangor, along the banks of the Perak River and in Kedah. The last distinct immigrant group from the archipelago was formed by the Baweans. Mainly concentrated in Singapore, they spread into the Peninsula, principally associated with domestic service as chauffeurs or with horse-racing.

The Peninsular Malays
As a result of this penetration by Malaysians from across the water, the Peninsular Malays retained their predominance and coherence only in those states where they had been concentrated in the greatest numbers prior to the nineteenth century. The least affected and therefore the most Malay states in the Peninsula were Kelantan and Trengganu. Malay predominance was also apparent in Kedah and its former domain of Province Wellesley, in Negri Sembilan and Pahang, and to a lesser degree in Malacca Territory. In the other states where the Malay population had always been sparse, isolated and backward, they tended to be heavily outnumbered and continued to live a subsistence existence in riverine kampungs.[11] During the nineteenth century there was little tendency for the various Malaysian groups to come together either amongst themselves or with the Malays indigenous to the Peninsula. Despite the bonds of Islam, each Malaysian community kept to itself or showed as much jealousy and suspicion of others as did the rival Chinese clans towards one another in the tin fields. After 1900, however, with the growth of communications, the spread of modern education and with many Malaysians, regardless of origin, recruited into government service—particularly the police or the army—parochial attitudes began to disappear and a new consciousness of their common heritage developed.

They soon came to realize that this heritage was in danger for after three generations or less of British domination the Peninsula had become a 'demographic no-man's land'.[12] Yet out of the kaleidoscope of races that found themselves thrown together in the Peninsula, an unmistakable pattern had already emerged. By 1931 nearly nine-tenths of the total population of all races was concentrated on the tapering coastal terrain of west coast Malaya in a rash of new towns and villages unknown in 1850, laced together by roads and a trunk railway line which functioned as the main artery. This new Malaya was part and parcel of the wider world of international capital and commerce for which it produced its wares and it 'exhibited in rather an extreme form the demographic characteristics of a colonial society' whose wealth and material progress depended on a predominantly male immigrant labour force. The new Malaya was in fact a multi-racial society where the indigenous Malay population was outnumbered by the immigrants of the last few decades. The rest of the Peninsula, on the other hand, remained predominantly Malay.[13] This was the traditional peasant world with its subsistence economy primarily devoted to the cultivation of food crops and little touched by the bustling commercial and industrial life of the new Malaya.

This dichotomy did not only exist in a geographical sense. For while the developed, urbanized west coast was generally far more prosperous than the rest of the country, there was also an economic division based on race which cut straight across the Peninsula. Wherever the Malays happened to be (in fact the majority of them were also concentrated on the west coast), they were markedly worse off than the Chinese and Indian immigrant communities in their midst. The Malays were predominantly employed in 'agricultural pursuits', that is as peasant cultivators, and as such were involved in the least remunerative sector of the economy.[14] The pattern of urbanization itself highlighted the contrasts between the indigenous and immigrant elements in the population. While the percentage of town-dwellers steadily grew, this took place almost entirely in the west coast states of the F.M.S. and Johore and the new urban population was overwhelmingly Chinese. Outside this area only Kota Bharu and Kuala Trengganu could number more than 10,000 inhabitants apiece prior to 1941. Not only did the Malays remain the poorest of the inhabitants of the Peninsula but they also became a racial minority into the bargain. The fact that alien enterprise did not penetrate effectively into the other Malay states of the Peninsula merely ensured that these states continued to stagnate in their poverty.

The poverty and backwardness of the Malays in the F.M.S., where the prevailing political and social pattern bore very little relation to their own, and in the non-F.M.S., which remained a world apart, developed into an increasingly serious social and political problem. Its origins lay in the laissez-faire optimism of the British Victorian world, which, equating progress with economic growth, put a premium on the latter. There were also the purely geographical factors—the fact that the tin, and in consequence the rubber, were located in general away from the main areas of Malay settlement. On top of this came the part played by official policies which, being fundamentally dichotomous themselves, helped to confirm and emphasize the economic and social dichotomy arising in the Peninsula under their aegis. Wittingly or not, the general policies of the British administrations, particularly those bearing on land and education, served to compound the basic problems emerging with the creation of a multi-racial and plural society.

The evolution of British policy

As Roff has observed,[15] British policy in the Malay Peninsula became 'schizoid' in its attempt to pursue what were basically two contradictory aims. On the one hand there was the aim of rapid economic exploitation, to be se-cured by the institution of a stable and efficient government. This had been the real motive behind the spread of British control over the Malay States after 1873. At the same time there was also the desire to promote Malay wel-fare and to protect Malay interests from the pressures of the new order which the British themselves were helping to create. This provided the justification for their presence in the Peninsula. The incompatibilities involved in the pursuit of these two aims became more evident as time went on but initially both ap-peared feasible since the areas of the most intense economic exploitation were the areas of lowest Malay concentration. So while promoting modern cap-italism, the British administrations ever more consciously strove to evolve a protectionist policy towards the Malay population as a whole, designed to shield them from the disruptive effects of the new economic order. The general result was to cushion successfully the impact of social and economic change on the Malay way of life and to prevent the dislocations so evident under similar conditions in Burman society. At the same time, however, the Malay world tended to remain in isolation and in ignorance of these currents of change and was therefore all the less able to adapt to them when the inevitable moment of encounter took place.

The first sphere in which a protectionist policy became evident was in that of land. The earliest measures to protect the position of the Malay farmer date from the 1880s but the seeds of protectionism were truly laid by W.E. Maxwell, who despite his doubts as to the worth of the Malay peasant (or perhaps because of them) took steps to provide for safeguards against the encroachments on Malay lands by business-minded outsiders. However laissez-faire pragmatism still ruled the day and within a year the safeguards had been swept away by Swettenham's strong broom.[16] In consequence a 'pro-Malay' protectionist policy became effectively established only after the first decade of the rubber boom. The alarming speed with which Malay lands were being engulfed in the tide of rubber prompted the passing in the F.M.S. of the Malay Reservations Enactment of 1913 designed to preserve the ownership of large areas of land in Malay hands for their present and future needs. In practice, however, while protecting the Malay farmer's ownership rights, it failed to prevent him from slipping into further debt and deeper im-poverishment. More fundamentally still, it was the first of those measures that identified the Malay with a particular form of agriculture and hindered his entry into other fields. It encouraged his innate conservatism and main-tained if not strengthened the more unprogressive aspects of Malay society but did nothing towards enabling him to raise his standard of living or to adjust to the new economic forces unleashed in the Peninsula.[17]

The policy of creating Malay land reservations quickly became identified with that of encouraging Malay rice cultivation. By the beginning of the twentieth century the logic of capitalist economics had already imprinted a clear social formula on the population structure of the Peninsula, each community having its appointed role. The Europeans (and the Chinese) were the purveyors of capital, technique and equipment; the Chinese (and the Indians) furnished the pool of cheap, hired labour; and the Malays remained the sons of the soil, the tillers and harvesters of the fields. The Malay destiny to be a race of peasants was implicit in the 1913 Reservations Enactment itself which specifically sought to preserve good rice lands from alienation and even if from time to time rice cultivation by other races was proposed or even initiated, within the next two decades, rice became established as a virtually exclusive Malay sphere of activity.

The general evolution of British policy was severely shaken by the Great Depression. The Depression exposed the deficiencies of the policy towards the land, revealed with yet greater clarity the unfavourable position of the Malays and showed that up to date, at any rate, protectionism was not really achieving very much. With the general collapse of prices and with them of profits, the pressure of creditors for the settlement of their debts mounted rapidly and the full extent of Malay rural indebtedness was bared. This resulted in a new campaign to promote rice cultivation and in an intensification of the general policy of shielding the Malays from the blasts of *laissez-faire* economics. Apart from the new rice campaign itself, the most important step taken was the establishment of the Malay Reservations Committee by the F.M.S. government in 1931, the fruit of whose work was embodied in the Malay Reservations Enactment two years later. The new enactment prohibited the transfer of Malay holdings to non-Malays under any circumstances and moneylenders were expressly forbidden from setting up Malays as nominal owners.[18] The implementation of this and other measures in the 1930s signified the clear emergence of the basic contradictions inherent in British policy under increasing economic pressure. Whilst the government committed itself more deeply towards protectionism for the Malays, such policies began to impinge on the other goal of unimpaired economic development. The government showed itself growingly reluctant to alienate land for the expanding oil palm industry and the like and the growing restrictions on Chinese and Indian penetration or access to land started to become a political issue.

The protectionist policy was of course a highly conservative one aimed at preserving the traditional nature of Malay society and as such tended to enjoy the support of the Malay ruling class. However, during the 1930s a growing number of Malay intellectuals were beginning to question the desirability of such a policy and to challenge the assumptions upon which it was based.[19]

The contradictions in British policy were most apparent in the F.M.S. where the Malays were already in a minority and their position was most obviously threatened. But the same policy was also at work in the non-F.M.S. where, apart from Johore, the Malays were in a majority. A comparison of

the pace of development between these two groups of states throws the Malayan dichotomy into high relief. In the non-F.M.S. (with the general exception of Johore which was far more closely linked with the new Malaya),
the absence of the economic pressures of the intensity encountered on the
west coast enabled British administrators to indulge their fancies regarding
the virtues of a pristine, rural society and to permit development to proceed
at its own speed. So while British power was universal, in the non-F.M.S. it appeared to rest much more lightly because there was a real difference in the spirit
of policy. In these states Malay interests were put first, or nearly so, and not
sacrificed on the altar of 'progress', as was undoubtedly the case in the F.M.S.
This meant much slower economic growth and a much less sophisticated
administration, but 'On the other hand the Government and the people have
remained Malay, foreign economic interests and immigration have been negligible and neither the Rulers nor their British Advisers have any wish
to change.'[20] As a result, the non-F.M.S. were predominantly rice states,
although rubber made its impact even in those states.

The intensification of protectionism after the Great Depression was felt as
much in the non-F.M.S. as elsewhere. The creation or extension of Malay
land reservations in those states matched the new impetus to that policy in
the F.M.S. after 1931. In Kedah new Malay reservations were quickly established to counter the large block of land alienated to rubber in the south
of the state, while in Kelantan almost 90 per cent of the land became gazetted
as a reserved area. In Kelantan there was also a determined effort to check the
swing away from rice to rubber.

The different accent in British policy in the non-F.M.S. sprang from the
circumstances under which British control was extended over them. The
British takeover in each case was accomplished against a background of
smouldering resentment which occasionally burst out into flames of open
opposition. This, the overwhelming Malay element in the states themselves
and certain other incidental factors[21] tempered British policy from the very
beginning. Clearly linked to this was the time factor: British control over the
non-F.M.S. was established almost a generation after the rest of the Peninsula.
By this time, something of the naive faith in the superiority of Western ways
had been eroded, while British administrators themselves had in front of
them an object lesson of how indigenous interests could be virtually drowned
by the waves of economic progress breaking in from outside.

Malay poverty and the co-operative movement
The general backwardness of the Peninsular Malays under British rule was
further compounded by the evolution of an educational policy designed,
especially after Winstedt, to keep the bulk of the Malays tied to the soil.
This formed a powerful factor in the failure of the Malays as a community
to improve their economic position or to raise their standards of living.[22]
Within the framework of a rural, rice-bound economy the chances of achieving a breakthrough were extremely remote. Rice cultivation had never
been profitable nor showed any signs of becoming so. Rural indebtedness
symptomized the padi-planter's plight, though its presence was constantly

underestimated by the British authorities. The Little Depression of 1919-21 provoked some attention but it was the great extent of rural poverty bared by the Great Depression of 1929 that showed government intervention to be essential if undesirable social and political consequences were not to follow. Peasant misery expressed itself in mortgaged titles, widespread tenancy with absentee landlords and the general prevalence of the so-called *padi kuncha* system.[23]

One obvious solution to the problem lay in finding a way round the credit system, as it operated through Chinese village shop-keepers and private moneylenders, by the establishment of government-sponsored co-operatives, as had been pioneered in Java and in British India. But as elsewhere, attempts to launch a vigorous co-operative movement ran into a whole host of problems, not merely economic but social, the overcoming of which called for far greater sums than a colonial government was willing or able to provide.

In the Malay States one of the first obstacles was formed by Muslim views on usury. This issue was the main reason why the proposal to set up co-operatives in 1911 was dropped and not raised again until 1922. By that time (1922) it had been decided that Malays could join co-operatives without endangering their spiritual well-being but the new department found that it 'always had to struggle and fight hard' against religious prejudices. Another impediment to solvency was fragmentation of land holdings. Subdivision of property went on from generation to generation, rendering holdings uneconomic, creating disguised unemployment and inviting the moneylender to step in. However the system was part and parcel of the Muslim law of inheritance which made the passing of ameliorative legislation very difficult, all the more so in view of the dictum laid down by the British themselves about not interfering 'with Malay religion and custom'. In the event it was Kelantan, the most 'Malay' state of all, that led the way in its Land Enactment of 1933 which prohibited subdivision of small plots of land.

But a greater impediment to economic progress than religious prejudice was the weight of tradition. In many instances, when the pressure was getting too great, the Malay farmer could simply have abandoned his land and settled elsewhere, probably to his profit. But his attachment to the land was very strong, regardless of its economic value. The social environment, too, which became increasingly the object of British policy to preserve, discouraged a change in his attitudes whilst preserving institutions which had diminishing relevance to the world beyond. Rice cultivation tended to be looked upon more as a way of life than as a means of making a living, and as such continued to be encumbered with an accretion of custom and ritual, which—as in the case of Malay mining—made it totally uneconomic. The government slowly succeeded in improving certain farming techniques but it proved an almost impossible task, in the context of the period, to alter Malay scales of social values which kept the peasant on the threshold of debt and incapacitated his chances of survival in an increasingly commercial world.[24]

Against this background, it is not surprising that the rural co-operative movement made slow progress after its institution in 1922. In the 1920s the movement expanded slowly and extended out of the F.M.S. (except Negri

Sembilan) into both Kedah and Johore. With the Great Depression, it went into decline. Official policy was to let improvident societies collapse; many did so, while others had to suspend their operations for a number of years. There was some recovery after 1936, largely as a result of the Strickland Report's recommendations of 1929.[25] The Report and the Depression brought about some reforms, but prior to 1941 the co-operative movement in the rural sphere had still made very little impact. But as Lim Chong-yah has pointed out, even at its best, co-operatives or any other means of providing cheap credit to an impoverished peasantry 'is but a palliative and cannot cure a serious disease...'.[26] Poverty feeds on poverty in a vicious cycle that can only be broken by massive outside intervention, mobilizing the resources of the nation as a whole. Malaya before 1945 was not yet a nation and the sort of economic effort needed would have been impossible within the colonial framework. British options were limited: one of them would have been to expose the Malays to the full blast of the new forces penetrating their country but this would have been opposed tooth and nail by the Malays themselves who would, with justification, have feared the total submersion of their identity. Massive state intervention on the Malay behalf was equally out of the question since the rapid economic development of the Peninsula, which alone could provide the means to help the backward areas, was dependent on the forces of alien free enterprise. A diversion of the Peninsula's resources for the salvation of the rural population would at this stage have impeded further development. But in the final analysis a policy of placing Malay needs first would have been to hamper British economic interests in the Peninsula quite apart from the threat it would have posed to the continuation of British rule—in short, such a policy was politically impossible. The inconsistencies and inequalities which emerged in the economic and social development of the country was the price that had to be paid under a colonial system whose own survival prevented a more radical solution.

Immigration and labour
Nevertheless in 1941, by comparison with the rest of the region and indeed most of Asia, British Malaya seemed to be an oasis of political calm and material prosperity. However, this Malayan prosperity (for some) and the Peninsula's spectacular development rested without doubt on the availability and ruthless exploitation of hordes of poverty-stricken workers imported from overseas who, because of the wretched circumstances in their own homelands, were prepared to submit to appalling conditions of maltreatment and abuse. No one will ever know with accuracy how many immigrants from China in the second half of the nineteenth century died in the tin-mines of Malaya for want of proper medical attention, or as the result of a violent discipline which included flogging. The death-rate was extremely high and it was only the hope—rarely realized—of striking a fortune that made so many willing to undergo the privations involved. The plight of the average Indian labourer, despite the plethora of official regulations passed to protect him, was still worse. In the nineteenth century government reports and enquiries present a tedious picture of sub-human conditions, cruelty and neglect. By

the third decade of the present century conditions had improved somewhat, particularly as far as the Chinese were concerned. The Indians, however, remained very badly off and in 1941 the average Tamil worker existed at little above subsistence level and faced starvation at any drop in the rubber price that would affect his wages.

Labour was clearly closely related to recruitment and immigration. In the nineteenth century in particular, when nearly the entire labour force in the country consisted of immigrants, labour conditions were directly linked to the prevailing mode of immigration and the laws associated with it. In the twentieth century conditions of labour became a subject in their own right as did the official to deal with them in the peninsular states. In fact, administratively speaking after 1911 labour in the Colony and in the Protected States came under a common control, so that the only differentiation between the two entities lay in the type of labour dominant in each. Official policy evolved on two separate though parallel lines as far as the Indians and the Chinese were concerned. This was partly the outcome of political considerations but, more largely, sprang from the great distinctions in the social structures of these two communities. On top of that, the Chinese always remained much more of an unknown quantity to the British administrator than did the Indians, as a result of which they were left to a considerable extent to their own devices. The British connexion with India itself made it both easier and more necessary to establish a close official supervision.

Indian immigration not only sprang from the British connexion but was also indispensable to it. The demand for Indian labour existed from the moment that Francis Light set foot on Penang Island in 1786 and by the end of the next century had become insatiable. By this time the system of immigration had gone through three transformations and was on the point of undergoing a fourth. At first most Indian immigrants were either slaves or convicts but when slavery was abolished in the British Empire in 1834, contract or indentured labour took their place. From that date the sugar and later the coffee planters of the Peninsula imported Indian labourers at their own expense, usually through professional recruiting agencies in India itself. But by the 1870s the inadequacies of this system began to become a serious hindrance to the expansion of European agricultural enterprise in the Peninsula so that two new forms of labour emerged, both styled—in contradistinction to the indentured system—'free'. However, the more popular of the two, usually called the 'kangany system', was in fact merely a variant of traditional contract labour, with the kangany (the labour agent or foreman) playing a dominating and commonly sinister role.[27] The kangany system spread rapidly and was well established in the Straits and the Peninsula before the end of the century but it too soon proved inadequate to meet the demands of the mushrooming rubber industry. The new pressure for labour provoked a heated debate amongst officials and planters as to the relative merits of free and contract labour. The solution finally found was in a scheme of assisted immigration, the costs of which were met by a special fund set up by the governments of the Straits Settlements and the F.M.S. This fund (known as the Indian Immigration Fund and established in 1907) made it possible to provide free passages for all immigrant labourers travelling between India and the Peninsula. Meanwhile actual recruitment was still largely carried out under the *kangany* system, although now subject to official scrutiny and control. The *kangany* system remained the chief means of securing Indian labour up till 1929 but it was already in decline before the steady rise of free labourers, entering the Peninsula or local born. When immigration from India resumed as the effects of the Depression wore off, free labour gained the ascendancy. In 1938, when the *kangany* system was outlawed by the Government of India (together with a ban on the emigration of all unskilled labour) for political reasons, the system itself was dying for economic ones.

As with the Indians, by far the great majority of Chinese immigrants in the nineteenth century came as indentured labourers. Known as 'sin-kheh' (Hokkien) or 'san-hak' (Cantonese), the basic distinction between the Indian and Chinese contract labourer was that the former was recruited at the behest of a European employer whereas the Chinese became the creature of his own countrymen. In other respects the manner by which the Chinese *sin-kheh* was recruited and imported into the country was basically similar to that for the Indians. The Chinese method did not alter in its essentials until officially abolished in 1914.[28]

The general conditions under which immigration took place in the nineteenth century were appalling. For Indian and Chinese alike, the villain of the piece was the recruiting agent and his henchmen who lured unsuspecting and illiterate coolies from their villages with a whole series of spurious promises. The recruits were invariably charged for everything involved in the voyage—passage, maintenance and agent's fees—and were then transported in overcrowded, ill-provided vessels across the Bay of Bengal or southwards across the China Sea into the stifling heat of the tropics, crammed below battened hatches. At their ports of disembarkation, the new arrivals faced a bleak future of work without respite until they had paid off the inflated costs of their recruitment and passage. Those who survived eventually tried to make their way back to their homelands, often in broken health and still paupers, to die, or as in the case of the Indians, after their contracts had expired to be shipped back to their villages empty 'like sucked oranges'.

The first measures to protect labour were in fact measures to control immigration or rather the manner in which it took place. Up till the 1850s the British administrations in the Straits Settlements were content to hold the ring in the best liberal tradition, creating the conditions and providing the amenities by which the merchants of Singapore, Penang and Malacca could make their fortunes out of the toil and sweat of countless voiceless immigrants imported under the vilest conditions. After mid-century, however, changing circumstances forced the British authorities to take steps in the name of expediency, if not of humanity, to come to the rescue of the exploited.

The British failure to take earlier steps to control Chinese immigration is surprising as the overwhelming bulk of immigrants was made up of Chinese. But there was an abysmal ignorance of things Chinese amongst British officials, ncluding language; more decisively there was also the entrenched opposition of the mercantile communities of the Straits, both European and

Asian, which deemed their prosperity to rest on cheap labour and who there-fore regarded the principle of unhindered immigration as sacrosanct as the principle of free trade. Nevertheless this united front of traders ultimately crumbled when in the early 1870s Chinese merchants suddenly discovered the rise of the nefarious coolie traffic with the newly opened Culture Zone of north-east Sumatra cutting into their interests. Singapore had become the scene for the forcible abduction of Chinese coolies to Medan, causing a labour shortage and rocketing prices in the Straits. The subsequent outcry by the Chinese merchants for government supervision and control of immigration precipitated a prolonged and at times acrimonious public debate on the whole issue of the Chinese presence. The outcome was the establishment in 1877 of the Chinese Protectorate, a new government department to handle all Chinese affairs, and the promulgation of two important ordinances which subjected Chinese immigration to strict supervision and protected Chinese labourers from abduction. At first the work of the Protectorate was primarily concerned with the activities of the Chinese secret societies, for so long one of the principal instruments of coercion of Chinese employers. As British power spread over the Peninsula, similar offices were set up in those states where the Chinese formed a substantial community. By 1934, when the Chinese Protectorate in the Colony and that in the F.M.S. were merged to form the new Secretariat for Chinese Affairs, Malaya, with its headquarters in Singa-pore, this department had emerged as the most important link which the British colonial authorities had with the Chinese community.

The development of official control over Indian immigration—a parallel process to that over the Chinese—was determined by pressures from two sources. The primary one came from India itself, where from the middle of the nineteenth century the government displayed concern for the fate of its subjects who were recruited to work overseas, a concern which became ever more pronounced as the temper of Indian nationalism advanced. The other pressure was from the Peninsula, conditioned basically by the desire of Eu-ropean planters for an adequate and uninterrupted flow of cheap labour from South India, but increasingly impregnated by humanitarian considerations informed by enlightened self-interest. From the 1870s onwards every decade saw a major legislative enactment in response to one or other of these pres-sures, making the Indian immigrant labourer, on paper at any rate, one of the best protected workers in the world.

But there was always a wide gap between the law and reality. In general, at least up till the 1890s, the main characteristic of all labour legislation in the Pe-ninsula was its bias in favour of the employer and the almost complete ineffec-tiveness of its safeguards for the rights and welfare of the labourer. In the case of the Chinese, where most labour in the nineteenth century was connected with tin-mining, the main aim of government was to ensure labour's stability by upholding the sanctity of contract and by checking against gross exploita-tion. At all events great care was taken to interfere with Chinese mining prac-tices as little as possible for fear of killing the geese that laid the golden eggs. The main problem of the time was that of the absconding labourer and the principal solution was the penal sanction. As a result working conditions remained wretched and the average coolie continued to be little more than a debt-slave, with a brief expectation of life.[29] However, the lot of the Chinese mining labourer improved considerably from the 1890s as a result of changes within the economic and social structure of the tin industry itself. The tin crisis of the 1890s crippled the handful of pioneer Chinese towkays, who had once almost monopolized production from Larut and the Klang Valley, and in their place rose up a new class of small, independent mineowners. Labour became more valuable and less easy to control. By 1900 the *sin-kheh* was fast becoming a thing of the past, and new forms of labour, whether contract or not, were rising up, much better placed to secure reasonable terms. The labour shortage of the 1890s, which forms the background to this change, led the British authorities to go into the whole question. The result was the Labour Code of 1895 (in the F.M.S.) which 'made the Chinese labourer a free and independent man', followed by a series of other pro-labour measures culminating in the revised Labour Code of 1912. The Code of 1912 was a major law not confined to mining labour alone but embracing all the various ordinances that had been passed for the protection of Chinese, Indian and other labourers.[30] By the 1920s the Chinese miner was incomparably better off than in the evil days of the previous century, but by this time his kind was no longer a major element amongst labour as a whole, being outnumbered by agricultural labourers on the new rubber estates.

The lot of the agricultural labourers in general remained far less happy right up till 1941. The conditions of Chinese agricultural workers on the sugar plantations of Perak and Province Wellesley and on European estates in Negri Sembilan were exposed in all their crudity by the official commission of enquiry of 1910.[31] Even after the subsequent abolition of all Chinese contract labour in 1912, the labour contractor or foreman survived with most of his powers intact, a serious obstacle to further progress and an important factor in the grave labour unrest in the F.M.S. in the 1930s.[32] The Chinese urban worker, on the other hand, was from the beginning better off, particularly in the Straits Settlements. He was the chief beneficiary of the restrictions imposed on secret society activities after 1890 and played a leading role with his greater expertise and sophistication in the incipient trade movement in the 1920s and 1930s.

Despite the minutiae of government regulations passed in his favour, the position of the Indian labourer never substantially improved prior to 1941 and by all counts he remained far worse off than his Chinese counterpart. The Chinese worker's more independent position and his general preference for piece rates were reasons for this, but the Indian's plight was rooted in the official paternalism which at once cocooned and smothered him. Despite the host of legislation passed from the 1870s onwards stipulating the rights of the labourer, most of it was as much loaded in favour of the employer as were the far more frugal labour laws for the Chinese and until the twentieth century stayed ineffective for want of proper supervision.[33] The distressing picture painted by the report of the Labour Commission of 1910 prompted a new spate of attempted reforms over the ensuing two decades, nearly all of which foundered on the rock of employer opposition. Even the comprehensive Labour Code of 1912 which was the main fruit of the Commission's efforts, represented, as far as the Indians were concerned, another advance made largely on paper. When in 1923 this Code was revised, there were some tangible benefits for Indian labour for the first time.[34]

From this time onwards till 1941 the main issue at stake revolved around wages, in particular the establishment of a legal minimum wage. A working arrangement in this regard was reached for Indian estate labour in 1927, to be wrecked by the Great Depression two years later, and the failure to resolve this problem was a major factor in the Government of India's ban on the emigration of all unskilled Indian labour to Malaya in 1938. This decision, whatever its demographic implications, proved an undoubted boon for the local-born Indian labourer who was now no longer liable to be undercut by the arrival of new immigrants. Indeed, signs that the general conditions of Indian labour were beginning to improve were evident in the Srinivasa Report of 1937, although its favourable findings reaped a whirlwind of nationalist criticism.[35] European planters always argued that Indian workers in Malaya were incomparably better off than they would have been in India itself, but this was only relatively true. The average Indian labourer in 1941 still lived in the shadow of destitution, engaged in a never-ending struggle with rising prices, while any savings he made were made at the expense of his daily living and of his health.

Only a very small proportion of Malaysian workers fell into the category of organized labour thereby coming under the purview of the Labour Department and subject to the Labour Code. Amongst this minority, especially at the start of the present century, the Javanese formed not only the most significant group but were also the only Malaysian community to be engaged under any system of contract labour. Such labour was officially abolished in 1932 by which time there were very few Javanese still employed in this manner.

As far as the Peninsular Malays were concerned, the greatest single British contribution to an improvement of conditions of labour was the abolition of all forms of slavery and forced labour.[36] Both were well established institutions in pre-colonial Malay society and the early British attempts at reform were important factors in the uprisings against them in Perak, Pahang and Kelantan. After a salutary experience in Perak, however, British officials hastened more slowly and following the sagacious pattern laid down by Hugh Low in Perak itself, slavery—in particular the custom of debt-slavery—was finally ended, while compulsory services were replaced by taxation.[37] The eradication of slavery and of forced labour amounted to a social revolution in Malay society and was perhaps the one major British contribution to Malay welfare.

The growth of secondary industry and protectionism
While the labour force in the country was substantial, only about one-thirteenth of the total working population was involved in industrial enterprise. In fact Malayan manufactures had an insignificant role in the economy, apart from those connected with the processing of rubber, tin and, to some degree,

pineapple. There was no heavy industry at all. There were a handful of substantial Western and Chinese firms with branches in major centres in the Peninsula, but the great bulk of Malaya's secondary industry consisted of family concerns or individual enterprises. Malayan secondary industry fell into four broad categories. Taking pride of place in terms of value and age came the processing industry, associated with tin, rubber, timber and foodstuffs. In the second category were service maintenance occupations, characterized by various forms of light engineering closely linked with the tin and rubber industries and with the needs of transport and irrigation. The third category comprised the manufacture of simple consumer goods with a high demand on the local market, while the fourth was represented by cottage industries and traditional handicrafts which absorbed the largest percentage of hands—nearly one-third of the whole—but was by far the least progressive or remunerative.

On a small scale the pattern of these secondary industries faithfully reflected the economic dichotomy imposed by the primary ones. Most manufacturing was concentrated in Chinese hands on the west coast. The Chinese formed from 80 to 90 per cent of the industrialists in the country (the Indians made up the remainder) and accounted for three-quarters of the labour force. At the other end of the scale were the cottage industries of the country, by definition part-time occupations for an agricultural population idle between harvests, found mostly in the east coast states of Kelantan and Trengganu, which were wholly Malay, with meagre profits and bleak prospects for real expansion.

The failure of secondary industry to develop on a large scale in Malaya before 1941 lay as much in circumstance as in policy. The Peninsula lacked suitable raw materials for the growth of industry or resources of energy with which to feed it. On top of this, the domestic market was too small to make the encouragement of local industries worth-while. The colonial mould into which the economy of the country was cast further diminished its prospects. Malayan revenues were mainly derived from tin and rubber and were then used to import the manufactured goods and the foodstuffs that the population needed. Much of the available capital was absorbed by the primary industries. Local manufacturers could not hope to compete with foreign-manufactured goods in a *laissez-faire* economy, except in those areas where material advantages such as immediate availability, close links with the primary industry concerned, suitable location and low transport costs operated.

Nevertheless the impact of the Great Depression coupled with the rapid penetration of Japanese goods into the Malayan market, and the stabilization of population which followed, forced Britain to adopt protectionist policies in order to safeguard its own traditional preserves. At the same time, confronted with the growing reality of a settled urban society in the Peninsula itself, the local colonial administration began to think for the first time in terms of protection for local industry.

The first official proposal to create a customs union embracing the Malay States and the Straits Settlements was made by Governor Clementi in 1931. However, his initiative failed to overcome the strong free trade prejudice of merchants and businessmen in the Straits Settlements and, more surprisingly, was rejected by business interests in the F.M.S. as well, on the grounds that as the trade of the federation was mainly with the colony and little inter-state trade was involved, such a union would not serve any real purpose. Loud opposition to the scheme came from Kedah and Johore whose largely rural populations could not see why they should bear the burden of increased prices just to benefit a handful of local manufacturers. The scheme was also strongly opposed by influential manufacturing interests and agency houses whose profits came from the importation of goods into the Peninsula.[38] As a result, faced with virtually unanimous opposition from all sides, Clementi had to retreat.

An alternative proposal for a customs union to comprise the Malay States and the mainland areas of the Straits Settlements (namely excluding the islands of Singapore and Penang) was put forward in 1934. The committee appointed to consider this matter decided that it would be wiser, on the whole, to preserve the *status quo* except for the Dindings which on its recommendation was retroceded to Perak the following year. So Clementi's scheme for a customs union for the whole Peninsula was ultimately lost, and since it concerned an issue of only local importance in which imperial interests were not involved, the question was allowed to rest.

In the meantime the concept of Imperial Preference which originated with the British Home Government and in which imperial interests were very definitely implicated was successfully carried through. The new policy marked a sharp break with the long tradition in the Straits of not discriminating by tariff on goods according to their origin and met with a mixed reception. In general, the F.M.S. together with Trengganu and Kelantan applied imperial preference to the widest range of goods, followed more reluctantly and on a more limited scale by Johore and Kedah. In the Straits Settlements themselves opposition was the strongest and compliance the least.

Apart from anything else, the issue of tariff protection threw into relief the rapidly growing divergencies of interest between the Peninsula as a whole and the Straits Settlements, especially Singapore. Awareness of these differences made the Malay States more receptive to Imperial Preference as a means to promote their own interests and there was little sympathy with the struggles of the mercantile community of the Straits to preserve intact their free trade integrity. From the point of view of the Malayan manufacturer, however, Imperial Preference, by ensuring entry of overseas manufactured goods, particularly British ones, was an impediment to his own expansion and diversification. In fact, he lost both ways. The exigencies of imperial interest resulted in the imposition of this system of imperial protection, while the relative unimportance of Malayan affairs in the grand, imperial scale of things meant that the customs union plan died by default.

Health and social welfare
Closely related to general economic progress in Malaya was the question of health. In the nineteenth century the Peninsula was one of the unhealthiest areas in the tropics. The serious consequences of this on economic develop-

ment revealed themselves in the devastating toll of human life which accompanied the rapid opening up of the country in the second half of the century. Traditionally disease and death amongst all communities had been accepted as part of fate and the prevailing philosophy was to seek the cure rather than the cause, so that preventive health measures received scant attention. However, the development of the tin and rubber industries, embracing large tracts of land and great numbers of men, made the situation intolerable. After 1900 there was a remarkable improvement in health conditions throughout the country. The twin scourges of beri-beri and malaria were tamed, while in the big towns, above all in Singapore, earnest attempts were made to deal with the problems of slums and overcrowding. Between 1900 and 1950 the death-rates for adults and infants were halved and in one decade (1910-20) the mortality amongst estate labourers was reduced by two-thirds.

This achievement was brought about by a fortunate combination of circumstances including the application of far-sighted and systematic policies by the colonial authorities. The country produced great wealth during the period in question, which provided the necessary funds, and the British administrators were able to take full advantage of the valuable experience that had been gained and of the important new discoveries that had been made in medicine, particularly in the fields of bacteriology, epidermiology and the effective prevention of tropical diseases.

The victories over beri-beri and malaria were achieved almost simultaneously in the 1900s after a generation of mistaken assumptions. It was a triumph of medical research which relied in the first instance on government backing; however, official efforts would have been inadequate (particularly in the case of malaria) without the active participation of private enterprise. The government's parsimonious attitudes cost it the services of Watson, who had played the leading role in the eradication of malaria in the Peninsula, and blighted the promise of the Institute of Medical Research, established in 1901.[39] On the other hand, government played a pioneer and constructive role in the field of curative medicine and if the high mortality rates of the second half of the nineteenth century suggest otherwise, much, in fact, was achieved: the inadequacies were due to largely uncontrollable factors. The first public health measures were taken in Singapore as a result of the severe cholera outbreak of 1851. In the 1850s the first sanitary regulations were passed and immigrant health controls were established in 1873. The first public hospital in the Malay States was opened at Taiping in 1880 and after that date there was fairly rapid expansion in the provision of medical services. This progress was substantially supplemented both in the Straits and in the Peninsula by private donors and charities but much effort was wasted on account of the general prejudice against Western medicine.

After 1900 the medical services were greatly extended, a process temporarily held up by the Great War but resumed with greater intensity after it. In the 1930s the medical and health services of the Colony and the states were combined into a single Malayan Medical Service. One of the most significant developments in the Straits was the foundation in 1905 of the King Edward VII College of Medicine, with the primary task of recruiting and training local practitioners. Other specialist centres were set up in Malaya after 1909 for mental health, leprosy and for the decrepit. By 1941 about one-third of all the hospitals in the country were government institutions but they contained about two-thirds of all the beds. Other hospitals were maintained by estates (by law), by missionary societies and Chinese philanthropic organizations.

However, the quality of the medical services was uneven and their distribution unbalanced. Estate hospitals in particular left much to be desired. The bulk of the medical facilities were to be found in the urban areas so that the predominantly Malay-inhabited rural areas of the east and the north were the least served. The basic reason for this imbalance lay in the lack of sufficient resources, so that the natural tendency was to try and do the greatest good for the greatest number, which implied paying attention to the greatest centres of population. It must also be conceded that at first the health problems of the towns appeared far worse than those of the countryside. However, by 1941 the discrepancy was the other way round.[40]

In Singapore the problem of public health was intimately connected with over-crowded housing. In 1938 the population of Singapore Town was crammed into about half the area its numbers demanded, the outcome of a century without town planning. Raffles' imaginative layouts had long been swept into oblivion by the febrile growth of the city after the 1860s. In this *laissez-faire* atmosphere row upon row of cheap dwellings rose back-to-back with no heed for ventilation or sanitation, proper cooking facilities or adequate lighting, thrown up to accommodate crowds of indigent, illiterate immigrants who had known nothing better where they came from and did not know how to protest when they arrived. By 1900 Singapore was 'the possessor of first-class slums'. This awesome legacy did not receive official attention until 1917 and it took another decade of leisurely deliberation before effective action was taken. In 1928 the Singapore Improvement Trust was finally established with a mandate to eradicate the slums that existed and to plan so that new ones should not arise. Once formed, the S.I.T. set about its tasks with impressive energy, although by 1940 it had only started to nibble at the problem. Provision was also made for slum clearance in Penang and Malacca in the 1920s and 1930s, but the problem was far less severe in those two settlements.

Other social problems tended to reflect the idiosyncracies of each particular community. In any case the other social welfare services before 1941 were very limited, largely supported on a voluntary basis by charitable organizations of one sort or the other, representing piece-meal attempts to deal with the problems of orphanage, destitution and old age. For the Chinese, social welfare problems appeared to pivot around opium, gambling and brothels, and the role of government was, if anything, to institutionalize these activities rather than to suppress them. In the circumstances of the nineteenth century these vices lay beyond the power of the colonial administration to control. Prostitution in particular presented many complexities.[41] Brothels were permitted and prostitutes allowed entry into the country up till 1927 when puritanical British parliamentarians finally succeeded in closing down the former and imposing a ban on the latter three years later. But since the 1870s the Chinese Protectorate had taken steps to prevent the slave-traffic in women and young girls, and in 1873 founded the *Po Leung Kok*, an organization providing a home for those in need of protection. Changed conditions and a more balanced sex ratio amongst the Chinese population after 1930 helped to ameliorate the situation.

In human terms the most serious problem was opium. During the nineteenth century no effort was made to curb the habit of opium-smoking; indeed, many towkays did all they could to encourage it as the best means of keeping their labourers in perpetual debt, while it proved a useful source of government revenue to a generation of British administrators. The moves to control opium-smoking in Malaya began in the 1900s, a result of the British puritanical conscience now rampant in colonial affairs, a new spirit of Chinese nationalism which also had strong puritanical overtones and allied to a nice sense of where their true interests lay on the part of European (as opposed to Chinese) mining entrepreneurs. Nevertheless, in spite of the inauguration of a vigorous anti-opium movement in 1905 and the setting up of an official Opium Commission the following year, it was not until the 1940s, in the midst of the Pacific War, that opium-smoking became officially prohibited. Government opium farms, however, were abolished in 1910.[42]

The social problems of the Indian immigrant labour community were far less sophisticated than those of their Chinese counterparts. The predominant problems were associated with alcoholism. Toddy-drinking, not so prevalent in India itself, under Malayan conditions became virtually synonymous with Indian estate labour assuming a role somewhat analogous to that of opium amongst Chinese mining coolies. Producing grave social effects on the labourers themselves, it became a source of profit to planter and government alike. However the drawbacks of having a drunken, spendthrift labour force soon made themselves apparent to estate managers and the lead to check toddy-drinking came from the Planters' Association of Malaya soon after its foundation in 1908. In consequence certain government measures were introduced, starting with the establishment of licensing boards the following year, to control the quality of the liquor sold. By the 1920s toddy sales had been brought under the effective control of estate managers and three-fifths of the profits were set aside for the benefit of the labourers. In the 1930s Indian nationalist sentiment gave rise to a campaign for total prohibition but this issue was still unresolved in 1941.

The Indian labourer was also seriously affected by the disparity between the sexes. The Chinese solution lay in the institution of the brothel, which were in copious abundance in all centres of population. Although such facilities were also open to Indian labourers, the isolation and self-sufficiency of the estate labour lines together with other factors tended to cut out that solution. In consequence amongst Indian estate labourers the sex crime rate was high and incidents arising from broken marriages and infidelities were frequent. Court action was rendered inoperable in most cases by the difficulty of establishing the legality of the marriages entered into. As was the case with the Chinese, the situation eased somewhat in the 1930s with the normalization of the sex ratios which followed the imposition of immigration controls.

The co-operative movement

All the three major communities in British Malaya were touched to a lesser or greater degree by the problem of indebtedness. In response the British authorities established a co-operative movement in the country, initiated by the creation of the Cooperative Societies' Department in 1922. In this field too—perhaps inevitably—things moved along communal lines. The first object of the Department was to come to the rescue of the Malay peasant farmer, so that the earliest co-operatives were the rural ones already noted. Another step came in 1929 when the first thrift and loan societies were instituted amongst Indian estate labourers. These societies, being placed under the control of estate managers who were feared rather than trusted, got off to a slow start. After 1932, however, and despite the Great Depression, there was a far greater response, so much so that the Department with its limited staff and resources was unable to keep up with the demand, and expansion accelerated still further as recovery from the Depression took place. To what extent these estate societies succeeded in overcoming the indebtedness of their members remains a moot point. The unofficial tontine run by the *kangany* was probably a more popular form of saving.

The most successful venture of the Cooperative Societies' Department up till 1941 was with its urban thrift and loan societies, the first three of which were founded soon after the launching of the rural co-operatives. Catering for clerks in government service and in private firms they were a rapid success, for their point and purpose were readily understood. They survived the Great Depression and by 1938 had doubled their membership and capital. Although these societies amounted to under a third of those on the estates, the capital subscribed totalled six times as much.

In many ways Malaya was a showpiece for the virtues of colonialism—the transformation of a territory from (economically speaking) isolation, poverty and backwardness into a flourishing, (largely) westernized community with international connexions. Yet British rule had created profound economic and social problems the solutions to which, increasingly obviously, lay beyond the colonial framework within which the interests of the colonial power itself must predominate. The answers to the problems of the dichotomous society of the Straits Settlements and of the Malay States would only come from that society itself, freed from its colonial restraints to choose its own destiny.

[1] viz., Charles A. Fisher, *South-East Asia: A Social, Economic and Political Geography*, Methuen, London, 1954, p. 172, et seq.

[2] In fact the rate of natural increase was even smaller than the actual figures suggest, since the turnover of migrants entering and leaving was so high.

[3] T.H. Silcock and E.K. Fisk, *The Political Economy of Independent Malaya*, Eastern Universities Press, Singapore, 1963, p. 63.

[4] As is pointed out below (see p. 237) in speaking of Malay population increase and immigration, one has to be careful with the use of one's terms. The term 'Malay' may be used to identify (a) the Malays as a distinct race; (b) Malay-speaking peoples; (c) peoples in the region of the same basic ethnic stock. Throughout this book, the term 'Malay' is used in the first sense, while the terms 'Malaysian' and 'Indonesian' are used in their

original ethnic sense to describe the ethnically related peoples of Island and Mainland South-East Asia as a whole.

[5]Silcock and Fisk, op. cit., p. 62.

[6]Included in the figures for the Peninsula here are the Straits Settlements of Penang and Malacca.

[7]The Hokkiens who predominate in both Johore and Selangor were the first to come in large numbers into the Peninsula; they tend to be mostly associated with trade and commerce in the towns. The Cantonese tend to predominate elsewhere and are engaged in most occupations, but have a large stake in tin-mining, shop-keeping and agriculture. The Hakka are also well distributed, with interests in mining and agriculture while the Hainanese are particularly associated with domestic service, and food shops in the past.

[8]R. Emerson, *Malaysia, A Study in Direct and Indirect Rule*, University of Malaya Press, Kuala Lumpur, 1964, p. 29.

[9]The use of Indian convict labour was restricted to the Straits Settlements.

[10]The Sikhs actually formed the largest group in this minority, many of them serving with the police, or working as night watchmen and surreptitious moneylenders. Other elements included English-educated Jaffna Tamils who, at one stage, virtually monopolized English-medium schools and government offices, the chettyars, and the Sinhalese, most of whom were shop-keepers.

[11]The major exception to this generalization was the Perak River Valley, where the indigenous Malay population continued to predominate, although with significant admixtures of Bugis and Achinese.

[12]A phrase coined by Vlieland in his report on the Census of 1931.

[13]i.e. the northern and eastern parts of the country, or the non-F.M.S. without Johore.

[14]According to the 1931 Census, the Malays living in the F.M.S. were totally excluded from tin-mining which was a European and Chinese preserve; their stake in the rubber industry was limited to smallholdings which despite their number accounted for only about 22 per cent (1957 figures) of the total smallholding acreage. They had no share in large business concerns, nor did they manage small ones which was a field for Chinese and Indians; they did not even, on the whole, participate in the modern world as employees, for the majority of the clerks in the offices, the conductors on estates and the workers in the factories were either Chinese or Indians again.

[15]William Roff, *The Origins of Malay Nationalism*, Oxford University Press, London, 1967, p. 13.

[16]For the background to land policy in this period and the controversies raised, see Philip Loh Fook Seng, *The Malay States, 1877–1896: Political Change and Social Policy*, Oxford University Press, Singapore, 1969, esp. Chapter IV.

[17]Indeed, it has been observed that in 1945 the Malay farmers of Province Wellesley for whom no land reservations were ever provided were no worse off than Malay farmers elsewhere in the Peninsula who had been 'protected' by the land reservation policy.

[18]In its report, the Committee recommended that in no state in the F.M.S. should the ratio between cultivable lands in the Reservations and cultivable lands in the state as a whole be allowed to fall below 60 per cent. Neither the Committee's Report nor the attitude of the government towards it was ever made public, but apparently this recommendation was accepted, although it was already impossible to apply in either Negri Sembilan or Selangor where half the available land had been alienated for forests or to foreigners. By the Malay Reservations Enactment of 1933 Malaysians from overseas were regarded as Malays for its purposes.

[19]e.g. see Roff, op. cit., p. 240.

[20]Quoted by Lennox Mills, *British Rule in Eastern Asia*, Oxford University Press, London, 1942, p. 108.

[21]i.e. especially the outbreak of the Great War, in which the Ottoman Empire (Turkey), the doyen of the Muslim powers, was ranged against Great Britain and her allies.

[22]"The aim of the Government is not to turn out a few well-educated youths, nor anum-

ber of less well-educated boys; rather it is to improve the bulk of the people, and to make the son of the fisherman or peasant a more intelligent fisherman or peasant than his father had been, and a man whose education will enable him to understand how his lot in life fits in with the scheme of life around him.' 'Annual Report of the Director of Education, F.M.S. for 1920', quoted by Roff, op. cit., p. 127.

[23]By the *padi kuncha* system, the planter got his credit from the padi dealer—usually the village shop-keeper, a Chinese—against a portion of his crop when it was harvested, the rub being that the value of the padi to be given generally far exceeded the sum originally loaned. This system doubtless had its origins in the days before the spread of a commercial economy, when loans were only raised for special needs such as crop failures, illness, weddings, funerals, etc., and where, to cover himself against the great risks involved, the creditor needed to charge high rates of interest. Such exorbitant rates, however, had little justification with the wider use of money and the greater availability of credit. But since the planter was poor and needed credit during the six months between sowing and reaping, he had little choice but to make use of the sole source open to him. The Chinese shop-keeper, on the other hand, was an essential part of this system—essential for credit, and essential as the only link with the outside world which only he knew how to deal in.

[24]Perhaps the greatest achievement of government was to wrest from the *pawang padi* such vital functions as determining the times of planting, transplanting and harvesting the padi and placing them in the hands of government officials.

[25]The Report was very critical of the rural co-operative movement and pinpointed its cheeseparing approach as one of its basic deficiencies. It also criticized the scarcity of properly-trained European officers and the failure to carry out a comprehensive survey of the extent of rural indebtedness.

[26]Lim Chong-yah, *Economic Development of Modern Malaya*, Oxford University Press, Kuala Lumpur, 1967, p. 172 et seq.

[27]The *kangany* system was introduced from Ceylon, probably by European coffee planters from that island, who came to seek their fortunes in the Peninsula. By this system, the estate owner sent his own recruiting agent (the *kangany*), selected from amongst his own labour force, to India to recruit fresh labourers there at a certain fee per head. The *kangany* was given the responsibility for choosing the labourers and for paying their passages, and was allowed to reimburse himself out of their monthly wages on the estates they worked.

[28]In principle the recruitment of the Chinese immigrant was in the hands of a professional recruiting agent, at one of the South Chinese ports, who was responsible for finding and engaging the volunteer, paying his passage to the Straits Settlements and usually for providing a small cash advance besides. On arrival in the Straits, the recruit was either handed over directly to the employer who had commissioned the agent in the first place, or, as was more usual, was held until some prospective employer came along and purchased him. To pay off the costs of his passage and advances, the *sin-kheh* was required to work for a year under his employer, who would supply him with food and clothing during that period and grant him a small allowance. In the early days Chinese merchants in the Straits chartered their own vessels to bring back the immigrants, and often sailed as supercargoes, procuring their own agents for recruitment on arrival at the South China port. On return to the Straits the *sin-kheh* so procured were either held on board the junks they had arrived in or were shepherded to some depot on shore to wait for their buyers to come. The recruiting agents received a flat rate per head for each new recruit dispatched, but the *sin-khehs* themselves fetched different prices according to their skills and state of health. Before the days of steamships, the coolie trade was seasonal.

[29]For the greater part of the period 1850–1900 mining labourers, indentured or free, found themselves enmeshed in a self-perpetuating credit racket known as 'the Truck System', the essence of which was that they received their basic daily provisions on credit for which they were ultimately charged at exorbitant rates. For details of how this system worked to the disadvantage of the employees and to the great profit of

the employers, see Wong Lin-ken, *The Malayan Tin Industry to 1914*, University of Arizona Press, Tucson, 1965, pp. 74–6.

[30]Other enactments embodied in the Code of 1912 were the Labourers' Wages Priority Enactment of 1899 which made wages the first charge in the settlement of unsecured creditors for a mine which had failed; the Anglo-Chinese Labour Convention of 1904 which defined minimum conditions for indentured labour, and legislation in 1908 and 1909 severely restricting the Truck System and prohibiting the supply of opium and alcohol as remuneration to labourers. For the reaction of employers to all this labour legislation, see Wong, op. cit., pp. 181–5 and pp. 206–8; see also C. Gamba, *The Origins of Trade Unionism in Malaya*, A Study in Colonial Labour Unrest, Singapore, 1962, p. 29.

[31]For details of this report and a description of labour conditions in general, see R.N. Jackson, *Immigrant Labour and the Development of Malaya, 1786–1920*, Government Press, Kuala Lumpur, 1961, esp. pp. 151–4.

[32]For the background to the labour troubles of the 1930s, see J. Norman Parmer, 'Chinese Estate Workers' Strikes in Malaya in March, 1937' in *The Economic Development of South-East Asia* (ed. by C.D. Cowan), George Allen & Unwin, London, 1964; and also M.R. Stenson, *Industrial Conflict in Malaya*, Oxford University Press, London, 1970, esp. Chapter 2.

[33]See Jackson, op. cit., pp. 103–4.

[34]The most significant advance under the 1923 Code was the appointment of a representative of the Government of India in Kuala Lumpur, known as the Indian Agent, in order to look after the interests of Indian labour in conjunction with the Labour Department. Most of the penal sanctions for labour offences were abolished, the principle of a standard wage accepted and employers were now required to provide educational and welfare benefits.

[35]V.S. Srinivasa, a member of the Executive Council of the Government of India, made his report in 1937 on labour conditions of Indian immigrants in Malaya at the behest of the British Malayan authorities.

[36]In the Malay world, slavery—especially debt-slavery—was a custom sanctioned since time immemorial, even though opposed to the tenets of Islam. At the same time it was usually not so tyrannical as the variety which flourished amongst Africans brought to the West Indies, as most British observers were prepared to admit. The extent and degree of the practice varied from one state to another.

[37]In Perak Hugh Low brought about the abolition of debt-slavery within eight years. He began by confirming that all who were slaves or debts-bondsmen on his arrival remained as such, but no fresh enslavement was permitted and debt-slaves were to be freed when they had paid their debts; any slave, the victim of abuse and maltreatment, would be freed at once. From here the next step was to establish the amount of debt involved and a rate of monthly work by which it could be reduced. Finally the government stepped in and brought about the manumission of the bondsmen by compensating the owners. In this last process a certain amount of quiet pressure and bribery was also employed. Although no official line was ever formulated, in other states British Residents acted in general along the same principles, adapting themselves to local conditions. In Selangor the emancipation of bondsmen was effected through district officers or magistrates by directives on terms of compensation to owners. No law on the subject was ever passed in the State Council. In Sungai Ujong debt-slavery was apparently ended by the general influence of the first British Resident who 'strongly discouraged' any claims on hereditary debtors, while a decade later it was reported from neighbouring Sri Menanti that the conversion of the debtor into the hired servant of the former slave-owner had proved the most practicable solution to the problem. At the first meeting of the State Council of Pahang under the new regime in 1889, a ceiling was put on the amount that a debtor could owe and provision made for its reduction by work computed on a monthly basis. Registration of slaves was also introduced. With the passage of time, together with the new emoluments and allowances the territorial chiefs now received, the institution melted away. In Kelantan debt-

slavery was brought to an end before the official British take-over, in 1909 through the influence of Graham, the (British) Thai adviser to the state; in Kedah George Maxwell persuaded the State Council to register all slave-debtors and within a couple of years reported that the handful of creditors remaining had been paid off out of state funds and so ending the system. The last state to abolish debt-slavery was Trengganu which was also the last state in the Peninsula to come under effective British control.

[38]Rubber and tin interests as well as many British officials in the Malay States were also concerned with the need to keep down the cost of living which, they argued, would be impossible with the imposition of the proposed customs union. In their view since the prosperity of the country so largely depended on those two commodities, imported goods should be cheap to keep labour cheap and enable the exports to compete effectively on the world market.

[39]Dr. Watson resigned from government service in 1907 so as to be able to devote himself fully to the problems of malarial control, for despite his signal services in this field being already evident the government could not see its way to permitting him to carry this out on a full-time basis whilst in its employ. For the thwarted and chequered career of the Institute of Medical Research which owed its foundation to the vision of men like Joseph Chamberlain and Frank Swettenham, see Chai Hon-chan, *The Development of British Malaya: 1896–1909*, Oxford University Press, Kuala Lumpur, 1964.

[40]By 1941 the bulk of the medical services were concentrated in the urban areas, not the rural ones, and the work of the Medical Department was far more elaborate in the thickly populated states of the west coast than in the east coast states. Furthermore, by virtue of the fragmented nature of Malayan administration prior to 1941, resources were operated on a state basis, with the result that the incomparably wealthier F.M.S. and Johore could afford far better services than the rest and there was no central government for the Peninsula as a whole to ensure equitable distribution. All this was clearly reflected in the allocations, establishments and services provided by the various states.

[41]One of the complexities was the *mui tsai* system, the *mui tsai* being a girl placed by her own family to live with another family and act as a domestic servant, without regular wages and not free to leave the household at her will. Her employer was obliged to look after her and to marry her off when she came of age. The system was made illegal in Malaya in 1938.

[42]At the same time (1910) government took over the monopoly of importing, preparing and selling opium through its newly-created Monopolies Department. This led to a policy of very gradually suppressing the opium traffic.

Books and articles for further reading

BOOKS

Arasaratnam, S., *Indians in Malaysia and Singapore*, Oxford University Press, London, 1970.

Blythe, W., *The Impact of Chinese Secret Societies in Malaya*, Oxford University Press, London, 1969.

Gamba, C., *The Origins of Trade Unionism in Malaya*, A Study in Colonial Labour Unrest, Singapore, 1962.

Jackson, R.N., *Pickering: Protector of Chinese*, Oxford University Press, Kuala Lumpur, 1965.

Kernial Singh Sandhu, *Indians in Malaya: Immigration and Settlement, 1786–1957*, Cambridge University Press, 1969.

Netto, G., *Indians in Malaya*, published by the author, Singapore, 1961.

Roff, W., *The Origins of Malay Nationalism*, Oxford University Press, London, 1967.

Stenson, M.R., *Industrial Conflict in Malaya*, Oxford University Press, London, 1971.

Wong, C.S., *A Gallery of Chinese Kapitans*, Dewan Bahasa dan Kebudayaan Kebangsaan, Singapore, 1963.

ARTICLES

Arasaratnam, S., 'Social Reform and Reformist Pressure Groups', *JMBRAS*, XXXX, 2, 1967.

Blythe, W.L., 'A Historical Sketch of Chinese Labour in Malaya', *JMBRAS*, XX, 1, 1947.

Comber, L., 'Chinese Secret Societies in Malaya', *JMBRAS*, XXIX, 1, 1956.

Gamba, C., 'Chinese Associations in Singapore', *JMBRAS*, XXXIX, 2, 1966.

Khoo Kay Kim, 'Biographical Sketches of Certain Straits Chinese', *P.S.*, 2.2.1967.

Quah Chooi Hon, 'The Chinese in Malaya, 1786–1941', *JHSUM*, XXXX, 65–6.

C. Sarawak

'...Any government...must be directed to the advancement of the native interests and the development of native resources, rather than by a flood of European colonization to aim at possession only, without reference to the indefeasible rights of the Aborigines.'
James Brooke, Prospectus for an Expedition to Borneo, 1838.

'After my life the future will remain with you to be independent and free citizens or to be a humbled and inferior class without pride in yourselves or your race. You must choose between the two, the owner or the master on one side or the dependent and coolie on the other. It is for you to see that whoever rules this land that the land is not granted away to strangers....'
Charles Brooke, to the Council Negri, Kuching, 1915.

IN northern Borneo, 400 miles across the China Sea from the Straits, lay three other British territories, the most singular of which was the principality of Sarawak, ruled for a century by an English family which ran it like a vast private estate. The Brookes administered their property in the best paternalistic traditions of a squierarchy, deliberately discouraged the introduction of Western enterprise, except where essential, and did their best to shield their subjects from the ill-effects of modern commercial exploitation. The price that had to be paid for this paternalism was a far slower pace of economic growth and whatever progress was achieved under Brooke rule was largely brought about by permitting the substantial immigration of Chinese traders, farmers and miners, as indeed had happened elsewhere in the archipelago. In 1941 Sarawak economically speaking was still a very backward country. Three-quarters of the land was covered by virgin jungle and on the remaining quarter the great bulk of the population subsisted by farming. Kuching was the only town of any size, serving as the main port through which the country's exports flowed to Singapore. Amongst those, only oil possessed any real significance for the outside world, although for brief spells antimony, gold, gutta percha and pepper had their day. Communications were rudimentary and there was virtually no local industry of consequence at all. But Sarawak's slow development was not entirely the result of Brooke policy. The country itself was inherently poor.

Oil, rubber and timber—the major exports
Ironically enough in view of Brooke precepts, Sarawak's leading export in the 1930s was entirely in the hands of a large Western concern, Royal

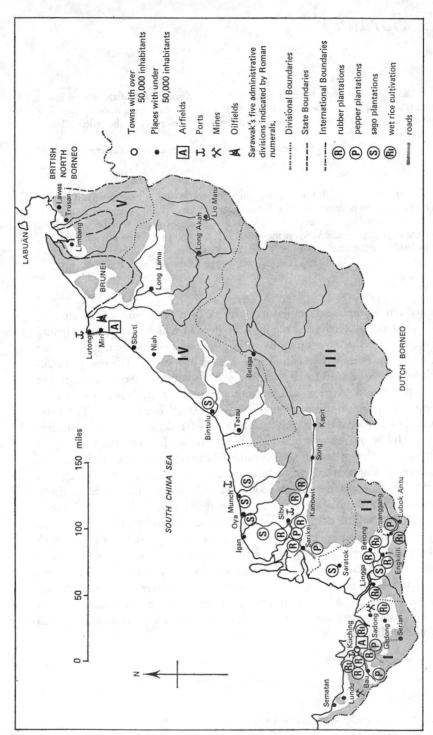

Legend:

○ Towns with over 50,000 inhabitants
● Places with under 50,000 inhabitants
Ⓐ Airfields
⊥ Ports
✕ Mines
ᐃ Oilfields

Sarawak's five administrative divisions indicated by Roman numerals,

.... Divisional Boundaries
— — — State Boundaries
———— International Boundaries
Ⓡ rubber plantations
Ⓟ pepper plantations
Ⓢ sago plantations
Ⓡᵢ wet rice cultivation
roads

LABUAN

BRITISH NORTH BORNEO

BRUNEI

DUTCH BORNEO

SOUTH CHINA SEA

0   50   100   150 miles

N

Lawas
Trusan
Limbang
Long Lama
Long Akah
Lio Matu
Lutong
Miri
Sibuti
Niah
Belaga
Bintulu
Tatau
Kapit
Song
Kanowit
Igan
Oya
Munch
Sibu
Sarikei
Saratok
Lingga
Betong
Simanggang
Lubok Antu
Engkilili
Gedong
Sadong
Kuching
Bau
Lundu
Sematan
Serian

I II III IV V

21. General Map of Sarawak

Dutch Shell. The existence of oil in the state had been known since the 1870s, but it was not until 1907 that effective steps were taken to do something about it. By this time it had become quite evident that the deposits were worthwhile, but since they could not be developed without heavy capital investment from outside, Rajah Charles reluctantly agreed to open negotiations for their exploitation. In 1909 a concession was granted to the Sarawak Oil Company, a newly created subsidiary of Royal Dutch Shell, and operations commenced the following year. Production rose rapidly for over a decade, topping 550,000 tons annually by 1923, the year in which the mineral, displacing gold, became the country's leading export. Four years later production reached its peak, after which output entered into a long, steady decline. In the brief span of its heyday in the 1920s and 1930s, the oil industry brought welcome wealth to Sarawak, formed the mainstay of Brooke revenues, and accelerated the pace of development, calling into existence in particular Miri which grew into the third largest town in the state.

Rubber, Sarawak's second most valuable export and the most important of its cash crops before 1941, was also an innovation of the twentieth century, but in this case the Brooke prejudice against Western enterprise prevented the growth of large estates and ensured that it remained predominantly a smallholders' crop. In 1941 well over 90 per cent belonged to smallholdings of less than four acres apiece. The crop covered over half the total area of cultivated land in the state and accounted for more than half its agricultural exports; in fact, Sarawak was the largest producer amongst the British territories in North Borneo.[1]

Basically the history of the rubber planting industry in Sarawak followed the same pattern as elsewhere in South-East Asia. The first seedlings were planted at Kuching in 1881 but no serious planting was done until the boom frenzy of the 1900s. Although large commercial enterprises were not encouraged, the lead was taken by the Borneo Company which planted 2,500 acres with rubber in 1902, importing Javanese labourers for the purpose. But a more important role was played by the Chinese settlements in the Rejang Basin which from 1905 onwards turned to rubber for their salvation. The first rubber exports from Sarawak in 1910 coincided with the height of the rubber boom and stimulated a fresh rash of planting in the following decade, much to the concern of Rajah Charles. The Little Depression of 1919 proved the first confirmation of the Rajah's gloomy prognostications and deterred further planting for a season. But the recovery of prices in 1923 led to more planting and increased exports. The Great Depression of 1929 was much more serious as it took place just as the majority of the trees planted in the early 1920s were maturing. As a result many holdings were neglected or abandoned. In 1934, Sarawak experimented unsuccessfully with a tapping holiday, then in 1938 tried out a coupon system, similar to that adopted in the Malay Peninsula, but with better results. At any rate Sarawak's smallholders were far less affected by these fluctuations on the world market than the much more heavily capitalized planters elsewhere, and in consequence despite its low rating overseas rubber came to be a sheet anchor to its growers and provided them with a steady income. In fact rubber in Sarawak assumed an immense local importance. It attracted a fresh influx of settlers from China and Indonesia and considerably modified the pattern of population and settlement in the country. Kuching and Sibu were confirmed as the main foci of economic development, while the isolation of scores of fishing villages and longhouses was ended as immigrant and indigene alike turned to the planting of the new crop.

After rubber, timber came next amongst the state's exports in terms of value. This was another twentieth-century development, for although the state contains large reserves of commercially exploitable forest, neither opportunity nor demand were available till the late 1890s when some Chinese merchants in Kuching started exporting timber overseas. The new industry remained under Chinese domination and its first real expansion took place after the Great War and continued steadily up till 1941.

Pepper, sago and other cash crops
Two of the country's traditional crops, pepper and sago, not only retained their importance but expanded in the twentieth century. Pepper, which at one period had been the mainstay of the revenues of the Brunei Sultanate, was no longer planted in Sarawak by the 1850s. However, its cultivation was revived by Rajah Charles who provided the Chinese pepper and gambier planters of Singapore with free passages to Kuching and granted land to certain local merchants for pepper gardens. By the late 1870s this project was already proving very successful, the main area of planting being in Ulu Sarawak. There the Singapore immigrants and underworked Hakka gold-miners from Bau planted it together with gambier, a combination already proven profitable in Singapore and Johore. By 1885 the prospects of the twin crops seemed sufficiently good to attract the Borneo Company. Gambier which held the upper hand in the 1880s and 1890s rapidly declined after 1900, but pepper went from strength to strength. Its output almost doubled in the same period and its cultivation spread into the Rejang Basin. In the twentieth century, pepper's career was checked by the rise of rubber which virtually displaced it around Sibu, although the crop was extended to Binatang and Sarikei with the opening of new Chinese colonies there after 1910. Pepper also became subjected to severe price fluctuations which affected its development, but there was a marked recovery after 1929 and between 1935 and 1937 Sarawak became the world's second greatest pepper producer. Up till 1941 pepper remained an exclusively Chinese affair.

Sago was traditional to Melanau country on the Igan, Oya, Mukah and Bintulu rivers, and throughout the nineteenth century was Sarawak's most important agricultural export. After 1861, following Brooke intervention into the area, planting entered into an era of unparalleled expansion, a leading role in which was played by immigrant Malay traders who became its principal exporters to Kuching. Induced by the progress of the trade, the Borneo Company opened a mill at Mukah and in the 1870s advanced money to cultivators to plant their own trees. Production rose swiftly in the 1880s; by the end of the decade Sarawak was reckoned to be producing half the world's total output. Exports continued to soar into the twentieth century but then became overshadowed by those in pepper and rubber.

The sago industry played an important role in the development of the state's economy. As far as the Melanau producers were concerned, its expansion ended their subsistence way of life, took them out of their longhouses and gave rise to ribbons of individual, river-bank holdings. Sago also helped lay the foundations of the fortunes of the Hokkien shop-keepers and traders of Kuching, who became the commodity's middlemen and exporters. By 1941 probably some 90,000 acres were under the crop, mostly in Melanau territory.[2]

The only other cash crop of significance was the coconut, four-fifths of which was grown by the Malays on smallholdings in the coastal areas of the First and Second Divisions. The growing of coconut palms for commercial purposes probably started in the 1830s and spread with the establishment of the Brooke regime and with the intensification of Malay settlement.

As for jungle produce, the various products of the Bornean forest had long formed one of the traditional sources of attraction for foreign traders, and throughout the nineteenth century continued to enjoy considerable local importance. After 1900, however, they were completely eclipsed by the rise of oil, pepper, rubber and timber. Certain items held specialized markets: in the middle of the nineteenth century, Kuching was one of the principal sources of gutta percha; jelutong survived as a minor export, centred on Bintulu, well into the twentieth century with its market in the United States; nipah palm was used as a source for sugar, some of which was exported, and the unpredictable illipe nut provided occasional windfalls for its Iban harvesters. Indeed, the real importance of all these minor products lay in the part they played in the subsistence economies of the peoples who gathered them.[3]

Amongst the wide variety of domestic crops, rice was by far the most important, accounting for the largest area under cultivation and involving nearly half the population. It remained, however, primarily the occupation of the inland peoples. Farming methods were very primitive, domestic animals and water control virtually unknown, the minute average holding prevented the development of economic techniques, and two-thirds of the crop came from the far less productive dry rice cultivation. Another factor behind Sarawak's failure to grow enough rice for its own needs lay in the lack of incentive for planters to produce a surplus, for the Malays and the Chinese of the towns had become accustomed to eating imported rice, a pattern not modified until the rice shortage which came in the wake of the Great War.[4]

Sarawak minerals
During the days of the Brooke regime, the known extent and yield of the country's mineral resources were disappointing, and would appear to have been more important for the role they played in shaping its destinies than for the benefits they brought to the economy.

Antimony, for instance, played a leading part in the events surrounding the creation of the modern state. Singapore's emergence after 1819 as a new entrepôt for the trade of the archipelago provided it with a market, and four years later the first antimony mines were opened at Bau. Antimony's swift rise excited the attention of Brunei's *pangerans*, lay at the root of Governor

Mahkota's tyranny over his non-Malay subjects and prompted Bonham, the British governor of Singapore, to persuade James Brooke to call at Kuching in 1839. The demand for the metal on the Singapore market made antimony Sarawak's main export and provided the state with its chief revenues for forty years, but after 1885 started to decline in quantity and importance and by 1916 had ceased to be of any significance at all. The main deposits were all found on the Sarawak River and were worked by primitive methods by both Malays and Chinese. The Borneo Company established a smelting plant at Kuching in the 1840s and another near Bau two decades later.

Gold, likewise found along the banks of the Sarawak River, attracted the Chinese gold-miners from their exhausted Sambas fields and led to the growth of the famous *kongsi* near Bau which launched the abortive rebellion of 1857. However, the gold they mined never assumed significant proportions and the rebellion nearly ruined the industry altogether. Desultory panning was continued by a generation of Chinese, Malay and Iban miners, but by the 1890s it was obvious that primitive methods no longer sufficed, so in 1896 the Borneo Company introduced modern equipment for extraction, opening up its own mine at Bau two years later. The company's efforts gave Sarawak's gold a new lease of life and gold-mining entered into its most productive period. During the next twenty-one years, the state exported nearly 1 million ounces of gold and the metal was its leading mineral export. However, having exhausted all the profitable deposits, in 1921 the company withdrew from goldmining completely, and the industry went into a new and permanent decline.[5]

Coal and mercury both had comet-like phases of importance before lapsing into complete insignificance. Coal actually became the country's leading mineral export for ten years after 1889, when the government finally managed to work the colliery at Sadong, while mercury led the field between 1874 and 1879. The existence of other minerals was known of, but either their deposits were insufficient to be worth-while opening up or they proved too inaccessible and therefore too costly to exploit.[6]

The development of communications

Against this background of limited economic potential, the absence of a well-developed system of communications other than by water is hardly surprising. The building of roads through the swamps of the lowlands or through the densely-jungled hills of the interior was a very expensive undertaking, made all the more difficult by the great scarcity of good quality stone, particularly in the Rejang Basin, and not visibly justifiable in terms of the returns that could be anticipated. The few roads that were built were naturally centred on Kuching. The earliest road in the country joining Kuching to Penrissen was started in 1883 and by 1900 there were still no roads outside the First Division. Proposals, prompted by Rajah Vyner himself in 1921, to extend the road system aroused strong opposition, and the subsequent work to link Kuching to Simanggang had not got beyond the forty miles to Serian by 1941.[7] By that time there were still barely 100 miles of metalled highway in the whole state and over two-thirds of all motor vehicles were to be found within the area of the capital. The country could boast a railway line, if only briefly. A pet scheme of Rajah Charles was to join Kuching to Bau. This line was completed in 1917 but, never proving an economic proposition, was closed down in 1932 during the Great Depression.

In the meantime the sea and rivers served, as they had always done, as the main channels of communication and commerce. In fact, the key role in promoting Sarawak's development from the moment James Brooke established himself at Kuching in 1841 was played by the sea-lane between his capital and Singapore, and as the country's export trade gradually grew over the years, so the lane broadened, converting Kuching into an outport of Singapore and Sarawak into its economic dependency. Indeed the control of the sea-lane to the outside world became the key to the economy of the world within the state. By the 1870s Sarawak's export trade had sufficiently expanded to make feasible the establishment of a local steamship company, based on Kuching. Founded in 1875 with the active encouragement of Rajah Charles, it was financed by the leading Chinese merchants of the town—mostly sago millers and exporters—and by the Borneo Company which provided the management.[8] Known as the Singapore and Sarawak Steamship Company, the new venture got off to a flying start with a complete monopoly of the sea route, and was able to pay handsome dividends from the first year of its formation. The company continued to flourish for the rest of the century and in 1908 its sphere of operations widened when the government handed over its own local steamship services and all the coastal traffic eastwards from Kuching as far as the Limbang and Baram rivers.[9] In 1919 a group of Chinese merchants in Kuching, led by the prestigious Ong Tiang Swee, the Capitan China of the Sarawak Chinese, bought out the Borneo Company's interest, and reorganized the firm under the new name of the Sarawak Steamship Company.

By this time, however, the company faced serious competition on its Singapore route from the Straits Steamship Company, while the coastal and river services to the east had always been an economic liability. Immediately after his takeover, Ong tried to vamp up the eastward services by starting a new line between Kuching and Sibu, but without success. In the 1920s the company faced mounting overheads because of aging vessels and expanding maintenance costs, while a new boat built to order in British shipyards in 1927 was only possible through a substantial loan from the Sarawak government. Then with the Great Depression which hit company and government alike, the Straits Steamship Company was able to take advantage of the situation to acquire shares in the Kuching firm and finally a controlling interest in it. After 1931, as a subsidiary of the Straits Steamship Company, the firm was reorganized, its services interlocked with those of the parent concern, and a new era of efficiency and profits resulted. Its control was extended over the small Chinese businesses that operated between Singapore and Sarawak and local coastal services, and by 1941 it held a predominant position in the import-export trade of the country by virtue of a series of exclusive agreements with all the leading merchants in the state. So, as far as Sarawak's water-borne communications were concerned, not only were they reasonably well developed, but they were also effectively monopolized by the dominant economic interests in the country.

As for air communications, these literally had not got off the ground prior to 1941. In 1929 an abortive attempt was made to inaugurate a government air service within the state. Kuching's airport was not completed till the 1930s and in general the age of air transport had to wait till after the Pacific War. Modern radio communications, on the other hand, were introduced well before 1941. The first telegraphic cable between Kuching and Singapore was laid in 1897 and the capital joined to the outlying Baram district by 1908. The first telephone was installed in Kuching in 1900, its first radio transmitter was functioning in 1916 and a regular broadcasting service was established in 1919. By 1941 Sarawak possessed thirty-four post offices. Limited as they might have been, the development of these facilities provided a mighty impetus to development.

Brooke policy and the pattern of Sarawak's commerce

Sarawak's economic development would have been faster had the Brooke family not consciously eschewed Western enterprise. However, the first Rajah's gentlemanly instincts against the world of Western trade and commerce were immeasurably reinforced by his unhappy dealings with his London agent, Henry Wise, during the pioneer days of his rule. Wise's idea was to float a large public company in London (in which he would hold a controlling interest), buy Sarawak from James and then run it as a purely commercial profit-making concern, a vision far removed from the Rajah's who regarded his mission primarily in terms of ending oppression and misrule, curbing piracy and suppressing headhunting. But James needed money and so in 1847 consented to the formation by Wise of the Eastern Archipelago Company with exclusive trading rights in Sarawak (and Labuan). The new enterprise was ill-managed from the start, was soon bogged down in its attempts to mine Labuan's mediocre coal deposits and was finally dissolved in 1852, largely as a consequence of the Rajah's quarrel with Wise over other issues. The whole episode, together with the complications which followed in its wake, intensified James' natural mistrust of all businessmen; by the same token it also made business and commercial circles in both London and Singapore profoundly wary of him and of Sarawak.[10]

Nevertheless it was obvious that there could be no development in Sarawak at all without the aid of some outside capital, so that within four years of the untimely demise of the Eastern Archipelago Company, Rajah James had given his sanction to the formation of the Borneo Company (1856) as the sole public company in the state with the right to exploit the government monopolies over antimony and coal, to organize the commerce in sago and gutta percha, and to finance other official schemes of commerce. Although it had a very chequered career both commercially and in its relations with the Brooke family, the Borneo Company played an important role in the development of Sarawak's economy. It did not make any profits at all out of its Sarawak ventures until 1898, having tried its hand in nearly every aspect of commercial enterprise in the country with mostly disappointing results.

However, it became the banker to the state government, gained control over a good share of the state monopolies and as we have seen was responsible for providing Kuching with its only regular means of communication with Singapore and the rest of the outside world. In the twentieth century the company also acquired an early interest in the rubber planting industry, and in general benefited from the general expansion in trade and commerce.

Other Western concerns were able to establish a foothold in the country after 1900, notably the Sarawak Oil Company (a subsidiary of Royal Dutch Shell) in 1909. The Chartered Bank of Australia, India and China became the first (and only) Western bank to open up a branch in the country at Kuching in 1924. However, the basic Brooke policy of discouraging large-scale Western enterprise prevailed, contributing to the fact that rubber developed primarily as a smallholders' crop and that the bulk of Sarawak's trade in general resembled a 'transmission belt' which linked the big concerns of Singapore with the individual shop-keepers in the countless, tiny bazaars scattered along the country's great rivers, dominated by the Chinese and held together by a trade-credit relationship which existed at all its stages along its length. Western firms could only fit into this system by using the Chinese as agents for their products and by serving as a source of credit as well, and as such they formed a limited but vital link in the country's trading structure. The scattered and lonely bazaars of the riverways, the lack of good communications and the shortage of capital conditioned the evolution of Sarawak's trade and commercial organization.

The population pattern

The presence of the Chinese reflected the one area in which Brooke practice seemed at variance with the theory of ruling in the interests of the indigenous folks and of protecting them from undue exploitation from outside. For the Brooke dispensation followed the pattern set by more orthodox colonial regimes and deliberately permitted and encouraged the (comparatively-speaking) large-scale immigration of an alien race in order to boost the development of the country.

From the earliest days of Brooke rule the Chinese were welcomed to the country and were invited to settle down there. From the end of the nineteenth century they did so in increasing numbers, so that by 1936 they accounted for nearly one-quarter of the total population. Apart from a small group of Indians, the remaining two-thirds of Sarawak's population could be regarded as indigenous, in the sense of being native to the region if not actually to the country itself. According to the official classification of 1941, eight main groups were considered native to the country.[11]

Taken as a whole, the indigenous peoples were overwhelmingly engaged in agriculture, most of which was of the shifting hill-padi type. The Ibans held first place by virtue of their numbers, forming the largest single ethnic group in the state and mostly concentrated in the Second and Third Divisions —almost entirely subsistence farmers, still holding on to their traditional way of life associated with large longhouses of up to fifty families and more. Then came the Malays, only half as numerous but carrying greater weight in terms of power and influence, mainly located in the First and Second Divisions as well. During the course of Brooke rule, the Malays lost their position as the second major ethnic group in the country to the Chinese, but compensated for this by dominating the lower echelons of government service. Although still predominantly a rural people, nearly one-third were to be found in urban occupations. The other indigenous groups were considerably smaller. The Land Dayaks were practically all confined to the hill region of the First Division where they subsisted on dry padi, while some also found employment in the Chinese gold-mines around Bau. The Melanau, on the other hand, were spread along the coastline of the Third and Fourth Divisions and were the country's principal planters of sago, which formed their staple diet. All the other groups could be numbered in terms of thousands. The Kayan, the Kenyah, the Murut and the Kelabit all lived by the headwaters of the great rivers, planting dry padi and hunting. Small groups of Bisayans farmed in the Lower Limbang, Kedayans farmed the coast around Sibuti and in Limbang and Lawas, while deep in the interior following their age-old ways as nomad hunters, the Punan or Penan people lived out their lives.

Although the various indigenous peoples of Sarawak were distinct from one another and held their own special features and customs, distinctions which were sharpened under Brooke rule by conversions to Christianity and by growing economic pressures, they all shared a common cultural base (in many cases with a common ethnic origin), rooted in what was still mainly a subsistence economy. Communal life was dominant, women enjoyed a high social status, slavery was an established institution, and a general belief in the spirit world held sway. Private property was recognized, and wealth measured in terms of livestock owned and in the possession of ornaments and of the ancient ceremonial jars. The Land Dayaks were exceptions to some of this, and the Malays were also generally apart, separated by origin, political privilege and religion.[12]

Growth and change in the population pattern
Even within the cautious framework of Brooke rule, the peoples of Sarawak experienced important changes, including an overall rise in numbers, the penetration of Christianity into the remotest corners of the country, and some important shifts in population distribution.[13]

Compared to the growth rates of neighbouring lands, the increase in Sarawak's population between 1841 and 1941 was hardly spectacular, yet it was significant enough. A rough though probably exaggerated estimate of 1841 put the total population at around 20,000; by 1936 it was approaching half a million. By this time, however, the area of the state had extended out of all proportion and the composition of its inhabitants was drastically altered. In fact, the population growth rate was slow, markedly so amongst the Ibans who only increased by just over one-third between 1848 and 1939. Limited medical resources and unchecked diseases, together with—in the 1920s and 1930s—the effects of economic depression, were the main contributory factors.

By 1941 one-third of the people were concentrated within the First Division, focused on Kuching, the centre of the greatest economic development.

There were also important shifts of population elsewhere less connected with the Brooke regime than with traditional forces working within the country. The main centre of population change outside the First Division was in the Rejang Basin caused by the pressure of Iban migrants.[14] For centuries the Ibans had been pressing their way northwards from the heart of Borneo. Up till 1840 they were still confined to the upper waters of the Sungai Ai, but were beginning to move further north towards the Seribas and Krian rivers. Soon after they were finding their way down the Batang Lupar and the Seribas, eastwards to Kanowit and westwards along the coast to Lundu. Then pressed by Rajah James' raids on their strongholds in the Second Division, they started to cross over into the Third.

The main Iban penetration of the Rejang Basin took place during the 1850s and 1860s. At first affected by the fresh Brooke campaigns against Rentab and by the needs of their own shifting agriculture, which drove them into conflict with the long-established Kayan and Kenyah peoples for the farming land along the Rejang, after 1863 the Ibans found themselves allies in the Brooke attempts to pacify the Kayans of the area. The outcome was to enable the Ibans to consolidate their control and occupation over the whole of the Middle and Upper Rejang. In the meanwhile other large groups of them moved up the Entabai, while yet more penetrated towards Sibu. In the 1870s the needs of shifting agriculture again caused an Iban drive northwards, bringing about a new spate of tribal warfare. By the 1880s they were settled on the headwaters of the Mukah and Oya rivers, and at the turn of the century along the waters of the Baliangan, Tatau and Kemena systems. Brooke's attempts to arrest this process met with only momentary success. In the meantime the Kayan and the Kenyah were driven remorselessly further towards the north-east. But it was not until the great peace-making ceremony held before Rajah Vyner in Kapit in 1924 that the Iban presence was accepted by the other peoples.

On a far more restricted scale the emergence of the Kelabit and Murut peoples onto the Sarawak scene was also the outcome of migrations in the Brooke era. One group whom Brooke rule possibly saved from extinction were the Land Dayaks. Largely leaderless and defenceless, they had been steadily losing their farms in the rich low-lying country around the Sarawak River to their more aggressive neighbours and retiring to the hilltops their numbers had entered into a fixed decline. With the establishment of Brooke authority in Kuching, the pressure against them was lifted and they were able to expand once more, and their numbers have increased accordingly.

The Chinese of Sarawak
Apart from the great Iban migrations, the most significant change in the country's population after 1841 was the coming of the Chinese. Mainly settled by the mid-twentieth century in a thick belt between Kuching and Serian and around the townships of Sibu, Sarikei and Binatang, they were without doubt the most dominant community in Sarawak. Nine large Chinese firms virtually monopolized the import-export trade and most of Sarawak's commerce was in their hands. They lorded over the production of the state's prin-

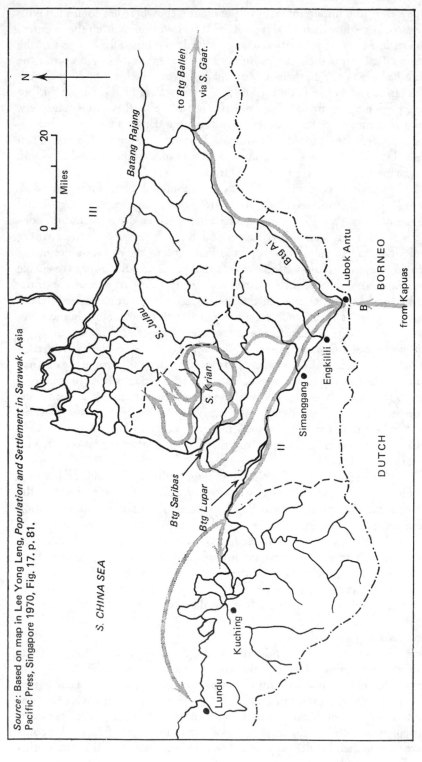

Source: Based on map in Lee Yong Leng, *Population and Settlement in Sarawak*, Asia Pacific Press, Singapore 1970, Fig. 17, p. 81.

22. Sarawak: Iban Migration Routes in the Nineteenth Century

cipal cash crops, grew wet padi, were the shop-keepers, tradesmen and the country's main craftsmen, and owned the transport services on water and on land. Chinese were to be found as clerks in government offices and private firms, and provided the bulk of the labour, skilled and unskilled, in the oil fields and elsewhere.

By 1945 over half of the Chinese in Sarawak were local born, although the preponderant mass arrived within the early part of the present century.[15] Chinese contacts with the country, however, go back to the dawn of history, as archaeological, literary and circumstantial evidence testifies. There was an early Chinese settlement at Santubong, and although this and other such permanent colonies disappeared after the Mongol collapse in China itself, the trading links were preserved. A small Chinese trading community was already established at Kuching when James Brooke first appeared on the scene, furnishing the Governor Mahkota with the only reliable force of fighting men at his disposal to cope with the rebellion that he confronted.

The attitude of the Brooke regime towards the Chinese presence was generally favourable, although the rebellion of the Chinese gold-miners of Bau in 1857 marked a set-back which had the effect of cutting off the flow of substantial immigration for the rest of the century. Rajah James himself had at first formed a good impression of the Chinese, all the more so as they were his loyal allies in the events which led to his securing power, and he encouraged them, albeit warily, for he realized that they would bring much needed elements of skill and enterprise to his sparsely-populated and backward province.[16] The establishment of the Brooke regime correspondingly attracted Chinese to Sarawak. The immigrants up to 1857 consisted of three main elements. One comprised the small but expanding colony of merchants, mostly Hokkien, living in Kuching, who were law-abiding, co-operative and useful in various trades. A second group was represented by the more numerous and restive Hakka gold-miners from Sambas, settled in the neighbourhood of Bau. The third group consisted of Teochew and other pepper and gambier planters around Kuching, and of small colonies of miners and traders who moved into the territory east of the Batang Lupar opened up by the acquisition of 1853.

The Hakka miners of Bau presented problems from the very beginning and became more troublesome still in and after 1850 when their numbers were suddenly augmented by the arrival of about 3,000 refugees from the Sambas troubles. Nevertheless the Rajah's officials actively encouraged their coming, for the state's revenues tripled overnight. The rebellion of 1857 destroyed James' faith in the Chinese, resulted in an exodus of the Hakka population from Bau and reduced immigration to a mere trickle. Nevertheless the Brooke administration never lost sight of their usefulness and even the Rajah himself remained objective enough to contemplate encouraging a fresh wave of settlers in the 1860s. So Chinese immigration continued, but it remained a fitful and spasmodic affair until the closing years of the century. Prejudices aroused by the Rebellion played their part, but more important was the existence of far more tempting opportunities and more effective organization for Chinese seeking their fortunes in other territories overseas. In the meantime the Chinese already in the country began to spread out, opening up small bazaars for jungle produce in the lee of government forts built at strategic centres across the land.

Rajah Charles clearly favoured the Chinese and took active steps to induce them to come. In 1880 he promoted the settlement of 500 Chinese on the Lower Rejang; the scheme attracted more settlers and by 1887 there were some 7,000 Chinese in the country. The Rajah gave his full backing in 1900 to a second settlement on the Rejang, this time based on Sibu. By this time the Chinese were becoming established; Sibu itself had already grown into a town and there was a flourishing bazaar at Kapit, further upstream. In the decade which followed the trickle became a flood and the Rajah's efforts were rewarded. But the great influx which now ensued was not on account of those efforts alone; it was also a consequence of deteriorating circumstances in China and of the contracting markets for Chinese labour within South-East Asia as a whole.

The new Chinese settlement at Sibu of 1900 was led by Wong Nai Siang. Consisting of 1,000 Foochows, it marked the onset of the flood. The new settlers faced a host of problems including the hazards of the environment, crop failures and treachery from within their own ranks. However, they survived, a testimony to their toughness, but partly due to the efforts of the local administration and of Hoover, an American missionary, who was largely instrumental in 1906 in getting them to turn to rubber which proved their salvation. After this the Foochow community at Sibu never really looked back. They were hit by the Little Depression of 1919 but prosperity returned with the recovery of the rubber price in 1924. By this time Sibu had become transformed into the second largest town in the country. Stimulated by the initial success of the Sibu settlement, in 1901 the Sarawak government permitted the immigration of 5,000 Cantonese into the area, followed in 1911 by a large batch of Heng Hua. With this steady influx of settlers and the economic growth they brought with them, Sibu waxed prosperous; firms dealing in groceries and other consumer goods sprang up, sawmills, rubber mills and rice mills were built, the town acquired its own steamship line and became the centre of the greatest concentration of Chinese in the state.

During these years similar settlements were started elsewhere—at Binatang, at Sarikei, Song and Kanowit, at Rejang and Baram, at Kapit and at Bintulu—all founded by Foochow men from the focal point of Sibu itself. There was also mounting immigration paid for by private Chinese settlers in Sarawak who sent for their relatives. By 1941 there were Chinese settlements in every district of Sarawak. All of them were run on a variant of the kangchu system which had evolved in Johore the previous century.

In fact, there were three main waves of Chinese migration into Sarawak between 1900 and 1940. The first was that associated with Wong's settlement at Sibu. The second between 1910 and 1919 was closely connected to the rubber boom and ended with the Little Depression after the Great War. The last wave came between 1924 and 1930 when larger groups than ever before started coming into the state either to escape the ever-worsening conditions in China or to seek alternatives to the failing openings in the Straits and the

Malay Peninsula. Up till 1930, as in Malaya itself, no attempt was made to restrict or discourage such immigration, but after 1931, confronted with the realities of the Great Depression, no male immigrant was allowed entry unless sponsored by a member of his community. Such restrictions were maintained up till 1942.

In Sarawak, as much as elsewhere, the Chinese evolved a complete and self-contained community which embraced the whole spectrum of society from the richest to the poorest. At the top of the inevitable pyramid were a few big towkays who dominated the economic life of the community—and of the country—while at the base were 'the huge majority of Chinese planters and labourers, the workers by whose sweat and lives primary jungle had been transformed into cultivated land'.[17] In between was a fairly large class of small merchants, traders and middlemen who formed the vital links between the primary producers and the large wholesale exporters. However, the real economic power was concentrated in the hands of men drawn from specific communities, as a recent study has shown.[18] Of the seven major Chinese speech groups in the country, two—the Hokkien and the Teochew —effectively dominated the scene. The rise of these two communities was closely related to the economic activities which they pioneered. The career of the pioneer Hokkien leader, Ong Ewe Hai, who arrived in Kuching in 1846, is a case in point. He laid the foundations of his family's fortunes by handling the export of pepper, sago and jungle products in exchange for textiles, food-stuffs and hardware from Singapore. He then set up one of the first sago refineries in the country, which consolidated his grip over the export trade. From this, his family naturally extended its interests into shipping and real estate. When he died in 1899, Ong was rich, recognized and rewarded; he had been appointed Capitan China by the Brookes, a title which passed along with his fortune to his son, Tiang Swee, on his death. In general, the Hokkien sago-millers of Kuching played a role analogous to that of the Chinese tin-smelters in the Malay Peninsula, serving as advancers, wholesale dealers and distributors. They dominated the newly-formed Chamber of Commerce in Kuching in 1873 and have continued to play a major role ever since. The rise of the Teochew community, on the other hand, had its beginnings in their role as market gardeners and farmers, particularly in the early days when gambier was one of Sarawak's major exports. From market gardening to groceries was a natural step, and as the latter formed a large item in the country's links with Singapore, this brought the Teochew their entry to wealth and influence.[19]

Rich or poor, the achievement of the Chinese settlers in Sarawak was certainly remarkable. Not only did they arrive desperately poor, but many of them were sick and further weakened by the torrid, tropical climate. Yet they survived and after a fashion flourished. Initially they owed everything to the close clan or district solidarity which had ensured their passage and kept them going in the early days; as individuals they could have got nowhere and would have soon succumbed. They were also extraordinarily tough. Those who prospered did so by sheer hard work, and maybe through a break in their luck; those who had succeeded were immeasurably helped further by government boons such as the gift of a monopoly farm which helped to make or confirm the fortunes of the merchant class. But this was far removed from the countless, nameless, ordinary labourers and farmers who sweated away their lives in poverty, to return penniless to China at the end of their days, or to die paupers in the land of their adoption.

The importance of the position held by the Chinese amidst the peoples of Sarawak was reflected in their distribution. The bulk of the Chinese were concentrated in the First, Second and western part of the Third Divisions where three-quarters of the entire population of the country was to be found. Furthermore the Chinese predominated in the urban areas, 75 per cent of which was represented by the towns of Kuching, Sibu and Miri.[20]

Brooke land policy

The absence of population pressure presupposes the absence of a land problem, but in fact even in sparsely-peopled Sarawak a land problem did develop with mounting intensity in the early decades of the twentieth century. For although prior to 1941, probably not more than 5 per cent of the total land area was under actual cultivation, the widespread practice of shifting agriculture and the relatively restricted area under sedentary cultivation created problems of their own. Shifting agriculture involved most of the indigenous peoples in the state and was carried out over a very considerable proportion of land. The state's low average density of fifteen persons per square mile could easily tolerate a system of shifting cultivation based on a fifteen-year cycle, but under Brooke rule this basic ratio was lost in certain districts. The great Iban migrations of the nineteenth century upset the balance, the migrants assuming densities twice the norm and cutting down the rotationary cycle by two-thirds in the regions where they settled, while the Brooke administration, putting a premium of security, encouraged the trend by attempting to confirm concentration in these areas.[21] The problems caused by over-population in such areas could only have been surmounted by improved farming techniques which were difficult to obtain under the existing circumstances. At the same time the total lack of pressure in other areas where shifting cultivation was practised meant that there was no stimulus to improve the techniques of traditional farming there either.

The wide demands of the shifting cultivator for land also impeded the growth and expansion of sedentary agriculture by restricting the land available for the latter and by making the institution of an effective land tenure system difficult if not inoperable. This affected the Chinese who took up farming. They faced no problems regarding techniques or efficiency but faced an uphill struggle against their environment. Their settlements tended to be isolated, rendering the disposal of their produce difficult and uneconomical, while the soils they worked were usually poor in quality. Despite the marginal support given by government to pioneer settlements, the policy of total *laissez-faire* prevailed so that the Chinese farmers were left to prosper or to fail on their own. But their choice of land was restricted by the traditional system of land tenure which gave inalienable rights over padi lands to the occupier and pre-empted vast areas to the nebulous claims of shifting cultivators. As a result the Chinese agriculturalist found his prospects blighted by cramped and increasingly overcrowded landholdings which could not be expanded, while the great confusion of boundaries caused by shifting cultivation formed a fruitful source of litigation for Iban planters. By the 1920s the growing complexity and intensity of these problems forced themselves on official attention and in 1933 a Land Settlement Ordinance was passed providing for the creation of a new land register based on the Torrens System. But it was not until after the Pacific War that the system of land classification was put on a legal footing and that an up-to-date and comprehensive Land Code was passed.

Social welfare under the Brookes
In general Sarawak was a country of low living standards and of cheap labour. To all intents and purposes the only organized labour in the state was confined to the Chinese and it remained enclosed within the cocoon of that society.[22] Most Chinese labourers up to 1941 arrived under the traditional credit-ticket system which was as much open to abuse in Sarawak as elsewhere, and although such contracts were officially forbidden, they were made all the same. However, in an economy where most people were self-employed growing food or as cash crop smallholders, the numbers of regular labourers were few, and hired labour was largely casual. Those who worked in the towns were better off than those in the countryside but the general standard of remuneration remained very low. A Labour Department was created in the 1920s but its scope and administration were very limited.

The greatest achievement of the Brooke regime in the social field was the abolition of slavery, a long-standing institution amongst the Malays as well as amongst the Iban, Kayan and Melanau peoples. As elsewhere in the Malay world, the slaves themselves were more often than not well treated and to have abolished the system overnight would have entailed serious economic and social, and ultimately political consequences. The campaign against slavery was conducted by Rajah Charles, in person, who moved slowly but deliberately. He initiated laws to protect the slaves from abuse and to improve their conditions. Cases of maltreatment could be brought to the courts and the traffic in slaves was expressly forbidden. By the 1880s slave-ownership was becoming an uneconomic proposition and legally cumbersome. In 1883 a law was passed providing for the manumission of all slaves within five years; three years later it was withdrawn as no longer necessary.

In other fields of social welfare the role of the Brooke administration was limited by the vastness of the country, the poorness of communications and above all by the scarcity of funds. As a result the brunt of the effort of providing social services like medical centres, orphanages, public relief and education fell on Christian missionary organizations which were in fact responsible for introducing the first modern medical facilities into the country. The first dispensary was opened in Kuching in 1849 by McDougall, the founder of the Anglican mission in Sarawak, who was also a qualified doctor and largely instrumental in getting the first hospital established ten years later. Government efforts to promote health facilities were painfully slow, but there was greater progress after 1900. A lunatic asylum was founded at Kuching in 1909, a leper colony in 1925 and a new general hospital the following year. Outside the capital, however, health services remained rudimentary. In 1913, Sibu, already the second largest town, only possessed 'a converted shack' as a hospital and one government medical officer, and the place did not get a modern drainage system until it had been largely destroyed by the great fire of 1928. In the countryside, tending to the sick and dispensing medicines were left to the amateurish hands of district officers and their assistants, who did as best they could with their elementary knowledge and bare facilities, fighting a hopeless struggle against ignorance and superstition. The principal diseases were cholera, smallpox, goitre, yaws, malaria and tuberculosis.[23]

All other aspects of social welfare in Sarawak prior to 1941 were still in their infancy. Limited resources and political considerations resulted in little being done to eradicate anti-social customs. No official attempt was made to control opium-smoking until 1924, and that as a result of international pressure. There was no law regulating gambling houses until 1945, neither was there any co-operative movement introduced until after the Japanese War. The other great Brooke achievement, after the ending of slavery, was undoubtedly the suppression of headhunting, an exhausting and protracted operation started by Rajah James but not effectively completed until the 1920s.[24]

In all the Brooke experiment was weakest at the very point closest to its intent, the social welfare and well-being of the inhabitants of Sarawak. In the light of the Brooke philosophy of letting things develop at their own pace, all this was possibly justifiable. But the world would not wait for Sarawak, and when outside events carried the country into the maelstrom of world politics, the people of the principality found themselves backward and ill-prepared.

[1]Nevertheless the total area under rubber in Sarawak was only one-tenth that of the Malay Peninsula.

[2]Singapore was sago's immediate market; at first it was transhipped straight to the Colony but in the early 1850s the first sago refinery was opened at Kuching itself and the product was thereafter processed in Sarawak.

[3]By 1941 jungle produce accounted for only 2 per cent of Sarawak's exports.

[4]To cope with the acute rice shortage felt throughout South-East Asia in 1919, a Committee of Food and Supply Control was set up, purchasing supplies on behalf of the government and chartering vessels to bring them to Kuching. Rationing was introduced in the larger towns. The high price of imported rice and the stimulus to local production as well as the turning to other foods as substitutes caused imports of rice to drop by 75 per cent. Under the Brooke regime rice exports from Sarawak were prohibited.

[5]The Borneo Company's interest in gold-mining began in the 1870s when it assisted local miners by loaning them equipment; in 1892 the company erected a mill at Bau to crush the ore and a couple of years later was lending pump-engines to the Chinese miners. After the company's withdrawal in 1921, small Chinese companies took over, many managed by former employees of the company. With their efforts production reached a peak of 28,000 ounces a year in 1934-5, but thereafter declined.

[6]Amongst these other minerals were the bauxite deposits of Sematan which were not exploited until 1957.

[7]For details of this controversy, see A.B. Ward, 'Rajah's Servant', Data Paper 61, Southeast Asia Program, Department of Asian Studies, Cornell University, New York, 1966, p. 199.

[8]Prior to the 1870s the Rajah's own yacht served as the sole regular link between Kuching and Singapore, but was joined in 1865 by the Borneo Company which provided a steamer of its own. Rajah Charles was largely instrumental in bringing about the formation of the Sarawak Chamber of Commerce, which played a leading role in the establishment of the new shipping line.

[9]Instant and unchallenged success bred complacency and inefficiency and in the 1890s Rajah Charles was again stirring up the merchants of Kuching, canvassing for the formation of a rival line; but no one was prepared to take the risk. However a little later competition appeared when the German Norddeutscher Lloyd, based in Singapore, extended its services to Kuching.

[10]For James' relations with Wise and the involved quarrel between them, see Sir Steven Runciman, The White Rajahs, Cambridge University Press, 1960, esp. pp. 93 et seq. The Rajah also had a disagreement with another (far less influential) trader called Burns.

[11]viz. the Ibans, the Malays, the Land Dayaks, the Kayans, the Kenyahs, the Melanaus, the Muruts and a heterogeneous group classified under the heading of Kemantan. The occasion for the classification was the promulgation of the state's first written constitution in 1941. The Indians in the country were the descendants of Muslim-Indian cloth merchants who had cornered this particular branch of trade, of Sikh soldiers and guards, and of Tamil labourers who had entered under Brooke auspices in the nineteenth century.

[12]The origin of the Sarawak Malays is obscure. Some claim to have come from Sumatra, others from Celebes and the rest of local stock. In any case there is evidence of large admixtures of Melanau, Iban and Land Dayak. The distinctions evident among the other indigenous peoples is often clearly enough the result of circumstance. There was a kinship, for example, between the Kayans and the Kenyahs on the one hand, and the Muruts and the Kelabits on the other; but the Kayans and the Kenyahs came to depend on the river rather than the land for their livelihood and failed to develop the experienced and advanced farming techniques of the Muruts and Kelabits. In a similar way, the Melanau people of the coast were of Kayan ancestry but evolved a distinctive way of life as they adapted themselves to the alien sea and to the cultivation of the sago palm, unknown in the hills of their forebears.

[13]According to the 1960 census, just under one-sixth of the population were Christians and just under a quarter Muslims. Islam was of course traditional amongst the Malays and was also followed by other groups closely connected with them, such as the Kedayans and Melanaus. Christianity came in with the Brooke regime which tolerated its propagation amongst non-Muslim races. The most prominent group among the Christians were the Chinese, many of whom were converts before entering the country—indeed this was one of the reasons why they did so. There were quite a number of Iban converts, and some amongst the Land Dayaks. The Muruts and the Kelabits, amongst the hill peoples in particular, fell under the influence of the Borneo Evangelical Mission.

[14]'By any standards these great Iban migrations into the Rejang and beyond were the most momentous happening in the social and economic history of nineteenth century Sarawak.' J.D. Freeman, Iban Agriculture, quoted by Lee Yong-leng, Population and Settlement in Sarawak, Asia Pacific Press, Singapore, 1970, p. 173.

[15]In 1900 the Chinese still formed a mere 10 per cent of the total population.

[16]See Victor Purcell, The Chinese in South-East Asia, Oxford University Press, London, 1965, pp. 366–7.

[17]Ju-kang T'ien, The Chinese of Sarawak, Lund Humphries, London, 1953, p. 69.

[18]Ibid.

[19]For a full analysis of the Chinese community in Sarawak, see Ju, op. cit.

[20]The greatest concentration of people was in the First Division, in particular Kuching

itself, which contained one-fifth of the total population of Sarawak. The pre-eminence of the First Division lies partly in the historical accident that led James Brooke to settle there and make it his headquarters. It was a natural magnet, serving as capital and chief port and acting as the focal point for agricultural and mining activity. The rest of the country remained sparsely populated, with the exception of one or two subsidiary centres on the Batang Lupar (Simanggang), on the Rejang (Sibu) and at the oil fields in Baram (Miri).

[21] As part of this policy, a government decree specified that no longhouse should accommodate less than ten families within it.

[22] The major exception to this was at Miri where the oil company employed the largest labour force in the country. This force was multi-racial.

[23] For graphic descriptions of disease and its treatment under primitive conditions, see Ward, op. cit., pp. 35, 95–6 and 109.

[24] Amongst other social welfare measures, the first orphanage was opened in Kuching in 1849 for Land Dayak children, and extended to Chinese in 1850. Similar institutions were started at other mission stations subsequently but their capacity was very limited.

Books and articles for further reading

BOOKS

Cooper, A.M., *Men of Sarawak*, Oxford University Press, Kuala Lumpur, 1968.

Emerson, R., *Malaysia: A Study in Direct and Indirect Rule*, University of Malaya Press, Kuala Lumpur, 1964 (reprint).

Fisher, C.A., *South-East Asia: A Social, Economic and Political Geography*, Methuen & Co. Ltd., London, 1964.

Irwin, G., *Nineteenth Century Borneo*, Donald Moore, Singapore, 1955.

Jackson, J.C., *Sarawak: A Geographical Survey of a Developing State*, University of London Press, London.

Jacoby, E.H., *Agrarian Unrest in Southeast Asia*, Asia Publishing House, Bombay, 1961.

Lee Yong-leng, *Population and Settlement in Sarawak*, Asia Pacific Press, Singapore, 1970.

Leigh, M.B., *The Chinese Community of Sarawak*, Malaysia Publishing House, Singapore, 1964.

Mills, L.A., *British Rule in Eastern Asia*, Oxford University Press, London, 1942.

Purcell, V., *The Chinese in South-East Asia*, Oxford University Press, London, 1965.

Robequain, C., *Malaya, Indonesia, Borneo and the Philippines*, Longman Green, London, 1958.

Roth, H.L., *The Natives of Sarawak and British North Borneo*, Vols. I & II, University of Malaya Press, Kuala Lumpur, 1968.

Runciman, S., *The White Rajahs*, Cambridge University Press, 1960.

Ju-kang T'ien, *The Chinese of Sarawak*, Lund Humphries, London, 1953.

Ward, A.B., *Rajah's Servant*, Data Paper 61, South-East Asia Program, Dept. of Asian Studies, Cornell University, Ithaca, New York, 1966.

ARTICLES

Docring, O.C., 'Government in Sarawak under Charles Brooke', *JMBRAS*, XXXIX, 2, 1966.

Tarling, N., 'British Policy in the Malay Peninsula and Archipelago, 1824–71', *JMBRAS*, XXX, 3, 1957.

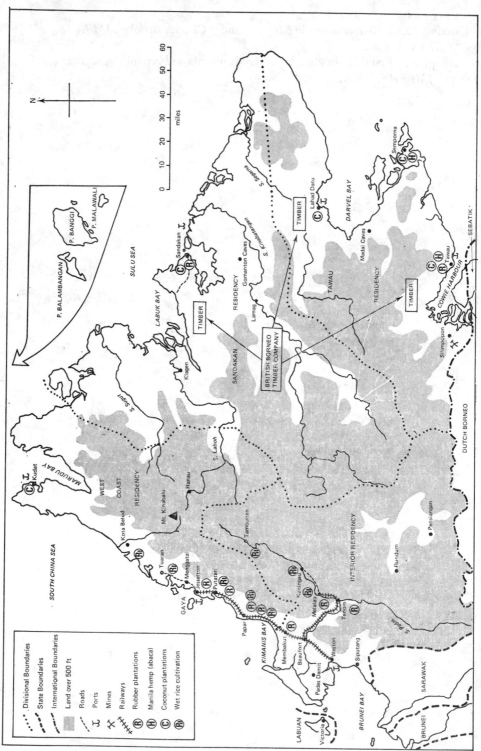

23. General Map of British North Borneo, 1941

D. British North Borneo

'As might be supposed, the Company has had much opposition and many difficulties to contend with...and grave doubts of the wisdom of granting the Royal Charter were expressed in Parliament and in the press; but the policy has been completely vindicated by the energy and liberality which have distinguished the Administration and which have brought the territory into a state in which its public revenues are more than equal to its expenditure, while the previously unknown territory has been explored and mapped, and security have succeeded to the piracy, slave-dealing, headhunting and oppression which prevailed long after the time when I first saw the country fifty years ago.'

Sir Hugh Low, *India, Ceylon, SS, British North Borneo and Hong Kong*, 1899.

The large hunk of territory of over 29,000 square miles which came to be administered by the Chartered Company of British North Borneo after 1881, at the expense of Brunei and to the chagrin of the Brookes in Sarawak, was run on entirely different lines to the domains of the latter. Yet the end results were remarkably similar. British North Borneo was managed avowedly for profit but did not prove to be very profitable. In 1941 the dependency was as little developed as Sarawak and on the whole less prosperous. In contrast to Sarawak its failure to develop at a faster rate was not a reflection of official reluctance to make it do so, but along with the Brooke principality, British North Borneo also acquired the problems inherent in the creation of a multi racial and economically differentiated community.

The quest for minerals
British North Borneo was the child of speculation, a creation of the Chartered Company, nurtured on the hopes in Sabah's economic potential. Ever since the days of Magellan, Europeans had been prone to believe in the fabled mineral wealth of the interior, particularly of gold, a belief which initially was shared as much by Dent and Cowie as by anybody else. In fact the Sabah of 1880 was very largely an uncharted and unknown land as far as the outside world was concerned, and it was not until the first decade of company rule that the country was systematically explored and the absence of minerals and the emptiness of the interior conclusively revealed. The aim of this exploration was primarily geological and was carried out by the servants of the company. The discovery in 1885 of gold grains in the sands of the Segama River served to lend credence to the myth and precipitated a minor gold rush; but within two years the deposits were exhausted. The Segama experience, however, did nothing to diminish the faith of government official and prospector alike that somewhere at the headwaters of one of Sabah's rivers lay rich gold reefs waiting to be discovered. In 1897 a new effort was launched by the Brit-

ish Borneo Gold Syndicate, only to be abandoned six years afterwards. The syndicate's mission was then taken over by the newly-formed British Borneo Exploration Company which in turn was liquidated twelve years later, after two fruitless expeditions up the Segama River. Other attempts by individual prospectors in 1928 and in the 1930s proved equally as unsuccessful.

Apart from gold only two other minerals excited serious attention during the period of the Chartered Company's rule, namely coal and manganese. The mining of manganese was another shortlived, speculative affair which aroused great hopes amongst the directors of the British Borneo Exploration Company but in the end involved them in serious loss. In the event coal proved to be the only paying mining enterprise attempted under the company. The first outcrops were found in the Sandakan area in 1880 but none were of commercial importance. Nevertheless the discovery of a large field of 'considerable economic importance' on the Silimpopon River in 1903 brought about the formation of the Cowie Harbour Coal Company which from 1906 until 1930 kept the field in regular production. Even so, the going was not smooth. Profits barely met overheads and the Chartered Company itself had to give frequent subventions to enable the coal firm to continue. In 1922 the colliery reached the peak of its output, but within a few years the industry was in irremediable difficulty. Between 1926 and 1930 the value of the company's coal exports fell by nearly half. The onset of the Great Depression caused operations to come to a complete standstill, never to be started again.[1]

Fleeting hopes were raised by rumours and reports of other mineral deposits, including iron, copper, tin, chromite and antimony, but none of these were in any quantity. The greatest disappointment of all was the apparent absence of oil deposits in the territory, the abundance of which in neighbouring Brunei and Sarawak justified hopes that North Borneo would have its share. Indeed oil seepages did exist, particularly in the Klias Peninsula which first attracted attention in 1890 and led to a most favourable report by a government engineer the following year. From this date on up till 1941 a series of investigations was carried out by a succession of interested parties, including inter alia Royal Dutch Shell. But none produced satisfactory results; even the Shell search which was far more thorough and systematic than any other taken so far had no success, and was interrupted by the outbreak of the Pacific War.

The rise and fall of tobacco
North Borneo's lack of mineral resources was matched by a lack of human resources which meant that labour was forever to be at a premium and its shortage to act as a serious impediment to faster development. However Borneo was famous for its forests and ultimately timber was to become the mainstay of the economy. In the meantime two other products—tobacco and rubber—played an important role in the country's development.

Without tobacco the Chartered Company might well have gone into early liquidation. It was the first major export under company rule and apart from enabling the new regime to balance its budget in 1887 for the first time, it stimulated the first wave of Chinese immigration, focused economic development on the east coast and blazed the trail which rubber planters and timber loggers were to follow. The establishment of the tobacco growing industry, however, was largely a matter of chance. Of all the crops planted at the government's new experimental station at Silam in 1881, tobacco was notable by its absence. Its launching as a commercial crop was largely due to Saunders, 'a penniless and opinionated' planter from the Culture Zone of East Sumatra, who, employed by a pioneer Chinese enterprise in the territory to plant sugar, was allowed to experiment on tobacco instead when the sugar venture failed. The first tobacco bales arrived in London in 1884 where they got a good reception, and the following year Saunders' tobacco was being quoted at a higher rate on the prestigious Amsterdam market than the famed Deli leaf itself.[2] With that the tobacco rush was on. Within ten years the value of tobacco exports rose from virtually nothing to over $1 million a year. By this time (1895) there were well over sixty estates in the country, mostly run by experienced German and Dutch planters from the Netherlands Indies, attracted by light duties, a liberal land policy, minimum official interference and optimum market prices. The peak year came in 1903 when export values passed the $2 million mark. The tobacco estates were concentrated along the great rivers flowing down to the east coast, and around the ports of Lahad Dato, Sandakan and Tawau.

However, the young industry was soon confronted with serious difficulties, including the acute shortage of labour which was only partially solved by recruiting Chinese from the Straits or Hong Kong, more often than not at unnecessarily exorbitant rates. More serious still was the imposition in 1893 of a discriminatory tariff against tobaccos imported into the United States.[3] This ended land sales for tobacco estates in North Borneo and presaged fiercer competition in a narrowing world market. There was an immediate drop in prices; a number of estates were abandoned and in London the company made moves to merge its interests with those of Sarawak. Despite a temporary recovery, soon after the turn of the century, it became clear that the days of tobacco were numbered. Floods and disease added to the hazards of the tobacco planter, while the advent of rubber, giving faster returns for far less effort and cost, sealed the issue. By 1910 there were only twelve tobacco estates left in the country; there were still four in production in 1922, by 1928 there were only two and in 1929 production ceased entirely.[4]

The rise and the role of rubber
In the 1900s rubber replaced tobacco as North Borneo's major cash crop, thereby ensuring the continued solvency of the Chartered Company and the development of the country. Like Sarawak, North Borneo never became a major world producer but as far as the domestic economy was concerned rubber held a very important place. By 1941 it was easily the most important export in terms of value and as a crop covered a larger acreage than any other.

Unlike Sarawak, on the other hand, nearly half the area under rubber was owned by large Western estates. By the same token the estate owners gained considerable influence over the direction of economic affairs in the country.

This large Western stake in the rubber planting industry was the direct outcome of the 'absurdly' attractive terms offered by Cowie, Chairman of the Court of Directors, in 1905 to prospective rubber planters, which placed a very heavy burden on the state.[5] As such, Cowie's move has been severely criticized, but tobacco was failing, minerals were proving non-existent and the future of the timber industry was as yet undivined. The territory had little else to turn to and without some spectacular concession little with which to attract the potential investor. The economy was also staggering under the heavy burden of paying for another of Cowie's concepts—the west coast railway which joined Jesselton to Beaufort and ran over the Crocker Range to Tenom and beyond. However, the existence of this line became a major factor in making the prospects for rubber in the territory feasible, for it ran through virgin soils ideal for the planting of the new crop. At any rate Cowie's offer, together with the railway and the willing support of the administration which cleared and prepared suitable sites along the line for new estates, produced the desired results. Fifteen new companies took advantage of its terms within the first five years and started planting forthwith. By 1917 there were over 35,000 acres under the crop while exports topped well over 2,000 tons. By 1928 exports had tripled again, despite the effects of the Little Depression, with thirty companies in the field, and in 1940 rubber exports stood at around 17,640 tons. Chinese and indigenous planters also joined in the rush to plant rubber and their numbers steadily grew. By 1928 smallholdings already formed between a third and a half of the total area under rubber; ten years later they had surpassed the estates. Three-quarters of the rubber planted was to be found on the plains of the west coast and in the interior along the railway line. There was also a substantial acreage around Sandakan and Tawau.[6]

In its origins and development, rubber planting in Sabah followed the general pattern set elsewhere. The first rubber seedlings were introduced from Singapore in 1882, to be 'greeted with indifference'. The first crop actually produced was in 1899 at Tenom, but in 1902, on the eve of the great rush, there were still only 100 acres under rubber in the whole country. From the early 1900s, planting in North Borneo underwent rapid and uninterrupted expansion until the end of the Great War when it was hit by the Little Depression. As the rubber price plummeted, companies economized, large numbers of rubber workers lost their jobs and some estates closed down altogether. A number of planters attempted voluntary restriction, without great success, and the influence of the European planters secured North Borneo's participation in the Stevenson Plan.

The Great Depression was a far greater blow, and resulted in a much stricter restriction scheme being implemented. In 1934 the Western planter interest ensured that the territory adhered to the International Rubber Regulation Scheme and abided by its provisions which involved smallholders for the first time, very much to their disadvantage.[7] The approach of the Second World War helped to lift prices and by 1940 the rubber industry of North Borneo was apparently headed for a new era of high production and profit.

The rise of rubber brought about a great influx of Chinese and other im-

migrants into the country, shifted the focus of economic development from
the east coast to the west and had an important effect on many of the people
of the country. It attracted many of them as labourers, still more as smallholders. It also altered their living patterns, ending the traditional isolation
of coastal fishing villages, hill settlements and longhouses and bringing them
into direct contact with the immigrant groups along the coast. All this was
reflected in the steady decline of the population of the interior after 1910 as
many of the indigenous inhabitants moved into the growing centres of population on the west and east coasts.

The rise of timber
However the industry destined to hold premier place in the territory's economy was the one most natural to it—timber. In 1941 British North Borneo ranked third in the British Empire as a timber exporter and Sandakan
had become one of the great timber ports of the world. Yet only about 34
per cent of the country's forests are of commercial value, mainly located
within twenty miles of her east coast shores which on account of their sparse
population who are primarily concerned with the sea have been preserved
from the ravages of shifting cultivation and settlement that characterize the
western seaboard.

The origins of Sabah's modern industry lay, like that of tobacco, in a quirk
of fortune that early in 1885 turned de Lissa, a sugar planter from Australia,
into an exporter of seraya wood instead. His first shipment to Australia marked
the beginning of a regular trade, but Hong Kong became the territory's
main market, though Australia remained important. By the turn of the century timber exports came second in value to tobacco and by 1910 they stood
at twelve times the 1890 figure. But this growth rate was not fast enough.
The timber trade was in the hands of four firms but despite this none of them
had sufficient capital to be able to afford large-scale operations or up-to-date
methods, so that from time to time they lost part of their concessions for
failing to work them as laid down in their lease terms by government. This
situation prompted the Chartered Company at the end of the Great War to
create a new timber concern with monopoly rights and far greater capital
resources with which to exploit the jungles. This new deal, in the shape of
the British Borneo Timber Company formed in 1920, and largely en-
gineered by West Ridgeway, the company's chairman, was as bold and
extravagant a gamble as Cowie's famous tax-free offer to rubber planters in
the 1900s. It saddled North Borneo with a heavy commitment which proved
very expensive to resolve a couple of decades later, and also aroused the active resentment of the existing timber concerns. At the same time the desired
end of injecting new capital into the industry was achieved and accordingly
the industry as a whole developed. By 1930 the territory's timber exports had
nearly doubled their value within a decade and by the peak year of 1937 they
had tripled in volume since 1922. The main market was still Hong Kong,
followed by Japan, Britain and Australia. However, the British Borneo Timber Company's monopoly perhaps cushioned its directors too well, for
despite their large profits and minimal taxes, extraction operations were still

conducted by old-fashioned methods, and mechanization was not introduced until 1950.

The disadvantages of this monopoly were also reflected by the effect it had
on the development of forest policy. The dangers of uncontrolled felling had
become apparent in the 1900s and finally led to the creation of a Forest
Department in 1913. At first the new department concentrated on gathering
revenue from timber concessionaires. Its later efforts to conserve resources
were crippled by inadequate funds, and after 1920 in particular by the terms
of the British Borneo Timber Company's concession which virtually converted the department into its agent. Even after 1936, when a comprehensive
forest ordinance was passed, the position was little changed.[8]

The role of timber in the development of the territory under the company
was important. It soon became one of the mainstays of government revenue
and kept the east coast ports of Sandakan, Tawau and Lahad Dato alive when
the collapse of the tobacco industry left them bereft. It was also responsible
for a considerable movement of peoples on the east coast, particularly Filipinos
and Indonesians. On the other hand the existence of extensive timber concessions in the region hampered other forms of development.

Forest and other products
Apart from timber, the forests of Sabah had traditionally been famed as a
source of other jungle produce which continued to constitute a minor but
locally important element in trade. Indeed in its early years the company
was glad to rely on the exports of birds' nests, rattans and gutta percha in particular, the combined value of which in 1885 mounted to more than a quarter
of that of the total export trade. Another forest product which acquired considerable importance under the company was cutch. The industry came to
be monopolized by the Bakau and Kenyah Extract Company, founded at
Sandakan in 1892, and expanded steadily up till 1941, by which time its value
as an export ranked next to rubber and timber.

As in Sarawak, the Chartered Company's administration experimented
in great ignorance and hope with a wide variety of other potential cash crops
in the pioneer days of its rule with little or no success. Only abaca (Manila
hemp), coffee, coconuts and their products, and sago acquired some significance. The abaca industry came to be a Japanese affair, although the first
attempts were conducted by Pryer at Sandakan in the 1880s. When the leading Japanese concern in Sabah, the Kuhura Company, acquired its land near
Tawau a small section was allocated to the crop and a first experimental shipment made in 1919. But Kuhara did not take the crop seriously until the
Great Depression forced the rubber price down to uneconomical levels. A
good deal of the Tawau estate was turned over to abaca after 1929 and exports
quickly rose in quantity and value. More important, both for local consumption and export, were coconuts and their associated products. Apart from
coconuts grown purely for domestic use, the industry was almost entirely
in the hands of smallholders, mostly Chinese or Bajau. Exports of copra and
coconuts rose from a mere $935 recorded in 1887 to a peak of over $750,000
in 1929 on the eve of the Great Depression. Like the coconut, the sago palm

was a traditional product of the country, centred on the Padas-Klias Peninsula which had served as a source of supply for Labuan and Singapore for many decades. The coming of Chinese sago millers, the demarcation of individual plots by government survey, and the appointment in 1925 of a special officer to watch over the industry all helped to boost production. However, ingrained habits and an uncertain outside market prevented sago cultivation from being developed to its full capacity.

Rice cultivation

Rice was by far the most important domestic crop both in terms of acreage and population. As in Sarawak, most padi planters consisted of the people of the country (in this case especially the Kadazans), the rice grown was insufficient for the territory's needs, methods were traditional, yields uncertain and a great proportion produced from dry padi, associated with shifting cultivation. The policy of the Chartered Company was in general to encourage local rice production but in a manner which would not conflict with the promotion of revenues through trade. The administration, for example, was quite prepared to draw labour away from the rice-fields, as the price of imported rice was cheap; in fact an attempt by Governor Beaufort in 1895 to impose a tariff on imported rice as a device to meet the costs of the new railway aroused such an outcry from those affected and had such a drastic effect on immigration which fell to a trickle, that the tax was lifted in 1903. In any case as a measure to stimulate local rice production, the tax was totally ineffective since the Kadazans and their kind still belonged predominantly to the world of subsistence agriculture and were beyond the demands of the local rice market.

On the whole, however, in the twentieth century the administration did what it could within the severe limits of its resources to increase local cultivation, with the result that the acreage under wet padi increased both in relation to that under dry and in total area. But the effect of this increase in production was nullified by the growth of population, so that in 1941 the territory was still importing about half its rice needs. Measures to curb shifting cultivation, a practice as widespread and as inevitable in Sabah as in Sarawak, were not very effective prior to the Pacific War.

Communications: the Sabah railway

Prior to 1941 communications in Sabah were as sparse and as inadequate as they were in Sarawak, and for the same reasons. However, relatively speaking, Sabah was better off and the Chartered Company showed itself prepared to invest more in their development than did the Brooke regime in Kuching.

This is witnessed in particular by the 116 miles of railway line on the west coast which has the distinction of being the only track in the whole of Borneo. Quite fortuitously the railway came to play a vital role in the economic development of the country within the first years of its construction, though it was built at unnecessarily high cost as a result of over-hasty planning.

The concept of the railway and its implementation came from Cowie, the grand speculator who dreamed of a trans-Bornean line running from Brunei

Bay to Sandakan and beyond to Tawau. A start was made on the first section from Weston on Brunei Bay to Beaufort twenty miles away in 1896 and by 1905 the line extended northwards up to Jesselton and another branch ran inland through the Padas Gorge to Tenom. This was as near to Sandakan that Cowie's line ever reached, but once built it proved very useful and eventually paid well.

Nevertheless the costs involved were tremendous and nearly sank the Chartered Company. Cowie's original estimates proved hopelessly unrealistic. He expected the line to cost no more than £107,500, but by 1905 it had already cost five times that amount. There were serious errors of judgement in planning and administration. The whole project was put into the hands of West, an engineering friend of Cowie, whose experience in railway construction was limited to light tramways. The choosing of a suitable port-terminus proved a costly exercise. As for the construction of the line itself, Cowie finally left it to the Chartered Company to hire a private firm of contractors to do the job, but also allowed the firm to be responsible for checking its own work. The inevitable consequence of all this was that when completed the railway was in a highly unsatisfactory state. Nothing was done until after Cowie's death in 1910 when the new governor, Sir West Ridgeway, immediately called for a detailed technical report. The report, prepared by two railway experts from Malaya, was devastating and the line was condemned from practically every point of view. Nearly complete reconstruction was necessary, work on which was started in 1912 but not fully completed until 1923.[9]

However, once properly completed, the railway paid off. From 1924 onwards it showed an annual profit, except for two years during the Great Depression. Even before this, however, the railway had justified itself by the role it played from the earliest years in assisting the spread of rubber planting, in opening up the rich farmland over the Crocker Range, and in encouraging settlement along the western coastal strip up to Jesselton and beyond.

Road and other communications
Cowie had had equally grandiose schemes for the roads of North Borneo as he had for the railway but from the outset the physical and economic handicaps presented by the rough, thickly-jungled and thinly-populated terrain made it clear that the building of trunk roads spanning the country from end to end would have to bide its time. In fact up till 1919 the territory had virtually no roads at all. For the want of something better, Governor Birch in 1902 introduced a system of bridle paths which were developed and extended on an annual basis under the direction of district officers. By 1920 there were already several hundred miles of such tracks looping the countryside, although mostly serving the west coast; by 1941 there were over 600 miles.

In the meantime the construction of a proper road system was begun. In 1920 plans were drawn up for developing three main road patterns, one based on Jesselton (Kota Kinabalu), a second on Sandakan and the third in the interior focused on Melalap. The most important of these systems was that based on Jesselton which was joined to Tuaran, twenty miles to the north, in 1924. By 1940 there were 103 miles of metalled road in the country which were supplemented by about a hundred miles of laterite feeder roads.

Granted the difficulties of developing overland communication by road and rail, the advent of telecommunication was eagerly grasped as the best solution to the problem of maintaining effective links between the various scattered outposts of the company. In this field, also, Cowie impetuously involved the Chartered Company in yet another extravagant scheme with his project of an overland telegraph line to link the west coast with Sandakan in one direction and with the world outside via Labuan and the submarine cable to Singapore in the other. Work was started in 1894 and the line finally opened in 1897. Once constructed it proved extremely expensive to maintain and brought in a meagre revenue. The opening of radio links between Jesselton and Sandakan barely seventeen years later (in 1914) obviated its need altogether, and so it was closed and the wire salvaged. Radio stations were quickly established at all the main centres within the next few years. By 1941 postal services operated from the towns, all of which had post offices, while all settlements with government offices had postal facilities. The company issued its own stamps. Limited telephonic communications were also established between 1919 and 1941.

Prior to 1941 the air age had not reached North Borneo, and although sites had been surveyed at Jesselton, Kudat and Sandakan there were no airfields in the country.

Sea communications

In all, the territory remained predominantly dependent on water-borne transport. This was particularly true of the east coast where the regular links were maintained by river and sea craft. It was also true for most of the country's new immigrant population who depended on imported food in order to survive, a point strikingly brought home in 1914 with the sudden and total disappearance of the services provided by Norddeutscher Lloyd which used to maintain the only regular links with Singapore and Hong Kong, and by the wartime shortage of shipping which followed, causing the introduction of four years of rice rationing from 1916.

However, the administration had made it clear from the beginning that it was not going to involve itself in the risks of shipowning and the development of the territory's sea communications were left entirely to private enterprise. After a precarious beginning, the bait provided by the rise of the tobacco industry in the mid-1880s soon attracted the interest of established British, Dutch and German firms. In the ensuing competition the Norddeutscher Lloyd came out on top and from 1899 until the outbreak of the Great War the shipping links between Sabah and the outside world were virtually a German monopoly.

The vacuum caused by the sudden disappearance of the German fleet in 1944 was eventually filled by the Straits Steamship Company. After the war was over, Straits Steamship expanded its services, absorbing in the process the Sabah Steamship Company, the sole local firm. The only other shipping company of significance prior to 1941 was the Indo China Steam Navigation Company which ran a regular service between Sandakan and Hong Kong, much used by Chinese immigrants.

The pattern of trade and commerce

Although the Chartered Company was basically a commercial concern, dedicated to the proposition of selling North Borneo as a good field for foreign capital investment, the pattern of trade and commerce that developed was very similar to that in Sarawak under the cautionary Brooke regime. The import trade was dominated by a few European firms together with a group of Chinese merchants. They also handled most of the export trade which was not sent directly by its native producers. The retail and distributive trades were a Chinese monopoly and fashioned by the demands of a subsistence economy market, by high prices and easy credit along a transmission belt system linking small shop-keepers with the merchant agents of the five ports. As for the Chartered Company itself, it never became a great source of profit to its shareholders.

From the outset the Chartered Company determined to keep itself out of direct participation in commercial ventures and to depend on its profits from the revenues that general development carried out by others could bring. However on occasion when a particular concern whose viability was considered essential for the general interests of the territory was in difficulties, the company was prepared to step in. Up till 1921 when a state bank was established, the company used first the firm of A.L. Johnstone, then Guthries of Singapore as its financial agents. No private bank was set up in the country until after the Pacific War.[10]

Population growth

Throughout the sixty years of Chartered Company rule the population remained small and in 1940 the total estimate was only between 250,000 and 500,000 people. Of these, immigrants accounted for over a quarter, and amongst the immigrants the Chinese represented by far the largest and fastest growing element. The rest consisted predominantly of Filipinos and Javanese.

The most outstanding feature of the demographic evolution of the country under company rule was not its growth rate, which was below the average for the region as a whole, but the establishment of a substantial alien minority and the sharp differences which marked it from the indigenous peoples.[11]

Population growth was slow and uneven. The first census held in 1891 recorded a total population of just over 100,000 people while the population estimates for 1941 put the total figure at around three times that amount. But in fact the rise in population was probably far less than these figures indicate; furthermore the growth rate varied greatly from community to community. In fact whilst numbers in general gradually rose, the percentage of indigenous peoples in relation to the whole steadily declined. In 1911 they accounted for over four-fifths of the total population but by 1931 had dropped to three-quarters. The major factor behind the rise of the immigrant population, particularly that of the Chinese, was immigration itself, but the dependence of population growth on immigration meant that it was affected in years of trade recession. Health was another important factor which differentiated the growth rates of the indigenous from those of the immigrants.

Labour and Chinese immigration

From the earliest days immigration appeared essential to the Court of Directors of the Chartered Company in order to get their piece of real estate on the move. It also soon became obvious to them that the population of the territory was very sparse indeed, added to which they had a general reluctance to use indigenous labour on the new tobacco estates, mindful of the critical eyes on their administration. So from the outset the company's officials set out to recruit labour from whatever outside source it could. The most natural and popular choice was the Chinese.

Chinese immigration into Sabah under the company fell into three main phases. The first which started in the early 1880s and petered out in the middle of the next decade was largely associated with the tobacco boom. The second, in the early 1900s, was connected with the rush to plant rubber, and the third phase originated in the general economic and political circumstances of the 1920s and 1930s. Most Chinese immigration up till the 1920s was state-assisted since, unlike Malaya or East Sumatra (or to a lesser degree Sarawak), there were few natural inducements and no established Chinese merchant class to stimulate and finance the movement. The official efforts to encourage Chinese immigrants were marked by serious blunders and needless extravagance, and yet without them the territory would not have been able to develop at all.

The appointment of Sir Walter Medhurst as Commissioner for Chinese Immigration in 1881 marked the first government attempt at recruitment and ended in almost total failure. The situation created by Medhurst's haphazard selection of emigrants in Hong Kong and his failure to liaise with the authorities in North Borneo was made still more difficult by the competition of Straits Chinese, who far better acclimatized to local conditions had come of their own accord, while the current policy of retrenchment inspired by London shut out the possibility of employment on public works. Within a year Medhurst's immigrants were on their way back to China and by the end of 1883 there were very few of them left in the territory. After this débâcle the administration left the recruitment of labour to the planters themselves for the next few years but intervened again in the 1890s, both to protect the planters from breach of contract and to counter the increasingly bad name the territory was acquiring for the treatment of labour. But a second attempt to recruit labour itself, made in 1894, this time by using official channels at Hong Kong, was also completely unsuccessful.

By this time, however, the immigration position had considerably improved as labour conditions in the country became much better. Missionary enterprise was responsible for a small but significant trickle in this period. In 1883 ninety-six Christian Hakkas settled as agriculturalists at Kudat and became the fore-runners of the largest speech group amongst the Chinese to settle in Borneo. Sabah also attracted the attention of a group of Chinese capitalists which resulted in the formation of two Chinese companies with concessions covering 50,000 acres of land between them. In 1878 there had been but a handful of Chinese in the territory; by 1883 there were some 3,000 and by the end of the century they numbered nearly 14,000.

Nevertheless the flow of Chinese immigrants came to an abrupt halt with the imposition of Beaufort's rice tax in 1895. At the same time Cowie, now Chairman of the Court of Directors in London, refused to sponsor any scheme of Chinese immigration. In 1902, with still no Chinese coming in, yet another tax was imposed to help pay for the new railway; with this the exodus of Chinese 'became noticeable'. Meanwhile a number of official and unofficial attempts to recruit fresh Chinese labour from overseas all failed. Finally in 1903 the unpopular rice tax was lifted.

The lifting of the tax ushered in the second phase of Chinese immigration. This time, although government attempted to play a large role, Christian missionaries took a greater share and the amount of unassisted migration increased substantially. The prime factor behind this second wave was the sudden upsurge of rubber planting, stimulated by Cowie's fantastic offer. The first batch of immigrants to arrive in 1903 received government assistance. When at the end of that year the administration was forced to economize because of the railway, conditions were sufficiently attractive to bring voluntary migrants in at their own expense. In 1911, the administration made another attempt to go into the recruitment business at Hong Kong, but W.S. Young Riddell who was appointed as the second Commissioner for Chinese Immigration and put in charge of all recruitment for the territory as well as of the organization of an agricultural settlement scheme proved as disastrous a nominee as Medhurst. This marked the last direct intervention by the administration into labour recruitment. In the meantime more and more planters were recruiting on their own account, many turning to a Chinese variant of the *kangany* system. An important contribution which received official support was also made by Christian missionaries. By 1911 there were nearly 28,000 Chinese immigrants in the territory and ten years later the figure had risen to 39,000.

In the 1920s and 1930s the pace of Chinese immigration accelerated, marking the third phase. One factor behind the increased flow was a new scheme introduced in 1921 by which freeholders in the territory were granted free passages to bring over their wives and relatives. Despite a slow start, the number of free passages granted under this system mounted rapidly, reaching a peak in 1929. The Great Depression caused numbers to fall off and in the 1930s the number of passes issued each year was restricted. After 1921, however, there was also a marked increase in unassisted immigration, stimulated by generous new land terms announced in 1923 and by the poverty and instability endemic in South China. From 1924 the demand for contract labour on the estates also began to fall off and more immigrant labour became available on the local market. From 1927 the number of immigrants who paid their own passages steadily increased and in the 1930s became a flood, forcing the administration for the first time to think of the economic, social and political consequences. The numbers coming in were now far in excess of local labour needs. In 1936 deportation powers were issued and two years later the money required to be in the possession of Asian immigrants on entry was raised, which reduced the flow by two-thirds. The volume of unassisted immigration was also now affected by the outbreak of the Sino-Japanese War. In 1941 the number of Chinese in the territory was estimated to stand at around 60,000.

Javanese immigration

However the company did not depend on the Chinese alone. Another important group who was encouraged to come in and did so in fairly large numbers were the Javanese, who were employed largely on the big estates. Unlike the Chinese they were transitory visitors and the great majority returned to their homeland having completed their contracts. The earliest recorded Javanese to enter the territory under Company rule were seventy labourers who were sent to the new experimental station at Silam in 1892. Dutch tobacco planters occasionally imported Javanese to work on their estates during this period as well. In 1890, the first official attempt was made to recruit Javanese labourers direct from the Netherlands Indies, but permission was only granted by the Dutch authorities in Batavia in 1907 after years of negotiation. However planters did not show real interest in Javanese labour until the cutting off of indentured labour from China was foreshadowed by the abolition of contract labour in Malaya and Hong Kong in 1910. A fresh agreement allowing Borneo planters to recruit their labour in Java was signed by the company's administration and the Dutch in 1911, with effect for twenty years. Recruiting under this agreement continued up till 1932, then the company stopped recruiting contract labourers. Two years later contract labour was abolished in Java itself.

Between 1914 and 1932 nearly 10,000 Javanese entered North Borneo; about 7 per cent died there and another 11 per cent settled down—most of them women. In 1938 a new agreement was reached with Batavia, this time for the recruitment of free labour, but as it coincided with the flooding of the labour market by Chinese immigrants, planters failed to avail themselves of this opportunity. From the point of view of employers the great drawback of the Javanese as a labour force was their insistence on going back home as soon as their contract was completed. For the same reason the Javanese influx under company rule never assumed the same significance as that of the Chinese.

Other immigrants

The next most numerous group to come into the territory were the Filipinos, but this was mostly on an independent basis. In fact the extent of Filipino immigration is hard to gauge as so many of them were blood-relations of the inhabitants of Sabah themselves. On three occasions official schemes for Filipino colonization were proposed but none came to anything. The last of these proposals came in 1935 when a plan for settling a colony of Filipinos on the east coast was discussed by officials 'in a somewhat academic way', but was never put into practice.[12]

Another seemingly obvious source of cheap labour was India, and the administration, spurred on by planters standing on the threshold of the tobacco boom of the mid-1880s, looked at Malaya and opened negotiations with Calcutta for the recruitment of Tamil labour. In 1891 the Indian Government gave its consent, but the anticipated flow never materialized for the Malay Peninsula was on the way. For the same reasons fresh attempts to attract Tamil labour in 1913 and again in 1926 also failed.

On the other hand one source of immigration which was welcomed with increasing reluctance but which came steadily more persistent was that from Japan. In the early years the need for labour was compelling, so much so that in 1893 Governor Creagh, having met with failure from India and China, approached Tokyo and got an immediate response. However the first group of Japanese colonists, who settled on the east coast, were all dead within twelve months of their arrival, and for many years to come there were no more immigrants from Japan. Tokyo itself was far more interested in its adventures on the Asian mainland. Japanese interest revived in the 1900s and resulted in the establishment of a small colony at Tawau in 1915, its activities centring on the enterprise of the Kuhara Company. The Tawau settlement became stabilized at around the thousand mark and concentrated on rubber, dried fish and, after 1931, abaca. However after the Great War Japanese interest was no longer so welcome in Sabah, and it became official policy to discourage the establishment of fresh Japanese colonies in the territory.[13]

Population: distribution and occupation

The influx of settlers into the country created new patterns of settlement and a marked differentiation between the immigrant and indigenous peoples. Although the territory had a very low average density of population, it was very unevenly distributed, nearly half being crowded together on the west coast, particularly around Jesselton, with pockets elsewhere around the inland townships on the high plains beyond the Crocker Range and around the east coast ports of Sandakan and Tawau. The immigrant population was predominantly to be found in these areas, while there was also a discernible trend away from the sparsely populated districts of the interior to the west coast.

Economically speaking the Chinese formed by far the most dominant section of the population and predominated in the main centres of settlement. The towns in other words were largely Chinese, as were most of the shop-keepers, tradesmen, technicians, artisans and clerks. Nevertheless the majority of the Chinese themselves were engaged in agriculture, especially as rubber or coconut planters. A fair proportion were logging on the east coast and they provided the bulk of estate labour. Very few were involved in rice production, an industry most of them had shied away from since the first days of the company. Chinese miners formed the greater part of the labour force on the Silimpopon coalfield.

The Chinese connexion with Sabah dates back to the seventh century A.D. During the Ming period (1368-1644) there were regular trading links be-

tween South China and North Borneo and colonies of Chinese pepper planters on the shores of Brunei Bay. In Company days the first Chinese to come
into the country were mostly Cantonese, who found employment on the
tobacco estates or set themselves up as shop-keepers and traders. At first the
Cantonese were the leading speech group in the territory, but later on gave
way to the Hakkas who owed their rise to the emphasis given to agricultural
settlers in the 1880s and 1890s. The Hakkas came to form the majority
amongst the Chinese in every district in Sabah, their dialect became the lingua
franca of the territory, and as a group they acquired a better sex ratio than
any other Chinese community. The other major speech groups in the territory were the Hokkien, Teochew and Hainanese.

Of the other immigrant groups, the Indonesian (Javanese) descendants of
the indentured labourers of the 1914-34 period were the most prominent,
although in the timber industry on the east coast Filipinos predominated.

Most of the indigenous races, on the other hand, remained tied to a subsistence way of life with the exception of the Kadazans, Bajaus and Brunei
Malays. The Kadazans who formed the largest single racial group in the
country were mainly on the west coast and on the inland plains of Ranau
and Tambunan where they planted padi and represented the chief rice producers in the state. Some of them, however, went in for estate labour with
the opening of rubber plantations along the new railway line, and subsequently took up smallholdings themselves. The Bajaus were to be found along both
the east and west coasts as fishermen, farmers and cattle-raisers. Their evolution into agriculturalists amounted to a social revolution, since as recently
as 1881 they were still a nation of sea-gypsies living on their boats. The Brunei Malays and their cousins the Kedayans came next in importance in economic terms amongst the indigenous peoples. Settled in a line from Brunei
Bay to Jesselton, they too were mainly fishermen and padi planters, generally
at little more than subsistence level.

The Murut people stayed as a group far less involved in the modern world
of commerce introduced by the company to Sabah, living in remote villages
and longhouses in the more inaccessible parts of the territory. Theirs was a
primitive existence based on a shifting agriculture of tapioca and hill-rice,
hunting and an occasional trade in jungle produce. Some ventured onto estates as seasonal labourers and eventually became like the Kadazans, smallholders along the railway line. After 1921 in particular there was a discernible
movement away from the hills to the plains. The Orang Sungai were the
only other significant indigenous minority group. They too lived a simple,
subsistence existence.

Taken as a whole the bulk of the working population was engaged in primary industry, nearly half in rice production and another considerable number in rubber planting. In both cases the people concerned were mainly indigenous. Logging absorbed some 10,000 workers and 7,500 people were
involved in coconut planting. The remaining fifth of the working population was divided between business, manufacturing and transport, the public
services and domestic employment. The number of urban dwellers was therefore small and the growth of towns and townships a recent phenomenon;

Jesselton trebled its inhabitants between 1921 and 1951; the growth rates of Sandakan and Tawau were similar.

Apart from the small but distinct trend towards urbanization, particularly after 1920, the other most significant social change under company rule was the de-peopling of parts of the interior, a trend associated with the overall Murut decline and with the pull of rubber along the west coast.

Land policy

Sabah possessed vast reserves of land, of which a mere 5 per cent was reckoned to be in productive use. The existence of these vast tracts and the fact that the Chartered Company was less inhibited in its policies than the Brooke regime at Kuching meant that the territory basically faced no land problem of the kind caused by extensive native land reserves constricting economic expansion. In fact in 1928 the administration moved in the opposite direction by abolishing the restrictions on Europeans and immigrant Asians who wished to acquire land in certain 'native' areas. The land problems which did exist were created by over-generous concessions to foreign enterprises and by the aversion of the indigenous peoples to any form of land tax.

The company's liberality with regard to land concessions sprang from its initial dependence on land sales as a source of revenue. However this did not prevent the establishment of a rational land policy based on two forms of tenure, one, ordinary leasehold available to anybody, and the other heritable and non-transferable native titles. Land under shifting cultivation was not included in these provisions but was treated like all unalienated land as the property of the state. About one-third of the land area of the territory was held under lease by foreigners. The land under native title was far smaller, being under two-fifths of the area held under ordinary leasehold. On the other hand, despite the absence (after 1928) of any means to prevent immigrants from settling anywhere they wished, the Company's record in protecting existing indigenous land rights was creditable. Right from the very beginning the administration set out to defend indigenous land rights from unscrupulous Western concessionaires. Indeed the zeal of the government in this regard was one of the principal factors behind the formation of the Planters' Association of North Borneo in 1888, which in turn provoked the promulgation of more detailed land regulations in the native interest the following year.[14]

In 1903 Governor Birch, alarmed by the imminent rush for rubber lands, reinforced this legislation by making provision for the issuing of native titles to land, fearing that without them existing indigenous rights could not be established in a court of law for lack of evidence. However this move, sound as it was, brought to the fore the problem of the land tax. In fact Birch himself also proposed the progressive substitution of the existing poll tax by a land tax with the double aim of encouraging permanent land settlement and of raising government revenues. The new land policy quickly ran into opposition. There was a general reluctance by the Kadazans or Muruts to take advantage of the possession of title. A more technical problem was caused by the frequently highly complex and intricate property rights involved.

Nevertheless the economics of the rubber boom which forced up land prices and made titles valuable soon brought about a change of attitude. After 1909 began an ever-increasing demand by Kadazan chiefs for surveys, demarcations and title-deeds. At the same time government did not press for its land dues which were in any case very light. A further fillip to native registration of title came in 1937 when the land laws were amended so as to encourage padi-planting. By this time there was a growing political awareness of the importance of these land rights, reflected in the growing demands of the Native Chiefs Advisory Council for the strengthening of indigenous land rights.

Conditions of labour

Labour conditions in Sabah were fundamentally similar to those which prevailed in Malaya, and labour legislation, almost entirely based on that of the Straits Settlements, was likewise paternalistic, limited in its protection of the labourer and generous in its regard for the employer. The evolution of labour policy in the territory was dictated by the shortage of labour itself, and the strong desire to present a good image before the suspicious eyes of the British House of Commons so as to preserve the confidence of the company's investors.

However, at the beginning, this image was somewhat tarnished by the unscrupulous methods of the pioneer tobacco planters, while the administration on occasion proved little better, particularly during the period of railway construction in the early 1900s when a large proportion of the labour force, mostly Chinese, succumbed to the appalling conditions and inadequate diet.[15] The worst abuses as usual were connected with indentured labour and the steps taken to combat these evils followed faithfully in the tracks laid down by the Straits Settlements.

The earliest piece of labour legislation was the Labour Code of 1882, modelled on the Straits Settlements Ordinance of the same year. The following year this code was superseded by a new one based entirely on the Straits Settlements Indian Immigrants Ordinance of 1881, which created a Protector of Labour with wide powers of administration and inspection. Designed to stimulate a flow of Tamil labour from the South of India which never materialized, its beneficial effects nevertheless remained. By the mid-1890s general labour conditions in the territory had greatly improved. Employers had come to realize that better treated employees made better employees while government supervision was more organized and effective. Twenty years later matters were markedly better, with the death-rate reduced and desertions an increasing rarity.

During the twentieth century the Labour Code was considerably improved upon, mostly in connexion with contract labour, in which policy Malaya largely set the pace. The revision of the Labour Code of the F.M.S. in 1908 brought similar changes in Sabah and two years later further modifications were made in response to criticisms from the Straits Settlements. In 1916, 1927 and 1929 the conditions governing labour contracts were further tightened and amended in favour of the labourer. In fact contract labour no longer enjoyed official support, was banned in neighbouring territories and was losing popularity amongst local employers. Finally in 1932 all such labour was abolished in British North Borneo.

In the meantime steps to protect the labourer from the system of advances which could ensure his permanent indebtedness were also taken, despite mounting opposition from foreign planters.[16] In 1936 the labour laws of the territory were incorporated into a new labour code, based as usual on that of the Straits Settlements and covering all aspects of conditions of labour.

The elimination of slavery

One of the greatest achievements of the Company's regime was the elimination of slavery within its territory. The problem was evident in the slave-raiding endemic along Sabah shores in the early 1880s and in the institution of slavery itself amongst the population. Anxious to avoid the interference of the British government, the Court of Directors was determined to ensure that these practices should cease.[17]

To break the back of the slave-raiders force was the only way. In 1878 the sinking of every pirate vessel in sight in Sandakan Bay and the destruction of the slave-raiders' base at Tungku successfully brought large-scale raids to an end, but raids on a smaller scale, kept alive by the still flourishing slave marts at Lawas and in the Sulu archipelago, continued for another twenty years. But as the Company strengthened its hand the practice gradually died down. In 1891 a Straits Settlement Ordinance was adopted which made it an offence for any village to harbour slave-dealers or newly captured slaves. The work of district officers in following up all reports of slave activities brought about their eventual suppression. In the new century there were only spasmodic incidents of minor importance.

In the meanwhile the administration also took cautious but effective steps to abolish the institution itself amongst the inhabitants of the territory. Slavery, particularly the custom of debt-bondage, was prevalent along the west coast. It also existed amongst the peoples of the interior, although on a much more reduced scale as poverty and nomadic habits would not permit their maintenance. Human sacrifice was not unknown. The first successful steps against slavery were taken by Pryer in Sandakan in 1878, but elsewhere Company officials made little progress. The first firm legislation on the matter was promulgated by Treacher in 1881, forbidding all foreigners to possess or to import slaves at all. It was necessary, however, for the administration to be circumspect, since its officials were thin on the ground and it could not have coped with any widespread uprising which too hasty or too sweeping anti-slavery measures might provoke. However in 1883 Treacher followed up his initiative with more drastic legislation, including the provision that all children born of slave parents after 1 November of that year were to be considered free-born. This cut off the last traditional source of supply, since recruitment by war was already out of the question, and the institution of slavery started to wither. It took time to die. Implementation was difficult because of too few officials, limited naval support and the existence of too many loopholes in the law. In 1902 all forms of slavery were formally abolished but it was another ten years before this measure could be effectively enforced.

Health

As far as health measures were concerned, the Chartered Company was at first motivated by purely utilitarian considerations, doing little beyond trying to protect its own employees. This was followed by a period under Cowie who held public health very low on his scale of priorities. Finally after 1913 there took place a marked change of attitude so that although in 1941 the territory's health services left much to be desired, they nevertheless compared favourably with those in Sarawak.[18]

However, outside the main centres of population health conditions remained extremely primitive. The territory was not to know a water-borne sewage system until the 1950s, while malaria, dysentery, beri-beri, tuberculosis and pneumonia were still as potent as killers at the end of the Company's rule as they had been at the beginning. Added to these were cholera, smallpox, yaws, leprosy, enteric fever and hook-worm. Of all these, however, malaria and beri-beri were the most deadly, if only because their causes stayed undivined in the nineteenth century.

The administration achieved some signal successes, particularly with regard to the reduction of cholera, smallpox, hook-worm and yaws. By 1941 both smallpox and yaws had been virtually eliminated and hook-worm reduced to a negligible figure. The attempt to overcome beri-beri was less successful. In 1940 a steady stream of beri-beri victims were still being admitted to government hospitals, of whom a fair proportion inevitably died. The malarial problem was unresolved in 1941 although much had been done to reduce its effects. The North Borneo administration was not left out of the discoveries about the origin of malaria which had been made elsewhere and was able to take full advantage of the work of Watson at Klang in Malaya, but unfortunately the Sabah carrier was not the same as in the Peninsula or as in other parts of the archipelago, a fact not realized until 1938. The provisions made to care for and cure lepers were nothing short of scandalous.[19]

The first area to which health measures were effectively applied were the estates. After an initial period of wanton neglect, employers with enlightened self-interest changed their attitudes towards the health of their labourers, while in the 1890s the government was able to initiate regular inspections of the estates. In the years that followed there were further improvements in estate health, with the advances in medicine and with the greater accessibility of the estates themselves, particularly after the opening of the railway line. The general result was that death-rate amongst estate labourers had been reduced from about 30 per cent in the 1890s to $2\frac{1}{2}$ per cent by the end of the next decade. Up to this point, however, government health measures had been very limited. In the 1880s and 1890s there was no regular medical department and official measures were left in the hands of the Protector of Labour. During the Cowie era the attitude of the administration became even more parsimonious still.

The establishment of an embryo medical service to cater for all the peoples of the territory took place on the initiative of Cowie's successor, Ridgeway, who in 1912 called for a report on the question. As a result of the report there was a reorganization of the medical department and a more liberal allocation of funds. By 1940 there were nine government hospitals together with ten sick rest houses at major centres. There were also twenty dispensaries in villages throughout the country and two mobile ones, reaching between them more than a quarter of a million people. The dispensaries were crude affairs, consisting of a simple attap hut with a bench, a table and a wall on three sides— 'primitive but popular and approved of by the League of Nations'. Steps to reduce infant mortality were also taken after the Great War, although at first difficulty was found in securing recruits for midwifery. On the eve of the Pacific War more extended measures for infant and maternity welfare were being introduced, largely on the recommendations of the Shircore Report.

One basic problem was the fundamental lack of interest of the indigenous population in Western medicine, although there was a marked change of attitude after the successful campaign against yaws in the 1920s. Another problem was the steady decline of the Murut population. For some time the high death-rate amongst this people was obscured by ineffective administration which rested in the hands of illiterate headmen and overworked district officers, but when an efficient system of registration was established, the true situation was exposed. For many years the official explanation for this phenomenon was that it sprang from the drinking habits of the Muruts. Their decline was also ascribed to the increasing employment of Muruts as estate labourers which produced visibly bad social effects. Finally, in 1936 a new governor, Jardine, appointed a commission headed by Dr. J.O. Shircore to go into the whole matter. The Shircore Report stressed malaria and gonorrhea as causes for Murut sterility, recommended research into the former, the setting up of maternity and infant welfare clinics and the creation of a rural health service. The Report was a very useful one and became the basis for the steps taken after 1945 to rectify the situation.

Social welfare
Provisions for social welfare in general were rudimentary, while the administration depended for a considerable proportion of its revenues on the proceeds from the opium and gambling farms held by the Chinese. Up till 1907 the two farms were run separately, but in that year they were, to the government's greater profit, combined. Steps to arrest these social evils were only taken as a result of outside pressure. When the F.M.S. government in Kuala Lumpur took over the opium farms in 1910, British North Borneo followed suit in 1914. In 1927 moves were taken for the suppression of opium smoking entirely. In the same year gambling was made illegal for everybody in the territory, except for the Chinese who were granted a period of grace.

The great majority of the population continued to live at subsistence level. Indebtedness was widespread, although this was a matter which officialdom tended to make light of until Jardine became governor in 1934.[20] But despite his efforts to tackle this problem, it was left basically unresolved by the time of the outbreak of the Pacific War in 1941.

In general British North Borneo under the company remained a backwater as far as economic development and the process of westernization were concerned. The basic contradictions evident in other British colonial territories were latent but not visible as the period of their germination had not yet arrived.

[1]The Silimpopon coal industry was affected by the same factors that eventually forced the closing down of the Sarawak Sadong colliery. The low grade ores needed to be mined in larger quantities than the equipment available could handle in order to pay its way. Coal prices in general declined and as ships converted from steam to oil demand fell as well.

[2]By this time, alas, Saunders had been dismissed and his sponsors, the Sabah Land Farming Company, had passed into oblivion.

[3]The McKinnon Tariff of 1893 was passed in order to protect the United States home industry. Its effects were immediate, and the ensuing crisis prompted Cowie and his assistants to try and introduce a version of the Dutch Culture System onto the lands at the foot of Mount Kinabalu where a coarse local crop was grown. A superintendent of tobacco culture was appointed and district officers directed to order the cultivation of tobacco for disposal by the government. By 1896 it was already clear that the experiment would not work.

[4]However, production was revived by the government and taken over by the Imperial Tobacco Company on a small scale after 1933.

[5]By this offer, the North Borneo administration was prepared to offer tax exemption on exports for 50 years to all companies formed to plant rubber in the territory, with a guaranteed 4 per cent return on their investments for the initial six years.

[6]The Chinese, who, in 1903, had been the first to plant the new crop, formed the overwhelming majority amongst the smallholders.

[7]According to Tregonning 'the smallholders were treated worse than in any other rubber producing territory'. K.G. Tregonning, A History of Modern Sabah; 1851–1963, University of Malaya Press, Singapore, 1965, p. 91; cf. the fate of smallholders in the Peninsular Malay States and in Indonesia.

[8]Nevertheless some progress was made. In 1923 the first forest reserves were marked out in the teeth of strong opposition from all the timber concerns. Under the forceful Keith as Conservator of Forests in the 1930s, the Forest Department built up firm guidelines as to administration and established facilities for proper training and research. However in 1937 barely $1\frac{1}{2}$ per cent of forest land in the territory were under reserve, as compared to the Malay Peninsula's 27 per cent.

[9]For the background to the construction of the Sabah Railway, refer to Tregonning, op. cit., pp. 56 et seq.

[10]The company produced its own currency.

[11]The question as to whom should be regarded as 'indigenous' to the country is as complex in British North Borneo (Sabah) as in Sarawak, and necessitated a legal definition by the Interpretation (Definition of Native) Ordinance of 1952 to clarify the position. According to this Ordinance, the indigenous people of Sabah fall primarily into two groups—the tribal peoples who have inhabited the country over an indefinite period of time, and settlers from other parts of the archipelago who culturally and even ethnically have much in common. Within the first group are found the Kadazan or Dusun, the Bajau, the Murut/Tidong and the Orang Sungai; the second category embraces the natives of Sarawak and Brunei, and of the Sulu archipelago who have lived in the country for three years, and also natives of the Malay Peninsula, Indonesia and the Philippines who have lived there for five.

[12]The earliest of these proposals is connected with the hero of Filipino nationalism, José Rizal, who in 1892 suggested establishing a colony for Filipino patriots on Marudu Bay.

[13]The company in this period was warned by the British Foreign Office not to discriminate but not to encourage either. The Court of Directors turned down one scheme for a Japanese agricultural colony during the period of the Great War (1914–18) and later rejected two more proposals, made with much greater insistence, for the establishment of a colony of Japanese rice farmers in the Kota Belud Valley in 1937 and again in 1940.

[14]From the outset, all land deals between natives and Europeans were forbidden, government setting itself up as intermediary for such transactions. While this measure was doubtless designed to protect the company's own interests as much as those of its subjects, the intention of the detailed land regulations of 1889 was clear: no land transactions to European interests could take place without full consultation with and the approval of the local community concerned, while district officers were empowered to investigate and ensure what existing native rights were on their own account. Certain basic land rights were laid down and all land deals were subject to the scrutiny of the governor himself, to whom the native landholder was granted the right of direct appeal.

[15]For an example of the excesses that could occur on the pioneer estates, see the excerpts quoted from an official report of enquiry of 1891, quoted by Tregonning, op. cit., pp. 135–6.

[16]Such measures were all the more necessary as larger numbers of Kadazans and Muruts entered the labour market, being far more vulnerable to this form of exploitation than their Chinese counterparts. In 1924 the first steps were taken to cut down the amounts legally advanceable to a Murut or any other indigene, and by the next year this totalled no more than $5. These measures brought forth protests from the North Borneo Planters' Association in 1927, but without effecting any change in official policy.

[17]See Tregonning, op. cit., p. 187.

[18]In the late 1930s Sabah had more hospitals and double the number of inpatients compared to Sarawak, and had effected far more widespread measures against diseases like yaws and smallpox. Perhaps, however, this superiority owed much to the pattern of distribution of Sabah's population which was, comparatively speaking, grouped together in more accessible areas, while the distances involved were not as extended as in Sarawak.

[19]For details of the leper settlement in Sandakan Bay and its history, see Tregonning, op. cit., p. 172.

[20]For more background on the problems associated with indebtedness, see Tregonning, op. cit., pp. 124–5.

Books and articles for further reading

BOOKS

Baker, M.H., *Sabah: The First Ten Years as a Colony, 1946-56*, Malaysia Publishing House, Singapore, 1965.

Emerson, R., *Malaysia: A Study in Direct and Indirect Rule*, University of Malaya Press, Kuala Lumpur, 1964 (reprint).

Fisher, C.A., *South-East Asia: A Social, Economic and Political Geography*, Methuen & Co. Ltd., London, 1964.

Irwin, G., *Nineteenth Century Borneo*, Donald Moore, Singapore, 1955.

Jacoby, E.H., *Agrarian Unrest in Southeast Asia*, Asia Publishing House, Bombay, 1961.

Lee Yong-leng, *North Borneo: A Study in Settlement Geography*, Asia Pacific Press, Singapore, 1965.

Mills, L.A., *British Rule in Eastern Asia*, Oxford University Press, London, 1941.

Purcell, V., *The Chinese in South-East Asia*, Oxford University Press, London, 1965.

Robequain, C., *Malaya, Indonesia, Borneo and the Philippines*, Longman Green, London, 1958.

Roth, H.L., *The Natives of Sarawak and British North Borneo*, Vols. I & II, University of Malaya Press, Kuala Lumpur, 1968 (reprint).

ARTICLES

Tarling, N., 'British Policy in the Malay Peninsula and Archipelago: 1824-71', *JMBRAS*, XXX, 3, 1957.

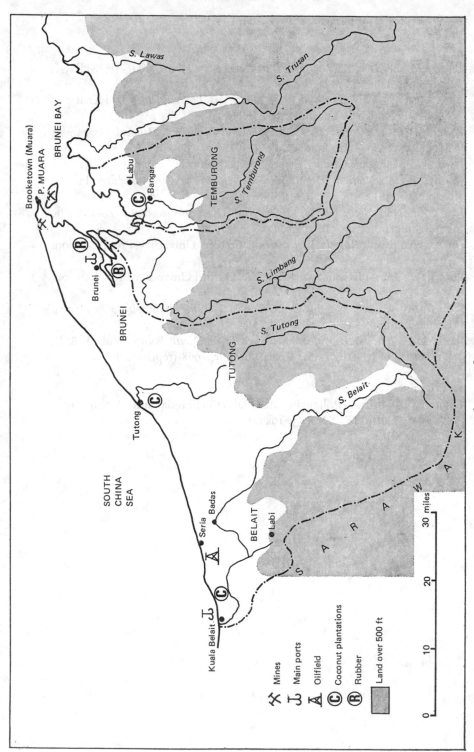

24. General Map of Brunei, 1941

E. Brunei

'Called the Venice of the East, Brunei, Butterworth suggested in 1923, might be "more appropriately called the Vienna of the East, the biggest Malay city of the world and the capital of a Sultan having only a little bit of country left on which to support its dignity...." '

Nicholas Tarling, *Britain, the Brookes and Brunei.*

'The Residents have been busy in getting a system of law into force, applying as a general rule those provisions of the Federated Malay States' laws which are suitable to the circumstances of Brunei, and generally doing what they can in a state where there is little or no money.'

Sir R.E. Stubbs, Memorandum on the History of Brunei.

THE 2,226 square miles of land which was all that was left of the ancient sultanate of Brunei when it received a British Resident in 1906 was the only one of the three British territories in North Borneo to be administered along orthodox Colonial Office lines. The Resident was posted there more with a view to safeguarding British interests in the region rather than in the expectation of gaining large economic returns, in spite of the sanguine views of the sultanate's potential entertained by officials like Weld and others. That the state should eventually become the richest oil producer in all Borneo was an unanticipated irony of fate.

In fact, however, the existence of oil within Brunei territory had been discovered before the British takeover, and was a possible factor in the British move.[1] However, it was not until the 1920s that the rich Seria deposits were located—much richer than those of neighbouring Miri just across the border of Sarawak. Royal Dutch Shell immediately showed interest and in 1927 its subsidiary, the British Malayan Petroleum Company, went into production. The exploitation of the new oil field was slowed down by the onset of the Great Depression two years later as well as by the general policy adopted by the Shell group of companies during the ensuing decade to maintain prices by preventing too much of its resources coming onto the market at once. But even with the moderate output of some 2,400 tons a day or 700,000 tons a year (1941), Brunei was able to clear its national debt and introduce 'agricultural improvement of all kinds'.

Up till the 1930s, on the other hand, Brunei was hard put to it make ends meet. The main exports were gambier, rubber, jelutong, hides and horns, some sago, pepper, and brass and silverware. Of these rubber was the most important. As gambier faded out in the 1900s, Brunei joined the rubber boom in a minor key and several estates, as well as smallholdings, were opened up. In the opening years of the British Residency a number of timber concessions were granted, but although three-quarters of the country are covered by forest, logging never acquired more than a domestic importance, and in fact the exportation of timber was expressly prohibited. As for pepper, despite the sultanate's past renown as a pepper mart, the product played a fitful role in the twentieth century, flowing and ebbing with the world market. Of domestic crops only a small area was given over to padi which was far from sufficient to meet the needs of the state, although the new administration made some efforts to improve quality and output by the introduction of new varieties and better methods. Other crops grown included coconuts but none was planted on a large scale.

Mineral deposits of significance, apart from oil and coal, were non-existent, and the coal of Brunei was as disappointing as that of Labuan. The Muara deposits played their role in Brunei's history, but they proved to be of more importance politically than economically, for they never realized a profit. Even if they had done so, it would have been largely lost to the sultanate for in 1882 Sultan Abdul Munim granted the mining concession in Muara Damit to Cowie. This concession which became the centre of a triangular dispute involving Sarawak, British North Borneo and the British government itself eventually fell into the hands of Rajah Charles of Sarawak who ran the mines for two decades at a loss. Finally in 1921 Sarawak gave up and handed back the profitless Muara concession and all rights over other coal deposits in the state to Brunei. The collieries closed down at once and the area reverted to jungle.

In other fields of development Brunei got nowhere. Apart from the oil field, prior to 1941, the total sum of industry in the state was represented by a cutch factory and two samsu distilleries. Communications except by water were virtually non-existent. There were no roads beyond the three towns of Brunei, Kuala Belait and Seria, and the state's only link with the outside world was by the Straits Steamship Company's ferry across Brunei Bay to Labuan. There were three radio telegraph stations and six post offices in the state.

Until the oil boom the administration had little opportunity to promote faster development. Official efforts were made to encourage handicrafts and to find a market for Brunei silverware, without much success. At first the British Resident was entirely dependent on loans from the prosperous F.M.S. of the Malay Peninsula in order to carry on. The bulk of the money borrowed was used to liquidate existing concessions granted under the old regime which tied up all the state revenues and on occasion involved more than one concessionaire for the same concession. Their redemption ensured the state of a modicum of income, but it was oil that saved the day.

In all other respects Brunei's administration and development followed in miniature the pattern laid down in the Malay Peninsula, particularly in the east coast states. Brunei's own population was predominantly Malay, according to the 1931 census, amounting to 80 per cent.[2] There were also some 2,500 Chinese (about 8 per cent) and a handful of Indians, Europeans and Eurasians. The Chinese had been a permanent element in the population of Brunei (meaning Brunei Bay) for centuries, and their trading contacts dated back even further. But their numbers waxed and waned according to fortune, both local and in their homeland.[3]

As always this small community enjoyed an importance out of all relation to its numbers and held the keys of the sultanate's economy in its hands. In the middle of the nineteenth century they monopolized the sago trade and

also that in jelutong; they were also inevitably the revenue farmers and moneylenders of the state, and it was reported that they formed an important
element in the opposition to the British takeover of 1906, fearful for their
own future under the new dispensation. To this merchant colony were added,
in the 1930s, a larger population of skilled and unskilled Chinese labourers
who immigrated to work in the Seria oil field.

The Chinese were mainly to be found in the three towns but the predominantly Malay rural population was concentrated along the river-ways
and coast as farmers and fishermen. The Malays also predominated in government service. The rest of the sultanate's inhabitants was made up of other
indigenous groups who pursued their livelihoods in the hills.

If Brunei derived any advantage by virtue of being administered along
orthodox colonial lines, it was that its economic and social policies were attuned to the more systematic and progressive practices adopted in Malaya.
Hence only four years after the appointment of the first British Resident,
a new land code provided for the registration of land titles granted before its promulgation (in 1909) and for the issuing of new titles subsequent
to it under the Torrens System. Titles were limited to surface rights—minerals
remained state property—and unless special conditions were granted, land
was allowed for agricultural purposes only. Nevertheless land administration
in Brunei met the same snags that it had encountered in the Malay Peninsula;
shortage of trained staff hindered speedy and adequate surveying and the
business of registering titles.[4]

Brunei's adherence to the Malayan pattern also ensured that the elemental
social welfare services conformed closer to those of the Peninsula rather than
to the slower and more haphazard measures in Sarawak and British North
Borneo. Slavery was brought to a speedy end soon after the arrival of Mc-
Arthur as the first Resident; gambling and opium smoking were restricted
to adult male Chinese. On the other hand, there were virtually no labour
laws in the sultanate prior to 1941, although it must be said that there was
also little need for any except on the oil field which was managed on
enlightened, paternalistic lines by the Shell subsidiary.

Brunei's history in the nineteenth century was one long record of unrelieved
disaster, and at the end of it the sultanate's prospects, economically as well as
politically, had never looked bleaker. Under the British Residents, although
manifestly not because of them, fortune smiled more kindly, and by virtue of
its oil resources, limited area and small population Brunei in 1941 appeared
headed for a prosperous future.

[1]The oil was found on Pulau Berembang, off Muara, in 1903, during shafting operations
on one of Raja Brooke's coal mines. Work was begun soon afterwards but discontinued
when the boring machine broke down.
[2]The Malay total included other indigenous groups such as the Kedayan, Kadazan, Iban
and Murut.
[3]In the seventeenth and eighteenth centuries there were probably several hundred
Chinese terracing the low hills around Brunei Bay with the pepper vine. By the nineteenth century the pepper planters had vanished and in 1889 Treacher estimated that

the total Chinese population was no more than 80 out of an estimated 12,000–15,000 inhabitants.

⁴The situation became so bad that in 1954 alienation of state land was virtually suspended so as to enable the Land Department to catch up on a backlog of work that stretched back to 1936. In 1969 it was estimated that barely 2 per cent of all the land in the state had been alienated under the Code; of that amount the most substantial share was in the hands of the Brunei Shell Petroleum Company.

Books and articles for further reading

BOOKS

In general reference should be made to the books and articles listed under Sarawak and British North Borneo. In addition, refer to:

Tarling, N., *Britain, the Brookes and Brunei*, Oxford University Press, Kuala Lumpur, 1971.

ARTICLES

Black, I.D., 'The Ending of Brunei Rule in Sabah. 1878–1902', *JMBRAS*, XXXXI, 2, 1968.

Leyes, P., 'Observations on the Brunei Political System, 1883–1885', *JMBRAS*, XXXXI, 2, 1968.

Stubbs, Sir Reginald Edward, 'Two Colonial Office Memoranda on the History of Brunei', *JMBRAS*, XXXXI, 2, 1968.

IV. FRENCH INDO-CHINA

IN November 1887 the French established the Indo-China Union, bringing together the three distinct historical entities of Vietnam, Cambodia and Laos into one political unit under a French governor-general resident at Hanoi. Flattering as the Union may have been to Vietnamese nationalist sentiment, it never bore any relationship to ethnic, economic or geographical realities, and as events after 1945 were to demonstrate, possessed little political validity either. For the Union involved three major races who had little in common and whose economic and social circumstances were entirely different from one another. In reality, each nation within the Union continued to develop along its own lines, notwithstanding the common French tutelage, and in the fullness of time each went its own way. Likewise, in studying the development of the countries of French Indo-China, we have to consider them separately in turn.

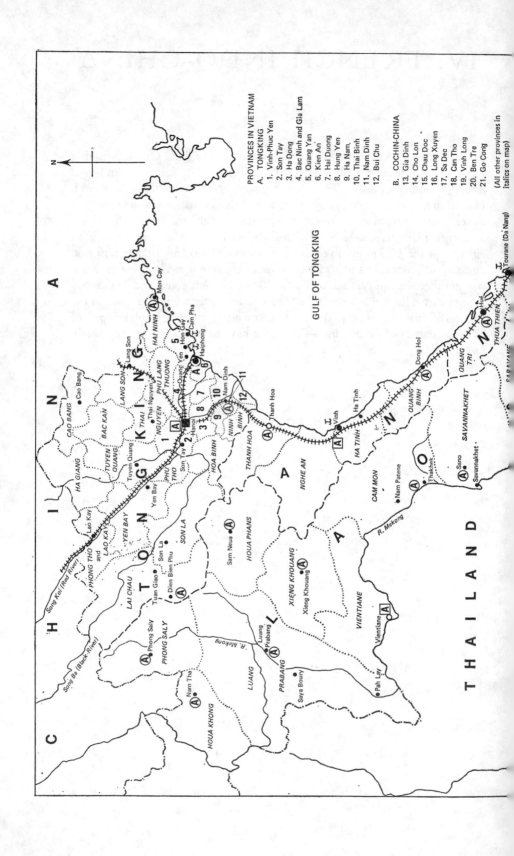

PROVINCES IN VIETNAM

A. TONGKING

1. Vinh-Phuc Yen
2. Son Tay
3. Ha Dong
4. Bac Ninh and Gia Lam
5. Quang Yan
6. Kien An
7. Hai Duong
8. Hung Yen
9. Ha Nam
10. Thai Binh
11. Nam Dinh
12. Bui Chu

B. COCHIN-CHINA

13. Gia Dinh
14. Cho Lon
15. Chau Doc
16. Long Xuyen
17. Sa Dec
18. Can Tho
19. Vinh Long
20. Ben Tre
21. Go Cong

(All other provinces in
italics on map)

GULF OF TONGKING

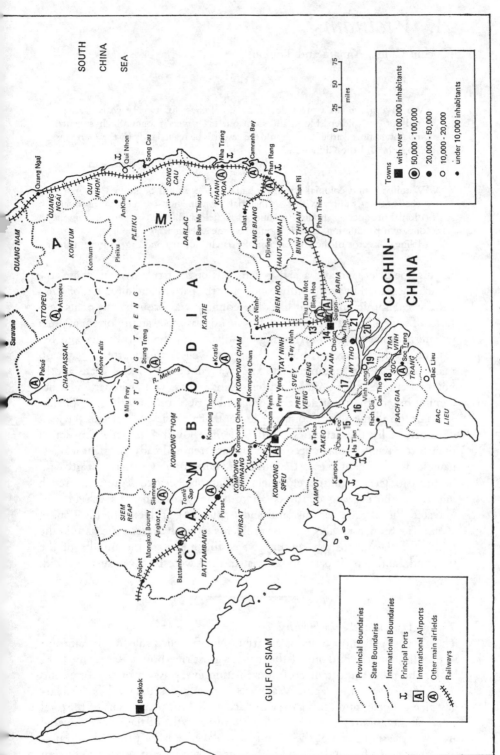

25. General Map of French Indo-China, 1941

A. *Vietnam*

(Cochin-China, Annam and Tonkin)

'We have given up a great deal for the colonies; for twenty years we have poured out our soldiers' blood and spent our tax-payers' money. Such sacrifices should not go unrewarded nor should the rewards be reaped only by the Germans, the English, and the Chinese....'

L. Ferry, *Le régime douanièr de l'Indochine*, Paris, 1912.

'Within a sound colonial system, colonial produce must be limited to supplying the mother-country with raw materials or with non-competitive products. If colonial production should step out of this field and offer competition ruinous to our own production, then it should become a dangerous opponent.'

Meline, Director of the Association of French Industry and Agriculture, 1910.

During the brief two and a half generations of their rule over Vietnam, the French succeeded in profoundly modifying the pattern and direction of Vietnamese economic and social life. The country was brought out of its centuries of self-sufficient economic isolation and was made an important adjunct of international trade, contributing one-quarter of the world's rice and becoming its third largest rubber producer as well as an exporter of cement, maize and coal.[1] It acquired a trunk railway and a network of roads and its population more than doubled within seventy years, Tonkin in particular becoming one of the most densely populated regions on earth. In spite of this, Vietnam of all the major countries in South-East Asia was perhaps the least transformed by the activities of the colonial power. The chief impact of French rule seems to have been to accentuate trends already incipient in Vietnamese development rather than to create entirely new patterns of growth. In stimulating economic development to an unprecedented degree, the French intensified the existing contrasts between the north and the south and aggravated the already serious land and population problems of the Tonkin Basin. The fundamental economic problems which had faced Vietnam in the middle of the nineteenth century were still present in the middle of the twentieth, and even if partially alleviated, they were by no means resolved.

The development of the rice industry

The greatest and most obvious contribution of French rule to Vietnam was to turn the country into one of the region's great rice-bowls. Rice came to be by far the most important crop, dominating every aspect of economic and social life. Prior to the Pacific War, Vietnam ranked as the world's third largest rice exporter and up till 1931 rice accounted for 65 per cent of the total value of the country's exports. It took up five-sixths of the total cultivated area, was the staple diet of the country and played a major part in the domestic economy as a fuel and as a fodder for livestock. Vietnamese rice production increased five-fold between 1870 and 1930 and at least three-quarters of the population depended on rice for their livelihood in some form or other.

The two main centres of rice production were the delta of the Song-koi (Red River) in the north (Tonkin) and that of the Mekong in the south (Cochin-China). A much smaller amount of rice was also grown in the northern estuaries of Annam. Tonkin, the traditional home of the Vietnamese people, was the oldest centre of rice cultivation in the country and produced the highest yields per acre, but over half the country's rice was grown in the south which provided over 90 per cent of the grain exported. Cochin-China became the main exporting region of Vietnam because it was the area of most recent development and therefore far less densely populated, whereas traditional Tonkin had to support a huge population which absorbed the bulk of its crop. Indeed from time to time both Tonkin and Annam had to import Cochin-Chinese rice to meet their own needs. Apart from the wet rice grown in the great deltas and coastal estuaries, there was also a certain amount of dry padi grown in the hills by the peoples of the interior, who practised shifting cultivation. However hill rice played no part in the export economy of the country.

The emergence of Vietnam as a major rice exporter was the result of 'French intelligence and application'.[2] Vietnam had the potential to export rice before the French arrived but the emperors of Hué preferred to keep the rice at home, actuated partly by political considerations and the Chinese principle of the 'ever-even granary' but also to ensure their own supplies, since by the middle of the nineteenth century the court was dependent on the south for its rice, as Admiral de Genouilly well knew when he attacked Saigon.

Rice in Cochin-China

In fact rice cultivation in the Mekong Delta had been known for nearly as long as in the north and had formed the economic base for the early empire of Fu-Nan and the great Khmer kingdom of Angkor which eventually evolved from it. But unlike in the north conditions in the delta did not favour the growth of a large population and intensive farming; not only was the rainfall less and temperatures higher but the monsoon season was unreliable and the annual inundations of the Mekong amongst the deltaic swamps uncontrollable. Up till the middle of the eighteenth century the area was still predominantly inhabited by a sparse Khmer population, the bulk of them farming in the much easier conditions offered further upstream. Vietnamese infiltration started in earnest around 1700 but 150 years later they were still only substantially settled east and north of the Bassac River. The Vietnamese brought with them better methods of cultivation and the important innovation of floating rice, but it was left to the French using modern scientific and technological methods to irrigate the vast lands to the south and west of the Bassac (the Trans-Bassac) and open them up to the growing of rice. Starting in the 1860s, under the French work progressed in the Trans-Bassac at the rate of 110 square miles a year, done almost entirely by manual labour. With increasing mechanization at the turn of the century the pace quickened so that by 1937 over 3,500 square miles were under padi. Impressive as this progress

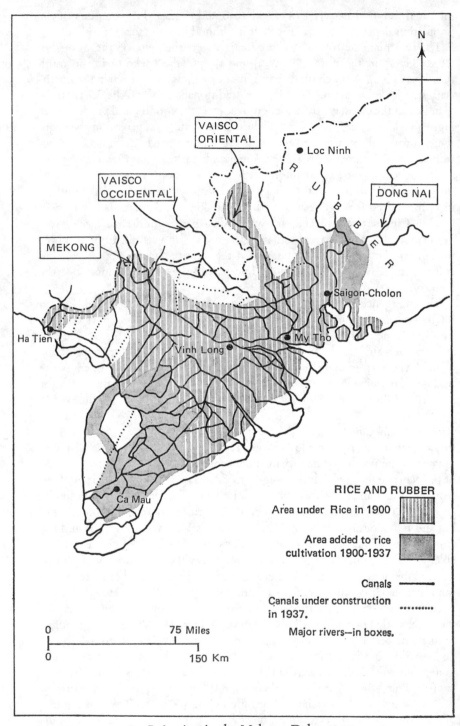

26. Irrigation in the Mekong Delta, 1941

was, it was still not enough. The principal arteries still remained unlinked to the secondary and tertiary streams so that effective use of tides and surplus waters was not possible. The French had anticipated that landowners would extend the government works into the interiors of their own estates and so enhance their agricultural value, but circumstances made most landowners speculators rather than farmers and they did not choose to invest their capital in this way. Consequently, despite the canal network, a good proportion of the rice lands of Cochin-China were not properly irrigated at all. Nevertheless the net result was the successful conversion of Cochin-China into one of the new rice-bowls of South-East Asia. Rice took up 90 per cent (and in some districts 100 per cent) of the cultivable land in the delta, while between 1880 and 1940 land values rose to above three times the expenditure on them, the population nearly tripled and Saigon's rice exports increased five-fold.

The development of rice production in Cochin-China has an obvious parallel with that in lower Burma during broadly the same period, and as far as the welfare of the peasants involved was concerned the consequences were almost identical. But whereas in Lower Burma the British sought to create a stable, independent class of peasant smallholders, in Cochin-China the French aimed for a stable, prosperous class of landowners who would work their properties through the medium of tenant farmers. The French justification of this policy was their high expenditure on draining the swamps, settling farmers and developing Saigon's port facilities which was far greater than what the British had found necessary in Lower Burma. To obtain quick returns which politically were essential, large blocks of newly opened rice lands in the Trans-Bassac were sold off at bargain prices to the first bidder. As a result large areas of this region came to be divided up into rice estates of considerable size. In the area of older Vietnamese settlement on the east side of the Bassac, holdings tended to remain much smaller. But even here landlordism crept in, largely through the manipulations of moneylenders, as the whole of the south became overshadowed by the new cash economy and the demands of the rice export market.[3]

The direct French share in all this remained strictly limited, although at first rice growing appeared to them to be the only economic activity which could guarantee steady returns. In the Trans-Bassac, French colonists acquired only a fraction of the total cultivated area. Most of the French estates were medium or large and were worked, like those of their Vietnamese counterparts, by tenant-farmers.[4]

This meant that the great majority of actual padi-planters in Cochin-China were tenant-farmers working on these various estates. They numbered two-thirds of the total farmer population in the delta, paying an average of 40 per cent of their crop as land rent and usually dependent on their absentee landlords for both cash and their own rice, which they could obtain at high rates of interest.

Rice in Tonkin and Annam
There was a striking contrast between the conditions of rice cultivation in

the south and those that prevailed in the north, especially in Tonkin where 90 per cent of the cultivated land was also devoted to the crop. In the north the rice was grown almost wholly for local consumption and the land was not divided up amongst large estates but into miniscule landholdings, 70 per cent of which were—in the 1930s—estimated at less than one acre each. As in the south production depended on extensive water control but in this instance not in order to obtain a surplus but in order to survive.[5] To overcome the seasonal flooding of the Song-koi and the annual variations in rainfall, an elaborate system of bunds or dykes had been built up over the centuries. The foundations of this 'hydraulic civilization' was the gift of the Chinese, and within the defensive arms of the bunds ingenious though primitive Chinese techniques of irrigation and cultivation had been maintained by generations of Vietnamese peasants, enabling some 5,800 square miles of delta land to support a huge population. However as time passed by, the bed-level of the Song-koi itself rose steadily, caused by silt deposits, so that the guardian bunds, once three feet above the high water mark in the flood season, no longer sufficed. Another fundamental problem was that the bund system helped to sweep the surplus rich silt out to sea instead of letting it be deposited on the floor of the delta.

Faced with these inescapable problems, French engineers in 1883 began to raise the bunds above flood-water level, which at once brought up the larger question of what should be done next. One school of thought pressed for the destruction of the bunds so as to let the silt carried by the flood waters fertilize the soils of the delta and at the same time remove a major burden from government and people alike. But the cost would have been astronomical and the dislocation of the existing patterns of settlement too vast. So it was decided to continue with the policy of strengthening the bunds and of developing within their confines a modern system of irrigation. After carrying out the essential preliminary survey work, construction started in 1905. The first irrigation works were located upstream in upper Tonkin to take advantage of the smaller rivers. By the early 1920s two major systems affecting over 61,000 acres had been completed, and an even larger one affecting an even larger area started. Each system consisted of a holding dam, one main canal and a series of secondary and tertiary canals which brought the water to the fields by gravity alone.

However, the inadequacy of these efforts was revealed by the increasing occurrence of serious flooding in the years that followed. The climax came with the epic flood of 1926 which inundated one-third of the Tonkin Delta and wrought incalculable damage to life and property. This disaster prompted a far more comprehensive scheme of water control which was carried out within the next ten years. The main bunds were widened and raised, the larger ones being also made to serve as roads; they were also strengthened at crucial points by adding clay and rocks and by correcting dangerous curves. By 1937 the programme of reinforcement of the bund system was considered completed, although floods in that and the previous year north of the Delta made further measures necessary. The years after 1926 also saw an intensification of the irrigation schemes. By 1939 three major systems were ready and a fourth was in process. In the eastern part of the delta where the threat to the rice lands came from the sea, embankments were also built to contain the tides at the estuary of the Song Thai Binh.

The French achievement in water control in Tonkin was at least as notable as that in the south. By 1936 nearly half the total rice acreage in the delta had come under double cropping and the average yield per acre was also the highest for all Indo-China. But rice production still failed to keep pace with population growth and imports from the south were frequently necessary. The scope of the achievement also failed to impress the Vietnamese peasant who was hard to shake out of his traditional fatalism. In short, despite all the efforts made by French engineers, the net result was merely to preserve the *status quo*, not to find a solution. More radical measures would have struck at the roots of traditional Vietnamese society, a task manifestly beyond the will or capacity of the colonial power. What France did was the best she could do within the framework of existing institutions.

In Annam, conditions were basically similar to those in Tonkin, but rice cultivation was on a smaller scale, and irrigation works and flood controls were more restricted as the rivers involved were smaller in size. The largest water control scheme comprising dams and canal networks was constructed in the dangerously overcrowded Thanh Hoa and Nghe Tinh deltas and around Phu Yen and Phan Rang. Similar schemes were in progress in the provinces of Quang Nam and Quang Ngai. After 1935 a policy of building small irrigation systems in the region was adopted as this seemed more in line with the conditions of the countryside, broken up as it was by the mountainous ribs of the Annamite Chain.

Because of the general circumstances prevailing in the north, French participation in rice cultivation was still more limited than in Cochin-China where there were large tracts of virgin land for sale. An enterprising bid to bring back deserted rice lands north of the Song-koi on the fringes of the delta under cultivation by means of French-owned and capitalized estates employing Vietnamese sharecroppers was launched in the 1890s but abandoned within the same decade.[6] In the 1930s only some 75,000 acres of land were French-held in Tonkin.

Features of rice production under French rule
The application of French capital, technological expertise and administration to rice cultivation in Vietnam during the eighty years of colonial rule increased the area farmed and raised production substantially, enabling Tonkin and Annam to survive and Cochin-China to export its surpluses for the world market. But all of this was of little benefit to the padi-planter himself. In the north he remained an impoverished smallholder on his ever-dwindling plot and in a land of rice had to eke out his inadequate ration with maize and tubers. In the south the tenant-farmer was, comparatively speaking, better-off, but he also lived at little more than subsistence level and probably remained a debtor all his life. The conversion of Vietnam into a rice-bowl kept the peasant a pauper and only benefited the merchants (mostly Chinese) who monopolized

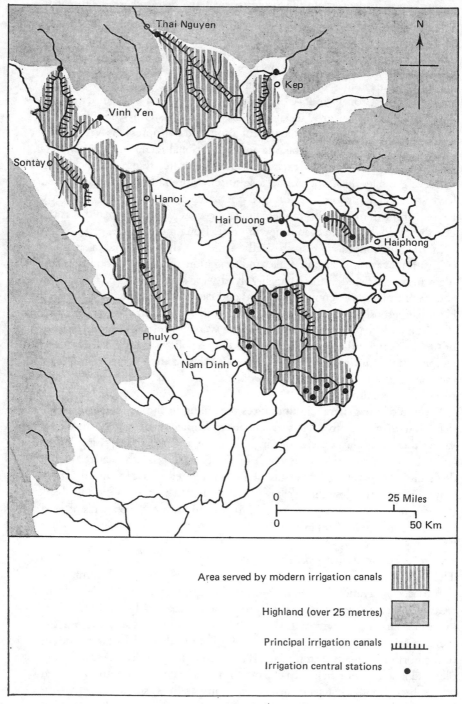

27. Irrigation in the Tonkin Delta, 1941

the rice export trade and the landlords (usually Vietnamese) who thrived on the misery of their tenant labourers.

The rice export trade was virtually a Chinese monopoly, acquired through their role as transporters, millers and marketers. Cholon was the rice capital and formed one of the great rice marts of the world, containing by far the greatest concentration of rice mills and distilleries in the country. As such it was the Cholon Chinese who really dominated the rice business, owning most of the huge junk fleets that bore the crop along the canals of the delta to the mills of the city, most of which were also theirs. However, the Chinese millers were not entirely alone in the field and in the 1930s, hit by the Great Depression, there were signs that their long unchallenged predominance was coming to an end. They also faced growing competition from smaller Vietnamese-run factories which milled entirely for local consumption. As for the French, they owned four large rice-mills, two of which were in Cholon.

One feature of rice production under the French was the generally poor quality of the rice grown, which placed French Indo-China a very poor third as far as the great world rice exporters were concerned. In terms of yield per acre Vietnamese production lagged far behind that of either Burma or Siam, and the quality of its rice exports was considered far inferior to that of its two main rivals. Part of the reason for this was to be found in the appalling congestion and poverty in which the average padi-planter lived. He was the heir to antiquated and inefficient methods of tillage; he suffered from lack of fertilizers not only because he had no cash or credit facilities but since even natural manure was denied him as population pressure restricted pasture land and so limited the number of livestock available; neither did he have any opportunity to acquire better seeds for his crop. In consequence the average cultivator adopted a completely fatalistic attitude and while incapable of taking the initiative to make improvements himself was also most reluctant to accept changes proposed by people from outside.

The low quality of Vietnamese rice was also the result of poor milling which resulted from the wide variety of grains grown in the country. It was not economic to sort them all out at the collecting centres. The husking, bleaching and polishing machines of the mills could only be adjusted to deal with one type of grain and so the end-product was inevitably a mixture containing much broken and waste rice. Attempts to overcome this problem by setting up sorting workshops failed because the machines used could not do the job efficiently enough while the cost of implementing refinements was too high. Apart from that, very few landlords bothered to assemble the crops of their tenants for dispatch direct to the millers. The only solution lay in reducing the number of varieties grown. In general, the poor yields and low quality of Vietnamese rice considerably offset the great technological achievements of the French in promoting rice production under their rule.

In 1930 a Rice Bureau (L'Office Indochinois du Riz) was established in an attempt to meet these problems, together with two experimental stations and a number of advisory centres. The Rice Bureau immediately turned its attention to the problems of low yields and poor quality. Basing itself largely on Japanese experiments in the same field, the Bureau had made some progress by 1941, carrying out research in its own laboratories, supervising the growing of selected seeds on its provincial farms and distributing the fruits of its labours throughout the countryside by means of its propaganda department. The advisory centres mainly served as centres for the giving of practical advice to local farmers.

However, with or without these efforts, there were clear indications in the 1930s that rice was losing its position as the major export of the country. Between 1913 and 1937 rice and rice products dropped from contributing two-thirds to only one-third of the total value of Vietnam's exports. Although exports tended to fluctuate a lot as the result of local or world market conditions this decline reflected the growing domestic consumption as population outstripped production, as well as the growing value of other products. There was a significant change in markets too following the Great Depression.[7]

Rice products: alcohol

About three-fifths of those engaged in the foodstuffs industry were employed in various ways connected with the preparation of padi for local consumption, but the most important single by-product of rice was its distillation for alcohol. The distillation of alcohol or rice-wine has been carried out in the villages of Vietnam since time immemorial, some of them specializing in the trade. So the decision of the French authorities in 1902 to place the distillation of all alcohol under official control and to ban all local unlicensed distilling was very unpopular from the start. This unpopularity increased with the contemporaneous rise of the Société française des Distilleries de l'Indochine which with its scientific techniques soon dominated the market. Many village distilleries went underground and illegal distilling became widespread, which provoked official raids and repression. During the Great Depression contraband rice-wine began to flood the country, the fall in rice exports causing more to become available on the domestic market and available for wine. Faced with an uncontrollable situation, in 1933 the colonial administration amended its laws and permitted distillation under licence. Two years later, to make these measures more effective, the price of manufactured alcohol was lowered and a small centre set up at Bac Ninh where distillation could be carried out by traditional methods.

These changes did not seriously affect the position of the Société, for by this time it had built up a great commercial empire which besides rice-wine itself dealt in such by-products as fuel alcohol, vinegar, starch, glucose and so on. It also processed sugar-cane into rum and produced a carburant which could be added to petrol. The Société was easily able to maintain its dominating role in the alcohol market by virtue of its experience and superior organization and resources, although by 1941 there were fifty other distilleries in the field.

Rubber

The second major French contribution to the Vietnamese economy was the introduction of rubber planting. In 1941 Vietnam (together with Cambodia) was the world's third largest producer of natural rubber, which was at the same time the country's most important plantation crop. Within the space of twenty years rubber production rose to become Vietnam's second most important export.

In the process rubber helped to accentuate the dichotomy between north and south, already marked out by the different rice regimes of Tonkin and Cochin-China. For rubber, as the result of the dictates of climate, soil and circumstance, was a southern crop, and nothing but stunted trees and low yields could be expected above An Khe (14° Latitude) in Annam where the most northerly rubber estate was located. Rubber planting in the south was also favoured by the existence of a narrow belt of rich, red basaltic soils stretching in an arc across South Annam into Cochin-China from the coast towards the Cambodian frontier. Called by the French the 'terres rouges' or red lands, they were to prove ideal for rubber cultivation and became the centre for the new plantation industry.

Perhaps the most remarkable feature of rubber cultivation in Vietnam was the rapidity of its rise. Rubber in Vietnam was a late starter, for the industry was not taken really seriously until after the Great War. However this turned out to be a major advantage since French planters were able to benefit from the experience and the mistakes of the rubber pioneers in British Malaya and the Netherlands Indies. They also derived the maximum benefit from Dutch researches into rubber clones which were imported 'at great expense' into the country but were then used to good effect. By 1936 well over a third of the total area under rubber was planted with the new buds, making Vietnamese rubber the best-yielding in South-East Asia. After 1930 important research work into bud-grafting and clones was conducted in Vietnam itself both by certain large French rubber-plantation companies and also under government auspices by the Institute of Agronomic and Forest Research.[8]

Indeed large estates and huge combines were characteristic of the Vietnamese rubber industry, which seemed 'conducive to improved methods and increased yields'. In Indo-China as a whole 68 per cent of the planted area was owned by only twenty-seven companies while one-third of the estates in the Union were more than 100 acres each and accounted for 94 per cent of the total acreage. In fact the trend towards monopoly was even greater than figures indicate as many of the companies themselves were inter-related or dominated by the same holding concerns. This became evident from the mid-1920s onwards but was greatly accelerated by the Great Depression which brought about the downfall of many firms. Those that survived saw that their interest lay in improved technology and efficiency which in turn pointed to merger.[9] Another factor which assisted the trend towards monopoly was the general aura of protectionism which permeated French colonial policy and became overt in the 1930s. To start with, the entire Indo-Chinese production of rubber was easily absorbed by the French market so that problems of foreign competition could be side-stepped. As a result of the Depression which led to the adoption of a deliberate protectionist policy by France towards her overseas territories and the institution of the International Rubber Committee which France joined in 1934, the industry was guaranteed as a French preserve safe from outside competition.

By the same token it is not surprising that in great contrast to the situation in British Malaya and the Netherlands Indies, smallholdings never became a major element in the rubber industry of Vietnam. They accounted for only 6 per cent of the planted area (in Indo-China as a whole) and in Cochin-China were to be found concentrated in the grey lands around Saigon.

Rubber in Vietnam was a European affair and almost exclusively French, the consequence of laws which prohibited the granting of land concessions to non-citizens.[10] In its general development, the industry followed a similar pattern to that followed in Malaya and the Indies. Wild rubbers were known and exploited in the jungles of Vietnam in the nineteenth century. As elsewhere the revolutionary *hevea brasiliensis* was also introduced into the country before the end of the century, to be duly ignored, the French Ridley being Raoul, a navy pharmacist once stationed in Singapore. Although Raoul was responsible for introducing 2,000 hevea plants to the Botanical Gardens at Saigon in 1897, only one man, Belland, a perspicacious member of the Saigon police, went ahead the following year and planted some land on the outskirts of the city with 15,000 trees. His foresight paid off in 1905 when the trees gave forth their first latex, giving Belland the first bonanza out of rubber in Vietnam with frs. 100,000 net profit. This triumph won speedy converts and from that date onwards rubber planting grew steadily in Cochin-China.

The first plantations, mostly smallholdings, were opened up in the grey lands around Saigon which offered the most favourable conditions for the assorted army of petty speculators who now rushed to advance their milleniums.[11] As a result the bulk of the smaller estates (under 250 acres apiece) were to be found within a fifty-mile radius north and east of the city. However better soils were to be found further away in areas of low population and heavier jungle, and being correspondingly more expensive to clear became the first field for the operations of joint-stock companies. The fertile red lands lay in still more difficult territory and were even more remote, so that prior to the 1920s little had been done to develop estates in this region. By the end of 1921 there were an estimated 70,000 acres under rubber in Cochin-China, and about frs. 40 million had been invested in the industry. Up to this point production had grown steadily, from the time the first yields from the estates planted in 1906 came onto the market six years later.

The Little Depression imposed a momentary check on the industry which was overcome with the aid of government subsidies. But French Indo-China benefited immediately afterwards just as did the Netherlands Indies in consequence of the imposition of restrictions under the British-controlled Stevenson Plan. Rising prices and the rubber boom in the Indies quickly restored confidence and by 1925 had promoted a great wave of speculative investment which emanated for the first time from France itself. Between 1925 and 1929 investments in rubber totalled frs. 700 million and the area under the crop increased to a quarter of a million acres. This great expansion was centred on the red lands of the Moi Plateau. However despite the fertility of the soil and the liberality of the concessions obtainable, the opening up of this region posed grave problems. Much of the new area was barely explored and many of the Moi hill people were hostile. Malaria was to prove an even greater threat while the general inaccessibility of the region and the absence of local labour sent up costs. The solutions were found in the formation of heavily-capitalized firms which tended increasingly to merge, and in the recruitment of a contract labour force from the over-populated provinces of Tonkin and North Annam.

The Great Depression of 1929 came as a severe blow to the industry, and without the active assistance of the French government it would probably have entirely collapsed. The rubber companies were the worst hit, as they were just beginning to get in the returns on their capital expenditure, and a large number went into dissolution. The colonial administration staved off total disaster by creating a special loan fund for planters in 1930 and by setting up in 1931 an Indemnification Fund which saved those estates which had to sell their rubber below cost price.[12] By 1934 the worst was over. Prices started to recover and France's adherence to the International Rubber Agreement the same year worked out very much to her favour.[13] The International Agreement was extended for another four years in 1938 and Indo-Chinese planters were permitted to increase the area of their estates under rubber by another 5 per cent. Yet despite these concessions and the spectacular rise in rubber output which accompanied them, the actual acreage under rubber increased very little from what it had been in 1931. The great increase in output was accounted for by new trees yielding and by the improvement in yields through the use of new clones and replanting.

There was very little development of rubber manufactures in Vietnam prior to 1941. In that year there were only two small factories producing miscellaneous rubber goods, one in Saigon, and the other, started in 1938, at Hanoi.

Coal

A wide variety of other products was to be found or cultivated within the confines of Vietnam, but none of these assumed the significance of rice or rubber, and most were primarily for domestic consumption. Amongst the secondary exports coal, cement and maize were the most outstanding.

Coal was by far the most important of all the minerals of Vietnam. Accounting for from 63 per cent to nearly 90 per cent of all mineral production in the country in the 1930s, output in 1937 (a peak year) amounted to over 2 million tons, two-thirds of which were exported, thus making Vietnam, after Manchuria, the largest exporter of coal in the Far East. Moreover Vietnamese coal was of good quality. The great bulk came from Tonkin which in 1939 produced 90 per cent of all the coal in Indo-China. The main Tonkin coalfield lay in the hills of Dong Trieu, north of Quang Yen; there were two smaller fields in the region, both located north of the Song-koi, and some small deposits near Ninh Binh lower in the delta and in Central Annam, some forty miles south-west of Da Nang.

The deposits of the Quang Yen field had been surface-worked for centuries by Chinese miners; the mines at Hon Gay had been one of the objects of Garnier's schemes in the mid-1870s and played their part in precipitating French intervention and conquest in the following decade. Subsequently the development of this coalfield and of other deposits became an entirely French affair, because only the French could provide the capital and technology to work them on a commercially profitable scale. The first scientific survey of the region had already been carried out two years before the French occupation began, while the court of Hué had also made grants to French entrepreneurs for land in the area before it came under actual French control. One of these concessions was confirmed in 1887 by the new French establishment at Hanoi, and marked the beginnings of the Société des Charbonnages du Tonkin, the first of the two great French concerns which were to dominate the industry. But despite all efforts to encourage mining by way of legislation and other means, in 1900, after fifteen years of French rule, only some 9 million francs had been invested in the mines and coal formed barely 1 per cent of the total value of Indo-China's exports. However, with the turn of the century coal output steadily increased until by the 1930s exports had exceeded the 1900 figure by over one million tons.

The lead in coalmining in Tonkin was taken by the Société des Charbonnages du Tonkin. It faced serious drainage problems in its early days and had to make a heavy capital outlay, so that it was not until 1900 that the company could pay its first dividends to its shareholders. After that year, however, it made steady progress, absorbing some of its rivals and by 1937 controlled over 70 per cent of Tonkin's production. Most of the remaining 30 per cent came from the mines of the Société des Charbonnages du Dong Trieu which appeared on the scene in the Dong Trieu Basin in 1916, but was not producing effectively until the end of the Great War. There were also a number of smaller firms in the field whose output amounted to a few thousand tons a year. The Quang Yen field was the scene of the most successful exploitation of coal, with Haiphong serving as its chief port. As for the other fields, their production was very limited and the mines often unsuccessful. Conditions in the less accessible fields of Phan Me and Tuyen Quang were in general not so favourable. Lignite was worked at Tuyen Quang from 1915 onwards while small pockets of coal in the Phan Me field were worked intermittently after 1910. Work on the strip of coal around Ninh Binh 'had to be suspended' in 1931, while the sole deposits in central Annam, which were in production when the French assumed control in 1885, were finally abandoned in 1920 when the surface seams became exhausted.

The coal mined in Tonkin was always far in excess of Vietnam's own needs, so that the bulk was marked for export. The problem was markets. Japan became Vietnam's best customer by the 1920s, taking up to half of total exports by the eve of the Pacific War. Some coal also went to the Philippines. A much more unlikely market was France itself, which nevertheless grew in the 1930s under the pressures of the Great Depression and the imposition of overt protectionist policies by the Paris administration.

Other minerals

Tonkin was the main source of all mining activity in Vietnam. Amongst the deposits to be found were wolfram, lead, zinc, silver, tin, antimony, gold, phosphate, graphite, haematite and magnetic iron, but of all these only two were worked on a commercially significant scale apart from coal, namely tin and zinc. The existence of this mineral wealth was well known to the Vietnamese and to the Chinese and was used to fan the fires of intervention by French apostolics in the 1850s.

Nevertheless it was not until the 1920s that the rush for minerals began. The first official regulations regarding mining on the other hand date back to the first years of the French occupation. A commission appointed to look into the matter in 1885 recommended that the North American practice of staking claims be adopted and this principle formed the basis of the first mining code issued in 1912. The new code was liberal and vague; concessions quickly became permanent after few formalities and without any safeguards against speculation or failure to work the land. Special provisions however were made for oil and natural gas, rights over which could only be obtained at a public auction. Non-citizens were not allowed to own or run mines but there were no restrictions on foreign investment. This code continued without change until 1937 when it was modified by introducing clauses to prevent lessees from restricting development 'in a manner detrimental to the public interest' and to ensure government participation if and when desired.

In practice the role played by government in developing mining was negligible. Liberal as the mining code was, it could not compensate for the difficulties of mountainous, jungle terrain and an unhealthy climate which made prospecting hazardous and the construction of access routes costly. Nor could it make up for the absence of suitable labour in the remote areas where the minerals were to be found. Hence prospectors did not arrive in large numbers. Prospecting licences did not exceed 300 a year prior to 1914 for the whole of Indo-China, although hardly any prospecting was actually carried out beyond Tonkin. In 1900 the total contribution of mining activities was valued at 2 million piastres and had only reached eight million sixteen years later. Mineral exports never amounted to more than $3\frac{1}{2}$ per cent of the total export value prior to 1938.[14]

The boom in mining in Vietnam which developed in the 1920s and was reflected in the sudden rise in prospecting permits issued (no longer confined to Tonkin) and in the rash of new companies floated to mine copper, gold and tin, was the consequence of the contemporaneous boom in rubber which made their Indo-Chinese empire something more than an abstraction in French minds. There was 'a widespread infatuation with Indo-Chinese business'[15] which ended up in many cases with disappointment and even disaster. Besides the natural obstacles which all prospectors and miners in Vietnam had to face, there was also the background of unwise speculation and manipulation on the stock market of Paris. Provincial stock-holders were lured by cleverly staged advertising campaigns to invest in a country they had never seen and in an industry they knew next to nothing about. Between 1925 and 1928, 240 million francs were invested in the mining industry, a sum which nearly equalled the total amount invested in the previous three decades. Then came the Depression which, causing losses calculated at well over 100 million francs to the mining industry, quickly cut down the competitors in the field. This started the trend towards monopolistic control by a handful of big corporations, so typical of the evolution of French enterprise in Indo-China. By 1937 six concerns controlled 90 per cent of total mining production in the country and nearly half of this was in the hands of one company. Along with the process of merger by which this had come about there was also a great increase in efficiency which resulted in the growing contribution of mining towards export production.

French domination of mining in general was as complete as it was for coal in particular. Apart from sporadic activities carried out on a very small scale by Vietnamese interests, the development of mining was financed entirely by French firms which alone could provide the necessary capital resources. The Vietnamese, on the other hand, provided the great majority of the 50,000 workers employed by the industry on the eve of the Pacific War.

Tin came next after coal as Vietnam's most important mineral product, accounting for nearly 30 per cent of total Indo-Chinese mineral output in 1937. The main mining centre was in Tonkin in the northern Pia Ouac Range whose deposits were 'rediscovered' by the French at the turn of the century, having been abandoned by Vietnamese and Chinese miners years previously. The principal mines near Tinh Tuc were under the management of the Société d'Exploitation des Etains et Wolfram du Pia Ouac; they were opencast and from 1905 onwards produced the bulk of Tonkin's tin which in turn contributed about two-fifths of total Indo-Chinese output in 1937.[16] The smelting was originally done locally but after 1930 nearly all of it was sent for refining in Singapore. Tonkinese tin mining, being on a small scale, was not severely affected by the Great Depression but French Indo-China nevertheless adhered to the International Tin Agreement of 1934, which was renewed in 1937. Virtually all tin produced was exported.

Zinc which came next after tin in terms of export value in 1941, but prior to 1928 had stood before it, rose up as a mineral export during the same period. In 1906 three companies were floated to work the deposits just found in the Thai Nguyen-Tuyen Quang area. From the start, however, zinc mining was at the mercy of a volatile world market. The high points were 1916 and 1926; the lowest (before 1941) was in 1920 when Vietnam's miners felt the repercussions of the Russian Revolution on the international market.[17] After 1926 zinc mining was again affected by falling prices. By this time the industry was largely in the hands of the Compagnie Minière et Metallurgique de l'Indochine, which in 1920 had acquired the rich Cho Dien beds in Bac Kan province. During the Great Depression mining of zinc was confined to this area. In 1937 Vietnam's output of zinc totalled some 10,000 tons.

Other minerals were exploited with fleeting or limited success. Wolfram, associated with the Pia Ouac tin deposits, prospered briefly during the Great War as tungsten fetched inflated prices, and showed signs of revival after 1934. Attempts by French miners to emulate the Chinese who had mined the lead deposits found alongside zinc in the Pia Ouac Range were on the other hand a total failure.

Some antimony was mined intermittently near Mon Kay and Hon Gay but the enterprise of a French company in working the far higher grade deposits in Thanh Hoa province, North Annam, was doomed within a few months of opening in 1931 by a collapse in market prices. Iron mining might have played a more significant role if the problems of transportation, processing and marketing had been properly resolved. Some goldmining was done, albeit on a very small scale. For Vietnamese in Tonkin it was a seasonal occupation yielding very small returns. Between 1895 and 1919 a number of French firms, well furnished with the most up-to-date equipment, tried their luck while many other companies were formed but never commenced operations. There was also some mining of graphite and phosphates. Hopeful searches were carried out for oil without any success.

The only industry in Vietnam of significance which was a by-product of mining was that of cement. Vietnam was the region's largest cement exporter, half of which found markets in China, Siam, British Malaya, the Netherlands Indies, the Philippines and Madagascar. It was also the mainstay of the port of Haiphong where it had been manufactured since the end of the nineteenth century by the Société des Ciments Portland Artificiels de l'Indochine. The Société was floated in 1899 and its success ensured by the selection of Haiphong as the site for its factory, the availability of the nearby coal, clay and limestone deposits and the port's easy accessibility by sea and river. The first cement to be exported was in 1905 when 400 tons were sent overseas. By the late 1930s exports totalled 120,000 tons. Domestic demand also grew, stimulated by increasing constructional work.

Maize and other agricultural products
Of the wide variety of other agricultural produce grown in Vietnam, apart from rice and rubber, maize stood far ahead. The total value of maize from Indo-China as a whole in 1938 was nearly 18 per cent of all exports. The greater quantity of this came from Cambodia but a substantial proportion was also grown in the Tonkin Basin. The rise of maize was a recent development, almost wholly due to French initiative and policy which created the conditions necessary for its expansion. Traditionally a staple food of the hill peoples, up till 1905 it was grown entirely for local consumption. After that it was deliberately cultivated for the French market which by the late 1930s absorbed 90 per cent of Indo-Chinese production. The turning point for maize in Vietnam came in 1930 when the planting of the crop became more profitable per kilo than an equivalent amount of rice, although this reflected more the increased area under cultivation than improved techniques.

The rise of maize as an important export is a good example of the hot-house methods by which the French developed certain aspects of Vietnam's economy.[18] But despite its dependence on the French market, the industry remained outside French hands. It was predominantly grown by Vietnamese peasants, being easy to plant and giving quick returns, while the financing, transporting and marketing were largely done by Chinese and Indians.

The rest of the crops grown in Vietnam can be divided between those grown for commercial and industrial purposes and those grown merely for domestic consumption. In the former category coffee and tea were the only two of significance. Coffee was cultivated before the French conquest especially around Hué where it had probably been introduced by Roman Catholic missionaries. It soon attracted French capital, the earliest estates being opened in the late 1880s in lower Tonkin. From here it gradually spread over the next two decades southwards into Annam. At the turn of the century the first coffee estate was started in the fertile red lands belt of the Moi Plateau, but the real development of coffee estates in this area had to await the arrival of more French capital after 1923.

In the meantime coffee planting progressed slowly and had little to show for 'the half century of effort' which had been put into it. In 1938, 32,000 acres yielded a bare 1,500 tons, only a third of which was exported. From the beginning the French planters faced problems and although they were tough enough to persevere, their shortage of capital and inexperience of tropical conditions told heavily against them. Many of the early estates were sited on poor soils and the general scarcity of land ruled out the large-scale plantation with its Brazilian-style slash-and-burn methods. This problem could only be met by fertilizers, but green manure would not support a crop once it was bearing and animal manure in a region of dense human settlement was at a premium. On top of all this the climate was often unfavourable; in fact, Tonkin with its winters was at the extreme limits of coffee's natural zone. Conditions were generally more favourable further south, particularly on the Moi Plateau, but here too there were specific difficulties to be faced.

The French coffee estates nevertheless survived; in Tonkin and north Annam they represented the only European estates of importance. In south Annam the combined effects of the initial difficulties and the impact of the Great Depression led to quite a lot of company coffee land in the Moi Plateau being abandoned between 1930 and 1931 but there was a recovery after 1934. Although predominantly a French affair, there was an increasing number of Vietnamese smallholders who went in for the crop. Vietnamese also provided the bulk of the labour force—in Tonkin often as sharecroppers—on the French estates. Smallholder coffee was poorly tended and its quality mediocre; the general quality of estate coffee, however, was high.

Tea is indigenous to Vietnam but its successful development as a commercial crop did not take place till the 1920s. Found in many wild strains in the hills before the French period, tea was grown in gardens or in small plantations, particularly in central Tonkin and northern Annam, but its cultivation was both primitive and careless and its quality poor. The tea so produced was used for local consumption but the wealthy preferred to drink strains imported from China.

The French were quick to turn their attention to the crop but all their efforts to promote it as an export commodity met with failure prior to 1924 when the first large tea estates were started in the red lands of the Moi Plateau. The pioneer French tea planters had insufficient capital and experience to make their projects prosper, and it was not until 1893 that the first tea shipment was sent to France. By this time the French colonists had given up their attempts at growing tea for themselves and had turned to processing instead as a means of raising the quality of the crop. Several French tea factories were established in Quang Nam which helped to improve local production. But their efforts were largely frustrated by the wiles of the Chinese middleman who practised adulteration of the crop on a sufficiently large scale to ruin the good name of Annam tea. Plants were imported from Assam and Ceylon and in 1917 a research centre was set up in the heart of the Tonkinese tea-growing region at Phu To, but little progress was made until the opening up of the highly-capitalized estates on the Moi Plateau in 1924.

After that the rise of Vietnam's tea production was spectacular and it soon outstripped coffee in importance as an export crop. In 1938 the country's tea exports totalled about 2,000 tons, two-fifths of which came from the new estates. The launching of these estates on the Moi Plateau was difficult and expensive; suitable strains had to be found and the techniques of planting at higher altitudes mastered. Production costs were also much higher than in the lowlands — the land had to be cleared and guarded from erosion in an area where labour was scarce; processing factories had to be built and constant care and attention paid to the cultivation of the crop.

Nevertheless the new estates survived the Great Depression which struck before they were producing on a large scale, and by 1940 they covered over 7,400 acres with an output which accounted for two-fifths of the total tea crop in the country. In terms of world production, Vietnam remained a small exporter but her exports played an important role within the French imperial framework, without which the country would probably not have been able to export at all. Through a combination of skilful advertising, the enhanced quality of the local product and a special tariff, France itself came to absorb nearly 40 per cent of Vietnam's tea exports. The original dream of catering for France's North African colonies was also moving towards realization, although there was plenty of room for expansion.

Attempts made to cultivate other crops for the commercial market, although on a very limited scale, included pepper, sugar, cinnamon, coconut and kapok. Of these the greatest development was in sugar-cane, a traditional crop in Vietnam, some of which was exported to China. Most of it was grown in Annam but although some French planters went in for the crop at the beginning of the twentieth century, heavy French capital investment in the industry did not start till 1918 when a French company acquired a concession in Cochin-China. This marked the spread of sugar cultivation along the Dong Nai, Saigon and Eastern Vaico rivers, none of which were liable to severe floods. In 1940 there were some 100,000 acres under sugar throughout Vietnam, of which well over half were in Annam, nearly a third in Cochin-China and the balance in Tonkin.

The growth of the new sugar industry was yet another example of hothouse development under special conditions created by protectionist policies. In this instance the French leaned heavily on Dutch-Javanese experience to set the new industry going so that in organization it followed largely on the Javanese pattern.[19] But the Javanese miracle was not repeated. Although the area under cultivation amounted to half that under sugar in Java, the yield per acre was barely one-twentieth that of the Javanese fields and production was still insufficient to meet local needs. One of the factors behind this comparative failure was lack of incentive as per capita Vietnamese consumption was amongst the lowest in the world. Another factor was poor cultivation techniques, particularly in the main sugar-growing regions of Annam. An attempt to introduce mechanization in Cochin-China also proved a failure. Without the protection of the tariffs the industry would have not been able to survive at all.

Sericulture was another traditional occupation which the French tried to foster, in this case with signal lack of success. Exports of raw silk, mostly to China, amounted to 185 tons in 1899 but had dropped to 3 tons by 1937. Certain villages in Annam specialized in the industry, either by raising silk-worms or by selling the leaves of the mulberry to neighbouring villages of silk-growers. In an effort to develop the industry between 1920 and 1930 government spent half a million piastres on sericulture in Tonkin alone. But despite this, local methods remained outmoded and unclean and the product could not compete with Chinese raw silk or Japanese rayon. The attempts of the administration were vitiated still further by the conflict of interest between French industrialists and millers in the country, on the one hand, and those of the Vietnamese growers and weavers on the other.

The coconut industry formed a small but thriving part of the economy. The principal area of cultivation was in the Mekong Delta where plantations sprang up around the turn of the century around My Tho, Ben Tre and Vinh Long. Copra was the most important by-product from the coconut but exports were badly hit by the collapse of world market prices after 1930.[20] Most of the copra came from central Annam. By 1941 most of the coconut plantations were past their prime while actual methods of production were far from satisfactory.

Kapok was grown in Cochin-China in a disorganized manner by the Vietnamese; the crop caught the attention of some French planters and as a result sales tripled in the 1930s. Other Vietnamese products such as cinnamon and lac reached specialized markets. Some small quantities of pepper were grown in central Annam and some pineapple for export in Cochin-China.

The other agricultural products of the country had only a domestic significance serving to supplement local incomes but not assuming the status of cash crops. Amongst these was tobacco and also various American plants, probably introduced during the seventeenth century which helped eke out the peasant diet, particularly in the lean months between the remnants of the old rice crop and the harvesting of the new. Fruits abounded in Cochin-China and Annam, but had to be imported into Tonkin.[21]

Livestock, forestry and fisheries
Despite all their efforts the French never succeeded in developing a livestock industry in Vietnam. Pigs and poultry were ubiquitous and an essential element in the domestic economy. Elephants were used for timber and forest clearing. But the introduction of distinguished breeds of sheep by the French made little impression and their attempts at cattle-breeding together with coffee cultivation as an antidote to the shortage of manure were ultimately defeated by shortage of land and low quality pasturage. Their efforts to im-

prove the local breeds of horse by importing well-known stocks from abroad and setting up breeding stations at various points were likewise frustrated by the racing industry which bought up the best imported breeds.

The forests of the Indo-Chinese Union which covered about one-third of the total area formed an important natural resource. They contained a wide variety of hardwoods which could be used in the construction of ships, soft-woods and other lower quality timber which were of use for firewood, char-coal and the manufacture of matches. There was also a considerable range of forest products. Of these forest resources Vietnam was the main provider. Ninety-seven per cent of the bamboo came from Vietnam, together with two-thirds of the constructional timber and four-fifths of the firewood.

However, although two French firms were established soon after the turn of the century, the exploitation of the jungles remained a largely Sino-Viet-namese affair. They felled the logs in the deep of the jungle and brought them by buffalo to the assembly points to be collected by the agents of logging firms and floated downstream to Hanoi, Saigon or lesser ports in the lowlands. Lumbering was done by Frenchmen only as a sideline, usually out of the ne-cessity to clear land for a new plantation, cutting the costs of doing so in this way and keeping the labour force occupied in the slack season. For from the French point of view lumbering was hardly worth-while, since most of the timber was used locally and little of it could find an overseas market. Like-wise forest products were only of local importance; significant to the econo-my of the gatherers but contributing only a few million francs to the value of the country's exports.

Up till 1900 the domestic market itself was limited and exploitation of jungle resources conducted on a small scale. However in the new century there was a rapidly growing demand for timber and firewood, stimulated by the industrial development of the deltas, the growth of towns and the building of railway lines. In fact by far the greater demand was for firewood. Unfortunately the increase in demand was accompanied by haphazard and thoughtless decimation of acres of valuable timber lands by Vietnamese and Chinese profit-seekers who despoiled at will, virtually unchecked by a skele-ton Forest Department.[22] A report of the mid-1930s revealed the extent of these depredations which were seen to have reached crisis point. For years there had been 'expert warnings' but the Forest Department continued to be understaffed and manned by junior officials of 'questionable competence' who had neither the resources nor the know-how to promote forest preservation. At last in the late 1930s the first large forest reserves were established and other measures taken to remedy the situation, and within the short span of time before the Pacific War something had been achieved.

The traditional fisheries of Vietnam, always important, expanded under French tutelage. Fish products nearly doubled in quantity between 1900 and 1937. Most of the fish exports consisted of dried fish, salted and smoked by Chinese fishermen in Along Bay and the Mekong Delta for the markets of Singapore, Hong Kong and China. Fishing was carried on throughout the length of the Vietnamese coast but not on such a large scale as natural conditions would have led one to expect. In Tonkin only a very small fraction of the population was involved in the industry; a greater proportion was engaged in Annam, but the fishing industry was most highly developed in Cochin-China, greatly influenced by the annual out-flow from the protein-rich waters of the Tonlé Sap. Freshwater fisheries were important for the domestic economy, being a round-the-year occupation in parts of the Tonkin Delta and widely practised in the south.[23]

Features of Vietnam's economic development
After seventy-five years of French domination Vietnam had developed two distinct economies. In the north there was the traditional self-sufficient subsistence economy of the padi-fields where in 1936 some seven million souls were packed together in an area of some 5,800 square miles, with a resultant density of population which was the highest in South-East Asia and one of the highest in the world. Enmeshed in an elaborate system of dykes and dams which both ensured their survival and perpetuated their poverty, the peasants of the north were joined by 4½ million more who lived in the adjoining narrow coastal strip of Annam and eked out a living in similar circumstances. In the south, on the other hand, was a different kind of economy established in a newly-opened region. The economy of Cochin-China bore all the classical hall-marks of colonialism—an area where production was geared to export cash crops and where the nexus of finance and administration was ordered in the interests of foreign capitalism while the labour and toil were provided by the people of the country at little benefit to themselves.

These characteristics developed out of French rule but the French impact itself was considerably modified by the existing circumstances of the Vietnamese economy; in other words a basic dichotomy between north and south had long been apparent. In 1850 Tonkin was already an over-populated province waging a perennial struggle for survival while Cochin-China was still the scene of recent Vietnamese colonization only partially completed. The French naturally concentrated on the development of the south where there was much more scope for their capital and enterprise. The densely populated provinces of the north were unsuitable for capital investment except in terms of industry, and for a variety of reasons this was never encouraged in a true sense.

Indeed the pattern of population distribution was an accurate reflection of the basic problems of the Vietnamese economy as well as an illustration of its evolution under French rule.

Population growth and distribution
The uneven distribution of Vietnam's population was as marked at the end of French rule as it had been at the beginning. Out of a total population estimated in 1870 at about 11 million, 9 million were concentrated in the Tonkin Basin and along the narrow coastal plains of Annam, while the remainder were spread over portions of the Mekong Delta. At the same period the population density of the north was about ten times that of the south. The manner of this distribution was directly related to rice production and the slow historical process of the movement to the south which had been going on for genera-

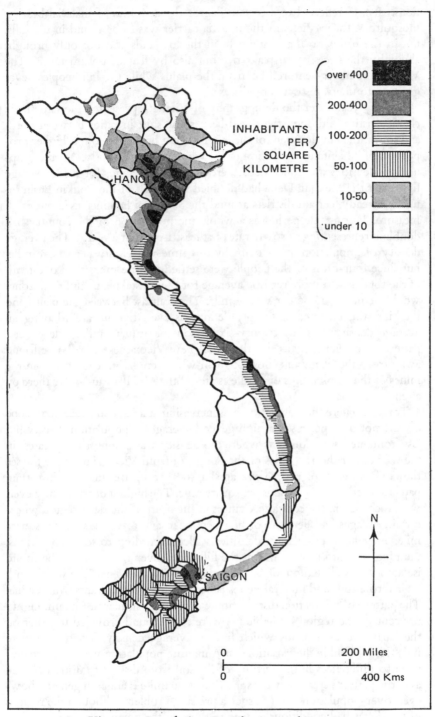

28.   Vietnam: Population Distribution and Density, 1931

tions. It also reflected to a certain degree the activities of malarial-bearing mosquitoes, for in Vietnam the malaria carrier was to be found in the hills, not in the plains, so that settlement in the lowlands was not only brought about by the necessity to plant rice but also by fear of upland fevers. The Vietnamese never ventured far from the plains while the hill peoples never grew in numbers, restricted by disease.

Seventy years later the demography of Vietnam presented the same basic characteristics, although there had been some shift in ratios between north and south, the development of the latter having brought about a higher proportion of inhabitants in relation to the whole than previously. As far as population densities are concerned, there was little change, for if the average figure for the Mekong Delta had doubled while that of the Tonkin Basin remained steady, certain districts around the Song-koi had increased out of all measure. During the period as a whole the population of the country had doubled, representing a growth rate of at least 1 per cent a year.[24] The average density of population in Vietnam by this time was eighty per square mile, but since four-fifths of the people were settled in little more than one-tenth of the total area, a more realistic average for the coastal plains and delta zones would be nearly 1,000 per square mile. The contrast between the plains and the hills still remained as sharply defined as ever, the hill areas having an average density of some twenty-six persons per square mile. The general pattern of settlement was also the same. Few Vietnamese were to be found away from the plains and most of them who were living elsewhere—in the mines of the Tonkin hills or on the estates of the Moi Plateau—were there on a temporary basis.

Tonkin, where the population was increasing at an average rate of 100,000 a year, not only possessed a high general average of population density but also contained some districts where the density was amongst the greatest in the world. For the 100 miles of the Song-koi from Viet Tri down to the sea the concentration of people averaged 1,560 per square mile and in certain patches reached 2,664 persons per square mile. The highest densities, however, were recorded in the coastal provinces in the heart of the delta region where certain villages had densities of between 4,240 and 6,360 persons per square mile. In general population densities varied according to local conditions, thinning out into low figures in the hill areas. Even there were to be found isolated valleys like those of Cao Bang, Lang Son and That Khe which with their fertile soils and mineral deposits had attracted immigrants from China. The pattern of population distribution was basically similar in Annam. Eighty per cent of the region's inhabitants were to be found crowded together on the narrow coastal plains which had an average density of 780 per square mile. As in Tonkin the variations in Annamite population were also attributable to differences in the fertility of the soil from district to district as well as to the patterns created by the sprawling Annamite Range. In general, however, over-population was not such a pressing problem, although the regions of the deltas had conditions similar to those in the north.

The factors that lay behind this growth and distribution of population are not altogether understood, particularly where the areas of highest density occur. That the high fertility of the soil in such areas was a cause is obvious; the effectiveness of some of the French irrigation projects in the Tonkin Basin was equally apparent. In Annam, areas where double-cropping could be practised and where fishing was a major occupation were the main centres of concentration. More general factors were also at work, amongst which the contribution of the French in checking diseases like malaria, cholera and small-pox which had once ravaged the countryside was important, as was also the comparative stability and peace brought by their rule.

In Cochin-China, after the initial expansion which accompanied the establishment of French rule there in the last quarter of the nineteenth century, the growth rate of population was slower than in either Tonkin or Annam, and the distribution of people was less dense and more even. After 1913 (up till 1930) the average population increase a year was reckoned at around 60,000, one-third of which was brought about by immigration from the north (mainly) or overseas, the rest being the result of natural growth. The average density of population for the whole of Cochin-China was 158 per square mile, but in the actual delta region it stood at around 260 per square mile, a little more than a quarter of the Tonkin average. However, there were also some districts where densities soared to over 3,900 persons per square mile. In general the most thickly-populated region was in the Mekong Delta proper and along the valleys of the lower Vaico and Saigon rivers which contained between them 70 per cent of the total population at an average density of 368 persons per square mile. The reasons for this rise in population lay in the opening up of the region to large-scale rice production by French capital and enterprise, and also in the development of the red lands to the north-east. In both cases this economic expansion attracted immigrants from the over-crowded north, but most of the development was carried out by the inhabitants of Cochin-China itself. In fact after 1920 the number of northerners who entered the region never exceeded 4,000 a year, a small proportion of the total increase. During the Great Depression between 1929 and 1934 the labour force was predominantly drawn from the people of Cochin-China.

The Chinese in Vietnam

The Vietnamese made up about 87 per cent of the total population of the country, while other indigenous groups made up the bulk of the remainder. Immigrants from other lands constituted barely 1½ per cent of all the inhabitants. Amongst the immigrants the Chinese formed by far the largest group and, as elsewhere, filled a role of great importance out of all relation to their numbers.

Nevertheless the position of the Chinese was highly paradoxical. The great influence of China in Vietnam is obvious, yet the actual Chinese presence was minute. Paradoxically again, the largest concentration of Chinese in the country was not in the north, on the borders of the homeland itself, but away in the Mekong Delta at the farthest extremity of Vietnam. In 1936, of the 217,000 Chinese in the whole country, 80 per cent lived in Cochin-China.

However, this was natural enough in terms of economic development.

Consistent with the colonial nature of its economy, Cochin-China under the French attracted the Chinese immigrant, since development was fast, labour scarce and opportunities in trade and commerce good. Tonkin on the other hand was a region already over-populated, well impregnated with Chinese techniques and possessing its own self-sufficient, involuted subsistence economy which gave little scope for the expansion of trade. Annam was difficult of access and could not produce enough for its own needs.

In Cochin-China the Chinese were able to play their classical role of middlemen, serving as the medium between European importer and native consumer, and as the initiators of a chain system of credit which linked exporter and processor of raw materials with their village producer. They were concentrated in the towns, particularly Saigon-Cholon, where about one-third of their numbers were located, and were the compradores of French banks and firms, the financiers, rice merchants and millers, junk-owners, shopkeepers, petty industrialists, and tradesmen. Apart from the rice industry which they virtually dominated up till the 1930s, the Chinese also had the lion's share of the trade in cotton, sugar, cardamom, cinnamon, silk and tea.

In Cochin-China, however, the Chinese owed their pre-eminent position to their domination of the rice industry. They arrived at this position by the time-honoured method of combining trade with usury. The Vietnamese padiplanter, rendered as indigent and as improvident as were his counterparts in the region by culture and circumstance, was soon at the mercy of the Chinese trader who bought his rice and made him advances in cash or in kind. The harvest was thus collected by a host of sub-agents throughout the delta to find its way by the junks of the rice merchants to Cholon or Saigon. There was only one significant difference from the usual pattern: the rice merchants, of whom there were about one hundred in Cholon alone, succeeded in maintaining their independence of the miller by forming syndicates which ensured that rice producers could not sell their produce directly to the mills. In other respects the system worked, as it did all over South-East Asia, based on credit which 'descended like a cascade', enriching the capitalist-merchant and perpetuating the poverty of the peasant producer.[25] The Chinese also played a predominant role in the copra industry through similar means and circumstances.[26] The minor trade in jute rice-sacks imported from British India was another profitable Chinese preserve; they all but monopolized the pepper grown around Ha Tien—although this was more of an adjunct to the Cambodian economy; they had a large share in the silk trade at Saigon and were ubiquitous market gardeners on the outskirts of towns and cities. They were also well represented in trade and industry; they carried on a whole variety of industries of all sizes and were conspicuous as artisans.[27] In all, the Chinese community in Cochin-China contained within its ranks the whole gamut of society from the very rich to the very poor.

However, despite their own background of rice cultivation, in Vietnam they shied away from padi-planting, which in any case was the natural field of the people of the country.[28] The French, particularly in their pioneer days in Saigon, tried to induce the Chinese immigrants to turn to agriculture, but to no avail. But the French themselves removed the most tempting bait by refusing to allow Chinese (along with other 'non-citizens') to obtain land grants, thus alienating the Chinese investor. Chinese labourers, on the other hand, were held to be too expensive by landlords, who preferred to exploit the cheap and abundant though less efficient pool of Vietnamese peasants. Besides this, there was also the natural reluctance on the part of immigrants coming south in search of a fortune to turn to back their old, back-breaking and scarcely remunerative occupation on the land.

The general French policy of restriction and discrimination against the Chinese was also responsible for the absence of Chinese participation in the rubber and mining industries. The Chinese stake in rubber was confined to smallholdings around Saigon since they were not permitted to hold concessions in the much more fertile lands further north, and they were totally excluded by law from acquiring any stake in the mining industry.

Despite these limitations the Chinese unquestionably attained under French rule a key position in the Vietnamese economy. The reasons for their success are merely a repetition of the factors which led to their rise in the other lands of colonial South-East Asia.[29]

However, the Chinese community remained small and tightly knit, both in Cochin-China and in Vietnam as a whole, and in the 1930s there was a growing challenge to their dominance. They were badly hit by the Great Depression of 1929 which, according to Robequain, 'decimated' the Chinese colony.[30] Not only did emigrants outnumber immigrants for the next three years but the Chinese grip over the rice trade was shaken and their monopoly over various others broken. Rice-husking, in particular, passed into French and Vietnamese hands and for the first time Chinese rice-millers began to face serious competition from French firms. Apart from this, an increasing number of young Vietnamese technicians were appearing, the products of the new system of education, who were able to occupy places once unknown to any except the Chinese, while the growing orientation of Vietnamese trade with France itself placed the Chinese entrepreneur at a disadvantage and helped to dislocate the world of Chinese commerce.

Outside Cochin-China the Chinese role was basically the same, although far more restricted. They largely dominated the sugar-cane industry of Annam by the same methods that gave them control over the rice trade of Cochin-China and played an important part in tea, silk and cotton. On the Tonkin coast near Mon Kay there were twenty fishing villages producing nearly 6,000 tons catch a year in the late 1920s. At Mon Kay itself the local Chinese specialized in ceramics; at Haiphong they were dominant in machine and boat construction.[31]

The economic prominence of the Chinese could not be denied; their economic value constantly was. In the official French eye they were more often than not regarded as tax dodgers and law evaders who ruthlessly exploited the advantages they gained under the security of French rule at the expense of government and native subject alike. Their role in creating wealth was overlooked, their speculations and facility at profiting from the poverty of others were emphasized. References to the 'Chinese cyst' or 'the Chinese excrescence' were commonplace as was also the image of the 'Chinese stranglehold on Indo-China'. As the ones who in fact had the stranglehold over the country's economy, the French attitude was understandable, for if unchecked and uncontrolled the Chinese might indeed have ousted the French from their position. The French feared lest the Chinese should swamp the local population, discourage or drive out French business and most of all indulge in political subversion, fears which indeed were shared by all the colonial administrations in South-East Asia to a greater or lesser degree.

On the other hand the workmanlike qualities of the Chinese were recognized and by some they were welcome as far better labourers on estates and mines than the 'indolent' Vietnamese. As a result French policy towards the Chinese community in general and to the question of Chinese immigration in particular was inconsistent, at times contradictory and on the whole counterproductive.

From the outset the Chinese in Vietnam—initially in Tonkin—were subject to special laws and special taxes. At first the French imposed a heavy poll on all Chinese residents under their jurisdiction, but in the face of protests from the imperial Chinese government at Peking in 1874 this was modified to apply to all Asians, with very much the same effect. In the decades which followed a whole spate of legislation ensued 'which looked splendid in Paris but worked badly in Saigon' to control and tax the Chinese,[32] but by the end of the century many of these laws had been lifted or lightened as the need for Chinese skills and labour was felt in the newly-opening mines in Tonkin. By the 1930s Chinese residents in fact had considerable freedom in Vietnam.[33] However they were still controlled through the communal associations known as 'congregations'[34] in Cochin-China, whose headmen held wide police powers and served as the principal tax assessors and collectors of the French administration. There was considerable feeling amongst local Chinese against this system but the prolonged Franco-Chinese negotiations which took place between 1930 and 1935 provided no relief. In an attempt to pierce the secrets of Chinese business in 1927 the French authorities required all commercial books and transactions to be kept in Roman script and Arabic numerals; but this was abandoned three years later in face of widespread criticism and a compromise solution was found to take its place.

The strictest regulations were those applied to immigration itself. In 1876, as a first step, the Service de l'Immigration was set up at Saigon, specifically to watch over Chinese immigrants and as far as possible to control them. All Chinese entering the country were subjected to stringent conditions which were nevertheless successively modified in the light of experience in the succeeding years, which tended to make them easier. In 1906, however, a new decree placed fresh restrictions on Chinese immigrants and after this date French policy was generally opposed to their entry.

The oscillations which characterized the evolution of French policy towards the Chinese in Vietnam were probably due, as Purcell points out,[35] to distinctions of purpose between the various rulings affecting revenue, population and immigration. In practice, despite the formidable prejudice in French minds against them, the Chinese were 'grudgingly tolerated', subject to strict supervision and control, but the effect of these policies was to restrict the scale

of Chinese immigration so that it never assumed the proportions that it did
in Island South-East Asia, and to make it much more selective in character.
Nevertheless the Chinese still came, their numbers grew, and notwithstanding the wall of official prejudice they faced, they survived and seemingly
prospered 'because of their supreme adaptability'.[36] The volume of immigration was in fact determined more by general conditions than the vagaries
of French policy. Apart from a handful of rich merchants who travelled in
style in the hope of becoming yet richer, the great bulk of the immigrants
came 'in picturesque, ill-smelling groups on the decks of small boats', usually
Chinese or British. On arrival they passed through the customs, got their
papers and then were taken over by the various guilds which represented
their home districts, and so on to their employers. Between 1906 and 1921
the flow continued, considerably reduced and now almost wholly pre-
arranged by their families already in the country or by Chinese firms which
preferred to employ Chinese staff. The general fillip to the economic growth
of Vietnam which followed in the wake of the Great War brought a new
increase in immigrants, but the Great Depression immediately afterwards
slashed the influx and reduced Saigon-Cholon's Chinese population by one-
third. After 1933 immigration picked up once more, so that entries surpassed
departures, but prior to the Pacific War the volume of the 1920s was never
attained again.

Until the 1920s, at any rate, the majority of Chinese immigrants to Vietnam were birds of passage who hoped to make good and then return home,
as was reflected by the low percentage of women immigrants. Events in
China itself and the aftermath of the Great Depression brought about a much
higher flow of women in the 1930s.

The pressures of competition and new social and economic circumstances
brought about by the French caused a distinct change in the traditional Vietnamese attitudes to the Chinese community. In the twentieth century attacks
on isolated individuals were no longer a rarity while communal disturbances
occasionally broke out, amongst the most serious of which were the Haiphong
riots of 1927. But the Chinese connexion went back to the dawn of Vietnamese history, the people had imbibed deeply of Chinese culture, and their
presence had come to be accepted not merely as a political necessity but as a
profitable asset.

The earliest Chinese immigrants, somewhere around the third century B.C.,
were probably itinerant pedlars. An imperial edict of the Han dynasty in
the second century B.C., placed a ban on the exportation of iron or metal
goods to Nam Viet, and from various Chinese sources thereafter came constant references to the value and importance of Chinese trade with the provinces of Vietnam. Faifo owed its origins in the sixteenth century to Chinese
merchants who made it their site for a fair. The first Europeans in the country
found Faifo the principal port and all trade virtually in Chinese hands. The
European presence stimulated this trade still further so that towards the end
of the next century (i.e. in 1786) Faifo contained nearly 6,000 Chinese and
its stores and markets were full of Chinese wares and even some Western
goods which they had brought to exchange for the local products of the

country. But of course the impress of Chinese civilization and influence in Vietnam did not come primarily through trade but through direct contact and conquest. The historical background of the Chinese occupation which laid the foundations of modern Vietnamese culture has been sketched elsewhere. Suffice it to say that, following Coughlin,[37] one can divide the Chinese connexion with Vietnam into three periods, starting with the prehistoric era when the primitive Vietnamese acquired from their more advanced neighbours knowledge of metals and of other properties and skills. The second period is associated with the actual period of Chinese domination. The Vietnamese success in overthrowing their overlords in the tenth century, itself proof of the extent to which they had become sinicized, marks the start of the third period, which lasts up to the French occupation. This period was the one in which, having won their freedom from the Chinese giant, the rulers of Vietnam self-consciously made China their model so that 'it could well be said that the Vietnamese became more Chinese after the departure of the Chinese administration than before'.[38]

Chinese immigration and settlement were directly affected by events within China itself. There was considerable Chinese settlement in Tonkin during Han times, the next wave coming with the collapse of the Sung before the Mongols in the thirteenth century. The pattern was repeated with the downfall of the Ming dynasty in the late eighteenth century, which led to the formation of the first Chinese colonies in the south. These were at Bien Hoa and My Tho, which became the nuclei for Chinese colonization in Cochin-China. In 1715, Mac Cuu, an adventurer from Kwangtung, made himself master of Ha Tien, having successfully taken advantage of Vietnamese-Khmer enmity. In 1778, in an attempt to evade the repercussions of the Tay Son revolt, the Chinese merchants of Bien Hoa moved to Taingon or Tingan, which, as Cholon, became the greatest Chinese centre in all Vietnam.

China held for the rulers of Vietnam the same place that Greece and Rome held for the princes of Europe. It was the source of their political system and institutions, of their cultural beliefs and values, of their art and literature. In fact, the only area in which Vietnamese originality was detectable at all was in the language. Accordingly the Chinese in Vietnam were by tradition more than tolerated. In Annam where Chinese residents were organized into communal groups called 'bangs', their leaders were treated on the same basis as Vietnamese officials of equivalent rank. In Cochin-China, the leaders of the Chinese 'congregations' enjoyed similar status and privileges. The general Vietnamese attitude was reflected by the treatment of the Minh Huong, the progeny of mixed marriages between Chinese immigrants and Vietnamese women. Such unions were common and in general welcomed by the Vietnamese. After 1829 the Minh Huong were officially regarded as Vietnamese instead of Chinese, as had hitherto been the case.

Other alien groups
The other immigrants in Vietnam formed very small minorities. The largest of them consisted of the Europeans, predominantly Frenchmen, who numbered between 40,000 and 50,000 on the eve of the Pacific War. By virtue

of their political position, they played a very significant role in the life of the country, holding the key-posts in the administration and dominating important areas of the nation's economy. The Europeans could be divided into three categories, namely Frenchmen and French citizens, Europeans of other nationalities, and 'assimilés', who enjoyed the legal status of Europeans although they were not of European origin.[39] The European community had the same characteristics as those in other colonial territories. The Europeans were concentrated by and large in the towns, were highly impermanent, and had a very uneven sex ratio. However the pattern of occupations was somewhat different. In Vietnam over half the employed European population was made up of members of the army and the navy, while the total number of those engaged in any field of commerce, agriculture or industry was smaller than those in the liberal professions; but those in these professions were less than half the number of Frenchmen in the administration. The Great Depression reduced the number of functionaries, however, by as much as 25 per cent.

Amongst other aliens in Vietnam the Indians were the most prominent. Of the 6,000 Asian foreigners in Indo-China in 1937, most were Indians who had come to Saigon as cloth merchants and chettyars soon after the French conquest and were rarely found outside Cochin-China.

The Vietnamese and other indigenous groups

All this left the Vietnamese in the usual colonial syndrome where in their own homeland they not only constituted the great mass of the underprivileged labouring population but were effectively denied any significant share in the sources of wealth and power which had been developed by foreigners and remained basically in foreign hands. 'Everywhere the Annamites work as helpers of the Europeans', Robequain observes,[40] 'in jobs which the latter plan and direct'. The Vietnamese were regarded 'as the most adaptable, obedient, skilful and energetic of the peoples of Indo-China...' although this was qualified by the apparent lethargy which afflicted those who lived in the south, and by their showing in comparison with their still more active counterparts, the Chinese. Most Vietnamese were rural-dwellers—rice-farmers skilled in Chinese-assimilated techniques, fishermen, and also part-time woodworkers, spinners of cloth, weavers of baskets and craftsmen of lac. There was, however, the small but highly significant growth of a new landless, wage-earning class, not amounting to more than 1 per cent of the total population of the country to be found on European estates or in French-controlled industries—the line between landless peasant and industrial wage-earner more often than not being very hard to determine. There was an even smaller but still more significant Vietnamese middle-class whose presence first became noticeable in the 1920s, particularly in Cochin-China. Most owed their rise to education, although in the south shrewd speculation in land accounted for the emergence of many. The new bourgeoisie had the roots of its prosperity in the land, and although in the heady boom years of the late 1920s a number ventured into commerce and industry, the effects of the Great Depression soon revealed their essential dependence on their role as landlords. A few of this middle-class were also to be found associated with the traditional ruling elite in the administration and in the professions, but on the whole they remained prior to 1941 extremely limited in their roles. The majority of the Vietnamese people, however, stayed hopelessly poor, and were only affected by the forces of the outside world in terms of the new economic pressures which were brought to bear upon them.

If this were true of the Vietnamese as a whole, it was even more so of the other much smaller indigenous communities in the country, who, with one or two notable exceptions, were almost totally removed from the effects of the Western impact. Most of them consisted of the various hill peoples inhabiting the highlands of Tonkin and the mountainous spine of the Annamite Chain, who being thus placed outside the main areas of French economic activity did not feel its pressures. In Tonkin they numbered between a quarter and a half million comprising Thai, Man, Miao and Lolo, all pursuing a traditional mixed economy as they had done for centuries but differentiated from one another by the altitudes at which they lived.[41] In the centre and the south were located the Moi who practised shifting cultivation over a wide area[42] and closely linked to them in the foothills of the Moi Plateau of south Annam were the remnants of the great Cham race, totalling no more than 100,000 on the eve of the Pacific War. Finally there were over a quarter of a million Khmer still scattered in self-contained groups amongst the immigrant Vietnamese population of the Mekong Delta.

Of all these peoples it was the Moi who were brought into closest contact with the French, coming face to face with Western civilization when French planters invaded their ancestral lands to sow coffee, rubber and tea in the 1920s. This encounter led the French to start studying the habits and background of the Moi 'just at a time when their native traits were being threatened with rapid disappearance...'.[43] The study neither changed the Moi way of life nor improved their fortunes prior to the Pacific War, any more than French efforts to persuade them to abandon their prohibited but profitable cultivation of the poppy bore success.

Vietnamese poverty and French policy

According to Albert Sarraut, 'Indochina is, from all points of view, the most important, the most developed and the most prosperous of our colonies'.[44] Reading 'Vietnam' for 'Indochina' one can add that the Vietnamese were at the same time extremely poor, a condition which was not new to them but certainly became accentuated during the brief period of French domination. 'There was real competition between man and beast', one observer has stated. 'Animal labour is as expensive as human labour, as man does not earn much more than is strictly necessary to feed himself, and the feeding of an animal is as costly as the feeding of a man.'[45]

This appalling poverty was reflected in the exiguous landholdings and almost universal indebtedness of the countryside, and in the miserably inadequate wages of the workmen in the towns. Conditions were worst in Tonkin, in Annam things were little better. The fact that nearly every Vietnamese farmer found himself in varying degrees of debt is hardly surprising. The

Tonkin peasant remained a smallholder everlastingly in debt, with his goods and harvests pledged long in advance; in the Mekong Delta where tenancy was the general rule, though land pressure was less intense, poverty and indebtedness were as rife.[46] Between 1900 and 1930 rural indebtedness in the south quadrupled and indeed usury was such a rewarding profession that it became a way of life for the landlords of the region who were much more concerned with the interest on their advances than in the yields from their crops. In the towns the wage-earner was as poorly rewarded as the peasant and his position was even more precarious. The average wage rate for the whole of Indo-China in the 1930s represented less than a twelfth of that of his French counterpart; wages in Tonkin stood well below this low overall average. His employment was uncertain—no daily-paid worker could expect to be employed for more than half the days in the year—and every piastre borrowed cost ten days' labour to pay off. Usury was as rampant here as in the countryside and it was not uncommon for the debtor to put one or more of his children to live and work for the advancer.

The factors behind this degrading poverty were an obvious compound of population pressure, landlordism and usury, as seen above, together with the spread of a money economy, the breakdown of traditional social safeguards against penury, old-fashioned attitudes and practices, and official land and fiscal policies. All these individual factors were interlinked and bound together within the nexus of French colonial policy.

To the outsider that policy tends to appear more ruthlessly exploitative and selfish than that of any other colonial power in the region. The French made little attempt to disguise the fact that they regarded their colonies as the sources of raw materials for home industries and as markets for their manufactures. Such motives, voiced explicitly by Jules Ferry, and echoed by French leaders down the decades which followed had their origins in the mercantilist concepts of the eighteenth century.[47] In fact, all imperialisms have been equally exploitative in intent; circumstances made the French more open and direct. Late starters in the age of industrial imperialism, they could not afford the luxuries of liberalism. They needed to gain an exclusive economic hold over their Indo-Chinese domain and succeeded in doing this so well that, apart from Chinese capital, foreign investments in these territories were minimal. Private enterprise played the leading role but it nevertheless received a large measure of official protection by means of tariffs and quotas and favourable legislation. So Vietnam became enveloped in 'the most protectionist system in South-East Asia'[48] and her economy became largely dependent on the interests of France herself. Such a course had its advantages for the Vietnamese but bore with it greater drawbacks, depriving Vietnam of her natural markets in the region and raising the cost of living for the inhabitants of a poor country. There was an over-emphasis on the production of commercial crops and a deliberate failure to advance industrialization. While most Vietnamese still did not have enough to eat, Vietnam became one of the world's major rice exporters.

Nevertheless French colonial policy was inspired by as high a sense of moral purpose as that which equally as ineffectually informed the colonial policies of Britain, Holland and the United States of America. French statesmen, heirs to the egalitarian doctrines of the French Revolution, were infused with the concept of France's 'mission civilisatrice' which was implied in the term 'assimilation'. The basic aim was to raise or modernize the standards of living of the colonies so that they could merge as extensions of the metropolitan Republic.[49] That such a goal was unattainable under the conditions existent in Vietnam without a vast expenditure which the French tax-payer could never accept took time to become apparent. When it did, official policy modified itself from 'assimilation' to 'association', which presupposed a period of partnership between the subject and the ruling races until the former were ready for absorption as Frenchmen.

The concept of 'assimilation' was initially spelled out in 1870 but the idea of developing Cochin-China as a 'limb of France' when its principal product fetched no market in the home country meant that the practical implementation of the policy had to wait. Barely ten years later, however, French industry was sufficiently developed to be eyeing with concern the few world markets which were still accessible to it, and agitation for a protectionist colonial policy, which 'assimilation' implied, rapidly grew.[50] The new French industrialists finally succeeded in canonizing their interests in the tariff law of January 1892, which declared Indo-China to be an 'assimilated' colony and which established, at least in theory, complete free trade between colony and mother country. This act confirmed the protectionist principle and served the interests of the French home industrialists faithfully for the next three and a half decades. Although the law provided for the possibility of adapting the tariff to meet local needs, home interests effectively succeeded in preventing any modification from taking place. However a protectionist policy manipulated solely in the interests of the home country involved all sorts of contradictions. It also aroused mounting opposition in Vietnam, which became increasingly effective as local French interests became established in the country, and as the French colonial administration became more and more concerned about the political consequences of a policy which sent up the cost of living. The new French awareness of the potential of Vietnam as a field for investment and the ensuing flood of French capital into the country in the mid-1920s finally brought about the rescinding of the 1892 Act in favour of a new law. The law of 1928, by placing the fixing of tariffs with the local colonial authority, now put control over tariff policy in the hands of French colonial interests in Vietnam itself instead of in those of the industrial interests in France.

The campaign to abrogate the Act of 1892 was conducted in the name of Vietnam's own interests, and indeed there was a strong case to be made. While French goods entered Vietnam protected by substantial tariffs, Vietnamese exports to France either had to compete with foreign goods on the open market or pay duty only slightly less than those on rival products. But when the 1928 law came into effect, local French interests turned out to be harder task-masters than those in France itself. Protectionism became more of an established fact after 1928 than it had been before, and its effects on the Vietnamese domestic economy more marked. This trend was greatly strengthened by other developments, in particular that of the Great Depression which forced the French administration to resort to a complex system of bonuses, compensatory funds and special quotas to enable the country's new export industries to survive. The subordination of Vietnam to the imperial economy was confirmed by the Imperial Economic Conference of 1934-5. Despite some benefits, the overall cost in terms of Vietnamese (as opposed to French colonial) economic development was high. Items which the country needed in order to develop its own economy were exported to France, while in exchange she received French luxury articles that rarely percolated beyond the limited upper strata of Vietnamese society.[51]

To sum up, the economic interests of the Vietnamese people were subordinated to those of France to a marked degree, with the result that the problem of Vietnamese poverty had to dance attendance upon the exigencies of French industry and commerce. Commercial agriculture was encouraged; industrialization was not. Trade was artificially channelled to serve the needs of the mother country and the interests of French colonial merchants. A money economy was introduced and spread at the expense of local institutions, which fostered the accumulation of wealth in the hands of a few while the great majority sank into deeper poverty. In an agrarian economy, the land itself became the domain of a small élite who commanded all the avenues to power and who exploited an impoverished peasantry totally subject to their will.

Vietnamese poverty and land policy

Since the roots of Vietnamese poverty lay in the land, French colonial policy made its greatest impact in the manner it handled the land problem. Indebtedness, usury and landlordism were equally as prominent in the north as in the south, but the factors behind them differed for each region. In the north the prime causes were over-population coupled with intense peasant conservatism; in the south the problem was more directly the outcome of deliberate land policies pursued by the French.

The first consideration in land policy under French administration was to make land a marketable commodity, which implied that as much land as possible should be opened up and exploited to the greatest possible degree. In practice the padi-planters of the south were the first to be affected, since Cochin-China was the initial area of French expansion and its vast swamp-wastes were awaiting their conversion into rice-fields. As 4½ million acres of swampland were dredged, drained and irrigated, the process of selling the newly-won fields was carried out either by making individual concessions of state land (all waste lands reclaimed fell into this category) to private buyers, or more often by selling it off at public auction, and by facilitating land mortgage under the law. This policy of deliberately creating a landlord class was based on the principle that land should only be given to those who had the capital to develop it, hopefully by using modern Western scientific techniques. The small peasant farmers in the eastern provinces of the Delta could not afford to participate in the resultant land-buying spree, and the new landlord class which was brought into being was drawn from wealthy Vietnamese in the towns

who either had the money or the influence to borrow some. The consequent
pattern of land tenure in Cochin-China was one where 80 per cent of the
rice land was held by landlords and where land-holdings in general were
larger than elsewhere.

However, the new landlords created under the French dispensation in
Cochin-China, instead of investing their capital in the development of their
new estates, preferred to sublet their lands to tenant-farmers (ta-dien) on a
one-family plot basis averaging between 7 and 25 acres apiece. Furthermore
most of them failed to take a direct interest in the farming of their estates,
but left their management in the hands of bailiffs 'with all the vices of middlemen' whose main function was to collect the rent. Nearly two-thirds of the
rice land in the south was leased out in this way and tenant-farmers formed
over half the total rural population. In the harvest season the tenant-farmers
were assisted by a large floating population of landless workers. Sharecropping might be a justifiable solution to the problem of managing a large estate;
absentee landlordism rarely is, and under the conditions by which it grew in
Cochin-China it ensured that the sharecropper himself was a poverty-stricken,
helpless individual. Although the returns on his produce were higher than
in the north, so was the cost of living, and as he had to pay between 40 per
cent and 50 per cent of his crop as rent in the first instance, he usually could
not make ends meet. So he was forced either to hire himself out as a labourer
or have recourse to the much easier solution of borrowing in cash or in kind
from his landlord, so ending up a permanent debtor. Indeed the average Cochin-Chinese landlord depended on his rents and on the interests of his advances to his tenants above all else; he was not interested in improving farming
methods or yields with the result that the rice industry of South Vietnam as
a whole was very inefficient, and the 'average income of a native farmer was
insufficient even to feed him, let alone allow him a decent standard of living'.[52]

The establishment of this landlord-tenant relationship in the rice lands of
Cochin-China was not entirely the product of French policies. It was also
assisted by trends already laid down in the process of colonization of the south
prior to the French arrival, whereby feudal-type mandarins organized colonies of soldier-settlers under their protection in newly-penetrated districts.[53]
But the French consolidated landlordism and followed a policy which consistently favoured the landlord. Not only were the landowners in the beginning able to obtain their estates at bargain prices but in case of need could
rely on the colonial administration for credit and support. The sharecroppers,
on the other hand, perennially in debt, had none to turn to save the usurious
moneylender. The final test of this policy came with the Great Depression
which laid bare the true extent of rural poverty, indebtedness and distress.
The colonial regime, however, failed to take this opportunity to launch a
programme of land reform which the bankruptcy of many large estate-owners
made feasible: instead it came to the rescue of the landlord class by creating
a special loan fund which stabilized and consolidated their position.

The rural poverty of Tonkin and Annam, on the other hand, was primarily
not the product of landlordism but of the relentless pressure of population on
land. The gravity of the problem forced the French to take immediate steps

when they took over the region in the 1880s, mainly by strengthening the existing water-control system, as we have already seen. They also introduced basic but effective health measures so that as a net result more people were enabled to live within the same crowded confines. Over-population ruled out the sort of land policies pursued in the south, but by encouraging the spread of a money economy and by giving land a new marketable value, the French contributed considerably to the process of fragmentation and concentration of wealth which characterized development under their rule.

Smallholdings in the north were traditional, dictated by the needs of irrigation and confirmed by social custom. Their existence was reinforced by the deep-seated conservatism of the northern peasant who felt tied to his ancestral lands, even when it could no longer support his livelihood adequately. Consequently as the population rose, which it did after 1890, sub-division of land took place on an intensified scale. By the late 1930s 62 per cent of the peasants of Tonkin owned less than nine-tenths of an acre each and 30 per cent of them far less than two-fifths of an acre per head. The average smallholding in the north was less than five acres and such holdings occupied over one-third of the total cultivated area.[54]

In pre-French times the misery which these small plots imply was offset to a fair measure by the strong co-operative traditions and institutions which existed in village society. Village land was divided between family and communal holdings and provision was made for the aged, widows and orphans and for the sick. There were rich and poor but the rich held their demesnes at the the will of the emperor whose natural interest lay in the prevention of the rise of over-mighty subjects. The tasks of the fields were done on a communal basis and water supplies were regulated by the village authorities.[55]

The French did not interefere directly with these village institutions, but the impact of their rule undermined them by weakening the authority of the village elders (who now found their power overshadowed by some French-trained government official) and by encouraging the use of money which came with greater stability, improved communications, easier credit and the expansion of trade. Those landowners who were already quite well established became better-off still, while the increasingly powerless local mandarins and village notables resorted to speculation and peculation in order to mend their fortunes. Communal lands imperceptibly shrivelled and in an era when the old values of communal responsibility and joint effort were giving way before the individualistic ideas of a Western capitalistic economy, the impoverished smallholder or tenant-farmer had nowhere to go.

So the tendency for wealth to become concentrated in the hands of a small landowning class whilst the mass of the peasant population sank into deeper penury was as true for the north as it was for the south, and in both cases French policy contributed largely to the end-result. The general poverty of the Vietnamese peasant cannot be solely attributed to the French. The traditional customs of peasants the world over, the lavish expenditure on social occasions, and the preoccupation with spiritual obligations were as characteristic of the Vietnamese as of any other peasant society. But the French administration itself did much to add to their burdens with its high taxes and the system of government monopolies, the effect of which was to send up prices of the commodities concerned. The burden of taxation on an already over-burdened peasantry was one of the bitterest grievances of Vietnamese nation-alists against French rule.[56]

The development of credit institutions and co-operatives

The French were of course not blind to the whirlpool of poverty which was spinning at their feet, nor to the dangers for the stability of their own position that it represented. The proper solution probably lay, at least as far as the north was concerned, in some radical measures such as the wholesale expropriation of the land and its redistribution, but such basic steps were hardly feasible within a colonial framework, and so recourse had to be had to measures which would improve or modify existing institutions. In general, what the French did in their attempts to combat poverty and relieve agrarian distress was limited, ineffective and very overdue.

The most obvious target for reform was the widespread evil of money-lending or usury. As Jacoby points out,[57] 'In Indo-China, as elsewhere, the landlord-moneylender is the worst influence on the general agricultural de-velopment'. Yet his existence had been encouraged by the French; he abound-ed everywhere and in the end could always turn for French backing to help him out of his troubles. He charged exorbitant rents, added to which he in-variably had the power to dispose of his tenants' crops and demand of them quasi-feudal services. This left the tenant with just about enough for his own needs but with no resources in the event of an emergency. The emergency al-ways came—in the guise of a wedding or a funeral, of a crop failure or some other natural disaster, or as the result of a rise in the price of the goods he bought or of a fall in the price of the crop he grew. The tenant's first source of credit was his landlord, whether for cash or for rice. The interest charged was steep: at least 50 per cent over a period of eight months to one year, often rising to 70 per cent. If professional moneylenders were involved, the rates were higher still.[58] Landlordism, usury and general indebtedness were all pervasive in Cochin-China. The landlord's main interest was to increase the number of his tenants by subdivision, which helped ensure the perpetuation of primitive, traditional methods of agriculture—quite the opposite to the French design; it also encouraged the rounding-off of estates through forfeitures, demeaning the cultivator and destroying all incentive. The system was not as compre-hensive in the north but its effects were the same.

There were two possible approaches to this problem. One was to restrict the usurer; the other to furnish alternative sources of credit. The French tried both with signally little success.

The attempt to limit chargeable rates of interest by law was as ineffective as it was late. No active government steps were initiated against usury till the late 1920s and it was not until 1934 that a decree fixed the legal rate of interest at between 5 per cent and 8 per cent, a measure reinforced by two more de-crees a couple of years later designed to prevent evasion. But as legislators in other usury-ridden lands have discovered, there is no practicable remedy by law to what is basically an economic and social problem.

French measures to develop alternative sources of credit, on the other hand, look very impressive, at least on paper, although these too were somewhat belated in their introduction. Credit institutions were longest and best established in Cochin-China. The first attempts to provide credit for agriculture were made there in the 1870s but they were a failure, and it was not until 1913 that a second and more successful effort was made by the creation of mutual loan associations. By 1920 these societies were established in all the provinces of Cochin-China and played an important role in the expansion of padi-planting in the trans-Bassac region between 1925 and 1930. However, the system pre-supposed the existence of rice cultivators with assets of their own to put into the common pool; as such the associations only served the interests of medium and large estate owners and remained beyond the reach of small-holders, let alone tenant-farmers. Such associations could not be formed at all in Annam or in Tonkin where there was no group of landowners numerous or rich enough to support them, and until 1927 when the colonial adminis-tration considered other methods by which credit might be made available, these two regions were totally neglected. In July 1927 a new type of credit institution was set up for the whole country. Known as the Caisse Indigène de Crédit Populaire Agricole (C.P.A.), it was modelled on the Dutch-Javanese pattern of agricultural banks, local banks, provincial banks and a central fund. The local banks were formed by committees made up of leading local citizens and were controlled by the provincial banks of which there were thirteen by 1930 and twenty-four by 1933. The Central Fund, however, was not created until 1932, and in the meantime the Banque de l'Indochine was made to act as the source of funds when called upon to do so. The C.P.A. never operated in Cochin-China, although it was planned that it should.

All these credit institutions were badly shaken up by the impact of the Great Depression, and without the active intervention of the colonial govern-ment they would undoubtedly have collapsed. As a result of this experience they were centralized under a new body called L'Office Indochinois du Crédit Agricole Mutuel (C.A.M.), the mutual loan associations of Cochin-China being 'laboriously liquidated'. After this reorganization the C.A.M. appeared to be placed on a better footing and the starting of a co-operative movement which was affiliated to the credit societies at the same time augured more positive progress.

On the whole, however, as the highest French officials were prepared to admit, the elaborate and expensive apparatus of credit institutions which were set up in the twentieth century did not achieve anything more than weakening 'to a certain extent...the influence of the native usurers who formerly had a stranglehold over a large part of the agricultural population.' In fact, all the evidence suggests that the position of the Chinese, Indian or Vietnamese moneylender was little affected. An official enquiry into indebted-ness in 1930 showed indeed that Chinese and Indian usurers often advanced the difference between the value of the security offered and the amount given against it by the official institution. Vietnamese landowners were also known to have obtained credit from agricultural funds solely in order to advance it at much higher rates to their tenants. But the greatest weakness of the system of agricultural credit was that it never reached down to the needy padi-planter himself.[59]

Another basic weakness, as the International Labour Organization (I.L.O) of the League of Nations pointed out in a report of 1938, was that the whole credit system was based on government funds and support and gave no scope for the development of thrift or initiative by the farmers themselves. This, nevertheless, was inevitable in the circumstances, as the farmer had no means by which to improve his own position; he borrowed in order to stave off immediate disaster, not to improve his lot. In any case, while the smallholder and tenant-farmer whose needs were greatest were left to sink in the quicksands of their own poverty, colonial credit institutions materially benefited the more prosperous medium and large estate owners and thereby encouraged still further the concentration of land and wealth into those hands. The role of French policy in this respect was never more clearly in evidence than at the time of the Great Depression when the whole credit structure was threatened with imminent collapse and the landowning class as a whole faced disaster.[60] In the French view, the landowners had to be rescued if the price of rice was to be maintained and even more widespread economic and social dislocation avoided. So stop-gap measures were taken to ensure wider and easier distribution of credit by expanding the existing institutions, enabling them with financial backing and guarantees to offer more credit, and also by creating new credit agencies. One of the latter, set up in 1932, was the Land Loan Office, whose specific function was to save the indebted landowner from his creditors. The policy of the Office was to bring about an adjustment of the outstanding debt by 'mutual agreement' between creditor and debtor, which although not particularly appreciated by creditors, saved the day for those landowners who were in debt. The financing of this huge rescue operation was an enormous and intricate task and represented a great triumph for French fiscal ingenuity.[61] The credit crisis was controlled and the rice export industry of Cochin-China was saved from collapse. But the plight of the poverty-stricken peasant was in no wise lightened. The whole credit operation went on above his head and benefited those who were his principal oppressors.

No doubt the best way to reach the peasant himself was through the medium of a co-operative movement, particularly as co-operative institutions were already familiar in Vietnamese society. However, incredibly enough, it was not until 1934 that the first modern co-operative made its appearance, and although the number had risen to about twenty by 1941 they were still fundamentally on an experimental basis. The new co-operatives were inspired by both European models and by the Dutch experience in Java. They were closely linked to the reorganized rural credit organization (C.A.M.). Loans were made to the co-operatives from the Central Fund and the money was then distributed as appropriate amongst their members. The agricultural co-operatives also set out to educate their members in ways and means of improving the quality and quantity of their harvests as well as in collecting their crops and selling them at the best possible terms on the market. Apart from agricultural co-operatives, co-operatives were also established on a pilot basis for various other products such as tobacco, sugar, tea, coffee and the mulberry in Annam and Tonkin, and plans were drawn up for the establishment of co-operatives in handicrafts. The co-operatives theoretically raised their capital from the shares of their members but in fact they had to be subsidized by the C.A.M. which usually provided their administrators as well. The progress made was encouraging on the whole but peasant ignorance and apathy coupled with the opposition of vested interests remained formidable obstacles.

Land tenure and land survey
Another problem which hindered the efforts of the C.A.M. in establishing its co-operatives was the difficulty of obtaining a satisfactory security on loans made because of the lack of an adequate land survey or of a proper land register. An effective and efficient survey of holdings was a prerequisite to land reform. As it was, ownership rights to peasant land were obscure and muddled, thus hindering the development of easy credit. However, once again the French administration seems to have been extraordinarily slow in getting down to the problem at all. A country-wide cadastral survey that could serve as the basis for unchallengeable land rights was proposed in 1915, but it was not till ten years later that the opposition to this proposal was overcome and work on the actual survey was commenced.

In the event the cadastral survey had only been partially completed by the time that French rule came to an end. In Annam it still covered little beyond the towns; in Tonkin it was applied to lands selected for concessions and although the greatest progress was made in Cochin-China where the survey set out to cover all lands regardless of status, priority was given to newly-drained rice lands in western Cochin-China which it was intended to alienate permanently and to the thinly-populated areas further east designed for planters of rubber, tea and coffee. By 1940 only one-third of the arable land in Cochin-China had in fact been surveyed, most of it owned by French concessionaires and Vietnamese assimilés, whilst the smallholder and tenant-farmer were once more left to fend for themselves.

Similarly most of the colonial land legislation in Vietnam was passed to facilitate the acquisition by French planters or miners of state or public lands. Even this came late. The first comprehensive law standardizing official practices came in 1913. The policy laid down was simplicity itself. Free grants were restricted to small and medium concessions not exceeding 750 acres. Grants up to 2,500 acres could be made on a contract basis by the local senior official (the Resident-supérieur) or by the governor-general if between 2,500 and 10,000 acres. Concessions of more than 10,000 acres had to be approved by the Colonial Minister in Paris. The conditions laid down for concessions were basically designed to ensure that the land obtained was developed, and a formal title to the concession was not granted until it had been ascertained that this was the case.

These land laws were generous to capitalist-investors but also ensured that French interests should prevail, since only French citizens and protected subjects were entitled to hold concessions. So the rubber, tea and coffee firms and the mining enterprises for whom the land policy was shaped were all French or French-controlled. Some additional legislation passed in the 1930s aimed at giving government itself a greater say in new land concessions.

The Vietnamese padi-planter neither benefited from nor was harmed by this development of colonial land policy which affected areas where he did not dwell. It was of concern, however, to the hill peoples, especially those of the Moi Plateau who ranged vast tracts of 'fallow forest land infrequently used' as they moved from place to place. As the opening up of the fertile red lands in this region was getting under way in 1926, a systematic survey was carried out to determine which lands could be opened up for the planters in each province. Safeguards for native rights and interests were laid down in each contract of concession. It was at first reckoned that about one-third of the red lands—some 2 million acres—could be reserved for French tea and coffee estates without harming Moi interests, but later it was found necessary to revise this estimate, and limit some of the earlier concessions.[62]

The general evolution of credit policy

The manner in which the colonial administration in general looked after its own in the matter of the land survey and neglected the interests of the great mass of its subjects who needed the most urgent attention, reflected the general trend of official policy towards economic development. Thus while the French evolved a credit system which served the interests of the land-owning class but which failed to cater for those of the actual cultivators themselves, they also assisted in the elaboration of a financial machine which worked exclusively for the interests of the French investor and entrepreneur and which in fact was able to manipulate the entire Indo-Chinese economy at will. The kingpin of this machine was the Banque de l'Indochine, founded by a consortium of French banking houses in 1875. The new bank was granted the privilege of issuing currency for twenty-five years, a concession which was subsequently renewed for similar periods. With the creation of the Union of French Indo-China in 1887, the Banque de l'Indochine assumed the functions of a state bank. Although it was now in charge of the economic interests of the whole country, it remained a private concern which, owing to its favoured position, was unchallengeable. Its capacity as the sole note-issuing authority in Indo-China gave the colonial administration a source of funds for its purposes free from the interference of ordinary commercial banks and helped to prevent the rise of any Vietnamese banking institution. But the bank itself enjoyed an advantage over the colonial administration in that its management never changed hands whereas officials in Saigon and Hanoi were as impermanent as the governments in Paris. In these circumstances the bank was able to pursue its own course with very little outside interference. It developed its interests not only in Indo-China itself but also overseas, to the extent that it was accused of pursuing more profitable investments elsewhere at the expense of local development. It was also criticized for being too cautious in advancing credit, for overcharging interest and for being excessively harsh with defaulters. Be that as it may, the bank played a major role in the great expansion of French investment and in the growth of French enterpries which took place in Vietnam, particularly after the Great War.[63]

During the Great Depression the Banque de l'Indochine was used by the colonial administration to prop up the local credit system. It was also used to save the French coffee and rubber planters who had been badly hit by the use of its reserves to meet special loans made on mortgages on rubber and coffee estates. During the period of the crisis nearly 10 million piastres were advanced to this group of planters alone.

Transmigration

Besides financial aid, directly or indirectly given, the French colonial administration in Vietnam attempted to deal with the problems of gross over-population (in the north) and of general poverty by transferring people from over-populated to underpopulated areas. However the French soon discovered, like their Dutch compeers, that transmigration was fraught with difficulty. The Vietnamese peasant, bound by the cult of his ancestors and the communal traditions of his village, was not prone to become an individualistic pioneer in a new environment. There was also the question of which underpopulated areas to choose from. The hills were there, open but uninviting, and requiring heavy expenditure to enable the immigrant to settle down and adapt to his new surroundings, quite apart from the problems raised by establishing permanent settlements in areas of traditional shifting cultivation. The undrained marshlands of the Mekong Delta were also open, but in many ways were equally as unattractive. Although the north and south had rice cultivation in common, actual farming conditions were not the same, while the inhabitants were different in outlook and attitudes. There was a general dislike of Tonkinese immigration in the south; the Cochin-Chinese feared lest an influx from the north together with the natural rise in the local population would duplicate the overcrowded conditions that the Tonkinese had left behind them. Southern landlords did not favour northern workers who would form self-contained colonies and not conform with the general docile pattern of their own local tenants. Another alternative for resettlement was offered by the new strips of land being formed in the deltas by alluvial deposits from the rivers; in this case the only drawback was that their area was limited and could only therefore provide a partial solution.

The French at first turned their attention to the hill areas of Tonkin, since in the 1880s the population problem of the north was not so pressingly apparent and the south needed capital, not labour. Government confined itself to facilitating transmigration without actual promotion of any scheme. An order of 1888 made free land grants to any Vietnamese who applied to be resettled in the middle region of Tonkin, but the response was poor. No new attempt was made till 1925 when, with an eye on disgruntled, demobilized Vietnamese soldiers who had fought in the French armies in the Great War, new conditions for free land grants were made which limited their size but made their permanent acquisition easier. The administration also gave more positive support by setting up migration committees and providing subsidies, but the response continued to be meagre, and even as a temporary solution to the now urgent population problem completely ineffective. By the end of the decade, French officials were admitting as much and turning to other methods of encouraging transmigration.

However, there was one hill region where transmigration met with greater success. This was in the Moi Plateau of south Annam which was easily accessible from the plains around Binh Dinh and Phu Yen and where Vietnamese settlements had already been established at An Khe and around Kontum before the French arrived. The opening of the nearby red lands provided the stimulus for official efforts to encourage fresh Vietnamese settlement there. From 1926 onwards the administration helped develop the region by constructing roads and improving health conditions, and by making free grants of land to new colonists. By 1939 there were some 15,000 Vietnamese settled around An Khe and Kontum, most of whom originated from central Annam. In the 1930s successful but less advanced Vietnamese colonies were established in neighbouring hill areas, notably near Pleiku and Ban Me Thuot and on the Lang Biang Plateau, to cater for the development of Dalat as a European health resort. Parallel to this, Vietnamese migration of a different character was taking place in those parts of the red lands given over to French estates, at an average rate of 7,000 a year between 1919 and 1934. But most of these were young bachelors, attracted by the high wage packets on the French estates, and over half of whom, having saved some money and completed their contracts, went back to their ancestral homes.

By the end of the 1920s it was clear that the limited progress achieved so far and the efforts of individual enterprise would never achieve the desired results. In 1930 as a new alternative all alluvial lands along the entire coastline were declared land reserves for resettlement, but the area involved was minimal and the beneficiaries were the inhabitants of the nearby estuaries. Attempts were also made in the 1930s to encourage, under government initiative, group settlements on the lines which some French Roman Catholic missionaries had already pioneered with success. But these moves, although promising, were necessarily limited. To bring about more tangible results an all-out campaign with full government backing was finally launched in 1936, largely inspired by contemporary Dutch experiments in the Indies, to resettle northern Vietnamese in the Mekong Delta on a large scale. A Tonkinese Colonization Commission, instituted to look into the whole question, contemplated a scheme for mass colonization in the southernmost provinces of Rach Gia and Ha Tien. Seventy thousand acres of land were set aside for the purpose and the main irrigation canals completed. The Commission also proposed a far larger scheme for the trans-Bassac which would cater for 50,000 migrants from Tonkin. But in the event neither scheme was implemented before the outbreak of the Pacific War. Other measures to encourage transmigration in the same period included the setting up of resettlement offices in all the provinces of Annam in 1936 and the creation in the following year of a Conseil Supérieur de Colonisation to look into the problems of and supervise the progress of resettlement.

Another option open to the Vietnamese of the north was migration to other French colonial territories overseas. Between 1920 and 1930 over 16,000 left the shores of Vietnam for the French Pacific, particularly New Hebrides and New Caledonia, but of these three-quarters had returned by 1937.

In all, transmigration or resettlement remained largely an idea on paper. The significant shifts in population which did take place under French rule—mainly in the Moi Plateau—were a result of the expansion of regional centres of colonization rather than of anything planned on a national scale. Indeed, there were many in influential business and commercial circles in Tonkin who were opposed to the whole concept of transmigration on the grounds that the northern economy would be damaged by a loss of manpower, and as usual the administration dragged its feet. When at last positive measures were taken, they were overtaken by events.

Industrialization

The failure of the French to relieve the problem of poverty by bringing about a greater degree of industrialization may be ascribed to the conflict of colonial interests with those of the local people. Without question Tonkin in particular possessed all the primary factors necessary to enable modern industrial development to take place. Its teeming population could supply ample reserves of labour, the Quang Yen coalfield had abundant resources of fuel for factories and there was an ever-ready market both at home and in neighbouring lands. But the classical concept of a colony existing solely for the benefit of the mother country as a source of raw materials and as a guaranteed market for manufactured goods died hard in French minds. In fact, the working of the Tariff Law of 1892 ensured that French home industrial interests were effectively protected for three and a half decades, and the hollowness of the agitation for greater local economic autonomy was revealed after the new tariff of 1928 enabled a fresh generation of French industrialists in Vietnam itself to impose a more rigid protectionism than ever before, not to promote Vietnamese industry but to bolster up their own. Only at the eleventh hour under an unusually liberal or percipient new colonial minister was a start made at encouraging the development of Vietnamese manufactures in the teeth of strong opposition from vested French interests, and even these were carefully selected to avoid competition with French imports.

In consequence the predominant form of industry in Vietnam prior to 1941 was the traditional cottage industry. Robequain described traditional handicrafts as 'an essential factor in rural community life';[64] in 1938 over one and a quarter million people depended for their livelihood on such industries and this number was swollen by those for whom handicrafts were a part-time or supplementary occupation. The most important of the cottage industries in terms of employment was food processing, but in terms of value it was textiles. Handicrafts such as woodwork and carpentry and ceramics came next. One general feature of the pattern of traditional industry in the country was the high degree of specialization in the making of even the simplest articles. Traditional industry was less common in the south. Because of more recent settlement, its population was smaller and there was less abject poverty. Furthermore foreign competition had been more forceful and direct.

Only about 4 per cent of the people of Cochin-China (half that of the north) were dependent mainly on traditional industries for their livelihood.

Of those engaged in food processing, three-fifths were involved in preparing rice for local consumption; second in food processing came the distillation of alcohol. Textiles and ceramics were important in Tonkin and north Annam. Carpenters and joiners were to be found in every Vietnamese village but there were also gangs of craftsmen who toured the countryside, offering their skills as sawyers, lacquerers, turners and carvers in the making of household furniture and of agricultural implements. In general, the traditional handicrafts, particularly in the north, were able to produce enough to meet virtually all village needs.

Although the widespread survival of these various cottage industries was a token of the limited economic development of the country and of the low living standards of its inhabitants, official policy was to encourage such industries as they were regarded as 'one of the best methods of combating the rural pauperism resulting from overpopulation'.[65] For all that, French efforts to develop handicrafts were not markedly successful. Workshops for mat-weaving and silk weaving were set up in one or two places in the north by the administration and there was the example of a French miller in Binh Dinh who encouraged local industry by leasing out looms and yarn to rural workers and buying their product for export processing. But these efforts were not concerted nor were they sustained, possibly for want of confidence in the ultimate future of handicrafts in a technological age.

For despite the entrenched opposition which existed against the establishment of modern industry in Vietnam, some progress was made and more was bound to come. In 1939 there were some 120,000 workers employed in mining and manufacturing in the country, a very low figure in comparison with other occupations but representing a steady increase of 2,500 a year since 1890. In fact, Vietnam's distance from France enabled her to develop a greater diversity and value in her industrial production than any other French colony. The principal areas of development were in the processing industries, although there was no apparent expansion in them after 1929. These industries were concentrated around Hanoi and Haiphong and were naturally closely linked to the coal and other deposits in the vicinity. The great irrigation projects of the 1920s and 1930s greatly stimulated the growth of these industries as it did also a variety of lesser manufactures. In the country as a whole there was also some development. A good deal of the processing of agricultural products (apart from rubber) was left in the hands of village workshops, but some firms specialized in preparing cash crops for overseas. Sugar refining became significant after 1920 as also did tobacco manufacture which developed at a faster rate within the same period. Oil-extracting factories and soap works also grew up after the Great War. Another processing industry originally started to cater solely for European needs was that in aerated waters, beer and cold storage—with plants at Hanoi and Haiphong, and also at Cholon. By the 1930s their products were finding a growing market amongst Vietnamese as well.

More surprising still in view of the conflict of interests involved was the emergence, albeit limited, of a Vietnamese textile industry. Vietnam of course had all the natural requirements for developing textile manufactures, and the facts of economic geography made it impossible for the French to prevent the introduction and establishment of modern spinning mills for cotton and silk. For some years the colonial administration tried to make imported French fabrics competitive in the local market by imposing a discriminatory tariff on the cheap Indian yarns imported for rural weavers. However, this proved useless, so it was decided to set up modern factories in Tonkin itself, using French capital and exploiting to the full the cheap labour and materials locally available. The first French mill was opened at Hanoi in 1894, followed by two others at Haiphong and Nam Dinh. In 1913 the three concerns merged to form the Société Cottonière de l'Indochine. Efforts to develop a modern silk industry were less successful. Two silk factories were actually established but one was forced to close down after 1929 in face of the general decline in local sericulture which followed the rise of rayon and the intrusion of Chinese silks. Other ventures in textiles included a rug factory at Haiphong and a cotton fibre sparterie works also in Tonkin.

Maintenance industries absorbed a fair proportion of industrial labour. The Saigon arsenal played an important role in training skilled labour: the main railway assembly and repair workshops were at Vinh; there were also shipyards at Haiphong for barges, river launches and cargo boats and plants for providing specialized equipment for estates and mines. Amongst other miscellaneous industries were a French-owned tannery established at Hanoi in 1912, four explosives manufactures, button factories, a candle-making factory, two oxygen plants, some varnish and paint factories and numerous small Vietnamese shoe and leather workshops.[66]

From all this it is clear that the foundations for industrialization had been laid, but it is equally clear that much more could have been done, and that the main obstacle in the way of doing so lay in the exigencies of French economic interests. A serious programme of industrialization could have reduced the cost of living and raised the purchasing power of the people.

The development of modern communications

The development of modern communications in Vietnam was actuated as much by political as by economic considerations. For this reason the French first paid their attention to the development of railways, since their construction seemed indispensable both to the economic growth and to the political unification of the country. There was also the great bait of the China market. These were the over-riding factors behind French railway policy which gave rise to the 'Doumer scheme' in the form of two great interrelated projects— the 'Transindochinois' which was to stretch from the Chinese frontier in the north to Saigon and Cambodia in the south, and the Yunnan line which would link Hanoi and its port of Haiphong with Kunming, the capital of the Chinese province of Yunnan. Another major project was a route across the Annamite Range from central Annam into the valley of the Mekong in Laos. The Transindochinois would tighten the bonds between Tonkin and Cochin-China, facilitate inter-regional trade and hopefully stimulate a flow

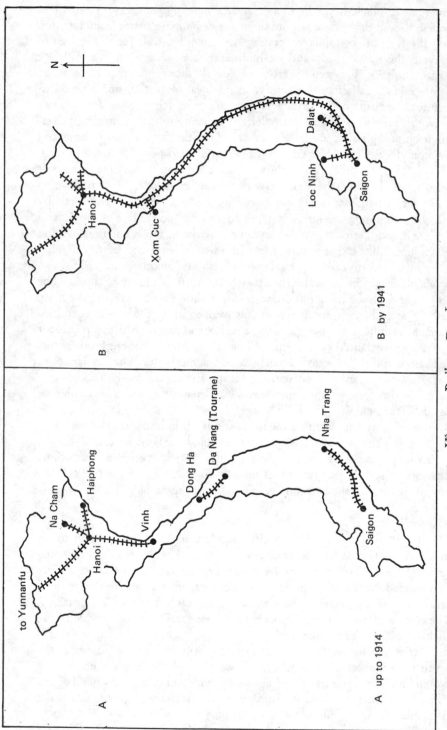

29. Vietnam: Railway Development

of migrants southwards, while the Yunnan and Annamese lines would serve as useful feeders. The first to be completed was the Yunnan line in 1910; described as 'one of the most remarkable feats of railway engineering' it certainly became the most profitable and the greatest asset in the Vietnamese railway system. The Transindochinois commenced at the beginning of the century was not completed till 1936. The line planned to cross the Annamite Range into Laos was not finished at all.

The carrying out of this grandiose scheme of railway construction clearly stood beyond local resources. The capital needed was raised by the issuing of government bonds, first in 1896 and again in 1898, which were eagerly subscribed to by French capitalists, attracted by the guaranteed dividends and by the promise of new markets for building materials. Up to this point railway construction had been limited to a line joining Saigon to My Tho and by a narrow gauge military line which served the colonial garrisons at Lang Son and Cao Bang on the Chinese border.

Priority was given to building the Yunnan line, which was seen as a magic trail by which the Chinese province could be transformed into a kind of vast hill resort for Europeans in the Far East and the huge market of China itself could be tapped. The engineering involved was full of challenges and by the time the 290 miles of the line were completed, over 3,600 engineering works had been built including 172 tunnels and 102 bridges. Work began on the line in 1898; it had reached Vietri by 1903, Lao Kay on the frontier by 1906 and took another four years to reach Kunming.

The main project, the Transindochinois, also entailed considerable engineering feats as it was tunnelled through the spurs of the Annamite Range and crossed flood-prone estuaries and plains. The line was built in two main stages. The most rapid development took place between 1898 and the outbreak of the Great War in 1914: during this period the Langson line was broadened and extended to Hanoi, and from there extended to Vinh by 1905. In Annam the section between Hué and Da Nang (Tourane) was opened in 1906 and extended to Quang Tri two years later. In Cochin-China the line north from Saigon had reached Nha Trang by 1913. The second stage was ushered in after 1922 with new loans. By 1927 the link between the Tonkin and Annam sections was completed with the building of the stretch between Vinh and Dong Ha and the last section, which also proved to be the most difficult one, between Da Nang and Nha Trang, was opened in 1936.

The third main project was the construction of a railway line across the nnamite Range from Tan Ap in central Annam to Thakkek in Laos. The route via the Mu Gia Pass was surveyed and twelve miles completed from Tan Ap to Xom Cuc, while a start on the permanent way was made from Thakkek. But then 'budgetary difficulties' ensued, causing an indefinite suspension of work, and it was never resumed.

Apart from these trunk routes two other branch lines were built, both being completed in 1933. By 1941 the railway mileage of Vietnam amounted to 1,250 miles, which had been built over some extremely difficult country at a great cost in lives and money. It is a moot point as to whether it was worth it. Only the Yunnan line was able to pay its way and show a profit;

all the other lines barely made ends meet and between 1932 and 1935 ran at a loss. The Yunnan line paid because there was no competition and in later years with the mounting pressure of Japan it acquired a tremendous strategic importance. But the Transindochinois itself was handicapped by competition from road and sea; freight was limited because inter-regional trade was small, and the anticipated increase in the movement of settlers from north to south never took place.[67]

Although at first railway development was given preference, it was the roads which made the greater contribution in the end. Up till 1923 road building was conducted at provincial level without there being any comprehensive overall plan. The birth of the motor-car and the coming of the Great War, however, together with the delays and difficulties experienced in the construction of the trunk railway changed all this. The problem of road development was studied in detail during the course of the War and at its end in 1918 the classification of roads into two categories—local roads and colonial highways—was established.

Up till 1913 the only overland route in existence between north and south was the famous 'Mandarin Road', which was in fact more of a trail than a road, leading the traveller with his caravan of baggages and porters along rice-field tracks, across river mouths, over mountain passes and amongst the sand-dunes of the Annamite shore till it eventually brought him to the Mekong Delta. In 1913 only certain sections were passable to two-wheeled traffic. This traditional route formed the basis for the first colonial highway (Colonial Highway One) which from 1913 was progressively extended. The modernized route retained its ancient importance as the medium for unity, as a means to combat famine and as the main artery of the land; but it contained few fast stretches and the average journey between Hanoi and Saigon took three days.

The greatest amount of road building took place in Cochin-China. The Saigon area was well served long before 1913; subsequently roads were extended into the centre of the region and then westwards towards the delta. Colonial Highway One was pushed into Cambodia and another main road linked Saigon with Ha Tien. Road building also had an early start in Tonkin, dictated more by strategic than economic considerations. The needs of a densely populated region, of new mines and remote but fertile valleys promoted further development after the Great War. Some of the greatest French achievements in road construction took place in Annam. By 1941 three routes had been built across the Annamite Range into Laos and the opening up of the red lands of the Moi Plateau to rubber and other crops after 1925 led to the construction of roads from Colonial Highway One into the interior. These main roads were interlinked by the local roads whose standards varied from the up-to-date to the old trails of the countryside. The costs of road construction were high as the stone for the roads was usually to be found far removed from the main centres of population, but by 1941 Vietnam was served well by over 16,000 miles of highway, more than three-fifths of which were metalled.

However, the traditional means of communication in Vietnam were by water and as far as the delta regions were concerned, waterways still played an important role in the conveyance of the internal traffic in merchandise and export materials to the ports, and although coastal shipping had to meet the competition of the new trunk road and rail routes, this also expanded.

River navigation was most important in the Mekong Delta where conditions were ideal for the use of the waterways, a fact long appreciated by the pioneer Vietnamese colonizers of the region who had built a number of canals to facilitate water-borne traffic before the French occupation. Realizing that the pacification and exploitation of the land could sooner be brought about by extending these waterways than by undertaking the construction of roads in vast swampy plains where stone was non-existent, the French took over and accelerated the good work. From 1866 when operations were begun up till 1893 when powerful mechanical equipment was used for the first time, each year under successive French governors thousands of labourers helped to elaborate the canals and build defences against erosion. By 1941 there were over 800 miles of main canals criss-crossing the Cochin-Chinese countryside which added to the rivers amounted to 2,500 miles of navigable waterway in the region. In the twentieth century the new canals became important as much for the development of irrigation, agriculture and settlement as they were for transport. Yet they still served as the most convenient means for the conveyance of rice, maize and charcoal from Camau, to the mills and wharves of Cholon-Saigon, and stood fair to hold this position despite the growing competition of road-based traffic.

In general the navigation of the waterways of Tonkin was far less favourable, so that the great network of canals developed both before and after the arrival of the French were built primarily for irrigation rather than navigation. But the stabilization of the water supply by the building of barrages, and the extension of irrigation works helped make the navigation of the main streams easier. By 1941 there were over 2,000 miles of navigable waterway in the region.

The waterways of Annam were the least extensive, although their navigable mileage did not fall far short of that for Tonkin. In fact Annam was the only part of Vietnam where water traffic declined during the French period. The ancient arroyos and canals which, sheltered from storms and pirates, had formed the main coastal route, lost their importance with the building of the trunk road and railway inland, with the growth of modern coastal shipping and the decline of piracy, and they fell into disuse and silted up.

The long Vietnamese coastline was not inviting to coastal shipping because of its lack of natural harbours between Haiphong and Saigon and its exposure to the storms of the South China Sea and the Gulf of Tonkin. Nevertheless the stability and expansion of commerce brought with French rule stimulated coastal traffic and both Haiphong and Saigon became regular ports of call for the two main French shipping lines in the Far East. Indeed the rise of these two ports in the French period was primarily because of their function as the main outlets for the produce of the regions they served, as Vietnam became part of the world system of trade. Saigon's development as a port paralleled that of Cochin-China as a rice-bowl. By the 1930s it had become the country's largest passenger port and was the scene of the biggest European settlement. Despite being some forty miles upstream, Saigon enjoyed several natural advantages as an ocean-going harbour with its relatively silt-free tidal waters and easy approaches. When the American John White was there in 1819, he found it already well established as the major port of the Mekong Delta, a straw-hut town stretched along the river bank. Fifty years later (i.e. in 1860 when Admiral Page declared it open to international trade) it was still 'only a collection of rather sordid quarters', but after that its growth was swift. Haiphong's development at the other end of the country, on the other hand, presented some difficulties. Its main problem was that it was subject to severe silting, a problem only partially overcome by the completion of the 4,500 feet Dinh Vu Cut in 1902, so that heavy and expensive dredging remained a perennial necessity. But its ideal location ensured the port's rise. In 1874 it became one of the treaty ports under Harmand's agreement with Hué and in 1882 was the point of disembarkation and main supply point for the French expeditionary force which conquered Tonkin. In the years which followed Haiphong grew into the natural distribution centre for all of northern Indo-China and the leading industrial centre of Tonkin. It acquired a population of 70,000 who lived in a city which rested on thousands of bamboo piles and stakes plunged into a 164 feet mud base—'an outstanding example of human willpower—one might even say, human obstinacy'.[68] Nevertheless the high cost of keeping the port open led to a constant search for alternatives in Along Bay. Finally in 1930 the last of a series of experts who had been sent out from France to consider the problem opted for Haiphong on the basis of extensive port improvements. The Great Depression hit Haiphong hard. A lot of trade was lost and businesses closed down as a result of the new protectionism which followed in its wake and from the curtailment of the China trade which was a consequence.

Saigon, Haiphong and Hon Gay (also in the Tonkin Delta) were the only three Vietnamese ports with a substantial foreign trade. The rise of other major ports along the long Vietnamese coastline was checked by the competition of road and rail services as well as by the narrow hinterland which they could serve.[69]

The coming of the air age was of the greatest significance to Vietnam, situated as it was at a natural cross-roads of air routes, although this advantage was offset to a certain extent by difficult terrain. The first landing fields were built in 1918 and ten years later a programme was launched to develop international airports for the benefit of Air France at Hanoi and Saigon, followed later by Da Nang, Hué and Vinh. By 1941 the country had become an important link in the ever expanding network of air communications. There were three fully equipped international airports, of which Hanoi was the most important. The country also possessed a string of landing grounds and airstrips from Saigon northwards along the Annamite coast to Tonkin.

As for other means of communications, by 1940 there were two broadcasting stations in the country as well as forty wireless transmitter stations (in the Union as a whole) directly linked to important centres throughout the world. Vietnam was also linked by the British submarine cable from Singapore to

Hong Kong via Cape St. Jacques. There were well over 300 post offices in the country (i.e. Indo-China) of which two-thirds were to be found in Cochin-China and Tonkin, and the mails were carried by road and rail, by river, by horse, by courier, and somewhat irregularly between Hanoi and Saigon by air. There were over 12,000 miles of telegraph lines in the Union, usually following the road and rail routes, and a telephone service of about half that length.

The French and Vietnamese labour

The great strides in economic development which undoubtedly took place in Vietnam under French rule were based, as throughout colonial South-East Asia, on the effective and ruthless exploitation of cheap labour. This labour had always been cheap. In traditional terms forced labour was an institution under the Vietnamese emperors. Every able-bodied man used to be required to do public works for so many days each year and in every village certain communal obligations such as the maintenance of the bunds and the upkeep of roads had to be carried out. The French saw to it in the name of humanity and with the enlightenment of self-interest that such illiberal practices were replaced by dues or taxes, but this process was remarkably slow. The system of forced labour was not effectively lifted throughout the country until the 1920s and it was not until 1937 that the substitute dues became commutable.[70]

The place of traditional forced labour was taken by a modern wage-earning proletariat which multiplied at a steadily increasing rate after 1900. This modest but significant development was actively encouraged by the French authorities, despite the generally poor opinion held of the working qualities of the Vietnamese labourer himself. For labour was necessary, whatever its quality, and granted the vast surplus of manpower which existed in the north and French misgivings about the wisdom of permitting unrestricted immigration of Chinese coolies into the country, the colonial problem of overcoming labour shortages which held up development could be solved in the case of Vietnam within the confines of the country itself. Vietnamese colonial labour, as elsewhere, fell into two broad categories—contract and free. At first, contract labour was the more prominent, but as the twentieth century advanced it steadily lost ground to the growing pool of 'free' labourers.

Shortage of labour was felt most acutely by the French in the south where vast tracts were underpopulated and the greatest scope for capital investment and exploitation existed. Contract labour developed and became of paramount importance during the 1920s as more and more estate land was opened up in the red lands of the Moi Plateau. Between 1919 and 1934 some 104,000 contract labourers disembarked at Saigon, the annual figures rising sharply between 1925 and 1930. The actual clearing of the land was mostly done by local Moi tribesmen who excelled at this job and were well acclimatized to the surroundings, but who were also sparse in number and totally unreliable. So the labour force on the new estates turned out to be predominantly Vietnamese, recruited under contract from the north.[71]

Although the rise of this form of labour took place half-way through the third decade of the present century, the whole system was permeated with abuse and corruption. The demand for labour was so great and the power of the planters so complete that it took time for the administration to be able to take effective measures to control matters. It was the same dreary story, which had already been enacted so many times in other parts of South-East Asia, of gross deception and exploitation on the part of labour recruiters and employers alike; the recruiters profited from their recruits at every turn and planters often administered their own summary justice in remote areas where civil authority was barely represented. The existing laws solidly backed up the planter, sanctions against desertion being particularly severe. Matters reached scandalous proportions. Desertions became commonplace and suicides frequent. Popular resentment against the system of recruitment and conditions of work for the contract labourer provided fertile ground for the burgeoning nationalist movement to work on and provoked some of the more sensational political atrocities of the decade.[72]

Under these pressures the French administration was forced to take steps. In 1927 a General Labour Inspectorate was instituted for all Indo-China while new labour regulations were promulgated, the wording of contracts made more precise, and the enforcement of their terms supervised more strictly.[73] For the first time recruitment came under official scrutiny and basic conditions of work in terms of minimum wages, rations, housing and hygiene were laid down. Penal sanctions against defaulting labourers were, however, still enforced and in many other respects the new controls left much to be desired. On the other hand, after 1928 things were certainly better for the contract labourer than they had been before. An indication of the improved state of affairs was afforded by evidence in the late 1930s that more and more contract labourers were opting either to extend their contracts or even to remain and continue as free workers on the estates where they were employed. Living conditions had also improved considerably. But the majority were still drawn back to their ancestral homes and the percentage of women in the total contract labour force, an important element for stability, still remained at around one-fifth of the whole. Home-sickness, dislike of the oppressive environment of jungle and mountain, and resentment of estate discipline helped sustain a fairly high desertion rate, although this fell from the peak years of the 1920s. Nor did the new dispensation improve average output for 'Labour regulations could not suddenly develop, in the Indo-Chinese, an interest in his work and a desire to labour diligently'.[74]

The labour regulations of the late 1920s only concerned contract labour. The 'free' labourer still remained immune from official protection and employer influence successfully prevented any steps from being taken in the direction of helping him until political events in France itself in the mid-1930s forced a change. In fact 'free' labour formed the greater part of the total number of workers in Vietnam. Much of it was organized on a group basis and this enabled the labour contractor, the familiar villain of the piece throughout colonial South-East Asia, to play his ambivalent but largely indispensable role.

Amongst the various groups of 'free' labourers, those involved in industry, in particular, mining, were the best off. Although the mines of the

Quang Yen Basin were often referred to as the 'hell of Hon Gay', the needs of modern industry led French employers to realize what benefits lay in a more enlightened policy. During the 1930s the mining companies of Tonkin transformed the conditions of work of their employees. Model mining villages replaced the old company lines, hospitals and schools maintained by the firms themselves were built and sports facilities established. Alongside this there was a general rise in standards of technical proficiency amongst the Vietnamese themselves, and in 1930 the largest of the mining companies opened its own school for training Vietnamese mining superintendents. In the surface mines working conditions remained primitive, but high standards of skill and safety were upheld on all underground works.

It was also the industrial workers who benefited most from the second wave of labour legislation which came in with the victory of the Popular Front in France in 1936.[75] A decree of the end of that year extended protection to all categories of labour, but only in the industrial sector was it easy to enforce. The new regulations laid down compulsory minimum wages for free labour, new health and safety laws and provision for more effective inspection. These new measures met with considerable resistance from amongst plantation-owners and led to various incidents, sometimes involving bloodshed, on estates. Nor did the new laws reach to protect the day labourer who was still the prey of the overseer, shop-keeper and moneylender. Trade unionism was officially never recognized. Yet, for all this and although certain vested interests, mainly French, delayed the implementation of labour legislation, labour conditions in Indo-China as a whole, according to an I.L.O. report of 1937, compared favourably with those of other Asian lands.

Health and social welfare
A source of pride to Frenchmen was the substantial contribution made towards improved standards of health under colonial rule. The country was subject to the whole gamut of tropical diseases common to the whole region, and prior to the introduction of Western concepts of hygiene and scientific medicine the defences against them were virtually non-existent. The greatest enemy of all was malaria which was more prevalent in the foothills and the mountains than in the deltaic plains. For this reason malaria took a heavy toll of life amongst the Chinese and Vietnamese labourers working in the upper valley sections of the Yunnan line in 1904 and 1905. In the 1920s as the red lands were opened up 'Gangs of coolies from the lowlands melted away in a few months' as they fell victim to the disease, while labourers working on the mountain road from Saigon to Dalat the following decade deserted wholesale before they should succumb. The initial failure of the French to deal effectively with the problem despite the experience which had been gained in British Malaya and the Netherlands Indies was largely due to the peculiarities of the disease. The most dangerous carrier in Vietnam was the *anopheles culicifacies*, a rare breed found only in the back country of Nghe An in North Annam and around Lai Chau in Tonkin, while another variety, the *anopheles minimus*, flourished in the clear-running streams which watered the deep

valleys of upper Tonkin. However, after 1920 measures introduced by the Pasteur Institute were applied and continued with ever growing success. Dalat was freed from the disease as the result of drainage built when the town was developed into a hill resort. Protective measures on the rubber estates of the red lands reduced the casualty rate amongst estate labourers by over four-fifths.

The French achievement against other epidemic diseases was less spectacular. Massive inoculation campaigns were carried out against cholera which swept the country several times between 1900 and 1940. Constant measures against rats and widespread vaccination reduced the incidence of plague and cut down the death toll to a figure well below the 50 per cent which was the average amongst those afflicted in 1914. Relapsing fever which was on an epidemic scale at the start of the century was brought under control but other epidemic diseases such as amoebic dysentery and smallpox remained endemic. Other widespread diseases which were only partially curbed included hookworm, beri-beri, tuberculosis, leprosy and venereal diseases. As usual the infant mortality rate provides the best clue to the general standard of health in the country. The lowest figures were for Cochin-China which had the best medical services; they were higher in Annam and Tonkin where Western medicine had not permeated the countryside to such an extent. The rates for the big towns fell, but they were still well above those of other urban centres in South-East Asia.

However, in assessing French achievements in this field, one must bear in mind that when they started there was nothing in the way of modern medicine, hospitals or practitioners. The first Western hospital was the Cho Quang, opened at Saigon in 1864, but lack of doctors prevented the establishment of proper medical and health services up to 1914. In the following twenty-five years much was done. By 1935 there were over twenty-five general and more than seven specialist hospitals in Vietnam quite apart from the numerous dispensaries and lying-in wards scattered throughout the length and breadth of the country. In addition there were two Pasteur Institutes for medical research, one at Saigon and the other at Nha Trang (the latter being mainly veterinary) and vaccine institutes and public health laboratories at Hué and Hanoi. All this was under the control of the Inspector-general of Public Health for Indo-China who had under him provincial health officers and their staffs. There was no distinction in general between medical and health services and all treatment was free. By 1938 proper drainage, the introduction of modern sewage systems and pure piped water supplies reduced the dangers of overcrowded cities, particularly in the north, and made them healthier places to live in. But impressive as the French contribution was, it remained pitifully inadequate when compared with the magnitude of the problem.[76] The urban centres of population benefited most, the villages least. The overwhelming poverty of the great bulk of the people compounded the problem, to which may be added the effect on general health conditions of the three staple government monopolies, particularly that on salt. Even the fact that an increasing number of young Vietnamese were graduating as doctors themselves had not—prior to 1941—alleviated the situation. Too many of them put their personal fortunes first and preferred to go into private practice or even to retire to France than to serve in their own country.

Yet limited as it may have been, the French made their impact felt in medicine. Most other fields of social welfare, on the other hand, were sadly neglected or even adversely affected by official policies. The slow and belated progress in improving conditions of labour has already been noted. There was also entrenched opposition, especially from resident Europeans, to other measures of social welfare, despite which some progress was made by Roman Catholic missions with government subsidies in protecting the aged and the orphaned.[77]

In all, perhaps more than in any other territory in South-East Asia, colonial rule, despite all its technological achievements and the veneer of high Gallic civilization which it imparted to a small élite of upper-class Vietnamese, proved an expensive enterprise which deepened the poverty and misery of the common man.

[1]As far as rubber is concerned, production has been reckoned in terms of output for French Indo-China, as a whole, and therefore includes Cambodian production.

[2]Charles Robequain, *The Economic Development of French Indo-China*, Oxford University Press, London, 1944, p. 219.

[3]The bulk of the new rice land in the Trans-Bassac was taken up by well-to-do Vietnamese living in the towns and by some who were already professional moneylenders and speculators; other purchasers included Frenchmen and a handful of Indian chettyars.

[4]For details of French enterprise in rice-planting, see Robequain, op. cit., pp. 192–3.

[5]The peasants of Tonkin were in fact caught up in the same sort of process which Geertz, writing of the sugar provinces of Java, described as 'agricultural involution'. Water control was essential in the first instance in order to ensure the production of the crop on which survival depended and this could only be brought about by mass social co-operation; success not only ensured survival but also population growth, predicating in turn more intensive farming techniques and a still greater reliance on water control. When the French arrived on the scene, there was already plenty of evidence that the existing system was on the verge of breakdown as a consequence of mounting population pressures and the use of antiquated techniques.

[6]The co-operative land scheme of 1893 was launched by granting French colonists abandoned lands in the area which they then rented to Vietnamese sharecroppers whom they supplied with loans of buffaloes, food, tools, seed and manure. However in most cases the sharecroppers, having made full use of these advances, disappeared by returning to their former villages. The French landlords were at times to blame, behaving as demandingly as their traditional Vietnamese counterparts and requiring an exorbitant interest on their capital.

[7]i.e. traditional customers like China, Japan and the Netherlands Indies reduced their imports from Indo-China while France rose to become Vietnam's principal customer. In 1939 France was absorbing half the country's exports and could take in no more.

[8]The Institute was set up in the early 1930s and unified the administration of all experimental stations in French Indo-China.

[9]The most powerful group of rubber interests was the Société Financière des Caoutchoucs, whose progenitor was Hallet of oil palm fame. In 1935 four rubber companies joined together to form the mammoth Indo-Chinese Hevea Plantation Company with an initial capital of 29 million francs, a sum which doubled two years later when three more companies joined.

[10]Citizenship was restricted to native Frenchmen and to those who acquired it by naturalization; the latter concession was never extended to the Chinese who did not even participate as labourers in the rubber industry as French employers found Vietnamese workers both cheaper and easier to manage. Since the boards of rubber companies also had to have a majority of citizens on them, rival Western interests were also effectively excluded.

[11]This 'army' consisted of merchants and government officials from Saigon—clerks, pharmacists, architects, magistrates, registry officers, professors and others—attracted by the accessibility of the lands, the low overheads involved and the cheap labour readily available.

[12]Despite the activities of the Special Loan Fund Board, nearly half the total capital invested since 1924 was lost during the years of the Depression. The loans issued were secured by mortgages on estates and the capital raised by drafts on Indo-Chinese budget reserves. The Indemnification Fund was maintained by a special tax on French imports of raw and manufactured rubber, and the proceeds paid in the form of bonuses to colonial exporters, the sum being reduced in proportion to the rise in the price of rubber.

[13]This was because, in the first place, Indo-Chinese production fell short of French consumption so that the International Rubber Committee agreed that there should be no restriction on production up to 30,000 tons. When in 1936 this ceiling was reached, the Committee then recommended that Indo-China be allowed to increase its production to meet French demand. This meant doubling the maximum production limit, the new ceiling being reached in 1938.

[14]The Indo-Chinese piastre, like the Straits dollar, had its antecedents in the Mexican dollar which was in wide use in the ports of Vietnam prior to the French occupation. In 1885 the first French trade piastre was issued which became the official coinage of the country.

[15]See Robequain, op. cit., p. 163.

[16]Production from the Nam Patene tin-mines in Laos overtook Tonkinese output in the 1920s.

[17]The chief effect of the Russian Revolution was to shut off the profitable Russian market to the Japanese metallurgical industry, which was Tonkin's best customer. In general the world market in zinc was very sensitive to freight rates, tariffs and currency manipulations. The industry was probably saved from complete collapse as far as Vietnam is concerned by the development of flotation and electrolysis after 1926, techniques which made possible the working of lower grade ores.

[18]i.e. maize enjoyed a protected position on the French market but in fact was inferior in quality to the Rumanian and Argentinian varieties.

[19]i.e. the sugar fields were tilled by sharecroppers or smallholders, under contract to their local factory to supply the cane, in return for fertilizers and cash advances. They also formed the bulk of the labour used in the factory at harvest time.

[20]Other coconut products included oil, cordage, brushes and rugs made for domestic consumption in various Annamite villages.

[21]Market gardening tended to be a Chinese monopoly on the outskirts of the towns, while Vietnamese smallholdings below Dalat became an important source of fresh vegetables in Cochin-China.

[22]See Robequain, op. cit., p. 272.

[23]Before the French occupation, fish had ranked next to rice as Vietnam's leading export.

[24]Official statistics must be treated with caution. Based on the estimates and statements of local officials, they also suffer from the close relationship between the census and taxation. Robequain recommends an allowance of 10 per cent either way for error.

[25]For a detailed description of the organization of the Chinese rice business in Vietnam, see Victor Purcell, The Chinese in South-East Asia, Oxford University Press, London, 1965, pp. 196-7.

[26]For a French economist's viewpoint on the deleterious effects of Chinese enterprise in this field, see Purcell, op. cit., p. 202.

[27]The trend to Chinese domination in industry was accentuated in the late 1930s with the

influx of women from war-torn China who stimulated the spread of small workshops in the big towns.

[28]The only exception were the Hakka who had settled down as farmers and fishermen in the border uplands of Tonkin.

[29]See Robequain, op. cit., p. 37 for his assessment of the Chinese role.

[30]Ibid., p. 43.

[31]On a smaller scale, they dominated the export trade in Moi cinnamon, aided by Vietnamese middlemen, through Annamite ports. They also played a leading role in the exporting of fish and hides.

[32]See Purcell, op. cit., p. 137.

[33]They were entitled to freedom of movement and trade, could acquire property (save for mining land), tender for public contracts and held certain other legal rights.

[34]The origin of the 'congregations' of Cochin-China apparently lay in the traditional associations based on dialect and district found amongst the Chinese throughout the region. They were known as 'hueys' or 'kongsis' in the Straits, and 'bangs' in Annam where they were accorded civil rights and placed on par with the Vietnamese themselves by the court of Hué. The Emperor Minh-Mang extended this system to the south but placed the congregations under much stricter supervision. The French on taking over elaborated the system. As elsewhere the congregations, apart from the duties imposed upon them by the colonial administration, looked after the general interests of the local Chinese community, managing schools, temples, cemeteries, hospitals and the like.

[35]See Purcell, op. cit., p. 188.

[36]Ibid., p. 189.

[37]See M. Coughlin, 'Vietnam: in China's Shadow', *JSEAH*, VIII, 2, 1967, pp. 240–1.

[38]Ibid., p. 243.

[39]Amongst the 'assimiles', the most prominent were the Japanese.

[40]See Robequain, op. cit., p. 74.

[41]The Man, Miao and Lolo all originated from China Proper having moved, some time from the thirteenth century onwards, from their exhausted lands and the pressure of their Chinese neighbours. The Thais probably formed part of the general Thai movement southwards into the region around the same period, their further advance being blocked by the Vietnamese themselves. The Thais occupied the floor of large valleys, living as rice planters; above them in the hills at heights ranging from 1,000 feet to 3,000 feet were to be found the Man practising shifting cultivation of rice, maize, cotton and vegetables, while the Miao 'who appear unable to acclimatise themselves to heights much below 900 metres' cultivated rice on high mountain terraces, as well as maize, a wide variety of vegetables and raising livestock. Only the Lolo lived at any altitude, though most often were found side-by-side with the Thais.

[42]'Moi' is a Vietnamese term for 'savage'. The Moi people, properly speaking, are divided into many tribes and sub-tribes, amongst which the most important were the Kha Khatang, Kha Pakho and Boloven living in the hills north-north-west of Hué, the Roungrao, Jarai, Sedang and Bahnar in the centre and east, the Brae in the west and the Rade, Muong and Stieng in the south. One Moi tribe, the Churu, were heavily influenced by the Chams, living in the broad valleys south of the Djiring Plateau, in working irrigated rice fields. Most of the Moi tribes kept small granaries which were depleted by July, after which they resorted to hunting and collecting to stay alive until the next harvest three months later. Moi crafts included iron-mongery, weaving, basketry and pottery-making. They traded in jungle produce and, like their counterparts in inner Borneo, laid great significance on ritual jars and gongs.

[43]See Robequain, op. cit., p. 190.

[44]Quoted by Ellen J. Hammer, *The Struggle for Indo-China: 1940–1955*, Stanford University Press, 1966, p. 11.

[45]See Hammer, op. cit., p. 69; quoting Pierre Gourou, *Land Utilization in French Indo-China, 1940*.

[46]For more details and some telling quotes about rural poverty, see Erich H. Jacoby,

Agrarian Unrest in Southeast Asia, Asia Publishing House, Bombay, 1961, pp. 163–4.

[47]Ferry proclaimed that 'Colonial policy is the daughter of industrial policy...', a dictum which would have been most acceptable, if slightly unfamiliar with regard to industrialism, to Colbert, Louis XIV's brilliant minister of economic affairs in the latter half of the seventeenth century. It was Colbert who identified the promotion of trade and commerce with state enterprise, monopoly and protection, the hall-marks of mercantilism, and it was Colbert who bequeathed to France her first empire, subsequently lost through misunderstanding and neglect. See H.A.L. Fisher, 'The Ascension of France' in *A History of Europe*, esp. Book II, Chapter 20.

[48]See Jacoby, op. cit., p. 150.

[49]The French concept of empire as an extension of the body politic of France itself—'La France d'Outremer' (France Overseas)—was a consequence of the extension of French authority over the countries of the Maghrib (Morocco, Algeria and Tunisia) on the shores of the Mediterranean opposite to the homeland. French imperialism was also stimulated by the desire to redress the balance of power in Europe upset by the emergence of a united Germany at French expense in 1871.

[50]By the 1880s the British and the Americans had pre-empted the China market while in South-East Asia itself—apart from the lands of Indo-China—the field was dominated by Dutchmen, Britons and Germans. The desire to safeguard the primacy of French interests in Tonkin was a major factor behind the French forward movement into the area between 1882 and 1885, and two years after it was all over, Waddington, the foreign minister of the hour, was telling the French parliament that the industrial progress of France could only be secured by gaining a protected market for French goods.

[51]In order to support French home industries and to promote French industries newly established in Vietnam itself, special concessions, long granted to Chinese and Japanese imports (which catered specifically for the low purchasing power of the Vietnamese themselves), were swept away to the permanent loss of the people who could not afford the French substitutes.

[52]Dennis J. Duncanson, *Government and Revolution in Vietnam*, Oxford University Press, London, 1963, p. 133.

[53]The mandarins in question were usually appointed for this purpose by the emperor and were allowed to collect and hold the taxes during their lifetime. In this way, jungles were cleared, irrigation systems built and settlements formed behind the protection of bamboo pallisades.

[54]For detailed figures regarding land holdings and population densities in Tonkin, see Jacoby, op. cit., p. 158.

[55]For a detailed description of traditional village organization prior to French times, see J. Adams and N. Hancock, 'Land and Economy in Traditional Vietnam', *JSEAS*, I, 2, 1970.

[56]For details, see Hammer, op. cit., pp. 68–9.

[57]See Jacoby, op. cit., p. 163.

[58]Ibid., p. 162.

[59]Ibid., pp. 166–7.

[60]The sudden drop in world market prices brought about a corresponding reduction in the value of rice lands, which threatened creditors with ruin as the value of the mortgages they held was drastically cut down. Debtor landlords, on the other hand, could no longer afford to pay back their debts at the new local market rates for their crops and so faced eviction from their properties.

[61]For further details of the crisis and the fiscal measures taken at the time by the colonial administration, see Robequain, op. cit., pp. 175–6.

[62]See Robequain, op. cit., p. 189.

[63]Prior to 1875 the financing of Cochin-China's trade with South-East Asian ports was solely in the hands of British-owned banks.

[64]See Robequain, op. cit., p. 243.

[65]Quoted by Jacoby, op. cit., p. 154.

[66]For details about the development of modern industry in Vietnam, see Robequain, op. cit., Chapter VII.

[67]The costs of construction were a heavy burden on the people, for these had to be met by the government who had to ensure that taxes remained high and the burdensome official monopolies retained. An indication of the people's poverty is seen in the fall in rice consumption per head from 620 lb. a year in 1906 to 400 lb. a year in 1937.

[68]See Robequain, op. cit., p. 119.

[69]The fine natural harbour at Cam Ranh Bay was used by the Imperial Russian Fleet on its way to disaster in the Tsushima Straits in 1905 and, in the 1960s, was developed by the Americans as one of their main supply bases for the Vietnamese War. But during the French period strategic factors did not seem to justify its development.

[70]Even so the old ways lingered on amongst the Muong and other hill peoples of the Annamite Range, while in parts of Tonkin human porterage also survived as a compulsory service, though now subjected to strict legal safeguards.

[71]For detailed figures of Vietnamese labourers on the Red Land estates and their places of origin, see Robequain, op. cit., p. 214. An attempt to employ Javanese labour was not successful.

[72]The Vietnamese nationalists had an unlikely ally in the Tonkin Chamber of Commerce which also opposed contract labour, as it tended to create local labour shortage in the north and send up labour costs.

[73]The earliest labour legislation was introduced in the form of decrees in the three separate territories between 1896 and 1913. In 1910 the central government (i.e. in Hanoi) prepared a labour code for the whole of Indo-China, placing labour recruitment under the control of the local administration and setting up a supervisory and inspecting service. In 1918 the 1910 Code was replaced by more comprehensive regulations: the 1918 Decree remained the basis for all subsequent labour legislation.

[74]See Robequain, op. cit., p. 79.

[75]In the French general election of 1936 a coalition of left-wing parties, known as the Popular Front, emerged with a clear majority with a programme of radical social reform.

[76]However, evaluations differ. Contrast Duncanson (op. cit., p. 107) with the assessment of Hammer (op. cit., p. 68).

[77]Certain social evils were actively encouraged. The smoking of opium which was illegal in France was licensed in Indo-China and formed one of the financial props of the colonial administration. (But the official monopoly kept the price so high that it lay beyond the reach of the ordinary peasant and remained a vice of the well-to-do.) Other government monopolies bore down more directly on the population since they affected indispensable commodities such as salt. The revenue from these monopolies and other forms of indirect taxation accounted for 40 per cent of colonial receipts in 1936 and provided fertile ground for fraud, corruption and speculation, whilst adding considerably to the general cost of living.

Books and articles for further reading

BOOKS

Duncanson, D.J., *Government and Revolution in Vietnam*, Oxford University Press, London, 1968.

Fisher, C.A., *South-East Asia: A Social, Economic and Political Geography*, Methuen, London, 1964.

Hammer, E.J., *The Struggle for Indo-China: 1940–1955: Vietnam and the French Experience*, Stanford University Press, California, 1954.

Jacoby, E.H., *Agrarian Unrest in Southeast Asia*, Asia Publishing House, Bombay, 1961.

Lancaster, D., *The Emancipation of French Indo-China*, Oxford University Press, London, 1961.

Robequain, C., *The Economic Development of French Indo-China*, Oxford University Press, London, 1944.

Purcell, V., *The Chinese in South-East Asia*, Oxford University Press, London, 1965, 2nd. ed.

Steinberg, J. (ed.), *In Search of South-East Asia: A Modern History*, Oxford University Press, Kuala Lumpur, 1971.

ARTICLES

Adams, J., & Hancock, N., 'Land and Economy in Traditional Vietnam', *JSEAH*, I, 2, 1970.

Chan Hok-lam, 'Chinese Refugees in Annam and Champa at the end of the Sung Dynasty', *JSEAH*, II, 2, 1966.

Cotter, M.G., 'Towards a Social History of the Vietnamese Southward Movement', *JSEAH*, IX, 1, 1968.

Coughlin, M., 'Vietnam in China's Shadow', *JSEAH*, VI, 2, 1967.

B. Cambodia

'We have tried to give to the Khmer people a new stimulus to instil in them the self-confidence which they have lost, and to confer upon them that spirit of national solidarity and initiative which they lacked. We have not wished to be their masters...but, as the Cambodians say, their teachers and their guardians.'
Adhemar Leclere' (former French Resident in Cambodia), *A History of Cambodia*, Paris, 1914.

The limited impact of French rule on the economic and social development of Cambodia stands out in strong contrast to its impact on neighbouring Cochin-China and other parts of Vietnam. Having made the discovery that the Mekong River could never become a new highway of trade into China, the French evidently regarded Cambodia as an area of low economic opportunity and relegated its affairs to the enthusiasms of their amateur archaeologists and scholar-administrators. In consequence, while the cultural impress of France has been considerable, particularly amongst the traditional ruling class of the country, economically there was little change. The Cambodians remained a nation of peasant smallholders, and whatever development did take place under French rule was as a result of the country becoming an extension of the new French economic order centred on Saigon. As such Cambodia came to make its modest contribution to the world market as a producer of rice, rubber, maize and pepper, commodities which were almost entirely in alien hands. The role of France in Cambodia was somewhat analogous to that of Britain in northern Borneo; in each case the colonial power self-consciously strained to safeguard indigenous interests while at the same time facilitating the consolidation and expansion of alien forces within the country —in this instance, Vietnamese and Chinese. When Cambodia regained her independence in the 1950s the Khmer people found that they were still what they had been for centuries—'either rulers, priests or peasants'[1] and that the economic life of the country was by default, as it were, the prerogative of foreigners.

Maize, rice, rubber and pepper
Of the four major commercial crops prior to 1941 rice was the traditional mainstay of the country's economy and of its people's livelihood, although in fact in the 1930s it was superseded by maize, another traditional crop, as Cambodia's most valuable export. Rubber came third and represented the only area where Western (French) interests predominated, while much further down the scale in terms of export value but high in historical significance came pepper, which was virtually a Chinese monopoly.

Besides becoming the country's leading cash crop, maize also made Cambodia the leading producer in Indo-China. Maize came next to rice as the country's most common dry crop and was to be found everywhere grown in the traditional manner. Its conversion from a subsistence into a cash crop

30. General Map of Cambodia, 1941

was a direct consequence of French rule and provides yet another example of hothouse development under colonial auspices, since its rise was only possible by the French effort to create a specialized market inside metropolitan France itself. By the 1930s 90 per cent of all Indo-Chinese maize was being absorbed into this protected market, a development achieved and maintained despite the notoriously inferior quality of the Cambodian product, which resulted from the scant attention paid to the selection of grades for export.

If the rise of maize was founded on artificial conditions created within the nexus of French colonialism, the rice export trade had a far more substantial basis. It had been the staple of the economy of Angkor and before and was traditionally the country's most important export. It was also Cambodia's principal occupation, taking up 80 per cent of all cultivated land, engaging the energies of the bulk of the Khmer population, forming the basic element in their diet, and providing the most important source of industrial and commercial activity in terms of processing and marketing. In 1937 some two million acres were under padi, of which the largest concentration was in the triangle formed by the Mekong and Bassac rivers and the Tonlé Sap, a region of rich silt-laden soils subject to the annual inundations of the Mekong. The second largest rice region lay to the south near the Cochin-Chinese frontier, but the so-called Cambodian rice-bowl was in a smaller third area found in the west along the borders of the Tonlé Sap itself. It was from here, especially Battambang, that Cambodia's rice surpluses sent down to Saigon for milling and export came, a region of less dense settlement and with extensive tracts of cultivation which gave the highest yields.

However Khmer farming techniques were neither advanced nor efficient and the yields were well below the average for South-East Asia as a whole. Shifting cultivation which had predominated in Angkorian days had long given way to wet rice, but attempts at controlled irrigation were minimal, and only one crop a year could be grown. One-quarter of the rice-lands lay fallow—a condition ascribed to 'underpopulation and the minimum interest most Cambodians show about exerting themselves to get the maximum production from their land'.[2] In fact most Khmer farms were small family holdings of 10 acres apiece or less and their owners lived hidebound by a tradition which abhorred innovation and regarded the pursuit of wealth as ignoble. Environment did not pressure change; there was plenty of land for a limited population and the annual floods of nature disposed of the need for elaborate irrigation works. On top of this the rice earmarked for export was as a result of inefficient harvesting and collecting of markedly low quality.

Although rice growing was virtually a Khmer affair, the rice trade was a Chinese monopoly. Indeed the rice trade of Cambodia as it developed under French auspices was nothing more than an offshoot of that of neighbouring Cochin-China, and the principal Chinese rice firms of Phnom Penh before 1941 were agents for or subsidiaries of parent concerns established at Saigon-Cholon. The Chinese share was guaranteed by the fact that all Cambodian rice passed through Saigon for export and up till 1921 it was also milled exclusively there.

Rubber in Cambodia, like rice, represented an extension of the Cochin-China economy, in this case the expansion of French enterprise in the red lands. As elsewhere the high costs involved in development meant that rubber planting in Cambodia began as an essentially Western undertaking, and the manner of its evolution ensured that it continued that way. The first rubber estate in the country was started in 1921 on the Chup Plateau, but the Cambodian industry was confined to its 45 acres until the boom period of 1925-9 led to the opening up of the red lands in general. By 1927 the actual acreage under rubber had reached its peak and thereafter did not increase substantially at all. In 1941 there were about 80,000 acres under rubber, nine-tenths of which lay on the eastern side of the Mekong. Shortly after its establishment, rubber planting in Cambodia became caught up in the same vortex of forces which determined the general course of the industry throughout South-East Asia. The Great Depression prevented further expansion in planting; official protectionist measures saved the planters from collapse and the implementation of international agreements with their quota systems and price controls guaranteed recovery. In 1937 Cambodian rubber production stood at some 17,000 tons a year; its subsequent growth was not the result of extended acreage but of research, replanting and improved techniques.

Rubber gave France her most significant economic stake in Cambodia but it hardly affected the tenor of Khmer life. The plantations were situated in a desolate, underpopulated and remote part of the country, and the French, partly from circumstance and partly from design, preferred to rely on Vietnamese labour.[3] After the initial years the estates were well appointed and the living standards of those who lived on them, manager and labourer alike, were well above those of the rest of the country. Apart from the large French concessions only about 20 per cent of the total acreage under rubber was accounted for by smaller estates and holdings, many of which were run by Chinese, operating through Khmer 'straw men'.[4] Rubber smallholdings played no significant part in the economy of the indigenous peoples themselves.

Pepper likewise was a sphere in which the Khmer population took no part. Although wild pepper had been collected by Khmers since the days of Angkor, a nation of peasants, they had never had the resources to develop the crop on a proper commercial basis. The commercial production of pepper is primarily associated with the Chinese colony established at Ha Tien in the eighteenth century, which as it faded as a centre for commerce turned to pepper cultivation instead. The date of the earliest pepper plantations is not known but the industry was well established by the time the French appeared on the scene. The tending of the pepper vine is an elaborate and delicate affair but the Chinese skill as cultivators enabled them to completely dominate the industry even after French power was established.

Nevertheless the French provided a valuable stimulus to the pepper industry. The original market for Cambodian pepper was China but towards the end of the nineteenth century a new market started to open in France, encouraged by the lowering of French import tariffs in 1891-2. In 1892 itself, pepper exports amounted to a mere 500 tons; by the end of the century they had risen to 2,000 tons a year and more than trebled again within the next decade, by which time Cambodia had become the world's second largest producer. But world market prices were kept constantly low by the competition from British Borneo and the Netherlands Indies, and despite the country's leading position as a pepper producer, pepper's export value never exceeded more than 10 per cent of Indo-China's exports as a whole. Furthermore it became necessary to support the industry by granting special tariff protection on the French home market. By the 1930s Cambodia's pepper exports were averaging 4,000 tons a year of which about three-quarters were absorbed by France.[5]

The cultivation of pepper remained concentrated within the area of its origin; and was responsible for the rise of Kampot from an obscure Khmer fishing village to the country's chief pepper port. Pepper served as the mainstay for the original nucleus of Chinese settlers in Cambodia. The labour on the pepper estates remained exclusively Chinese throughout.

Other agricultural products

Like its neighbours Cambodia abounded with a wide range of other crops,[6] but very few of them were tried out for commercial development; in general they were cultivated on a family basis, catering for local needs and occasionally supplementing local incomes. The Chinese developed some market-gardening around Phnom Penh and other towns. The French made one ill-starred attempt to establish a large cotton plantation in the red lands of Kompong Cham in 1919, but the high overheads of opening up unirrigated and underpopulated soils ended the venture within a year with an almost total loss and destroyed all Western interest in this direction. Locally produced cotton was grown in a small area on the banks of the Mekong but its prospects were ever bleak, as apart from a short season and poor quality it also fetched low prices on the market by comparison with other cash crops. Nevertheless on the eve of the Pacific War, Cambodia was producing some 1,500 tons a year.

The cultivation of the mulberry and the rearing of silk worms was also done by a number of villages to supplement their incomes and the product was exported in its raw form. Kapok cultivation, according to Robequain,[7] 'is growing in Cochin-China and Cambodia and is even meeting with favour among European colonists', and in the 1930s there was a general increase in production. But as was the usual case, Cambodian production was limited, its preparation crude and its quality low. Its chief use was for the making of gunny sacks. Ramie, jute, hemp, and Malacca cane were also produced in small quantities for the making of rope, bags and nets. There were about 2,400 acres under sugar-cane in the country but the demand was as low as the yield, so that there was little stimulus to improve techniques. Even so local output was insufficient to meet local demand. Some tobacco was grown in the province of Kompong Cham and catered for a growing local market. The Chinese found a variety of uses for the *kachang* plant and attempts were made at starting tea plantations.

From all this, however, it is clear that the other agricultural products of Cambodia were of little significance to the country's economy except for the role they played in maintaining the self-sufficiency of the village.

Fisheries, livestock and forests

Amongst the greatest of Cambodia's natural resources are her waters which teem with fishes, her ample pasture lands which can support large herds of cattle and her forests which cover over half the country. Before the Pacific War Cambodia provided the bulk of Indo-China's fish exports, and was the main centre for cattle breeding and livestock in the Union.

Cambodia's greatest asset was the Tonlé Sap, whose annual ebb and flow over flooded forest land provided its fish with a richer diet than anywhere else in the world. The yield of the Tonlé Sap together with that of freshwater fish from other streams and of the sea fish off the coast 'valued for their great size and weight' gave the fishing industry a very important place in the subsistence economy of the country. As a means of livelihood fishing came next to rice cultivation and nearly every Khmer was at least a part-time fisherman. But the value of fish as an export was low. In the mid-nineteenth century the export of fresh and dried fish was the mainstay of the country's economy, but although a hundred years later Cambodia was still Indo-China's chief fish exporter, these only accounted for $2\frac{1}{2}$ per cent of total export value. As such it was not an industry to excite Western capital, and the French were content to let fishing remain a Chinese monopoly, as it had been before they came. Before French rule, fishing revenues were farmed out by the Khmer ruler to the highest bidders who were invariably Chinese so that the trade was firmly under their control. The French perpetuated this system, merely changign its form, leasing out the fisheries by public auction every four years. The leases were keenly contested by the Chinese and Sino-Cambodians.

Most of the fish exported from Cambodia was dried, mainly for the Singapore and Malayan markets. Average overseas shipments nearly doubled between 1900 and 1941. The predominance of dried fish as a commodity, even within the country, was the result of poor communications. The entrance to the Tonlé Sap was hampered by the silt-banks at Snoc Trou, so that the great flat-bottomed barges in which the fish were transported had to be pushed over the mud to reach the river of Tonlé Sap itself which carried them downstream to Phnom Penh. This meant that the entire Tonlé Sap catch had to be smoked or dried before export. Important by-products also came from the fish, such as fish-oil from offal, fish paste and sauce, and fish meal which was often used as a fertilizer.

By the 1930s there was increasing evidence that the waters of the Tonlé Sap were becoming over-exploited, as reflected by a fall in the catch and a decline in production. To counteract this, the Institut Océanographique set up observation posts around the lake but the need for closer controls and restrictions was obvious.

With its ample land reserves and dry climate, Cambodia also became the chief cattle-raising country of French Indo-China. The most suitable pastures were to be found on the fringes of the rice lands close to the Mekong and its tributaries and the Tonlé Sap. There were also settled jungle clearings where cattle pastured around the village, while in the remoter jungle areas buffaloes were left free to roam as they willed. But despite these advantageous conditions full use was not made of them. Only a fraction of the livestock of the country was exported. Most animals were used simply as beasts of transport or for drawing the plough. Scant heed was paid to improving or increasing stock and out of carelessness and indifference herds of cattle were allowed to be ravaged by epizootic diseases or even allowed to die for want of sufficient food and water. Livestock breeding for commercial purposes was a virtual monopoly of Muslim Cambodians—Chams and Malays.

The sudden rise of the Philippines market at the beginning of the twentieth century briefly spurred the rise of a brisk export trade in Cambodian cattle. By 1910 cattle exports had reached a peak of 40,000 a year, but then the Philippines market collapsed and after 1911 cattle exports fluctuated in tune with the variable Philippines tariff, while the alternative markets of Singapore and Hong Kong proved poor substitutes. Exports of raw hides proved more constant in terms of value; dressed hide exports on the other hand steadily declined as local industry grew.[8]

Cambodia was the possessor of large tracts of forest land which provided one-third of the constructional timber and formed the second largest total forest reserves in French Indo-China. But this great natural asset was both neglected and abused. Much of the forest land is inaccessible and although the forestry service of the Union set aside large reserves and passed strict regulations against reckless methods of exploitation, these had little effect as they went largely unheeded. Prior to 1941 several tree species were nearing extinction as the result of inadequate supervision and care. A parallel negligence undercut the value of forest exports. Marketing problems arose in particular for want of standardization.

The chief exploiters of the jungle and its products were the Chinese. Since pre-colonial times they had been the principal concessionaires, and they continued to hold their predominant position in the industry. The Chinese also monopolized the saw-milling industry which had considerable local importance. Elephants were often used for hauling the timber to river or road heads, and the Mekong, the Tonlé Sap and other rivers formed the highways along which the timber rafts were floated down to Phnom Penh and eventually Saigon. In the last days of French power, however, the great potential of Cambodia's forests still awaited development.

Mineral resources and mining
Cambodia's greatest economic deficiency was in the paucity of her mineral deposits. It is true that a proper and adequate survey of these resources has never been undertaken, but of the wide range of minerals found in the country none appears to exist in sufficient quantity to justify large-scale investment and exploitation. Cambodia was touched by the wild fever for prospecting which swept the other states of French Indo-China in the 1920s but apart from confirming the presence of minerals already known, this led to no substantial result. The most significant and promising deposits are the iron ore

veins found at the hill of Phnom Dek, north of Kompong Thom. These have been worked for generations by the Kouy who manufacture tools from it which have a high reputation amongst the Khmer. Plans were drawn up in the 1930s to start mining this iron on a commercial scale, a total production of some 60,000 tons a year being anticipated. But there were serious problems of transportation and by 1941 the scheme had been dropped, never to be seriously reconsidered by the French again. Sapphires and other precious stones were mined at two centres, one at Pailin south of Battambang near the Thai frontier, and the other at Bokeo in the province of Stung Treng. The Pailin mines were apparently flourishing in 1900 when the district was still under Thai sovereignty with a local population of 10,000, but production subsequently declined. However, the most constant source of mineral wealth probably came from the phosphate mines of Battambang and Kampot. A phosphate processing plant was built at Battambang itself and produced a small quantity of fertilizers. There was some salt of mediocre quality manufactured by the evaporization process and some marble and quartz mining.

Mining labour was provided mainly by Burmese and Thai who worked the mines of Bokeo and Pailin and by the Kouy who worked the Battambang iron-mines. The Chinese by law were excluded from all mining enterprise.

The nature of French policy

When the French took over Cambodia in the early 1860s, they were stimulated by the belief that they were gaining control of another back-door route into China as well as securing the approaches to their new colony of Cochin-China. The illusion of the new Chinese back-door was speedily dispelled by the Lagrée-Garnier expedition of 1866-7 up the Mekong which demonstrated the unnavigability of that great river, and by the time fifteen years later that the French had consolidated their hold over the country, they had reconciled themselves to the fact that whatever her past glories may have been, Cambodia was in the last quarter of the nineteenth century a land of very limited economic opportunity. Her strategic importance, however, remained and it was this that caused France to render what was probably her greatest service to the Khmer by saving them from permanent partition and eventual extinction at the hands of the Thais and the Vietnamese. At the same time, in a manner reminiscent of British policy towards the Peninsular Malay States, the French persisted with the contradictory attempt at welding the Khmer nation into a union with the other states of Indo-China, thereby opening the country to Vietnamese (and Chinese) penetration and economic domination. Any economic development which took place under French rule was directly linked to the expansion of commercial and business interests in Cochin-China, while the growth of modern communications was related to the French design for the whole of the Indo-Chinese Union. Above all, the peaceful establishment of sizeable and influential Vietnamese and Chinese minorities inside the country was a direct consequence of this French policy.

The development of communications

The introduction of the railway to Cambodia was part of Governor-general

Paul Doumer's grand scheme to link Tonkin with Cochin-China, and Cochin-China with Thailand. In the end, plans to complete the link between Saigon and Phnom Penh were shelved indefinitely in view of the great expense involved in traversing the network of canals and riverways that make up the Delta, and of the severe competition offered by boat and later by road transport. However when the first railway line was built in Cambodia itself, joining Phnom Penh with Mongkolbourey to the west, its ownership and control were vested in the Indo-Chinese State Railways. This line, covering 205 miles and completed in 1935, was built to overcome the problem of transporting rice and fish from the region of the Tonlé Sap during the dry season and to meet the French fear that Cambodian trade might be drawn overland to Bangkok rather than downstream to Saigon. Nevertheless the line had been extended to the Thai frontier by 1941, which gave Cambodia 236 miles of railway track. Financially the new railway paid off. It was constantly in use for the carrying of freight to and from the Thai border and it experienced a boom every rice harvest in Battambang.

The trunk road system of the country was likewise developed as part of the grand design for Indo-China as a whole. Colonial Highway One was continued west from Saigon to cross the Plain of Junks and enter Cambodia via Soairieng (Sveyrieng) and lead straight to Phnom Penh. From Phnom Penh it then went westwards splitting into two branches, the straighter and faster route going north of the Tonlé Sap while the other branch passed south to tap the Battambang rice-bowl. Both routes rejoined at Sisophon and continued as a poorly metalled track right up to the Thai border. Another Colonial Highway (Twenty-two) crossed the border with Cochin-China further north and to the south roads linked Cambodia with Cochin-China near Ha Tien and Chau Dek, while another main route within the borders of Cambodia itself linked Kampot to Highway One. In the 1930s an important extension of the Cambodian road system was built northwards over the Laotian border from Kratié along the eastern bank of the Mekong.[9] Besides these trunk highways there were a number of other roads of varying standards, making a grand total of 3,389 miles in 1939. The only road which bore heavy traffic was Colonial Highway One which supplemented the waterways with the freight brought by rail from the west. As was the case with the rest of French Indo-China, there was very little road development prior to 1914. In 1910 there were reportedly only 750 miles of metalled roads in the entire country. Most of the building took place in the 1920s and 1930s. Almost half the total metalled highway was done between 1927 and 1940 and the construction of the Monivong Bridge across the Bassac at Phnom Penh was completed within this period.

As befitted an economic backwater, Cambodia was left far behind in the application of more sophisticated forms of communication. The telegraph and telephone came first, following on their introduction and extension throughout Cochin-China. A direct telephone link existed between Phnom Penh and Saigon before 1941 and Saigon also served as Cambodia's sole channel for radio-telephonic communication with the outside world. The country was similarly lacking in air communications. Only Phnom Penh and Siem-reap had proper airfields before the Pacific War and neither was fully equipped. There were, however, a number of landing grounds or airstrips.

Hence up to 1941 waterways still held their traditional place as the main and most important arteries of communication in the country. The great Mekong and its many branches formed the highways along which the bulk of the rice and other exports were conveyed to Saigon-Cholon, the Mekong itself bearing 'a lively navigation' as far upstream as Kompong Cham, while smaller vessels could make their way for good stretches beyond. The heavy river traffic of Cambodia was all but monopolized by the Compagnie Saigonnaise de Navigation, whose antecedents dated back to 1890. Phnom Penh itself, superbly placed at the junction of four rivers, primarily owed its existence to the Mekong and could handle (in the rainy season) small ocean-going vessels of up to 8,000 tons.

Population and its distribution

In fact in 1936 Phnom Penh was by far the largest of the three Cambodian towns which could boast a population of 10,000 or more. Its establishment as the country's principal port followed its selection as capital in 1434 which also marked the beginnings of Cambodia's dependence on world trade. Phnom Penh remained the largest urban centre in the country up to the time of French rule. According to a Portuguese account, in the early seventeenth century Phnom Penh's population numbered 20,000, although Mouhot reported in 1859 that it was only half that amount. By 1936 the capital had over 103,000 inhabitants. The second largest town before 1941 was Battambang, although less than one-fifth of the size of Phnom Penh. Battambang was the centre of the richest rice province of the country and had expanded rapidly since its transfer from Thai hands in 1907. Close to Battambang came Pursat, another market town with a population in 1936 of roughly the same number. In other words Cambodia's population was overwhelmingly rural, which was underlined by the fact that 80 per cent of the people were engaged in agriculture.

Cambodia stood out in great contrast to her neighbour, Cochin-China, in the low density of her population. Over three-quarters of her land was cultivable but much of it had not been brought under cultivation. On the eve of the Pacific War the mean density of population stood at 42 persons per square mile, although the mean density of different areas ranged from 12 to 175 per square mile. So while the overall average was low, the population tended to be concentrated within certain districts. It was estimated that about four-fifths of the people lived within about one-third of the total area. The greatest concentration was to be found along the banks of the Mekong from the Co-chin-China border northwards as far as Kompong Cham and Kompong Chnang while another thick belt of people lived in the extreme south along the line of the Ha Tien-Chau Doc canal. A much less densely populated belt went thinly around the Tonlé Sap, while the rest of the country—the Cardomon Mountains and the Elephant Range, the narrow coastal belt between

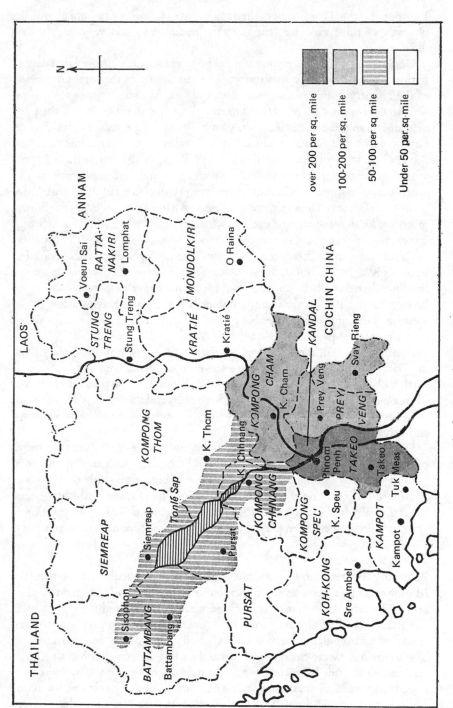

31. Cambodia: Population Distribution, 1935

over 200 per sq. mile

100-200 per sq. mile

50-100 per sq mile

Under 50 per sq mile

Kampot and the Thai frontier, the jungle and savannah of the north and the plateaux of the Annamite Range to the north-east—was very largely desolate.

Under French rule there were not any appreciable shifts in population distribution and only slow population growth. In the 1930s the total population of the country numbered around three million. Accurate figures are impossible to obtain since up to 1941 no thorough or systematic census of the population had ever been carried out. Cambodia was a protectorate of France, not a colony, and of marginal economic importance. A census of sorts had been held in 1921 which counted nearly 2½ million inhabitants and in 1937 provincial governors had been required to submit rough and ready estimates of the numbers of foreigners in their respective provinces. As in the rest of Indo-China, the French estimates were not based on a head-count but on the figures given by local authorities to each provincial centre, as a result of which observers regard a 10 per cent margin of error probable. In these circumstances any reckoning of population growth must be highly speculative. Following figures given by Willmott, the total number of inhabitants would appear to have nearly trebled between 1899 and 1940, although this increase was partly brought about by fortuitous circumstances such as the reacquisition of the western provinces of Battambang and Siemreap in 1907, which added another 250,000 people to the whole.

As already noted, the great bulk of the working population was involved in agriculture, most of whom were self-employed smallholders, although a small and distinctive minority made up the labour force on the French rubber estates and Chinese pepper plantations in the east and the south. Various forms of industry absorbed the rest and a small minority made up the professional and governing classes.

Ethnically, the Khmer easily predominated, forming well over two-thirds of the total population. The Vietnamese and Chinese who made up the great majority of the immigrant races constituted about one-tenth of the total, while the rest comprised other indigenous groups. In line with the general pattern established by colonial rule throughout South-East Asia the immigrant minorities, however, played the key role in the economy of the country.

The Vietnamese

Politically castrated but preserved under the protection of France, the Khmer retained a keen sense of their national identity and resented this alien presence, particularly that of the Vietnamese who, although mostly farmers and fishermen, had also managed 'to squeeze into the empty occupational cracks of Cambodian society as clerks, small shop-keepers and factotums'.[10] The Vietnamese were clearly regarded as the most dangerous threat to Khmer survival, an attitude burned deep into the national consciousness by more than three centuries of Vietnamese pressure and penetration. The earliest Vietnamese settlers in the Mekong Delta who came as padi-planting soldiers were easily able to take advantage of the sparse population and of the absence of any defined frontiers to extend their colonies upstream towards Phnom Penh. By the beginning of the nineteenth century, the riverine provinces of

Cambodia had become heavily infiltrated while around the shores of the Tonlé Sap a sizeable community of Vietnamese fishermen also sprang up. Insult was added to injury by the way in which the immigrants tended to displace rather than to assimilate with the local Khmer population.[11] Under the French this process was deliberately accelerated. After 1875 they came 'in a steady stream', occupying the more fertile lands along the Mekong. The French apparently seeing the Khmer as an indolent, easy-going peasant race whose identity for political convenience could be preserved but who could not be expected to be trained for the chores of running a colony, turned to the Vietnamese to supply the clerks and petty officials needed by the new administration, and encouraged the entry of Vietnamese carpenters, mechanics, and plumbers. Vietnamese immigration received a new fillip with the opening up of the rubber estates in the east of the country in the mid-1920s. By 1940 when all legal immigration came to a halt, the Vietnamese had grown to about 5 per cent of the total population, having increased by over a third since the beginning of the century.

By this time the Vietnamese population in Cambodia fell into four distinct groups, the most substantial of which were the farmers who now not only dominated the rice-lands of Prey Veng and Soairieng, but were also in considerable strength in neighbouring Kandal and Takeo. The fishermen, a second group whose origins in Cambodia preceded those of the French, formed the majority of the commercial fishermen around the Tonlé Sap, a position which they had maintained since the nineteenth century, although the trade itself was in Chinese hands. The third group was made up of the Vietnamese who lived in the towns and formed an entity quite apart from the rest of their countrymen. Most of them were French educated and Roman Catholic, many of them holding white-collar jobs or professional posts, although there were a considerable number of artisans amongst them.[12] The fourth group belonged to the great rubber plantations where they formed about four-fifths of the total labour force.

Despite the concentrated patches which characterized Vietnamese settlement in Cambodia, nowhere did they form a clear-cut majority, but along with the Chinese held a dominating position in trade and industry and constituted (with the Chinese again) the middle-class of the country. Their presence was alarming to the Khmer because of their high birth-rate and the fact that under the French dispensation they were placed legally on the same footing as the Khmer themselves.[13] To all intents and purposes they were regarded by the French as indigenous to Cambodia, with the same rights and privileges as the indigenous inhabitants of the country.

The Chinese and their role

If the national bogey-man of the Khmer was the Vietnamese immigrant, he should have been at least as much concerned about the Chinese who were settled in even greater numbers and had in fact a far more substantial grip on the economy of the country. However, for a variety of reasons, the Chinese were accepted, tolerated and even liked. In the first place China was held in high prestige by the average Khmer, as the fount of civilization. The Chi-

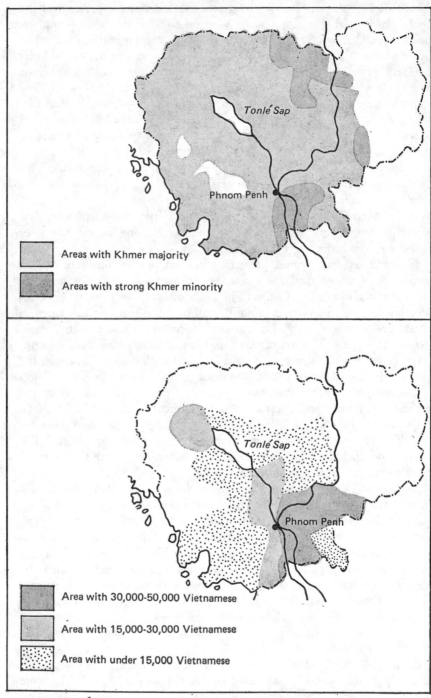

32.   (A) Khmer Distribution   (B) Vietnamese Distribution

nese were also quick to identify with the Khmer population, as reflected by the frequency of intermarriage between the two races and by the growth of a sizeable number of Sino-Cambodians. On top of all this came the cool relations between French officialdom and the Chinese community in Cambodia. The wealthy Chinese in the country had enjoyed close and profitable connexions with the court of Phnom Penh and resented the French intrusion which gave them a common bond with the Khmer themselves, and which was strengthened all the more by their shared distaste for the partiality the French administration showed to Vietnamese immigrants.[14]

Owing to the vagaries of French methods of census-taking, it is difficult to be precise about the actual number of Chinese settled in Cambodia before the Pacific War. According to the 1921 census there were some 91,000 of them in the country, representing about 6 per cent of the total population. In the late 1930s in general about one-third of all the Chinese in French Indo-China were to be found in Cambodia.

To a large extent the Chinese presence in Cambodia was an overspill from Cochin-China, facilitated by easy communications between the two regions and the complete indifference of the Khmer themselves to commerce. The general expansion of trade and business under the French after 1875 accentuated the trend but Chinese commercial links with Cambodia stretched far back into the past. The earliest evidence dates back to the first century B.C., and there is firm witness to Chinese trade with the proto-Khmer empire of Fu Nan. However, it is clear that the beginnings of a permanent Chinese community in Cambodia belong to the middle of the fifteenth century when the Khmer court started to establish links with the world market. From its earliest days Phnom Penh saw foreign merchants settling there, amongst whom the Chinese were by all accounts preponderant. A second great impulse to Chinese settlement in Cambodia came with the collapse of Ming power in China which led to the establishment in the early 1670s of a Cantonese colony in the Mekong Delta, followed a few years later by an influx of Hailam colonists who settled on the coastline of Kampot and southwards, led by the legendary Mac Cuu. His headquarters at Ha Tien grew into a great trading centre and when he died in 1735 it had already become Cambodia's main seaport.[15] Ha Tien held this position and served as the capital for the principality of the same name under the Mac family for the rest of the century, flourishing until its eclipse by Cholon and the advent of the clipper and steamship. The third phase in Chinese immigration and settlement came with the French themselves in the second half of the nineteenth century. The Chinese were the full beneficiaries of the slow but solid expansion in trade and other economic activities brought about by French administration. In 1886 they represented about 3 per cent of the total population. By 1921 the percentage was almost double and within the next decade, stimulated by the opening up of new lands, the building of roads, the new railway and the general growth of trade, it rose again by another 50 per cent, which was the largest total increase for any one community in all French Indo-China.

This expansion took place despite the vagaries of French policy towards Chinese immigration into the country, which affected Cambodia as much as other parts of the Union. For the first half of the 1870s and again within the first few years of the new century, Chinese immigrants were exempted from the usual taxes imposed upon them. But from 1907 onwards they were subjected to a special impost which would have effectively prevented all further immigration had not the Chinese 'bang' come to the rescue by developing a loan-credit system. In the event immigration continued, but the restrictions and limitations upon Chinese entry were amongst the subjects of the Franco-Chinese negotiations which culminated in the Nanking Treaty of 1930. Thai measures in closing their eastern provinces to Chinese settlement in 1941 caused an influx of Chinese overland across the Thai-Cambodian border, but with the outbreak of the Pacific War and the subsequent Japanese Occupation at the end of the same year, all Chinese immigration came to an abrupt halt.

Prior to 1941 the sex ratio amongst the Chinese in Cambodia was unbalanced, although not to the same degree as in British Malaya and other lands which used a high proportion of Chinese labour. As elsewhere there was a distinct trend towards normalization and permanency in the 1920s and 1930s.

The Chinese held a key position in the Cambodian economy. They dominated finance and credit, the internal trade of the country, both wholesale and retail; they monopolized the coastal fishing trade virtually by default and in the only sphere of agriculture in which they had shown interest or been given a chance to participate, namely pepper, they were the sole producers. On the other hand there were very few Chinese contract labourers in the country—the figure probably never amounted to more than 15,000 throughout the French period. By virtue of their position, the Chinese community also had a substantial financial stake in the economy. The size of their investments came next to that of the French and their financial and credit operations were widespread.

The origins of this predominance lay in Cambodia's proximity to Cochin-China which even before French days was starting to make the territory upstream its economic hinterland. Apart from the pepper enterprise in Kampot, the Chinese penetration of Cambodia proper was through the rice trade and, typically, the main agent of that penetration was the ubiquitous village shop-keeper. There was scarcely a village without its shop and there was scarcely a shop whose owner was not Chinese. He fulfilled the same role of middleman and moneylender, as his countrymen throughout South-East Asia, genially exploiting the Khmer peasantry year in and year out.[16] He was likewise at the end of the long chain of credit and exchange which linked the peasant with the world market. In other fields, the Chinese preponderated in fishing, market-gardening and manufacturing. Under the Khmer kings they were the traditional holders of the fish farm and under the French they and the Sino-Cambodians were the sole contenders for the periodical auctions of fishing rights. In the development of vegetable gardening as a cash-crop industry around the towns and markets of Cambodia, the Chinese emerged as monopolists, and such industry as evolved in the country prior to 1941 was either in Chinese or Vietnamese hands.

Chinese participation in industry was merely an extension of their hold over certain staples of commerce. They owned the handful of rice mills, the sawmills scattered throughout the countryside, and were the manufacturers of soft drinks, ice and soya sauce. Their enterprises were invariably small-scale family affairs, often indistinguishable from purely commercial firms since they did their own retailing as well. After 1930 the Chinese also moved into banking.

Despite the concentration of Chinese interest and activity in trade and commerce, a large proportion of Chinese settlers in Cambodia were country-dwellers. Over 40 per cent lived outside the towns, not, as we have seen, as farmers (except in Kampot) but as itinerant vendors and village shop-keepers. There was as marked a distinction between the urban and rural Chinese as there was between the urban and rural Vietnamese in the country. Broadly speaking, like their Vietnamese counterparts, the rural Chinese were poorer, quicker to assimilate and of different background to the Chinese of the towns. They were nearly all Teochew, whereas Cantonese and other speech groups tended to preponderate in the urban areas. In contrast to the Vietnamese, however, the urban Chinese represented the group of longest standing in the country. Probably the oldest Chinese settlers were those of the Cantonese colony at Phnom Penh itself. In fact the Cantonese were the predominant Chinese community in Cambodia up till the coming of the French, and continued to maintain that position under the new regime as a result of their close links with Saigon. The Great Depression, however, destroyed their power and from that date they took second place to the Teochew.

The other three main speech groups formed a mere fraction of the whole. The Hainanese held third place, essentially identified with Kampot and pepper which had once been their exclusive preserve. The Hakka and the Hokkien formed two small groups of about equal strength. The Hokkien connexion went back a long way and they counted amongst them some of the richest families in Cambodia. They were predominantly urban. The Hakka on the other hand were closely associated with the Teochew influx from Swatow. Like the Teochew they were to be found mostly in the rural areas as vegetable farmers, rubber smallholders and shop-keepers. Apart from this, there was also a very small group of northern Chinese in the country, accounting for no more than one thousand. They were all urban dwellers and mainly professional men.

The Sino-Cambodians formed a peculiar group of their own. They were in an anomalous position, so that it is difficult to distinguish them as a separate community or to know when they have or have not been added to the total figures for the Chinese. However, the 1921 census established that there were at least 68,000 belonging to this group, a figure well over two-thirds that of the pure Chinese in the country. Most of the Sino-Cambodians were farmers, emphasizing the fact that the rural Chinese amongst whom the sexual imbalance was greater were more prone to intermarriage with the Khmer. There were those who, like James Brooke in Sarawak, enthused greatly over the potential of 'this new race' but in fact, although the French created a special division for the Sino-Cambodians when they extended the congregation system to Cambodia in 1891, this did not last and the subsequent treatment of the Chinese as a distinct and alien entity in the country forced the Sino-Cambodians to identify with one group or the other. In the days of Khmer rule, Sino-Cambodians born in the country and conforming to Khmer custom had been regarded as Khmers. However, as French policy evolved, the position of the Chinese and the status of mixed offspring became more rigorously defined. The adoption of the congregation system in 1891 marked the establishment of the basic means of controlling the position of the Chinese community as a whole.[17] The position was tightened under the new Civil Code of 1920 which stated that all Sino-Cambodians were to be regarded as Chinese unless their parentage was three-quarters Khmer, while the revised Code of 1934 abolished their right to opt for Cambodian nationality but made this status open to those one of whose parents was Khmer.

As for the pure Chinese, although designated as 'foreigners' in Cambodia under successive French laws, their position still remained ambiguous in certain respects, mainly because of their preponderant economic stake in the country. Under the Khmer kings they had been the traditional holders of the royal tax farms in revenue, gambling and lotteries, opium, alcohol, fishing, and so forth, which gave them an indisputable voice in the country's affairs. With the coming of the French, things were not much different. The revenue farm disappeared into the arms of the French administration with the financial reforms of 1884 but all the other farms survived, emerging in new guise as leases, government monopolies and the like. In any case they still remained in Chinese hands and although the Chinese were subjected to property restrictions which prevented their participation in mining or in the opening up of rubber estates, they were allowed to engage in other activities including teaching, printing and hotel-keeping, all of which were denied to other aliens.

In fact, the French were still aware, despite their distaste for Chinese commercial cunning and competition, that they formed a 'most precious leaven' in the colonial cake. It was difficult in practice to treat the Chinese simply as 'foreigners', even though they were classified as such and from time to time subjected to discriminatory acts against them. The application of the congregation system to Cambodia by the royal decree of 1891 was one such blow, destroying the special position which the Chinese had built up for themselves under the Khmer kings. The alien status of the Chinese under the French protectorate was confirmed by a decree of May 1898, which made them subject to all the laws which had been applied to their compatriots in Cochin-China. Official alarm over the spread of Chinese landholdings resulted in the decree of 31 October 1924, restricting ownership of freehold urban property to French citizens, subjects or protégés, which in 1929 was extended to rural holdings as well. Subsequent legislation making all children born in French Indo-China French subjects, passed in 1933, was apparently not made applicable to the Chinese in Cambodia, although in 1940 detailed procedures on how to acquire Cambodian nationality were laid down. But perhaps all this did not matter, since a steady trickle of Chinese found a way of 'disappearing' from the rolls of their congregations and becoming merged into Khmer society.

The Chinese did not accept the various discriminatory moves against them without protest. Their opposition to the congregation system was vocal and prolonged. The legality of the restrictions on landownership was contested in the courts of France itself, while the whole issue of the status of Chinese nationals in French colonial territory was taken up at the highest diplomatic levels in the negotiations which led to the Franco-Chinese Convention of 1930. But nothing substantial was achieved, which was to some degree a reflection of the purposes of the new nationalist (KMT) regime in Peking as well as that of the French themselves.

Other aliens in Cambodia

Apart from the Chinese, the Vietnamese and the French—the lattermost exerting an influence out of all proportion to their numbers—other foreign minorities played a very small role in Cambodian life. The French, of course, occupied the key administrative posts in government and were prominent, if scarce, as business executives, plantation owners and managers and as military personnel. They formed by far the greatest number of Europeans in the country. There was also a small but interesting Eurasian population, part of which was of Portuguese and Filipino origin, retaining few physical traces of European blood but holding important posts in the civil service, while the rest sprang from the French connexion, likewise to be found in the administration or in other white-collar occupations. The only significant alien minority was made up of Indians, most of whom owed their presence in Cambodia as French subjects from the French settlements in India. According to the 1921 census there were some 6,000 of them in the country at that time. Most of the Indians were to be found in Phnom Penh where they plied their traditional trades as cloth merchants and moneylenders; those who were not French subjects were controlled through the congregation system.[18] There were two Burman settlements in the country, one at Pailin near the Thai border and the other at Bokeo in the north—both connected with the mining and trading of precious stones. Twenty thousand Thai and Lao farmers were to be found in parts of Battambang and Siemreap provinces, the vestiges of the Thai occupation of these areas.

The Khmer and other indigenous peoples

If it was the French intention to preserve the Cambodian way of life and, in the manner of the British 'pro-Malay' policy in the Malay Peninsula and Borneo, to shield them against the inroads and evil effects of modern industrial civilization, then they were remarkably successful. For the people of the country remained not perceptibly different in the way they lived from what they had been before the French protectorate was established. Of the Khmer themselves it has been said—'One sole activity is truly national—agriculture'.[19] Even in the late 1950s barely 3 per cent of the Khmer population lived in towns. They preferred to live by farming and fishing in small, self-contained settlements. The few who were not involved in this idyllic but subsistence-level existence were mostly in the administration which in its higher echelons was a Khmer monopoly. The top-ranking civil servants were

almost invariably drawn from the small, aristocratic élite which surrounded
the throne and which likewise dominated the upper reaches of the Buddhist
hierarchy. An incipient middle-class of lesser officials was forming, the product of the exclusive French schools in the protectorate. Khmer society as
such was still divided broadly between the members of the royal family, the
nobility, the monkhood, freemen (peasant smallholders) and—formerly—
slaves; but since the differences in landed wealth were not great, class distinctions were not evident.

The Khmer were evenly spread over the face of the land, forming the
overall majority everywhere except in the remote easternmost provinces
which were occupied by hill peoples. In the days of the Angkor monarchy
they had covered a much wider area—from the plains of the Menam Chao
Phaya to the estuaries of the Mekong—then had retreated before the tides of the
Thais from the west and of the Vietnamese from the east. As a result of their
prominent past, the Khmer had brushes with many different races in the region, acquiring in the process a wide ethnic blend so that today wide variations in physical traits are noticeable in the people. Some of the Khmer ethnic
groups never merged or assimilated with their neighbours, but remained in
their jungle-hill fastnesses, preserving a racial purity and remaining culturally
far more backward. Regarded as uncivilized relatives and known deroga-
tively as Phnong or more politely as Khmer-loeu (upper Khmer), these hill
peoples, numbering some 50,000 in all, were scattered in the deep jungle of the
high Moi plateaux in the east, and in the uplands of the Cardomon, Elephant
and Dangrek Ranges, where they followed an existence well removed from
the mainstream of Cambodian life, keeping fleeting contacts with the outside
world by trading jungle products with itinerant Lao or Chinese pedlars.
They subsisted by slash-and-burn (ray) cultivation or by trapping elephants,
hunting, and gathering forest products. All property was held in common
save for gongs, which were highly prized, and weapons; wealth in general
was measured in terms of great earthenware jars borne from neighbouring
lands and also from as far away as China itself. The Khmer-loeu were divided
up into various groups, all speaking dialects akin to Khmer. Other hill
peoples whose dialects are closer to Cham are probably of earlier negroid
ancestry. In all, up till recently, thirteen distinct tribal groups have been cate-
gorized amongst the hill peoples, of whom only the Rhadé, Jarai and the
Stieng are comparatively well known.[20] Another group of Khmer-loeu, the
Kouy, live more closely to their civilized cousins of the plains and have become specialists as iron-smiths. Other hill peoples have contributed to the
traditional Cambodian economy as craftsmen and labourers and became good
soldiers under French arms; but they rarely intermarried with other Cambodians.

A third category of indigenous Cambodians comprises small minority
groups which history has left as tight little islands of their own in the midst
of the Khmer sea. The most significant amongst these were the Chams whose
fall from greatness has been even greater than that of the Khmer themselves.
As they fled from their Vietnamese oppressors at the end of the fifteenth
century, they ran into the Malay raiders who were invading Kampot, and

became converts to Islam. Today all the Cham people within Cambodia are Muslims and having merged completely with the Malay interlopers form together with them a compact 1 per cent of the total population, and rank fourth amongst the racial groupings in the country. The Malay-Cham are to be found principally in Kompong Cham province where they live as farmers growing a variety of crops. They are also prominent as cattle-breeders and engage in commerce and fishing. The Cham element is still distinct on account of language and within their own community uphold their elaborate high etiquette and ritual, an echo of their past days of greatness. Another group of Malays, the residue of ancient Malay incursions, are to be found along the coast as fishermen. In 1936 this group was put into one congregation along with the Javanese and the Arabs.

Khmer society and the land

Cambodia was, or at least appeared before the Pacific War to be, 'the one area in Indo-China least likely to welcome the end of French rule',[21] a result of French shrewdness in buttressing the traditional Khmer establishment socially, in checking (at least from the political angle) the encroachments of aliens, and in maintaining peace and a modicum of prosperity. The countryside might be poor but it was—to the foreign observer—picturesque and calm. The Khmer themselves were apparently 'a quiet hospitable folk, not remarkable for their industry, indifferent farmers, and as traders inferior to both Chinese and Annamites... and also intensively conservative, a characteristic usually attributed to the all-pervasive role of Buddhism in Khmer life and to the compact self-contained nature of Khmer settlement.[22]

The basic factor for Khmer conservatism and the bucolic calm which encompassed the countryside under the French protectorate prior to 1941 was almost total absence of pressure on the land itself. Only 10 per cent was under continuous cultivation with another 30 per cent consisting mostly of tracts of savannah, subject to sporadic farming. The rest of the country was taken up by dense jungle and water. In these circumstances the land problems usually associated with South-East Asian countries were conspicuously absent. Tenancy and sharecropping were virtually non-existent and the agricultural labourer a rarity. Communal lands were unknown. Land was not even a source of wealth, but 95 per cent of the Khmer were peasant smallholders. Indeed there was no merit and little inducement to become a large landowner. Buddhism frowned upon the acquisition of material wealth; labour was hard to come by and since farmers depended upon the seasonal floods rather than irrigation to do their work for them, large-scale social co-operation was not called for. The lack of land pressure also meant low productivity. Despite French efforts the Khmer farmer could not be persuaded to adopt more efficient methods of irrigation in the name of progress, profit and higher yields.[23]

The traditional land system too discouraged landlordism and contributed to the complacency of the peasantry. All land belonged to the king—at least till 1904 when the French caused the custom to be changed—while traditionally uncultivated land came under the ownership of whosoever cleared and tilled it, and (where necessary) enclosed it. All this was unacceptable to the French who sought to make land a marketable commodity and so wished to impose a uniform land system for the whole of Indo-China. The first hint of change was contained in the text of the Franco-Cambodian Convention of 1884, which was followed up by the introduction of land registration, a procedure alien to the Khmer imagination. In consequence actual land registration made very slow progress. By 1931 only one-third of the total land area had been surveyed. Despite the establishment of a Board of Surveys a combination of peasant attitudes and official red tape still ensured that progress was slow. However French laws made possible the alienation of land, so that the land grant system already functioning in neighbouring Cochin-China was extended into Cambodia, enabling the opening up of the red lands in the eastern provinces to French rubber plantations. At the same time, the failure of land registration to make effective headway became a factor in the growing problem of rural poverty and indebtedness.

Rural poverty

Despite the calm of the rural scene and the absence of a landlord problem rural poverty in fact was both present and increasing before 1941. The origins of this situation lay in the same factors that blighted the lives of the peasant farmer elsewhere in South-East Asia, as he became progressively ensnared in the nexus of a spreading money economy. His subsistence economy did not provide for the extraordinary such as natural disaster, domestic calamity or unheralded social demands. In such circumstances in the past the Khmer peasant turned to his neighbour and offered his land as collateral for aid in kind. Since land was not transferable, the creditor was allowed to take over the land and work it until the debt was paid. The commercialization of rice and the introduction of a money economy at village level (marked by the arrival of the Chinese shop-keeper) caused the traditional system to be bent to serve new purposes. The shop-keeper who was inevitably also the rice-broker became the obvious and easiest source of credit. But his terms were high: apart from charging usurious rates of interest, the shop-keeper now took over the entire surplus harvest of his client. At the same time he paid the farmer's taxes and disposed of the harvest to his own profit. By way of further guarantee he also received a written undertaking from the farmer to the effect that he would be entitled to succeed to the ownership of the land should the debt remain unliquidated. As things stood, this was an empty promise which could only become redeemable when the lengthy process of land registration was complete, but the vision of eventually coming into this inheritance buoyed more than a few Chinese. As for the indebted smallholder who had already been converted in this way into a virtual farm labourer, he often found a solution in abandoning his lands and settling elsewhere. The role of the Chinese moneylender amongst Khmer and Vietnamese fishermen was similarly baneful.[24]

As elsewhere in French Indo-China, official credit institutions proved unable to remedy the situation. In the first place they were late in being established. It was not until the end of the 1920s that the Caisses Indigénes de Credit Agricole Mutuel was set up in the Union. This was superseded by the Office du Credit Agricole Mutuel which by 1936 had succeeded in setting up only seven credit banks in Cambodia. The slowness of the land registration prog-ramme had a serious effect on the efficacy of these new credit institutions as the farmer was denied the means of getting the credit he needed because of the administration's understandable reluctance to lend money to unregistered landowners. There was altogether too much red tape connected with bor-rowing from the government's credit institutions.

Industrialization

As much as anything else the problem of rural poverty was the result of the lack of effective pressures either on the Khmer farmer himself to rouse him into action to improve his position or on the French administration to stimu-late more thoroughgoing efforts on his behalf. Under the security of French rule and amid the bounty of nature which shielded him from starvation, the average Khmer smallholder was content with his lot, and if things got bad there was plenty of virgin land to run away to. French administrators, on the other hand, had no urge to and saw no profit in transforming the somnolent Khmer economy. Industrialization did not seem worth-while. Cambodia had been cast in the role of supplier of primary commodities for the imperial econ-omy. There was a notable dearth of raw materials suitable for the develop-ment of industry and the Khmers themselves appeared to possess little aptitude for and less interest in industrial-type employment. As a result Cambodian industry before the Pacific War was a very limited affair, confined to the pro-cessing of the country's primary products for export and to some traditional handicrafts, and it rested almost entirely in alien hands.[25] The factories of Cam-bodia comprised a few sawmills, a couple of medium-sized rice mills, some sugar refineries and one distillery at Phnom Penh. Even then, as far as rice which was a virtual Chinese monopoly was concerned, much of the actual processing was done in Saigon-Cholon. In fact, the conversion of padi into polished rice was the country's principal industry, but while rice for domestic consumption was dealt with locally, rice exports were usually husked at large plants in Kompong Cham, Soairieng and Kandal provinces before being sent to Saigon for final processing and shipment overseas. Cambodia acquired its first rice mills in 1921 when these were constructed at Phnom Penh. Sawmills were more widely spread, wood being very commonly used in a land short of other basic fuels such as coal and oil; these were all Chinese-owned, for it was the Chinese who were the principal collectors of forest products and timber—mostly small family concerns except for the handful of larger mills found at the capital. Sugar production was dominated by the French-owned Société des Distilleries de l'Indochine which enjoyed the alcohol monopoly. On a number of rubber estates of Kompong Cham there were processing plants which cured the rubber and produced sheets of this and crepe for export. Fish processing was an industry of considerable local importance, centred on the provinces of Kandal and Kampot. Cottage industries and native handi-crafts were more widespread than in neighbouring Cochin-China although the degree of specialization typical of Annam and Tonkin was absent. Cot-ton spinning was a typical such industry found all over the country with each district famous for its own particular designs, but attempts by Chinese entre-preneurs to start cotton manufacture on an international basis were not very successful. Other traditional crafts included cloth-making, embroidery, the making of fish-nets, basket-making, carpentry and metalwork. The standard of traditional Khmer craftsmanship was very high but at the beginning of the century became debased due to commercialization. The establishment by the French of a School of Fine Arts during the reign of King Monivong attempted to check this fall in artistic standards and achieved a marginal success. There was a small pottery industry in Chinese hands, itself little removed from cottage industry levels.

Labour
With a little-developed industrial sector, the ranks of Cambodia labour were similarly limited. About 80 per cent of the country's labour force was self-employed on the land, so that the conditions and problems of the re-mainder who were employed as wage labourers in some form of industrial enterprise were marginal as far as the bulk of the population was concerned. The fact that the bulk of the industrial labour force was made up of Chinese and Vietnamese aliens also meant that there was no undue pressure on the French administration to be concerned for their welfare. However, in fact by far the best cared for workers in the country were the Vietnamese contract labourers who worked on the great French rubber plantations in the east of the country. They were the beneficiaries of the labour laws which had been passed for all Indo-China for contract labour in 1927, and if at the beginning they had been the victims of the same exploitation at the hands of the 'cai' who recruited them and the planters who employed them as their compa-triots in Annam and Cochin-China, by the mid-1930s they were governed by eighteen-month agreements which ensured them free medical, educational and recreational facilities and a wage scale which compared favourably with any other group of workers in Cambodia.[26] Other Cambodian workers had to wait until the labour decrees of 1936 which extended the 1927 legislation to 'all wage-earning and salaried employees'. The 1936 decrees dealt with the regulation of apprentice labour, conditions of health, safety and employment of the labourer, and a scheme of compensation for those involved in industrial accidents. Its implementation was provided for by the supervision of the Labour Inspectorate which had been initially set up in 1927. In practice the effectiveness of this new legislation is questionable. The Labour Inspectorate in Cambodia always lacked sufficient staff to carry out its duties effectively and the staff available lacked adequate training. In addition the whole system was highly paternalistic. Trade unions were never allowed, probably because of French fears of subversion by nationalist or communist elements and also as a result of the strong political influence and pressure of the leading French entrepreneurs in the country. As a kind of foil and more directly as a means of raising the standards of Cambodian handicrafts and of promoting facilities for their marketing, the French administration did sponsor the formation in 1920 of 'guilds' which were empowered to discuss questions of quality of production, wages and other matters related to the industries they represented,

but which fell short of holding the right to strike or any other of the independent prerogatives of a trade union. Many workmen clearly still remained beyond the reach of the authorities to protect them, especially as most industrial workers as such were members of small family concerns. Nevertheless in 1931 the average earnings of a worker in Cambodia were reckoned to be on par with those in Cochin-China which in turn were the highest in the French Indo-Chinese Union.

In general all this labour legislation left the Khmer workman himself unaffected, as he did not fall into any of the categories it provided for. At the same time the deeply entrenched opposition of the Khmer ruling class prevented the disappearance of slavery, in the forms of serfdom and debt bondage, which were traditional to the country. The friezes of Angkor and the witness of contemporaries testify to the ancient origins of these institutions. In the days of Angkor the serfs were probably hill tribesmen but in the days of Khmer decline, forced labour became generalized for the whole population. Every able-bodied man between the ages of twenty-one and fifty was liable to do up to as much as three months a year on the construction or maintenance of royal projects and public works. Debt slavery was regarded as equally important in the eyes of the Khmer aristocracy. According to King Norodom it was 'one of the foundations of the Cambodian state. Our subjects reduced to that servitude are the happiest of all'.[27] Be that as it may, debt slavery was clearly regarded as an essential prop of the ruling class. Like the British in the Malay world facing a similar situation, the French trod carefully. In the name of nineteenth-century progress and humanity, the institution had to go, but instead of resolving the problem through stealthy commutation, the French permitted it to continue in disguised form; they promulgated the end of forced labour but substituted it for contract which in the form it was organized was more or less the same thing.

Health and social welfare
In other fields of social welfare, the most important of which was health, even by comparison with Vietnam services were poorly developed and standards were generally low. This was reflected in the high death-rate which was one factor contributing to Cambodia's slow population growth. The country was visited by all the major diseases to which the region was prone but particularly serious were dysentery, malaria and tuberculosis, at least one of which was bound to afflict a Cambodian during the course of his life. Amoebic dysentery was one of the major causes of infantile mortality and of the general debility of the population. Malaria was 'almost an occupational disease' for the countryman, as the rice fields and the forest abounded with a host of malarial mosquitoes, two species of which thrived in extraordinary abundance. Phnom Penh was early recognized by the French as one of the three permanent centres of plague in Indo-China, largely associated with the China-town of the port. Yaws was commonplace particularly amongst the Khmer, and trachoma was a major disease. Smallpox was endemic, there being particularly serious outbreaks in 1917-20 and 1924-5. Diphtheria, scrub typhus and hookworm were common, leprosy was not unknown and syphilis, scarlet fever

and measles—all Western importations—occasionally made their appearance.

The prevalence of disease and the low standards of health were fundamentally the outcome of inadequate preventive measures. This was very obvious in the case of water supplies which up to the 1930s were cholera infested and very largely defenceless against pollution. After 1931 a concerted effort was made to improve matters so that by the time of the Japanese Occupation all the major towns and a good number of the lesser ones possessed pumping stations and purifying plants. But the supply and distribution of purified water still remained totally inadequate, especially in the rural areas where people had to rely on polluted rivers, irrigation canals and ponds to meet their daily needs.

Prior to 1931 all the sanitation measures that had been taken under the French administration were extremely primitive. The first medical and health services came with the invading French army in Cochin-China in the early 1860s and, limited as they were, were extended to the civil population not long afterwards. But it was not until 1914 that a Public Health and Medical Service for all Indo-China was established to cater for both military and civilians and not till 1931 that the Inspector-general in charge, who was stationed at Saigon, was made solely responsible for the civilian side. In the meantime the most notable achievement in the field of medicine was the establishment of the Pasteur Institute at Saigon in 1890, at the specific request of Louis Pasteur himself. In other respects health measures lagged behind. There were no large-scale attempts to combat cholera or smallpox by vaccination until after the Great War, but when applied for the first time such measures proved dramatically successful. In 1930 the Cambodian Sanitary Code was adopted and after that more definitive progress was made. There was a general though limited expansion of health services under the Director of Health Services at Phnom Penh.[28] Evidence that some headway was being made came in 1936 when the inoculation of well over half a million Cambodians checked the severe cholera outbreak in neighbouring Thailand from spreading into the country. Before 1914 there was not a single regular civilian hospital in Cambodia at all: in that year a general hospital was built at Phnom Penh and subsequently others at each of the provincial capitals. Phnom Penh also came to possess a vaccine institute and a public health laboratory and served as a quarantine station for immigrants. Its notoriety as a plague centre was also reduced by widespread vaccination and a campaign against rats. A leper settlement was built at Treong and throughout the rural areas maternity centres, dispensaries and first aid posts were set up. Some provision was also made for the training of nurses, midwives and public health officers.

But for all that was done, it was still far too little. The medical and health services in general were inadequately staffed. As a result senior personnel did not have the time to inspect progress outside the towns and they were hampered still further by insufficient equipment and funds. The almost total lack of any health education programme, particularly important for a country where the bulk of the population was still governed by superstition, meant that the scientific basis of Western medicine was never grasped.

If medical and health services left much to be desired, other forms of state social welfare were almost non-existent. Care of the aged, the sick, the destitute, the maimed and the orphaned was left to traditional Cambodian means. Fortunately within the compass of a Buddhist society the tradition of social welfare was a strong one, as is attested by decrees of Angkor's monarchs, and the pagoda was the customary source of assistance. The Buddhist ethos also played its role, undisturbed by the colonial presence, in maintaining the steady tenor of Khmer life. Murder and sexual assault were rare, alcoholism almost unknown, and the prevalence of petty theft probably a reflection of the loose concept of private property in Khmer society. Drug addiction, especially opium, was common enough in the towns and was hard to control since the opium itself was kept on as a profitable government monopoly, but the addicts were nearly all Chinese and Vietnamese, who were also of course the principal consumers.

In general, the Khmer lived in a simple, rustic poverty, but their society was coherent and compact. Food was cheap and abundant, needs were moderate and limited and the moneylender was always available for an emergency. Social life centred on the pagoda in the villages. For as long as Khmer society remained within the French cocoon, there seemed no reason why its calm and complacency should not continue undisturbed.

[1]David J. Steinberg (ed.), *Cambodia: Its People, Its Society, Its Culture*, HRAF Press, New Haven, 1959, p. 22.

[2]See Steinberg, op. cit., p. 198.

[3]The French preferred Vietnamese labour for it was supposedly cheaper and also available in large numbers from penal institutions.

[4]'Straw men', equivalent to the Malay 'Ali Baba'; in other words Khmer surrogates who acted on behalf of the real Chinese owners by law denied such rights in rubber producing areas.

[5]This dependence on the French market helped to bring about the disastrous collapse of Cambodian pepper which followed in the wake of the Pacific War and the Japanese Occupation. Cut off from its guaranteed market, the industry withered and in the highly competitive conditions which prevailed after 1945 failed to make an effective recovery.

[6]See Steinberg, op. cit., p. 27.

[7]Charles Robequain, *The Economic Development of French Indo-China*, Oxford University Press, London, 1944, p. 235.

[8]The expansion of the Philippines market was connected with the rapid growth there of food and plantation cash crops which put draught and beef cattle at a premium. At the time of the collapse of this market, the Philippines was absorbing 70 per cent of Cambodia's cattle exports.

[9]In fact this road was a continuation of Colonial Highway Thirteen which originated in Saigon and was destined to reach Vientiane and Luang Prabang. By 1937 the southern section had got as far as Paksé in southern Laos, the distance from Kratié having been completed in a record time of two years (i.e. three dry seasons) with the help of 8,500 coolies.

[10]See Steinberg, op. cit., p. 41.

[11]For more details of the Khmer attitude towards the Vietnamese, see William E. Willmott, *The Chinese in Cambodia*, Publications Centre, University of British Colombia, 1967, pp. 34–5 and also Robequain, op. cit., p. 48.

[12]The distinction between the urban and the rural Vietnamese was therefore religious as well as economic. The rural Vietnamese were mostly Buddhist and had come into the country by themselves; the urban Vietnamese owed their positions to French patronage.

[13]By the Decree of 31 December 1891, which established 'congregations' for alien Asians living in Cambodia, provincial heads for the Vietnamese community were also provided for as well as their registration throughout the land. After this the Vietnamese were made to pay the same personal taxes as the Khmer.

[14]The Chinese attitude towards the French in Cambodia stands out in contrast to that of the Chinese merchants of Saigon who actively connived for the extension of French imperialism into that country.

[15]Mac Cuu first appeared at the Khmer capital of U Dong in 1675 at the age of 17 and proceeded to make a fortune for himself through trade, mining and the management of the gambling farm. In 1709 he was made a provincial governor by the Khmer king but when a few years later Khmer power sagged under Thai pressure he judiciously switched allegiance to Hué and became established as the autonomous governor of Ha Tien, a post he held till his death in 1735.

[16]See two quotes from French sources, describing the Chinese role, in Willmott, op. cit., pp. 59 and 60.

[17]The French tax law of 1884 had already stipulated that the children with Khmer fathers were to be considered Cambodians without making any mention of mothers. This clearly implied that the children with Chinese fathers were automatically considered Chinese by the French. On the other hand, a decree of King Norodom in 1900 permitted any mixed child with one Cambodian parent to be placed on the Cambodian tax register, provided he abandoned Chinese dress and hairstyle. The Chinese were also the only aliens permitted to bid for contracts, such as the construction of public works or for the provisioning of army or civil organizations, under the French administration. This right was bitterly resented by French commercial interests who kept up a constant agitation against the Chinese presence and their privileges. In 1900 the French Resident-Superieur in Cambodia gave in to the demand of the Cambodian Chamber of Commerce that Chinese be excluded from official tenders, but the ban did not last long.

[18]The French defined the non-French Indians as 'Asian aliens' along with the Chinese. An ordinance of 1891 further divided these Indians into two new congregations, one Muslim and the other Hindu. However by 1941 only one congregation survived.

[19]Jean Delvert, 'Le Paysan Cambodgien', Paris, 1961; quoted by Willmott, op. cit., p. 44.

[20]The dialects of the Rhadé and Jarai are closer to Cham and they have been identified by French anthropologists as being probably of earlier negroid ancestry. The Rhadé inhabited the jungles on either side of the Cambodian-Vietnamese frontier; the Jarai were found more or less in the same region as well as in southern Laos and had similar traits to the Rhadé and to the Stieng; the latter enjoyed a reputation as elephant hunters and trainers and dwelt in the forests north of Kratié.

[21]John F. Cady, Thailand, Burma, Laos and Cambodia, Prentice-Hall Inc., New Jersey, 1966, p. 114.

[22]Only the more discerning, such as Robequain, suspected that beneath this placid surface lurked other potentials. See Robequain, op. cit., p. 75.

[23]The empire of Angkor had flourished on account of a sophisticated and extensive system of water control, the neglect of which was probably one of the major factors for its fall. The French started to reconstruct some of the ancient irrigation works and building new ones after 1900 but comparatively little was achieved. The most important project was the harnessing of the flood waters of the Mongkolbourey River so as to irrigate part of the drought-prone Battambang Plain. Khmer irrigation methods were extremely primitive.

[24]For a French view of the role of the Chinese moneylender, see Pierre Gourou, Land Utilization in French Indo-China, 1940, quoted by Purcell, op. cit., pp. 202-3.

[25]Another source of Cambodian economic weakness was their almost total lack of capital. In any case industry touched barely 2 per cent of the total population, while

government confined itself to granting concessions to and collecting fees from those who undertook the exploitation of the country's natural resources.

[26]The 1927 legislation also laid down standard conditions for recruitment, minimum housing and food standards and other welfare schemes to guarantee their welfare and future.

[27]Quoted by Steinberg, op. cit., p. 183. Debt-slavery in Cambodia is supposed to have originated from the ransoms paid by prisoners-of-war to escape perpetual slavery for themselves and their descendants.

[28]At the same time a local health officer, reporting to the Director, was made responsible for each province and reported to the Director. The Medical and Health Services supervised health control at the frontiers and at other points of entry, were responsible for mass vaccinations and inoculations, inspections, general sanitation work and hospitals and generally reviewed the development of health plans and budgets.

Books and articles for further reading

BOOKS

Cady, J.F., *Thailand, Burma, Laos and Cambodia*, Prentice-Hall Inc., New Jersey, 1966.

Dauphin-Meunier, Achille, *Le Cambodge de Sihanouk*, Nouvelles Editions Latines, Paris, 1965.

Fisher, C.A., *South-East Asia: A Social, Economic and Political Geography*, Methuen, London, 1964.

Jacoby, E.H., *Agrarian Unrest in South-East Asia*, Asia Publishing House, Bombay, 1961.

Lancaster, D., *The Emancipation of French Indo-China*, Oxford University Press, London, 1961.

Purcell, V., *The Chinese in South-East Asia* (2nd. ed.), Oxford University Press, 1965.

Pym, C. (ed.), *Henri Mouhot's Diary*, Oxford University Press, Kuala Lumpur, 1966.

Robequain, C., *The Economic Development of French Indo-China*, Oxford University Press, London, 1944.

Steinberg, D.J. (ed.), *Cambodia: Its people, Its society, Its culture*, HRAF Press, New Haven, 1959.

————, *In Search of South-East Asia: A Modern History*, Oxford University Press, Kuala Lumpur, 1971.

Willmott, W.E., *The Chinese in Cambodia*, University of British Colombia, 1967.

ARTICLES

Willmott, W.E., 'The Chinese in Cambodia', *JSEAH*, VII, 1, 1966.

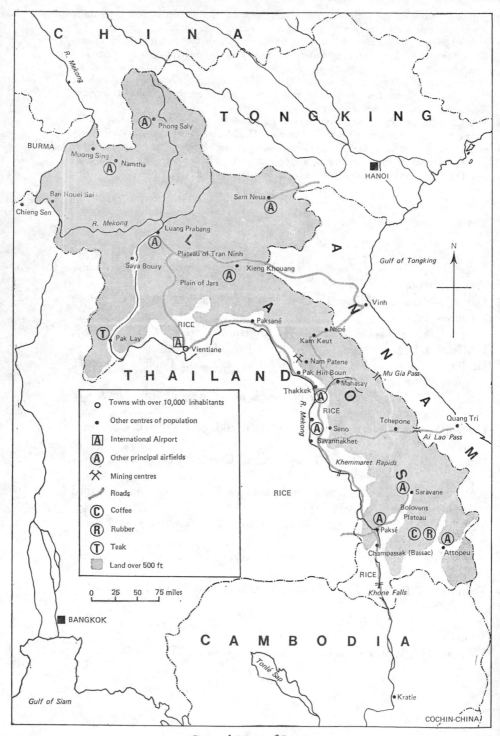

33. General Map of Laos, 1941

C. Laos

'Some historians, particularly British historians, see France's colonization of
Laos as the result of a single-minded French determination to occupy as much
territory as possible before the British could get to it, or to set up a solid bulwark
against the British in Burma. But this explanation misses the most note-worthy
fact about France's involvement in Laos: It had no positive aim.'

Arthur J. Dommen, *Conflict in Laos*, London, 1964.

For many Frenchmen Laos was another world, remote from the pressures
of the age, alien to the economic realities of the twentieth century, a realm
apart, peopled by a simple rustic folk who had to be preserved against the
corrosive influences of the West and where one could escape and live the life
of a happy eccentric. In other words French rule dwelt lightly on the Lao
states so that despite their economic potential, correctly surmised by Pavie,
they remained little exploited and therefore little developed. Laos was economically the most backward state in the Indo-Chinese Union, and whatever
development did take place there was in the context of the Union as a whole.
In the twilight of French rule the country and its people were little changed
from what they had been two generations earlier when the French presence
was foisted upon them, a nation of subsistence farmers.

This state of affairs was the product of various factors, the two most evident
of which were the general inaccessibility of the country from the outside world
and the French preoccupation with their more rewarding provinces of Co-
chin China and Tonkin. The Lao states had been acquired by default, largely
through the ambitions of one man. The economic gains to be won were
never obvious and had already been largely discounted by the findings of the
Lagrée-Garnier expedition of 1866 up the Mekong. In the event Laos remained an anomaly. It was not even treated as a political entity, being ruled
as half colony, half protectorate, and on at least one occasion French administrators were seriously toying with the idea of annexing the country to Annam.[1]
There was no attempt to treat the country as a viable economic unit and the
colonial administration was content to allow the annual deficits to be covered
by the surplus revenues of the other states in the Union. The only apparent
step in terms of positive economic policy ever made was to strengthen the
country's links with the rest of Indo-China in an effort to check the natural
drift of Laotian commerce and economic growth into the Thai orbit.

The development of communications

This problem was the main rationale behind the road building programme
launched after the Great War which represented the most significant French
contribution to the economic development of the country. The most important of these roads was Colonial Highway Thirteen, which was started in
1935 and completed during the Pacific War. It was designed to open a direct

land route between Saigon and Luang Prabang with the aim of securing for the Cochin-Chinese capital 'the largest possible share' of the Laotian trade and of emasculating the economic bonds between Laos and Bangkok. Apart from this route, there were three other major roads which crossing the Annamite Chain forged direct links between the Lao states and Annam. The first of these was Colonial Highway Nine which joined the Mekong town of Savannakhet to Quang Tri on the Annamite coast. A second route linked Thahkek on the Mekong with Vinh in north Annam, and in the 1930s was supplemented by a branch to connect with the cable railway at Ban Na Phao. The third route was built to join Luang Prabang via Xieng Khouang to Tonkin. These roads, together with a fourth metalled all-weather road which connected Paksé with Saravane constituted all the metalled highways in the country, covering some 1,477 miles. The French had plans for a great trunk frontier highway stretching from the Gulf of Tonkin along the Chinese border to Luang Prabang, but by 1945 only certain sections in Tonkin had been completed. The reasons for their failure to develop roads in Laos further lay in the rugged terrain, particularly in the north, low population densities and the generally poor prospects of quick economic returns.

For the same reasons Laos could not boast of any railway, apart from some four-odd miles of narrow gauge track which crossed the mid-Mekong island of Khone. The scheme in the 1930s to join Thahkek with Da Nang (Tourane) in Annam by rail was stopped owing to shortage of funds, although on the Vietnamese side the branch line from the Transindochinois was constructed as far as Xom Cuc, from where a cable line was built to hoist materials and supplies up the Mu Gia Pass to Ban Na Phao on the Laotian side. The Xom Cuc-Ban Na Phao cable line became a regular route for conveying merchandise which was then hauled by truck or bus to the Mekong Valley.

The existence of the brief Khone Island railway underlined the inescapable role of the Mekong as the key factor in the economic development of Laos. On the middle Mekong between Kratié (in Cambodia) and Savannakhet there are four major natural obstacles which make transhipment unavoidable, of which on the Laotian side the first and most formidable are the double falls at Khone. In 1891 a French river steamboat company based on Saigon made the first attempt to get a vessel through the barrier but after two years of failure, it was decided to build the line across Khone Island instead. This was in use by the end of 1893 and provided the means by which the first gunboats and steam launches reached the middle Mekong. The second barrier formed by the rapids of Kemmarat starts some thirty miles below Savannakhet as the Mekong enters a canyon. The 310 miles between Savannakhet and Vientiane constitute the only true navigable stretch on the middle Mekong, though the river is navigable by lighter craft up to Luang Prabang and beyond. The overall effect of these natural impediments was to make travel into Laos tardy and tedious. More serious still the narrowness of some of the passages limited the size of vessel which could be used and severely restricted the cargo capacity of river traffic.[2]

Nevertheless the bulk of the population of Laos was concentrated along the banks of the Mekong and its tributaries, which formed the main highways for their needs. Combined they accounted for nearly a thousand miles of navigable waterway, open to barge and launch, although much greater distances could be covered in pirogues and sampans. The French too found the river the most economical means of communication and so improved upon its navigation. After 1910 more powerful launches were introduced onto the middle Mekong above Savannakhet to replace the pioneer vessels brought in the 1890s, and the number of transhipments was gradually lessened. Motorized canoes introduced between Vientiane and Luang Prabang in the 1930s marked another improvement. However, when the contract of the Compagnie Saigonnaise de Navigation et de Transport expired in 1937, the former regular service between Paksé and Savannakhet was suspended and modifications took place in the services further upstream.

As for more sophisticated communications, Laos was predictably left far behind. Prior to 1941 there were five government wireless stations in the country but none of them for broadcasting, and although telephones had been introduced there were only a handful. Laos possessed one fully equipped airport, that at Vientiane.

French commercial investments: tin and coffee

The absence of a good system of communications in Laos and the difficulties involved in trying to create one go a long way to account for the French failure to embark on the exploitation and development of the country's natural resources. In fact only tin and coffee attracted French investors and came to make a marginal contribution to the commercial economy of the Indo-Chinese Union as a whole. Of these two, tin was by far the more important.

Tin was the country's most important export prior to the Pacific War and was the only mineral to be extracted by the French on a commercial scale. Although tin contributed only some 2 per cent to the total value of Indo-China's exports in the late 1930s, it formed 29 per cent of total mineral production in the Union of which Laos provided nearly two-thirds. The whole of the tin production of Laos came from Phon Tiou and Boneng in the basin of the Nam Patene River, whose alluvial deposits had been worked for centuries by Laotians and started to be mined by Frenchmen in the early 1920s. By the end of the same decade Laotian tin production was topping that of Tonkin and averaged an annual output between 1923 and 1941 of 1,800 tons with its peak year in 1938.

All the tin mined in the Nam Patene Basin before the intervention of the French had been carried out by primitive, traditional methods which produced an average of ten to fifteen tons a year, mostly destined for Siam to be used as ballast for fishing nets. Modern methods and large-scale mining came with the first systematic operations of the Société d'Etudes et d'Exploitation Minières de l'Indochine in 1923. The mounting fever of mining prospecting which swept Indo-China between 1926 and 1929 led to the formation of other French companies which ended up by getting their grants worked for them by the Compagnie Fermière des Etains d'Extrême Orient. This second concern opened mining operations around Boneng in 1933. Production rose steadily and, like other small producers, these two French firms with their guaranteed market in France benefited greatly from the terms of the International Tin Agreement, which granted them a minimum quota already above their maximum production, to be doubled again when the Agreement was renewed in 1937.

The French adopted open-cast methods of mining as the deposits were alluvial and not deep below the soil's surface. Expensive machinery was imported and installed to separate the ores. However the scarcity of local fuels and the impurities of the ores themselves meant that smelting on the spot was impracticable, and so the entire production of the Nam Patene Basin was sent to Singapore for refining, either via the Mekong and Saigon, or overland by truck via Thakhek or Savannakhet to Da Nang (Tourane). There was also a labour problem. The mines were situated in a thinly populated region whose inhabitants—mostly hill tribesmen—were not likely to provide suitable workmen for modern mining conditions. So right from the beginning recourse was had to coolies imported from Vietnam; in the late 1930s there were some 6,000 Vietnamese mining labourers working in the Basin, most of them from the province of Nghe Tinh in Tonkin.

The employment of the Vietnamese illustrates the almost complete eclipse of native Lao participation in the tin-mining industry. Lao or Indonesian workers had never been very numerous. After the arrival of the French some Laotians still dug their own ores on the new concessions, selling their tin to the French companies. Some others were employed for prospecting and clearing the land and for pulling the small wagons that transported the ores.

Coffee was the only other product in Laos in which French investors took any significant interest. Evidently coffee would flourish in the rich, virgin soils of the Bolovens Plateau, but although in the 1930s it was reported that 'coffee plantations are increasing rapidly', they were still in their infancy and their contribution to the colonial export economy was very restricted. All the coffee exported went to France. The failure of coffee cultivation to catch on in the Bolovens Plateau was another reflection of the poverty of communications and the general inaccessibility of the country.

Other exports: teak, cattle and jungle produce
The only other commodities to find a market outside the country were benzoin and a handful of other jungle products, some teak, cattle, and, unofficially, opium.

One of the great natural resources of Laos lay in her vast, sprawling forests which covered almost two-thirds of the land, and at least half of which were of economic value. Forest products formed an important element in the economy of classical Lang Chang, and played an essential role in the traditional subsistence economy of the people. From the French point of view, however, the most significant forest product was teak, only found growing amidst the crystalline rocks near Pak Lay but in sufficient quantity to make it a worthwhile commercial proposition. All the same, the French lumber company holding the sole teak concession found it brought poor returns, overshadowed by the far more bountiful resources of neighbouring Thailand and handicapped by the high costs of transportation.

More promising although not fully exploited were the prospects in livestock. Laos seemed suitable for cattle-breeding, particularly in the south, and surplus cattle were regularly exported to both Annam and Cochin-China during the French period. The French were also successful in introducing sheep-rearing which became an established industry on the Plain of Jars. However, for the people of Laos as a whole their heritage of livestock was yet another supplement to their subsistence way of life. Fine herds were wasted through disease and want of adequate pasturage, both the consequence of primitive techniques and sheer neglect. In 1941 the livestock population of the country was reckoned at over three-quarters of a million head.

Marginal attempts were made to grow rubber. A few plantations were cleared on the fertile Bolovens Plateau and a trickle of rubber was exported from them in the 1920s and 1930s. Wild natural rubber, on the other hand, had been long one of the traditional forest products, and the French pioneers in the country, before the era of *hevea brasiliensis*, were quick to establish collecting centres at Vientiane and Luang Prabang for the wild product.

Of all the jungle products for which the Lao states were famed amongst their neighbours, the most important was benzoin, a resin used as a fixative for perfumes. About 30 tons a year were exported, almost wholly to France itself. Another jungle exotica which acquired some economic significance was sticlac or gum-lac used in the preparation of varnish and shellac, and with a good market in the West. Gathered in several provinces by hill peoples, exports from Laos (and Tonkin) averaged 340 tons a year at the turn of the century, most of it being sent overseas via Bangkok. By the 1930s output had slightly decreased. Other jungle produce included some amomum and cardamom, 400 tons of which were gathered annually from the mountains of Lower Laos in the 1930s for export. This, as most jungle produce, was collected by the hill people and sold by them to dealers in the village markets or towns or to itinerant pedlars who came their way.

Nevertheless by no standard did jungle produce assume real economic importance beyond that of being a welcome addition to the hand-to-mouth existence of the hill peoples involved. The effective exploitation of the Lao forests was not only held back by lack of communications. The French made no attempt at their systematic development, and of the five states which made up the Union of French Indo-China, Laos alone did not possess a forest service at all. While all forest land was regarded as state property, in the established tradition of the region, its exploitation was left entirely to a handful of isolated private interests on lease.

Mineral resources and their development
The mineral potential of the country was similarly neglected. Apart from the tin deposits of the Nam Patene Basin, nothing was done to work other known mineral deposits, and although spasmodic surveys of various districts were carried out, by the end of the French period no full-scale geological survey had ever been attempted. On the basis of what was known of the country's

mineral resources up till 1945, it would appear that Laos possessed considerable mineral wealth waiting to be developed, the bulk of it in the northern half of the country. Workable and commercially viable deposits of antimony, lead and zinc have been found near the royal capital of Luang Prabang and around the provincial capital of Xieng Khouang on the Plain of Jars. Prospectors have also detected sizeable deposits of copper near Luang Prabang and silver near Xieng Khouang. Gold was once well known on the Bolovens Plateau although exhausted by the 1850s, but alluvial gold is still panned in Xieng Khouang and near Ban Houei San. Zircons and sapphires are also found in water courses near Ban Houei San and copper near Nam Tha itself. There is gypsum in Phong Saly province as well as some antimony; anthracite beds of considerable extent exist in the same region and also near Luang Prabang and in the Nam Khiep Valley east of Vientiane. Lignite has been found in Nam Tha and Sayaboury provinces. Rich iron ores have been detected south of the Plain of Jars and iron pyrites in Sam Neua to the north. Salt deposits near Vientiane are worked by evaporation. However, as one moves further south, the traces of mineral deposits become scarcer.

The presence of all these minerals has been known to the peoples of Laos for centuries and exploited by them for their own needs. The salt deposits have been worked since time immemorial; smitheries of gold, copper, iron and tin have long been established as traditional crafts; anthracite, sulphur and limestone have been made to serve local uses and precious stones have formed an element in local trade and barter. But without capital, labour and more recently security, the mineral deposits of Laos have had to await their proper exploitation.

Agriculture and fisheries and the subsistence economy
If Laotian exports were limited, in terms of a subsistence economy the country was bountiful. Most important of all the food crops grown for home consumption was rice, the staple of the Laotian diet. In fact the cultivation of rice for the average Laotian 'is both an essential economic activity and a way of life closely interwoven with the supernatural',[3] but although Laos has the potential for self-sufficiency in the crop, before 1941, not enough was grown to meet the growing demands of the incipient towns, so that supplies had to be imported from Thailand.

The rice crop of Laos fell into two distinct categories, wet rice and dry rice, corresponding to the differences between the sedentary agriculturalists of the lowlands and the shifting cultivators of the hills. The wet rice lands are found mostly in the narrow flood plains bordering the Middle Mekong, with smaller pockets in the gorges of the upper reaches and along its tributaries, the Nam Tha and the Nam Hou. Wet rice-farming methods are very similar to those practised in the Malay Peninsula. The cultivation of dry rice in the hills, on the other hand, closely resembles the methods employed amongst the nomadic peoples of North Borneo, producing similar results. In general, rice production under French rule continued to be conducted along traditional lines, with little or no improvement in method or technique. Growing nothing beyond the needs of their own communities, Laotian farmers were always subject to instant disaster, brought about by unruly insects or an untimely drought. In the 1940s the average production of rice stood at around 386,000 tons a year.

After rice the most important food staple was maize, grown however on a much more limited scale. About two-thirds of the crop was grown in the northern provinces of the country and being associated with those areas of shifting cultivation where the rice crop was likely to fail or to prove insufficient, was essentially a hill tribesmen's crop. Like rice, maize was wholly a subsistence crop and no single large area was devoted to its cultivation. Since the 1930s production has been falling steadily.

All other crops served merely to supplement the subsistence economy. Laotians completely depended on vegetable oils for their cooking and cultivated the appropriate plants for this purpose. They also depended on home-grown textiles and as such cotton plays an important local role. In the higher valleys and on the plateaux ramie and hemp were also grown for local use and consumption. Tobacco was another widespread crop grown purely for local needs.

The last element in the subsistence economy of the country lay in fishing which as much as farming was part of the Lao way of life. The waters of the Mekong and its tributaries yielded each year an ample harvest of fish which supplied the fishermen and their families and also found a market in the villages and townships.

One product of Laos which held a place of unique importance was opium. Under the French opium was a state monopoly throughout Indo-China and a great source of profit to the administration. In Laos it was the single greatest source of revenue up till 1945, but although the French permitted its production by the Meo tribesmen who were its principal growers, they did not encourage its extension on account of the serious erosion caused by its cultivation on the hillsides. But all official efforts to convert the Meo people from roving opium and maize cultivators into settled rice-farmers were a failure. Opium production before the Pacific War was estimated to stand at around 40 to 100 tons a year. Although it found a ready market outside the country, it was also consumed on quite a large scale by the Meo themselves and by other hill tribesmen.

Population growth and change
The undisturbed tenor of Laotian life was nowhere revealed more explicitly than in the almost complete absence of change in the population pattern, whether in terms of growth, composition or distribution. In this respect Laos is unique amongst the countries of South-East Asia. Whatever changes did in effect take place within the three generations of French tutelage were mainly brought about by traditional pressures, although there was a slight trend towards urbanization and the ruling class became markedly gallicized.

As with the rest of Indo-China, the evidence of population growth is conflicting and unreliable, all the more so in the case of Laos since no formal census was ever held by the French, the sole official estimates being those of 1921 and of 1937. According to the 1937 figures there were then just over 1 million inhabitants, from which the ethnographers have concluded that the growth rate was small and little affected by external factors. By the same token it is believed that there was little change in the various ethnic ratios of this ethnically most complicated country and that, untypically for South-East Asia, sex and other ratios held quite even. The main French contribution was apparently to have prevented a further decimation of population such as that occasioned by the wars of the first quarter of the nineteenth century. Hence the peoples of Thai stock still held their narrow primacy in numbers which they had had since the days of Fa Ngum in the fourteenth century, accounting for over one-half of the total population of Laos, while those of Indonesian affinity amounted to about one-quarter.[4]

The broad pattern of distribution was also probably the same, although certain local modifications took place under the steady pressure of tribal peoples from Yunnan continuing the centuries-old process of southwards infiltration. Most notable was the arrival of the Meo or Miao who made their first appearance in northern Laos in the 1850s. The Indonesian tribes also had a tendency to shift around from district to district. However, the general picture remained unaltered.

The great bulk—some 96 per cent—of the population were subsistence farmers, scattered in 9,000 villages over an area of 91,000 square miles, representing at four per square mile the lowest average density of any nation in the region; but in reality they were mostly concentrated on the flood plains of the Mekong and its tributaries, particularly in the four provinces of Champassak, Savannakhet, Saravane and Vientiane where over half the people of the country lived. The rest of the population consisted of the roving tribesmen who eked out a living amongst the inhospitable hills. The only appreciable population shift induced by the French was in the tin-rich Nam Patene Basin which led to the rise of a series of mining villages in what had been previously a sparsely inhabited area.

Lao and Thai

The overwhelming bulk of the Laotians who made up the settled farmers in the country were the Lao themselves, the major element amongst the peoples of Thai stock in Laos. They occupied the valley of the Middle and Upper Mekong and its tributaries, forming the heartlands of the principalities of Luang Prabang and Vientiane and covering the most fertile regions of the country. Although apparently distended along the length of the river banks, the Lao formed the most coherent and compact ethnic group in Laos and also (together with the other Thai groups) were in a majority in every province save for two of the three northern ones. In any case, the Lao were accepted as the leaders of the country by all the other groups. Forming part of the great Thai migrations southwards between the sixth and thirteenth centuries, they shared close similarities with the Thais of Siam proper. The Lao were predominantly wet rice farmers, with fishing, hunting, boat-building and weaving as basic subsidiary occupations.

Although the other ethnic Thais found within the borders of the country came from the same basic stock as the Lao and indeed took part in the same migration southwards, circumstances kept them apart and resulted in marked differences. The other Thais were all located in the area between the Red River in Tonkin and the Mekong, particularly around Muong Sing and Dien Bien Phu. Living in this difficult mountainous region, they remained broken up in small, distinctive, self-contained communities just as they had arrived, spaced out over the decades, and today are known by Lao names based on the distinctive colours of their traditional costumes, location or 'some other real or imagined identifying characteristics'. The best known of them are the Thai Dam (Black Thai), Thai Kao (White Thai), and Thai Deng (Red Thai). Not surprisingly these various groups were never able to develop any racial cohesion amongst themselves, and as a result of being widely dispersed fell under different influences, the most important of which was Vietnamese. Like their Lao cousins, the Thai hill tribesmen were also mainly wet rice cultivators but some depended as much on maize and millet, dry rice and even wheat. The greatest difference in cultural terms between these Thais and the Lao was in religion; while the Lao were universally Theravada Buddhists, most of the Thai hill peoples were basically animist, with a Chinese-type admixture of Buddhism, Taoism and Confucianism. Some of the Thai tribes exhibited very distinctive characteristics of their own. The Thai Dam, for example, were generally regarded as more conservative than the rest, reflected in a strong feudalistic social pattern—a consequence of their relative isolation. The Nung and the Nhang also tended to be distinguished from the other Thai groups in their traces of Chinese cultural influence, the outcome of their comparatively recent exit from that country.[5]

The other hill peoples

The remaining inhabitants of Laos were also made up of hill peoples, all of distinct ethnic origin from the Thai and generally termed collectively by the Lao as 'Kha'.[6] Although the term 'Kha' is considered by most anthropologists to embrace all those ethnic groups in the country which speak Mon-Khmer tongues and have affinities with the Malaysians/Indonesians of Island South-East Asia and elsewhere, it covers about sixty different tribal groups. What these groups have in common is their supposedly shared origins, appearance and a history of exploitation by the other races in Laos. This is particularly true of those Indonesian hill tribesmen in the north who were constantly exposed to conquest, enslavement and forced labour by the Lao and other Thai groups. On the whole, therefore, the Indonesian peoples were the main beneficiaries of French rule, since the colonial administration brought the slave-raids and the extortion practised against them to an end. In other respects the Indonesian groups remained unchanged, except for their locations. Scattered all over the mountainous regions, totally lacking any social, political or even cultural cohesion, the fact that in certain areas they formed collectively a majority was totally without significance. Some Indonesian groups were brought into such constant contact with the Lao that they became largely assimilated by them, even to the extent of adopting the Lao tongue. Others suggest, with their darker skins, broad noses and crinkly hair closer affinities with the various Negrito groups in South-East Asia rather than with the

Malaysian-Indonesian family. The best known of the Indonesian tribes were probably the Kha Mou or Khmu and Kha Katang, Kha Pakho and the Bo-loven in south Laos. But in way of life the Indonesian hill tribesmen were very similar to one another. Mostly animists, they subsisted on a shifting cul-ture of rice or maize; they grew cotton, tobacco and—on the Bolovens Plateau—coffee, and they lived in longhouses on stilts, their interiors 'par-titionless and smoke-blackened'.[7]

Two other distinct ethnic groups were the Man and the Meo who, con-centrated in northern Laos, had strong cultural affinities to the Chinese.[8] Of the two groups the Man was the longer established but the fewer in number; they were the leaders of the migrations into Laos which started in the thirteenth century and included the Meo and the Lolo as well. The Man settled on mountain slopes between the 980 feet and 3,000 feet contours, to be followed by the Meo four and a half centuries later who never settled below 3,000 feet. The Man were distinguished by their cult of the dog as a totem animal, the cultivation of cotton and the manufacture of gunpowder, together with their close social links with neighbouring Thai tribes with whose way of life they shared much in common. The Meo, on the other hand, were more numerous and more aggressive. They had had to fight their way into the country and to their present locations against the bitter opposition of both the Thai hill people and the Man. Numbering from a quarter to half a million, they were mainly found in the province of Xieng Khouang and in parts of Luang Pra-bang, Sam Neua, Phong Saly and Nam Tha. Possibly the most sophisticated of all the hill peoples, growing wet rice on irrigated terraced mountainsides, as well as maize and vegetables, they kept various livestock, were the principal opium-growers in the country and manufactured gunpowder and fire-arms. Like the Man, they maintained close social links with the Thai, but unlike most of the other hill peoples they had neither a developed patrilineal social system nor an elaborate system of ancestor worship.

The Vietnamese, Chinese and other aliens
As was the case in Cambodia, French rule brought with it the intrusion of aliens into the country, particularly the Vietnamese and the Chinese, but al-though aliens occupied a pre-eminent position because of the general lack of development, they did not come to acquire such a deeply vested interest as elsewhere. The most numerous were the Vietnamese who numbered around 27,000 in 1937 but probably never exceeded 30,000 at any stage. Most of them were town-dwellers, although there were a number of Vietnamese fishermen and padi-planters in the south. The Vietnamese influx into Laos was the direct consequence of the establishment of French control and the incorporation of Laos into the Indo-Chinese Union. In the event not many Vietnamese took advantage of this situation as there were no obvious pros-pects for advancement, but after 1893 a steady flow of minor functionaries, clerks, traders and professional men came into the country, and in the 1920s Vietnamese labourers were recruited for the Nam Patene tin mines. As a result the lion's share of Laotian commerce fell into Vietnamese hands, and they constituted a good proportion of the artisans, service operators and

shop-keepers to be found in the country. Placed on an autonomous footing, as in Cambodia, the Vietnamese presence was as unpopular amongst the Laotians as it was amongst the Cambodians.

The Chinese presence, in marked contrast to that in most other South-East Asian lands, was much smaller, and during the period 1921-31 when their numbers were increasing phenomenally in Vietnam and Cambodia, the Chinese actually dropped by over half in Laos. The low number of Chinese in the country can be attributed partly to French policy, but the key factor lay in the backward state of the economy, the scattered population and poor communications and hence the limited scope for making a fortune. In 1945 it was estimated that there were about five to six thousand Chinese in Laos, a little less than the number reported before the decline of the 1920s. However, limited as their numbers may have been, the Chinese played a key role in the Laotian economy. They were the middlemen par excellence, in the towns as shop-keepers and traders, in the rice-growing areas of the countryside as millers, moneylenders and itinerant pedlars. They were also the harvesters of the wild tea known as Tran Ninh tea, gathered from the mountain slopes of the Phousang district and marketed by them throughout the country. They ran their affairs in the same manner as elsewhere in South-East Asia.

Of the other aliens in Laos, all were present in very small numbers. The European group of course was the most significant, particularly the French. Most of the Frenchmen in the country were colonial administrators, supplemented by a handful of professional men, planters, traders and missionaries. European contacts date back to the seventeenth century when Laos was in its late glory under Souligna Wongsa. The most significant Western contribution was French culture, which was deeply imbibed by the Lao ruling class though leaving the ordinary people untouched. Apart from Europeans, there were some Indians and Pakistanis, most of whom lived in the towns as merchants and moneylenders, and a few Malays, Burmese and others besides.

Land

The lack of any substantial economic development and the highly conservative nature of French policy meant that the problems normally associated with Western colonialism hardly emerged in Laos. Urbanization was in its infancy in a country 96 per cent of whose population was rural. Vientiane was the only town which could count more than 10,000 inhabitants before 1941. There was no land problem in the sense of the Mekong or Red River Deltas. Although Laos was subject to the same land regulations as imposed on the rest of the Indo-Chinese Union, their application was nugatory amongst a nation of subsistence smallholders and roaming hill tribesmen. All land in Laos, true to the traditional pattern of the region as a whole, was held to be the property of the ruler. In practice land ownership followed local custom, so that existing systems of land tenure varied, ranging from individual or family holdings to tribal and communal systems.[9] Despite the legal fictions they introduced, the French did not interfere with existing land practices very much. Only in the vicinity of the towns or townships did land begin to assume the functions of a marketable commodity and did sharecropping develop, but even so up to 1945 registration of title was neither proposed nor enforced.[10] Perhaps the most positive French contribution to the land question was their ban on the acquisition of land and land rights by aliens, a measure designed to check land alienation to (Vietnamese and Chinese) moneylenders, and quite effective in doing so. In any case indebtedness was extremely limited by the narrow scope of the money economy. The country's products were largely marketed by the producers themselves and mainly restricted to the domestic market where barter still remained supreme, while imports were usually handled by the foreign importer who acted as his own wholesaler and retailer. The only general exception to all this was the rice trade; this was largely in Chinese hands, from the mill owner to the shop-keeper who was collector, distributor and moneylender. When social circumstances forced the Laotian peasant to borrow, it was to this source that he turned, paying the usual exorbitant rates. No alternative sources of credit were in fact available. Government credit institutions founded elsewhere in Indo-China were not extended to Laos. However the country was allowed to benefit in part from the creation of the co-operative movement of the 1930s.

Industry

The lack of economic development also meant the absence of industrialization on any significant scale. The only industrial enterprise in the country before 1941 which resembled anything of the sort to be found in the West was that of the tin mines of Nam Patene. Apart from this, modern industry in Laos consisted of a few rice mills, a number of sawmills, garages, brickworks and carpentry shops, all on a family basis and employing a few hands each. Traditional industries, however, thrived as seen in the widespread production of handicrafts which formed an integral part of the self-sufficient village economy, with a degree of specialization in brick and pottery ware, iron-work and cotton and silk weaving. Even more specialized were the small colonies of lacquer workers, silversmiths and goldsmiths, particularly around Luang Prabang, who primarily catered for the court but also found an exclusive market abroad. Altogether it has been reckoned that traditional cottage industries absorbed about 4 per cent of the total population.

The lack of modern industrialization was linked to the other factors which kept Laos economically backward and prevented it from more rapid exploitation. Above all was the country's isolation and want of good communications both internally and with the outside world. To this were related the lack of capital and skilled labour, the low population and small domestic market, and also the lack of power resources.

Labour

In this context it is not realistic to talk of labour in Laos except in the traditional sense. In most parts of the country wage labour was simply unknown and amongst Laotians prior to 1941 there were no skilled workmen of any kind at all. Whatever need for skilled mechanics or technicians that existed was met by Vietnamese or Chinese immigrants. Hence the labour legislation passed for Indo-China as a whole was scarcely applicable in Laos. The only true labour force in the country was that on the Nam Patene mines—and the only beneficiaries of the Labour Code were immigrant contract Vietnamese workers.

In the rest of the Lao states labour needs were met by traditional means. Aliens were invariably employed through the labour contractor (or cai) who was granted a lump sum by the prospective employer and then recruited his own labour gang, more often than not becoming its mandor.[11] For Laotians themselves provincial chiefs often filled the role of purveyors of labour; but they merely served as channels for the hiring of labour, not for the imposition or observation of conditions of work which was a matter between the individual workmen and the employers involved. Sawmill owners were amongst the most common employers of such labour, much of which consisted of indentured hill tribesmen. Indentured labour was but a step away from forced labour, pure and simple. In time of harvest failure the hill peoples, whether Thai or Indonesian, had no choice but to seek employment for a mere pittance in the sawmills and lumbering camps of the Chinese and Vietnamese, or in the rice-fields of Lao peasants. Often their poverty and their inability to support themselves converted these people into little more than debt slaves, and there were no officials to check on their situation or to rescue them from their dilemma. Slavery and forced labour were in any case well established institutions amongst the hill peoples, especially the Indonesians. The latter were traditionally looked down upon by the sedentary Lao as suitable prey for servitude whenever the need arose and when they themselves were not being harried and enslaved by Lao raids into the hills, the Indonesians were carrying out slave-raids of their own on others. Indeed the French attempts to stamp out slavery and slave-raiding amongst the Boloven was the principal cause of the six-year-long rebellion which burst out against them in 1901.

As for forced labour, far from abolishing it, it was institutionalized by the French who in 1914 issued a decree calling for the assessment of taxes in the form of labour on Laotians and 'other assimilated Asiatics'. This 'very unpopular' order remained in force up till 1941, largely through force of circumstances because of the general absence of a money economy and the remoteness of many of the peoples so assessed.[12]

Health and social welfare
As far as public health was concerned, the French contribution was rudimentary, as was to be expected in the general economic context. However, in so far as what the French did in the way of fighting disease and in promoting public health was completely new, it represented a significant advance. Before the French takeover Western medicine was totally unknown and public health a private concern. In 1937, when, according to official figures, Laos enjoyed the lowest infantile mortality rates of all five states of the Indo-Chinese Union, it was still probably the unhealthiest country to live in with the highest incidence of disease per head of population. It was certainly the most poorly served by modern medical facilities. The usual list of tropical diseases ranged the country, the most serious of which by far was malaria. Three main types of malaria, allied to different regions and altitudes, accounted for over

90 per cent of the cases. In 1937 28 per cent of the hospital inmates in the country were suffering from this disease.[13]

For the average Laotian disease was a matter of fate, dictated by the innumerable *phi* of the spirit world. Fundamentally therefore little could be done to ward off sickness and whatever remedial aid was offered was given within the framework of the village community. From the Western point of view health conditions were being continuously jeopardized by the false cleanliness of people who insisted on taking frequent baths in polluted waters and who practised insanitary habits with regard to food and the disposal of human waste. Overcoming these deeply-entrenched habits lay well beyond the resources which the French had at their disposal.

Having to work on a shoe-string, the French administration directed its efforts to providing a skeleton framework of public health services and facilities for the country as a whole. As in the other states of the Union, Western medicine was first introduced by the French army which gave help and medical aid to the local inhabitants of whatever area they were operating in.[14] Later, also in line with the rest of Indo-China, Laotian health services were placed under an Inspector-general of Health, Indo-China, who had his headquarters at Hanoi, while a European doctor was placed in charge of each province in the country. The medical establishment in Laos was supplemented by four other European doctors who ran the government laboratories and mobile health units. Much of the routine work was done by 'Indochinese doctors'—invariably Vietnamese graduates of the Hanoi Medical School who worked under the supervision of their European chiefs. In addition to this the services of the Pasteur Institute in Vietnam, the Hanoi Medical School and other health facilities to be found elsewhere in Indo-China were open to those Laotians who could avail themselves of them. Inevitably such a skeleton service was chiefly of benefit to the towns where the health facilities were centred. Prior to 1941 the French had built hospitals at Vientiane, Luang Prabang, Xieng Khouang, Savannakhet, Thahkek and Paksé. However, the rural areas were not entirely neglected; dispensaries, some maternity centres and first aid stations were set up in the countryside. The army continued to play an invaluable role for the hill peoples amongst whom its units were usually stationed, and in general hundreds of thousands of rural folk were the beneficiaries of occasional vaccination and other immunization campaigns. Totally inadequate as they were in relation to the health needs of the country as a whole, the French efforts served to make Laotians aware of the effectiveness of Western medicine.[15] The greatest single French achievement in the medical field was their sanitization of the Nam Patene Basin, once known as 'Death Valley'; however, typically enough, this affected hardly any Laotians at all. In the 1930s a campaign directed under the guidance of the Pasteur Institute largely eradicated malaria and other fevers and ended the notoriety of the district.

In other fields of social welfare (apart from education) the French contribution was barely perceptible. Laos had to pay the price of having a colonial administration which prized the preservation of traditional values and ways above all else. Left to slumber on under its Buddhist mantle, there were no disruptive forces creating economic and social change to muddy the tranquillity of traditional village society. The only element of Western social welfare in Laos was brought by Christian missionaries who working amongst the hill peoples were responsible for the establishment of orphanages and leper settlements. Opium was a state monopoly and considerable numbers of the Meo and other hill peoples were addicts, but in Laotian terms this did not represent a social problem.

In all it can be said that while Laos under French rule remained a largely untouched haven of the traditional world of South-East Asia, it stood in 1941 on the threshold of great changes and willy-nilly was to be thrust by international power politics into the modern world of the twentieth century for which it was woefully unprepared.

[1]The French protectorate of Laos consisted of the kingdom of Luang Prabang itself (comprising the three provinces of Luang Prabang, Houa Phan and Phong Saly) and seven other provinces, the shells of the former principalities of Xieng Khouang, Vientiane and Champassak. In the kingdom of Luang Prabang French authority was administered only indirectly, the actual reins of government remaining in the hands of the king and his royal council. In the other provinces French officials exercised direct power. The proposal to annex the country to Annam, made largely on economic grounds, was shelved because of patent Lao opposition.

[2]It took longer to travel from Saigon up to Luang Prabang by river than it did to sail from Saigon to Marseilles in the south of France. The French succeeded in cutting down the time involved by two-thirds between 1900 and 1937 but it still took more than a month upstream and the best part of a month downstream.

[3]F.M. Lebar and A. Suddard (eds.), *Laos: its people, its society, its culture*, HRAF Press, New Haven, 1960, p. 201 et seq.

[4]Only the 1921 estimates accounted for ethnic composition and omitted all reference to non-indigenous groups such as the Vietnamese and the Chinese. The estimates were derived from questionnaires handed down to officials at all levels as far as the village.

[5]The Nung and the Nhang established themselves in Laos around the sixteenth century. Both peoples were skilled traders, pedlars and caravan men and cultivated *inter alia* the anise tree.

[6]Known as 'Kha' in Laos, they were the same as the 'Moi' of Vietnam and the 'Pnong' in Cambodia—all collective and derogatory terms.

[7]Arthur J. Dommen, *Conflict in Laos: The Politics of Neutralization*, Pall Mall Press, London, 1964, p. 5.

[8]The Man are the same people as the Yao of southern China. The languages of the Man and the Meo, which are interrelated but not mutually intelligible, appear to be closer to those of certain tribal groups in Yunnan than to either Lao or Thai.

[9]In general there was a distinct contrast between the land tenure systems of the hill peoples and those of the plainsmen. Amongst some of the Thai hillsmen, a feudal-type social organization prevailed where the land was held by noblemen and worked by commoners; amongst some of the Kha tribes land was village property and was allotted to individual families by the village council. As for the Lao of the plains, in principle, property of all kinds was divided equally amongst all children but, in practice, sons appeared to be favoured for rice lands and daughters for house sites. The trend towards the fragmentation of property was often met by judicious marriages between second cousins.

[10]Rights over forest land were also obscure, although in theory the laws which obtained for the Union as a whole obtained in Laos as well.

[11]This system was beset by the usual abuses: the labour contractor paid the workers under him, having deducted his own fee first from each man's wages. He was naturally out to get as much as he could for himself.

[12]A similar system existed with regard to porterage which continued to be carried out on a forced labour basis as late as the 1950s.

[13]This leaves out of account the many more cases which went unreported and untreated.

[14]The chief beneficiaries of this type of aid were the hill peoples.

[15]The French introduced the first sanitation laws and the use of quinine and vaccination. They provided aid in time of natural disaster and epidemics and they helped to end the concept that local communities should rely solely on their own resources.

Books and articles for further reading

BOOKS

Cady, J.F., *Thailand, Burma, Laos and Cambodia*, Prentice-Hall Inc., New Jersey, 1966.

Dommen, A.J., *Conflict in Laos: The Politics of Neutralization*, Pall Mall Press, London, 1964.

Fisher, C.A., *South-East Asia: A Social, Economic and Political Geography*, Methuen, London, 1964.

Jacoby, E.H., *Agrarian Unrest in South-East Asia*, Asia Publishing House, Bombay, 1961.

Lebar, F.M. and Suddard, A. (eds.), *Laos: its people, its society, its culture*, HRAF Press, New Haven, 1960.

Purcell, V., *The Chinese in South-East Asia*, Oxford University Press, London, 1965.

Robequain, C., *The Economic Development of French Indo-China*, Oxford University Press, London, 1954.

Steinberg, D.J. (ed.), *In Search of South-East Asia: A Modern History*, Oxford University Press, Kuala Lumpur, 1971.

V THE PHILIPPINES

'Our principal aim had always been that of converting the Indies and the Tierra Firme to our Holy Faith, sending to them prelates, missionaries and other learned persons to instruct them, educate them and teach them good manners.'
Isabella, the Catholic, Queen of Spain. Last Will and Testament, 1604.

'We regard ourselves as trustees acting not for the advantage of the United States but for the benefit of the people of the Philippine Islands.'
Woodrow Wilson, President of the United States of America. Message to the Filipino people, 1913.

'We built well in the Philippines. Our work is a monument to American idealism and enterprise, a living monument of fifteen millions rescued from tyranny, rebellion, ignorance, poverty and disease, and set upon the path of free government, peace, education, prosperity and health. With all seriousness, no nation in the world can boast of so grand a monument.'
Paul V. McNutt, last United States Commissioner to the Commonwealth of the Philippines, Radio address, 1938.

AFTER three and a half centuries under Western colonial rule, the economic and social situation of the Philippines reflected the familiar picture of great productivity set amidst great poverty. The Islands held a virtual monopoly of the world's output of abaca, were the world's largest single supplier of copra and other coconut products, and ranked as the fifth largest producer of sugar. At the same time the bulk of the Filipinos were living in conditions of poverty and squalor while the problems of rural indebtedness and land hunger were amongst the most acute of the entire region. In other respects, the Philippines experience was unique amongst the colonial territories of South-East Asia. Not only had the country been the longest subjugated to colonial rule but it also had undergone the tutelage of two very different colonial powers—first Spain, then the United States of America. In consequence, despite their ethnic and cultural roots, Filipinos today are amongst the most estranged in the region from the ways of life and attitudes of their ancestors, and have come the closest to assuming the attributes and values of Western civilization. The modern features of the Philippines economy have been acquired within the course of the last one hundred years, particularly during the period of the United States regime; nevertheless, as we shall see, it was under the slow, prolonged administration of Spain that the Islands acquired their Christian base and that the foundations of their modern society were laid.

Monopoly and the galleon trade
Although the Philippines was ruled by Spain for over three hundred years, a commercial cash crop economy geared to the world market did not begin

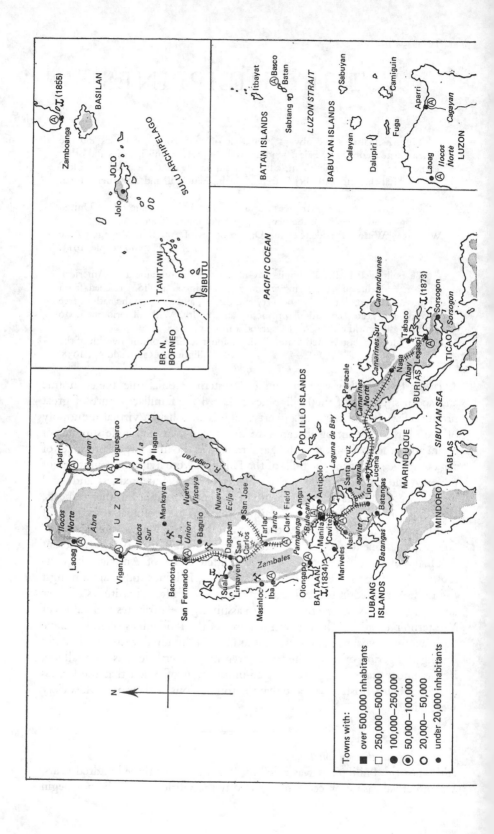

Towns with:

■	over 500,000 inhabitants
□	250,000–500,000
●	100,000–250,000
◉	50,000–100,000
○	20,000–50,000
•	under 20,000 inhabitants

N

BASILAN

Zamboanga Ⓐ (1855)

SULU ARCHIPELAGO

JOLO

Jolo

TAWITAWI

SIBUTU

BR. N. BORNEO

BATAN ISLANDS

Itbayat

Ⓐ Basco

Sabtang Batan

LUZON STRAIT

Sabuyan

BABUYAN ISLANDS

Calayan

Dalupiri Fuga

Camiguin

Aparri Ⓐ

Cagayan

Laoag Ⓐ

Ilocos Norte

LUZON

PACIFIC OCEAN

Aparri

Cagayan

Tuguegarao Ⓐ

Ilagan

Isabella

LUZON

Ilocos Norte

Abra

Mankayan

Nueva Viscaya

Baguio

La Union

Laoag

Vigan Ⓐ

Ilocos Sur

Nueva Ecija

San Jose

Bacnotan

San Fernando Ⓐ

Dagupan

San Carlos

Tarlac

Tarlac

Clark Field

Sual

Lingayen ○

Masinloc

Iba Ⓐ

Zambales

Olongapo Ⓐ

BATAAN ⚓ (1834)

Mariveles

Naic

Pampanga

Angat

Bulacan ✕

Manila ■

Cavite

Antipolo

Ⓐ

Laguna de Bay

POLILLO ISLANDS

Santa Cruz

Laguna

Lipa

Cavite

Batangas

Batangas

Lucena

LUBANG ISLANDS

MINDORO

R. Cagayan

Paracale

Camarines Norte

Camarines Sur

Cantanduanes

Naga

Tabaco

Albay ✕

Legaspi Ⓐ

BURIAS

TICAO

Sorsogon

Sorsogon

⚓ (1873)

SIBUYAN SEA

MARINDUQUE

TABLAS

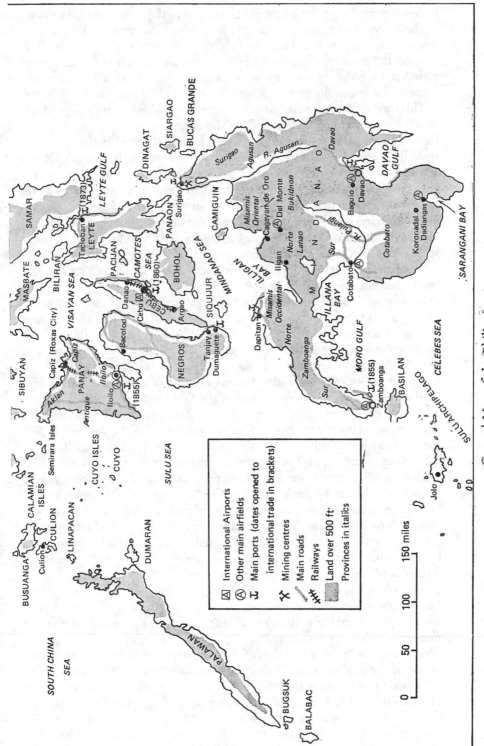

34. General Map of the Philippines, 1941

Legend:
- ⊠ International Airports
- Ⓐ Other main airfields
- ⚓ Main ports (dates opened to international trade in brackets)
- ⚒ Mining centres
- Main roads
- Railways
- Land over 500 ft·
- Provinces in italics

Seas and bodies of water:
SOUTH CHINA SEA, SULU SEA, VISAYAN SEA, CAMOTES SEA, MINDANAO SEA, SIBUYAN, CELEBES SEA, MORO GULF, ILLANA BAY, ILIGAN BAY, DAVAO GULF, LEYTE GULF, SARANGANI BAY, SULU ARCHIPELAGO

Places and provinces:
BUSUANGA, Culion, CULION, CALAMIAN ISLES, LINAPACAN, DUMARAN, PALAWAN, BUGSUK, BALABAC, Semirara Isles, CUYO ISLES, CUYO, Aklan, Antique, PANAY, Capiz (Roxas City), Capiz, Iloilo, Iloilo (1855), MASBATE, SAMAR, BILIRAN, Tacloban, LEYTE (1873), PACIJAN, Danao, Cebu, CEBU (1860), Argao, BOHOL, PANAON, SIARGAO, BUCAS GRANDE, DINAGAT, Surigao, Surigao, CAMIGUIN, SIQUIJUR, Tanjav, Dumaguete, NEGROS, Bacolod, Misamis Occidental, Dapitan, Norte, Sur, Zamboanga, Zamboanga (1855), BASILAN, Jolo, Misamis Oriental, Cagayan de Oro, Del Monte, Bukidnon, Lanao, Norte, Iligan, Cotabato, Cotabato, MINDANAO, Agusan, R. Agusan, Surigao, Davao, Davao, Baguio, Koronadal, Dadiangas, R. Pulangi, Mi, Sur

Scale:
0   50   100   150 miles

to develop until after 1750. In striking contrast to the single-minded servants of the Dutch East India Company in Java who soon converted themselves from merchants into landlords, the Spanish colonists of the Philippines, their eyes on the trade of China and the Americas, did not care to look beyond their Manila godowns to the hinterland and islands beyond, which they were content to leave to the proselytizing efforts of the Roman Catholic Church.

This obsession of the small Spanish oligarchy in Manila with the rich trade which flowed through their port from China to the Americas was the prime factor in their failure to undertake the development of the Islands. In fact this trade became their lifeline but it brought no returns to the Spanish Crown and was of little relevance to the Philippines as a whole. Their preoccupation with the China-Pacific trade sprang from Manila's swift rise as a leading entrepôt for the commerce of the Far East. Within a few years of the Spanish capture of the city, it had become a focal point for the vessels of China and Japan, India and Malacca, Ayuthia, Java, Cambodia and the Moluccas, crammed with wares to offer in exchange for the silver of Mexico. At first there were no restrictions on the traffic across the Pacific, and all seemed set for Manila to become one of the great emporia of the region, leading in turn to the development of the Philippines themselves. But the mercantilist philosophy of the age and the jealousy of the Spanish interests in the trans-Atlantic trade precluded any such development. As early as 1585 at the behest of the merchants and manufacturers of Andalucia, King Philip II was attempting to cut off Manila's China trade, and finally in 1593 he succeeded in imposing a royal monopoly over the entire Spanish commerce across the Pacific. This marked the beginning of the voyages of the famous 'Manila galleon', which annually over the course of the next two centuries carried with it the hopes and fortunes of nearly the entire Spanish community in the Philippines. But for the Islands themselves the establishment of this royal monopoly meant the stifling of any hopes of economic development through trade, since Manila's role was merely to serve as a collecting centre for the Chinese goods so in demand in Spanish America in return for the silver of the mines in Mexico.

As long as the galleon trade lasted, it signified security and profit for the Spaniards of Manila and helped to perpetuate Manila's place amongst the premier ports of the Far East. Its holds stuffed with Chinese silks, cottons, and linens, or porcelain, spices, amber, musk, scented woods 'and other Asian rarities', and with a passenger list of some four hundred on board, the Manila galleon ploughed its dangerous course in a wide arc across the waters of the Pacific to arrive at Acapulco some six and a half months later. The return voyage was quicker, taking well under half the time, borne by the trade winds on a more southerly route via Guam, arriving to the great joy of Manila laden with silver, Western luxuries and the official mail. But the annual departure and arrival of the galleons was of little consequence to the Islands as a whole. The only direct repercussions the trade had on the local economy was in the form of requisitions of labour to provide timber, sails and rigging for the galleons themselves. There was no demand for Philippines products to stimulate development, while the fact that because of the monopoly Manila had become a closed port meant that there was no possibility of future economic development through the spread of free trade. So whilst the Spanish establishment in the city waxed rich, the Islands could not produce enough to support it, with the result that as a colony the Spanish Philippines was run at a loss which had to be borne by the Spanish Crown.

In other words for the sake of the galleon trade the economic development of the Philippines was held in abeyance. Being the easiest and most obvious source of enrichment, officials and merchants alike placed all their hopes and investments on the galleons. It was a highly speculative affair which encouraged corruption to the benefit of a few and to the impoverishment of many. The provinces were regarded merely as a source of tribute and labour to meet the needs of the Manila establishment. As such the Filipinos themselves were given no incentive to produce more than they were forced to in order to meet the demands of their masters and their own needs. The administration outside Manila was left in the hands of a scattering of officials and an army of Roman Catholic missionaries. The main function of the latter, in the eyes of Manila, was to hold the loyalty of the subject Filipinos and to expand the existing subsistence economy sufficiently to maintain the Spanish presence. In the process the friars resettled large numbers of people, founding new villages and townships, introduced new crops, improved methods of agriculture and in general played a major role in moulding the economic and social order on which Filipino life in the nineteenth and twentieth centuries came to be based. They also served to justify the continuance of Spanish rule in the Islands to Madrid, for the Spanish Court was prepared to foot the bill for the administration of the Philippines, despite the heavy burden that this entailed, in the conviction that by so doing it was promoting the interests of Christendom.

The decline of the Manila galleon and the rise of international trade

However the winds of change which were eventually to sweep mercantilism away completely and to bring in an era of unprecedented expansion in trade and production started to be felt towards the middle of the eighteenth century. By the century's end they were exercising a decisive influence on the pattern of development of the Islands and promoting the emergence of a cash crop economy tied to overseas markets. The source of change lay in the encroachments of the rising industrial imperialism of Britain and the emergence of the United States as a new, expansionist power in the Americas which were fast undermining the very bases of the galleon trade. Even in the 1750s the Mexican market was being ruined for the merchants of Manila by the activities of Anglo-Saxon smugglers, while English and other European adventurers were rapidly gaining access to Manila itself through the corrupt laxities of the monopoly system.

Matters were brought to a head by the outbreak of the Seven Years War[1] and the subsequent British occupation of Manila (1762-4). The British occupation proved a turning-point in the economic development of the Islands. Manila was flung open to world trade and the Spaniards, on their return, were never able to close the door effectively again. The galleon trade, in particular, was dealt a mortal blow although it lingered on for another fifty years: the intervention of the European traders in the Chinese market of Manila raised the value of Chinese goods while the British left behind a colony looted and bankrupt and racked by rebellion. Recovery could not be brought about by dependence on the galleon trade alone which in any case ran into a very bad spell of fortune within the next decade. After 1764 it had become obvious to Spanish governors, if not to the Spanish merchants of Manila, that if the colony were to survive the old monopoly system would have to change and that the time had come to develop new routes of trade and to start on the development of the Islands themselves. Whilst the forces of the new industrial age had started to gnaw at the roots of mercantilism, the ideas of the Enlightenment[2] which had already made their mark at the Spanish court were now employed to try and find a solution.

The movement to convert the Philippines into a productive and paying colony dates back to the first half of the eighteenth century. Under the influence of his capable minister, José Patiño, King Philip V (1700-46) decreed the formation of a Spanish merchant company which would hold the right to trade directly with Manila via the Cape of Good Hope. But the scheme was thwarted by the dynastic imbroglios of the Spanish court in Europe and by the vigorous opposition of the merchants of Manila, so that it fell to the monarch Charles III, a generation later, to lend his ear to a powerful lobby advocating the abandonment of the galleon monopoly and the development of the Islands. These advocates of change got their opportunity with the British occupation of Manila. Its restoration to Spanish hands prompted one of them, Leandro de Viana, to present his famous memorial the following year, proposing amongst other things the establishment of direct trade between Spain and the Philippines, the formation of a trading company in order to promote this, and the encouragement of agriculture and industry in the Islands themselves, stimulated by Spanish immigration and the opening up of plantations. Leandro's arguments initially fell on deaf ears (probably because he was still in the Philippines at the time he made them), but a couple of years later the first direct voyage by a merchant vessel was made between Spain (Cadiz) and Manila. Although this first attempt proved totally unprofitable, royal frigates continued making the annual voyage via the Cape of Good Hope up till 1783 with the blessings of the king himself. Finally in 1785 the reform lobby carried the day with the promulgation of a new venture, the Royal Company of the Philippines. Floated with an initial capital of 120 million reales and backed by the leading financial institutions of Spain, the Royal Company was specifically designed to promote direct trade between the motherland and the Philippines and at the same time to develop the natural resources of the Islands. It was granted the monopoly of all Spanish-Philippines commerce, thereby ending the 200-year-old privileges of the Manila merchants in the galleon trade.[3]

In the meantime in the Philippines itself, in the wake of the disaster of the British occupation, the first steps were being taken to move towards a self-supporting economy. The way was opened by the first governor to be appointed after the occupation, José de Basco y Vargas, who arrived in Manila in 1778. A disciple of the Enlightenment and soon proving himself 'the most economically minded of all Spanish governors-general', Basco launched a vigorous campaign to enable the Philippines to stand on its own feet and break in particular its financial dependence on Mexico. To this end he drew up plans for the promotion of agriculture, commerce and industry. On his initiative the cultivation of indigo, pepper, abaca, sugar and tobacco—the three last-named destined to become the staples of the Philippines economy within a few decades—as cash crops for export was seriously undertaken for the first time. He also imported mulberry trees into the Bicol area to stimulate the rise of a local silk industry and tried to promote farming in general by the establishment of the Agricultural Society which granted prizes to enterprising landowners, printed texts on the techniques of cultivation and publicized the study of agronomy. Even more far-reaching was his creation in 1781 of the Economic Society of Friends of the Country, a direct imitation of a movement started in the Basque provinces of Spain in the mid-1760s and instituted in Madrid itself a decade later. Under Basco, the Economic Society became a powerful force for the implementation of his ideas. Under its auspices encouragement was given to entrepreneurs in all fields, particularly to the efforts of the remarkable Francisco Salgado, information was circularized and legislation passed to protect the farmer. The Society was also responsible for the establishment of two government monopolies—one for wine and the other for gunpowder manufacture.

All this activity both in the Philippines and in Spain was proof that official policy had decisively turned away from dependence on the traditional galleon trade towards the establishment of a productive Philippines economy by the end of the eighteenth century. Yet the initial efforts, which were still based on traditionalist mercantilist lines reinforced by the statism of the Enlightenment, did not prove successful. Of all Basco's economic measures, only one, the establishment of the tobacco monopoly in 1781, turned out to be efficacious, carrying with it as it did the seeds of the Culture System adopted later on by the Dutch in Java. The profits of the tobacco monopoly, wrung from the sweated labour of the Ilocans, freed the Philippines from its thrall to the Mexican subsidy. On the other hand, all his other measures, including the Economic Society, failed to mature. Meanwhile the great project of the Royal Company of the Philippines, launched by the grandees of Spain themselves, soon proved an empty boon to the economy of the Islands and was unable to emulate the successes of its older rivals, the Dutch and English East India Companies.

The ultimate failure of the Royal Company stemmed from a combination of factors including poor management, the bitter hostility of the galleon merchants of Manila and a galaxy of unpropitious circumstances. Its directors in Manila were 'improperly selected as well as ignorant and rapacious...'[4] and despite a few years of initial success soon plunged the Company into irremediable debt. In any case the Manila directorate was severely hampered by the powerful opposition of the established merchants of the city who had an entrenched position inside their own council. It was this vested opposition which had prevented the circulation of Leandro de Viana's schemes of reform in the 1760s, had caused the failure of the first direct trading voyage between

Spain and the colony and which had constituted what Basco once described as 'the massive mountain of prejudice that stands in the way of the enlightened purposes of the central government'. These merchants played a major role in the failure of the Royal Company to develop its Manila trade. Perhaps equally as important, however, was the fatal allure of the opium trade with China which caused many of the Company's servants to spend their official time and facilities in the pursuit of their personal fortunes in this field, with the result that even after 1794 when the power of the Manila merchants was broken, no real interest could be worked up for the Philippines trade. In fact, after 1790 the Company concentrated on the direct links between China and the Americas and barely paid lip service to its trade with the Islands. On top of all this, outside events intervened fortuitously to impede further the original designs for success. A series of political crises starting with the Nookta Sound dispute of 1789 and culminating in the Napoleonic Wars and the worldwide dislocation of trade which followed in their wake put paid to all hopes of promoting the Philippines trade and accelerated the downfall of the Royal Company.[5]

Nevertheless the episode of the Royal Company provided signal service for the cause of the economic development of the Philippines. Above all it opened up Manila to foreign trade on a permanent basis, gave the first real stimulus to the production of local merchandise and laid the foundations for future economic development. It also played an important role in bringing about the final collapse of the galleon trade which had paralysed the development of the Islands for so long.[6] Lastly, the very failure of the Company itself also served a purpose since it demonstrated conclusively that the future of the Philippines did not lie with state monopoly but with private enterprise and free trade. In fact, the Company's abolition in 1834 was made the occasion for the promulgation of Manila as a free port open to world commerce.

Manila as a free port and the rise of an export economy
That the Philippines economy could best be built up by free enterprise and that the colony in this way be made to pay its own way had been apparent to a number of Spanish officials for some time, including the governor, Berenguer de Marquina, who in 1790 memorialized the Madrid government with his 'Plan of Reforms for the Government of the Philippines'. The validity of the argument became more painfully explicit with the economic crisis which ensued after the ending of Spanish rule over Mexico and the subsequent bankruptcy of the Manila Consulado. Now completely cut off from Mexican trade or subventions, the entire economic system of the Spanish Philippines needed to be overhauled, but the Spaniards themselves lacked the wherewithal—the capital, the commercial expertise, and even the will—to carry out the operation. The opening of Manila in 1834 implied a recognition of these facts but it was not for another ten years that the Spanish administration committed itself wholeheartedly to the liberal experiment by finally doing away with the commercial perquisites of its high officials.[7]

The consequences were both what the supporters of free trade had hoped for and its opponents had feared. After 1834 the Philippines economy expanded rapidly and as the rise in trade shows, the Islands prospered. Between 1839 and 1870 the value of exports increased by forty-four times, but the bulk of the trade fell into non-Spanish hands. British, American, Swiss, French and other Western firms, starting as simple import-export agencies, paying on commission, soon became the main advancers of credit for the cash crops of the smallholders of the Islands and as such were transformed into sophisticated merchant banking and credit houses with their agents throughout the archipelago. They 'hooked the Philippines into the world community', trading in pounds sterling and American dollars rather than in the peso, and forming ties with the great trading and banking institutions of the Western world. Overnight the traditional Spanish merchant oligarchy of Manila, short in numbers, capital and ships, lost its favoured position. This situation alarmed Madrid and led to the appointment in 1842 of Sinibaldo de Mas, a distinguished diplomat and economist, to investigate the state of affairs. His three-volume report published the following year condemned the vestiges of mercantilism still present in the colony and recommended more liberal measures still. One of his most important recommendations—the opening of other ports besides Manila to foreign trade—was acted upon and by 'one of Spain's rare strokes of economic sagacity'[8] six such ports were eventually opened. Predictably the process of foreign domination over the export economy of the Islands was accelerated so that by 1879 the Philippines resembled 'an Anglo-Chinese colony flying the Spanish flag'[9] but Spanish interests too benefited in the general expansion of economic activity, which helped to justify the policy. At any rate, the liberal experiment had finally given the Philippines a cash crop economy geared to the world market.

Sugar under the Spaniards
Up till 1941 the product that played the leading role in the new cash crop economy was sugar. But although sugar came to dominate the economy during the American period and was a prime factor in the evolution of United States-Philippines relations, the foundations of the industry were laid under the Spanish regime. It was the first of the major cash crops to be exported on a commercial basis and by the end of the nineteenth century was firmly established as one of the staples of the colonial economy.

Sugar itself has been grown in the Islands from early times, introduced from India either directly or by one of the China ports. Its cultivation spread considerably around Manila soon after the Spanish conquest but it had no commercial significance until the last quarter of the eighteenth century when with the British occupation of the capital, foreign merchants were able to establish themselves there for the first time. Even so in 1835 sugar exports did not amount to more than 12,000 tons a year, and the industry was still very much a primitive affair, the cane being processed in crude mills and the product sold or bartered as muscovado or panocha.

The real growth of the sugar industry came with the liberalization of trade which followed the opening of Manila to world commerce in 1834, and more particularly with the opening of Iloilo as a free port just over twenty years later (1855). In this the leading role was taken by foreign merchants who had indeed from the very beginning been a crucial factor in the stimulation of sugar exports. Since the days of Basco, the Spanish authorities had attempted to sponsor the fledgling industry, but they had been hampered by their own restrictions and regulations so that it was the British, French and American import-merchants who, driven by the necessity for profitable return cargoes, stimulated the industry by advancing loans to sugar planters against the delivery of the crop. The pioneer of the modern industry of the Visayas was an Englishman, Nicholas Loney, who, with a background of experience with a British merchant house in Manila, set up shop in Iloilo the year it was opened to foreign trade, and started financing local sugar planters. He worked through the traditional advance system but made his greatest contribution by introducing modern machinery for production.[10] The first steam sugar mill on Negros was set up through his efforts shortly before his death in 1859. Others soon followed. Between 1857 and 1861 the first three modern mills were erected on Panay and by 1861 also the number of steam mills on Negros had risen to thirty. Within the same period the number of European planters (mostly Spaniards backed by foreign capital) rose from two to thirteen and production rose commensurately thirteenfold. At the same time a new element in the industry was introduced with the influx of large numbers of Chinese mestizos from Iloilo itself who, having encountered increasing Chinese competition in the retail trade in piece-goods, sought to recoup their fortunes in the new and profitable field of sugar production.[11]

The mid-century upsurge in sugar production was also stimulated by other factors, chief amongst which were technological advances and the opening of the Suez Canal which quickened the pulse of trade as much in the Philippines as elsewhere in the region.

During the remaining half century of Spanish rule sugar cultivation developed in two main areas—on Negros in the Visayas which proved the most fertile and productive, and in the Luzon provinces of Pampanga and Tarlac. Negros was the original and during Spanish times the most important centre of production, which rose to a peak of 90,000 tons in 1893. Progress during the same period was much more limited in central Luzon where the producers were largely smallholders who could not afford the importation of modern machinery.

Tobacco, abaca and coconut during the Spanish period

The other three staples of the Philippines export economy which emerged in the nineteenth century were tobacco, abaca (Manila hemp) and coconut produce. All bloomed during the American period but all owed their rise, like that of sugar, to the opening of the Islands to foreign trade in the second half of the eighteenth century.

Of these three, tobacco played the most important economic role under Spanish rule and was unique in being the only major cash crop to have been introduced from outside and in remaining the only major industry under predominantly Spanish control in the twentieth century. Tobacco was brought to the Philippines from Mexico by Spanish missionaries soon after the Spanish occupation of the Islands and its cultivation was already widespread by the early years of the seventeenth century. In conformity with the general pattern of economic development, tobacco acquired no commercial significance till the end of the eighteenth century, the earliest shipment being in 1784. However, tobacco's emergence as an export cash crop was sudden and spectacular, and became the object of what was to prove to be the one commercial experiment undertaken by the Spanish colonial administration which really brought in profits. The establishment of a state monopoly over tobacco had been suggested by Leandro de Viana in his memorial to the Spanish Crown of 1766, and was put into effect some fifteen years later by Basco. Designed as one of Basco's measures to establish the economic viability and financial independence of the Philippines in view of the crisis imminent in the Americas, his measure proclaimed large areas in the Cagayan Valley, the Ilocos, Nueva Ecija and Marinduque exclusive for the cultivation of the crop, and achieved immense and immediate success. Within the first decade over one million pesos were remitted to Spain; proceeds from the new monopoly which ended two hundred years of deficits covered the costs of the administration with profit to boot for the following hundred and established the reputation of Philippines tobacco on the world market.

The achievements of the tobacco monopoly were brought about by the implementation of a thorough, ruthless, state-controlled system of forced cultivation. In the designated tobacco areas, each cultivator was expected to tend four thousand plants and sell the leaf at a fixed price to the government buying stations. The leaf was then transported to Manila for processing and manufacture into cigars and cigarettes which were sold, also at a fixed price, either on the domestic or export market. The whole system was placed under the authority of a special minister of tobacco who determined the times of ploughing and planting and other steps, and who had under him an army of provincial officials, crop and market inspectors and internal revenue officers to supervise and enforce the monopoly. Cultivators who failed to produce their annual quota were fined, their houses searched for hidden leaf, punitive expeditions were mounted against the unco-operative, surplus and low grade crops were destroyed. More than one observer regarded the operation of the system excessive, and it was indeed extremely unpopular in the Philippines amongst Spaniard and Filipino alike. Meticulous supervision ensured its success but at the same time led to frightful abuse. Searches for contraband tobacco were made an excuse by unscrupulous officials for pillaging the peasantry. Cultivators too often were not paid for their crops, the money being pocketed by those who should pay them, or they were given worthless promissory notes in lieu of the cash they should have received. As a result many fled the land for Manila and other urban centres; the decrease of population in the Cagayan Valley became particularly marked. In the meantime in Manila itself the system promoted still more corruption in high places. While the best leaf was exported or monopolized by the governor, his top officials and the monied few, a flourishing black market in the crop arose, accompanied by bribery and smuggling on a large scale. In the end the monopoly became increasingly counter-productive and inefficient. The costs of production, manufacture and administration bit deep into the profits and only the absolute certainty that a guaranteed revenue was forthcoming ensured that the Spanish administration did not abandon the monopoly altogether. But by the late 1870s the venality, inefficiency and scandal with which the tobacco system had become associated made its abolition inevitable and in 1882 it was officially brought to an end. The legacy of the monopoly was largely taken over the following year by the Compañia General de Tabacos de Filipinas, a concern newly formed in Spain.

In fact Spanish interests continued to predominate in the industry, but tobacco as an export crop went into decline after the 1870s, though it retained its importance on the domestic market. Its chief markets overseas continued to be Spain for leaf tobacco and Hawaii for cigars.

For the next forty years after the decline of tobacco, abaca held the field as the leading cash crop of the Philippines. Apparently a plant indigenous to the Islands, abaca—described as 'the strongest cordage in the world'—has been used since time immemorial by the Filipinos themselves for making ropes and even cloth, and early acquired a reputation and a market amongst world mariners for the rigging of their ships. The Spaniards soon made use of the fibre for their own galleons on the Acapulco run and for their men o'war used against the Dutch, while the friars encouraged and stimulated cultivation. However, in common with the other staple exports of the Philippines, the true stimulus for the cultivation of the plant for commercial purposes only came with the opening of the Islands to world trade towards the end of the eighteenth century. Basco's Economic Society contributed to the development of the crop by rewarding Lopez Diaz who invented a machine for cleaning the hemp in the 1780s, but it was the growing American demand for abaca which led to its rise as an important export after 1830. By the 1850s most of the Philippine abaca crop was being shipped to New England for manufacture into rope, while at the same period a small American cordage factory was opened in Manila itself. Abaca exports reached their apogée in terms of position during the last decade of Spanish rule. The chief centres of production were in the Bicol provinces of Albay and Sorsogon with some cultivation taking place on Leyte and Samar where the most ideal conditions prevailed.

The last of the four staple cash crops in the Philippines to emerge was also indigenous although not exclusive to the Philippines, namely the coconut. A basic element in the traditional economy, serving as a source of food, fuel and shelter, coconut produce was to rise by the mid-twentieth century to become the main export of the Islands and the Philippines the world's greatest single producer. But it was the last of the cash crops to emerge onto the world market. Coconuts were not exported on a commercial basis until the 1870s, but they started to become available for export as with the other staples in response to the opening of the Islands to world trade. The area initially affected was the waist of Luzon, just south of Manila from around the Laguna de Bay to the Tayabas coast. Its easy accessibility, rich volcanic soils and suitable climate brought this region into prominence as an almost exclusively coconut growing area, so much so that even though later on several of the

Visayan islands and Mindanao further south also became important coconut centres, the Luzon region continued to hold about one-third of all the coconut palms in the Philippines. Of all the staple cash crops, the coconut was the least subject to interference by the colonial authorities and remained essentially a smallholders' affair.

The Spanish period: other cash crops
Amongst the plethora of new plants and crops introduced to the Islands by the Spanish friars, there were a few which became the object of attempts at commercial development when the Philippines was opened to world trade. Of these the most notable was indigo which at one stage seemed set fair to become a major product of the colony.

Indigo was introduced to the Islands within the first decades of Spanish rule but like the rest had to await its opportunity till the last quarter of the eighteenth century when the growth of foreign trade and the schemes of Basco stimulated commercial agriculture. In direct consequence the cultivation of indigo in Ilocos was encouraged and the first reported cargo of the crop for overseas market left Manila in 1783-4. For the next few years considerable efforts were made by the colonial administration to promote indigo planting. Under Basco, the Economic Society, already responsible for the first shipment of the produce, urged on all those interested in the crop. A few years later the newly-formed Royal Company of the Philippines was actively supporting its exportation. But the major role was played by the Chinese mestizos of Rizal who, building on the foundations of the Augustinian friar Matias Octavio at Malabon, spread its cultivation to Bataan and found a market for it in Manila. So successful was the mestizo monopoly over indigo cultivation through the traditional system of advancing to the farmers, that the Manila authorities became alarmed and tried to break their grip. However the fate of the industry was determined by other factors. Near the turn of the century production was hit by the conscription of a large number of the cultivators into the militia. Heavy overheads, inadequate capital resources and primitive techniques further hampered the efforts of the smallholders and by 1840 it was reported that manufacturers in the Islands were not producing more than one ton a year each, and most of them much less.

Other commercial ventures during the Spanish period were still more fruitless. Efforts (by a Franciscan friar) to establish coffee planting were a total failure. Basco's Economic Society made a determined effort to promote a local silk industry as well as cotton, cinnamon, pepper and tea.[12] The Royal Company made similar efforts, besides essaying the planting of spices in the Bisayas and the manufacture of salt. Attempts were also made to cultivate wheat and cacao with equally unsatisfactory results.

The domestic economy under the Spanish regime: rice
The rise of cash crops brought about important shifts in the general economic pattern. In particular to be affected was rice which now acquired a commercial value. But though production rose swiftly in the course of the nine-

teenth century, it did not do so sufficiently in order to keep pace with growing demand.

Although by comparison with most other lands in the region the area of
cultivated land under rice is low, rice was the most important food crop in
the Islands. In 1609, according to de Morga, rice was 'the daily mainstay for
the entire country'.[13] Three hundred years later over two-fifths of the land
tilled was under the crop and it formed the staple diet for nearly three quarters of the population. Most of the rice grown was wet rice and there were
three distinctive modes of production which had persisted since pre-Spanish
times. Of these the least significant were the slash-and-burn methods (kain-
gin) practised by the remote hill peoples, which as elsewhere were extremely
primitive and provided small yields. The other two methods comprised the
traditional wet rice cultivation of the lowlands and the highly sophisticated
terrace rice farming of northern Luzon.

Of the two the terraced rice fields of the Ifugaos, Bontocs and other peoples of
the north represented the older and technically superior way. Owing nothing
to the Spaniards, this remarkable system of terraces climbing the hill face to
heights of 5,000 feet, was probably introduced to the Islands by the second
wave of Indonesian immigrants between the seventh and fourth centuries
B.C. Why the system should come to be confined to northern Luzon is not
properly understood, but it is clear that the terraced fields were closely related
to the intricate and unique socio-economic patterns of the peoples involved.
In contrast rice cultivation in the lowlands where the plough had been known
from the remote past and where Spanish influence had brought marginal
improvements in irrigation and other techniques remained a simple, primitive
affair, virtually identical with the rice culture of other Malaysian lands,
characterized by the use of the buffalo (carabao), hand transplanting, fields
watered by impounded rain and perennially low yields. In the nineteenth
century, however, as whole districts were given over to the cultivation of
specific cash crops, the demand for rice rose together with the price, and
there was a marked extension of the area under the grain. Rice farming in
the traditional areas for production in the central plains of Luzon increased
and spread to peripheral areas such as the Cagayan Valley and Negros. Rice
production in central Luzon itself was also considerably stimulated by the
construction of the railway line northwards from Manila in the closing years
of the century. The increasingly commercial nature of rice production
brought important social consequences in its train. Dealing in rice proved
another profitable field for mestizo enterprise and accelerated the growth of
large landed estates, tenancy and sharecropping, and the shaping of a crisis
on the land.

But demand outstripped supply. The rice-bowl of the country remained
central Luzon with Pampanga the most fertile province yielding two crops
a year. The provinces of the plain were able to send their surpluses to feed
Manila and other parts of the country, but by the end of the century Ilocos
on the mainland and Panay in the Visayas were the only other centres with
a surplus to spare. The Ilocos rice was sent to Manila while the surplus from
Panay was usually earmarked for the Spanish garrisons and fleets watching

Mindanao and the Moluccas. On the other hand since the early days of Spanish rule Cagayan and the Camarines produced no food surplus and Cebu had to depend for its rice supplies on imports from neighbouring Leyte, Samar and Bohol. By the middle of the nineteenth century crisis point had been reached and after 1870 the Philippines had to import rice every year to meet the needs of its peoples.

Other Spanish contributions: maize, yam and manioc

Apart from their contributions to the commercial economy of the Islands, the introduction of new plants by the Spaniards also played an important role in the domestic economy. The most important crops in this field were maize, yam and manioc, all brought to the Islands by Roman Catholic missionaries. Maize became by far the most important, although it did not win acceptance in the principal rice-growing regions. But up till the nineteenth century at any rate the wet rice areas were limited and well defined, and in the rest of the Islands where rice cultivation did not predominate maize became without much difficulty the staple crop of the people. Cebu developed as the chief producer of maize in the Islands and the crop also became the mainstay of the diet of the shifting cultivators in the hills.

The yam or sweet potato became an important staple food in certain areas of the country, particularly in the northern part of Luzon, while in the south, especially in the Sulu archipelago, a similar role was played by manioc or cassava.

The Philippines economy: the Spanish role

From what has been said it is clear that during the three centuries of their domination, the Spaniards made an appreciable impact on the economy of the Islands and eventually succeeded in linking it to the system of international trade. However the impact was strictly limited. In effect, the Spaniards did not transform the pre-colonial economy; they merely supplemented and reinforced it. Their presence imposed a burden on the existing subsistence way of life which would have been unsupportable alone. The introduction of maize, yam and manioc probably prevented mass starvation and economic collapse, but these did not end the basic Filipino dependence on their rice and root crops, their fishing, hunting and game. The domestic economy remained essentially agricultural, tradition-bound and static. Even in the field of export crops, the modes of cultivation and production stayed primitive and entrenched within the traditional framework. Production increased under the pressure of outside events such as the Dutch Wars of the seventeenth century and the penetration of foreign trade, especially after 1834, but this increase was in terms of numbers and area rather than in productivity and techniques. Only in the last years of Spanish rule did the colonial government start to take active and effective steps to promote agricultural development, but these efforts were swiftly overtaken by political events which brought Spanish rule itself to an end.[14]

In other fields of economic activity the Spanish contribution was still more limited. The Spaniards barely tapped the vast reserves of forest land with their rich array of hardwoods, resins and other jungle produce. They built their galleons with the timber of the forests around the Laguna de Bay but there was no systematic exploitation or administration of the forest lands until the time of the United States administration. More attention was paid to the possibilities of livestock in the Islands. The Spaniards were responsible for the introduction of cattle and horses as well as various wild fowl. A particular effort dating back to the sixteenth century was made to develop a cattle-raising industry. By 1606 there were some 24,000 head of cattle in the Islands, but they failed to thrive. In most places there was no suitable pasturage and the climate was against them. Apart from that, the industry could offer no great profits as the market was limited to the Spanish colonists themselves. They also experimented with donkeys and oxen, sheep, goats and kids with a similar lack of success. Horses were used—Japanese and Chinese breeds were found to acclimatize far better than Mexican varieties—but they did not create a revolution in transportation. Meanwhile the native water buffalo remained supreme. Water buffaloes had been used for ploughing long before the advent of the Spaniard but their use in this capacity was restricted to the rice fields of Luzon and Panay until well after 1750. Elsewhere animal power was not employed at all. It was not until the 1880s that official attempts were made to experiment in animal breeding by setting up special farms. As for fishing, which played a major role in the subsistence economy of the Filipinos, the development of this industry into a major affair also had to await the arrival of the Americans.

A major factor which affected the whole course of Spanish policy towards the Philippines and its development was the apparent scarcity of minerals. For the Spanish conquistadores the Islands were not another Mexico or Peru with fabled riches of gold and silver to seize and hold. If the Spaniards had suspected otherwise, the colony's hinterland would not have been left to the friars alone to carry out their purposes. The Spaniards were well aware of the existence of certain iron, copper and gold deposits, all of which had been worked since time immemorial. The gold caught the attention of Legazpi and other Spanish pioneers, but exploitation was difficult. These minerals, let alone the others as yet undivined, lay in remote and inaccessible places. Mining would have required capital and techniques which only became available in the twentieth century. So even the mining of gold remained a primitive and limited enterprise, which made only a small contribution to the economy of the Islands.

Underwriting the general Spanish failure to develop the Philippines economy until the closing years of the nineteenth century was the restricted and rudimentary system of communications that evolved under their rule. In 1898 the Islands possessed only 900 miles of road and 117 miles of railway track, while a handful of companies whose vessels 'meandered among the islands' provided the elements of a shipping system. Nevertheless these land and sea links, limited as they were, represented a fair amount of progress in the nineteenth century and the Philippines was beginning to participate in the world revolution in transportation.

Inevitably water-borne transport played the leading role in the communications of the Islands, dictated by environment and the abundance of cheap labour. From the beginning the Spaniards relied upon the sea, without appreciably altering the local pattern till the advent of the nineteenth century with its technological innovations. They exploited the craft of the Filipino boatbuilder and probably improved his skills, but they did not revolutionize the ships he built. The great innovation of the nineteenth century which led to a swift improvement in sea communications and added a new dimension to Spanish power was the introduction of the steamship. The first such vessels, purchased from their English builders, arrived in the Philippines in 1848. A couple of decades later with the opening of the Suez Canal the time between Manila and Europe had been reduced by steamer to only one month. In the meanwhile a number of Manila firms had opened up regular inter-island services in small, slow but serviceable vessels, so that on the eve of American rule, the basic network of inter-island steamship routes had been laid.

The development of land communications also had to wait until the nineteenth century before a real start could be made. Prior to 1800 travelling overland was rendered difficult by the terrain of hill, swamp and sea, and was unnecessary in view of the lack of economic development. Those who had to travel did so by mule or by horse, or were borne in litters by human porters; 'the ordinary folk just walked'. The greatest Spanish contribution during this period was the introduction of horse transport, and it was the missionaries who were the pioneer road builders. Using forced Filipino labour they built hundreds of miles of roads and tracks, together with bridges. The rise of a cash crop economy and the expansion of trade in the nineteenth century brought about direct government participation. For the first time in the 1830s there was a 'road-building governor', Pascual Enrile, who with his engineer nephew promoted an extensive state road building programme. But the first car did not appear on the streets of Manila till Spanish rule had passed away and the earliest form of mechanized transport in the Philippines was the railway. The first railway line was started in 1891 to join Manila with Dagupan in the north. Completed three years later, it was built by a British engineer and owned by a British firm. By 1898 Manila itself boasted a horse-drawn tram service, started ten years earlier and run by a Spanish-Filipino company. The nineteenth century also saw the introduction of postal services and the first telegraph, cable and telephone links, which replaced church bells (also a Spanish contribution) as the heralds of news, good and bad.

The American impact
So at the end of the century when Spanish rule gave way to that of the United States of America, the transformation of the Philippines from a self-contained subsistence economy to one tuned to cater for the world market was virtually complete. The basic elements of commercial agencies, credit facilities and trunk lines of communication were already there for the Americans to make use of, which they at once proceeded to do. The short epoch of American domination saw a decisive expansion of the economy in all directions. Economic development was galvanized by the philosophy of a na-

tion dedicated to *laissez-faire* capitalism, individual initiative and free enterprise, although the tenets of free trade were applied in a somewhat special way which enmeshed the economy of the Islands with that of the United States domestic market. By 1938 80 per cent of Philippines overseas trade was with the United States, while a similar or greater proportion of her imports came from the American mainland, with the result that the Philippines had become more dependent economically on her colonial master than any other Western dependency in South-East Asia. At the same time her four staple cash crops grew tremendously in output, particularly sugar and coconut.

The sugar industry under the United States administration

The most spectacular development amongst the cash crops was that in sugar. During the United States period (i.e. up till 1941) sugar production increased six-fold and by the 1930s was firmly established as the country's leading export, its value being twice that of those for tobacco, coconut and abaca combined. However, the rise of sugar was not an immediate consequence of the American takeover. In fact sugar cultivation remained in a depressed condition from the start of the century till the 1920s when production exceeded Spanish norms for the first time. The sudden change in the fortunes of sugar after 1920 was one result of the Great War which greatly increased demand. It was also helped by the introduction of modern methods and technology, in particular with the institution of huge and costly centrifugal mills[15] and the existence of the new railway line which ran north from Manila and opened up the plains of Pampanga. But the decisive role in the expansion of the industry was played by the evolving tariff policy of the United States to the Philippines.

At first sugar imports from the Philippines were subject to a crippling tariff which effectively excluded them from the American market.[16] In 1909 the tariff schedules were altered (the Payne-Aldrich Tariff Act) which opened a market for sugar in the United States by permitting a certain quota to be imported duty-free. Four years later, by the Underwood-Simmons Tariff Act of 1913, this quota was lifted entirely and sugar granted free entry to the United States market. But the measure which really boosted Philippines sugar at the expense of its competitors was the Fordney-McCumber Tariff of 1921 which nearly doubled the existing tariff rates on other sugar imports and thereby placed the Philippine product in an unassailable position. The consequences were quickly seen. Production rose rapidly and between 1920 and 1934—the latter the peak year for pre-1941 production—output doubled and the area under sugar cultivation increased by 50 per cent.[17]

But there were other consequences as well. The tariff policies of the United States also had a decisive influence on the way in which the sugar plantation industry of the Islands themselves developed. In the first place sugar interests in the United States used their power to prevent the Philippines industry from raising a serious threat to their own position. Thus for many years these interests were responsible for preventing the importation of machinery duty-free into the Islands, fearful lest this would lead to keener competition from Philippines sugar millers.[18] American sugar manufacturers were also quite successful in opposing any liberalization of Philippines land laws so preventing the growth of large sugar plantations which once again would represent a threat to their interests. As a result, as in Dutch Java, the cultivation of sugar in the Islands remained basically in the hands of the peasant smallholder. The problem of organizing production on a large scale for the United States market was overcome, especially in central Luzon, through the establishment of sugar centrals—large, modern refineries set in the midst of the sugar plots which yielded the crop.[19] The cultivators themselves were more often than not the tenants of large estates whose owners contracted with the mill managers for their labour. In this way an unholy alliance arose between the American or Filipino capitalists who financed the central refineries and the traditional landowners of the countryside, giving rise to 'sugar barons' whose lands grew along with the establishment of the centrals, leaving the peasant in his customary state of near serfdom and perennial poverty. Furthermore the protection of the American tariff, by providing a guaranteed market in the United States where prices were well above the average world level, allowed the Philippines industry an artificial growth which sustained the 'sugar barons' with great profits but which did not provide the incentive for modernization and efficiency. In fact the efficiency and productivity of the Philippines sugar industry was well below that of its main rivals and its product was priced right out of the world market.

By the end of the 1920s virtually the entire Philippines export crop of sugar was being imported by the United States, thereby putting the economy of the Islands in a very dependent position in relation to the colonial power. The precariousness of the Philippines position was amply demonstrated in the political debates of the early 1930s which accompanied the presidential elections and the protracted negotiations over the Islands' autonomy.[20] The tough negotiations which led to the establishment of the Philippines Commonwealth in 1935 provided for the progressive imposition of quotas and tariffs on all Philippines products. The future for sugar on the eve of the Pacific War looked bleak indeed. Faced with the closing doors of the American market and a total inability to compete at world market levels, it was clear that the industry would have to undergo radical transformation in order to survive.[21]

The coconut industry under the United States regime
The rise of the coconut industry under the United States regime was also spectacular. The establishment of American rule provided an immediate fillip to the industry since there was a ready market in the United States itself. However tariff policy played as critical a role in the case of coconut as it had in that of sugar. The real expansion in coconut products began in 1910, the year following the passing of the Payne-Aldrich Tariff Act which established partial free trade between the two countries. During the course of the next nine years there was a rapid increase in the export of coconut products, especially of coconut-oil and copra, accompanied by a corresponding increase in planting and production in the Islands. Coconut exports were

further stimulated by the Fordney-McCumber Tariff Act of 1921 which left copra still untaxed and coconut-oil competitive on the United States market. By 1934, when 17 per cent of Philippines exports consisted of coconuts and their derivatives, two-thirds were being absorbed by the United States. But in that same year the extreme vulnerability of the Philippines export economy to the vagaries of American tariff policy was demonstrated once again when an amendment to the Tydings-McDuffie Act threatened ruin to Philippines coconut producers.[22] In the event disaster was averted by a timely drought in the United States which raised the prices of oils and fats all round. Hence in 1941, by which time coconut products had grown to claim nearly one-quarter of all Philippines exports, the coconut industry was flourishing and still growing.

The chief coconut products marketed were copra, coconut-oil, desiccated coconut and copra meal. Of these copra was the most important. Its production had increased nine-fold since 1900 and since it commanded a better market in Europe (while coconut-oil had a better market in the States), processing was more suitably done in the Islands themselves, giving rise to an important local industry. Nevertheless the general quality of the copra exported was poor. It was largely processed by smallholders who lacked the resources, techniques and know-how to prepare, dry and store. A large amount of the oil produced was retained for local use but nearly all the desiccated coconut was exported, mostly to the United States. In general processing and exporting was foreign (mainly American) controlled. Although there were many small, independent mills for the oil and its by-products, the two major coconut-oil plants which catered for the overseas market were owned by international companies. Similarly plants for desiccating coconut were few in number and foreign-owned. The limited number of foreign firms, mostly American ones, in the coconut processing and exporting business made collusion between them simple and price-fixing an established practice.

As in the Netherlands East Indies, although the exportation of the crop was controlled by foreigners, its cultivation remained a smallholders' affair.[23] Most coconut plantations were no more than $12\frac{1}{2}$ acres apiece and of the $2\frac{1}{4}$ million acres under the crop, a bare 1 per cent was controlled by large estates. Most large plantations were to be found in the more recently developed areas, particularly Mindanao. The vast area under the crop—representing two-thirds of the total area devoted to commercial export crops in the Islands—together with the large numbers of people involved, made the coconut industry the leader amongst the cash crop industries of the Philippines. The great expansion in coconut cultivation which took place in the American period altered the production map of the Islands. Although southern Luzon remained the greatest single producing region, in terms of output, it yielded to the Visayas and Mindanao. In Mindanao coconut cultivation spread rapidly along the north coast and southwards towards Zamboanga on the eastern side and to the Gulf of Davao on the western side. By 1941 the Visayas were the greatest source of production and soon after 1945 Cebu supplanted Manila as the chief centre for the collection and processing of the crop.

Abaca and tobacco under the United States

When the United States took over control of the Philippines, abaca was the leading cash crop of the Islands. Under American rule it continued to hold its position as one of the mainstays of the export economy although it lost its predominance to sugar in the 1920s and fell to a much reduced role in the following decade. In addition the Philippines retained its place as virtually the sole supplier of the crop for the world market; in 1941 it produced some 95 per cent of total world output. Production also continued to increase and the area under cultivation to expand. Between 1900 and 1941 the yield more than doubled and its cultivation spread, particularly around Davao in east Mindanao. Davao became the centre for an active colony of Japanese planters and entrepreneurs who extended the land under the crop from 6,300 acres in 1903 to 270,000 acres some thirty years later, an area which represented one-third of the total amount of land under abaca. In the twentieth century Davao along with the two Bicol provinces of Albay and Sorsogon were the main centres of production. The Davao region was particularly suitable for its cultivation with its soils enriched by the volcanic ashes of Mount Apo. Japanese enterprise in the region made abaca more of a large-scale affair than the cultivation of any other cash crop, but beyond Mindanao the industry still rested predominantly in the hands of smallholders.

The fortunes of the abaca trade during the American period were as much dominated by tariff politics as was the rest of the Philippines economy. Although the Payne-Aldrich Act of 1909 permitted the duty-free importation of abaca into the United States, the actual duty was nevertheless collected and then refunded to the *importers*! This concession to the cordage manufacturers of the United States had aroused nationalist ire ever since it was first granted, and finally in 1913 with the passing of the Underwood-Simmons Act the offending duty was lifted entirely. After this episode abaca enjoyed free access to the United States market and its fall from leadership amongst the cash crops of the Philippines was qualitative, not quantitative. Production and exports continued to expand, and although the American market was by far the most important, absorbing about half the total output of cordage and a quarter of that of abaca itself, the crop had important customers elsewhere. Cordage production in particular rose spectacularly from the mid-1920s and increased by 200 per cent within the decade prior to its peak year of 1934. The success of Philippines cordage within the American market aroused increasingly strong opposition from domestic competitors in the 1930s.

In the meantime tobacco, the star crop of the nineteenth century, never recovered its former glory although it remained an important adjunct to the economy of the Islands. As an export crop its value sharply declined, until it reached the point in the late 1930s when it accounted for only $\frac{3}{4}$ per cent of their total value. Philippines tobacco was granted access to the United States domestic market under the various tariff Acts which characterized American colonial policy; in particular by the Acts of 1909 it was accorded a duty-free quota which was comfortably above actual export levels. In reality the different smoking tastes of the United States consumer were the most effective barrier against the penetration of the Philippines product, and by the 1920s it was the Philippines tobacco industry that was being challenged by American Virginian tobacco within the Islands themselves. As time went by Filipinos showed a growing preference for American blends, to the extent that it became profitable to plant Virginian tobacco in various parts of the Islands. Nevertheless the production of the local tobacco doubled during the period of United States rule, more and more of which was consumed on the domestic market. Although taking up about 1 per cent of the total cultivated area, it was grown in small amounts almost everywhere and contributed a substantial fifth to the internal revenues of the country. The Cagayan leaf still held its primacy for cigars and the Ilocos coast for cigarettes.

The United States regime: rubber and other crops

Although much was done by the new United States administration to improve agriculture in general, no new major cash crop for export was successfully developed nor was there any appreciable increase in the importance of any other crop already cultivated apart from sugar, copra and abaca. In this respect perhaps the most surprising development was the failure of the Philippines to cash in on the rubber boom which swept the Malay world at the beginning of the twentieth century, especially since the United States itself was from the very start the world's greatest consumer of rubber. In fact, interested parties made considerable efforts to found a rubber industry in the Islands, particular attention being paid to Mindanao and the Sulu archipelago where the most suitable conditions obtained. The main barrier to the implementation of such designs was the principled adherence of American colonial officials to certain policies aimed at protecting Filipino interests. First amongst these came American land policy; the American administration in Manila deliberately fashioned restrictive land laws with the specific purpose of thwarting capitalist entrepreneurs who were only too eager to establish large plantations at the expense of the native farmer. Colonial land policy in the Philippines in fact became a major factor in discouraging large-scale foreign investment in rubber in Mindanao. Foreign capital was also put off by the absence of a suitable, cheap labour force. Once again in defence of Filipino interests, the American administration maintained strict controls over Chinese immigration, thereby confining the labour market to the islanders of Mindanao who for various reasons were not interested or suitable, and to migrants from the Ilocos and the Visayas. Exasperated by the denial of rich opportunities in the south, a group of American capitalists interested in the development of a rubber plantation industry, even went so far as to advocate the separation of Mindanao and the Sulu archipelago from the rest of the Philippines, to be placed under a distinct American administration. Such a plan was actually discussed during the administration of Governor Leonard Wood (1921–7) but it aroused such a storm of nationalist opposition that it was quickly dropped.[24] These various factors prevented the rise of a large rubber planting industry in the Islands; in 1941 there were only half a dozen or so large rubber estates, nearly all on Mindanao itself. The largest of these was the Goodyear plantation in the Zamboangan Peninsula, covering some

12,000 acres; this estate was also the only one to be run on entirely scientific lines, its trees all having been cloned in Sumatra.

Amongst other cash crops there was one huge pineapple plantation of 15,000 acres, also on Mindanao, wholly geared to the export market. Sisal fibre was grown in small quantities, while ramie had local importance around Cotabato and Davao.

The output of domestic crops expanded, but this was more a reflection of the increase in area brought under cultivation than of greater productivity. The three main domestic crops still remained rice, maize and yam which between them covered approximately 70 per cent of the total area under cultivation. Amongst these the most remarkable expansion was shown by maize whose production increased more than that of any other crop, particularly after 1937. Rice production also increased by five times between 1900 and 1941 but this was not fast enough to catch up with the still greater increase in population. Under United States rule the goal of regaining self-sufficiency in rice, lost to the Islands since the middle of the previous century, was never attained. The main American contribution in this field was the construction of a large number of irrigation schemes which raised the area under controlled irrigation from a mere 67,000 acres in 1900 to over $1\frac{3}{4}$ million acres by 1935, a sum which represented four-fifths of the total area under rice, the great bulk of which was grown in swamp land. In common with the rest of Philippines agriculture, rice productivity was low. Naturally the most productive regions were those where the irrigation works had been extended, in particular the Central Plain of Luzon where one-third of the fields were located and two-fifths of the harvests of the Islands were obtained. Beyond this the second most important region in the Islands was on thickly populated Panay, while the coastal plains of Ilocos came third.

The United States regime: agriculture, forestry, livestock and fisheries
Despite the fact that agriculture was the main occupation of the people of the Islands, even under the far more progressive rule of the United States it remained basically primitive, traditional and static, especially in the domestic sector. Farming was largely a subsistence, family affair, providing small yields, a condition governed by a total lack of capital, poor soils and primitive techniques. The Americans, however, laid the foundations for improvement by establishing an organizational framework. In 1902 the Bureau of Agriculture was established, the first government department to be set up under the new regime. Scientific methods of cultivation were encouraged by the creation of model and experimental farms. New strains of rice and livestock were imported, weights and measures standardized, modern farm machinery introduced from the United States and effective measures taken against pests and diseases. These steps were insufficient to solve the problem of agricultural backwardness which was itself intermeshed with the whole nexus of rural poverty, to achieve a solution for which mere technical methods could not suffice; but at least they paved the way for the administration of the Commonwealth which was to follow.[25]

Another field of great potential which though developed by the Americans still remained comparatively neglected was that of the Islands' vast forest reserves. Exploitation of these increased by six times under the United States regime but the real expansion only took place after 1945. Once again the main American contribution was in the organization of the foundations for future expansion. A forest bureau was set up, which together with the implementation of strict land laws protected this great natural resource from undue and unscrupulous exploitation. On the other hand, the colonial administration made a major contribution to the livestock industry and to fisheries. The number of animals, particularly of water buffaloes, cattle and pigs, quadrupled within forty years and livestock rearing became for the first time an important industry. The fishing industry also expanded to take on a significant role in the economy, especially with regard to deep sea fishing and fish canning. Up to 1941 these two operations were virtually monopolized by the Japanese.

The development of mining under United States rule
Under the American regime there was a significant increase in mining activity and production, although this came as a late development. Moreover prior to 1941 the full mineral potential of the Islands was not realized, and apart from gold, mineral production made only a minor contribution to the national economy. Nevertheless right from the very beginning the First Philippines Commission had its eyes on the possibility of developing the mineral resources of the Islands, but as was the case with the forest reserves, the new administration acted cautiously to avoid unscrupulous exploitation. Thus the First Organic Law of the Philippines (the Cooper Bill) of 1902 denied to the administration the right of disposal of public lands known to be mineral areas. Governor Taft the following year proposed that interested parties be allowed to file more than one mining claim on lode or deposit, but the initial mining laws based on United States practice were withdrawn in 1904 and replaced with a new act reinstating Spanish law so as to end the confusion that had arisen over such claims. In the event, however, there was no mining fever in the Philippines until the 1930s when a gold rush precipitated by the devaluation of the United States dollar in 1933 and an increase in the fixed price of gold took place. Prior to 1928 gold production never exceeded in value more than four million pesos a year, most of it coming from the old, established mines at Paracale in Camarines Norte. Output started to rise with the opening of the Baguio mines which soon became the chief gold-mining centre. The gold rush proper started in 1933 and lasted for the best part of four years, culminating with a peak output of 900,000 ounces in 1937. As a result of this expansion minerals were pushed up to second place amongst Philippines exports by 1941. Gold of course was the main element, placing the Philippines sixth amongst world producers; in 1940 there were forty-two mines in operation, run by fifteen companies and engaging more than 40,000 workers. However the peak had been passed in 1937 and after that date began a decline which was accelerated by the war itself.

Up till 1941 there was also some though far more limited expansion in other mining activities. The most spectacular development was in chromite.

Commercial production from a large mine in Zambales started in 1935, the great bulk of which was shipped to the United States. By 1939 the Philippines was already the world's fifth largest producer. Manganese mined by small-scale operators on Luzon, Masbate, Bohol and elsewhere, reached its peak production in 1938, with its principal markets in Japan and the United States. Copper, obtained from what was for many years the largest mine in the whole of the Far East, located in the hills of northern Luzon, was shipped in its unprocessed state to smelters at Tacoma, Washington, United States. Substantial iron-mining, exclusively for the Japanese market, commenced in the mid-1930s was exceeding 1 million tons a year from 1938, reaching its pre-war peak the following year. Some silver was obtained as a by-product of gold, copper or lead. The Islands also possessed coal reserves variously estimated at between 25 to 40 million tons, but the seams were thin and mining costs high; the only mines in production before 1941 were on Cebu and Mindanao and they produced barely one-tenth of the Islands' needs. Traces of oil were detected here and there without any commercial finds before 1941, and a considerable range of other minerals was also exploited, but on a very insignificant scale.

The growth of communications under the United States
The most tangible and substantial part of the American legacy to the Philippines was in the great extension of communications which took place after 1900. The Americans were swift to build on and to extend the Spanish foundations and provided the Islands with their first proper infrastructure on which later economic development could be based. The lack of effective communications had indeed been forcibly impressed on the new colonial administrators by the difficulties this caused in executing the military operations against the nationalist forces in the American-Filipino struggle of 1899-1902. As a result the very first act of the Philippines Commission was the appropriation of a large sum of money to construct roads and bridges in 1900. Subsequently a network of modern roads was developed, particularly in central Luzon. More than half the all-weather roads in the Philippines came to be built on Luzon itself, most in a closely-meshed system amongst the rice fields of the Central Plain. Beyond this, metalled roads remained far more limited; two lonely roads, one via the Ilocos coast and the other by the Cagayan Valley, linked Manila with the north of the island. The only other islands which came to possess a coherent road system at all were Panay, Cebu, Negros, Leyte and Bohol, while on the large island of Mindanao the total mileage of all-weather highway did not amount to more than a tenth of the roadways in the Philippines as a whole. The greatest era of road building was during the administration of Governor-general Harrison (1913-1921), although his predecessor, Cameron Forbes, acquired the sobriquet of the 'American road-building governor-general' on account of the large allocations made under his administration for this purpose. In 1935 there were over 12,000 miles of roads and 8,100 bridges, and by 1941 this total had been raised by another 9,000 miles. The road system of the Islands on the eve of the Pacific War was still far from adequate but represented all the same a substantial achievement.

The railway system also underwent considerable expansion after 1900, although the ambitious plans laid down in 1904 by the Philippines Commission never came to fruition. The Commission believed that the development of the railway system was essential as a means of promoting pacification, consolidation and trade. But their proposals aroused a great deal of controversy in the United States. The controversy had its origins in the 1903 proposal of Governor Taft that all investors in railway development should be granted a government guarantee of a 4 per cent return on their investment. This proposal received the support of the Republican Party in the United States but was condemned by the Democrats as 'an unwise, impolitic and unpatriotic scheme of colonization'.[26] But the Republicans were in power and won the day. The Philippines Bill of 1905 incorporated the 4 per cent guarantee amongst its clauses and on this basis railway concessionaires were invited to submit their tenders without delay. Two companies obtained concessions, and by the following year (1906) actual construction had begun. One of these companies, the Philippine Railroad Company, was awarded a contract to build about 300 miles of track on the islands of Panay, Cebu and Negros. Construction on the Panay and Cebu lines was completed by 1910, but in view of the poor returns these new lines showed in operation, the plans to build on Negros as well were abandoned. The other concern, the Manila Railroad Company, contracted the right to build some 452 miles on Luzon without any government guarantee. By 1917, in which year it was taken over by the Philippines government, this firm had extended the Manila line northwards beyond Dagupan to San Fernando, and southwards to Batangas, Santa Cruz and Lucena, besides joining Naga to Legaspi and Tabaco in the Bicol provinces, and adding some important branch lines in the Central Plain. Subsequently the Luzon line was joined together into a single 550-mile stretch from San Fernando in the north to Legaspi in the south. With this by 1941 there were some 837 miles of track, not counting more than a dozen privately-owned industrial lines, especially on Negros which mostly served sugar plantations.

Railways in the Philippines did not prove as profitable as had been anticipated. The Bisayan lines never prospered at all; construction costs over difficult terrain were high; they were located in settled belts of population so did not serve to open up new land and they had to face the direct and pressing competition of established sea routes. The rise of road transport only added to the difficulties. Conditions in Luzon were more favourable and the main line played an invaluable economic role as the principal carrier of rice, sugar and copra for Manila.

But the nature of the Islands dictated that despite the improvements which had taken place in land communications, the seaways still held their primacy. As a result of the dislocation caused by the Filipino Revolution, the collapse of Spanish rule and the nationalist struggle against the United States, the inter-island network of communications completely broke down. The need to revive trade and the economy made their immediate restoration a prime necessity for the new American regime. One of the first acts of the Philippines Commission was to declare 196 Philippine ports open to shipping.

After 1906 there was a swift restoration of the sea-borne links between the islands together with a great improvement in their regularity and reliability. The Americans paid attention to the construction of harbour facilities, breakwaters and lighthouses, especially for Manila which acquired all the attributes of a modern ocean-going port of call. Manila naturally retained its position as the chief port of the Islands, serving as the collecting and distributing centre for the bulk of the inter-island traffic in rice, abaca, copra and tobacco, but although it was the primary international seaport of the country, it came to be overshadowed by Cebu as the main focus of the domestic inter-island trade. Cebu in general was the next most important port of the Islands, serving along with Iloilo as the collecting centre for Negros sugar and as the collecting and distributing point for the commerce of the Bisayas, Panay and northern Mindanao. By 1940 there were fifteen companies engaged on the inter-island shipping routes, beside innumerable individual operators, while an estimated 3,000 craft ranging from steamships to sailing vessels plied these waters. By and large this network of services covered all the Islands and was sufficient for their needs.

However, the organization and efficiency of this sea-borne commerce left much to be desired. To fill the gap left by revolution and war in the early 1900s, United States coastguard vessels had at first been used, then specific routes contracted out to individual private concerns as trade picked up once more. Thereafter the development of the inter-island shipping routes was left to private enterprise, with officialdom exercising only the most general kind of supervision. Despite the abundance of vessels that were available, the lack of regulation resulted in wasteful competition and high labour costs caused by the need for frequent transhipment. In fact the inter-island service might have been far more efficient and of a far higher quality had United States Shipping Laws been extended to the Philippines, but all attempts to do this were successfully thwarted. The imposition of these regulations would have ensured higher standards and greater efficiency for local shipping services, but it would have also entailed the establishment of a monopoly by American shipping interests over inter-island trade and much higher costs to the detriment of general commerce with the Philippines. It was on these grounds that the Philippines Commission itself in 1902 successfully appealed for the postponement of their application to the Islands for two years. In 1904, once again at the instance of the Commission, the American Congress deferred the issue for another two years and passed a bill authorizing the Manila administration to regulate inter-island shipping. In the meantime United States shipping interests campaigned for the extension of the laws to the Islands, but when their moment arrived in 1906 American shipbuilders proved unable to supply vessels so that the Islands won a further deferment until 1908. The situation in 1908 remained unchanged, with the outcome that Congress deferred the issue indefinitely and granted further powers to Manila over local shipping by granting it full control over locally-owned vessels.

After 1908 no more attempts were made to extend the Shipping Laws to the Philippines for over a decade, by which time as a result of the Great

War a large American merchant fleet had come into existence and powerful voices in Congress were raised once again, calling for the step to be taken. In early 1920 a new bill was passed extending the laws to all American possessions, but in the case of the Philippines it was not to be enforced until 1922 and then was to be subject to the proviso that a presidential commission should establish whether an adequate Philippine marine service existed or not. The year 1922 passed without further action being taken, and the matter was raised again for the last time seven years later. On this occasion, Henry L. Stimson, who had just returned from the Islands as governor-general, argued effectively against the extension of the laws on the grounds that, apart from any other consideration, such a step could lead to retaliatory measures by other colonial powers in South-East Asia which could prove very detrimental to United States commercial interests.

The fact that the Shipping Laws of the United States were not extended to the Islands was without doubt to the benefit of local Philippines shipping interests in particular and to the economic development of the Islands as a whole. But it was an issue which was waged between conflicting United States interests—the American manufacturers, importers and exporters on the one hand, and American ship-building interests on the other. Throughout the American connexion, the former group always maintained the greater influence over the evolution of policy, but in this instance their victory was also a victory by proxy for the interests of the Filipinos themselves.

The two most important innovations in the realm of communications that were introduced by the Americans, apart from that of the automobile, were radio and aircraft. The first aeroplane to make its appearance in the Philippines was in 1911 during the Manila Carnival, followed by a military craft the following year. But the development of civil aviation was limited and slow until after 1945. Although the first inter-island flight took place in 1919, it was not until 1930 that a regular internal air service took shape, and not until another five years later (1935) that the first international links by air were established when the Philippines became linked to California and to the Chinese mainland by a flight of Pan-American Airlines. By 1941, however, air links had been extended to Singapore, Batavia (Jakarta), Tokyo, India and Spain.

Wireless telegraphy came in with the United States armed forces. Wireless communications within the Islands and beyond were established by the army and the navy which set up their own radio stations, followed later by the Bureau of Posts and several private wireless companies. By 1935 there were four private broadcasting companies, three with stations in Manila and one at Cebu. In 1941 there were some 30,000 registered radio sets in the country.

The older established postal and telegraphic communications were greatly extended under American rule. By 1941 there were over 1,000 post offices in the Islands, along with 5,000 miles of telegraph line and four foreign cable companies. The first modern telephone system in the Philippines was installed in Manila in 1905 with equipment imported from the United States, to be followed by similar systems at Cebu, Iloilo, Davao and elsewhere. Manila became the first city in the whole of the Far East to have an automatic central exchange installed (i.e. in 1918) and in 1933 was linked by radio-telephone directly to American and European cities.

Population growth and distribution
Despite the obvious impact on the economic development of the Islands of American rule in the twentieth century, its effects on the Filipinos were reflected not so much in the rise of the general standard of living, which was in fact negligible, as in the marked growth of population. The basic pattern of distribution and densities of the peoples of the Philippines, on the other hand, laid down during the Spanish period became more deeply imprinted under the United States regime. Under the Spaniards the basic subsistence economy was expanded sufficiently to enable it to support the colonial host in its fabric; the economic expansion generated by the Americans proved just adequate to cater for the upsurge in the numbers of people.

The demographic development of the Philippines under the Spaniards has been described as 'evolutionary rather than revolutionary'; until the eighteenth century the population of the Islands was virtually static and only started to increase markedly after the 1750s. During the nineteenth century, the population expanded seven-fold, and in the twentieth century (i.e. up to 1939) it more than doubled itself again. The links between the growth pattern of the population and the economic evolution of the Islands are obvious. The long period of demographic stability which lasted till the middle of the eighteenth century was clearly associated with the primacy of the galleon trade, during which period the Islands merely served as the backyard of Manila. During this period the absence of economic growth was so marked that on occasion outside pressures brought about a decline in numbers, particularly during the seventeenth century when the Spanish Philippines was enduring the challenge of the Dutch. From the figures available, unreliable though they may be, the Filipino population under Spanish control in the first half of that century fell by roughly 100,000 and at the end of the same century the total figure was scarcely much higher than it had been at the beginning.[27] The hardships, exactions and shortages caused by the Dutch wars were the direct cause for this, and the gradual recovery which took place after 1650 shows the effect of their termination. Likewise the ever-accelerating rise in population which became evident after 1750 was manifestly related to the opening of the Philippines to world trade, the great expansion in economic activity during the nineteenth century, and the galvanizing effect of United States rule in the twentieth. Not least amongst the contributions of the Americans was the efficacy of their health programme which greatly cut down the death-rate; in a land where the birth-rate was already high and immigration of little significance in terms of numbers, this was a factor of the highest importance.

The pattern of population distribution and settlement was a distinct legacy of Spanish times. In general the pattern was very uneven. The overall population density of the Islands in 1939 was 140 per square mile; reckoned in terms of cultivable land, however, the figure jumps to 223 per square mile, while in terms of land actually cultivated rises to 984 per square mile, putting

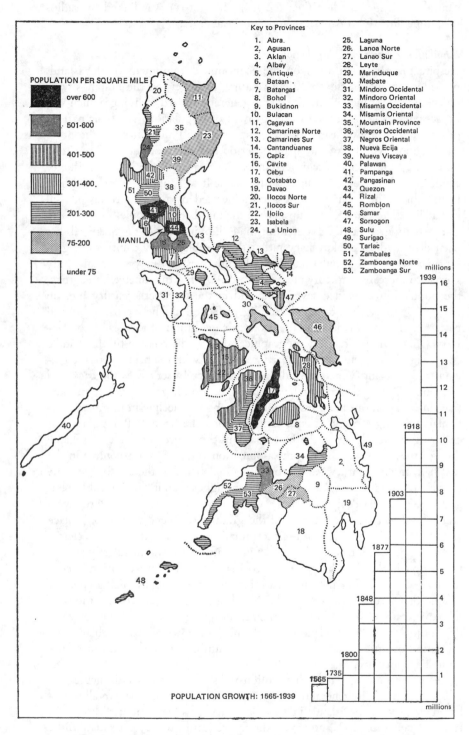

POPULATION PER SQUARE MILE

- over 600
- 501-600
- 401-500
- 301-400
- 201-300
- 75-200
- under 75

MANILA

Key to Provinces

1.	Abra.	25.	Laguna
2.	Agusan	26.	Lanoa Norte
3.	Aklan	27.	Lanao Sur
4.	Albay	28.	Leyte
5.	Antique	29.	Marinduque
6.	Bataan .	30.	Masbate
7.	Batangas	31.	Mindoro Occidental
8.	Bohol	32.	Mindoro Oriental
9.	Bukidnon	33.	Misamis Occidental
10.	Bulacan	34.	Misamis Oriental
11.	Cagayan	35.	Mountain Province
12.	Camarines Norte	36.	Negros Occidental
13.	Camarines Sur	37.	Negros Oriental
14.	Cantanduanes	38.	Nueva Ecija
15.	Capiz	39.	Nueva Viscaya
16.	Cavite	40.	Palawan
17.	Cebu	41.	Pampanga
18.	Cotabato	42.	Pangasinan
19.	Davao	43.	Quezon
20.	Ilocos Norte	44.	Rizal
21.	Ilocos Sur	45.	Romblon
22.	Iloilo	46.	Samar
23.	Isabela	47.	Sorsogon
24.	La Union	48.	Sulu
		49.	Surigao
		50.	Tarlac
		51.	Zambales
		52.	Zamboanga Norte
		53.	Zamboanga Sur

POPULATION GROWTH: 1565-1939

millions

1939 — 16
1918
1903
1877
1848
1800
1735
1565

millions

35. Density and Distribution of Population in the Philippines, 1939

the Philippines into the same league with Java and North Vietnam. Within this general framework there were great variations. In general the population density of the Islands tapered off from north to south and from west to east. The greatest areas of concentration of people were to be found in the urbanized and intensely-farmed provinces of the Ilocos coast, the Central Plain of Luzon, and on the islands of Cebu, Panay and Negros, while the northeast highlands of Luzon, the interiors of Palawan and western Mindoro and the great expanses of Mindanao which covered nearly one-third of the total area of the Islands were thinly peopled. Nature itself dictated that of the 7,000 islands a mere 26 per cent should account for 96 per cent of the area and 97 per cent of the population. The actual centres of concentration, nevertheless, were faithful reflections of the exigencies of Spanish rule. The focal points of Spanish power and the areas most directly under their control were the areas of heaviest settlement—especially Manila and its environs with its granary, the Central Plain of Luzon, and the island of Cebu which with its neighbours in the Bisayas formed the centre of Spanish activities in that region. Despite its great potential, Mindanao lay undeveloped, largely beyond the Spanish pale. Those areas already well established continued to attract more settlers and stimulate further development as the Philippines moved into the orbit of world trade.[28]

Transmigration and emigration

Even in Spanish times over-population was emerging as a distinct problem both in Cebu and in central Luzon. It became increasingly serious under American rule and by 1948 had reached the stage where in five provinces there were densities of over 2,000 per square mile. One obvious solution, as in the Netherlands Indies, appeared to lie in fostering transmigration from the over-populated areas to the empty spaces to be found particularly to the south. Indeed necessity had already induced such a movement to begin of its own accord in Spanish times from the overcrowded coasts of the Bisayas to the shores of northern Mindanao. The process became intensified in the twentieth century. Ilocanos overflowed into neighbouring provinces and into the Cagayan Valley; there was some migration from Luzon via Batangas and from the Visayas to empty northern Mindoro, and Mindanao again attracted more settlers as the activities of American road builders helped to open up that island. It was Mindanao which became the object of official American attempts at mass transmigration. Their first attempt which took place in 1913 to form a settlement in the Cotabato Valley, the heartland of the old Magindanau sultanate, was a complete failure, mainly for political reasons. But in 1917 15,000 people, mostly from the Bisayas and Ilocos, were successfully established in the Koronadel Valley. This represented the seventh such settlement made on the islands since 1913, and was followed by a number more within the next two decades. Between 1918 and 1934 some 34,000 migrants from the over-populated centres of Luzon and the Bisayas received free transportation and other help on their way to new destinations, mostly on Mindanao but also in the Cagayan Valley, Bohol and Mindoro. Many others made their way unaided. The pace quickened after 1938 as the Commonwealth administration reacted to the growing Japanese presence in and around Davao. The new administration set up the National Land Settlement Administration which forthwith proceeded with the colonization of more people in the Koronadel Valley. Within three years (1939-41) the Administration had settled 11,000 migrants in this area, 'a promising start', and by 1939 an estimated thousand settlers a month were arriving at Cotabato or Davao to take advantage of the lots cleared for them along the roads of the future granted by government. The whole process was peremptorily halted by the outbreak of the Pacific War.

Nevertheless the volume and pace of transmigration merely scratched the surface of the problem and itself bore many problems of its own. The same resistance with which Dutch officials had become familiar in Java, was encountered in Luzon and the Bisayas when attempts were made to persuade families to abandon their cherished but uneconomic plots of soil. Malaria played a baneful role, robbing life and weakening enterprise. With or without government aid, resettlement was expensive and the move was made to regions of unintelligible dialects and different customs. On Mindanao in particular these social and cultural aspects were rendered more serious by the traditional hostility between Christians and Muslims. The Christian newcomers were often high-handed in their dealings with their old, established Muslim neighbours. Land grabbing and other excesses were not infrequent and the seeds were being sown for the mistrust and antagonism which was to become a national problem after independence.

The other avenue open to Filipinos, who found local conditions caused by population pressure too difficult, was emigration. Under the Spaniards this was by and large out of the question, but under American rule many opportunities were opened. The main attraction was Hawaii which stimulated by the rise of the sugar industry there in the last decade of the nineteenth century became the leading centre for Filipino emigrés. A secondary centre was the United States mainland, in particular San Francisco and the Pacific coast.

Population: the alien element

Despite its heterogeneous nature, the population of the Philippines is overwhelmingly indigenous. In 1941 barely 1 per cent of the inhabitants of the Islands were of alien stock, although those of mixed ancestry accounted for just over a twentieth of the total population. The very low proportion of foreign settlers in the country was largely due to the policies pursued by both the Spanish and American colonial regimes. The largest alien element by far consisted of the Chinese who made up about three-quarters of the whole, while the rest consisted of various American, European and Asian groups. Amongst the last-named, the Japanese predominated.

Indeed in 1941 the Japanese formed the largest foreign minority in the Philippines after the Chinese, and although limited in numbers they played a significant role in the economy. The Japanese also played a significant role in the history of the Islands, especially during the opening decades of Spanish domination. The first Spanish contact with the Japanese was Goiti's encounter with a small colony of them when he captured Manila in 1570, but Japanese links with the Islands went back much further than that. There is evidence of at least two flourishing Japanese trading settlements established some time before the colonial period. The Spaniards themselves soon discovered Japanese settlements elsewhere, including one near Aparri at the base of the Cagayan Valley, ruled over by 'an audacious sea-hawk and swashbuckling pirate' called Tayfusa.[29] Legazpi and his immediate successors encouraged Japanese traders whose ships called regularly at local ports in Cagayan, Pangasinan and Manila Bay. In the early days of Spanish rule ships from Nagasaki started calling at Manila in October or March, bringing with them wheat, salted meat, cutlery, ironware (especially weapons), gold-lacquered goods, folding screens, cages of singing birds, paper fans 'and other knick-knacks', and bearing back gold, deer skin, beeswax, raw silk (from China), earthen jars, civet cats, Spanish wines, mirrors and sundry Western merchandise. This promising commerce stimulated the Spaniards to venture to the Japanese islands themselves. In 1584 the first Spanish vessels anchored off Hirado where they were well received by the local *daimyo*, and from that date the trade between the two countries steadily increased. So did the Japanese colony at Manila. It rose from twenty in 1570 to three hundred in 1592 and expanded rapidly thereafter as a result of the arrival of Christian refugees from Japan. However the total number of Japanese at Manila during this period never exceeded 3,000 and fell sharply once the Tokugawa regime established Japan as the Closed Country.[30]

The Japanese colony of early seventeenth-century Manila was turbulent and dangerous, but also useful to the Spaniards. There were four serious disturbances within this period, but more ominous still the Japanese residents of the city were involved in the famous Tondo conspiracy of 1587-8 which incorporated designs for active Japanese intervention from outside. On more than two other occasions plans were laid for the Japanese conquest of the Spanish colony. Nevertheless the Spaniards valued the Japanese presence for the trade it brought, for the reliability of Japanese auxiliaries, and for the excellence of the Japanese—as opposed to the Chinese—converts to Christianity. In consequence although the Japanese were segregated as were the Chinese and made to live in separate communities of their own, they were definitely better treated. However, events within Japan brought these budding relations to an end. In 1624 the Tokugawa shogunate banned further connexions between Japan and the Philippines and with the total seclusion of Japan after 1637, the Japanese colony at Manila dwindled in numbers, and through intermarriage lost its racial identity.

It was not until the fading years of Spanish administration that official contacts with Japan were re-established. In 1875 the new rulers of Meiji Japan sent a trade mission to Manila which was followed by a fresh influx of Japanese traders and businessmen. By 1889 Japanese interest in the Philippines was sufficient to justify the opening of a consulate in Manila. In the same year the Spanish Minister in Tokyo was suggesting to his government in Madrid that Spain should open the Philippines to Japanese colonization, a proposal which Madrid, however, wisely rejected. It was under the Americans that the Japanese presence became remarkable again. By 1939 there were some 5,000 Japanese settled in the Islands, most of whom had entered the country since 1900. Two-thirds of this number were to be found around Davao where, forming the largest Japanese colony in all of South-East Asia, they dominated the cultivation of and trade in abaca, and had interests in deep sea fishing, lumbering, retail shop-keeping and some industries. Although forming a much smaller group than the Chinese in the Philippines, they appeared to be far more settled; the sex ratio was more normal, mixed marriages were rare and they tended to be mostly associated with the land.

Apart from the Japanese and the Chinese (whose role requires to be discussed at greater length), the Europeans were the other important element amongst the aliens in the Philippines. As elsewhere they held a position in the economy of the country out of all proportion to their numbers.

Naturally the leading role amongst these was played by the Spaniards and the Americans. Despite their long connexions with the Islands the Spanish population was never large. Up till the nineteenth century it numbered no more than 3 or 4 thousand. This figure expanded after 1834 in line with the general economic development of the Islands but at no point did it exceed 34,000. The Spanish community was not unduly upset by the American takeover and continued to play a leading role amongst the entrepreneurs of the country, although there was a decline in numbers. In 1939 they still formed a noticeable element in Manila, where half of them lived, and as capitalists ranked third, with important stakes in tobacco and sugar.

With the fortunes of the entire Spanish community tied to the Manila galleon it was natural enough that up till the end of the nineteenth century, Spanish policy was strictly to exclude all possible competition, particularly from other European traders. With the gradual abandonment of mercantilism which followed the British occupation of Manila, foreign merchants began to find their way in, but Spanish prejudice against foreigners took longer to disappear. As late as 1840 a decree prohibiting foreigners from engaging in the retail trade or from trading in the Islands beyond Manila was re-issued, while even at this time the Spanish authorities were not averse to making scapegoats out of foreign residents. However in the 1850s Western traders started to establish a decisive influence in the Islands, with the French and English taking the lead. The first foreigner to set up outside Manila was the Englishman, Nicholas Loney, who moved to Iloilo in 1855 and played a key role in the development of the Negros sugar industry. By the end of the same decade there were fifteen foreign firms operating in Manila itself. Nearly a century later (i.e. in 1939) the British still retained an important minority role, although they were outnumbered by the Germans. French and Belgian residents formed much smaller communities.

In the twentieth century the Americans played the leading part amongst the Western groups. American contacts with the Philippines started in 1796 when the brig 'Astrea' called at Manila to load indigo, abaca, paper and sugar for the United States. In 1817 the first United States consul took up his appointment but he remained the sole American in the Philippines until 1825. After 1850 Americans became more numerous along with the rest, but their economic hegemony only began with the establishment of United States control. In the twentieth century American interests came to overshadow all others and American capital investment, although comparatively limited, became the highest. Nevertheless despite its increase in numbers, the American community in the Islands remained essentially transitory. In 1939 there were nearly 9,000 American nationals in the country, consisting of officials, businessmen and a handful of old soldiers 'found living here and there in out-of-the-way places with native wives'.[31]

The Chinese

By comparison with all the other alien groups in the Philippines the Chinese formed by far the largest group, yet their numbers were also limited, the smallest amongst all the Chinese communities in South-East Asia, including Burma and Laos. But the role they played in the economic evolution of the Islands was as great as anywhere.

Chinese relations with the Philippines long antedated the arrival of the Spaniards. The earliest concrete evidence dates back to the tenth century A.D. and within the next hundred years trade links became firmly established. Chinese commerce with the Islands continued to grow steadily in the centuries which followed, reaching a peak during the Ming period. That these trading contacts also led to the establishment of small Chinese colonies in the country seems to be without doubt, although exactly where and how important these colonies were has never been determined. The Spaniards found plenty of traces of Chinese influence, including in the more sophisticated political and social organization of various Filipino communities in Luzon.

The Spaniards were well aware of the importance of attracting Chinese trade and lost no time in attempting to do so. It was obvious that the future prosperity of the new colony would depend on it. That and the great mirage of the winning of China itself for Christendom propelled the Spanish pioneers towards the Chinese shore and led to a short-lived Spanish trading post somewhere near modern Hong Kong. The visits of the Chinese traders to Manila, on the other hand, proved from the very beginning a much more permanent affair. In 1574 six Chinese junks arrived in Manila Bay. By 1600 the annual number had risen to forty. With the establishment of the China trade, the Spanish position in Manila was secure. It provided the basis of their prosperity, laid the foundations of the galleon trade with Mexico and patterned the economic development of the Islands for the next two hundred years. And it was from those who stayed behind when the annual junks had departed on their return voyage home that the great majority of the modern Chinese community in the Philippines have their origins.

The China trade

The yearly arrival, around March, of the Chinese junks was one of the great events of the year. As soon as the first of them was sighted entering the bay, the news was relayed to Manila by great fires lit on the rocky promontory of Corregidor so that suitable preparations could be made for their welcome.

The junks stayed till May or early June and then set sail again early enough to avoid the typhoons. The Chinese merchants came primarily for the silver of Mexico which they took in exchange for cotton stuffs, together with some silks, porcelain, glassware, fresh fruits, domestic animals and birds, finely carved furniture and 'various trinkets' for the Manila oligarchy. A permanent resident Chinese merchant community quickly became established and by the early 1580s had already become the nerve centre of Manila's economic life. A municipal census of 1586 revealed that apart from the great majority who were shop-keepers, there were also some 300 Chinese residents who plied an amazing variety of trades. They were the principal artisans and la-bourers; they were to become the chief builders of the city's churches, con-vents and forts, and as craftsmen met the manifold needs of the Spanish com-munity. Some ventured into agriculture where they soon made their mark as well.

For as long as the Philippines economy remained under the thrall of the Manila galleon the Chinese community itself was largely confined to Manila, but during the eighteenth century with the loosening of the mercantilist bonds the Chinese quickly acquired a dominating share in the swiftly devel-oping carrying trade of the Islands and the South China Sea. By the 1750s, Chinese were handling the bulk of the inter-island trade of the Philippines as well as that of the Muslim sultanates of Magindanau and Sulu. They had long been present in the islands of the south and so were able to play a key role in extending the growing commerce in Indian and regional piece goods for the Manila galleon, as well as the traditional trade in Chinese wares. The same circumstances placed the Chinese in an ideal position to serve as the essen-tial link between Western importers and the Philippines market when the Islands finally became open to world trade. By this time the familiar chain which linked Chinese merchant in Manila with the itinerant pedlar or village shop-keeper in the provinces was already forged and provided the most suit-able channel for the Western importer to distribute his goods. As the cash crop economy of the Islands developed, the role of the Chinese expanded with it at the expense of all their rivals. The Chinese were also aided by other factors. When the Spanish administration finally dismantled the trappings of the old mercantilist economy, the Chinese were the first to benefit. In 1839 they were granted 'complete liberty to choose the occupation that best suits them', and subsequently were permitted to settle freely anywhere in the Is-lands. In 1844 Spanish provincial governors lost their privileges over local trade, an essential step towards establishing a liberal economy. Despite offi-cial desires to the contrary, the Chinese with their low overheads, capacity for hard work and well-developed credit system were easily able to fill the gap. By the second half of the nineteenth century as Spanish rule drew to a close, the Chinese were no longer merely the merchants extraordinary, the artisans and the craftsmen for the Spanish establishment. They had become the principal financiers of the smallholders who had become hooked to the new cash crop economy; they were also the chief millers of rice, refiners of sugar and processors of abaca for the world market and even had a stake in the tobacco industry.

Chinese immigration and Spanish policy

Up till the end of Spanish rule in the Islands the Chinese were treated as aliens and although official policy towards their entry and residence was forever fluctuating, it was constant in keeping Chinese numbers to a clearly defined low. Up till the eighteenth century there was no steady growth in the Chinese colony at all. From the 1720s onwards there was a perceptible increase which became much more marked after 1800. In the nineteenth century there were two main periods of influx—the first immediately after the opening of Manila to world trade in 1834 and the second between 1876 and 1886. But at no time did the Spanish authorities permit unrestricted immigration.

Spanish policy towards the Chinese was from the beginning torn between economic necessity and political prudence.[32] The importance of the China trade and the indispensable role that the Chinese residents of Manila so quickly assumed in catering for the needs of the Spaniards themselves were obvious. Equally understandable, however, was the Spanish concern for their own safety with such a well-organized, dynamic and apparently prosperous alien group in their midst. Within the first few decades of Spanish rule the Chinese of Manila often out-numbered the Spanish population itself, a situation which sometimes arose, as was the case in 1603, due to the laxity or short-sightedness of the highest authorities.[33] There were other sources of alarm. Within the first five years of the capture of Manila by Legazpi, the Spanish colony was confronted by the nearly lethal threat of Lim Ah-hong, a Chinese corsair who suddenly landed on Luzon with 4,000 men, borne by a fleet of some sixty war junks, and who all but stormed the city. Barely twenty years later a Spanish governor was assassinated by his own trusted crew of Chinese oarsmen, while in 1603 the arrival at Manila of three Chinese imperial commissioners who received with great state by the entire Chinese community led directly to the massacre which took place later in the same year. Then in the early 1660s came news of the impending assault on the Spanish Philippines of the renowned swashbuckler and adventurer, Koxinga. All these together with the obvious wealth and intelligence of the resident Chinese colony constantly fed and sustained the fears of the Spanish colonists.

Such fears and suspicions form the background to the massacres and expulsions which punctuated the relations between the Spaniards and the Chinese of Manila, and account for the policy of restriction and segregation, which despite its vagaries was fairly consistently adhered to throughout the whole course of Spanish administration. There were no less than five occasions when large numbers of Chinese were put to the sword, and many more but generally less effective decrees issued for their expulsion. Their net effect, nevertheless, was merely to lay bare the colony's dependence on the Chinese presence. Soon after the massacre of 1603, for instance, the Spanish citizenry of Manila began to feel the pinch—'they had no food, no shoes to wear, not even at excessive prices'.[34] The lesson was driven home every time. The Chinese, on their part, were always prepared to come back and to submit to the arbitrary regulations of the Spanish governors, for they too knew that only through the Manila galleon could they procure the silver of Mexico. In consequence the Chinese community survived, subjected as it was to vex-

atious supervision, great curtailments on individual liberty and discriminatory taxation. The most basic step was taken by Governor Gonzalo Ronquillo
de Peñalosa (1580-3) who in 1581 ordered all the Chinese in Manila to live
in a place just outside the city walls which became known as the Parian.
This in effect became the Chinatown of Manila, and as far as trade and business were concerned, its real heart. Within its bounds the Chinese were left,
in the manner traditional in South-East Asian lands, to their own devices
under their own leaders and officials. Beyond its confines their rights were
severely circumscribed. They were not allowed to travel freely in the Islands
nor even to go more than two leagues from Manila itself without express
authority. They were allowed within the walled city of Manila by day but
had to be back in their own quarter by nightfall. They were expressly prohibited from owning land, a restriction which lasted until the end of Spanish
rule. However, not all these laws were applied very strictly, their enforcement depending very much on the whim of officials or on the prevailing
sentiment at the time. More persistently applied, for the obvious reason that
they provided an ever-welcome source of income, was the wide range of taxes
to which Chinese residents were subjected throughout the whole period of
Spanish rule. Such taxes proliferated from the sixteenth century onwards, and
the Chinese were still being subjected to fresh taxation in the course of the
nineteenth century.

Apart from political considerations, there were two other major factors
which strongly influenced the evolution of Spanish policy towards the Chinese in the Philippines. One of these was the influence of Spanish mercantile
interests which while entirely dependent on the China trade in some of their
dealings, nevertheless strove to restrict Chinese competition wherever they
could.[35] In the early 1590s Governor Dasmariñas was writing to his monarch
complaining of the 'injurious' trade of the Chinese which led to 'great sums
of money' being taken out of the country; he followed up his complaint by
forbidding Filipinos to wear Chinese cloths and advocated a drastic restriction
on Chinese immigration, even though this would result in commercial loss.
Pressure from Spanish mercantilist interests led to intermittent attempts to
divert and confine Chinese activities to craftsmanship and agriculture, and
even as late as the opening decades of the nineteenth century, measures were
still being adopted to limit the Chinese to these fields. However such a policy
was never practicable and as we lhave already seen the pressures which forced
the Spaniards to liberalize the coonial economy after the 1820s presaged the
ending of most of the restrictions on Chinese movement and economic activity, even though it did not bring them relief from special taxation.

Despite the inevitability of such steps, the Chinese continued to meet with
the fierce opposition of established Spanish mercantile interests in the Islands.
The spectacular rise of Chinese trade and business after 1834 alarmed this
group. In tones reminiscent of Dasmariñas two and a half centuries earlier,
the outgoing governor, Fernando Norzagaray Escudero, in a long report on
the Chinese in 1859, argued strongly in favour of their exclusion even at the
expense of the impoverishment of the colony. A regular campaign for the
expulsion or exclusion of the Chinese was mounted in the Manila press dur-

ing the following decade which went on spasmodically until 1899, coupled with demands for Spanish immigration into the south. But such methods were no longer practicable and the Spanish business community had to turn to other devices. They attempted unsuccessfully to organize a network of provincial agencies to compete against the Chinese and also tried to dissuade foreign merchant houses in Manila from having dealings with them, equally unsuccessfully. Efforts by the Spanish authorities to check the mounting pace of Chinese illegal immigration via the Sulu archipelago during the last decades of the century likewise proved fruitless.

The other major factor which influenced Spanish colonial policy towards the Chinese was much more in their favour. This was the part played by the Roman Catholic Church. In the great debate which raged at the beginning of the seventeenth century as to the merits of the Chinese presence, the leading churchmen spoke out clearly about the importance of their economic role and opposed measures aimed at their exclusion. Quite apart from this the Church viewed the Chinese from an entirely different standpoint. In the words of Bishop Salazar, 'Anxious for the conversion of the people, I soon cast my eyes upon them (i.e. the Chinese) and took precautions to see that they were well-treated.'[36] Indeed the aim of winning the heathens of the Orient for Christianity was the main *raison d'être* of the Spaniards being in the Philippines, and beyond lay the great prize of China itself. Accordingly special encouragement was given to Chinese Christian converts. They were granted the right to trade and travel in the Islands and assigned a special status in the community.[37] When the Chinese community as a whole was subjected to a bout of persecution, the Christians were (generally) excepted, a circumstance which helped to bring about a considerable number of expedient converts at such times. Most important of all, the Christian Chinese were allowed to establish separate communities of their own. The best known of these was that established at Binondo in 1594 by Governor Dasmariñas, who despite his fulminations against the Chinese as a whole, realized the necessity of not losing them altogether. Apportioned to the Dominicans as a parish, Binondo was made by them into 'a kind of acculturation laboratory'.[38] A secondary centre for Christian Chinese was established later on nearby at Santa Cruz by the Jesuits.

The rise of the Chinese mestizo
The concern of the Church for the souls of its Chinese converts was to have most far-reaching consequences. In effect it was the prime factor in bringing into being a new class, the mestizos, who were destined to play a major role in the evolution of the Philippine nation. The Chinese mestizos were the children of Binondo. There they dwelt as privileged subjects, the descendants of Chinese convert fathers and Tagalog mothers who had been granted land which was tax-free and inalienable in perpetuity. By 1700 Binondo had become an all-mestizo community and, apart from the Jesuit settlement at neighbouring Santa Cruz, remained the sole mestizo colony in the Islands.

By the middle of the eighteenth century the Chinese mestizos had emerged as a distinct class and were accorded by the Spaniards recognition as such.

From 1741 they were classified separately for purposes of taxation and services. They were now placed on a similar footing to the Filipinos themselves, for although they had to pay more tribute and higher taxes, they were free to move about, could own property and take part in municipal government. On the other hand it was not so easy for the mestizo to acquire the legal status of a Filipino; this was only possible through female descent and intermarriage with Filipinos; after 1880 such alliances were discouraged by law. But by this time the formal distinctions between the mestizo class and Filipinos had disappeared since the tribute was no longer demanded.[39]

By the 1760s the Chinese mestizos accounted for about 5 per cent of the total population of the Philippines, a ratio they maintained as their numbers grew right up to the end of Spanish rule. At the end of the nineteenth century they numbered around 200,000 souls. The bulk of the mestizos was obviously to be found in Manila itself but with the economic expansion which took place after 1750 they tended to spread out, although their distribution continued to be closely linked to that of the Chinese. In the 1800s when they numbered about 121,000, nearly one-third were still in Tondo and two-thirds concentrated in the central provinces of Luzon. Much smaller groups of mestizos, however, were also to be found in nearly every other province on the island, while 10 per cent were scattered in isolated groups at Cebu, Iloilo, Capiz and Samar. By the 1850s there had been some noticeable shifts in this pattern of mestizo settlement. While Tondo still held nearly one-third of the total mestizo population, their numbers had increased significantly in the north (Nueva Ecija) and in the Bisayas.

The expansion of mestizo settlement was the corollary of the extension of mestizo enterprise. Between 1750 and 1850 the Chinese mestizos emerged as a dominant economic force in the Islands. Their rise was directly related to the gradual conversion of the Philippines from a subsistence to an export cash crop economy. At first indistinguishable, as far as their economic role was concerned, from the Chinese themselves, with whom they were associated in various merchant enterprises, the Chinese mestizos soon found unparalleled opportunities opening up before them as the demand for Philippines produce rose. They were ideally placed to become the new middlemen between Western importers and the Filipino producers. Inheriting the business acumen and entrepreneurial skills of his Chinese forebears, the mestizo possessed the capital and experience which Filipino cheiftains did not, freedom of movement to collect the produce from the provinces which was denied to the Chinese, and greater incentive and more energy to actually collect it than Spanish officials who were content to limit their trading perquisites to the business of the Manila galleon. In these circumstances not surprisingly by 1850 the mestizos appeared to dominate the inter-island trade as wholesale merchants, moneylenders and middlemen, and through their association with the cultivation of cash crops were fast becoming substantial landowners as well. Their prosperity and influence were obvious, particularly in the chain of small provincial towns of central Luzon which linked Manila with its rice granary, and in the booming sugar regions of Cebu and Iloilo.

However the liberalization of the position of the Chinese in the second half of the nineteenth century caused important modifications in the mestizo position. As the Chinese merchant was freed from the network of restrictions which had hemmed in his enterprise, he soon provided competition in commerce that the average mestizo, short on capital and credit, could not match. In consequence after 1850 the mestizos yielded quite a good share of their stake in commerce to their Chinese and Western rivals and increasingly turned to their investments in the land and cash crop agriculture where they had already secured a firm foothold. Their landholdings continued to multiply on a great scale, so much so that one Spanish observer at the end of the century gloomily predicted that 'If no remedy is found, within a short time, the lords of the entire archipelago will be the Chinese mestizos'.[40] In fact the modified economic role of the mestizos had profound social consequences. They failed to flower into the new middle-class of the Philippines in the nineteenth century, somewhat contrary to the expectations of observers such as Sir John Bowring, but at the same time they became far more closely attached to the traditional Filipino aristocracy. It was from this new grouping to which some Spanish mestizos and even local born Spaniards became connected that emerged a new elite, known as the 'illustrados', who were to play a formative part in the rise of Filipino nationalism.

By the end of the nineteenth century the rise of the Chinese mestizo was viewed with considerable misgiving by the Spanish establishment, but for the greater part of Spanish rule they enjoyed official indulgence and favour. They were Christians, they made an essential contribution towards the functioning of the colony, and they appeared to serve as an admirable bridge between colonial master and Filipino subject.

The Chinese in the Philippines: the role of the United States
When the United States swept onto the scene at the close of the nineteenth century the Chinese were riding high in the economic field and the Chinese mestizos predominated in the political. The main American contribution was to confirm this situation while still maintaining a strict control over Chinese immigration. Like their Spanish predecessors, the Americans regarded the Chinese as aliens, denied them all citizenship rights or access to land, and imposed a heavy clamp on their entry.[41] At the same time the Chinese resident in the Philippines were far better off under American rule. They were never subject to persecution or to arbitrary taxation, nor was their stay made conditional on conversion to Christianity. As such they could grow in numbers and prosperity, which was what they did, under a free enterprise type of economy that gave them plenty of scope for profit. But United States policy towards the Chinese was heavily influenced by considerations of domestic (U.S.) politics and also by the need to temper Filipino nationalism. The application of strict immigration laws against the Chinese, for instance, was as much motivated by such political considerations as by concern for the future of the Filipinos.[42] Immigration policy became a hotly debated issue during the First Philippines Commission (1900-3) and the laws were strongly opposed by various commercial interests who wanted a cheap labour market. The Commission itself favoured some system of tightly controlled contract

labour on a five-year basis, but in the end the political argument won the day and the immigration laws were retained, since to admit the Chinese 'would be to invite a disturbing social, political and economic factor into the life of the Islands'.[43]

From the Filipino point of view this dicision was a welcome one and as the years went by there was increasing evidence of the American willingness to yield to nationalist clamour in order to quieten it. As a result the Chinese community became increasingly exposed to the attacks of Filipino nationalists eager to restrain its command over the economy. The Chinese had never been popular with the Filipinos, and in fact Filipino hostility towards them had been one of the factors which enabled the Spanish administration to keep the Chinese in their place.[44] The Filipino attitude was a mixture of envy and fear which the unchecked material progress of the Chinese, their propensity to keep to themselves and their failure to assimilate with the country of their adoption did nothing to dispel. In Spanish times popular resentment found an outlet in the periodical massacres; under the United States reactions had to be more subdued since the colonial authorities no longer lent their support. A number of anti-Chinese disturbances did take place after 1900 but most were on a minor scale. The most serious disorder occurred in 1924, which, originating in Cabanatuan, spread to Manila and had to be suppressed with the aid of the Philippine Constabulary.

Far more serious for the Chinese was the growing effectiveness of Filipino nationalism and the demands it made to end their economic preponderance. This was symbolized by the Book-keeping Act of 1921, aimed at turning Chinese merchants into honest keepers of accounts by compelling them to maintain their records in either English, Spanish or a local dialect. The Chinese resisted this measure as vehemently as their kindred elsewhere and finally carried their campaign to the Supreme Court of the United States which declared the 1921 Act unconstitutional. This led to the redrafted version of 1926 which this time was within constitutional bounds, but continued Chinese opposition 'made it unadvisable to enforce it'. Subsequent amendments to the 1926 Act passed in 1934 still failed to make it workable and even a revised Bill passed under the Commonwealth two years later was never implemented.

The Filipino nationalists started to come into their own with the establishment of the Commonwealth in 1935. In its brief span before the outbreak of the Pacific War a series of new laws was passed which sought to restrict still further Chinese immigration and to curtail the liberty of the Chinese businessman. The seemingly more liberal immigration law of 1940 which fixed a quota of 500 per country, regardless of colour, in fact implied a severe blow to Chinese immigration which had been going on at a level well above that now stipulated. The Naturalization Law of 1939, designed specifically for the Chinese, virtually spelt out Filipino resentments; citizenship would not be extended to those 'Persons who during their period of residence in the Philippines, have not mingled socially with the Filipinos, or who have not evinced a sincere desire to learn and embrace the customs, traditions and ideals of the Filipinos.' Under the Commonwealth the first steps were taken also to establish effective competition to Chinese business. In 1940 the National

Trading Corporation was set up, expressly 'to break the stranglehold of foreign retailers'.[45] In 1941 the Manila Municipal Board struck directly at the Chinese monopoly over the city's public markets by prohibiting alien participation, an action which aroused a powerful Chinese protest.

Nevertheless, despite all these measures, in 1941 the Chinese still held a dominant place in the economy of the Islands and the pace of immigration, both legal and illegal, did not appear to decline. In fact notwithstanding the strict immigration laws, the Chinese population of the Philippines trebled between 1900 and 1941, a rise which could not be attributed to natural increase alone. The actual immigration laws were subject to liberal interpretation, while the traditional flow of illegal unskilled immigrants from North Borneo via the Sulu archipelago or via the northern tip of Luzon still continued. Meanwhile the Chinese stake in the Islands was immense. They had a predominant role in both the wholesale and retail trades of the Philippines, with their salesmen and buyers penetrating every corner and their commercial and credit systems reaching out to nearly every business. The rice trade was largely in their hands, three-quarters of the 2,500 rice mills in the country being Chinese-owned. Ten per cent of the capital, 40 per cent of the annual output of the lumber industry together with nearly all the sawmills were Chinese-owned. They owned many salt-works, and a large number of small and medium-sized factories producing leather goods or processing food and tobacco. They also had a considerable share in banking, and their total investments, calculated at around US$100 million, came next to that of the Americans themselves. Apart from all this the Chinese played a leading role in the opening up of the undeveloped south, particularly in Mindanao. Chinese firms dominated Cotabato while it was the intrepid, lonely Chinese trader who ventured up unknown rivers, scouted remote jungle trails and penetrated to isolated coastal villages with his load of cotton and assorted goods which he would exchange for copra, abaca, gutta percha and other forest produce. And even if the acquisition of land and participation in agriculture was ruled out, this did not prevent enterprising Chinese entering into judicious marriages with Muslim or pagan women and buying up through them tracts of virgin territory.

This huge share in the economy compensated the Chinese for their lack of numbers. Through their associations they were able to exert considerable influence on public policy, and under the milder, more democratic American regime were given the opportunity to do so. In 1904 the Chinese Commercial Council was inaugurated which later under its changed name of the Chinese General Chamber of Commerce (CGCC) became the focus of Chinese business and social organization. Together with the Philippines branch of the Kuo Min Tang and the office of the Chinese Consul-general in the Philippines, it formed the mouthpiece of the Chinese in the Islands.

The traditional centre for Chinese settlement, finance and influence had always been Manila. In 1939 nearly 40 per cent were still to be found in that city or 45 per cent including its environs. In the provinces there were Chinese in all, save one (Batanes), but outside Manila there were only seven centres where the Chinese community exceeded 3,000 members. Of the total Chinese population in the Island, three-quarters were Hokkien and the remaining quarter Cantonese, the latter predominant in hotels and restaurants and in food stores. In terms of sex ratio the trends were similar to those amongst other Chinese communities in the region, with a marked progress towards normalization between 1918 and 1939.[46]

The Filipinos

As for the bulk of the people who make up the indigenous inhabitants of the Islands, colonial rule had a great impact. Although the great majority were of the same basic stock, the geography of the Islands diffused them into separate, proud, jealous communities, each with its own dialect, traditions and characteristics. History also played its part, divorcing by the device of religion the islanders of Mindanao and the Sulu archipelago from their blood-brothers to the north. The great achievement of the Spaniards, albeit not altogether intentional, was to make Filipinos out of most of these disparate groups, although they failed either by conquest or culture to bridge the gap between the Muslims of the south and their own Christian subjects, or for that matter to bring the older, remoter peoples of the hills within the fold. The Americans, aided by a superior technology, were able to achieve a union of all these elements but it remained a highly superficial one. Their main impact, as with the Spaniards, was on the already developed areas, but whereas the Spaniards operated through a culture (i.e. Christianity) to create a nation,[47] the American contribution was to bring about a refusion of the various elements amongst the population of the Islands by means of accelerated economic development. Under their rule the Tagalogs continued to predominate in terms of numbers, education and position but in the Manila of the late 1930s there were probably more Ilocanos, Bicolanos and Cebuanos there than in their own provincial capitals. The Ilocanos in particular spilled out of the confines of their homeland in the twentieth century, penetrating the Cagayan Valley and profoundly modifying traditional agricultural systems, and also moving in considerable numbers to Mindanao and the far south. As the Tagalogs on Luzon spread south-eastwards at the expense of the Bicolanos, the latter were moving over to Masbate, while Bisayans, traditionally coastal dwellers, had crossed to northern Mindanao and were penetrating the interior. Greater mobility of labour, seasonal migrations associated with the harvesting of sugar or coconuts or the rise of gold-mining tended to lead to permanent removal with new land acquired or rented. By the late 1930s it was possible for an observer to say that the lowland Filipinos 'are distinguished by their dialect rather than by their physical appearance or mode of life...', a statement that would have been less accurate a hundred years before.[48]

Nevertheless the term 'Filipino' itself still held a restricted meaning for most of the inhabitants of the Islands before 1941. It was taken to designate only the Christian peoples who admittedly had been subjected to the same imperialism and the same culture and had been modified with a constant infusion of alien strains. Although their Muslim or pagan neighbours might be of the same racial stock, there existed a great gulf in culture and outlook between the Christian and non-Christian peoples of the Islands. The latter were never really integrated at all.

From the point of view, however, of economic role and function, all of the indigenous inhabitants of the Islands could be placed on the same footing. After nearly four centuries of contact with colonial rule, their way of life and standard of living were little changed. In the classical colonial manner they formed the group that benefited least from the development of their homeland and their traditional social framework remained intact. This was obviously true of those Filipinos who had remained largely beyond the pale of Spanish imperialism; it was also basically true of those Filipinos who had been under direct Spanish control. The traditional aristocracy retained its position as the *principalia* of the Spanish administration and by virtue of the advantages they enjoyed were able to keep their superior status under the more liberal regime of the United States. The average Filipino stayed in his place as a subsistence farmer.

In the early 1940s the overwhelming bulk of the population was rural and engaged in agriculture. According to the 1948 census 70 per cent of the people were farmers. Amongst the 24 per cent who lived in the towns were to be found nearly all the foreigners. In fact the greater part of the urban population was concentrated in one city, namely Manila which in 1939 had over half a million inhabitants. The next most important urban centre was Cebu which had been the first Spanish capital in the Philippines but was quickly displaced in importance and size when it was transferred to Manila. Nevertheless Cebu still served as the economic focus for the central and eastern Visayas, meeting the needs of about a quarter of the population of the country. Its importance steadily grew in the twentieth century alongside its population which multiplied fourteen times between 1888 and 1940, and as a regional entrepôt and leading centre for the export of copra it actually overshadowed Manila as a port for domestic shipping. Its neighbour, Iloilo, with a population of 90,000 in 1939 owed its importance to Negros sugar. Davao rose with Japanese enterprise, particularly in abaca, while Zamboanga which acquired municipal status in 1937 had for long been the only Spanish settlement on Mindanao, its inhabitants since the eighteenth century living within its stockade, overshadowed by the citadel of stone and brick, and working their fields under the shelter of its cannon. The other towns and cities were creations of the friars, local market centres characterized by a central square with its church and town hall, together with the twentieth-century additions of public school, cinema and Chinese-owned rice mill. Manila was the great exception, 'the undisputed queen of the Philippines'. In terms of the vlaue of its foreign trade, it exceeded that of all the other international seaports of the Islands combined.

In general, the bulk of the people, still tied to the land, remained embogged in a subsistence economy whose hall-marks were grinding poverty and perennial indebtedness. These conditions persisted throughout the era of Spanish domination, a situation which up till the nineteenth century at any rate was understandable since the economy of the country as a whole was still basically at barter level. But with the opening of the Philippines to world trade in the nineteenth century and with the accelerated pace of economic growth in the twentieth, the conditions of the Filipino peasantry still remained unchanged.

The poverty of Philippines agriculture

Despite the great progress achieved in the commercial, cash crop sector after 1800, the state of Philippines agriculture continued to be characterized by low productivity, uneconomically small holdings and archaic methods. Underlying all this lay basically unfavourable conditions for farming in the Islands—poor soils eroded by primitive and wasteful farming techniques, inadequate seasonal rainfall precluding the possibility of double harvests, and a rough topography which permitted only about one-fifth of the total land area to be devoted to cultivation. Linked with these conditions was a lack of capital investment, resulting in a primitive technology and an outdated system of land tenure.

There were basically three types of landholdings in the Islands—estates, smallholdings and common land subject to shifting cultivation. The last-named was the least significant, being confined mainly to the peoples of the hills and of the interior who remained beyond the scope of the modern economy, while smallholdings easily predominated in both the commercial and domestic sectors. Although the census returns of 1939 and 1948 failed to give a complete picture, it is clear that amongst the smallholders tenancy was widespread. In 1939 tenant-farmers accounted for well over one-third of the total number, another sixth were part-owners, leaving only half the smallholdings in the hands of actual owners. In the principal rice and sugar growing areas the incidence of tenancy was much higher.

In other words most of the farmers of the Philippines were smallholders, whether they were owners or tenants and whether they grew cash crops for the export market or planted food crops for domestic use. Most of them wore the familiar face of poverty. The average peasant lived on a plot of land whose yield was insufficient for the needs of his own family; he was only employed for part of the year, probably for no more than two-thirds of it, and the absence of a diversified economy made it impossible for him to find alternative employment in the off-season; if he worked for others his wages were a pittance, and if he were a tenant on a large estate years might pass before a settlement of his earnings was made. His was a subsistence existence, burdened by perennial debts, a continual round of work and drudgery, lived out in a miserable shack on a diet of rice and vegetables he grew himself, supplemented by occasional fish and meat and with two suits of clothes and a hat to see him through the year. In general the per capita income from agriculture was half the national average and only a quarter or a third of that in other occupations. Since, according to calculations, one-fifth of the farmer's income accrued to non-producing landlords, most farmers were not receiving a quarter of the income of those in other fields.

Of course there was nothing new about this abject poverty. When the Spaniards first arrived, they had found a subsistence economy and, as we have seen, for 250 years they did no more than expand it so as to meet the needs of their own establishment in Manila. Indeed so narrow was the margin of survival that under pressure the situation became critical, as during the days of the Dutch assault on the Spanish colony in the first half of the seventeenth century.[49] But the poverty of the Filipino peasant became more obvious and less tolerable as the economy started to develop and the contrast grew between wealthy landowners on the one hand and the mass of smallholders and tenant-farmers on the other. In fact the rise of the landlords was symptomatic of the intensifying plight of the farmer, since landlord wealth was associated with higher land values, the cost of which was passed onto the tenant-farmer in the form of higher rents.

The friction and distress which this situation engendered manifested itself periodically down the centuries in the form of peasant disturbances and unrest, particularly on the friars' lands. As early as 1609 Miguel Bañal, a scion of Raja Soliman, was petitioning the king of Spain over the sequestration of his ancestral lands by the Church. It was the friars' lands again which became the centre of the agrarian unrest in the middle of the eighteenth century, causing the Spanish Crown to appoint a commission of enquiry which upheld the grievances of the peasants. The Calamba affair of the 1880s involved Dominican property.[50] In general, worsening landlord-tenant relations played an important role in the genesis of the Filipino nationalist movement in the nineteenth century and continued as a constant source of nationalist agitation under United States rule. It was the great stimulant behind the magic cry of 'Independence!' since in the minds of most Filipinos landlordism was synonymous with foreign domination. The agrarian crisis started to come to a head after the 1920s, particularly in the overcrowded, impoverished, grain-producing provinces of central Luzon. In 1931 and 1935 there were two serious uprisings which could not be lightly dismissed as outbreaks of 'religious fanaticism'. The Tayug incident of 1931 in Pangasinan resulted in the looting of the city hall and in the destruction of the local land records, while the Sakdal uprising of 1935 which involved several thousands was a movement of tenants against their landlords which was finally suppressed with considerable brutality by the police. There was some respite under the brief administration of the Commonwealth but President Quezon had to take account of the tenants and agricultural labourers of Luzon as 'an essential political factor'.

The rise of landlordism
Landlordism was one obvious factor in the poverty syndrome pinpointed by the nature of this agrarian unrest. Perhaps it was more of a symptom than a cause, since landlordism itself was the outgrowth of conditions created by colonial policy under both the Spaniards and the Americans. Although our knowledge of pre-colonial Filipino landholding systems is very limited, it is clear that the concept of land as a marketable commodity which could be privately owned is a Western one, introduced in this instance by the Spaniards. In pre-colonial days landowning tended to be a communal affair, vested in the *barangay*, and the source of wealth and power lay in manpower. Land rights as such were rights of usage, not of ownership, and land itself had vir-

tually no commercial function at all. When the Spaniards came, they declared all lands not specifically occupied or identified as belonging to a specific person or community to be the property of the Spanish Crown. By doing so land at once acquired a market value, and in view of the needs of a growing population became a future source of individual wealth.

The first instrument of Spanish land policy was the encomienda system. Dictated more by expediency than by the requirements of a carefully considered policy, the encomienda was not actually a grant of land but the grant of jurisdiction over a specific territory which carried with it certain responsibilities and rewards. The encomendero (i.e. the grantee) was held responsible for the defence of the land in question, for the upkeep of good law and order within it, and in a general way for the welfare of the inhabitants of the land. To this end the encomendero was also charged with the support of Christian missionaries who were operating within the territory and he was also expected to develop the land included in the grant. In return he was entitled to support himself from the territory and collect tribute from its people in the manner prescribed by the Crown. However the grant of the encomienda was neither permanent nor transferable. Legazpi, acting on royal instructions, granted the first encomiendas to his followers in Cebu in 1571, then once established in Manila, apportioned all the Spanish Philippines into encomiendas, allotting one-third to the Crown. In 1591 there were 257 encomiendas, but the grants were only valid for two generations, after which they reverted back to the Crown. As a result thirty years later (1621) the total number of private encomiendas had already dropped to 186, due to the death of their holders, and although the system persisted into the eighteenth century, it went into steady decline after the 1620s. This was partly because of the attitude of the encomenderos themselves who neglecting their duties preferred to stay in Manila and speculate in the galleon trade, turning into absentee landlords and failing to make their grants profitable. The decline was also a consequence of official policy which aimed at curbing the various malpractices to which the system gave rise; apart from that, having served its initial purpose of rewarding the pioneer colonists and of ensuring Spain's political control over her new subjects, it was desirable to prevent the rise of overmighty lieutenants. In the eighteenth century old encomiendas were only extended and new ones granted to religious and charitable organizations.

Although the encomendero could not strictly speaking be described as a landlord since he held his land in trust and as an agent for the Crown, the system itself established the principle of absolute ownership, in this case vested in the Crown itself, and made possible the gradual commutation of actual encomenderos or their representatives into de facto landowners. This transformation was virtually complete by the end of the eighteenth century. The chief beneficiaries of this process were the Church whose encomiendas formed the core of the 'friars' lands' of the nineteenth and twentieth centuries, and the native Filipino aristocracy who as local cabezas de barangay and agents of the absentee encomenderos were able to establish ownership rights by default or who took advantage of the Spanish concept of land ownership to convert communal land rights into individual ones.[51] The rise of the Filipino aristocrat as a landlord was also facilitated by the absence of large Spanish estates which would not have tolerated his competition. Landlordism in general after 1750 was immeasurably strengthened and expanded by the rise of the cash crop economy which gave land a real commercial and competitive value.

In the new landlord class which took shape after 1750 there emerged three distinct elements: the Church, the Filipino chief and the Chinese mestizo. The Catholic Church manifestly appeared as the largest landholder, but it was also the absentee landlord *par excellence*, leasing its domains to enterprising leading Filipino or Chinese mestizo families who invariably sublet again. But of all the cultivated land in the Spanish Philippines, the Church's share was only a fraction, largely concentrated in Tagalog country around Manila. The rest of the land—in the late eighteenth century—was still largely in Filipino hands. However much of it was already beginning to be absorbed by the rising class of Chinese mestizos. Their chief entry into the land market was via the tenancy of the Church (*inquilinos*) whose lands they turned to rice and then sublet at rates which more often than not exceeded their own rentals. Having thus laid the foundations of their fortunes, they then set about purchasing Filipino land (which as mestizos they were entitled to do), usually by exploiting the Filipino predisposition to indebtedness. The mestizos got round the laws shielding the Filipinos from usury by devising the legalistic formula known as the *pacto de retro*.[52] By the early nineteenth century the rapid growth of mestizo landholdings was already causing official alarm, but the process accelerated after the 1850s when with increased Chinese and Western competition in the field of commerce and with land values constantly rising as the new cash crop economy expanded, they entered into agriculture wholesale. The sugar industry of the Bisayas became virtually a mestizo monopoly and at the end of the century observers were speaking of the Chinese mestizo as the 'most bulky estate owners' in the country.

The scourge of tenancy

Commensurate with the rise of landlordism was the spread of tenancy. In general the tenure systems of the Philippines did not differ much in their bare essentials from those found elsewhere in South-East Asia. In practice there were two main systems, sharecropping and cash tenancy. The sharecropping system was by far the most widespread, the older and more persistent. It emerged in the eighteenth century and was favoured by wealthy Filipino landlord and the Church alike. Known as the *kasamajan* system, it represented the typical arrangement between a landowner who did not want to work his own fields and a landless farmer in search of security; the latter farmed the land of the former and then both shared the harvest on a fifty-fifty basis. The system quickly gave rise to the abuses likewise familiar throughout the region. The cultivator invariably lacked the money to make ends meet and had to borrow at usurious rate; in any case he received far less than his 50 per cent of the crop after various charges had been deducted. So began the perennial bondage of indebtedness. Under the Church the same system was followed, with the variation that its tenants—known as *inquilinos*—who were contracted on the same basis invariably sublet to Filipino peasants for far harsher terms, so that it was the *inquilinos* who were the real beneficiaries and the peasantry the victims. In fact in a sense the *inquilino* was at the same time the representative of the other system, that of cash tenancy. The cash tenant contracted to rent the land at a fixed rate. This was risky since his position depended on the successful harvesting of his crop, but it also had distinct advantages. He was more independent and could find his own market. The cash tenant system was naturally more limited since only those of substance could really afford to go in for it. Such tenants were usually townspeople with some established commercial interest who sought out lands in densely populated districts where values and returns were high. Apart from these two basic forms of tenancy, about a quarter of the tenants of the Philippines operated under some other system usually characterized by rent paid partially in kind.

The nineteenth century witnessed the rise of larger estates, averaging around 250 acres apiece. Associated with families or businesses that were already prospering with the expansion of the commercial export economy, such large holdings were nearly always connected with rice and sugar cultivation. These estates were the forerunners of the typical *hacienda* of the twentieth century which became a key unit in the development of the sugar industry and which through the arrangements between *hacendero* and sugar central tied a large number of tenants in the sugar districts of central Luzon to the demands of the cash crop economy. The general trend in the twentieth century was for tenancy to become more widespread. Apart from the developments in the sugar industry which led the central Luzon provinces to have the largest concentration of capital investment against the smallest percentage of owner-farmers, the general increase of large-scale cultivation of cash crops took place at the expense of independent smallholders. The opening of the United States market to Philippines produce gave a great impulse to commercial agriculture and stimulated wealthy landowners and firms actively to acquire fresh lands. They had the capital and the influence to do so, and thousands of once independent smallholders were reduced to the status of tenants or of landless peasants through the manipulations of the courts of law.

As much as the organization of the land system evolved in the Islands, the position of the Filipino peasant remained in relation to the master of the land remarkably close to what it had always been. In the days before Spanish rule he had been exploited as a peon or debt-slave on the fief of his feudal lord. *Mutatis mutandis*, he held a similar position and relationship under the Spanish encomendero—more often than not his native feudal master was still there, now the Spanish agent. In the eighteenth century the peasant was transformed into a tenant or a smallholder—the distinction was rarely perceptible—still exploited, whether by his own race or by the new class of Chinese mestizos, and still subject to a remarkable degree to ancient feudal exactions. In the twentieth century his lot was in no way changed, in fact by the 1920s had visibly worsened. A money economy was now firmly established, making the peasant more dependent on cash and placing him still further in the clutches of the landlord-usurer. At the same time, while the landowner had a natural interest in keeping his tenants indebted, their plight was worsened by the competition of the growing army of unemployed and underemployed agricultural labourers. So while land was at a premium, labour was cheap.

In the twentieth century other factors combined to aggravate the misery of the peasant cultivator. The size of his holding was constantly being reduced into a more uneconomical unit as the population multiplied, particularly in the overcrowded rice and sugar lands of Luzon and the Bisayas. He was also the victim of his own prodigal habits, squandering—in the manner of peasants everywhere—his wherewithal on all the *fiestas* in the calendar, on weddings and on funerals; innocent of birth control, he produced large families which he was unable to support properly, and ignorant of the ways of the world, he was always open to being cheated. There was no way out. Philippines agriculture was capital-starved. The typical landowner had no mind to innovate by investing in new techniques and developing his estate; he preferred to put his capital into urban property or into foreign enterprises while allowing population pressure to increase the number of his tenants and enhance the value of his holdings. The cultivator, on the other hand, was obviously in no position to invest in the improvement of his own farming as all his money was absorbed by the usurer. So agricultural techniques remained primitive, methods traditional and productivity low.

Rural poverty: the search for a solution
The ways to overcome the problems of rural poverty and peasant distress were easy to discern but difficult to implement. There was a patent need for land reform, for legislation to protect the tenant, for the provision of adequate credit facilities, and for measures to take the pressure off the land by redistributing the population and diversifying the economy.

In Spanish times no coherent attempt was made to do these things. This was partly because the problem did not reach crisis proportions till the twentieth century, but basically because such an effort lay entirely beyond Spanish resources and would have at any rate undermined the foundations on which their power was based. Whatever steps were taken were in response to specific threats which had to be met; there was no move to an overall solution. Hence when in the first decades of the colony's existence complaints reached Madrid about the excesses of the encomenderos, the Audiencia of Manila was ordered to remedy the situation. Governor Acuña revised the tribute system and by so doing 'tamed' the encomienda. As a result of the agrarian troubles of the mid-eighteenth century, a royal decree was issued ordering the confiscation of friars' lands allegedly usurped by them. Reacting to the rise of mestizo landlordism on the eve of the 1800s laws were passed against *pactos de retro*. But generally speaking such measures, due to the circumstances of the time, were short-lived or entirely ineffective. The friars eventually succeeded in winning back their title to the lands confiscated from them and the efforts to check the Chinese mestizo proved of no avail as Spanish officialdom could not match the latter in their influence amongst the Filipinos themselves.

With the dawn of the twentieth century and the American takeover, the situation on the land was fast becoming critical, and comprehensive action could no longer be delayed. The United States, with its far greater material resources, was in a position to take measures but in turn found their effectiveness curtailed by political considerations.

Rural poverty: land reform

To their credit the Americans faced up to the basic issue of land reform from the very beginning and the principle was established by the Organic Act of 1902 (the Cooper Bill) that 'all public lands and natural resources were to be administered and disposed of by the government for the benefit of the inhabitants'. By the terms of the same Act the Philippines government was given the authority to classify and regulate the lease, sale or disposal of public lands, apart from mineral and forest areas which were reserved for the sanction of the United States President and Congress. The Act also contained provisions for the acquisition of land titles by squatters and private purchasers, laying down important stipulations regarding the amount of land which individuals or corporations could acquire. Since the 1902 Act also authorized the compulsory purchase of the friars' lands, the new colonial administration was brought at once face-to-face with the most sensitive issue regarding land in the Islands at that time.[53]

This was not the first occasion that the sequestration of the friars' lands had been called for. Governor Simon de Anda, infected by the Enlightenment, memorialized the king in the late eighteenth century urging such a step. The nationalization of the Church lands was written into the Malolos Constitution. The American point of view, as expressed by Taft, was that on principle State and Church should be separated and that the acquisition of the friars' lands was one of the necessary steps in this direction.

The first problem was the opposition of the friars' orders themselves. The issue was confused since in several cases some of the lands had been made over to development companies, making the question of real ownership hard to establish. Furthermore the heads of the orders were reluctant to sell as they would not get the proceeds. An impasse was reached with the papal delegate in the Philippines (who was an American himself), and Taft was authorized to negotiate directly with the Vatican. As a result of an audience which he had in 1902 with Pope Leo XIII in Rome, Taft secured the agreement of the Church in principle to the transaction at a mutually agreeable price. The following year the deal was finally concluded after tortuous negotiations with all those involved and nearly half a million acres and 60,000 tenants passed into the government's hands for a price of over US$7 million.

However this was not the end of the matter. To begin with it proved impossible to reach an agreed price for some of the friars' lands located in heavily populated areas, especially around Manila, a problem which was still unresolved by the time of the Commonwealth in 1935. The administrative task of looking after the lands required re-apportioning them amongst tenants and securing the rentals raised problems of its own. The individual lots had to be surveyed and assessed, purchasers or lessees found; in the process loss to government was inevitable. Taft's desire to keep this loss to a minimum led to further trouble. The case of the Mindoro and Isabella estates which were sold under specially favourable terms to a group of American real estate investors in 1909 drew cries of jobbery and malfeasance. The report of the resultant Congressional investigation, published in 1911, showed that no case of malfeasance had taken place but it raised doubts as to the position of the friars' lands in relation to general land policy. In the same year a temporary ruling from the Secretary of War subjected the sale of the friars' lands to the same restrictions as those for ordinary public lands. Finally in 1916 the control over the unsold friars' land was handed over under the Jones Act to the Philippines legislature along with that of other public lands. With this the problem of the friars' lands became melded with that of official policy towards the public domain as a whole.

Having laid down the basic premise that all land and natural resources should be administered in the interests of the Filipinos themselves, the essential question was what was the best way in which those interests could be served. There were two schools of thought on this issue, which in fact had been a subject of debate ever since the First Organic Law was passed in 1902. The first school, which consisted of an unlikely combination of Filipino nationalists, American liberals and certain American capitalists, strongly advocated a restrictive land policy that would protect the natural rights of the inhabitants of the Islands. The reasons why the Filipino nationalists subscribed to this view-point are obvious. American liberals or anti-imperialists supported this view as being the best way to prevent the Philippines becoming dominated by foreign economic interests as had happened in other countries in the region. The third element which in fact was the most influential and the least concerned about Filipino rights comprised the leaders of the United States sugar-beet industry and its associates, who consistently supported any line which would hinder the rise of large, landed Philippines entrepreneurs who could offer serious competition to them. The second school of thought favoured more liberal land laws which would encourage foreign investment since this school believed that without the injection of outside capital the Philippines would not be able to develop at all. This argument naturally had the self-interested support of various other industrial interests in the United States, but it was supported with conviction by most of the top United States administrators in the Philippines themselves. They argued that without such investments the existing ratio of capital to population in the Islands was so low that the administration would never be able to provide basic social and welfare services to the people and that the economy would continue to stagnate, just as it had done under the Spaniards. It was argued in particular with regard to the sugar industry that successful sugar estates, supplemented by modern machinery, could work an economic revolution in the country and promote a higher standard of living for its people.

The great debate which took up the first two decades of United States rule ended with a victory for the restrictionists. The voice of the sugar-beet industry was heard loudest by a rather indifferent Congress in Washington, while the tide of sentiment which was flowing strongly against imperialism and for nationalism at the end of the Great War helped to determine the matter. In 1919, Act Number 2874 of the Philippines virtually limited the sale of public lands to Philippines or United States citizens and while raising the limits on the amount of land an individual might purchase, retained the existing restrictions on sales to corporations. Senior administrators continued to voice their disagreement with this policy, a judgement supported by certain sage historians. But the benefits for the Filipino interest were too patent, and this coupled with the deep-rooted popular sentiment against large foreign-owned landholdings which had been engendered in the first instance by the Church lands ensured that the nationalist movement would not have accepted any other solution. In consequence, apart from a handful of large foreign-owned plantations in undeveloped Mindanao, large-scale commercial enterprise in agriculture never became established in the Philippines.

If the problem of the correct land policy to adopt had been settled by the 1920s, the successful implementation of it had not. In no area did the land reform movement launched by the Americans achieve the results looked for. Perhaps the greatest disappointment was the case of the friars' lands. Although by 1918 the number of farms owned by former tenants of these Church lands had more than doubled, many of them were reabsorbed by large landowners and even by the Church itself because of the high rates of interest charged on their original purchase from the state. By 1925 about three-quarters of the friars' lands had been sold, but of this a considerable proportion went to American financial interests, quite contrary to the original intention. In the wider sphere of the American administration's attempts to create a nation of independent smallholders as envisaged by the Public Land Act of 1903, the results were equally as disappointing. Almost half the applications made for smallholdings within the thirty years of its operation were rejected or cancelled. Part of the trouble lay in the cumbersome machinery created to implement this legislation. Its administration rested in the hands of the ponderous Bureau of Lands and Forestry and no grant could be made without a proper survey and a certification from the Bureau that the land desired was 'disposable agricultural land'. Since the Bureau carried out its gigantic backlog of surveys at a snail's pace and the cost of private survey was well beyond the means of the type of settler the administration was supposedly catering for, little was achieved. The prospective smallholder was also deterred by insecurity of title[54] and a nearly complete lack of credit or marketing facilities. But the greatest obstacle in the way of genuine land reform lay in the existence of the entrenched opposition of the traditional landed classes in the Islands, whose position became strengthened rather than weakened under United States rule. Wealthy, influential and well-informed landowners were the first to know of new lands suitable for development and ruthlessly indulged in barely legal manoeuvres to acquire such sites for speculative purposes. As Jacoby observed, 'It proved extremely difficult to conduct a progressive land policy in an almost feudal environment.'[55]

This grave land question which the colonial administration of the United States proved unequal to solve therefore devolved in 1935 onto the nationalists themselves with the establishment of the Commonwealth. By this time more and more open agrarian unrest had made the problem urgent and a new Public Land Law gave to every Filipino citizen the right to apply for a maximum of 58 acres of public land, for which purpose a special survey was carried out by the Bureau of Lands. The Commonwealth government also passed measures for the appropriation of large estates and their redistribution amongst the former tenantry.

Legislation for tenants

Actual steps to right the wrongs of the tenants themselves and to protect them against the traditional excesses of their landlords only came within the last few years of direct American control. The Rice Share Tenancy Act of 1933, which was actually the first piece of legislation on the subject, stipulated long overdue safeguards against landlord rapacity: contracts were to be written in the local dialect; the contract period was not to be less than one year and the rent not to exceed more than half the value of the harvested crop; the rate of interest on loans was restricted to a ceiling 10 per cent and the tenant was guaranteed a minimum share of 15 per cent in his harvest, however deep he was in debt. But the Act contained the fatal flaw that its enforcement depended on the petition and the consent of a majority of the local council in each province where it was intended to apply. This safety device ensured that the measure remained inoperable since all the provincial councils were securely in the hands of the landlords. The Commonwealth government amended the Act in 1936 so as to empower the President to enforce it by decree where necessary, and by 1941, driven by unstilled agrarian unrest, President Quezon had promulgated the enforcement of the Act in ten provinces.

Despite the heightened strictness of Commonwealth legislation, landlords still found ways round it. Tenants who petitioned for their rights under the Act found themselves subject to eviction at the end of the season, a tactic which was met by a new law (Commonwealth Act No. 461 of 1939) prohibiting such evictions unless they were done within the meaning of the original Rice Share Tenancy Law of 1933 or 'for any just cause'. The tenant was also given the facility to appeal to the courts. This measure had some effect, but the Philippines administration was no more successful than its counterparts elsewhere in the region in preventing other landlord-moneylender wiles. The *pacto de retro* in fact was still employed, allowing the creditor to acquire pieces of land for the price of the debt. If the anti-landlord legislation had any value at all, it was in making the tenant more aware of his rights.

Commonwealth measures to break up large landholdings by compulsory purchase and redistribution formed part of the campaign to overcome the tenantry problem. A law for this purpose was passed in 1936 which gave the administration the power to expropriate portions of estates subdivided amongst tenants against the payment of a fair sum in compensation. The government was also empowered subsequently to lease large estates for periods of up to twenty-five years. To implement this legislation a body known as the Rural Progress Administration (RPA) was established in 1939 and further supplementary measures were enacted the following year. By 1941 the RPA had acquired the tenant areas of a considerable number of estates in central Luzon and had taken the leasehold on the vast Buena Vista Estate. But even these efforts bore disappointingly meagre results. Progress was of course prematurely interrupted by the Japanese invasion, but in any case the operation was on too small a scale. Barely 2 per cent of all tenant lands were touched and even on those lands that the government took over, it was unable to do much in the absence of complementary measures to improve facilities for credit and marketing.

Rural poverty and rural credit
It was in the field of providing adequate credit facilities that the American programme of land reform was weakest. In fact hardly anything was done at all. In 1906 a so-called agricultural bank was founded with the avowed intention of providing easy credit to the farmer and of breaking the grip of the moneylender. But although government provided certain guarantees, the capital raised was all private and in the event it was used not to support the farmer but to finance the sugar centrals and so facilitate the progress of the large capitalist. In 1916 under the stewardship of the sympathetic Governor Harrison, the Philippine National Bank was established with the idea of financing projects of national development, but in the early years at any rate it was badly managed and subject to far too much political interference. In the same year, however, rural credit associations were also started, specifically to help the small farmer. They grew modestly. In 1921 there were 527 such associations. By 1935 the number had increased by only 42. In 1940 the Agricultural and Industrial Bank was founded by the Commonwealth regime.[56]

In all it is clear that the attempts initiated by the United States colonial regime to bring about genuine land reform were signally unsuccessful. The basic reason lay in the existence of a powerful land-owning upper class in Philippines society which as Taft, the first American governor, anticipated but certainly did not desire, became the instrument of American policy and ultimately the inheritor of the American legacy.[57]

The agrarian economy and industrialization
Apart from measures of land reform and of population redistribution already discussed, another way out of the problems of rural poverty and distress lay through economic diversification, in particular through industrialization. However, in this direction little progress had been made prior to 1941. Under the Spanish regime, needless to say, industry was limited to the traditional crafts carried on in the barrios which merely served to eke out the means of a subsistence economy. Under the Americans a start was made with the introduction of modern industries but it was not until the five years of Commonwealth administration that a real attempt was made to give the country an industrial base.

Cottage industries and handicrafts were well established long before the Spanish conquest. The pioneer Spaniards found skilled jewellers, boat-builders and wine-distillers, besides the more prosaic basket and mat weavers, silk and cotton spinners, weapon-makers and tanners. The main Spanish contribution was to encourage such local industries and to introduce some new ones of their own, which they did in the general context of stretching the existing subsistence economy sufficiently so as to meet the needs of the new Manila establishment. The leading role in this was as usual played by the friars who *inter alia* stimulated the rise of the manufacture of salt, bricks and tiles, silk-worm raising and hat-making. A new fillip was given to local cottage industries towards the end of the eighteenth century as heralds of the new cash crop economy began to appear. Basco's Economic Society had the development of industries as one of its chief aims and to this end gave rewards and scholarships, while its early contemporary, the Royal Company of the Philippines, actually raised over sixteen million Spanish reales for various agricultural and industrial projects, opened a few textile factories and encouraged the manufacture of indigo, sugar and silk. However, as we have seen, these were fitful and spasmodic efforts which were far too limited in scope to have any impact on the economy of the Islands as a whole. The United States takeover led to a revival and expansion of handicrafts and local industries in the early twentieth century, and in the 1930s Filipino nationalists put much energy into their further development. Fired by the need to develop the economic interests of the Filipinos themselves, various nationalist or nationalist-sponsored groups started to organize associations and campaigns to promote local industries. The Bagong Katipunan was founded by Manuel Roxas in 1930 specifically for this purpose though 'after a brief but colorful existence' it 'died a natural death'. More effective was the National Economic Protectionism Association (NEPA) founded four years later which succeeded in popularizing a wide variety of locally-made goods. By 1940 cottage industries involved at least half a million people full time and many more on a seasonal basis. Amongst the principal products were pottery, shoes, various forms of traditional weaving and embroidery and the bolo. Some of these—in particular embroidery, which was probably the most important of all, and hat-making—directly benefited by the general development of modern communications but on the whole cottage industries were on the decline, especially those which faced the competition of imported manufactures.

The foundations of modern industry were really laid with the coming of the Americans to the Islands, but up till 1941 this was limited almost entirely to processing and consumer production. In 1935 there were 120,000 'modern' factories, mainly consisting of rice mills, sawmills and plants for refining sugar, or coconut-oil or for dealing with abaca and desiccated coconut produce. The longest established of these were the rice mills, mostly Chinese-owned and located in and around Manila. The ones representing the greatest capital investment and employing the largest amount of labour were the huge sugar-centrals. The first modern sugar factory was built in 1911 on Mindanao to cater for the produce of a large plantation, followed by a second one at San Carlos in eastern Negros which was in effect the first real central.[58] In 1935 there were forty-six sugar factories and four mechanically equipped refineries which between them employed 50,000 people. Factories for processing the oil from copra for the export market started to increase after 1918; once again they were mostly to be found in Manila. Factories making desiccated products such as coconut flakes and powder started to be built near the great coconut regions from 1922 onwards and by 1937 were processing 6 per cent of the coconuts harvested. Apart from this there were also some consumer

industries of growing significance, particularly that in boot and shoe manufacture which had its origins in the Great War. There were also cigar and
cigarette factories, manufactures of textiles, distilleries and cordage shops,
one large pineapple cannery and an important fish-canning industry, Japanese
controlled. In spite of all this, the development of consumer industries was
severely hampered by the ever-growing competition of imported manufactured goods from the United States.

Filipino nationalists were very conscious of this weakness and as their
movement gathered impetus they brought pressure to bear for the enlarge-
ment of the industrial sector. With the passing of the Jones Act in 1916 they
acquired some measure of power in the state, and took the first steps to encourage industrial development through the direct participation of the government, although it was not until the Commonwealth period that the principle
of active state support in the promotion of economic activity became firmly
established. In 1916, however, as we have noted, the Philippine National
Bank was created to deal in commercial banking, followed the next year by
the National Coal Company, thereby establishing a state corporation, a step
'unprecedented in American colonial administration and contrary to American political practice'. In the same year the government took over the Manila Hotel and also the British-owned Manila Railroad Company, and in
1919 set up the National Development Company as a mixed private-govern-
ment undertaking. A National Petroleum Company and a National Iron
Company also received legislative approval but were never organized. All
these government-owned enterprises were placed under a Board of Control
comprising the President of the Philippines Senate, the Speaker of the House
of Representatives and the American governor-general. However, up till
1936, this brave venture into state-sponsored economic development did not
achieve much. With the departure of Harrison in 1921, there was a reaction
amongst American officialdom. His successor, Wood, reversed many of
Harrison's policies, and in 1926 succeeded in abolishing the Board of Control
on the grounds of being 'unconstitutional'.

The establishment of the Commonwealth led to renewed efforts by the
nationalists to encourage industrialization with state support. The National
Development Corporation, now brought under full government control,
subsidized the opening of textile factories and a large cement plant at Naga
on Cebu, and private enterprise was encouraged to invest in new projects
such as paper mills, glass factories and breweries. But although there was
considerable expansion in economic activity in the five short years before the
outbreak of the Pacific War, there was little evidence of comprehensive
planning. A National Economic Council was set up in 1936 by legislation
of the previous year, but besides demonstrating an admirable awareness of
what was needed to improve the economy of the Islands, the creation of this
Council did not lead to any extensive economic planning prior to 1941.[59]

On the eve of the Pacific War modern industry still played a very minor
role in the economy as a whole. Any programme of industrialization in the
Philippines was faced with severe handicaps. First and foremost was the total
insufficiency of local fuel and mineral resources such as coal and iron. Indus-

trial development was also held up by the general difficulty and lack of communications. The domestic market was restricted by the general prevalence
of poverty, while the handful of the very rich still favoured investment in
real estate rather than in other forms of production and labour was in general
unskilled and inefficient. On top of all this to a very large extent the course
of economic development was determined by the evolution of United States
tariff policy, which by encouraging dependence on the American market
restricted the scope of local industry.

The evolution of United States tariff policy

The acquisition of the Philippines immediately posed for the Americans the
question of what should be the relationship between the new territory and the
United States itself. Colonialism was anathema to the American political tradition but statehood in this particular context was equally as undesirable. The issue was not merely one of ideology; from the economic standpoint
it raised the very practical consideration as to whether the Philippines would
become fully integrated with the economic and commercial system of the
United States or not. If the former were the case, this was tantamount to the
establishment of complete free trade between the two countries, which would
clearly be of benefit to some and detrimental to others. This issue was to
dominate United States–Philippines relations from 1898 onwards and was
to become the central theme of debate between conflicting groups of interests
within the United States itself as well as between the two main United
States political parties.[60] At the same time while the great discussion ranged
over four decades of American rule, the needs and interests of the Filipino
people were never allowed to determine the outcome at all.

The first and most basic step was to define the status of the Philippines and
the nature of its relationship to the United States. This was done largely
through a series of decisions by the U.S. Supreme Court made in 1900 and
1901 regarding Puerto Rico (another American acquisition resulting from
the war with Spain), which arose over the question of tariffs to be imposed
on Puerto Rican goods entering the United States, and vice versa. Known
as 'the Insular Cases', the Supreme Court ruled that Puerto Rico (and hence
by implication the Philippines) was to be regarded as neither 'foreign' nor
'domestic' territory 'within the meaning of the revenue clauses of the Constitution' but as territory 'appurtenant to and belonging to the United States'.
This Solomon-like judgement nicely left in the hands of the American Congress the question as to whether to permit free trade between a territory so
defined and the United States mainland or not. In the case of the Philippines
the issue was complicated still further by the terms of the Treaty of Paris
signed with Spain in 1899 which stipulated that Spanish ships and merchandise were to be admitted to the Philippines on the same terms as those for
United States ships and merchandise for ten years after ratification, which
meant that the establishment of preferential tariffs for United States goods
was for the time being out of the question.

Such was the background of the evolution of United States tariff policy towards the Philippines. By a series of Acts, the first of which were passed

in 1901 and 1902, trade relations between the two countries were progressively liberalized until by 1913 for all intents and purposes full free trade was established. But even after that date the great debate still continued and throughout its course policy was strongly influenced by the pressures of various groups which not only succeeded in gaining special concessions for themselves, but also played a great role in determining the issue of when the Philippines should receive its autonomy or independence.

The tariff Acts of 1901 and 1902 were the immediate response to the situation created by the Insular Cases which had left to the American Congress the issue of what tariffs should be imposed on trade between the two countries. These Acts established that Philippines goods exported to the United States would be subjected to 75 per cent of the normal tariff duty (the Dingley tariff rates) imposed on foreign merchandise, the 25 per cent difference being refunded to the Philippines treasury; that such goods being exported to the United States would be exempted from the normal Philippines export duties, the sum involved being refunded in turn to the American importer; and that there would be an average all-round deduction of 25 per cent on the former Spanish tariff schedules in the Islands which were at the same time also readjusted to lower the rates on necessities and raise them on luxuries. The immediate purpose of the 1902 Act was to protect American producers from the evil effects of competition from Philippines goods entering the United States duty-free. Proposals to establish free trade at once between the two countries were successfully rejected on the grounds of the blow this would be to the Philippines Treasury and the situation created by the special Spanish rights accorded by the Treaty of Paris, but although the alternative solution passed by the United States Congress was seemingly fair, in practice it was a solution geared to the particular interests of certain groups in the United States. The 25 per cent concession on the Dingley rates for Philippines goods was meaningless as far as the Islands were concerned since the tariff was still prohibitive for sugar and tobacco, the mainstays of the cash crop economy. On the other hand the abolition of export duties on Philippines goods destined for the United States represented a serious loss to the Philippines treasury since the duties for the two items in greatest demand on the American market—hemp and coconut—had to be refunded to the United States cordage manufacturers who in this way obtained their raw material at a much cheaper rate than normal world market prices at no benefit to the Philippines. At the same time American manufacturing interests eager to export their goods to the Philippines were able to get over the difficulties of the Paris Treaty by the device of 're-classification'.[61]

In fact the tariff Acts were very one-sided in the benefits that they bestowed and did not serve as a basis for building up the Philippines economy. This was not in line with the publicly professed intentions of Governor Taft and the Second Philippines Commission, and in the next few years they campaigned untiringly for a much more drastic reduction in the Dingley rates on Philippines imports into the United States and for the abolition of the refunds on Philippines export duties to American importers. The consequent tug-of-war between the Commission and the various commercial and industrial interests involved over tariff policy between 1902 and 1909 when the next great tariff Act was passed was reflected in several amendments to the existing law and in an equal number of rejected resolutions. Starting with Cooper's Bill of December 1902, a series of measures to reduce the tariffs on Philippines imports were defeated in Congress, usually in the Senate as a result of the opposition of senators from the sugar-producing states of the Union. The same sugar interests also defeated in 1908 a Bill which had the support of the American administration in the Philippines for the duty-free importation of agricultural machinery into the Islands. The pressure of American exporters and manufacturers (particularly textile interests) for a reclassification of the tariffs on their goods was the prime factor behind the amendments of 1905 and 1906.

The expiry in 1909 of the special clauses in the Treaty of Paris regarding Spanish trade in the Philippines provided the occasion for a thorough reconsideration of the 1902 tariff arrangements and resulted in the passing of fresh tariff legislation the same year. The new Act[62] which became the basic tariff law for the rest of the period of direct United States administration conceded the principle of free trade between the two countries by including the Philippines within the United States tariff area but in practice still held out special concessions for particular groups, notably American sugar, tobacco and cordage interests. Under the new legislation all United States goods were admitted duty-free to the Philippines while Philippines goods fell into three categories—those on the American 'free list' and not subject to any import duties; those duty-free under a quota system whereby after a certain level of imports had been exceeded they became subject to the full United States tariff—a category which included sugar, tobacco and hemp; and rice which formed a category of its own, being liable to the normal United States tariff rates. Despite a decade of pleas from highly-placed American administrators, however, local export duties on goods dispatched to the United States were still refundable to the American importers.

The free trade lobby finally gained complete victory in 1913 when as a result of the accession of the Democratic Party to power the previous year, a new tariff law, the Underwood-Simmons Tariff, was passed which terminated all the quota limitations on sugar, tobacco and hemp, and abolished all export duties on Philippines goods bound for the United States. With this full free trade between the Philippines and the United States was established, a state of affairs lamented by Filipino nationalists at the time for good cause and still opposed by United States sugar and other interests.

The great fillip given to the cause of Filipino nationalism during the liberal regime of Governor Harrison (1913-21), particularly after the passing of the Jones Act of 1916, created a new climate in the Islands where attainment of independence seemed practical politics. The American opponents of free trade relations with the Philippines found in this situation new opportunities to advance their cause and in the process became identified with the lobby which pressed for the early granting of autonomy or independence to the Islands. In this independence lobby sugar interests maintained their prominence, but they now received increased support from other agricultural groups, especially those connected with cottonseed and dairy farming, whilst other new adherents included racially-minded employers of labour and labour unions fearful of the competition of Filipino immigrants. In the protracted congressional hearings which started in the late 1920s over the issue of Philippines independence, the various voices of this lobby were loudly and persuasively heard as they presented the case for their particular interests—in the American fashion—with unabashed candour. Conducting the case for the other side were a handful of principled administrators and an equally wide spectrum of vested interests who stood to gain by the continuance of free trade relations.[63] The impact of the Great Depression of 1929, however, had a decisive influence in tilting the balance in favour of the independence lobby.

The outcome was finally seen in the Tydings-McDuffie Act of 1934 which provided the blue-print for Philippines autonomy under the formula of the Commonwealth. According to the provisions of this law the free trade relations between the Philippines and the United States were to be gradually dissolved after an initial period of five years, during which all Philippines goods would be admitted free, subject to certain quota limitations. American goods, on the other hand, would continue to be granted untaxed entry into the Islands indefinitely. The Act dramatically demonstrated how far the Philippines economy by this time depended on the United States and concern about the implications involved in the changed relationship felt by Filipino nationalists and various American interests led to a spate of amendments, starting within a few months of the passage of the Act itself. In accordance to the terms of the Tydings-McDuffie agreement and in response to widespread nationalist concern, in 1937 Presidents Roosevelt (of the United States) and Quezon (of the Philippines Commonwealth) set up the Joint Preparatory Commission on Philippines Affairs (JPCPA) to make a specific study of United States-Philippines relations and to make whatever recommendations for adjustment it deemed necessary. Its deliberations lasted over one year and produced an excellent survey of the state of the economic relations between the two countries. Its proposals represented a compromise between the goals of leaving the Philippines with a viable economy after independence had been granted and of affording protection for United States economic interests. Its most important recommendation that the period of progressive elimination of free trade relations be prolonged beyond the original date of 1946 up till 1960 was carried into effect by the Tydings-Koscialkowski Act of 1939.[64]

The impact of United States tariff policies

Though the prospect of the ending of the free trade relationship between the United States and the Philippines as foreshadowed by the Tydings-McDuffie Act of 1934 was unwelcome to nationalist opinion in the Philippines, its establishment in the first place had met with equally vehement nationalist opposition. The nationalists argued in the 1900s that free trade would make the Philippines too dependent economically on the United States and 'would in the long run be highly prejudicial to the economic interests of the Philippine people and would create a situation which might hinder the attainment of the independence of the same people'.[65] These sentiments were dismissed by W.

Cameron Forbes, the governor of the day (i.e. in 1911) as being political propaganda made primarily for domestic consumption and unrepresentative of Filipino feeling as a whole. Be that as it may, their accuracy as far as economic dependence was concerned had been well borne out by 1935, while the fact that autonomy became a concrete reality in that year had more to do with an American desire to be free of the Philippines than with nationalist pressures.

That free trade between the two countries stimulated a tremendous development of the Islands' economy is undeniable. The value of Philippine exports mounted from an annual average of P60 million in 1908 to a peak of over P297 million barely twenty years later, and with rising revenues the administration was able to effect great improvements in the social welfare services, and to promote a higher standard of living—at least for the new middle-class. At the same time in the process of economic expansion the Philippines became dangerously dependent on the American market, particularly after 1909 when Spain lost its commercial privileges. After that date the United States quickly became the Islands' best customer, an inevitable process greatly accelerated with the opening of the Panama Canal.[66] By 1938 72 per cent of the foreign trade of the Philippines was with the United States; the great bulk of this consisted of sugar, coconut products, hemp and tobacco which were almost completely dependent on their access to the American market. On the other hand the volume of American imports into the Philippines also steadily rose. The implications of these close links were, as we have just noted, forcefully brought home with the passage of the Tydings-McDuffie Act. Free trade relations with the United States also resulted in the Islands losing their natural markets elsewhere and in making Philippine products non-competitive on the open world market, since they were cushioned by guaranteed access to the United States where average prices were much higher. The same factor also meant that Philippines export production, whilst lucrative under such circumstances, was not efficient; the cultivation of cash crops was encouraged at the expense of food production, thereby rendering the Islands more dependent still on overseas imports, while the development of local industry was effectively deterred by the competition of American manufactured imports.

What made matters worse was the one-sided nature of the trade links with the United States, for while the very livelihood of the Islands came to depend on access to the American market, there was no corresponding dependence on the part of American industrialists and businessmen on the markets of the Philippines. Although in the early 1930s the Philippines ranked eighth amongst America's customers, the Islands only absorbed about 2 to 3 per cent of U.S. exports in terms of value, while the chief Philippines products were in direct competition with those in the United States itself. In these circumstances it is not surprising if the U.S. Congress tended to regard the Philippines as not essential to general American economic interests and so, within the framework of the basic American belief in the sanctity of *laissez-faire* economics, left the field open to the various committed pressure groups to have their say. The United States did much more than any other colonial power in South-East Asia to prepare its subjects for independence and showed much more genuine concern for their welfare, but much of this political idealism was melted in the boiling pot of vested interest. The outcome was that the vital interests of the Filipinos as a whole were neglected and that they were left in a state of as great weakness and backwardness as their neighbours in the region who were under the heels of less principled powers. It must also be observed that many of the measures of Congress which did prove of benefit to the Philippines were passed not out of concern for Filipino welfare but for the self-serving needs of people in the United States.

Labour and labour organization under the United States

The most positive side of U.S. colonial administration was clearly seen in the field of social welfare. Within the brief four decades of American rule, the foundations were laid for a system of public welfare affecting labour, health and education which placed the Philippines in general on a par with neighbouring territories in South-East Asia and in some respects ahead of them.

Nevertheless as far as labour is concerned, the American record was least impressive, partly because the big problem of slavery had been basically resolved under Spanish rule. The main development after 1900 was the growth of a labour movement which became increasingly effective during the 1920s and 1930s but no comprehensive legislation to safeguard the interests of labour was passed until the establishment of the Commonwealth in 1935.

The first attempt to organize a labour union followed on the heels of the new American regime and was followed not long afterwards (i.e. in 1902 and 1903) by two more bodies which represented the first genuine labour unions in the Philippines. Both these pioneer unions were short-lived but their emergence was the signal for a whole host of other unions to form. In 1913 when the first Labour Day was held in the Philippines, a National Labour Congress was convened in Manila but this and subsequent efforts to establish a national labour front all foundered on the rocks of mutual jealousy. By 1934 there were 144 labour unions with a membership of some 83,000 workers in the Islands.

The growing power of these unions and the mounting agrarian unrest which marked the opening years of the 1930s form the background to the comprehensive programme of labour legislation which was rushed through under the administration of the Commonwealth. Up to this point the labour laws passed under the United States colonial administration had been confined to measures regulating the use of women and child workers, compensation for industrial accidents and a scheme for free medical and dental treatment for certain categories of employees. Within a year of the inauguration of the Commonwealth, the beginnings had been made of a legislative programme designed to provide workers with adequate protection against exploitation and abuse by their employers. A series of Acts passed in 1936 established for the first time a basic minimum wage while another law of the same year laid down the eight-hour day. Another piece of legislation instituted a system of free legal advice for the poor in court. But probably the most far-reaching step that year was the creation of a Court of Industrial Relations to mediate in disputes between management and labour and empowered to consider tenancy as well as ordinary industrial disputes, and to fix minimum wages and rents. Supplementary laws enacted in 1936 and 1938 added to the Court's status and defined its powers more closely. The new court was swift to use its powers and had a drastic effect on the number of strikes and days lost through industrial unrest; it also proved helpful to weaker unions in securing for them wage awards which would have been quite beyond their own reach. Legislation revising the existing provisions for workmen's compensation and medical care was also passed. President Quezon capped all this legislative activity by launching in late 1937 his 'Social Justice Programme', declaring that it was his ambition 'that the Philippines shall become a country where poverty is unknown, where justice is the watchword and democracy and freedom the motto'.[67] This declaration was made all the more necessary in view of the ever-growing virulence of the labour movement which the administration was endeavouring none too successfully to control, but the President's desires remained far removed from reality. In 1941 on the eve of the Pacific War many of the reforms legislated by the Commonwealth remained paper ones only.

In any case the labour legislation of the late 1930s catered only for a fraction of the total labour force in the Islands, namely for industrial labour whose numbers did not attain a quarter of a million. The conditions of work of these industrial employees was indeed still far from satisfactory, but they were incomparably better off than the bulk of the labouring class which consisted of peasants whose circumstances were rooted in the syndrome of rural poverty and indebtedness, land tenure systems and low productivity.[68]

Slavery and debt peonage

As was the case with his role as a tenant, the average Filipino of the first half of the twentieth century found his condition as a labourer little different from that of his forebears 300 years before during the opening days of Spanish rule. The great Spanish contribution to human progress in the Philippines was the abolition of slavery as an institution amongst the Islanders, but their own exigencies helped to institutionalize forced labour and consciously or unconsciously to perpetuate the feudal powers of the traditional Filipino aristocracy.

When the Spaniards first arrived they found that slavery was well established in the Islands though not in the form of total servitude as understood in the West. In the Philippines it was fundamentally a reflection of the feudal relationship between lord and follower which often had its origins in obligations incurred because of debts, as was indeed typical of the whole of the Malay world. Slavery existed in various forms in the Islands but these could all be reduced to three basic types; one, a kind of serfdom permitting those subjected to it to be property-owners as well; the second, personal service which rendered the individual concerned a part of his master's household; and the third, debt-slavery pure and simple. In any event no Filipino slave could be described as a chattel slave, to be treated as common property, to work for no reward or to be liable to purchase and sale at will. A man might become a slave as the result of being captured in war, as a punishment for some heinous offence, through the accident of birth or, as was the common case, through indebtedness. Debt slavery was by far the most prevalent and doubtless had its origins in a moneyless, rice-based economy where the natural fertility of the rice-seed provided the justification for interest. In any case there were several paths to emancipation, including purchase, marriage and the voluntary action of the master.

Such a flexible and socially intricate system of slavery could not be removed overnight, by fiat or decree, as the Spaniards themselves were quick to appreciate, without arousing serious opposition from the slave-owners and undermining the very foundations of the traditional ruling class who by policy and circumstance were being converted into the indispensable agents of the Spanish Crown. However, although in the early years of Spanish rule some Spaniards acquired Filipino slaves, the presence of the Church ensured that official policy came out unequivocally against the practice. An Apostolic Letter issued by Pope Paul III in 1537 had clearly stated the Church's attitude on the whole question and the abolition of slavery in all Spanish colonies had been repeatedly promulgated by royal decree throughout the course of the century.[69] The famous Synod of Manila convened by Bishop Salazar[70] forced the attention of Governor Ronquillo to the apparent ineffectiveness of these edicts and urged further action. This resulted in yet another royal order, now in the name of Philip II, which was issued in 1589 and was reinforced two years later by a brief of Pope Gregory XIII, prohibiting slavery under any pretext whatsoever. This time firm steps were taken to end the institution, but prudence and experience made the Spanish authorities hasten slowly. Two decades of Spanish missionaries had tried to end slavery amongst their new flocks but everywhere had encountered formidable opposition from the owners, whose economic status was immediately affected, while the pressure of Spanish officials, denied the privileges of slave-ownership themselves, to deprive the Filipino *datus* of similar rights, helped precipitate the Tondo uprising of 1588. Hence the royal decree of the following year provided for the gradual emancipation of existing slaves alongside an absolute prohibition against the acquisition of new ones. By the end of the century the task of executing this policy had largely devolved on the Audiencia of Manila which as the highest tribunal of justice was able to limit progressively the scope of the existing system and so prepare the way for its eventual extinction. Progress was seriously hampered during the period of the struggle with Holland and debt peonage increased appreciably during this time, but with the ending of the Dutch threat the Audiencia came into its own. Between 1679 and 1692 'the whole dependent system was legislated out of existence'. After the latter date no slaves were transferable either through inheritance or purchase and all children born from that time on were free. By 1800 the Spaniards had succeeded in eliminating the institution of slavery in the Islands, by any standards a great achievement, wholly inspired by Christian idealism.[71]

But as far as debt slavery was concerned, its disappearance was rather in name than in reality. As the seventeenth century progressed, the serf of yesteryear became the penurious, indebted sharecropper of the new era. The demands of the Spaniards for manpower and supplies under the pressure of the Dutch threat resulted in increased power for the Filipino chiefs whose responsibility it was to secure them. The ordinary peasant, confronted with never-ending claims on his time and labour, had a thousand new ways to fall into debt. The nineteenth century, with the emergence of a new commercial value in land, saw the rise of the *kasamajan* system so that debt-slavery became fully merged with debt peonage and an inextricable part of the complex of agrarian poverty which has held the Filipino peasant captive up till the present time.[72]

Forced labour under Spain
While slavery as an institution was definitively abolished under the rule of Spain, forced labour became institutionalized and played a major role in shaping the poverty-ridden pattern of rural Filipino society. This was not so much the result of deliberate policy as of circumstance. In the early years, many Spanish voices, particularly those of Churchmen, were to be heard raised in pleas for free labour—or even for imported labour—until events showed their impracticability. In effect, despite official efforts to substitute the encomienda system with that of free labour, such a policy proved only feasible in Manila where in the seventeenth century there were some 20,000 Filipino wage-earners. On the other hand the employment of forced labour which had been used since the earliest days, was regarded by Spanish officials as one of the rights of sovereignty and as a signal of Filipino submission to Spanish rule. A question of principle was quickly dissolved into one of expediency under the threat of the Dutch sea-borne assault in the seventeenth century, and the tribute and compulsory labour services subsequently imposed became the 'life belt' of Spanish rule in the Philippines. In what was essentially a naval campaign, woodcutters and shipwrights, oarsmen, sailors and munition makers became vital components, and forced labour an essential institution, more far-reaching and effective than anything that had ever gone before.

On paper fair, in practice the compulsory services demanded by Spain were extortionate and highly oppressive. Under the system known as '*polos y servicios*', every Filipino male between the ages of sixteen and sixty was liable to perform labour on public works for forty days out of the year. Prior to the Dutch wars public works signified building and repairing roads and bridges, churches and other public buildings; with the Dutch threat it became a matter of requisitioning labour for forests and shipyards or for service with the auxiliary troops, which was done by establishing the Mexican system of *repartimientos*, whereby each village was made to supply its quota of able-bodied men. Such labour was rewarded according to an official scale and exemption could be purchased. The principal abuses which characterized the implementation of this system sprang from the inability of the Manila administration to pay for the services which it demanded. This led to the villages from whence the labourers came being forced to sustain the cost of their upkeep which in many cases brought about food shortages and high prices, followed by starvation and mass flight to the hills. On top of all this the government collectors (invariably members of the local Filipino aristocracy) responsible for the village contributions, too often pocketed the government's token payments instead of distributing them to the labourers. Equally as oppressive were the circumstances under which the impressed labourers had to work. Large numbers of men were taken away from their families for long periods of time, often never to return, sent to far distant places such as the forests of Batangas or the ship and artillery yards of Cavite and Pantao, or even further afield to fight the Moros in the waters of Mindanao. In general, conditions were appalling and resulted in the mid-seventeenth century when the system reached its peak in a steady decline of population and a harvest of revolt.

It cannot be said that the Spanish authorities remained indifferent to the excesses of the forced labour system. Prelates of the Church were as outspoken in their criticisms of forced labour as they were of slavery, and their pleas for reform were often joined by those of high officials including the governor himself. Madrid responded by issuing periodically a series of royal injunctions which included idealistic lists of safeguards against the abuses of the system. But for as long as the Dutch pressure lasted, all such promulgations and resolutions remained dead letters, leaving revolt the only means of protest left to the people. The disappearance of the Dutch threat soon led to a partial amelioration of conditions, as an order of 1657 cancelling the annual assessments visited upon the village treasuries shows, but by this time the damage had been done. Many Filipino peasants were now entered into a new variant of their former vassalage, having become the debt peons of their former lords.[73]

Health and social welfare

From the very beginning the United States colonial regime in the Philippines made substantial efforts to improve health and education, particularly the latter, and laid great stress on them in its development plans, with the result that the progress achieved was spectacular even if not quite as superior as sometimes claimed. The American achievement in these fields certainly stood out in stark contrast to anything that the Spaniards themselves had been able to achieve, but it has to be borne in mind that the United States possessed far greater material resources than Spain could ever muster and had all the science and technology of the twentieth century at its disposal. Indeed, the Spanish record in certain respects was equally as remarkable. The missionary zeal which formed such an important element in Spanish imperialism ensured that the Spanish Philippines was far ahead of its contemporaries as far as the provision of medical services was concerned, limited though they might be to Manila and other centres of missionary settlement and influence. The first hospitals in the Islands were founded in the late sixteenth and early seventeenth centuries, largely the work of the friars supported by slender appropriations from the administration. It was also the missionaries who provided the first modern doctors, introduced pharmacy, wrote the first medical treatises in the tropics and established the first sanitaria. Up till the nineteenth century in fact medical services were virtually the friars' monopoly. The first major government contribution was the introduction of vaccination in 1806, followed later on in the century by the establishment of offices of public health and 'after many years of planning and work' the provision of a drinking water system for Manila in 1870. The efforts of the friars as pioneers in the field resulted in the Spanish Philippines, by the seventeenth century, outstripping 'other nations in the care of the sick' and had placed Manila in particular 'far in advance of any city in the English colonies for more than a century and a half to come'.[74] However, during the following 200 years there was little further development and when Spanish rule was brought to an end, their American successors termed the state of affairs they found 'scandalous'. Whatever public health institutions the Spaniards had set up or health measures they had provided for were rendered ineffective through inefficiency, incompetence and indolence. 'Plague was creeping through the alleys of Manila'; 50,000 died each year from cholera, 'tens of thousands' more succumbed to beri-beri, malaria was endemic and quinine sold 'at fabulous prices'; lepers were treated as social outcastes, 'the insane were chained like dogs underneath houses', 'a single fracture generally meant deformity'. Apart from the diseases already mentioned, tuberculosis, smallpox, typhoid, diphtheria and yaws were as rampant, while the 300,000 people of the interior were entirely neglected. The only saving grace was the topography of the Islands which checked the spread of epidemics by virtue of a widely dispersed population separated by mountain and sea.

The new American regime wasted no time in taking measures to improve matters with the result that the death-rate fell, the birth-rate rose and the average Filipino added four inches to his stature within a period of forty years. In 1901 a Board (later Bureau) of Public Health was set up, whose activities were not limited to medical measures alone but also extended to a widespread campaign against ignorance and superstition conducted mainly through schools. Courses in public health and hygiene became established as a normal part of the school curriculum and specialists were sent out into the provinces to conduct propaganda in such matters in the barrios. A Philippine General Hospital was opened in Manila and other hospitals throughout the Islands, together with public health dispensaries and infant clinics. Within the same period a new quarantine service was established while nation-wide campaigns of vaccination and inoculation against the major diseases were launched. A Bureau of Science was also set up to carry out medical research. These steps soon paid off. By 1907 the death-rate had already been reduced by one-third and continued to decline steadily in the ensuing years. By 1915 the incidence of cholera mortalities had dropped from 100,000 to 820 a year and that of smallpox from 40,000 to 276 a year. The greatest progress under United States administration was made under the two most conservative of the American governors, Forbes (1909-13) and Wood (1921-7). Forbes in particular helped to lay the true foundations of modern public health and medical services in the Islands. Under his regime particular progress was made with regard to the major diseases, especially leprosy. In 1905 a start was made to establish a leper colony on the island of Culion in Halsey Bay, which was to become the largest settlement of its kind in the world. Later on Wood supplemented these efforts by promoting the scientific study of the disease. Under Forbes effective steps were also taken against malaria, whose unwelcome presence had soon been detected by American troops campaigning in the Islands, beri-beri, smallpox, cholera, bubonic plague and yaws. Wood, apart from encouraging scientific research, instituted a nation-wide programme of hospital-building, so that by 1935 there were some 154 hospitals and 1,000 dispensaries and infant welfare centres throughout the Islands.

In general the Americans succeeded in establishing an efficient, if limited, health service, and also did effective work in preventive and curative medicine and medical research. Amongst their other achievements were the extension of pure water supplies to over a million people in the major towns between 1899 and 1934 and the construction of artesian wells in the barrios which served another 3 million. By 1934 Manila, the largest city, had also become 'the most sanitary town in the Islands' with an infant mortality rate reduced to just over 150 per 1,000. However despite the considerable American effort, it was dwarfed by the enormity of the problem and with limited funds at their disposal, the American authorities also had to make the choice, so familiar throughout South-East Asia, of concentrating on the areas of heaviest population. The fact that the peoples of the Islands were widely dispersed over a large area made the extension of the public health programme all the more expensive. Hence, typically enough, the towns were the chief beneficiaries while the rural areas remained comparatively neglected. If the towns had their sewage systems by the 1930s, most barrios still depended on contaminated streams and infected wells and 9 million Filipinos were without such services. The problem was too large to contain within the means which even the Americans had at their disposal. In 1937 it was estimated that 70 per cent of the population were still affected by hook-worm. Bore-hole latrines predominated in the slums of Manila while medical and health regulations on estates remained very inadequate, even in well-known malarial areas. A 'promising' start had been made in infant, maternity and welfare work 'but much more was needed to be done'. The Americans also had to face, as much as the health officials of other colonial powers in the region, entrecnhed resistance to their measures, stemming from apathy, ignorance and superstition, which did much to reduce the speed and effectiveness of the health campaign launched in the Islands. Last and ironically not least, the politics of independence also played their part. After the passing of the Jones Act of 1915, most American officials were replaced by Filipinos, no doubt desirable politically but unfortunate as far as the replacement of skilled professional men was involved, since in the case of medicine it led to a marked decline in the health services of the country.

With regard to other aspects of social welfare the United States record was unsubstantial and it might well be argued that by comparison the Spanish record was qualitatively speaking better. This was primarily because of the role of the Roman Catholic Church whose missionaries assumed responsibility for social welfare in the Islands from the moment they first arrived. Under Spanish rule all the social services were left in the hands of the friars—hospitals, as we have just seen, and also schools and orphanages. From the earliest days some of the pioneer colleges also served the role of asylum for the homeless and orphans; in the nineteenth century various missionary bodies established orphanages and other institutions for charitable purposes.

Under the colonial regime of the United States there was undoubtedly an extension and improvement of social welfare activities, in particular by the administration itself, but this was hardly commensurate with the problems to be faced. A school for the blind was set up here, a mental asylum there and a home for juvenile delinquents somewhere else. Retirement schemes for government servants were initiated in 1903 and by 1925 similar schemes had been extended to the Philippines Constabulary, teachers and medical service personnel. Comprehensive government measures, however, were somewhat belated. It was not until 1915 that a Public Welfare Board was established, reorganized in 1921 as the Office of the Public Welfare Commissioner and later renamed the Bureau of Public Welfare. It was not until the 1930s that the last United States governor before the inauguration of the Commonwealth instituted public relief measures for the victims of natural disasters (as opposed to the limited annual handouts of earlier years), launched a campaign to clear the slums of Manila, and another to end unemployment, and introduced legislation to provide free legal aid for the poor. In any case a great deal was still left to private charity. Even under the Commonwealth only the fringes of the problem of social welfare were touched.

*　　*　　*　　*　　*

During the brief span of their rule, the Americans certainly effected many changes for the better amongst the peoples of the Philippines, and American policy itself was marked by a remarkable blend of altruism and self-interest. American achievements were largely blunted by the colonial syndrome of conflicting interest and by the fundamental inability, common to all colonial regimes, to provide the huge resources necessary to carry out an adequate programme of economic and social reform. For all that, however, as a result of the American contribution, when the time came the Filipinos were more equipped to stand on their own feet than any other race in South-East Asia.

[1]The Seven Years War (1756-63) was the latest in a series of European wars in the seventeenth and eighteenth centuries which had their roots in the dynastic ambitions of the Habsburgs and other great European families. In the war, as was indeed the general case, Britain was ranged against France and Spain. In fact as far as Britain was concerned this conflict served to enable her to increase her overseas trade and empire at the expense of her principal colonial rivals, namely France, Spain and Holland.

[2]The Enlightenment is a term used to describe an intellectual movement which dominated European thought during the latter part of the seventeenth century and the first half of the eighteenth. The movement was largely derived from the discoveries and scientific advances which characterize this period. It gave rise to a belief that human progress and human problems could find their solution in the application of the principles of rational thought to all spheres of human endeavour.

[3]For further details of the Company's charter and background, see W.E. Cheong, 'Changing the Rules of the Game (The India-Manila Trade: 1785–1809)', *JSEAS*, I, 2, 1970.

[4]i.e. according to the British diplomat, Woodford; quoted by Cheong, op. cit.

[5]The Nookta Sound dispute concerned English demands to trade with the Californian coast (then under Spanish control), which was not solved till 1791 and nearly led to war between the two countries. War between Britain and France broke out two years later and in 1796, Spain, now under the heel of the French Emperor, Napoleon I, joined in on the side of France.

[6]However, by the beginning of the nineteenth century the Manila merchants themselves had lost their faith in the galleon trade and as early as 1810 Governor Gonzales Aguilar was pressing for its abolition. In 1815 the Spanish parliament (Cortes) finally sanctioned a royal decree abolishing the monopoly and throwing open the ports of California, Mexico, Peru and Ecuador to Philippine commerce, with an immediate and substantial increase in Manila's export trade as a result. The loss of Mexico in 1821 destroyed the *raison d'être* for the monopoly.

[7]The *indulto de commercio* (trade exemption), instituted in 1754, a device whereby provincial governors in the Philippines were allowed to indulge in private trade by paying a fine in advance! It was abolished in 1844.

[8]G.F. Zaide, *Philippine Political and Cultural History*, vol. II, Philippine Education Company, Manila, 1957, p. 67.

[9]Quoted by Steinberg (ed.), *In Search of South-East Asia: A Modern History*, Oxford University Press, Kuala Lumpur, 1971, p. 159.

[10]The advance system was operated through middlemen known as *personeros*, who dealt with the Filipino and mestizo growers in the *pueblos* (villages) and received a 5 per cent commission on crops delivered.

[11]The mestizos brought in with them families of workers from other areas to settle down and work on their estates 'on the usual system of proportionate share of profits'.

[12]Despite its strenuous activity and efforts, the Economic Society declined after Basco's retirement, fading out altogether in 1809. It was resurrected in 1811, its constitution revised in 1820 and again in 1826, but remained largely inactive till the 1880s when it was finally dissolved.

[13]Antonio de Morga, 'Sucesos de las Islas Filipinas', quoted by Teodoro A. Agoncillo, *A Short History of the Philippines*, Mentor, New York, 1969, p. 23.

[14]After 1887 various experimental farms to do research in new plant varieties, animal breeding, tillage and the extermination of crop pests were set up. The first experiments in scientific agriculture and farming techniques were started on a new government farm in Negros in 1890 and a government agricultural monthly started in 1895. However, one must not overlook the earlier work of the Economic Society which founded a professorship of agriculture at the University of San Tomas in 1821 and established the first agricultural school in Manila forty years later.

[15]In 1920 the cost of building a centrifugal mill amounted to US$1 million.

[16]This was so despite the fact that the tariff was preferential and admitted Philippine imports into the American domestic market at 35 per cent below the normal rate.

[17]The great upsurge in production also owed much to better canes and better methods of cultivation.

[18]The American sugar lobby was aided and abetted by another American interest group who had invested heavily in the sugar industries of Cuba and Puerto Rico. This lobby became an effective force during the debates on Philippine constitutional advance in the 1920s and 1930s, strongly advocating Philippine independence. For further details, see below, pp. 481–2.

[19]The sugar cultivators who worked small farms of some 50 acres apiece (i.e. about three times the size of the average Filipino holding) were organized into 'mill districts' serviced by a mill of sugar central. Mechanization was limited, most of the cultivation being carried out by landless labour.

[20]The Republican Party in its election campaign for the presidency in 1932 stood for the

complete elimination of Philippines sugar from the American domestic market. Fortunately for the Philippines economy, the Republicans lost the election.

[21]To understand the American attitude towards Philippines sugar production, it must be borne in mind that actual American investment in it was minimal; for American investors there were better opportunities in Hawaii and Cuba, whereas in the Philippines the land laws were unfavourable and the political climate uncertain.

[22]The effect of the 1934 amendment was to double the price of the commodity on the American domestic market. Another subsequent amendment to refund to the Philippines the taxes collected on coconut-oil imports was of little consequence as far as producers were concerned.

[23]i.e. for the same reasons; a traditional crop, harvestable throughout the year and simple to process for the market.

[24]The implementation of the Stevenson Plan in Malaya led to proposals for new land legislation to encourage rubber planting and to the suggestion that Sulu and Mindanao should be separated from the rest of the Philippines to make this practicable.

[25]Under the Commonwealth a whole host of new government departments and agencies were created, and funds appropriated for agricultural development and research. Between 1935 and 1939 the area under cultivation expanded by 3 million acres.

[26]For details of the Republican/Democrat railway controversy, see Grunder & Livezey, *Phillipines and the United States*, University of Oklahoma Press, 1951, pp. 87–90.

[27]For the seventeenth and eighteenth centuries, the primary source for population figures comes from the tribute rolls; as a general rule one-sixth must be added to the totals they show to compensate for statutory exemption, etc.

[28]However, it is not always possible to generalize as to the reasons for the incidence of population density. The fact that Mindoro, after Palawan, is the least heavily populated cannot be explained in terms of situation or potential. Perhaps Mindoro was too open to pirate depredations, despite its nearness to some of the most densely populated areas of Luzon.

[29]See Zaide, op. cit., vol. I, p. 259.

[30]i.e. after 1639 and up till 1854 the Japanese authorities deliberately prevented regular contacts with the outside world, allowing neither Japanese to leave the country nor foreigners to enter—except for two trading posts maintained by the Dutch and the Chinese in Nagasaki Bay. The effect of this policy was to postpone for two centuries the natural expansion of Japan overseas; without the closing of Japan, the Philippines might well have fallen into Japanese hands long before the twentieth century.

[31]Charles Robequain, *Malaya, Indonesia, Borneo and the Philippines*, Longman Green, London, 1953, p. 295.

[32]'The Spanish dilemma was quickly apparent: unable to live without the Chinese, they were equally unable to live with them.' E. Wickberg, 'The Chinese mestizo in Philippine History', *JSEAH*, V, 1, 1964, p. 68.

[33]The decision of Governor Tello in 1598 to grant certain of his friends the right to issue residence permits to Chinese at 2 reales per head created this situation in 1602. When the facts became known in Madrid, control over Chinese immigration was taken out of the hands of the governor and placed in those of the Supreme Court (Audiencia).

[34]Quoted from de Morga by V. Purcell, *The Chinese in South-East Asia*, Oxford University Press, London, 1965, p. 514.

[35]However, in the great debate argued out in the seventeenth century as to the role and value of the Chinese, the Spanish merchants of Manila carried the day against those Spanish textile interests (i.e. of Madrid, Seville and Cadiz) who would curb the Chinese presence in order to safeguard themselves against the competition of Chinese silks.

[36]Quoted by Purcell, op. cit., p. 512.

[37]This included lighter taxation and the freedom to marry local girls.

[38]See Wickberg, op. cit., p. 69.

[39]The tribute or poll-tax was lifted in 1884.

[40]See Zuniga, quoted by Wickberg, op. cit., p. 75.

[41]However, the husbands of Filipino women were considered citizens.

[42]In fact, the new United States administration found Spanish laws against Chinese immigration insufficient in the light of American feeling about Chinese immigration on their Pacific coast.

[43]R.M. Story, 'Problem of the Chinese in the Philippines', *American Social & Political Science Review*, iii/1 (Feb. 1909), p. 30. Quoted by Purcell, op. cit., p. 538.

[44]However as Phelan points out, it 'cannot be said that the Spanish administration cold-bloodedly fostered this social-economic conflict in order to guarantee their hold over Manila.... Rather the hatred of both the Spaniards and the Filipinos towards the Chinese created a situation favourable to the maintenance of Spanish control.' *The Hispanization of the Philippines*, University of Wisconsin Press, 1959, p. 146.

[45]i.e. in the words of its president, 'The Corporation was set up with government capital and represented the application of the new constitution of the Commonwealth stipulating the restriction of the exploitation of the Islands to those enterprises whose capital was 60 per cent owned by Philippine nationals.

[46]In 1918 the ratio was one female for every eighteen males; by 1939 the ratio had dropped to one for every four.

[47]However the nature of Filipino Christianity is open to debate. See Phelan, op.cit., especially Chapters 5 and 6.

[48]See Robequain, op. cit., p. 278.

[49]The Dutch Wars caused the introduction of the system of compulsory draft labour known as the *polo*, and the still more vexatious system of compulsory sale of produce known as the '*vandala*' (Tagalog for 'purchase'). Under the *vandala*, annual quotas for supplies were assigned to each province and local chiefs were held responsible for their collection. But government, hardpressed for funds, proved less than prompt with payments and by 1819 owed Filipinos over 1 million pesos for supplies and services rendered. Pampanga and the Tagalog provinces in general were the worst hit; the effects on the population were reflected in its decline during this period.

[50]For details of these various disturbances, see Zaide, op. cit., vol. I, esp. Chapter XXI.

[51]For further details and a full discussion on land tenure under the Spaniards see Phelan, op. cit., pp. 116–20.

[52]By the *pacto de retro* or contract of retrocession, the Filipino landowner pawned his land for ready cash with the option to re-purchase at the price of the original loan; in practice, this he could rarely do, so that the land went by default to the mestizo.

[53]In fact the friars' lands only covered some 403,000 acres, as compared to the 60 million acres of public land and the 7 million acres of other privately-owned land; but the friars' lands were well placed, well developed and the best available. At least one-half of the friars' lands were in and around Manila. The popular resentment against the friars' lands, which made it into a leading nationalist grievance, sprang from the high-handed actions and excessive demands of many of the friars' agents, while in the many cases of disputed property which reached the courts, clerical influence determined the issue in favour of the Church.

[54]The failure of the cadastral survey—as elsewhere in colonial South-East Asia—to keep up with approved applications for land deprived the settler of any proper legal protection. In land disputes involving large landowners, the settler was at a loss and without recourse—a situation which according to Theodore Roosevelt Jr. the large landowner might be perfectly well aware of, letting 'the little man clear and improve the property for a number of years and then turn him off without remedy'. Quoted by Erich Jacoby, *Agrarian Unrest in South-East Asia*, Asia Publishing House, Bombay, 1961, p. 217.

[55]Ibid., p. 216.

[56]The first credit institutions in the Philippines were religious endowments made by wealthy citizens for pious purposes and managed by the religious orders. Known as Obras Pias they served as the earliest commercial banks and insurance companies and financed the galleon trade. The first was founded in 1594. In the 1850s their role was largely superseded by modern commercial banks, the first of which was established with government backing in 1851. In the same year the Obras Pias were reduced by

decree to four and then amalgamated into one. The first Western (non-Spanish) banks established their branches in Manila in the 1870s.

[57]See Grunder and Livezey, op. cit., p. 85.

[58]i.e. in the sense that with its completion, a system of 35-year contracts with independent planters in the neighbourhood was instituted, which later became general practice wherever sugar centrals were located.

[59]For more details of the purposes of the Council, see Frank M. Golay, *The Philippines: Public Policy and National Economic Development*, Cornell University Press, 1961, p. 347.

[60]Three main issues were at stake: (i) tariffs on United States goods entering the Philippines; (ii) tariffs on Philippines goods entering the United States; (iii) the question of United States coastal shipping laws and their applicability to the Philippines.

[61]By the process of reclassifying types of tariff, the United States could evade some of the consequences of the Treaty of Paris (1898) and encourage the importation of American goods.

[62]i.e. the Payne-Aldrich Act of 1909. This Act was never systematically revised and remained the basic tariff law of the Islands until independence.

[63]For a full discussion of the American debate on the issue, refer Grunder and Livezey, op. cit., Chapter XII.

[64]Ibid., Chapter XIII.

[65]Ibid., p. 116.

[66]The Panama Canal was opened in 1913.

[67]Quoted by Zaide, op. cit., vol. II, p. 331.

[68]Of industrial labour in 1935, over half was in miscellaneous modern industry including sawmilling; about a quarter was employed in sugar factories or in the gold mines. Labour conditions under the American corporations on Mindanao were markedly better than elsewhere, but represented only a fraction of the whole.

[69]For the text of the Apostolic Letter of 1537 quoted in extenso, see H. de la Costa, *The Jesuits in the Philippines: 1581–1768*, Harvard University Press, 1961, p. 638, note 15.

[70]The Synod was an assembly of the priests and friars in the Philippines convened by Bishop Salazar in 1581 to discuss problems and policies. It continued till 1586 and marked an important landmark in the history of the Roman Catholic Church in the Islands.

[71]However, abolition was confined to the Filipino subjects of the Spanish Crown. Spaniards (and Filipinos) were free to purchase slaves from other parts of Asia, including the Moro lands of Mindanao and the Sulu archipelago, as well as from Africa, with the result that in the seventeenth century Manila was dangerously crowded with foreign slaves. In practice very few Moros were ever captured and the supply of slaves from elsewhere was never sufficient to be economic. As for the Moro-dominated areas of the south, slavery was practised and widespread, and it was left to the Americans to eradicate slavery there. This was only accomplished effectively after the passing of special legislation in 1911.

[72]See Phelan, op. cit., p. 116.

[73]Some Filipinos borrowed to pay their way out of forced service and so sold themselves into a dependent status; others unable to meet the quotas of the *vandala* fell into debt with their local lords. The prevalence of this rural indebtedness became a major factor in the failure of an untied, wage-earning labour force to rise up in the sugar, rice, tobacco and abaca plantations of the Islands in the late nineteenth and early twentieth centuries.

[74]See Zaide, op. cit., vol. 1, p. 196.

Books and articles for further reading

BOOKS

Agoncillo, T.A., *A Short History of the Philippines*, Mentor, New York, 1969.
Corpuz, O.D., *The Philippines*, Prentice-Hall Inc., New Jersey, 1965.

Costa, H. de la, *The Jesuits in the Philippines*, Harvard University Press, 1961.
————, *Readings in Philippine History*, Bookmark, Manila, 1965.
Cutshall, A., *The Philippines: Nation of Islands*, Van Nostrand, New York, 1964.
Fisher, C.A., *South-East Asia: A Social, Economic and Political Geography*, Methuen, London, 1964.
Golay, F.M., *The Philippines: Public Policy and National Economic Development*, Cornell University Press, 1961.
Grunder, G.A. & Livezey, W.E., *The Philippines and the United States*, University of Oklahoma Press, 1951.
Jacoby, E.H., *Agrarian Unrest in South-East Asia*, Asia Publishing House, Bombay, 1961.
Phelan, J.L., *The Hispanization of the Philippines: Spanish Aims and Filipino Responses; 1565–1700*, University of Wisconsin Press, 1959.
Purcell, V., *The Chinese in South-East Asia*, Oxford University Press, London, 1965.
Ruiason, S.D., *English 'Country Trade' with the Philippines: 1644–1765*, University of the Philippines Press, 1966.
Robequain, C., *Malaya, Indonesia, Borneo and the Philippines*, Longman Green, London, 1958.
Steinberg, D.J. et al., *In Search of South-East Asia: A Modern History*, Oxford University Press, Kuala Lumpur, 1971.
Zaide, G.F., *Philippine Political and Cultural History*, 2 Vols. Philippine Education Company, Manila, 1957.

ARTICLES
Chang, Tien-tse, 'The Spanish-Dutch Naval Battle of 1617 off Manila', *JSEAH*, VII, 1, 1966.
Cheong, W.E., 'Changing the Rules of the Game (The India-Manila Trade: 1785–1809)', *JSEAS*, I, 2, 1970.
————, 'The Decline of Manila as the Spanish Entrepôt in the Far East, 1785–1826', *JSEAS*, II, 2, 1971.
Corpuz, O.D., 'Western Colonization and the Filipino Response', *JSEAH*, III, 1, 1962.
Gould, J.W., 'American Imperialism in South-East Asia before 1898', *JSEAS*, III, 2, 1972.
McHale, T.R., 'American Colonial Policy Towards the Philippines', *JSEAH*, III, 1, 1962.
Roth, D., 'The Casas de Reservas in the Philippines', *JSEAS*, V, 1, 1974.
Spector, R.M., 'W. Cameron Forbes in the Philippines', *JSEAH*, VII, 2, 1966.
Wickberg, E., 'The Chinese Mestizo in Philippine History', *JSEAH*, V, 1, 1964.

VI THAILAND

'We must take cognisance of the time. Anything that seems to us possible we should tackle first. In short, we need not decide to follow a definite pattern based on this country or that, but should decide which of the bad practices can be remedied first, and then pool our strength to achieve our objects one by one— and this will no doubt be truly beneficial.'

King Chulalongkorn (1868-1910): Essay on Unity.

THE rulers of the Chakri dynasty succeeded in their primary object, that of preserving the political sovereignty of Thailand, but this did not prevent— in fact was largely achieved by—the country becoming to all intents and purposes an economic 'satellite' of Great Britain in particular and an extension of the colonial imperiums of the West in general. In 1941, 70 per cent of the kingdom's export trade was with the British Empire, its principal outlets being via British colonial ports such as Penang, Singapore and Hong Kong. Britain held the public debt and lionized the great bulk of Thailand's business and financial undertakings, 95 per cent of which were in foreign hands. Western investments totalled some US$90 million in the late 1930s, only surpassed by the even larger Chinese stake in the country. The Thai economy bore other colonial hall-marks. The kingdom's revenues depended mainly (i.e. some 80 to 90 per cent) on the exportation of four primary products— rice, teak, rubber and tin—all of which were wholly foreign-controlled except for rice, the cultivation of which remained a Thai monopoly. At the same time, local industrialization was in its infancy and the kingdom's supply of manufactured consumer goods was almost entirely imported. Another typical 'colonial' feature was the marked differentiation between the productive sector of the economy which was virtually foreign-manned, and the traditional world of agriculture which remained the preserve of the indigenous Thais. Indeed, in the view of at least one observer,[1] the Thais in their hybrid state of political independence and economic subservience got the worst of all possible worlds, for as such they were denied the benefits both of development in social welfare which colonial rule brought in its train, and of protection from exposure to the rigours of the world market which the Western colonial powers could on occasion afford to their wards. In all, as far as the Thai people were concerned, the economic changes which took place in the country after the epoch-making Anglo-Thai Treaty of 1855 (Bowring's Treaty) were more apparent than real. A money economy spread without an appreciable rise in per capita income. A flourishing export trade tied to the world market sprang up, the chief beneficiaries of which were aliens. The traditional subsistence economy of the peasant gave way to one based on commercial cash crop production, but in a manner which marked little prog-

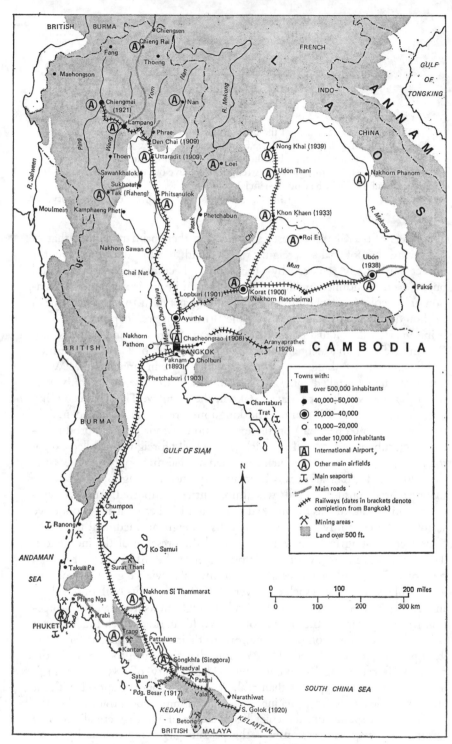

36.   General Map of Thailand, 1941

ress in terms of capital investment, new techniques or increased productivity.

But as much as the Thai response to the new economic pressures from the West which now penetrated the country was seemingly a passive one, the preservation of national sovereignty at least counted for something. The slower pace of change and modernization (by comparison with other lands in the region) was offset by the absence of the dislocation and disintegration of traditional society and of traditional values which characterized developments in neighbouring Burma and Vietnam. Indeed, the key factor in the pattern of the kingdom's economic development and evolution after 1855 was the reality of its political sovereignty remaining intact. If Thai policy after 1855 was one of marked deference to the demands and wishes of the Western colonial powers which resulted in the economy acquiring such a colonial tinge, it was also a policy of accommodation to the ineluctable conditions of the times and did not represent a sell-out to foreign interests. Thai policy above all was conditioned by the overriding fear of precipitating colonial intervention and control through failure to meet Western commercial needs or to protect Western financial interests already staked in the country. This was the rationale behind the ultra-conservative financial policies pursued by Thai administrations right up to the 1940s, the basic purpose of which was to protect the stability of the baht at all costs. Even when Thailand converted officially to the gold standard in 1903, the currency continued to be largely in silver and all proposals to reduce the weight or fineness of the coinage were rejected so as to avoid any loss of public confidence. For the same reasons, the paper currency introduced after 1902 remained fully convertible. The Currency Act of 1928, which is still in force today (1975), was, on the admission of its author, Sir Edward Cook, drawn up 'on particularly conservative lines' for 'obvious reasons'. As a result the baht became regarded as one of the strongest and most stable of currencies and Thailand possessed a substantial accumulation of liquid public funds.

The evolution of this conservative financial policy, which served Western interests so well, was probably inevitable in the context of the times. In the first place, from the 1850s onwards the government was heavily reliant on foreign capital and foreign banks. Of the eleven commercial banks in the kingdom in 1938, only four were actually incorporated in the country. This dependence on foreign bankers dated from the 1850s themselves when a decree of King Mongkut made foreign coins legal tender in order to overcome the acute shortage of Thai silver specie. For the next few decades, the handling of all foreign exchange and the financing of foreign trade lay in the hands of private (Western) traders and exchange merchants until this role was taken over by large foreign banks from the mid-1880s onwards. Four major banks between them continued to dominate the financial scene up till the 1940s.

From the start, the British had a preponderant share in all this. The first two large commercial banks opened in the country were the Hongkong and Shanghai Banking Corporation, which opened up a branch in Bangkok in 1888, and the Chartered Bank of India, Australia and China which followed in 1894. The strong British presence reflected the importance and volume of

British commercial interests in the country, and it was perhaps natural that when the government started to appoint foreign financial advisers from the 1890s, those advisers were invariably Britons. The financial advisers enjoyed considerable power over the direction of economic policy, and through them Great Britain was able to exercise a decisive influence on its evolution. The British, with their large stake in the import-export trade, their financial houses, their interests in teak and tin, and their political concern to preserve Thailand as a buffer state between themselves and their French rivals, had most to gain from a conservative financial policy which guaranteed the stability and the integrity of the Thai baht. Such a policy was pursued with consistency by a generation of British financial advisers, who in the name of stability discouraged the development of domestic credit facilities, delayed the recognition of the baht as legal tender, stood sentinel over the Currency Reserve, and resisted all proposals to establish a Central Bank till the late 1930s. At the same time, however, these British advisers were preaching to the converted, for conservatism in fiscal matters was what the Thai administration itself desired.[2]

In consequence the Thai economy, opened up by Bowring's Treaty which provoked 'a total revolution in all the financial machinery of the government',[3] was allowed to develop at the dictates of the world market, a *laissez-faire* system where the government acted merely as ring-master to secure the observance of certain basic rules. The conservative financial policy in particular ensured that the wealth of the country was used to preserve the international position of the currency and so secure the confidence of Western investors. At the same time, however, the effects of such a policy on internal economic development were less beneficial. Advantage was not taken of the existence of large government reserves to promote domestic economic growth or to meet the domestic need for an adequate, economic and social infrastructure which would itself help foster internal economic development. While Thailand's foreign trade grew apace alongside that of neighbouring territories, the economic and social level of the people themselves remained amongst the lowest in the region.

The development of communications

A more positive result of Thai political autonomy was reflected in the development of modern communications in the country, in particular in the construction of a nation-wide railway system which became the best in mainland South-East Asia. Thailand also proved a pioneer in the establishment of airlines in the region, but developed only a poor network of roads. In the event, railways played the decisive role, a bold decision by Thailand's rulers in view of the notorious role played by railway imperialism in other parts of the world. Indeed, a considerable amount of colonial rivalry and intrigue centred on bids to construct Thailand's railways, and it was the Thai achievement to build a national railway system on foreign capital and know-how without compromising the country's sovereignty any further. From the outset the driving factors behind Thai railway policy and the manner modern communications as a whole developed in the country were highly political, but they reaped ample reward in economic as well as in political terms.

As in every other land of South-East Asia before the modern era, travel in Thailand was dangerous, tedious and expensive, so much so that the earnest missionary, Pallegoix, thought it 'no wonder that the Siamese themselves did little travelling'.[4] It was only in the Central Plain that movement was comparatively easy with its network of rivers and canals. Travel beyond to the north and north-east was hampered by mountains, and the few rivers which flowed south of the watershed were strewn with rapids and were only negotiable in the high water season; in fact all overland routes, north or south, were difficult and prey to bandits. Until the railway was extended from Korat towards the Mekong in the 1920s a journey from that city to the Lao border took three weeks. In the late 1860s it took McGilvray, another pioneer missionary, three months to reach Chiengmai from Bangkok. It still took from three to six weeks by river in 1905 and over a week from the new railhead at Den Chai in 1911. In terms of expense it was probably cheaper (in the nineteenth century) to ship a ton of cloth from England to Bangkok than to send it from Chiengmai to Bangkok. Water was the most used medium of transport—even in the 1950s 75 per cent of internal freight traffic went by river or canal. In the pasture areas and foothills along the edge of the Central Plain, in the peninsular south and on the Korat Plateau the ox and the buffalo dominated as the means of transport. In the mountains of the north human porters and caravans mounted by 40 to 60 animals were the norm.

After 1850, with the mounting pressure of the West, the isolation, self-sufficiency and autonomy of the outlying regions had to be brought to an end, and the development of effective communications acquired a new urgency. Matters came to a head because of the international bickering over the proposal to build a railway line from Bangkok to Chiengsen and Chiengmai. The scheme started with the British who, reacting to the rise of French power in Indo-China, proposed the original concession; but when this was awarded to an English firm, it was opposed by the powerful German syndicate of Krupp and the British finally dropped the scheme altogether. In the meantime, foreigners had surveyed possible routes and explored the north, and by so doing awoke King Chulalongkorn to the dangers and the potential of railway-building. The outcome was the start made on building the first railway line in the kingdom in the following decade. The earliest and the first to be completed, the short line between Bangkok and Paknam opened in 1893 was purely a commercial venture which soon paid rich dividends. At the same time, work was started on the much more ambitious project to link the capital with Korat (Nakhorn Ratchasima), about 170 miles to the north-east. This important line was designed as a direct counter to the growing French presence on the Mekong and aimed to prevent the trade of the north-east being diverted from Bangkok to Saigon; the line was certainly not justifiable from a strictly economic point of view, as it ran through difficult and under-populated country. Similar considerations led to the construction of the line south-eastwards from Bangkok towards the Cambodian frontier, the first stretch of which was completed by 1908, while the northern line started in

1898 was intended to counteract the draw of Moulmein in British Burma on Raheng (Tak), and was lent further urgency by unrest in the north at the turn of the century. The construction of the peninsular line which eventually linked up with the F.M.S. Railways and Penang was largely the consequence of Anglo-German rivalries and of the British desire to have the ultimate influence in the Isthmus of Kra. At the same time, as the Paknam line swiftly proved, railways could be a profitable investment and railway construction, planned on the principle of direct return, increasingly formed a major element in the economic policies of the government.

By 1941 railways from Bangkok radiated to the four corners of the kingdom, leaving no place further than 150 miles from the nearest station, and totalling over 1,900 miles of metre gauge. The initial spurt of construction began in the 1890s, carrying over into the new century, but the great age of railway-building came in the 1920s and 1930s when a ten-year plan was drawn up for the unification of all the gauges and for the extension of the northern and north-eastern lines, complemented by appropriate legislation (passed under King Vajiravudh) providing for the acquisition of land, for passenger and freight regulations and for public safety measures. By this time all the lines were government-owned, a policy which had been prompted in the first place by the bitter and expensive experience of the Korat line whose construction had cost half as much again as the original estimates, taken three and a half years longer to build than anticipated, and had led to protracted quarrelling between its British and German contractors. After this, Bangkok invariably assumed responsibility for construction itself, with the aid of foreign loans, engineers and technicians. By 1940 the capital expenditure involved amounted to some 217 million baht, about one-fifth of which had been raised through foreign loans at the beginning of the century. In seeking such loans, the government took care not to rely solely on one source, and for preference chose the Germans who appeared to represent the least imminent threat to the country. High politics determined that the British financed the building of the peninsular line and the Germans forfeited their stake in the northern line with the outbreak of the Great War: but the government was prepared to spend large sums to maintain Thai control,[5] and as the lines proved increasingly profitable, found it later on easier to do so. The construction of the north-eastern lines was financed by Bangkok itself and built by Thai engineers alone, as by the 1907 treaty with France other powers (except for the French) were excluded. The profitability of the railways turned them into one of the government's principal assets and the main source of revenue from amongst the commercial services provided by the state. By 1932, 195 million baht had been earned from the railways against working expenses of 86.5 million baht, while the annual average value of freight carried came to 8 million baht. This success was brought about in the first place by deliberately neglecting the development of road communications so that there would be no competition, by imposing high and arbitrary freight charges, and by refusing to accept responsibility for any loss or damage en route. Unpopular as this policy was, it paid handsomely and amply justified itself. The profitability of the railways was further enhanced in the 1930s by the substitution of diesel engines for the ordinary wood-burning locomotives.[6]

In general, railway development had a profound effect on the evolution of the kingdom in the first half of the twentieth century. It was a major factor in promoting the authority of Bangkok in the outer provinces, particularly in those of the north, and so in unifying the country; it proved a major highroad for Chinese penetration into the interior where their numbers had been scarce before; and it served as a great boost to economic growth itself. More specifically in economic terms the railways pierced the isolation of the north and north-east and brought these regions within the orbit of world trade, whilst enhancing the value of land and making it more accessible. On the Korat Plateau in particular, the traditional caravan trade of the region was 'revolutionised', business in livestock and semi-precious stones stimulated, ancient river ports were abandoned for the bustling new stations along the line, and padi was exported to Bangkok for the first time. The new railways in fact represented a great boon to the rice industry, facilitating transportation and export. Even in the Central Plain, the railway vied with the canals to become the major padi carrier at a cheaper rate. Along with the provision of extensive irrigation schemes, the building of the railways was the government's major contribution to the conversion of the country into one of the world's great rice-bowls.

As we have noted, it was deliberate government policy to promote the railways and guarantee their success by guarding against competition from the roads. By the 1930s barely one-fifth of the money spent on railway development had been put into highway construction, and the principal roads which existed were mostly feeder routes to the railways themselves, apart from some development around Bangkok. Outside the capital the roads were little more than bullock cart tracks and were used as such, while interregional road connexions hardly existed. However, in the 1930s opinions began to change. The pressures of the motor age were mounting, the volume of traffic was greater and the demand for freight transport ever rising. These factors and the goadings of foreign experts made the new rulers of the country think again about the accepted policy of railways first and finally to abandon it. In 1936 a new road programme was announced and an 18-year plan to construct 9,000 miles of roads at an estimated cost of 153 million baht was launched. In that year, Thailand possessed some 2,000 miles of highway, of which a mere 75 miles were first class.

Seasonal trails had existed since time immemorial. Overland caravan routes trodden for centuries crossed from Thailand into Yunnan and Burma in the north, and other famous jungle routes—which were also the first to be used by Christian European missionaries—joined Raheng (Tak) to Moulmein and Phetchaburi to Mergui further south. Likewise numerous trails led across the Korat Plateau to the Mekong, of which the most important was that between Korat itself and Nongkhai. In the far south equally well-known routes crossed from the China Sea around Nakhorn Sri Thammarat (Ligor), Songkhla and Patani to reach into Kedah and to the Indian Ocean. Many of these peninsular routes became broadened into important local highways with the expansion of tin-mining and rubber planting in the late nineteenth and early twentieth centuries. In the Central Plain, Crawfurd observed in the 1820s that the two major roads in use were those between Bangkok and Ayuthia, and between Chantabun and Tungyai. The most important road construction which took place in the twentieth century prior to the 1930s was mostly in the north, in particular the Chiengmai–Lampang road, built in 1916, which was later extended up to the far north at Chiengsen and to the Burmese–Shan border at Mae Sai. This had the effect of bringing the caravan route from South China into direct connexion with the railhead at Lampang, opening up a hitherto remote region. Other important routes which were started in the 1920s included the Tak (Raheng)–Sawankaloke road, the Den Chai–Phrae Nan highway (started in 1919) and the Ubon–Paksé road, opened in 1931, which, in striking contrast to the other roads, was built in the record time of one year. Road building as a whole was slow, progress being held up by difficult terrain, floods and the impossibility of acquiring a permanent labour force. The same factors resulted in little of the 1936 road-building programme being completed by 1941.

In that year Thailand was still a country without roads in the sense that a national road network was still lacking. Bangkok was linked with neither Chiengmai to the north nor with Songkhla in the south, the second and third largest towns in the kingdom respectively. There were a thousand miles of first class, paved highway and 3,000 motor vehicles, of which over half were in Bangkok.

Along with the impressive achievements in railway construction and the more desultory efforts to build highways came other modern forms of communication such as postal services, telegraphs and telephones. Postal services on a courier basis had been known since the days of Sukhothai, which had absorbed the experience of the Khmers, and each township had its regular runners who knew the local routes and who were treated with great respect. But under the pressures of the nineteenth century this system was manifestly inadequate and up till the time the government finally established a modern postal department (i.e. in 1881), foreign merchants handled their own mail and correspondence from Europe was usually entrusted to the British consul. The new Post and Telegraphs Department was run under German supervision for its first ten years and then in 1891 was taken over by the government and made a branch of the Public Works Department. Up till 1916 the postal services were run at a large loss and were generally inefficient. Foreigners complained that the postal department continued to remain inefficient after 1916 as well, but services were improved and enhanced with the growth of rail and air links. By 1930 there were over 800 post offices in the country, compared to an eighth of that number a quarter of a century previously. Places along the railways were well served, towns on the east coast of the Gulf of Siam were visited by the Siam Navigation Company, and letters had been conveyed by air since 1922. But the modern post office was preceded by telegraphs. The nucleus of the telegraph services of the kingdom was created by the establishment of the Royal Telegraph Department in 1875, and the following year on government initiative the first lines were laid by student engineers between Bangkok and Paknam. Another pioneer effort was the laying of the

line between Bangkok and the royal residence at Bang Pa-in, later extended
to Ayuthia, and in 1883 the opening of the Bangkok–Saigon line along a
route which had been surveyed by the French adventurer and imperialist,
Auguste Pavie, gave the Thai capital its first links with the outside world.
During the next fifteen years the largely untrained staff of the Post and Telegraphs Department laboured through the routeless jungles to link up the capital with the main centres of population throughout the kingdom. It was
another of those unsung, unnoticed epics of human endeavour in the region
which finally produced a network of over 5,000 miles of cable, administered
by 684 telegraph offices. If the system had many shortcomings, perhaps these
were not surprising in the circumstances where the hazards of nature combined with the lack of competent or trained hands caused frequent breakdowns
and interruptions. The Thai telephone service also acquired a reputation for
poor service for similar reasons. The first telephone—solely for the use of
the military—was available in Bangkok in 1881, and the service opened to the
public in 1886. International phone links were started in 1930 and a dialling
system introduced in 1934.

In the advanced field of air communications, Thailand played a pioneer
role and led her neighbours in the region. While aviation was still in its infancy, three Thai officers were sent to France to study developments, returning a couple of years later to organize a flying corps with trained pilots and
mechanics without any foreign aid. In consequence when the country entered the Great War on the side of Britain and France in 1917, Thailand was
able to offer 500 fully equipped pilots for the Western Front. Immediately
after the war, in 1919, Thailand was one of the first signatories to the International Convention for Aerial Navigation, and the government maintained
its initiative in the pioneer days of civil aviation which followed. In 1922 the
Army started regular air services between Korat and Ubon and later between
Korat and Nongkhai which operated successfully for the next eight years
without any fatalities. In 1930 the military air service was taken over by the
newly (and painfully) formed Aerial Transport Company, with its headquarters at Korat, which immediately set upon a programme of re-equipment
and expansion. In the same year Don Muang airport just outside Bangkok
was converted into an all-season landing ground and quickly developed into
the main air hub of South-East Asia. New planes were bought and international air links established.

But the waterways remained supreme. In 1940 four-fifths of the rice trade
of the Central Plain was conveyed by boat, though the waterways of Thailand
cannot compare with those of either Burma or Vietnam. The waterway system of the Central Plain was considerably extended under King Mongkut
in the middle of the nineteenth century and to a somewhat lesser degree
under King Chulalongkorn subsequently. More important for water
communications and for Thailand's general economic growth was the modernization and development of the port of Bangkok. In fact, Bangkok never
acquired the importance of Singapore, Saigon, Manila or Rangoon as an
international port despite its being the focal point of the country's export
trade. One of its chief drawbacks was the great sandbar which screened the

mouth of the Menam Chao Phaya, causing two-fifths of the imports brought to the city to be transhipped and carried by lighters upstream. However, until the 1930s all proposals to deal with the bar and to improve Bangkok's facilities failed because of political factors. The lighter interest successfully foiled British and German plans to dredge the approaches to Bangkok prior to the Great War, despite the increasing necessity for action as the volume of international trade expanded. Likewise the farming interest successfully opposed various official schemes for digging a deep channel through the bar and upstream, but finally the pressures of the Great Depression and the coming into power of the new regime in 1932 enabled the matter to be considered again. Despite continued opposition from those who feared the effects of salinity on the adjoining rice lands, in 1932 itself the new government adopted in principle a trial dredging scheme expected to cost half a million baht, and to strengthen its hand called in G.P. Nijhoff, a League of Nations expert, to make a report. The Nijhoff Report fully vindicated those who favoured a dredging project as a means of developing Bangkok as an international port, drawing the rice market away from Singapore to the city, reducing costs and prices, and even as a means of encouraging tourism.[7] For all this, the project continued to arouse considerable opposition in the Thai parliament, and as a result Nijhoff's Report was not fully adopted. But the question of the management of the port of Bangkok itself was sufficiently serious to warrant certain other measures. The old port, which had been run on a monopoly basis by a Western undertaking over the past seventy years, was far from satisfactory. Its lack of proper wharves, godowns, modern machinery or any direct connexion with the railway system cost the country an estimated loss of over $3\frac{1}{2}$ million baht a year directly, and of 5 million baht a year indirectly. The new regime acted by breaking the foreign monopoly over pilotage; pilotage was made compulsory, fees were raised and a Harbour Association was set up to manage it. A 1937 law provided for the expropriation of land for the construction of new wharves and a contract for the construction of a new dock was awarded to a Danish firm. By 1941 a start had been made to the proper development of the port.

The rice economy

Within the framework of two basic policies—fiscal conservatism and the self-conscious and deliberate development of a modern communications network based on the railways—the Thai economy evolved from a subsistence one based on rice to one based on the production of rice as a cash crop for export. At all events, rice remained the foundation on which Thai culture and civilization had been built, and it continued to form the largest single element in the economy of the country. The cultivation of rice has been the principal occupation of the people from the earliest days of Thai settlement and formed the core around which the traditional social structure evolved. It was the chief source of civil dispute, and in foreign wars the main determinant in military strategy. In the mid-nineteenth century, on the eve of the Bowring Revolution, rice commanded the energies of almost the entire working population of the country and has continued to be the chief occupation of four-fifths of the nation up till the present time. As such, it has been the main source of government revenue—70 per cent in the late 1930s—and in terms of output placed Thailand fifth amongst world rice producers. By the same token, rice was consistently the kingdom's greatest export earner, over one-fifth of the annual crop being disposed on the overseas market; it also held a preponderant (92 per cent) share in the land devoted to the cultivation of crops.[8] But above all, the most significant and spectacular economic development in the hundred years following the opening up of the country to Western trade and influence was the great expansion in rice production and the conversion of rice into the major export crop. Between 1850 and 1950 the volume of Thailand's rice exports multiplied twenty-five times, a development which involved the greater part of the population.

If the rise of rice production in general was spectacular, it is the expansion in area under cultivation rather than rise in production and productivity that calls for remark, and serves as a pointer to the true nature of Thailand's emergence as a major rice producer. The rice revolution in Thailand was characterized by the spread of a wide-cast smallholder economy, without—on the whole—the attendant evils of landlordism, mass tenancy and universal indebtedness so typical of developments in Burma and Cochin-China. At the same time, while the area under rice expanded, there was no corresponding improvement in farming techniques and productivity as a whole tended to decline. In fact, although the land under rice increased uninterruptedly from 1855 up till 1941 (with the single exception of the years of the Great Depression), the total increase in production was little more than half of that in area. There are no reliable statistics to indicate with any degree of accuracy the actual extent of rice cultivation in the 1850s, but it has been estimated at around $2\frac{1}{2}$ million acres, compared with an annual average acreage of 7 million during the period 1935-9.[9] The rate of expansion rose sharply after 1920, doubling itself within a period of fifteen years. In 1941 at least 95 per cent of all the cultivated land was devoted to rice production, whereas in the 1850s more than 5 per cent was significantly enough probably devoted to other crops. Throughout the period the main centre of cultivation was the Central Plain, which produced about three-fifths of the total crop in the 1930s and prior to 1905 had been virtually the sole source of export rice. This was the outcome of all the natural advantages which the Central Plain enjoyed from the point of view of rice farming. In 1855 it was already the main focus of settlement, yet possessed large tracts unused and waiting to be opened up for cultivation. A combination of rainfall and the annual three-month flood season ensured the right conditions for farming and provided a cheap internal transport system. Above all, the region was easily accessible to outside, sea-borne trade. After 1905, however, with the penetration of the new railway into the hitherto isolated regions of the north and north-east, rice cultivation in these areas grew at a rate which was four times as great as that on the Central Plain itself. There was scope for increased rice cultivation in the peninsular south, but rubber and tin proved rival attractions and the railway link with the Centre was long and expensive.

As already noted, in contrast to the spread of cultivation, actual production

rose far more slowly and productivity, after 1900 at any rate, actually declined. Between 1905 and the mid-century, the average productivity per acre
dropped by one-third, the greatest falling off being in the Korat region, followed by the Central Plain itself. In general terms the reasons for this decline
lay in the gradual impoverishment of the soils caused by the almost complete
absence of artificial fertilizers and the general failure to improve farming
techniques. The failure to better farming techniques is one of the most outstanding features of the rice revolution in Thailand and was rooted in the
manner the great expansion of area under cultivation took place. With plenty
of land available and conducive land and fiscal policies, the small peasant
farmer had every incentive to devote himself solely to the cultivation of rice
which now (i.e. after 1855) fetched good prices on the market. So rice production for export became the preserve of the smallholders, who earned sufficient to meet their own needs but lacked either the capital or the inducement
to improve their methods.

The obvious cause for the rice revolution was the sudden emergence of a
large and constant demand for Thai rice from overseas markets. By the 1870s
the existence of this demand had become an established fact and so became
a permanent factor in increased production. This was the first fruit of Bowring's and similar treaties which followed, opening the Thai economy to the
world market [10] and leading to the penetration of Western goods, particularly
textiles, into the domestic market, creating a new need for cash. Starting
with a small demand for padi from the immediate vicinity of Bangkok itself,
which was handled by Chinese merchants, rice exports leapt from an estimated 5 per cent of total production in 1850 to 50 per cent by 1905. By the 1870s
an average of 200,000 tons a year was being shipped overseas, an amount
which had risen to $1\frac{1}{2}$ million tons by the 1930s, representing a twenty-five-
fold increase in volume and from 5 million to 95 million baht in value. Behind this rapid increase in world demand lay the development of cheap communications by sea which enabled Thai rice to compete effectively on open
overseas markets, and also the emergence of new markets as a result of the
Western impact within the region itself.[11]

In turning to the cultivation of rice for cash, the smallholder was given
direct encouragement by government.[12] The economic implications of Bowring's Treaty were such that if government was to recoup the loss of its traditional sources of revenue, it had no choice but to encourage the development of a dutiable export trade. King Mongkut had no doubt that the growth
of the rice trade would soon outweigh in its general benefits any anticipated
harm to domestic consumers, and he also believed that extending the acreage
under rice would help keep down the price. In order to do this, on the Central Plain the Chakri rulers pursued land and taxation policies designed in
the interest of the smallholder; they also set out deliberately to eliminate slavery and forced labour as economic impediments to the growth of a cash
crop export trade. It was left, however, to the governments of the post-1932
era to take further steps to help the farmer through the development of credit
agencies and technical services.

After 1855 the best padi lands in the Delta of the Menam Chao Phaya were quickly opened up by facilitating squatters to acquire land rights. Under the traditional system,[13] 'freemen' could acquire uncultivated land by due process of registration and payment of fees, after having worked it for three successive years, a right which was not abrogated up till 1941, although by that time the land laws in general had been altered and modernized. Land rights were also given to those who undertook to dig irrigation canals, subject to the proviso that the land so acquired be cultivated. King Chulalongkorn initiated the process of abolishing slavery and forced labour which had an important bearing on land rights as well as on the growing need for a labour force to handle the ramifications of the rice trade. Land taxation policy, though basically conditioned till the end of the century by Bowring's Treaty,[14] was also informed by the need to encourage the spread of rice cultivation, at any rate as far as the Central Plain and the southern provinces of the peninsula were concerned, for a law of 1857-8 exempted newly-cultivated lands from taxation for the first year, a provision extended to three years by King Chulalongkorn in 1874-5.

The role of the railways in stimulating the rice trade has already been mentioned. The growth of exports and the construction of rice mills in the north and north-east give ample proof of their impact. The inadequacy of road communications and the lack of facilities at the port of Bangkok, stressed by the Andrews Report,[15] highlighted the importance of communications in general in the development of the rice economy. The government's railway policy and the extension of irrigation, particularly on the Central Plain, represent its main contributions in the technical field prior to 1941.

A considerable amount of work on the extension and improvement of irrigation was done between 1900 and 1941, but it was not as much as could and should have been done. Despite the annual rains and floods, water distribution in the Central Plain was often insufficient to ensure a successful harvest over the whole area. Irrigation was therefore essential, a fact appreciated by the Thais, who, however, did not have the technological skills necessary to cope with water control on the scale required.[16] In the 1850s, whatever irrigation there was served the purpose of distributing but not of controlling the waters. Under King Mongkut, five new canals were built 'through thousands of acres of the richest rice-fields' of the Central Plain, and the early years of the reign of King Chulalongkorn witnessed some more desultory and sporadic effort at canal-building, without effective results. However, in the last decades of the century the needs of the rice industry made better communications and more effective irrigation mandatory, official recognition of which was evidenced by the concession granted in 1889 to the Siam Canals, Land and Irrigation Company to irrigate and open up a large tract of flat, swampy land north-east of Bangkok. Known as the Rangsit scheme, it quickly fell into difficulties. There was a total lack of proper planning and foresight. Although by 1910, 100,000 people had acquired land titles and settled in the district, the process had been attended by multitudinous litigation over land rights and by the ultimate downfall of the company. Failure to provide for the heavy seasonal rains caused the new canals to silt up quickly and led to insufficient water in drought years. As a net result, only about 40 per cent of the total cultivable area of 360,000 acres actually became productive.

The Rangsit débâcle led directly to the appointment of J.M. van der Heide, a Dutch irrigation expert, in 1899 as adviser on irrigation to the government, and later as head of the newly-formed Canals Department of the Ministry of Agriculture. In 1903 van der Heide produced his first report, having made a thorough study of the geography, economy and existing water systems of the kingdom. Described as 'a brilliant statement of the irrigation needs of Thailand and the solutions for them',[17] the Dutchman's scheme called for an estimated expenditure of 47 million baht spread out over twelve years, the principal features of which were the construction of a great barrage across the Menam Chao Phaya at Chainat, together with the sale of water and of public lands as an investment to help defray costs. The benefits which would accrue, van der Heide foretold, would improve rice yields, reduce crop failures, help diversify the peasant economy and assist the development of communications. But the scheme was rejected by government on grounds of expense and of the unacceptability of the proposal to sell water and land to the farmers. Undaunted, van der Heide came up in 1906 with a revised plan which called for a total expenditure of 24 million baht, designed to pay for itself from lock fees and land dues within nineteen years. Faced with the problem of how to populate the irrigated area and how to raise the money, the government postponed its decision for two years. In 1908 van der Heide put forward two smaller projects, costing no more than 8 million baht, which were also rejected on financial grounds, and when after a serious flood in the same year yet another scheme was rejected and the regular appropriation for the Irrigation Department was reduced (i.e. for 1909), he resigned in disgust. The Department of Irrigation itself, the functions of which had up to this point been confined to dredging existing canals and installing locks and sluices downstream, was abolished three years later.

A key role in the frustrating of van der Heide's projects was played by the Financial Adviser to the government, W.J.F. Williamson, a Briton who was laying down the orthodox conservatism which became the hall-mark of Thai fiscal policy prior to 1941. He made it clear in 1903 that he was opposed to any heavy expenditure on irrigation 'as rash in the extreme' and as unnecessary for the existing needs of the country. He probably advised against the adoption of van der Heide's 1906 scheme on similar grounds and came out against the projects of 1908 and 1909, being finally responsible for the reduction in the Irrigation Department's annual allocations. Apart from considerations of financial orthodoxy, Williamson was also concerned that all surplus funds should be earmarked for railway development, which was much closer to British strategic and economic interests.

Nevertheless, the need for irrigation was not to be ignored, as disastrous floods in 1909-10 and two ensuing seasons of drought between 1910 and 1912 soon showed. In the latter year King Vajiravudh announced in a speech from the throne that new drainage and irrigation works were to be carried out and a new adviser was appointed, this time shrewdly enough, an Englishman, Sir Thomas Ward. Taking up his appointment in 1913, Ward followed in van der Heide's footsteps in touring the country, subsequently producing a four-volume report elaborating his ideas. Ward's approach was that van der Heide's scheme, particularly the barrage at Chainat, was too elaborate in terms of the country's human and financial resources. He proposed in its stead work on a series of lesser schemes which would eventually be linked up together. Ward's plans envisaged the eventual controlling of the waters of the entire Central Plain including the Menam Chao Phaya at a comprehensive cost of 100 to 120 million baht, to be carried out in stages commensurate with population increase. He advocated as immediate projects five special minor schemes in order of urgency, which would entail an expenditure of some 23 million baht, and added proposals for the improvement and extension of the water supply and for the establishment of a co-operative credit scheme for the farmers.

Ward's proposals got a better reception than van der Heide's, if only because the situation demanded that something should be done. In 1915 the Irrigation Department was resuscitated, and the following year work began in the Rangsit area, which was one of Ward's projects although not the first on his list of priorities. However, the area was still suffering from the after-effects of the earlier mismanagement and government felt it better to deal with the problems in an existing populated area rather than start work in an unpopulated one. The new project, which centred around the construction of a barrage across the Prasak Canal at Rangsit (it was known as the South Prasak Canal Project) was completed by 1922 at a cost of 16 million baht, but whatever benefits it brought were short-lived as they were offset by a rise in the population and by the never-ending wrangling between landlord and tenant over water responsibilities and rights. After 1930 some more projects were undertaken, mostly in the Central Plain, in line with Ward's original proposals. The most important of these were the Jiengrak and Bang Hia drainage schemes which were complementary to the Prasak Canal Project; these were completed in 1932 at a cost of 9 million baht. Work was also started in 1927 on the Subhan River Project which had been the first on Ward's list. Outside the Central Plain in 1930 two million baht were allocated for work in the provinces of Chiengmai and Lampang.

By 1940 approximately one-fifth of the total cultivated area or 1.1 million acres were under irrigation, and by that time some 45 million baht had been spent on irrigation since the beginning of the century. This was not a very impressive figure, and even what had been done was inadequate, as van der Heide had warned, to avoid crop failures in years of abnormal flood. 'The strange reluctance' of the Thai authorities to push irrigation schemes harder seems at first hard to justify. The major role played by British influence is clear, particularly as shown in the case of Williamson who continued as Financial Adviser up till 1924. Railways were placed before canals in the allocations of the slender surpluses which the conservative fiscal doctrine or the day demanded. On top of this was the weight of tradition, and the natural conservatism of the Thais themselves. Not only did they lack full control over their own finances, but they were also hidebound by the outlook of a widespread, stolid peasantry. This was a major factor in ruling out the sale of water and land rights which van der Heide had proposed and which would have done so much to lessen the costs of irrigation. Furthermore, in a land of plentiful water, the dangers of seasonal drought were not readily apparent, although from the point of view of water distribution it often occurred.

Despite the progress made in spreading water control, by far the greater amount of rice cultivated in the kingdom was grown without the aid of modern irrigation. Rice production remained a Thai preserve, as it always had been, and in technique and organization showed little change. It was still essentially a smallholders' crop, farmed with tools and guided by methods which had their roots in Khmer times and were shared by all the peoples of the South-East Asian mainland. These traditional techniques were most evident and best preserved in the north whose narrow valleys lent themselves to the simple irrigation methods brought from Yunnan, and where short seasons, low rainfalls and light soils made intensive farming on a communal basis under the supervision of the village headmen essential. On the Central Plain, where conditions were different, transplanting was the general rule, following very closely the methods employed in the Irrawaddy Valley, although where the annual floods were too deep, direct sowing or broadcast methods were employed. Slash-and-burn techniques associated with shifting cultivation also persisted in the remoter hill regions, but formed an insignificant factor in overall production. Above all rice cultivation continued to be a seasonal affair in what remained basically a monocultural economy. The average farmer had nothing else to do while waiting for the harvest besides gambling or practising dacoity or succumbing to malaria. There was no incentive for him to improve his techniques nor the wherewithal to do so, with the result that his tools were still of the same primitive kind as had been used by his forefathers. Likewise the use of fertilizers, except for certain highly commercialized districts on the Central Plain, remained virtually unknown.

On the other hand, the opening up of Thailand to the world economy and the conversion of rice from a subsistence to a cash crop added a new dimension to the rice industry which from the outset grew outside the realm of the Thai peasant world and was dominated by aliens, mainly Chinese. This was the marketing side of the industry which developed rapidly with the commercialization of rice production after 1855, and, in sharp contrast to the production sector, was modern and sophisticated. Whilst the bulk of the Thai population continued to sow and to reap, the Chinese—as the ubiquitous merchants—provided the capital with which to purchase the crop, to finance its transportation and its milling and ultimately to ship the rice to its new overseas customers. The process began on a small scale, with individual Chinese brokers buying up the crop from the smallholdings 'by the basket'.[18] The main area where this happened was around the immediate vicinity of Bangkok, and gradually over a wider part of the Central Plain, and soon a pattern of marketing was established which in its essentials remained unchanged up to the 1940s. Inevitably the rice mills formed the heart of the system. As far as the rice destined for export was concerned, it was nearly all processed by the big mills on the banks of the Menam Chao Phaya in and around Bangkok, but like their counterparts in Cochin-China the middlemen who bought the grain from the peasants and transported it to the mills maintained their independence of the mill owners. But the rise of small, provincial mills with the penetration of the railway to the north and the north-east helped to modify the pattern at local level.

In response to commercial demand, milling itself became a major industry in its own right, which displaced handmilling and made way for the application of machinery. Bangkok was the natural milling centre, for it was there that the demand first arose and the first mills were supplied directly by the farmers themselves. In 1858 the capital had its first steam mill, an American enterprise which changed hands several times before finally paying its way under Chinese control. Within the succeeding years, the number of such mills grew rapidly, from five in 1870 to twenty-five in 1892 to fifty-nine in 1910 to over seventy by 1930. All the earlier mills were concentrated in and around Bangkok, with an average capacity of some 100 to 200 tons of padi a day. Small mills in the provinces with a daily turnover about one-third that of the city mills started to spring up a little later. The earliest reports of country mills date back to the late 1870s; in 1915 the first 'modern' mill was set up at Korat and within the next fifteen years another thirty-odd mills had sprung up in the north-east. In 1930 there were an estimated 500 mills of 30/40 tons a day capacity, two-fifths of which had been built since 1920 as part of a national attempt to ensure the quality of rice exported overseas.

In the beginning, the chief demand for Thai rice (as was also the case with the crops of Burma and Cochin-China) came from Western Europe, although important secondary markets opened up in the Malay Peninsula as it fell under British rule and in both China and Japan. But this pattern was profoundly affected by the Great War and its aftermath. In 1919 in consequence of inflationary demand and crop failure, the government was obliged to ban all rice exports for two years, the first time since 1855. Apart from the internal effects of this episode, the regional shortage of 1910–21 caused Thailand's neighbours to re-examine their own rice policies and to aim at greater self-sufficiency. At the same time the demand for Thai rice in the West shrank significantly, and the kingdom came to rely principally on its exports to the tropical world (i.e. 75 per cent of all rice exports in the 1920s and 1930s) and on her old, established markets in China and Japan. After 1921 the rice market continued to be unstable. As the impact of the Depression increased economic nationalism, Thailand found herself in an ever more exposed position, progressively being shut out of traditional markets and being unable to adapt to changing circumstances. The Chinese market in particular started to decline in value, if not in volume. War and banditry reduced China's purchasing power and depreciated her currency, a trend capped in 1933 by the political decision to impose a special tariff on Thai imports in retaliation for alleged discrimination against Chinese nationals in Thailand itself. Appeals for the lifting of the duty were to no avail and the French in Indo-China were able to strike a better bargain at Thai expense. Another blow at the same time was the sudden ban on Thai rice into Japan. Passed in 1934, it was temporarily lifted in 1937 owing to force of circumstances, but the Japanese market could no longer be regarded as secure. Similar nationalist considerations led India, the Netherlands East Indies and British Malaya to take steps to lower their dependence on Thai imports. Dutch rice controls in the Indies imposed in 1933 reduced Thai imports by nearly one-fifth of their normal volume within twelve months. India threatened to prohibit Thai rice imports in 1933 and though failing to do so, imposed a special duty on Thai rice two years later which enabled Burmese rice to recapture the Indian market and caused 'a serious, lingering strike' amongst the rice coolies of Bangkok. Malaya, however, remained a steady customer despite the launching of several schemes aimed at self-sufficiency. In general, the outlook for the Thai rice export industry looked increasingly bleak towards the end of the 1930s. Rice exporters picked up some crumbs of consolation in new, unanticipated markets in the Philippines, Peru and Tunisia, but in the open market the Thais lacked bargaining power. As economic nationalism was reflected in the spread of systems of imperial preference and tariff barriers, Thai rice exports continued to rise but they declined steadily in value in relation to other exports.

The only natural advantage that Thai rice had lay in its quality. But even this was in jeopardy. Although considered the best rice obtainable from South-East Asia, Thai rice also suffered like that of neighbouring lands from adulteration, which endangered its reputation. The villain of the piece was the Chinese middleman who invariably resorted to adulteration to guarantee a profit on his transactions which tended to be highly speculative, governed by the problems of petty dealings with innumerable smallholders, hoarding, improper storage and lack of satisfactory grading. Government's response to this problem which became acute in the early 1920s with the decline of the European market, lay in the programme to construct government provincial mills, aimed at sidestepping the middleman and ensuring better graded rice. The effort was not very successful owing to the many strains of rice to be graded, which lay beyond the competence of the machinery installed, and to the complexities of grading itself which gave ample scope for malpractice.

Teak, tin and rubber

While rice remained the staple of the Thai economy and represented a truly national enterprise in that it involved the greater part of the country and the bulk of its population, three other products also vied for paramountcy amongst the new exports. Two of these, tin and teak, were traditional products of the country, but in contrast to rice were entirely regional. The kingdom's tin was almost entirely located in the southern peninsular provinces, forming part of the great tin belt stretching between Yunnan and the Straits of Malacca, centred mainly on Phuket and other places on the western side of the Isthmus of Kra. Teak on the other hand was confined to the hills of the north where it took up about a quarter of the monsoon forest and was found particularly in the valleys of the Me-ping, Me-wang and Salween rivers. Rubber, the other major export, belonged to the twentieth century and was also regional, being grown mainly in the peninsular south. The export industries engendered by these three products were very largely alien-dominated, with minimal Thai participation.

Tin, which has always been Thailand's most important mineral, is also the oldest of her exports. Although credit for discovering and working the tin deposits of the Isthmus of Kra is usually given to Chinese traders operating along the ancient routes across the peninsula at the dawn of history, there is evidence to show earlier mining influences before the Chinese assumed a monopoly over the industry. The tin industry of the south in all essentials formed part of the tin industry of the Straits of Malacca (i.e. involving the tin states of the Malay Peninsula and the Sumatran tin islands of Bangka and Belitung as well), and its course flowed in rhythm with the rest of this area. Up till the twentieth century the industry in all aspects of production was in Chinese hands. Centred on Phuket, which emerged as a typical Chinese tin town, the Chinese mining community of the south was in reality an extension of the Chinese colonies on Bangka and Belitung and its politics a continuum of the politics of the other Chinese mining communities in the Straits.[19] Likewise the vicissitudes of the industry reflected the same factors which governed the ebb and flow of tin-mining in the Straits as a whole. As in the Straits, the principal market for Thai tin until the nineteenth century—apart from its domestic use—lay in China, and it served as the magnet for Chinese settlement in the region. Demand and supply fluctuated according to the pressures of the time which affected the whole of the Straits. Dutch activities, the visits of British and French privateers, the periodic upsurge of Malay 'piracy' or Malay revolts, and foreign invasion determined the volume and flow of the trade.[20] In the nineteenth century itself, the history of the industry continued to echo developments elsewhere. The pace of Chinese immigration into the mining areas of the Isthmus quickened in response to the new Western demand for the metal which became apparent from the 1830s onwards. By 1850 tin was joining rice as the kingdom's leading export. In the 1820s Crawfurd reported that there were about 20,000 Chinese miners of tin or gold in the country. By 1870 there were 28,000 Chinese on Phuket Island alone, mostly working in the tin-mines, and by 1884 this figure had almost doubled again. Indeed Phuket, which possessed the best deposits, served as the barometer for the state of the industry throughout the nineteenth and well into the twentieth century, as well as being the scene for the most significant developments. The recession on the world tin market in the 1890s was mirrored by Phuket whose mining population had dropped to 12,000 by 1897. In 1907 Phuket was the site for the first successful dredging operations which marked the triumphal entry of Western interests onto the scene. In general, the Thai tin industry continued to fluctuate with the tides of world trade, recovering from the recession of the 1890s to be buffeted by the erratic rise which characterized world tin production after 1907 and to share with all other producers the stresses and trials of the Great Depression which came in 1929.

The factors which account for Chinese predominance over tin-mining in southern Thailand up till 1900 and also account for the sudden upsurge of Western interests in the early twentieth century are virtually identical with those operating in the tin states of the Malay Peninsula. As in the Malay Peninsula, Chinese domination in the industry rested on their unrivalled knowledge of mineral deposits in the area, their superior skills and their low overheads. The system of financing mining activities was the same as in the Malay States during that period, whereby the towkay or capitalist was able to ensure himself of ample profits and of a steady, cheap labour supply by working hand in glove with recruiting agents in South China ports, and by controlling all provisions to his workers, including liberal supplies of opium. Powerful Chinese tin merchants rose up in this way in the southern provinces of Thailand, in certain cases acquiring office under the Thai Crown.[21] The existence of enlightened Chinese governors (who also proved able administrators) in the principal tin districts of the south was in fact an important contributory factor to the great increase in tin production in the nineteenth century, particularly during the reign of King Mongkut. Cheap labour and low overheads were also the main reasons why Western interests failed to break the Chinese monopoly over the industry, despite the acquisition of handsome concessions in the 1880s and 1890s. And, as in the Malay Peninsula, it was the application of Western technology—in this instance through the introduction of the tin dredge—that finally broke the Chinese hold and enabled Western interests to gain a major share in the industry after 1907. The introduction of the first tin dredge by an Australian firm at Phuket in that year opened the way for the rapid expansion of Western mining. Despite the high capital outlay involved, a dredge could mine large areas much more economically, going over alluvial ground whose superficial deposits had been exhausted by primitive Chinese techniques and whose deeper deposits lay beyond Chinese capacity to get. No Chinese miner, on the other hand, could afford to buy dredging equipment, so as the number of Western dredges in operation increased, the Chinese share in production declined. By 1930 there were thirty dredges operating in the south and the previous year's production from them had overtaken overall production from Chinese mines for the first time. By 1937 the output from Western dredges was more than one-and-a-half times that from Chinese mines. At the same time, as was the case in Malaya as well, the Chinese were not eliminated from the industry. As world demand expanded, Chinese production rose. They continued with their opencast mining and adopted the gravel pump as they had done in the Malay States.

Western technology also served to break the Chinese monopoly over tin smelting in the first decades of the twentieth century, the chief significance of which for tin-mining in southern Thailand was that it brought the Thai industry still yet further into the Malayan orbit. The orientation of the industry towards that of the Malay States had been implicit in the traditional links which bound the Chinese miners of Phuket with those on Bangka and Belitung and in the tin fields of Perak and Selangor. With the influx of Chinese immigrants into southern Thailand in the nineteenth century, the bulk of the new arrivals came via Penang, while Penang's links with the south were made closer with the opening of the railway line from Bangkok via Haadyai and Padang Besar. In Malaya the establishment of a Western smelting firm based on Singapore had been the first successful blow against the Chinese monopoly over the Malayan industry. In southern Thailand the extension of the same Western smelting interests at the expense of the local Chinese smelters was the inevitable corollary to the penetration of the Western tin dredge. The agents of Straits Trading and Eastern Smelting first appeared on the scene soon after 1900, but in 1907 more than half the local output was still being smelted by Chinese. After that date, however, the Western smelting firms with their ready cash and ability to corner the market made steady inroads into the local smelting industry and by 1922 nearly all the Chinese smelters had been driven out of business by Western competition. By the same token Thai tin exports increasingly took the form of tin ore, and by 1930 all exports were in ore, 90 per cent of which went direct to the Straits Settlements for smelting.

The close ties between Thailand's tin industry and its Malayan counterpart were clearly demonstrated during the Depression years following 1929. Western and Chinese miners in southern Thailand strongly opposed plans to restrict mining output, but Malayan interests desired that Thailand should conform with the international scheme, and the Bangkok government, conscious of the industry's dependence on the smelters of Penang and Singapore, perforce had to give way. In the event, however, restriction turned out to be highly favourable to the country's mining interests. The quota fixed for Thailand under the 1931 agreement represented 95 per cent of her actual output for that year. When the agreement was renewed two years later on the basis of the 1931 quota, Thailand was exempted from any further production curtailments imposed on other participants. When Thailand successfully held out for a nearly doubled quota, however, on the second renewal in 1936, a drop in world tin prices deprived her of much advantage.

By 1940 Thailand's tin industry, which now accounted for over 8 per cent of total world production, was dominated by Western interests, mainly British and Australian which between them operated some twenty to thirty mines (using dredges) and provided about two-thirds of total output. The rest came from around three hundred smaller Chinese mines, mostly employing the gravel pump, with an occasional Thai entrepreneur in between.

The almost complete absence of a Thai stake in the tin industry devolved basically from a traditional attitude of *laissez-faire*, coupled with a rentier approach to the mining activities of others. The typical South-East Asian concept of the ruler as 'the eater of the land' conditioned official thinking from the start and implied royal control vested over all mining and mineral rights. It became a feature of government policy not to aim at the expansion of production as a source of future investment, but merely to achieve an increase in royalties, and till as late as 1929 it derived its revenues from tin through licensing fees, tariffs and an adjustable scale of royalties without making any corresponding attempt to encourage or support the industry. As things stood, even without government support, the rewards were satisfying enough. In the second half of the 1920s the tin mines were yielding state revenues of over 3½ million baht a year.

Nevertheless, although tin was officially regarded more as a source of tribute than as an economic investment, the intrusion of the West meant that the old haphazard ways of granting mining concessions had to be amended. In the nineteenth century Chinese miners acquired their mining rights not from Bangkok but from the local governor, who in fact had the last word in the matter. Having got his concessions, the lessee was a completely free agent, subject only to the excise on all tin exports. He drew his own boundaries and in the event of conflicting claims might was usually right. Westerners were enabled to acquire mining leases as a result of the extra-territorial clauses of the Bowring and successive other treaties, but up till the closing years of the century, at any rate, it was clear that the terms granted to them were far less favourable than those granted to the Chinese. This too was probably due to the overriding influence of the local governor who was more likely than not Chinese or half-Chinese himself; it was also a reflection of the comparative ineffectiveness of Bangkok's writ in the outer provinces up till the end of the century. But in the 1880s more pragmatic considerations began to take charge, leading to the creation of a Department of Mines in 1891. The new department was designed to bring about greater official control over the country's mineral resources as well as to entice Western entrepreneurs. To this end new mining regulations were introduced in the following year, which fixed a sliding scale of royalties and for the first time imposed restrictions on actual leases. The latter move was highly necessary, for although by that date there were only thirteen concessions in Western hands, nearly all of them were held by speculators who laid claim to hundreds of square miles of land which they had no intention of working and who were subject to no legal injunction to do so. The 1892 regulations marked the first step towards taming the tin concessionaires; the mining laws of 1901 and 1919 completed the job. The 1901 law in particular limited the size of new leases, stipulated that the land so leased should be worked, and provided for the progressive abrogation of the old-type concessions. Although it met with a storm of protest from established interests, the obvious advantages stilled the protesters and were instrumental in bringing about a greater Western interest in the industry, culminating in the Australian breakthrough at Phuket in 1907.

From this time onwards for the next two decades, it was government policy to treat the area south of Chumphorn as the preserve of foreign firms and individuals and in general to encourage the promotion of tin exports by considerate treatment of the foreign interests involved. More active intervention or any attempt to promote Thai interests apparently lay beyond official contemplation until the onset of the Great Depression and the ensuing upsurge of nationalism embodied in the Revolution of 1932 changed the scenario. The Depression hit the country's tin industry hard because of its Malayan connexions, for while costs were met in Thai baht, profits were only realizable in depreciated Straits dollars. Fear of widespread mine closures forced the government to act, not—as we have already seen—in the manner that was desired by local miners at the time, but in a way which turned out to be in their best interests by becoming a party to international restriction. That and the recovery of tin prices saved the day and enabled firms in the south of Thailand to go on paying dividends of up to 15 per cent each year; the episode also made the government more conscious of the drawbacks of foreign domination of the industry, while the new nationalist mood demanded greater Thai participation. Bangkok's changing attitude was also probably influenced by the growing consolidation of Western interests, epitomized by the formation of the Siam Chamber of Commerce, a Western-dominated affair formed by 25 Western firms having a combined capital between them of 50 million baht. Royalties, concessions and restrictionist policies became hotly-debated issues in the new National Assembly in the mid-1930s, and for the first time voices were heard demanding a limitation on foreign enterprise and the promotion of Thai interests.[22] In 1935, the government declared that it had no intention of entering into mining operations itself, but four years later was announcing plans to mine on its own account. In 1940 the first government-sponsored mining attempts with Thai labour were carried out near Phang-nga and on Samui Island.

If tin was the king of Thai minerals, teak was the queen of the Thai forest. Reputedly the best in the world and at least on par with the teaks of Burma in quality if not quantity, teakwood in Thailand had long been an important commodity on the home market, mainly for the building of boats and bridges or for the decorative lintels of palaces and temples. However, it hardly featured at all as an export prior to 1855 and after that date was slow to acquire an overseas market. In fact, till 1883 the total value of teak exports (via Bangkok)[23] never rose much beyond half a million baht a year. Increases in production were soon absorbed by the domestic market, particularly for shipbuilding, houses and furniture, and foreign purchasers were put off by the poor reputation of Thai teak, its relative inaccessibility, and above all by the easy availability of Burmese supplies. It was only when this Burmese supply was interrupted (as happened with the outbreak of the Third Anglo-Burmese War in 1885 and the prolonged pacification campaign which followed) and the depletion of the Burmese reserves became evident that Western merchants started to pay serious attention to Thailand's own resources.

Up to this point, the teak forests had been the preserve of the remote Lao chieftains of the northern hills, providing them with their principal source of income. The actual felling of the trees and the extraction of the huge trunks by elephant out of the forest and down to the rivers for floating to the downstream markets was mainly in the hands of the Chinese—and later as the Burmese forests became exhausted—of Burmese operators who paid handsome fees for their right to do so to the Lao princes. Meanwhile the bulk of the labour was provided by hill tribesmen from Burma or the Khamus from Laos. European participation in the teak trade was limited to buying and marketing the received product at Bangkok or Paknampho until the 1880s, since until they acquired the right by treaty in 1883, no Westerners were allowed to cut the timber for themselves, and it was another five years before the first European firm started to work a forest concession on its own. But the possibilities for teak as an export had been already divined by an enterprising American merchant in Bangkok in the 1850s, and the Borneo Company in the early 1860s became the first Western firm to try and post its agents in the north, only to be confronted with 'a political situation ... of almost impenetrable confusion'.[24] These circumstances and the mounting activities of teak concessionaires became a source of growing alarm to Bangkok and led in 1870 to the first steps being taken to bring the northern provinces under closer supervision by placing the monarchy's own candidate in power in Chiengmai in that year. This was followed in 1875 by the posting of a permanent resident-commissioner there to keep an eye on the situation. When Western interest and participation became more pressing in the late 1880s, there was increased urgency for Bangkok's intervention on political and economic grounds. Indiscriminate concessions to Western concerns coupled with the internecine disputes between the Lao chiefs in the areas involved provided dangerous pretexts for Western intervention. A total absence of control over the activities of the concessionaires themselves had by 1895 led to a crisis, with the forests nearest the streams down which the timber was floated becoming virtually denuded. Undersized timber was being cut and no attempt was being made at re-afforestation. The seriousness of the situation was underlined by appeals for government action from the Western teak companies themselves, which by this time held a good share of the hundred-odd concessions in force. It was, in other words, high time for Bangkok to assert its authority effectively in the region.

The first measure by Bangkok in this direction was the establishment of a forestry department in 1895, which was advised starting from the following year by a British forestry expert from India named Slade, who was called by King Chulalongkorn expressly for this purpose. Under Slade's guidance, a series of royal decrees in the next couple of years were issued, controlling the granting of concessions, introducing compulsory conservation measures, and imposing a stricter surveillance over royalties. In effect Bangkok was taking over the rights of the Lao princes, granting them subsequently, by way of compensation, a 25 per cent increase in their timber revenues. The basic aim of the new department was—apart from the political considerations—to prevent harmful and indiscriminate felling. The emphasis was more on conservation than production. The result of the department's efforts was to improve the quality of teak exports and to promote the concentration of the industry in the hands of four or five European firms which from then on exercised a virtual monopoly over the exporting of teak. The small, scattered holdings of the years before 1890 could not survive under the conditions laid down by the new forest regulations, which necessitated a large capital outlay, and after 1897 in particular their number rapidly dwindled. By the end of the century there was some £2½ million invested in the industry, of which four-fifths represented British capital. By 1909 the extraction, milling and exporting of teak were all under Western control.

The direct consequence of Western interest and involvement in the teak trade after 1883 was a dramatic rise in teak exports from Bangkok which by the end of the century had placed the commodity amongst the four major exports of the kingdom. But in contrast to the domestic market which expanded steadily up till the eve of the Pacific War, the overseas demand was subject to unpredictable fluctuations. As an export, teak reached its peak in the period 1905-9 when it ranked second to rice in value and accounted for 11 per cent of all products sold overseas. Thereafter the export market went into decline, both in value and volume. By 1920 teak production amounted to only 4 per cent of total commodity exports, and apart from one brief two-year boom, never recovered in volume. In terms of value on the world market, teak prices in the 1920s were the same as those of 1914, although most other commodities had become dearer. In 1926 the world market in teak collapsed entirely, and after a brief recovery dropped another 65 per cent during the Depression years. The market rallied after 1933, and prices rose steadily up till the 1940s. The general weakness of teak exporters was their lack of flexibility. Tied to the terms of their fifteen-year leases, they could not easily adjust to the fluctuations of the world market. Within Thailand itself, exporters tended to be handicapped by competition from the domestic market, while the volume of production itself was dependent on such unpredictable factors as the sufficiency of rainfall which would ensure that the logs could be floated downstream in time to catch the most favourable market conditions.[25] As for overseas markets, these too were subject to constant change. Up till 1914 Europe was an important market for Thai teak, but that market rapidly declined during and after the Great War and fell by another 50 per cent during the Great Depression. In general, as with rice, after 1914 teak exporters in Bangkok suffered from the lack of a guaranteed market, although the main trend was clearly towards China and Japan. In 1919 one-fifth of all the teak sent out from Thailand was still destined for Europe or for the U.S.A., while the great bulk (three-fifths) went to India and Ceylon and about one-sixth to the Far East. Fifteen years later over half the country's teak exports were being absorbed by China and Japan.

As far as control over the industry within Thailand itself was concerned, there was little change between 1909 and 1941. In 1938, 88 per cent of the teak forests were being worked by European firms, six of which held the lion's share. The Chinese constituted about 7 per cent of the remaining lessees and owned about one-third of the large Bangkok mills, and nearly all the small handmills in the provinces. Direct Thai participation, represented by Forestry Department plantations, amounted to one-twentieth of the whole. Capital investment in the industry did not grow much after 1909 either and probably did not much exceed £3 million in 1941. At the same time, the preponderance of the alien share in the industry had very little effect on the actual areas of production. The sporadic, scattered nature of the teak forest, located in inaccessible areas which could only be served by hardy hill tribesmen and elephant transport meant that the basic conditions of felling, cutting and extracting remained unchanged. There were hardly any teak plantations, and even the large Western firms had no recourse but to take as their labourers a 'gaudy mixture of Burmans, Shan and Lao, Karen and hill tribesmen' who happened to live in the vicinity of their operations. The elephants continued to haul the heavy logs of teak through the jungle to the rivers which carried them downstream to Paknampoh and eventually Bangkok. Paknampoh itself, which served as the principal royalty-collecting station for foreign exporters, owed its existence initially to this traffic. Towns like Tak (Raheng), Sawanlok and Uttaradit also depended for their livelihood on their role as assembling points for the teak logs to be converted into rafts so as to continue their passage down to Bangkok. Until the extension of French rule over Laos cut off the supply, Khamu hill tribesmen provided by far the cheapest and best lumbermen in the forest, but subsequently were replaced by Lao and Thai, who also made up most of the elephant drivers. The work of the elephant drivers in particular was tough and required great skill, so they were well paid, receiving enough, we are told, 'to afford a second wife'.

From the Thai point of view, the teak trade was worthwhile. It yielded to government coffers an average of one million baht a year between 1897 and 1926, and for the ensuing decade the government was milking 67 per cent of the gross profits from the six leading Western firms in the industry. In the 1920s the licence fees collected at Paknampoh alone amounted to around two million baht a year. In line with general official policy prior to the 1930s, Bangkok was content to allow the industry to be dominated by aliens and took no steps to obtain greater Thai participation. The Forest Department stuck to its role of conservation and replacement, although at first somewhat tentatively in the face of prejudice and opposition from local producers. The Department was also handicapped by lack of capital and know-how. However, when the original leases sanctioned in 1897 expired in 1909, steps were taken to lighten the existing regulations (and to raise the royalties). In 1913 a new law created special forest reserves to protect the more valuable areas. In 1925 further restrictions were made regarding the felling of teak trees as the 1909 leases reached their half-way mark, and the royalties were raised once again. But when it came to specific problems such as the natural hazard of fire which affected about one-tenth of the teak crop each year, together with the ravages of insects, birds, elephants and fungi, little was done. Although about one-half of the country's teak resources were being reduced by excessive felling, only one-fifth of the forest's revenues were put back into the Department, with the result that its staff was overworked, too little research was carried out and no surveys were made. Another problem which never found a proper solution was the rampant incidence of theft. The teak firms regularly complained that they lost half their logs in this way, but government measures were generally ineffectual and sometimes boomeranged. This overall failure to invest adequately or to carry out research was reflected in the 1930s by a marked decline in the size and quality of the teak being exported, with a consequent reduction in the royalties obtained.

Nevertheless with the impact of the Great Depression and the new temper of nationalism in the country, both private entrepreneurs and government dropped their *laissez-faire* approach to the industry after 1930. The government especially for the first time showed interest in obtaining a greater stake in teak production, and plans were made for working more of the forests directly. This inevitably raised the question of the existing teak concessions which were due for renewal in 1940. A spate of rumoured intentions became rife as the time approached, which signified basic changes in the organization of the industry but in the event in 1940 itself five out of the six major Western companies gained a renewal of their concessions on the basis of working one-third of them each themselves, opening up one-third to local enterprises and leaving the remaining third as government reserves.

Rubber was the newcomer amongst Thailand's four major exports, and as in neighbouring Cambodia and Cochin-China appeared late onto the scene, a full decade after the rubber industries of Malaya and the Netherlands East Indies had got under way. On the other hand—in contrast to French Indo-

China—the Thai rubber industry was mainly a smallholders' affair, and even by the 1930s there were only a handful of estates. By the same token Western participation in rubber planting in Thailand was very limited—there were only two European-owned estates in the kingdom—while the smallholdings themselves were owned by Thais as well as by Malays and Chinese. The Chinese had by far the largest stake in the industry, not merely as smallholders and planters, but as labourers and capitalists, as rubber merchants, processors and exporters. Chinese holdings tended to be larger as well, and probably amounted to half the total acreage under rubber.[26] It was in fact Chinese immigrants from Malaya who introduced rubber planting to the south of Thailand, moving out of the Malay States on the eve of the Great War when conditions were beginning to prove not so favourable.

The peninsular south remained the principal area of planting which began against the background of the Great War as rubber reached a premium and prices were pushed to new heights on the world market. But the great period of expansion for rubber in Thailand came in the mid-1920s, stimulated by the recovery in world prices after the Little Depression of 1919-23 and considerably aided by the opening of the peninsular railway with its branches to Nakhorn Sri Thammarat, Patani and Padang Besar. Thailand never became a signatory to the Stevenson Plan but benefited from its side-effects in the same ways that the smallholders of the Netherlands Indies did. Production was adversely affected by the onset of the Great Depression, but the kingdom's adherence, after appropriate bargaining, to the International Rubber Restriction Scheme in 1933 worked out to the considerable advantage of local rubber planters. For, as was the case with tin, the Malayan desire not to leave Thailand out because of the problems that this would raise for the Malayan industry put Bangkok in a strong bargaining position and resulted in the kingdom receiving a quota well above her actual production. Furthermore the quota was put onto an annually rising scale and the maximum acreage permitted for new planting over a five-year period was comfortably beyond the country's growth capacity. Planting circles were highly critical of these arrangements until they were seen to work; in any case the manner restriction was actually implemented rendered it virtually meaningless.[27]

By the late 1930s rubber was the third largest export (after rice and tin) and accounted for more than one-eighth of their total value. The area under the crop had expanded twelvefold since 1920 to cover an estimated 362,000 acres in 1932. There was an army of about 70,000 tappers involved in the industry—predominantly Chinese—and the industry was serviced by Hokkien rubber merchants who sorted, graded, packed and exported. Nearly all the rubber produced was exported to Malaya up till 1940, one-third to Singapore for further processing and re-exportation, and the rest which was cured locally was sent for transhipment via Penang. But the Thai contribution to the world rubber market remained a very minor one. In fact, by Malayan standards, Thai-grown rubber production was inefficient and the product poor in quality. This was a result of planting being so largely a smallholders' affair with a complete absence of scientific techniques and with the existence of a very skeleton-like infrastructure of roads. The typical holding was planted between padi seasons and then left untended. The trees were planted too close together, parasites and weeds were allowed to flourish and soil erosion went unchecked. Production and marketing were quite unorganized, resulting in lack of standardization. In the meanwhile, government adopted its traditional *laissez-faire* approach, not even imposing licences or taxes on rubber till 1935. Official encouragement of the industry came in the form of easy land laws and light dues. It was not until 1939 that plans were announced for the construction of a government rubber factory and of a centre for training young Thais in the industry.

Sugar and other exports

Apart from the four great staples, the kingdom had long been renowned for other products which at one time or another had enjoyed great favour and prestige on the world market but which in the new economy which emerged after 1855 played only a marginal role. Amongst these traditional exports, pepper was particularly prominent, the monopoly of which was keenly vied for amongst the foreign merchants who thronged seventeenth-century Ayuthia and which had formed one of the most valuable of the gifts of Thai kings to courts abroad. Another was cattle-hides which were especially sought after by the Dutch in the same period. Thai salt enjoyed an old and valuable market in the Straits of Malacca and the archipelago. The kingdom was famous for its gamboge, lac and benjamin, for other timbers besides teak, such as sapanwood, for its tobacco and precious stones. However most of these products which were never yielded in great quantity belonged essentially to the pre-industrial trade in luxury commodities, whose scarcity was the lodestone of their value. With the penetration of the modern world of mass production and mass markets, they were swept to one side and continued to hold significance only in the domestic economy.

Sugar was the one notable exception to all this. As a commercial product, cane-sugar itself[28] was a novelty in the Thai economy, reputedly introduced by Chinese immigrants around 1810, but it swiftly rose to become a major export crop within the next couple of decades and by mid-century was the most important Chinese plantation activity in the country. Bowring confidently predicted that sugar would indeed become the kingdom's primary export in the second half of the nineteenth century and the circumstances of the time seemed to justify his prophecy. It was already the chief Thai export to Europe and it had also found a good market in the U.S.A. where it was readily exchanged for arms and ammunition. The new industry expanded at an even faster rate after the kingdom was opened to foreign trade in 1855. It doubled in acreage and output within one decade, and by the end of the 1850s accounted for 10 to 15 per cent of all Thailand's exports. The seemingly bright promise of the industry attracted investors, reflected in the spate of sugar mills built in the main sugar-growing districts. Following the pattern elsewhere, particularly in the Malay Peninsula, European and American firms began to get a foothold alongside the Chinese, forcing their way in with the lever of superior technology (and resources). In the 1860s when, as the British consul at Bangkok reported, 'native mills are springing up in all directions', the first Western steam mills made their appearance. The main areas of planting were all with-in range of Bangkok, around Cholburi, Chachoengso and Nakhorn Pathom, where the fields were full of Chinese labourers and the land was dotted with small mills employing some 200 workers apiece. The concession held by the British-owned Indochinese Sugar Company, covering some 30,000 acres of land and with its costly modern steam mill opened in 1870, symbolized the upsurge of the industry and the faith in its future.

But almost immediately this faith was shattered and the sugar industry went into sudden and irreversible decline. In fact, even prior to 1870 there had been signs of trouble, which now became marked. By the 1880s the best quality imported sugar was so cheap on the Bangkok market that local producers found it difficult to compete. The mills closed down, the fields were turned over to rice and by 1889 no Thai sugar was being exported at all. Only around Cholburi was the crop still cultivated to some extent.

The factors which brought about this sudden collapse of the kingdom's sugar industry are complex and debatable. In general it is clear that the Thai industry was the victim of the same pressures on the international market which nearly destroyed the Javanese sugar industry during the same period and crippled the sugar planters of North Malaya at the turn of the century. The emergence of European beet sugar was the prime factor in the world-wide decline in sugar prices in the 1870s and 1880s. Thailand was particularly vulnerable to such changes on the world market since she could not raise any protective tariffs, being tied by the foreign treaties which placed a ceiling of 3 per cent on all her import duties, and since she lacked the resources—let alone the will—to subsidize her own planters. In consequence the domestic market became flooded with cheap sugar imports from Java and the Philippines after 1880, making local commercial production profitless. Another major factor was the coincidental rise in the world market price of rice; in a manner that was analogous to what happened to coffee and rubber in the Malay Peninsula a couple of decades later, as sugar declined, rice rose. This saved many planters from disaster but ensured sugar's eclipse as an export cash crop in a free economy. Around Nakhorn Chaisi which had been the centre of the sugar industry, the land was swiftly turned over from sugar to rice as Chinese labourers flocked to the new rice mills where wages and conditions were better, and as Thai farmers turned their abandoned fields over to padi. Apart from planging sugar prices and competition from the rice industry, other factors usually cited are probably of marginal significance. Unfair and heavy imposts on the industry as a whole, inequitable land-rates and internal customs added to the burdens of the sugar cultivator but not sufficiently, if all else had been equal, to discourage him. The actual event which marked the demise of sugar as an export crop was the disastrous flood of 1871 which hit the richest sugar-growing areas of Nakhorn Chaisi hardest, broke the credit system and brought about a permanent decline in production.

Nevertheless sugar continued as an important domestic crop. In the twentieth century the industry underwent a revival, partly brought about by changing external factors but more largely induced by new nationalistic policies promoted by the government itself. The shortages created by the

Great War brought about a stimulus for greater planting and local production, as was seen around Cholburi where sugar was still being grown on Chinese smallholdings and milled in small Chinese mills. Between 1909 and 1921 the area under sugar cultivation expanded by about one-quarter, while output increased by about one-fifth. Cultivation was reopened around Nakhorn Pathom and extended in the 1930s to certain districts in the north and north-east, as well as in the south. By this time the government was no longer tied to the tariff stipulations of the unequal treaties of the nineteenth century and so was able to adopt a tariff policy which would protect local producers. As part of the new nationalist economic policy after 1932, government went into the industry itself by constructing its own refinery at Lampang. This venture did not prove a great success, and even with tariff protection the chances of sugar becoming a staple export once more remained remote. But its value in the domestic economy was maintained.

No other export after 1855 approached the four staples or showed the promise of sugar. Amongst those which still retained some importance were salt and pepper, and a new trade in livestock. Cotton, tobacco, various fibres and specialized jungle produce also played a minor part and were of some significance in the domestic economy. The kingdom's salt trade attracted the attention of the British envoy, John Crawfurd, in 1822, and led him to consider the prospects for finding a market for it in India. By the twentieth century the bulk of salt production was derived from the sea, extracted by a system of coastal dykes and ditches on the Gulf of Siam, from where it was then sent to Bangkok for shipment overseas or for distribution in the northern provinces. Surface deposits on the Korat Plateau formed an additional source, while salt wells in the north-east served as a staple in the local subsistence economy.[29] Pepper was one of the oldest of Thailand's products, the art of its cultivation being acquired by the Thais themselves from the Khmers. The traditional centres of cultivation were around Phuket and Chantaburi and continued to be so until the second decade of the twentieth century when the crop was steadily displaced by rubber. Pepper was one of the first articles of trade sought by Westerners when they irrupted into the region, the Dutch in particular seeking to corner the market. The Greek adventurer, Phaulkon, granted the French the monopoly shortly before his downfall, and in the mid-nineteenth century, despite a history of constant fluctuation, pepper was still numbered amongst the kingdom's leading exports, possibly the greatest of them all. The crop continued to rise and fall with the market well into the twentieth century. The problems of the pepper planter were compounded in the 1930s by the spread of a root fungus which affected whole plantations, while the reputation of Chantaburi pepper was ruined by unscrupulous middlemen who tampered with the crop. Government paid little heed to the plight of the industry, however, and took no steps to provide the foreign expertise that might have improved its prospects. The area under pepper was never large, its importance depending on its fluctuating market, and it was usually grown as a supplementary crop to rice. By the twentieth century pepper cultivation and processing were almost entirely in Chinese hands. Other spices were only of local significance.

Cattle-rearing, based on the Korat Plateau where half the kingdom's cattle and buffaloes were bred, had long been the source of Thailand's valuable trade in hides in pre-industrial days, and acquired a new importance with the rise of the Singapore market. After 1855 the exporting of cattle to Singapore, which at one stage in the nineteenth century derived its entire meat supply from the north-east plains, became a substantial sideline, reaching its climax in 1897 when 28,000 head of cattle were shipped out of the country via Bangkok. The trade was initiated and monopolized by Indians from the Straits Settlements who, making full use of the extra-territorial privileges enjoyed by all British subjects in Thailand after 1855, became the prime purchasers of livestock, stolen or otherwise. The proportions that this trade had reached by the end of the century created a public outcry, and led to the imposition of government measures to control the traffic and to eliminate its excesses, without however effecting the Indian domination over it. Bangkok's role as a cattle port diminished somewhat in consequence, but the trade as a whole continued to flourish to the profit of its Indian organizers. Cotton and tobacco, on the other hand, were two typical traditional products whose production expanded after 1855 but still suffered from the inroads of foreign imports. Cotton had always held a rather ambiguous place in the economy. While cotton exports were reckoned to account for 10 per cent of the value of all the kingdom's overseas trade in the 1850s, with a considerable market in Burma and the Andamans, as early as the seventeenth century the books of the European chartered companies showed cotton textiles amongst their major imports into Thailand. In the nineteenth century, prior to Bowring's Treaty, cotton textiles from India were being imported via the Straits. However, at the same time domestic cotton production was widespread, serving to clothe the bulk of the population, and it survived the competition of imported textiles. The wholesale commercial invasion of the country which took place after 1855 profoundly modified the role of the domestic industry and totally eclipsed it as an export product. Foreign textiles enjoyed several obvious advantages over local cottons. They were cheap, light and attractive. The handwoven product of the Thai peasant, on the other hand, was laboriously woven from inferior, insect- and disease-prone strains by primitive and inefficient methods. Its only virtue was that it was durable—much more so than the cheap, imported varieties, a factor which seemingly delayed the inevitable triumph of the foreign import. As the second half of the nineteenth century wore on, those areas most accessible to foreign trade witnessed the steady decline of local cottons. Although it took time, by the end of the century cotton production in the Central Plain was well on the way to extinction, unable to compete with cheap Western imports. The new tentacles of railway line which soon followed carried Western textiles into the more inaccessible domestic centres of production to the north and north-east and became well established in the markets of the larger towns. However the railway's impact had its limitations. Although the construction of the Korat line made foreign cotton a major import on the north-eastern plateau, trade was still very restricted and the use of local cottons common. Northern centres like Chiengmai, Phrae and Nan still remained beyond the pale of modern commerce, while the importation of German aniline dyes helped to boost the competitiveness of local cloth by giving it new colour. By the 1930s the general pattern which had emerged was of imported cottons dominating the areas bared to foreign commerce, as was the case in the Central Plain and in the peninsular south, while domestic weaving and consumption predominated in those areas less open to commercial penetration. In the north-east beyond Korat and Ubon, household wefts reigned supreme and were almost as widespread in the northern provinces despite the greater degree of commercialization there. While textiles in 1935 had become one of the kingdom's principal imports, steadily increasing in volume, domestic output and the area under cotton also expanded. The latter trend became apparent after 1920 and accelerated in the 1930s. This was partly due to the decline in the profitability of the rice trade in the same period, coupled with a drop in the price of yarn between 1921 and 1941 and the growing returns from domestic manufacture. Another element was growing government intervention and protection to boost the local product. As early as 1913, the Department of Agriculture imported modern machinery and seeds, in an attempt to diversify the economy, planting 2,400 acres around Pitsanuloke. This particular experiment failed, but the pressures of the Great Depression caused a revival of interest which was taken up by the new regime after 1932. The first efforts, made with Japanese assistance, again met with failure as a result of inexperience and inadequate backing, leading to harvest failure or poor yields. A second campaign was launched in 1939, spurred on by a private Japanese venture started the previous year near Nakhorn Pathom. That the local industry possessed potential was not in doubt, but its greatest problem in 1940 remained that of finding an adequate market to justify expansion. On the eve of the Japanese War the Thai cotton industry was flourishing, retaining its basic traditional characteristics, but nonetheless playing little part in the modern economy.

The story of tobacco in its essentials is similar to that of cotton. A crop native to the country, it was prior to 1855 widely grown throughout Thailand, with some being cultivated in every province and there being a small surplus for export. After 1855, foreign imports started to pour in, so much so that traditional smoking tastes and habits were altered. But the local product still prospered, and like cotton, even expanded. Finally, under nationalist pressures, in the late 1930s the government took measures to cut off foreign imports and to boost the consumption of the domestic product. Though universally grown, the main tobacco areas inside Thailand lay in the valleys of the north, where it served as a secondary crop during the dry season. As with cotton also, foreign competition after 1855 was most keenly felt in those areas easily accessible to Western commerce. Well before 1914, Chinese, British and American brands tended to dominate the larger towns and after the Great War began to challenge the local product even in the rural market. By the 1930s cigarettes represented the predominant form of tobacco consumption, the bulk of which came from Great Britain. Chinese tobacco also gained a good share of the market, particularly in the late 1930s when sales of Chinese brands in the country doubled. Until tariff revision in 1926, measures to protect the local industry were impracticable. However, from 1926 onwards, with increasing seriousness government took steps to encourage local cultivators and to popularize the domestic product. The first move was to impose a blanket 25 per cent duty *ad valorem* on all manufactured tobacco (1927); this was followed in 1931 by an amendment which subjected all tobacco, manufactured or otherwise, to a 50 per cent tax on their imported value (1934). These measures had their effect. Imports of manufactured tobacco fell at the expense of unmanufactured tobacco which initially rose until it was confronted with a new upsurge in domestic production. The reaction of the largest foreign tobacco importer, the British-American Tobacco Corporation,[30] was to turn to the cultivation of Virginian tobacco in Thailand, as had also been tried in the Philippines. The Corporation set up tobacco stations in the north and north-east, supplied seeds and dispensed expert advice to cultivators. The operation was a great success and stimulated the government itself to take similar measures. Whilst encouraging the Corporation's initiative, Bangkok in 1934 sent an official to Java to study the industry there. On his return, a methodical campaign to step up local production and to encourage local consumption was launched. Being a 'winter' crop, tobacco did not compete with rice cultivation, and the pest-free crops grown along the Mekong Valley invited official encouragement and support. Legislation was prepared to assist cultivators by imposing higher discriminatory tariffs against foreign imports and by lightening local taxation on the crop. This, together with the distribution of free seed, the activities of the British-American Tobacco Corporation, and a favourable upturn in world prices in the late 1930s, led to a considerable increase in local output and by the end of the decade production stood at over double the amount of tobacco imported. In 1941 government took one more decisive step by nationalizing the successful Corporation holdings for US$2 million and forming a Tobacco Monopoly in the same year to take over their management. By this time, Thai tobacco had largely replaced foreign brands on the domestic market.

All the other exports of the kingdom contributed only a fraction to the total value and were also only of local significance. Coconuts which had once flourished in the Central Plain and on the Korat Plateau as well as in the west and the peninsular south, were confined after the 1900s to the latter two areas, where they served as an adjunct to the local economy. Sporadic attempts were made to develop coconut plantations between 1900 and 1925, particularly in the south, but the uncertainties of the world copra market made investors cautious and prospects unsure. In the late 1930s the total value of the kingdom's copra exports did not amount up to half a million baht. The copra trade of the south passed through Penang, while that around Chantaburi and the west via Bangkok. Amongst forest products which enjoyed a reputation overseas (apart from teak), lac and gamboge were the most valuable.[31] The Danish East Asiatic Company and a couple of other firms carried on a minor but flourishing sideline in various medium and hard timbers, including sapanwood, rosewood, boxwood and ebony. Some bamboo was shipped to the Netherlands Indies, and Penang served as the local market for the timber, attap and charcoal derived from the long mangrove forests along the western shore of the peninsula. Besides cotton, other fibres which entered the international trade included kapok, jute, kenat (ambary), ramie and flax. Kapok in particular, whose growth is widespread, found a variety of modern applications, and some attempts at commercial production were made after 1919.

Natural resources and the domestic economy

Although the kingdom possessed within its borders a wide range of other resources and products, all of which helped to sustain in various ways the traditional self-sufficient domestic economy, their quantity, quality or circumstance determined that their role did not extend any further beyond. In fact, despite the economic penetration of the outside world after 1855, the traditional economy remained untouched to a remarkable degree.

Within this traditional framework, fish came next to rice. It was a perennial element in the food of the people, and its importance in the national economy was reflected in the large numbers engaged either directly or indirectly in fishing as an occupation, as well as in the old, established trade in dried fish with the southern ports of China and the sturdy excellence of the fishing craft which ploughed the waters of the Gulf of Siam and beyond. The fishing industry naturally fell into two parts—freshwater and sea. Only sea-fishing had any commercial significance, since only salted fish were exportable. But Thai methods of handling the catch were by and large the same in the 1930s as they had been for centuries, so that even within their home waters in the Gulf or in the Mergui archipelago, Thai fishermen were being successfully challenged by Japanese and other foreigners with cheap, efficient, modern techniques. In the first decade of the new nationalism after 1932, belated steps were at last taken to try and retrieve the situation. Japanese instructors on fishing methods were recruited for the first time in 1935; the following year a Fisheries Act insisted on three-quarters of all fishing crews being Thai nationals, and in 1939 legislation restricting fishing rights in Thai waters to Thais was passed. In the meantime the freshwater industry, which involved to some degree almost every single member of the population living inland, possessed only a local economic significance. Being completely non-profitable in a commercial sense, freshwater fishing was totally dependent on government interest and support in order to make any progress. However, government's interest up till the mid-1930s was purely a financial one, and its involvement in the industry restricted to levying a mild series of dues and export imposts. New circumstances after the Great War induced a change of attitude. In the early 1920s it became apparent that the kingdom's supposedly inexhaustible reserves of freshwater fish were facing serious depletion, even in the rich fishbowl of the Talé Sap, near Songkhla. Acting on these reports, in 1923 Bangkok called in Dr. Hugh Smith, an American fisheries expert, to make a study of the whole position. Smith's report and recommendations were echoed in the more general observations made by Andrews a decade later. By this time Smith had succeeded in bringing about the establishment of a separate Department of Fisheries, whose functions were far wider than the purely revenue-collecting activities of the Ministry of Finance which it replaced. As a result of the Andrews Report, reserve pond and swamp areas were designated and government showed signs of taking other more positive steps. It accepted in principle a policy of encouraging the pond breeding of freshwater fish, helping to finance experiments in fish-canning, and in 1939 plans to establish a School of Fisheries were announced. But many of these plans remained on paper or were inadequately implemented, because of lack of trained men and dependence on fishing monopolies.

In her livestock, Thailand possessed another resource of potential, but apart from the flourishing trade in cattle and hides, animals also played only a marginal role in the economy. They were regarded primarily as useful as beasts of burden rather than as a source of meat, manure or milk. Cattle and pigs formed the largest element in the animal population. Oxen and buffaloes acquired a new importance with the rise of the rice trade. Pig-rearing which had always been associated with the Chinese and remained a complete monopoly of theirs up till 1938, benefited from the growth of Bangkok and other urban centres. It also received a great stimulus with the opening of the peninsular railway line, which made the already well-established Singapore market more readily accessible. Government's role in the industry until the nationalistic 1930s was merely that of a revenue-collector, administered through a Pig and Poultry Farm started in the nineteenth century and replaced in 1902 by a simple but much more lucrative licensing system. Elephants made an important contribution to the timber economy of the north but fears that they might become extinct unless protected led to special legislation in 1900. In the 1930s the total (captive) elephant population amounted to some 12,000. Poultry (along with pigs) were also significant adjuncts in the northern economy, and use was made of horses as well as of bullocks on the Korat Plateau to transport rice or salt. In other words with proper development, expertise and capital, livestock could have made a far more significant contribution to the national economy, but as it was Thai knowledge of breeding and animal health were minimal, and livestock in general was poor in quality and quantity as a result.

Similarly, apart from teak Thai forests contained a wide range of products of commercial potential which nevertheless only found a local market. Mention has already been made of the cardamoms and resins, some of which held a place in the world market; there were also forty varieties of rattan, durian trees, areca and sugar palms and sources of specialist products such as the ipoh and cahulmoogra trees. Before 1850, in general, these forest products played an unknown and obviously minor role in the local economy, and after that date were subjected to the same official rentier approach.

In agriculture, as we have seen, rice completely dominated the picture, accounting for (in the 1930s) 93 per cent of total agricultural production. A choice range of fruits and vegetables served to bolster domestic self-sufficiency but little more. Maize and kenaf were prominent subsidiary crops in the north and north-east. Tapioca, introduced from the south by Chinese immigrants in the early twentieth century, had some use as animal fodder. Coffee was grown successfully by European and Chinese entrepreneurs, but failed to find a ready market outside the towns. Tea, native to the country, could likewise have been developed if there had been a market for it; as it was, it was chiefly grown by Lao hill people to serve as a stimulant (miang) or as an additive to fish paste and ginger curry. There was also some gutta percha, betelnut, groundnut and sesame from which oilseeds could be obtained, all of which possessed some potential but whose development remained restricted because of poor communications and other factors. In fact, after 1855 as self-sufficiency declined, so did these minor crops, while rice increased its domination. After 1920 for the first time government made various efforts aimed at rediversifying the economy and encouraging the minor crops. The emergence of a number of vegetable mills in the 1920s attracted official attention and led to a report by the Ministry of Commerce which underlined the lack of local demand as the principal obstacle to further development. In the 1930s the government launched a campaign to encourage the cultivation and export of local fruits, and on the eve of the Japanese War experimented with soya bean production.

As far as minerals are concerned, Thailand is poor. Prior to 1941, despite fabled resources, the kingdom proved to possess (apart from its tin) deposits of iron, copper, lead, tungsten, wolfram, coal, gold, gems and oil, but none of these in sufficient quantity to have any real commercial importance. Precious stones formed the core of most fables and the ancient mines at Chantabun remained a closely guarded secret for generations until revealed by French observers in the seventeenth century. Two hundred years later the deposits were still being worked on a small scale, but the gems were valued as charms, not jewellery, and a cutting industry had not developed. In the second half of the eighteenth century the Chantabun mines came under the control of a private Shan operator, who worked the gravels with Shan and Burmese labour until the whole area was leased to a British firm by the government in 1895. The Western enterprise failed to prosper, and with the loss of the neighbouring Pailin mines to French Cambodia in 1907 the Thai gem industry went into eclipse. There was a revival in 1918 centred on Kanburi, of sufficient dimensions to cause special clauses to be inserted into the Mining Act of the following year. The Kanburi concession eventually fell into the hands of an Italian who lived off the royalties of the diggings.

Gold was another mineral which excited higher hopes than proved justified. Although deposits are found and washed in river beds all over Thailand, the amounts obtained are small. From the 1870s onwards several enterprises were set up to mine gold, the most ambitious of which was the company formed to work the remote To-mah mines. This firm followed the rest by going bankrupt in 1893, defeated by heavy overheads, bad administration, poor communications and labour problems. A similar fate awaited the Kabin mines in the east, which had been taken over by a British firm and failed in 1902. Other failures followed involving British, French and Thai investors, but attempts continued to be made in various parts of the country right up to the Japanese War. The discovery of coal deposits in the peninsular south near Krabi and Trang led to the formation of a couple of coal firms; the Trang deposits turned out to be poor quality lignite and the firm concerned went bankrupt. The Krabi field became the preserve of the Siam Coal Mining Company Ltd. whose main distinction was that it was wholly Thai-owned and operated. But this did not save the enterprise from failing to make any headway. Crawfurd found iron cheap on the Bangkok market in the early 1820s, leading him to suppose that the mineral was in abundance. But although universal, iron was never found in substantial quantity and whatever industry existed based on local deposits was quickly killed by Western imports after 1855. The mirage of profitable oil deposits was also hopefully pursued. Some prospecting was carried out in the north in the 1920s and 1930s, and the government took the precaution of passing legislation that would ensure Thai control over the kingdom's own resources. Apart from this, the widespread occurrence of copper veins led the Danish East Asiatic Company into a false venture on the Korat Plateau in the 1900s; a British firm failed in its attempts to mine lead near Yala on the eve of the Great War, though the Chinese were successful in mining local deposits, smelting the copper and shipping it to China; a Swiss firm flourished briefly during the Great War itself, mining wolfram. There was also some mining of antimony and gypsum.

The domestic economy and industry
From the foregoing it is clear that even if Thailand's economy acquired a strong 'colonial' flavour after the country was opened to the pressures of the world market in 1855, it was not entirely due to those pressures alone. Basically the kingdom appeared to lack the essential ingredients for industrialization, amongst which lack of power sources was the most conspicuous. Added to this were the weak infrastructure of communications, an acute shortage of capital (partly the consequence of conservative fiscal policies) and scarcity of labour, since cheap immigrant labour was discouraged and the Thais themselves were unprepared for that kind of employment. Domestic production was inhibited by the limited capacity of the domestic market, whilst overseas markets were only open to a few staple products. The prospects for industrial growth were further confounded by the loss of control over tariff policy which was one of the most damaging features of Bowring's and other treaties with Western powers signed in the nineteenth century and not redeemed until the 1920s. There was also the absence of economic assistance from foreign sources (which at least colonial territories derived to a certain extent), a cumbrous and discouraging system of excise and duty, and last but not least uncompetitive attitudes both amongst officials and amongst the people as a whole.

As a result in 1941 Thai industry still largely conformed to the traditional pattern, characterized by a widespread cottage industry supplemented by an equally wide range of small workshops and family enterprises, and by an almost complete absence of heavy manufacturing. This was so despite the new awareness provoked by shrinking overseas markets of the country's dangerous dependence on a handful of primary products and the subsequent government drive to industrialize. Prior to 1932 Western-type industry had been rare in Thailand. In 1938-9 manufacturing accounted for less than 10 per cent of the gross national product and even thirty years later only involved 1.6 per cent of the total population.

Nevertheless, the traditional cottage industry of the countryside had been considerably modified since 1855. While it was still true to say that the average Thai household still did its own weaving and pottery-making, and made its own tools for farming and fishing, by the 1930s it was reckoned that no Thai family depended entirely for its living on handicrafts. The old craftsmen of yore employed in the temples or in 'the huge households' of the landed nobility were no more, while the market for handicraft products was now provided by the cash crop farmer, not by princely patrons. At the same time, although where rice now flourished as a cash crop the money economy gave the smallholder farmer the power to buy products instead of providing them for himself, he was still not rich enough to buy on a large scale, and so the market for specialization had not yet arrived. The importance of cottage industry was directly proportional to the degree of penetration by the new rice cash economy, as Andrews' survey of the mid-1930s tends to show. Boat-building, pottery-making, weaving and brick-making were the most prominent survivors amongst the traditional crafts, of which weaving appeared to hold in the 1930s the greatest potential for further growth. All had been affected in one way or the other by the impact of the new trade with the outside world. Weaving, for instance, almost completely disappeared as an industry from the Central Plain and the peninsular south, swept aside by cheap Japanese imports. The silk-weaving industry of Korat, the traditional centre for this in the kingdom, was badly hit by the opening of the railway from Bangkok at the turn of the century, which exposed the north-east to the competition of cheap European materials. But as we have already seen, both cotton- and silk-weaving survived and ultimately developed, both as a result of changing circumstances and of official encouragement. The Chinese played a major role in keeping local cotton production going around Korat in and after the Great War, and in 1936 government itself started to intervene with effect. The fate of Thai textiles was closely related to the development of the dyeing industry, the introduction of 'cheap, gaudy' imported aniline dyes virtually killing off Thai dye producers but giving new life to Thai cottons and silks, now rescued from the sombre local dyes of tradition. Pottery-making survived in the north but in a form debased from the high skills that had once made Sawankhalok ware so famous, and with only a limited domestic market. Boat-building, on the other hand, gained a new lease of life, mainly as a Chinese affair. Because of their dependence on local materials unfamiliar to outsiders, the handicrafts associated with rattan and bamboo hats, baskets and furniture continued to be of local importance. Traditional brick-making also survived, largely a Mon monopoly, with some commercial function in Bangkok and other towns. The making of lacquer ware occupied some 600 workers around Chiengmai in the late 1930s. Metalwork in bronze, silver and iron—never done on a large scale on account of limited materials—remained an artistic speciality, in particular niello work which was of high quality. The one traditional industry which did receive a considerable boost with the opening up of the country to foreign trade was the manufacture of liquor. In the first place Thailand had been flooded by cheap Western imports which were initially exempted from the standard 3 per cent import duty. Whatever the consequences on the population, the inflow of foreign alcohol had the effect of stimulating the local industry which quickly acquired the skills for distilling whisky, and brandy manufacturing beer besides the traditional rice wine (arrack). In 1936 government cashed in on this bonanza—the manufacture of liquor was already a government monopoly—by entering into the business directly itself, with gratifying results.

Apart from the distillery business, prior to the 1930s modern industry in Thailand was virtually limited to rice and timber milling, with the odd cement plant and paper mill. The rice- and saw-mills which required a full-time labour force were by far the most important form of modern industry and they maintained this position right up till the eve of the Japanese War. However, the pressures of the Great Depression gave rise to the urge to industrialize, which also seemed a natural policy to the nationalist-minded generation which took over power in Bangkok in 1932. Despite the obvious handicaps in the ways of industrialization already mentioned, it appeared to them that the problems of widespread if seasonal unemployment, the uneven distribution of development and resources, and the need to end dependence on foreign imports in an unstable world economy, could only be solved by industrialization and economic diversification at home. It also seemed to them important that government itself should play a leading role as entrepreneur so that the process of industrialization should remain a Thai affair and not become yet another field of foreign (including Chinese) predominance. The state-owned railways and airline were sufficient proof of government's ability to handle commercial enterprises, and after 1932 official participation in business expanded and intensified. For a start the Chulalongkorn School of Science was established to provide technical training and to supplement the activities of the Arts and Crafts School of Bangkok already in existence. Between 1935 and 1941 the government opened up a cotton mill at Bangkok, a paper mill at Kanburi, two modern sugar mills, a cannery at Pak-chang and various smaller undertakings elsewhere. At the same time tariff policy was modified to protect home industries. As a result, a whole host of light consumer industries—mostly Chinese-run—sprang up, amongst which match factories, cement works, paper mills and tobacco factories figured most prominently. The match industry had initially developed under foreign patronage, and after various vicissitudes caused by changing tariff policy, smuggling and cheap competition from Japan, was coming on the eve of the Japanese War near to capturing the entire domestic market. The cement industry, on the other hand, was the oldest established Western-type industry in the country, and prospered because of the availability of the necessary raw materials, proper location of the factory and royal patronage. The industry was more or less a monopoly of the Siam Cement Company which, founded in 1913, paid an average annual dividend of 12 per cent between 1915 (when its first plant was opened near Bangkok) and 1923. Protective tariffs after 1926 guaranteed the home market and safeguarded its continued profitability. The paper industry got off to a shaky start at the beginning of the century, but with the discovery that various types of bamboo were suitable for paper manufacture the industry started to develop on a large scale. In 1934 the Siam Paper Company was formed with government backing and participation, and a factory built at Kanchanaburi, which started to produce good quality material. However the most successful government enterprise was that in tobacco. The Siam Electric Company, floated in Copenhagen in 1898, became the proprietor of Bangkok's tramways and proved a profitable concern for all its various concessionaires until it was struck down by the Great Depression. Beyond Bangkok the spread of electricity was limited to a score of townships, where it was operated through the local municipality. A leather tannery at Lampang, a couple of aerated water plants and a soap factory completed the total of industrial enterprises in the country prior to 1941.

Obviously since 1932 in particular some progress had been made in setting up modern Western-type industry in Thailand, but the progress would have been much more impressive if all the plans announced since that date had actually been put into effect. The success that was achieved was primarily brought about by the creation of a home market guaranteed by a wall of protective tariffs. But although government itself began to emerge as a major entrepreneur in its own right, its record was discouraging. Government factories became notorious for their inefficiency and corruption, lack of proper planning and supervision and poor accounting, resulting in erratic production, unkept schedules and low puality products. And despite increasing government participation, modern industry as a whole still remained largely a Chinese preserve. In all, after nearly one century of being open to world trade and of developing a *laissez-faire* economy under its own political tutelage, 'it would probably be true', in the words of one observer, 'to describe pre-war Siam as commercially the least developed country in the whole of South-East Asia'.[32]

Population growth and distribution

In general consonance with Thailand's leisurely pace of development, the kingdom also had a comparatively slow rate of population growth. The population actually trebled between 1855 and 1941, a rate which betokened a steady rise but not a spectacular jump. Consequently the country was 'under-populated' in the sense that large areas were almost empty and even in the most heavily populated districts, the average was well below centres of population concentration elsewhere. In 1850 the average density was reckoned at around 25–30 per square mile; in the late 1950s the density had risen to 100 per square mile, a figure higher than that for neighbouring Burma but still below the regional average. Thailand's comparatively small population had its roots in a history of open frontiers, invasions and wars, and the ravages of disease. After 1855, all the same, the country tended to conform to the general pattern of population increase which took place throughout South-East Asia under the economic impact of Western colonialism. The rise of rice as a cash crop was a major factor, and population growth was primarily associated with the main rice-growing areas of the kingdom, to which natural increase, undisturbed by civil commotion or foreign attack and stimulated by improved diet and a falling death-rate, was an important contributory element. Immigration was also important although this

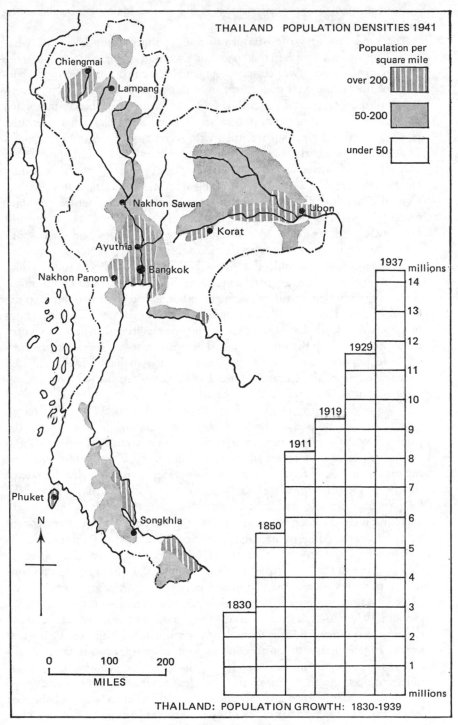

37. Population Density of Thailand, 1941

did not assume the proportions that it did in the Malay Peninsula or the Indonesian archipelago.

The predominantly rural nature of the economy made Thailand a nation of villages, of which in the 1930s there were an estimated 40,000, and the pattern of settlement was closely bound to rice cultivation. In 1939 four-fifths of the people were concentrated on the best rice lands, barely a seventeenth of the total area of the country. Naturally the most thickly populated region was the Central Plain, particularly around the Delta where densities reached 250 persons per square mile, with secondary concentrations around Lopburi and Singburi. Already in 1911, 30 per cent of the total population was to be found there, and a generation later this proportion had increased by another 10 per cent. This was in keeping with the historical pattern, for the Central Plain had always been the scene of the greatest settlement since earliest times. After 1855 this trend was merely accentuated. The next most heavily peopled area, but on a far smaller scale, was the peninsular south where tin and rubber rather than rice were the main factors at work. In general the population outside the Central Plain doubled between 1911 and 1947, a development largely attributable to the role of modern communications, especially that of the railways, in exposing the outer provinces to the world of international trade and commerce. In the north, the main centres of population tended to congregate along the traditional river-valley entry routes now used by the railway line. The north-east saw a similar great increase in population to that of the north, but it remained widely dispersed over the whole of the Korat Plateau. The other regions such as the west and the valley of the Mekong to the east remained far less densely settled.

In the midst of this village demography stood Bangkok which in size and significance had no peer in the kingdom. It was London-like in terms of the proportion of the population who lived there in relation to the country as a whole—9 per cent of the inhabitants of the Central Plain lived within the metropolitan area of the city in 1947—and was growing at twice the rate of the rest of the country. It was Paris-like in terms of its role in the life of the kingdom; as the sole, real urban centre its citizens were living in a world apart and it served as a great magnet, drawing the people from the provinces never to return. Bangkok had always played this role since its foundation as the royal capital in 1782. Even in the 1850s Bangkok was between 30 and 40 times the size of the next largest town. Built with the labour of 10,000 Cambodian prisoners-of-war on a site already occupied by Chinese traders, it owed its origins to its strategic advantages. Bangkok started to transform into a modern, Western-style city after the treaties of 1855, and was embellished through the efforts of King Chulalongkorn and King Vajiravudh. It grew rapidly in the nineteenth century and its population was nearing the one million mark in 1941. Beyond the city and its sprawling suburbs, in the mid-nineteenth century there were only a hundred other urban centres with populations of around 5,000 apiece, amongst which Ayuthia was probably the largest. By the twentieth century some new towns had arisen, notably Phuket which emerged as a result of the tin industry, the first town in the kingdom to have paved roads and motor vehicles. But in 1941 there were still only six towns (apart from Bangkok itself) in Thailand which could boast of more than 25,000 inhabitants each, led by Chiengmai whose population numbered probably about twice that amount.

In general (apart once more from Bangkok) there was no obvious trend towards urbanization in Thailand prior to the Japanese War. The abundance of land available and the absence of radical economic change for the bulk of the population meant that no major shifts in settlement or distribution patterns occurred. In fact the most significant demographic development was in the immigrant population and in the establishment of a sizeable and powerful alien minority in the midst of the indigenous Thai people. For by 1941 Thailand possessed the second largest Chinese minority in all South-East Asia.

The Chinese in Thailand

In 1941, at least 10 per cent of the kingdom's population consisted of ethnic Chinese, thereby making them by far the largest alien community in the country.[33] These figures represented a dramatic rise from those of 150 years earlier, when the total number of Chinese resident in Thailand did not exceed 1 per cent of the total population, and as was the case throughout all South-East Asia, the great influx of Chinese migrants took place after 1820. Indeed, in its main outlines the course of Chinese immigration and settlement in Thailand followed the same pattern as elsewhere in the region. The migrants were drawn substantially from the same coastal provinces of southern China and came in response to the same stimuli. The primary factor was trade and the sudden demand for labour which came from already established Chinese monopoly farmers, rice- and saw-mill owners, sugar planters and tin-miners as the kingdom's economy swiftly developed after 1855. As in the Straits Settlements the Chinese soon discovered that they had an essential role to play as intermediaries between the new Western import-export agencies and the world of the peasant producer-cum-consumer, and as in the Malay Peninsula Chinese enterprise was all the more encouraged by the unwillingness or inability of the local inhabitants to participate in the burgeoning world of commerce around them. The pace of immigration was likewise quickened by the rapid improvement in communications which took place after the 1860s, in particular with regard to the advent of the steamship, and Thailand was all the more inviting by virtue of being near, relatively underpopulated, and prior to the Great War at least offering the highest wage rates throughout the Far East (i.e. at Bangkok). The general volume of immigration ebbed and flowed as it did in the Straits, in the Indonesian archipelago and in neighbouring French Indo-China in response to fluctuating economic circumstances, and as was the case throughout the region there was a marked falling off in immigration as a result of the Great Depression. Long established in the country, Chinese numbers started to show a marked increase from the times of Tak Sin, who, half-Chinese himself, made great efforts to encourage Chinese settlement in the country. This policy was carried on by his Chakri successors, mindful of the importance of the China trade and bent on the enhancement of the royal trading monopoly, well into the nineteenth century. The

Chinese immigrants of this period helped to provide the base for the great increase in immigrants who came after 1850. From that time onwards their numbers steadily rose until the peak decade of the 1920s, when they were coming in at a rate of 95,000 a year.

The general social pattern of the Chinese community in Thailand followed that amongst Chinese settlers in the other lands of South-East Asia. Female immigration, for example, was very limited prior to the 1890s and of the handful of Chinese women who did enter the country before 1910, the great majority were destined for the brothels of Bangkok and of other Chinese centres. There was some increase after 1893 but 1910 marked the turning point. Between 1910 and 1917 the rate of female immigration went up to about 10 per cent of the whole, 'respectable women' constituting the majority for the first time. After 1920 the proportion grew steadily. However, male immigrants always maintained a substantial majority, and the sex ratio in the 1930s was still heavily unbalanced, with Chinese males still marrying Thai or Sino-Thai women 'both because of the shortage of Chinese girls and because of the lesser expense involved'. Nevertheless the increase in Chinese women immigrants brought about marked social consequences. Intermarriage between Chinese and Thais declined, the Chinese community as a whole gained greater coherence, and at the same time became less assimilable. Meanwhile Chinese society in general remained typically fluid and variegated, conditioned by the pattern of immigration. 'Most of the immigrants arrived with a roll of bedding, a few cash and a determination to make good,' as indeed they did at other ports throughout the region, but unlike in the Straits or in the Indies, most of them arrived unindentured.[34] The average immigrant was assisted by his own clansmen in the traditional manner and travelled under the same, scandalous conditions which characterized the whole of the vast 'coolie traffic' out of China in the middle of the nineteenth century.[35] Out of this amorphous pattern there emerged the main class groupings which typified Chinese emigrant society throughout South-East Asia. At the top were to be found an elite group of very rich merchants, many of whom had long connexions with the country and were the holders of one or more of the monopoly farms. Not far below them as the century advanced came a number of newly-rich rice-millers and compradores, followed by an ever-expanding middle class of tradesmen, shop-keepers and artisans, clerks, craftsmen and a few professional men. At the bottom lay the great mass of Chinese immigrants, about whose lives 'there was nothing particularly glamorous',[36] who made up the hawkers, rickshaw pullers, street actors, mill employees and dockers of the towns, and the coolies digging canals and planting sugar in the countryside. Chinese society in Thailand retained these broad characteristics well into the twentieth century but after 1900 became much more coherent and organized, especially in Bangkok. New leaders, whose wealth and influence were based on cosmopolitan interests such as shipping, banking and processing industries, in contrast to the traditional tax-farmers and secret society chiefs of before, arose. This new leadership tended to be less concerned with sectional, speech-group interests.

The great bulk of Chinese immigrants were concentrated in the towns, above all in Bangkok, or in other key centres of economic activity such as in the tin fields and rubber smallholdings of the peninsular south. In fact Bangkok stood out as much as the main focus of Chinese settlement and activity as it did as the first city of the nation as a whole. As the seat of the royal court and centre for the royal patronage of commercial and artisan skills, as well as a natural entrepôt for the junk trade, it already contained half the total Chinese population in the kingdom in 1850. A century later Bangkok and its environs remained the chief centre of Chinese concentration. With the spread of trade and commerce, other towns such as Korat, Lampang, Sukhothai, Uttaradit, Phitsanuloke and Roi Et, also acquired sizeable colonies of Chinese merchants and shop-keepers. Outside Bangkok, however, the next greatest concentration of Chinese was in the Isthmus of Kra which witnessed a steady growth after 1918, despite the two depressions which the local rubber and tin industries weathered better than did their counterparts in Malaya. The pattern of Chinese settlement was considerably modified with the extension of modern communications, in particular the railway. They seemed to move ahead along with the railway line under construction, and each new railhead became a new centre for Chinese business and commerce. Chinese numbers in the northern provinces tripled in the 1920s with the penetration of the railway line to Chiengmai in 1921, and with the construction of new highways to Chieng-rai, Phrae and Nan shortly afterwards. On the Korat Plateau the Chinese presence increased fourfold as the railway system in the north-east extended. The new line to the Cambodian frontier at Aranyaprathet helped to double the Chinese population in South-east Thailand between 1919 and 1941, and the lack of new communications in the south-west made that region the area of lowest Chinese growth. The development of modern communications also played a major role in redistributing the pattern of speech-groups in the kingdom.[37]

In general, the pattern of Chinese distribution in the country was marked by a gradual fanning out into the interior from the seaports which had formed the initial centres of settlement. In 1800 almost the entire Chinese population was to be found confined to the coastal regions in a line of towns which stretched from Trat to Saiburi, and mid-century there were still only six inland centres with Chinese inhabitants. A shift began to take place with the opening up of the kingdom after 1855, but in 1919 only 7 per cent of their number were to be found living in inland districts. After 1919, however, as we have noted, there was a marked influx of Chinese into the interior, so much so that the rate of increase was greater in inland districts than anywhere else in the kingdom, stimulated by the spread of communications and by the increasing difficulty of getting employment in Bangkok and other traditional areas of settlement.

The fact that the primary centres of settlement were on the coast is an obvious indication that Chinese immigration came predominantly by sea, although the existence of the ancient caravan trails from Yunnan into the northern provinces shows that, as in neighbouring Burma, there was also a long-established overland connexion. In fact it was the overland route along which came copper pots, silks, rock salt, tinsel, lace and other sundry wares to the old markets of Nan and Lampang, representing the oldest trade link between China and Thailand. As evidenced by the stream of embassies between the two countries which date back to at least the eleventh century, the origins and mainstay of the Chinese connexion lay in trade. The sea route, however, soon overshadowed the overland route in commercial importance and became the main highway for the Chinese immigrant. There is clear evidence of the presence of Chinese traders in the Gulf of Siam before the Thai occupation of the Menam Chao Phaya Basin, the numbers of whom increased with the opening of the first tin-mines in the Isthmus of Kra. There is also ample evidence of Chinese contacts with Sukhothai and after Ayuthia had been founded, the Chinese connexion became well established. By the time that the Portuguese arrived on the scene, Chinese traders and pirates were 'everywhere established in Siam'. By the seventeenth century there were major Chinese settlements at Ayuthia, Paknampoh, Chonburi (Bangplasoi), Paetriw, Thajin, Nakhorn Sri Thammarat (Ligor), Songkhla, Patani and Phuket. The largest and most important Chinese community was that at Ayuthia, followed by the turbulent and virtually autonomous Chinese colonies in the south, particularly the one at Patani.[38] As in Vietnam and in the Straits, the size and nature of the Chinese presence was closely related to developments within China proper itself.

One of the distinctive features of Chinese settlement in Thailand was the marked predominance of the Teochew amongst the various speech-groups which made up the Chinese community. As in island South-East Asia, the Cantonese and the Hokkien were the oldest established amongst the Chinese communities in the kingdom, but from the middle of the eighteenth century onwards the Teochew gained a clear ascendancy. In the 1930s the Teochew accounted for three-fifths of all the Chinese in Thailand and dominated the business and commercial world from their commanding position as rice-millers, import and export merchants, and local manufacturers, as well as being well represented in all strata of society. The Hokkien came next in importance though not in numbers, and were particularly prominent in the peninsular south, a consequence of the close links with the Hokkien community of the Straits. The Hainanese and the Hakka speech groups came to rank second and third numerically during the nineteenth century. The rise of the Teochew was primarily due to their connexion with Phaya Tak Sin, who reunified the kingdom after the collapse of the Ayuthia monarchy before the Burmese in 1767, and made his new capital at Thonburi, opposite present-day Bangkok. With his direct encouragement Teochews already settled near Thonburi flocked to Bangkok which thereby became and subsequently remained the main Teochew centre in the kingdom. From this base and under royal patronage, they quickly acquired a hold over the commercial life of the country. Teochew economic predominance was confirmed in the second half of the nineteenth century when the opening of the first two direct steamship services between Thailand and China linked Bangkok to Swatow and Hai-K'ou in 1886. These two ports continued to be the only ones to have a direct connexion with the Thai capital for the ensuing fifty years, with the result that the pool of immigrants was drawn from Teochew, Hakka and Hainanese sources. The extension of the railways to the four corners of the kingdom led to the spread of the Teochew throughout the land so that the predominance they had already acquired in Bangkok now became nation-wide. By the 1930s the Teochews remained the most prestigious and powerful group in the kingdom, especially in Bangkok and the north; in the peninsular south the Hokkien continued to lead. In other respects, however, the various speech groups tended to follow the occupational patterns which were generally associated with them throughout South-East Asia. Thus the Cantonese were largely connected with the professions, especially in medicine and dentistry, with hotels and catering, engineering and technical enterprises, and ranked third in business. The Hokkien were prominent as businessmen and merchants, particularly in the tea trade, and completely predominated amongst the tin-miners in the peninsular south. Equally typically the Hakka and the Hainanese tended to be found only at the lower occupational levels, as petty traders, lesser craftsmen, hawkers and labourers—the Hainanese being the poorest group of all.

The role of the Chinese in Thailand, the manner of their arrival, the factors behind their ascendancy, all had much in common with the Chinese communities in the other lands of South-East Asia, especially with those in the Philippines and in Malaya where numerically they held a greater significance; but nowhere else in the region did the Chinese achieve such a great degree of social penetration. Their economic predominance was almost absolute. Not only were 70 per cent of all the Chinese in the kingdom (ethnically speaking) engaged in some form of business or trade, but they controlled 80 per cent of that trade including a complete mastery over the rice industry from which nearly three-quarters of the national revenue was derived. Nor was this a new situation. They had been the mainstay of the foreign trade of Ayuthia, particularly after the eclipse of the Europeans in the second half of the seventeenth century, were the pioneers of silk-weaving and sugar-cane agriculture, and in effect formed the only effective middle-class between aristocrats and peasants under the old dispensation. The French missionary, Launay, ascribed the rapid recovery of the Thai economy under Phaya Tak Sin from the disasters of the Burmese Wars and the sack of Ayuthia in 1767 to the part played by the Chinese, and in the eyes of a twentieth-century American observer, 'There would have been no progress without the Chinese'.[39] The only sector of the economy in which the Chinese did not play a leading role was in agriculture, despite the fact that—unlike in most other South-East Asian lands—there were no barriers placed in their way against acquiring land and working it.[40]

The reasons for this remarkable economic ascendancy were on the whole the same as those elsewhere throughout the region. Trade and commercial conditions were generally in favour of the Chinese. The Thais were simply not interested in commerce and trade as occupations, leaving the field by default virtually unchallenged to aliens, while the Chinese themselves were equipped with the social organization and personal qualities which made successful merchants and entrepreneurs out of them. They naturally took up the role of middlemen and even in their competition with Western businessmen in the nineteenth century evolved a symbiotic relationship with them which was much to the advantage of either side.[41] What was not typical was the privileged position which the Chinese in Thailand held from early on in Thai society. Long before 1855 they had been treated as free agents in matters of trade. They could buy and sell without restriction, paid lighter import duties than other aliens and were free to move wherever they pleased, all of which placed them at a great advantage over all other foreign traders. They were also exempt from forced labour or from the poll tax which was universal amongst the ordinary Thais themselves—privileges which they enjoyed undisturbed until the end of the nineteenth century. In addition to being permitted to clear land and plant crops, they could open mines (when Europeans were not allowed to do so) and follow their own customs. It was this privileged position which gave the Chinese their greatest lever and ensured their economic predominance. Of particular importance was the part they played in expanding the royal export trade monopoly which developed in the first half of the nineteenth century under the early Chakri kings. Much of it was borne in Chinese junks, often built by Chinese shipwrights in Thailand itself, vessels which were captained and manned by Chinese; the Chinese also served as factors, warehousemen and as royal advisers on commerce. Through this trade Chinese immigration was stimulated and Chinese merchants gained direct access to and influence at the court, and when in the second half of the nineteenth century their dominance over the kingdom's overseas trade faded before the arrival of the Westerners and the advent of the steamship, they were handsomely compensated by the rise of the state monopolies and tax farms which were introduced after 1826 to counteract the effects of Burney's Treaty on official revenues.[42] Between 1826 and 1845 rich Chinese acquired some ninety state monopolies between them, the principal amongst which were those in opium, gambling, lottery and alcohol, thereby enriching themselves and solving the revenue problems of the state. Bowring's Treaty was of course a great blow to the monopoly system, but the tax farms survived, in particular those in opium and gambling, which were nearly wholly Chinese affairs anyway. By this time the Chinese grip over the burgeoning rice industry was already almost unassailable, but in general under the changed economic conditions which prevailed after 1855 the Chinese were thrown back onto their traditional role as middlemen, abandoning the heights of the export trade to the Westerners. Being middlemen was a role they were particularly well suited to fill and they also went on, as the century progressed, to consolidate their domination over tin-mining, and early in the twentieth century to gain a substantial stake in rubber planting.

While the great mass of Chinese immigrants into Thailand, as elsewhere during the nineteenth and early twentieth centuries, sweated out their time in hard toil as coolies, labourers and petty traders, there was also a small group of Chinese who were extremely wealthy, who were accepted by local society and who held responsible political posts and often enough married into the families of the Thai ruling class. As far as Thai monarchs were concerned, the Chinese presence seemed indispensable to the progress of the realm, and their unfettered immigration was encouraged. As late as 1907 King Chulalongkorn could proclaim that 'It has always been my policy that the Chinese in Siam should have the same opportunities for labour and profit as are possessed by my own countrymen. I regard them not as foreigners but as component parts of the kingdom and as sharing in its prosperity and advancement.'[43] This remarkable declaration certainly reflected the attitude of all the king's forebears, who from Rama I himself had actively promoted Chinese trade and immigration. King Mongkut saw the Chinese as one of his principal instruments in accelerating the modernization of the country. Royal policy did not stop at that. Until the end of King Chulalongkorn's reign, it was official policy to ennoble rich Chinese of ability in order to secure their allegiance and their services, a policy which served to neutralize potentially overmighty subjects by committing them to the needs of the state, at the same time in this way opening to the Chinese so favoured direct entry to membership of the Thai aristocracy. In the Chinese-dominated peninsular south such a policy smacked of expediency since in Songkhla, Trang, Phuket and other local centres the provincial governors, all of whom were Chinese, were in fact descendants of fortune-hunters who had established themselves by force of arms. Nevertheless by the end of the century even these local 'dynasties' had become definitely 'taih-icised' and despite their origins were totally loyal servants of the Bangkok monarchy.

One reason why Thailand's kings and the people at large did not regard the Chinese as foreigners in the same sense that they did other outsiders lay in the ease with which the Chinese became assimilated into local society. There are no strong physical differences in appearance between the two races, the Chinese easily adapted themselves to the Thai form of Buddhism, and they readily accepted Thai custom. Intermarriage was commonplace, particularly in view of the fact that (prior to 1919) Chinese women never amounted to more than 10 per cent of the total immigrant population. Liaisons were especially common amongst Chinese and members of Thai aristocratic families, including the royal family itself. Every Thai king since 1850 had some Chinese blood in his veins, and it has been reckoned that 90 per cent of King Vajiravudh's court (including the king himself) were of mixed blood. The frequency of intermarriage naturally gave rise to a new group of Sino-Thais, known as *luk-chin*, of whom the earliest mention dates back to the early fifteenth century. However the speed with which the Chinese themselves became absorbed into Thai society meant that until the quickened pace of immigration after 1850 upset the balance, the fourth generation of Chinese in the country had usually become indistinguishable from the general populace. In consequence until the end of the nineteenth century, the *lukchin* tended to be an evanescent community without any real identity of its own. They were socially acceptable to both sides but possessed no clear-cut role. Their numbers in the early 1820s were reckoned to stand at around 80,000, approximately one-third of those of Chinese origin in the kingdom at the time.

In general, until the twentieth century Sino-Thai relations were remarkably harmonious. But that does not mean to say that there was no friction. During the course of the nineteenth century there were a number of Chinese uprisings, the most serious of which was that centred on the sugar-growing districts around Nakhorn Chaisi, Thajin and Chachoengso (Paetriw) to the south-east of Bangkok in 1847-8. Such outbreaks proceeded from localized causes and were suppressed with great severity. Cantonese pirates in the Gulf of Siam caused disturbances from time to time, but the most constant source of trouble came, as elsewhere, from Chinese secret societies. Like the British in the Straits Settlements, at first the Chakri rulers tended to encourage these organizations as a means of controlling the Chinese community as a whole, and also as a way of combatting the influence of Christian missionary activities in the country. But during the reign of King Chulalongkorn the secret societies became increasingly troublesome and were responsible for at least four major riots in Bangkok itself. Attempts to follow the counter-measures taken by the British authorities in the Straits proved ineffective, and secret society activities in new guise were prolonged well into the second half of the twentieth century.

Nevertheless none of this affected the position of the Chinese community in the kingdom as a whole nor the good relations which existed between them and the Thais until the end of the reign of King Chulalongkorn. The death of the king in 1910 came at a turning point in the history of the Chinese nation, epitomized by the Revolution in China itself the following year, an event which marked the birth of modern Chinese nationalism and which had widespread repercussions amongst all the Chinese communities in the region. Almost overnight the generations of goodwill and mutual trust between Thai and Chinese vanished, and for the first time people spoke of 'the Chinese problem'. For the first time also the Chinese in Thailand became the objects of official discrimination and of public antipathy. This new anti-Chinese spirit was led by none other than Thailand's new monarch, King Vajiravudh.

It was the king who first pinpointed the 'Chinese problem'.[44] The 'problem' which the king depicted was no different from that described by Indonesian nationalists in Java, Vietnamese intellectuals in Hanoi and Saigon, or Filipino politicians in Manila with regard to the Chinese communities in their midst. The Chinese manifestly dominated the economy of the country and they were to be blamed for the failure of the Thais to share in the benefits of modernization and economic expansion. The royal theme was quickly taken up by other members of the Thai ruling class, many of whom had good doses of Chinese blood in their veins and became the battle-cry of the new nationalist movement which gained control over the country after 1932.[45] The anti-Chinese campaign reached its climax (i.e. prior to the Japanese War) during the first tenure of power of Phibun Songgram, who became effective ruler of Thailand in 1938. By that time the climate of public opinion had become completely attuned to the hostile Chinese line.

The origins of this new anti-Chinese sentiment lay in a combination of factors, all of which were common to those lands in the region with powerful Chinese minorities. The sudden flowering of Chinese nationalism promoted a patriotic Thai reaction.[46] While after 1910 the Chinese community in Thailand as a whole acquired a new sense of coherence and self-respect from the overthrow of the Manchus and from the heady propaganda of Sun Yat-sen and his fellow nationalists in China proper, new arrivals who were still coming into the kingdom in ever-increasing numbers tended to be less and less assimilable as the proportion of women amongst them also steadily rose. Thai sensibilities, on the other hand, had already been aroused by the growing intensity of secret society disorders towards the close of the nineteenth century. The point was driven home by the great secret society hartal staged in Bangkok shortly before King Chulalongkorn's death in 1910. Although the movement collapsed after three days, no number of protestations of loyalty made by Chinese community leaders at the new king's coronation the next year could erase from Thai minds the realization that the demonstration had been made solely in defence of Chinese sectional interests, occasioned by the ending of their privileged tax-free status. Western-educated Thais were already influenced by their experiences in Europe, while King Vajiravudh, with an English upbringing, was particularly susceptible to the anti-Chinese prejudices of his British advisers. From this time onwards, Thai and Chinese nationalism reacted upon each other like abrasives. The growing separateness of the Chinese community was aggravated by the mounting discrimination against them. The ever more apparent connexion between Chinese disturbances within the country and Chinese nationalist politics, such as the anti-Japanese boycotts by Chinese port-workers which paralysed the port of Bangkok in 1927 and 1928 exacerbated Thai nationalist feelings still further.[47] When after 1932 effective power in Thailand rested in the hands of the new middle-class of professional men whose interests were much more directly in conflict with those of the Chinese establishment than were those of the traditional Thai aristocracy, the die was cast for the Chinese in the kingdom.

The earliest measures aimed against the Chinese—although no Thai law ever specified any particular community—came in 1913 with the Nationality Act of that year.[48] The first attempts to control the flow of Chinese immigration were made in 1926-7, supplemented by other regulations in the 1930s,[49] but it was not until Phibun Songgram's accession to power that a coherent anti-Chinese policy was developed. The main aims of the anti-Chinese measures passed between 1938 and 1941 were to establish effective supervision or control over existing Chinese enterprises and to open up hitherto closed sectors of the economy to Thais by forcing out the Chinese. These twin purposes explain the spate of legislation which required the registration of all businesses, the keeping of all accounts in Thai, the establishment of new taxation schedules bearing down heaviest on alien (i.e. Chinese) enterprises, the laying down of ownership qualifications, employment ratios, conditions for the issuing of licences and, finally, the setting up of a variety of state corporations to enter directly into various commercial fields. Amongst the last named, the most significant steps were the formation of the Thai Tobacco Monopoly in 1939 and of the Thai Rice Company, which immediately acquired control over most of the existing foreign enterprises in these two fields. The whole programme was sanctified by the proclamation of the 'Ratha Niyon'—a statement of guiding economic principles for the nation enunciated in 1939.[51]

Although the Chinese community was reputedly 'stunned' by the plethora of legislation directed against it in the late 1930s, it soon recovered and found

ways and means around the new difficulties.[51] The legislation itself was similar
to though more comprehensive than similar measures enacted in the Philippines and French Indo-China, for the Thais were at least masters in their own
house (politically), but it suffered from the same defects and practical shortcomings. Bribery and ineffective implementation softened the blow. As far
as the new regulations regarding immigration and citizenship were concerned,
they stimulated a great increase in largely unstoppable illegal entries into the
kingdom, and even the higher literacy requirements were offset by a general
rise in the standard of education of the immigrants, so that the flow was not
at first seriously checked at all. The effectiveness of the laws aimed at Chinese
business and commerce was substantially reduced because of the inescapable
dependence on Chinese knowledge and expertise. The first state rice-mills
had to retain their former Chinese managers, it proved impossible to obtain
sufficient Thai labour to meet the 75 per cent quota stipulated by law, and
government efforts to encourage Thais to enter business were largely negated
by the traditional Thai preference for government jobs. But the Chinese
were hard hit. The Liquid Fuels Act of 1939, for instance, whose terms the
two Western enterprises chiefly concerned refused to accept, resulting in their
withdrawal from the country's petroleum industry, led to the Chinese sub-
agents who served as distributors having their contracts terminated at one
month's notice and their being entirely replaced by Thais. The Chinese also
had to bear a far heavier burden of taxation, and the proclamation in 1941 of
certain strategic areas in the east and north-east which were henceforth prohibited to alien residence, affected the Chinese living in such areas very badly
indeed. No doubt the traditional privileged position of the Chinese had gone
forever, and their future was an uncertain one.

However in 1941 they still represented a major economic and social force
in the country, and if now a community very much on the defensive, they
could still hold their own. Their contribution to the economic development
of Thailand lay beyond dispute—it had been tremendous. The cost for Thailand was tremendous, too, for in 1941 as much as in 1900 or in 1855 the kingdom's economy remained largely in their hands.

The Thais and other indigenous groups

For, if the Thais had not suffered as their neighbours had done from the opening up of their country under colonial domination, neither had they been
en masse the main beneficiaries of the economic changes that had taken place
since 1855, still less so the other indigenous inhabitants of the kingdom who
probably numbered just over one million on the eve of the Japanese War.
The non-Thai indigenes of the country consisted of small, scattered, disparate
communities, many of them representing the remnants of the original
occupants of the region who had faded into the hills before the Mon-Khmer
advance at the dawn of history.[52] Apart from these hill peoples, the Malays
in the peninsular south, groups of Vietnamese and Khmer to the east and
north-east, Karens in the west and a small Mon community in the Central
Plain itself formed the other non-Thai elements in the body politic of the
kingdom. The hill peoples continued to live their simple, subsistence, ani-

mistic way of life largely undisturbed—they were primarily shifting rice cultivators who maintained fleeting contacts with the organized society of the plains through the bartering of forest products for salt and rice. Amongst the other five non-Thai elements in the population, the Malays were the most numerous and potentially the least assimilable. They numbered at least half a million in 1941, mostly concentrated in the four southern provinces of Patani, Satun (Setul), Yala and Narathiwat where they accounted for four-fifths of the population.[53] For the most part padi-planters, rubber smallholders and fishermen, and being Muslims, they followed a way of life identical with that of the Malay inhabitants of the Peninsula south of the border, to whom they were often connected by family ties. In the east, there were some 200,000 Khmers and Vietnamese, the Khmers being found particularly in the foothills of the Dangrek Range adjoining Cambodia proper and distinguished from the Thais only by language. The Vietnamese (known to the Thais as Yuan) lived mainly around Chantabun and Bangkok itself, the descendants of Roman Catholic refugees fleeing the persecution of Annamite emperors, or of prisoners-of-war from former campaigns. In the remote hills of the western border with Burma, particularly in the province of Mae Hong Son, lived various groups of Karen, who tended to keep very much to themselves. From 60,000 to 100,000 Mon, mostly the descendants of refugees from Burmese fury in the Irrawaddy Delta but including some survivors of the original inhabitants of the region, lived in a few scattered villages on the Central Plain; they were fast losing their identity, having adopted Thai language and culture.

As for the Thais themselves, they too were sub-divided into four or five groups based on area of settlement, dialect and mode of life,[54] and as amongst the Thai-speaking peoples of Laos or the Khmers of Cambodia a broad distinction was to be drawn between the more sophisticated inhabitants of the plains and those ruder folks living on the plateaux and in the hills of the north. As has already been shown, the Thais were overwhelmingly agriculturalists. According to the 1937 census, 98.5 per cent of all cultivated land was owned and worked by Thais; apart from producing virtually the entire rice crop, they were well represented amongst the rubber smallholders of the south but provided only a fraction of the labour in the tin-mines. In fact, as has also been noted earlier, the reluctance of the Thais to go in for labour in non-agricultural pursuits created a shortage of general labour and gave it an expensive scarcity value. In other fields the Thais were only well represented in government service and the professions, the result of modern education becoming available to the ruling elite. The power of this ruling class which stemmed from the institution of the monarchy itself, and was only slightly broadened as a result of the Revolution of 1932, had of course remained intact throughout the process of economic transformation which the kingdom underwent after 1855. In consequence Thai society as a whole maintained its traditional conservatism and although the aristocracy lost or abandoned its feudalistic privileges during the second half of the nineteenth century, their position *vis-à-vis* their fellow countrymen in no wise changed, nor did the mode of life or the occupations of the people in general alter. Long discouraged by the old system from venturing into new fields of enterprise, villagers after

1855 found that with the new demands of the world market, rice cultivation paid, while there was no dearth of land to inhibit expansion.

Agrarian poverty and the land

The continued identification of the Thais as a people with the land was congenial to them; it was also in part the result of a deliberate policy conceived by the Chakri kings to be in their own best interests. Nevertheless, as things had turned out by the third and fourth decades of the twentieth century the Thais found themselves caught up in the same poverty syndrome as the bulk of the other indigenous inhabitants of South-East Asia. They were tied to the least rewarding sector of the new economy whose heights were firmly held by aliens. This was the source of the new nationalism which swept the country after 1932.

While the conversion of his country into one of the world's rice-bowls brought few tangible benefits to the Thai peasant, his plight was considerably milder than that of his counterparts elsewhere in the region. He was poor but lived above subsistence level and was not crushed down by an overwhelming burden of debt. Rural indebtedness existed and indeed was common and tenantry was increasing, but there was in general a marked lack of landlordism and much of the indebtedness was on a personal or family basis and interest free. According to Zimmerman's survey made in the early 1930s, just under half the farmers of the Central Plain were debtors, while the total extent of rural indebtedness was reckoned not to exceed 143 million baht.[55] On the Central Plain too it was estimated that a good third of the farmers were tenants. But tenancy could be as much a sign of prosperity as of poverty, for as van der Heide had noted as early as 1900, people were prepared to pay high prices in order to rent fertile strips of land such as in the Rangsit scheme area. Rents too tended to be well below the regional average, and even in hard times debts were rarely settled by foreclosure—in great contrast to what went on in the neighbouring Irrawaddy Delta. The reasons for these comparatively milder circumstances lay in the abundant availability of land and in the spread of the smallholder economy. The abundance of land and the traditional obligation of the occupier to cultivate it helped to keep land values low and the renting of it superfluous. In 1938 little more than 1 million acres were irrigated out of an irrigable area of some 16 million acres, while as late as the mid-1950s only about 16 per cent of the total land area was cultivated. After 1855 smallholdings multiplied while the large estates of the nobility declined, primarily because the process of extending rice cultivation was not heavily capitalized as in Burma or Cochin-China, either by government or private investors, and the slow development of irrigation schemes, also dictated by financial prudence, helped to prevent widespread land alienation. The rice revolution in Thailand was basically a peasant movement and as the number of smallholdings gradually increased, the great landowners whose estates had largely depended on the availability of conscript labour steadily declined, all the more so after 1905 when slavery in the kingdom was officially proscribed. The advance of the smallholder after 1855 was deliberately fostered by government and encouraged by evolving circumstances.

The traditional *sakdi na* system of land grants was discontinued under King Chulalongkorn. After 1900 the spread of organized, modern irrigation gave land a new value, made land squatting no longer permissible and necessitated the establishment of a proper survey to settle hazy ownership rights. The issue of title deeds based on regular cadastral surveys fastened the farmer to his land and strengthened the smallholder system. The implementation of a proper land survey was mooted in the early 1880s, but it was not until the end of the century that the Survey Department really got under way. In 1901 the old laws which gave the squatter absolute right over the land he occupied after three years of working it were repealed and a modified form of the Torrens System of land registration was introduced. Subsequent measures encouraged the growth of independent smallholders by providing for the auction of public lands on special terms so as to give 'the right kind of man' a stake in the country, and by enabling cultivators in general to acquire easily as much land as they 'could turn to profit'. The application of the Torrens land registration system which was made compulsory met with difficulties at first, but was later accepted and welcomed, and the Land Survey Department made ponderous but substantial progress at a rate of about 1 per cent per year, so that by 1941 one-third of the total land area had been covered. The net result of all this activity was to hinder the rise of landlordism on a large scale, to encourage cultivation and to confirm the smallholder in his heritage. Only in the peninsular south was the government faced with the problem of land speculation, behind which foreign interests were involved. The twin booms in tin and rubber in the 1900s together with the extension of the railway line southwards to the Malayan border led to large tracts of land changing hands at speculative prices around Haadyai and Songkhla to the enrichment of local officials and the benefit of local Chinese businessmen. This and foreign land speculation nearer Bangkok were finally checked by special legislation.

Although the general condition of the Thai farmer tended to be better than that of his immediate neighbours, the problem of rural poverty and indebtedness did exist and began to make itself inescapably noticeable during the 1920s and 1930s. The great crop failures of 1919 and 1920 did much to increase the burden of indebtedness, while the impact of the Great Depression was felt particularly amongst padi-planters on the Central Plain where production was closely linked to the world market, and in the north-east where the economy went back to subsistence level. It was also reflected in the statistics of the co-operative societies in the following couple of years, and in the spate of demonstrations and petitions by farmers themselves between 1932 and 1936. As was to be expected, the agrarian problem in general was centred in the most developed areas, notably the Central Plain and the districts around Chiengmai. It was reckoned that prior to 1941 four-fifths of all rural indebtedness was concentrated on the Central Plain. The investigations of both Zimmerman and Andrews in the 1930s confirm that the burden was heaviest and *increasing* in the Centre, whereas in the other regions of the country indebtedness was 'of minor significance'. The incidence of tenantry reflected a similar pattern.[56] The most heavily tenanted areas were those on the rich lands nearest Bangkok where in certain districts such as Klong Rangsit, 80 per cent of the farmers were tenants, paying their rents to local collectors for their landlords living in the big city. The disappearance of the smallholder in such districts was inevitable in the face of their close links with the inter-national rice trade, the proximity of wealthy merchant-landlords and the annual influx of seasonal labour from the north. The land itself was also at a premium and enjoyed a value that could not be found elsewhere. On the eve of the Great Depression the number of landless families on the Central Plain stood at well over one-third of the local population, more than double the national average. However this was as much an index of social change as of growing poverty.[57]

The general factors behind the growing poverty of the Thai peasant farm-er were the same as those which attended the growing impoverishment of the countryside throughout South-East Asia. As elsewhere, the Thai na-tionalists of the twentieth century found their scapegoats in the middlemen and moneylenders, most of whom were Chinese, although in the case of the moneylenders in particular, closer investigation revealed that Thai practi-tioners were the worst offenders.[58] The rise of the Chinese middlemen dated from the time of Bowring's Treaty and by 1900 they were nearly everywhere, playing the roles of merchant and advancer, transporter, landlord and rentier. But if the middlemen were well rewarded for their pains, as indeed they were, according to Doll, the Financial Adviser in 1937, their risks were also dis-proportionately high as a result of the absence of adequate credit facilities be-sides the lack of standardization in weights and measures in the country. In fact, the middlemen were as much at the mercy of the vagaries of a poor marketing system as were the farmers themselves, and since there were no alternative facilities they were an indispensable link between producer and exporter. Farmers and middlemen alike were also helpless before the fluctua-tions in the price of rice on the international market. Furthermore there was intense competition between the middlemen themselves which helped raise prices but as Jacoby points out, what determined matters for the farmer was the terms on which he received his advance from the middleman, with-out which he could not survive. Lack of credit in general was another typical feature of the poverty syndrome amongst farmers. No adequate system of agricultural credit was ever successfully established prior to 1941, forcing the farmer into the arms of the moneylender as a result, without any bargaining power of his own. Although Zimmerman and Andrews found that much borrowing was done on an interest-free basis from family or friends, recourse to the professional moneylender became increasingly frequent in the 1930s, and as always credit was only obtainable at rates more than double the offi-cially approved level. Farmers' ignorance of the market and the best way in which to obtain a loan compounded matters still further. Although tenancy on the whole had not assumed the dimensions of the social problem that it became in Burma, French Indo-China and the Philippines, it also bore with it the hall-marks of insecurity of tenure, high rents and the absence of incen-tive to improve the property.

One major factor in the generally worsening conditions in the countryside after 1920 was the failure of the government itself to take effective measures to come to the rescue of the farmer and to make the attempt to underpin his economy. The earliest positive government steps were not taken until the second decade of the twentieth century, and a serious, comprehensive approach was not adopted until after the Revolution of 1932. The first measures were directed towards building up a co-operative movement, which was initiated on very cautious, prudent and conservative lines. With backing from the Siam Commercial Bank, the first co-operatives were set up under the aegis of the Ministry of Commerce in 1916. By 1928 when the movement was placed on a firm legal basis, signalling an end of the experimental period, the original 60 societies had expanded to 219 groups with over 2,000 members. The movement continued to grow, still run on the most orthodox and careful lines, and expanded considerably faster after 1932. As a result, the societies which were established flourished and brought tangible benefits to their members—only three failed between 1928 and 1951—but their scope was far too limited to have a widespread impact on the general problem of rural poverty. Conditions of entry excluded the poorer farmers from membership, the movement was entirely dependent on central government funds, and those who did use the societies did so merely to advance their own private interests rather than to promote the spirit of joint effort. In fact in the 1930s the co-operative movement was one of the popular targets in the farmers' petitions of that decade—it was accused of red tape and corruption, and it was alleged, with some justification, that the co-operatives had strengthened the position of the middlemen rather than weakening it. A measure of the limited success of the movement is afforded by the fact that prior to 1941 only 2 per cent of the total sum of rural indebtedness was cared for by co-operatives. In the same period, however, government took steps to boost the movement. The Department was brought under the Ministry of Agriculture in 1932, which greatly increased the budgetary grants for co-operatives and made the movement part of its comprehensive plans to help the farmers.

After 1932, in fact, on a wave of nationalistic fervour, ambitious plans to deal with the problem of rural poverty from all angles were discussed and plans drawn up, but all really radical solutions were rejected. It was decided that a long-term approach should be taken and that in conjunction with a concerted effort in the rice trade to eliminate the middleman by providing a network of state agencies to take his place—plans which had actually been drafted before the Revolution—the port of Bangkok should be developed first and Thai participation facilitated by the extension of vocational and commercial training. However, the implementation of this scheme was dealt a lethal blow by the fall of Luang Pradit, following the rejection of his sweeping land reform programme in 1933.[59] The National Assembly followed this up later the same year by declaring that neither nationalization nor the employment of forced labour were to be used as tools of economic development. All schemes that smacked of socialism henceforth made little headway. In 1934 a Bill providing for the distribution of unoccupied lands amongst vagrants and paupers was crushingly defeated. In the same year the proposals of a committee to study rural indebtedness set up by the Ministry of Economic Affairs, which included *inter alia* the establishment of an agricultural bank to assume farmers' debts and to provide credit, were also rejected.

However, with the accession to power of Phibun Songgram in 1938 Thai politics took a national socialist tinge and a series of measures, which promised to bring about a real change in the situation, ensued. The first of these was the establishment of the Thai Rice Company in 1939, with the express purpose of striking at Chinese domination over the rice industry. The Chinese rice mills were taken over at once and the company also acquired a controlling interest in the co-operative movement. Direct purchasing from farmers was started later in the same year, state capital being used to procure good seed for planters, and in 1940 the first of a series of padi-buying stations was set up in the Rangsit area. Rentals on rice lands were reduced by one-fifth a few months later.

Nevertheless, despite all the sound and fury, the achievements of the new regime (i.e. between 1932 and 1941) in its campaign against rural poverty were limited. Much was spoken but too little was done. The co-operative movement failed to get off the ground. Although weights and measures had been officially standardized in the 1920s, these were still not in general use. Plans to establish storage silos throughout the countryside did not materialize. An attempt to set up state trading agencies at provincial level in the late 1930s failed, and the Thai Rice Company, despite its ample resources, did not succeed in affecting the general market. Many of the problems the government faced in its efforts were deep-seated ones, not liable to instant removal. The innate conservatism of the average farmer had to be overcome and his attitudes and values changed. Returns on farming investment were low.[60] The shortage of Thai agricultural experts hindered the implementation of measures to take over from the middleman and from time to time nationalist prejudice played its part, preventing the pragmatic use of foreign assistance when it could have been obtained. Above all, the pressures necessary to bring about radical reform were not yet strong enough.

Labour

Such pressures might have emanated from a new industrial proletariat brought into being by the opening up of the economy to world trade, but as we have seen, Thailand's economy remained basically agrarian and industrialization made little headway. In fact, reflecting the general division of the new economy between its modern, urban and commercialized sector on the one hand, and the traditional rural world of the farmer on the other, labour was similarly divided along ethnic lines. In any case, the element of a modern wage-earning working class was very small, probably no more than a bare 2 per cent of the total working population. The urban, commercial sector was overwhelmingly alien—predominantly Chinese, who were reckoned to make up from 70 to 90 per cent of all the non-agricultural labour in the country. The labour of the countryside was almost wholly Thai.

The roots of this ethnic division in labour which became a source of increasing concern to Thai leaders after 1932 lay both in cultural and economic circumstances. The Thai attachment to the land was deep, and after 1850 the land with the upsurge in the rice trade offered more and more opportunities and was in sufficient abundance for there to be no overcrowding. As the price of rice leapt up nearly tenfold in the second half of the century, there was no temptation to migrate to the city, and the overall trend within this period was for the Thais to leave more specialized occupations and go into farming. The whole process was encouraged by the generally slow development of the economy under the heavy hand of fiscal conservatism and the effects of the low tariff on imports imposed by foreign treaty, two factors which between them prevented the rise of rival attractions to rural labour. The Thai preoccupation with the land naturally created an intense scarcity in the new labour market which sprang up with the growth of trade and the commercialization of agriculture. This was easily and naturally met by the Chinese who, attracted by the (comparatively speaking) high wages induced by the shortage, quickly filled the new jobs created in building, transportation and processing. The Chinese also benefited from being exempt from the corvée and the poll tax, and even when these traditional imposts were abolished placing Thai and Chinese on an even footing in the labour market, it made no difference. The Chinese immigrant was still ready to work longer hours for little pay and under conditions intolerable to the Thai peasant; in any case Chinese skill and clannishness ensured that the wage labour market remained a virtual Chinese monopoly.

The continued Thai attachment to the land and the alien domination of wage labour were also intimately bound up with the steady emancipation of Thai society from the semi-feudal bonds of service and obligation in which it had been enmeshed for centuries. Indeed, without the establishment of individual freedom for the farmer, the new smallholder economy could never have arisen and the conversion of rice cultivation from a subsistence activity into a cash crop industry would never have occurred. This was realized both by King Mongkut who initiated the process of reform and by King Chulalongkorn who saw it through. The progressive abolition of all forms of slavery and the substitution of forced labour (corvée) by free labour represented a social revolution, brought about with a minimum of internal friction. It is to be numbered as one of the greatest achievements of the Chakri kings.

In 1855 slavery and the corvée were still basic institutions in Thai society, defining the relationships between people and government. There was a broad division between freemen and slaves, but all Thais were regarded as chattels of the king and subject to the corvée. Slavery probably had its origins in the ancient practice of enslaving prisoners-of-war and was nurtured by the chronic underpopulation of the country. By the nineteenth century the most common form of slavery was that of debt bondage. In the middle of the century, according to foreign observers, between one-fifth and one-half of the total population were debt slaves, many on a voluntary basis. The corvée, on the other hand, was imposed on all those aged over seventeen and required a specific time each year—by the 1850s this was three months—to be spent on public works, such as the construction or maintenance of roads, canals, fortresses and so on, at the behest of the local official. A variation on this theme was the institution of hereditary service, which was a fate reserved for craftsmen working for a patron, whose service was carried on by his sons. In the eyes of many observers, this institution was responsible for stunting the flowering of Thai craftsmanship, because it deterred Thai enterprise in applied skills and opened opportunities to the Chinese artisan.[61] Be that as it may, by the middle of the nineteenth century both slavery and the corvée were losing their *raison d'être*. The need to expand rice cultivation demanded greater social mobility. The farmer needed to be freed from his personal obligations to the state or to his patron and the wage labour market had a need for expansion. The growth of the export trade and the rise in land values undermined the basis of slavery as an economic institution and encouraged the landlord to count his wealth in other ways.[62]

The process of abolishing slavery and the corvée was undertaken in stages and cautiously. As early as 1805 the first steps to weakening the institution of slavery had been taken when the right to purchase redemption was extended to prisoners-of-war and to the children of slaves. The first positive measures, however, came in 1873 when King Chulalongkorn, as he came of age and assumed full kingship, issued his first decree promulgating the progressive abolition of slavery. No children born in his reign were to become slaves, and children who were already born into slavery were to be freed when they were twenty-one years old. This ensured that slavery would die a natural death. The next step to hasten its demise was the decree of 1897 which prohibited all traffic in slaves, including the right of the individual to sell himself into slavery. Finally in 1905 slavery as an institution was formally abolished. There was a time lag between the promulgation and complete implementation of the new law, particularly in the remoter regions of the north, but by 1910 the process was virtually complete. The ending of the corvée was also carried out by stages. King Mongkut paved the way by encouraging the use of hired labour on public works such as canal construction. For a long time, however, the general scarcity of labour (outside agriculture), quite apart from the opposition of powerful patrons, prevented further measures from being taken. But at the end of the century a series of Acts replaced all forced labour and other forms of personal obligation to the state with a capitation tax with provision for various exemptions. The new legislation also covered conditions for the use of convict labour and for military conscription.

The social consequences of these reforms were profound. They did not result in a cheapening of wage labour, in fact the opposite, but they confirmed the smallholder revolution. The average Thai farmer, freed from his traditional obligations, could turn to securing for his family and himself enough land for them to work for their own profit. The size of such holdings was limited by the absence of hired labour. At the same time, as farming became more individualistic the old customs of communal planting and harvesting were discontinued, and with the growing influx of seasonal workers coming from the north, hired labour for such occasions took their place. These trends took time to appear but they had become evident on the Central Plain by the 1900s. By the 1930s the spread of commercialized agriculture and the high value of land made the use of hired labour essential, and its prevalence was shown by the Zimmerman and Andrews' Reports. Such labour was invariably Thai, and agricultural labour was the one field in which the Thais dominated. It was unskilled labour, and labouring conditions were far worse than those in other occupations. But the labour of the fields was one of the traditional kinds and could not be compared with the new types of wage labour to be found in Bangkok and other towns. The continued Thai preference for the land placed such labour at a premium, and for the greater part of the period between 1850 and 1940 wage labour was chronically scarce.[63] The result was to make labour costs higher than anywhere else in the East.

This, however, did not mean that actual working conditions were any better than elsewhere. Even in the south where wages were highest, the Chinese mining coolie was exploited as mercilessly by his employer as were his counterparts in Malaya. The death-rate was high and the owner could usually recoup his expenditure from his monopoly over provisions and the supply of opium sold to his workers. But skilled workers were better off. The coming of the Great Depression brought matters to a head. The Thai sector was able to absorb the blow because of the flexibility of labour use in the fields, while the monasteries could take in a fair number of the unemployed; but unskilled labourers in other fields and the small but growing class of white-collar workers were badly hit. Even so, agricultural wages dropped by over two-thirds, and in the towns millers took the opportunity to cancel their workers' bonuses without making compensatory differences to the prices they paid to the farmers. For the first time unemployment represented a national problem.[64]

Up till this point, labour as such had not been a problem at all, and government had not undertaken any comprehensive measures to cater for labour's needs. Organized labour was small and almost wholly limited to the Chinese who managed their own affairs. The Depression and the new liberty which followed the Revolution of 1932 created a different situation. During the next four years there was considerable labour unrest, centred on Bangkok but by no means confined to the capital. The early strikes were confined to specific industries and involved distinct ethnic groups. By 1934 the issues were much broader. The strike by the mill workers in 1934 demanding a restoration of their bonuses and the railway strike of the same year were closely linked and involved both Thais and Chinese. The net outcome was to make the government more aware of the alien domination of wage labour and to take steps to improve the Thai position. Prior to this, government intervention in labour matters had been limited to individual crises. In 1913 what may be described as the earliest labour welfare regulations were drafted for Bangkok's rickshaw pullers, the first oblique blow at the Chinese.[65] Government relief measures were also mounted to cope with the rice famine of 1917. An attempt to establish a labour exchange in 1929 to deal with the growing unemployment amongst the educated middle-classes caused by King Prajadhipok's economies was a failure. The new regime set up labour bureaux at the end of 1932, partly to combat the activities of unscrupulous private agencies, although without much better results. In the same year a basic minimum wage was laid down for government employees, but not for manual labour who rejected the government's offer. These stop-gap measures were followed

by a more concerted effort to raise labour conditions up to international standards, and during the course of the rest of the decade a whole series of new
Bills were placed before the National Assembly, including laws to fix minimum wages, maximum working hours, sickness and accident benefits, and
health safeguards. However, none of these measures was passed, and it was
clear that the country's representatives were not interested in legislating
benefits for what was a predominantly alien labour force.[66]

Health

Nationalist sentiment was also a significant factor in the generally low standards and slow progress in the field of health. The kingdom's medical services
on the eve of the Japanese War were still in a skeleton stage, concentrated on
Bangkok and the few large towns, while the general health situation was
marked by appalling sanitation, a high infantile mortality rate and rampant
disease. Outside of the capital there were barely thirty-five hospitals scattered
throughout the provinces, mostly averaging fifty beds apiece, with the result
that hardly 5 per cent of the total population was within range of government medical treatment, while in 1941 the number of qualified doctors per
head of population was 1 in 10,000. Primitive unhygienic habits, conditioned
by a fatalistic belief in *karma*, made public sanitation a nightmare. In the
klongs of Bangkok flourished 'a bouillon of microbe cultures that would
make even a bacteriologist pale',[67] and the great, picturesque but highly in-
salubrious water pitchers that were to be found in every household helped
to perpetuate disease in the countryside. In 1938 over 46,000 babies died at
birth or within the first twelve months, setting an incidence of infant mortality which was amongst the highest in the region. In these conditions malaria, tuberculosis and dysentery ravaged unchecked amongst the people,
while the usual gamut of other diseases was also much in evidence.

As Jacoby has suggested, these conditions, perhaps, were the price that
Thailand had to pay for retaining its sovereignty and escaping colonial domination. Improvement of public sanitation and health (at least in the twentieth
century) was an integral part of colonial policy, at the very least as an act of
enlightened self-interest to guarantee adequate returns on investment made.
In Thailand, on the other hand, government was slow on the uptake in all
fields. The first state hospital was established only in 1888. Bangkok did not
possess a modern water supply until 1914. A Department of Public Health
was not set up until 1918 and only acquired legal powers after 1932. Government sanitary measures were for years totally ineffective and it was not
until the 1930s that a comprehensive programme to establish hospitals and
health centres in every province and to reorganize the existing sanitary
boards was undertaken. There were no trained female nurses prior to 1925—
a result of prejudice—the first clinic for venereal disease was set up in Bangkok a decade later, only vaccination against smallpox was made compulsory
for want of funds, and up till 1943 the treatment of leprosy was left entirely
in private hands. The first sanitary boards were set up in 1909 but were hopelessly understaffed, implemented ineffective and 'cheap half measures', had all
their priorities wrong, and were a monument to official corruption. The

situation was considerably improved after 1932 when for the first time their status and functions having been defined by legislation, the boards were placed under newly created municipalities with legal power and the long projected Sanitary Code was finally implemented.

The kingdom's public health services emerged slowly from *ad hoc* arrangements made towards the end of the nineteenth century. Before King Chulalongkorn founded the first public hospital in 1888, government assistance had been limited to times of epidemic when temporary hospitals were put up, as occurred for the last time in 1882. In the next decade Bangkok saw the beginnings of public sanitation when an American private practitioner in the city was asked to supervise health conditions. This was followed by the first Public Health Law passed in 1897, which provided for the appointment of a Medical Health Officer and City Engineer. This appointment and the establishment of a maritime quarantine station together with a medical depot and vaccine laboratory in 1901 marked the nucleus of the public health service, which up till 1918 remained incorporated in the medical department of the Ministry of the Interior. The Health Department primarily concerned itself with the combating of epidemics, health conditions in state prisons and with the supervision of the handful of public hospitals in existence. It was responsible for the Medical Law of 1914-15 which catered for the control of contagious diseases. However, up till 1932 the Health Department's efforts seemed to be limited mainly to poster campaigns, and it was only in the last few years of the 1930s that serious legislation was passed to regulate and to extend the medical services of the country. Amongst the measures taken during this period were the laws of 1937 that outlined the powers of the Medical Council and standardized the regulations for the medical profession. The first students from the Medical School of Bangkok, established by King Chulalongkorn in 1889, had graduated in 1893 and the School steadily expanded, amalgamating with the Chulalongkorn University in 1917 and being completely reorganized with aid from the Rockefeller Foundation in 1923. Five years later it issued its first medical degrees. Up till this point, the Bangkok School had been seriously handicapped by inadequacies of equipment, facilities and teaching staff; now things improved, the quality and the standard were raised, but with these also the cost. In the early 1930s as the Great Depression bit deeper into the economy, voices of criticism were raised against the expense of training, and led by Zimmerman it was argued that in line with the needs of a poor country 'junior doctors' with lower qualifications should also be trained. The ensuing controversy which involved the Medical School itself became a political issue and ended up in 1935 with the government adopting Zimmerman's scheme on a modified basis.[68]

In fact the general health services of the kingdom were so limited prior to 1941 that they appeared to supplement the efforts of private organizations rather than vice versa. Of that small proportion of the population to whom modern medical services were available at all, three-fifths were provided by missionary societies, the Red Cross and other private institutions. In 1941 there were eleven mission stations with a total of forty-three doctors in operation, offering treatment free or for a nominal charge. The Christian missions played the largest role and indeed had been the first in the field in introducing Western medicine into Thailand. The earliest known Western hospital was set up by a group of Christian missionaries in 1669 and the first medical missionary to arrive in the kingdom was a Jesuit father in 1676. It was Christian missionaries who first introduced vaccination, the application of surgery, the use of anaesthetics, blood transfusion, quinine and the first literature on Western medicine in Thai. They founded the first medical training school in the kingdom, took the first steps to ensure proper drug control and to take scientific care of lepers. Most of this was achieved by the wave of Protestant Christian missionaries who worked in Thailand in the nineteenth century, and it was the adoption of vaccination by the court of King Rama III (Nan Klao) in the 1830s which marked the first breakthrough against Thai prejudice and scepticism. Their overall contribution was impressive. The treatment of leprosy was their monopoly. The Medical School of Bangkok owed its fame and success in large measure to the support of the Rockefeller Foundation. The missionaries carried the main burden of combating disease and death in the countryside.[69] But for all that, their impact and that of Western medicine as a whole on Thai society was very limited. Thai medical lore was deeply ingrained in the beliefs of the people, and if some of its practices appeared exotic to Western notions, it was also on occasion effective. Despite the spectacular results sometimes achieved by missionary doctors, the Thais themselves remained unconvinced. Although the medicine of the missionaries checked the smallpox epidemic of 1772, the king contented himself with dispatching gifts to the Roman Catholic Archbishop but did not adopt Western remedies. There were similar instances in the Chakri court in the nineteenth century. The real problem was that the resources of the missionaries themselves were limited, and the numbers who benefited from Western techniques were far too few to make any substantial impression on Thai society as a whole.

As was the case throughout South-East Asia, disease played a decisive role in Thai history. Malaria, which was a probable factor in the decline of the Khmer empire of Angkor, helped to prevent the over-population of the kingdom. Epidemics which appeared with monotonous frequency carrying away thousands to their death also served to frustrate an early Chinese invasion from Nan Chao, turned the Burmese back from Ayuthia and caused the abandonment of at least two royal capitals. The prevalence and unpredictability of disease helped engender that fatalistic approach which rendered the Thais (and most other South-East Asian peoples) careless of steps to prevent it.

The greatest killer was malaria which destroyed an average of 40,000 persons a year, nearly one-third of whom were children under four, and in the north where its incidence was highest, it struck at the rate of one labourer each week. Up till 1949 preventive measures were limited to the distribution of drugs and the spraying of ditches and ponds on a spasmodic basis. The ineffectiveness of such measures was pointed out in the Anigstein Report of 1931, but either its recommendations lay beyond the means of the country to implement or its implementation lay too low amongst the priorities of the country's rulers for any action to be taken upon it.[70] In consequence the problem of malaria remained completely unsolved on the eve of the Japanese War. The absence of purified water and proper sewage disposal accounted for the very high level of intestinal diseases, amongst which diarrhoea and dysentery ranked as the most dangerous. Tuberculosis, linked to slum housing, was rife in Bangkok and other urban centres but its treatment was left entirely in the hands of private or voluntary agencies. Steps against yaws, particularly prevalent and serious in the south and north-east, consisted of the distribution 'of a small amount of arsenicals by a few rural clinics'. Plague which became endemic in Bangkok after 1905, spreading from there to other centres, remained unchecked in the face of inadequate health measures, as was also the case with hookworm. Despite considerable efforts by missionary doctors, probably only 4 per cent of all the lepers in the country were receiving treatment in 1941. The only major diseases which were effectively dealt with prior to that date were beri-beri, cholera and smallpox.

In all, compared with almost every other country in the region, Thailand's progress in combating disease and in improving public health prior to 1941 was very limited. Yet compared to what had gone before and in view of the chronic shortage of funds for the purpose in hand, what was achieved was considerable enough.

Social welfare
By Western or Western colonial standards, in the field of social welfare prior to 1941 Thailand was also found wanting. It was not until 1940 that a Department of Social Welfare was established, so that it can be said that in Thailand before the Japanese War social welfare services run by the state did not exist.

But neither did the problems. Throughout the provinces, society was secure within the traditional folds of the family and the temple. The great majority of the sick, maimed, aged or unemployed were taken over by their own families, and in times of local distress communal needs were met by the temple. Only in Bangkok was the traditional system inoperable. The capital, always disproportionately large, had swollen even further as it became the focal point of all economic development in the kingdom. Its population mounted, its slums multiplied and crime festered. Government steps to deal with these new social problems were as usual totally inadequate, but Bangkok was not typical of the country, and in the country as a whole no pressing need was felt. The concept of a state system of social welfare was still foreign to most Thai minds.

Much of what would have been considered baneful in the West passed as ordinary facets of human society in Thailand. Drinking, gambling, prostitution and the consumption of opium were not regarded as inherent social evils, but as tendencies which needed to be controlled and exploited to the public benefit. The main characteristic of official policy towards these human foibles was to tax them for the benefit of the state and for the curbing of excess. In 1941 the sale of liquor, the operating of brothels and the smoking of opium were all controlled under public licence, which was in fact a variation of the older device of farming them as tax monopolies to the highest bidder. State lotteries to capitalize on the gambling instinct were first started under King Mongkut, but were established more successfully by King Chulalongkorn and rose to become an important source of state revenue. Stricter controls over gambling were introduced after 1918 and the original monopolies and state-sponsored lotteries brought to an end, but in 1925 a new national lottery was instituted. The national lottery system underwent several vicissitudes in the 1920s and 1930s but survives to the present day. There was further legislation against gambling in the 1930s, most of it quite ineffective. Prostitution had always flourished. It tended to increase in the twentieth century as the result of legislation which reduced the traditional authority of parents over their children, and it became a lucrative investment for businessmen and even of government officials in Bangkok and provincial centres. But at the same time, steps were taken to reduce the traffic in women, particularly after 1928.

Opium smoking was a different kind of problem, and one which was viewed by Thai officialdom with some concern. Its spread in Thailand seems to have been connected with the Chinese in the early part of the nineteenth century, and after the failure of various attempts at its suppression it was finally made a state monopoly under King Rama III. King Mongkut likewise found that he could not avoid conceding the opium farm to the Chinese but deterred Thais from becoming addicts by fining them, forcing them to wear the Chinese queue and threatening them with execution. In fact, opium smoking remained primarily a Chinese addiction, but it created problems because of its international ramifications. King Rama III himself had got involved in a serious diplomatic crisis as a result of seizing opium-bearing vessels from the Straits. In the twentieth century, the problem was how to comply with the new international pressures for the suppression of the traffic. By this time the opium monopoly had become an important source of state revenue[71] as well as an ever more lucrative source for smuggling. Thailand participated in the initial International Opium Conference held at Shanghai in 1909, and was associated with all subsequent international conferences and agreements on the subject. But as international action effectively dried up the traditional sources of opium imports, new sources started to develop in neighbouring Burma and in the mountain areas of the northern provinces of Thailand itself. Efforts to check smuggling, originally hampered by the clauses of the Bowring-type treaties of the nineteenth century, were now hindered by the difficulties involved in checking supplies coming from overland or from territory occupied by remote mountain peoples, whose hostility Bangkok was not prepared to provoke. In the meantime, internal legislation tightened the controls over opium addicts in the country, but the problem as a whole still remained unresolved in 1941.[72]

Apart from this, various welfare organizations, mostly associated with Christian missions or with traditional Chinese welfare societies, catered for the comparatively few waifs and strays who felt outside the orbit of Thai social welfare.

The low standards or almost complete absence of a state system of social welfare could be interpreted, as Jacoby certainly would, as another indication of the price that Thailand had to pay for escaping from colonial tutelage. The calm cohesion of Thai society was an equally impressive reminder of the benefits of retaining one's sovereignty intact.

[1]Erich H. Jacoby, *Agrarian Unrest in Southeast Asia*, Asia Publishing House, Bombay, 1961. See in particular p. 55.

[2]See James C. Ingram, *Economic Change in Thailand: 1850–1970*, Oxford University Press, Kuala Lumpur, 1971, p. 173. The proposal to establish a Central Bank for Thailand was first raised in 1890 and in 1899 a consortium of Western bankers led by the Danes had reportedly obtained the concession to set up a national bank. This did not materialize. In 1915 a British expert was brought to Bangkok to study the project, even though the Financial Adviser of the hour (a Briton, Williamson) remained strongly opposed. The Central Bank was still a project on paper in 1932 when after the Revolution it became a hotly debated issue. Various proposals were put forward, then rejected; finally in 1942 the Bank of Thailand was established, taking over from the Thai National Banking Bureau set up under special legislation two years previously.

[3]Sir John Bowring, quoted by D.G.E. Hall, *History of South-East Asia*, Macmillan & Sons, London, 1967, p. 633.

[4]Virginia Thompson, *Thailand: The New Siam*, Paragon Book Reprint Corporation, New York, 1967, p. 496.

[5]The British, in particular, exploited the financial problems of the Thai government as a result of its efforts to keep the railways in Thai hands, in the process gaining an ascendancy over railway development, with the British Financial Adviser of the day playing a key role.

[6]The adoption of diesel engines was a major boon to Thai railways for diesel was far more economical and cut down the travelling time between Singapore and Chiengmai by five hours. Wood fuel took up a lot of storage space, was expensive in Bangkok, and the demand for it threatened to exhaust the kingdom's forest reserves.

[7]Nijhoff argued that the estimated 20 million baht which would be needed to carry through the project would pay handsome dividends and produce direct benefits in the form of compulsory pilotage and wharf charges.

[8]Between 1855 and 1945 rice consistently accounted for 60 to 70 per cent of total exports but contributed a mere 3 per cent to total world production. Burma was the world's largest rice exporter, her total output being greater than that of Thailand and French Indo-China combined.

[9]Ingram (op. cit., pp. 8–9) arrived at this figure for the area under rice in the 1850s by assuming that in view of the few changes in farming techniques or acreage per capita, productivity was roughly the same in the mid-nineteenth century as it was in the 1920s, the period whose statistics he took as the basis for his calculations.

[10]Under Bowring's Treaty, the exportation of rice was subject to the proviso that this would not be permitted 'wherever a scarcity may be apprehended'. In practice the Chakri kings never invoked this clause.

[11]The opening of the Suez Canal as a factor stimulating the Thai rice export trade is open to debate; despite the claims made for the Canal's impact by Thompson, Furnivall and others, the actual flow of rice to Europe does not seem to have increased appreciably after 1869. As Ingram (op. cit., p. 42) suggests, a possible side effect of the opening of the Canal may have been to divert Burmese rice from local markets to the West, thereby giving Thai rice fresh openings in the region. However, this point has not yet been proven either.

[12]However, this encouragement was limited to questions of land tenure. In terms of technical assistance, the government's record was very poor. Van der Heide's schemes were set aside; if they had been implemented, the disastrous crop failure of 1919–20, which alone cost the country more than the entire expenditure required for the irriga-

tion works, might have been avoided. Little or nothing was done to improve farming techniques, seed selection, to study soils and crops, to educate farmers about the market or market conditions.

¹³As was general throughout the region, Thai kings were regarded as the absolute proprietors of the land, a right which was extremely rarely exercised. In practice the abundance of land available made it possible for every freeman to acquire as much land as he and his family could cultivate but land grants in general were governed by the *sakdina* system, established in the days of King Trailok, which determined the amount of land a man could own according to his position. The relationship between freeman and patron by which the former had to perform services for the latter had no basic connexion with the land system since these were on a personal basis and not a territorial one. In the process of time, certain families who had received their first lands as gifts of the monarch for services rendered, acquired great estates ranging from 550 acres up to 250,000 acres.

¹⁴By Bowring's Treaty, land rates for British subjects occupying land could not be changed; in consequence all land rates remained static, as the government was not prepared to tax its own subjects higher than it did foreigners. However, at the turn of the century Britain modified this proviso so that land rates for British subjects should not exceed those prevalent for similar lands in Lower Burma. As a result, in 1905, the Thai land tax was completely revised.

¹⁵The two Rural Economic Surveys of Thailand serve as invaluable sources of information regarding the economic and social condition of the country at the period they were made. The first was carried out by Carl C. Zimmerman in 1930–1 and the second by James M. Andrews in 1934–5.

¹⁶The earliest irrigation works were in the north, as is evidenced in the ruins at Sawankhalok and Sukhothai. In the north where the land was hilly and floods too shortlived, irrigation was essential. Irrigation works consisted of primitive water courses and bamboo weirs built on a co-operative basis but usually regarded as the property of the local chief. Government on occasion took over and improved the weirs.

¹⁷Ingram, op. cit., p. 82.

¹⁸Padi was traditionally sold by the basket, its size varying from village to village and usually reached the mill in individual boatloads of 20 tons or less; only in the north-east was the harvested rice sold by weight.

¹⁹e.g. the Larut Wars of the 1860s involving the Ghee Hin and Hai San factions were in effect an extension of the feud which started in Phuket (the Malay Ujong Salang) in 1859. Refer to Volume I, note 28, p. 274 and p. 300.

²⁰In the reign of Phra Narai (1657–88) the French established a factory at Phuket and actually seized control of the port for a short period during the Phaulkon episode (refer to Volume I, p. 503). Mining activity was brought to a low by the troubles surrounding the downfall of the Ayuthia monarchy to the Burmese and by the resurgence of Malay power during the second half of the eighteenth century.

²¹A classic example of this is provided by the case of Hsu Szu-chang/Kaw Su-chiang, a Chang-chou Hokkien who rose to become appointed Phya of Ranong during the reign of Rama III (Nang Klao, 1824–51). For details of his background and career, see G. William Skinner, *Chinese Society in Thailand: An Analytical History*, Cornell University Press, New York, 1957, p. 151.

²²The two main issues debated were the proposal to raise royalties, which was hotly contested by the mining interests, and the question of new concessions. The Assembly decided that in future (i.e. from 1932 onwards) poor agriculturalists would be permitted to pan tin for lower fees and fewer formalities in the off-harvest season.

²³The teak from the northern forests was floated either down the Menam Chao Phaya to Bangkok or down the Salween to Martaban and Moulmein; the volume of teak via the Salween was sometimes as great as that down the Menam Chao Phaya but the value of the Bangkok exports was greater, being milled and processed there.

²⁴See Thompson, op. cit., p. 474. At this period Bangkok's writ in the north was still limited by the feudal nature of its authority over the northern chiefs, including the

Chao Phaya of Chiengmai, and it was not until the central government assumed direct control in the 1890s that the situation altered.

[25]In any case there was a time lag of nine months between the cutting and floating of a particular consignment of timber and the actual demand and price conditions.

[26]Statistics on the rubber industry prior to 1941 are inadequate as a result of loose government control over the industry and the large number of smallholders.

[27]For further details regarding Thailand's participation in the rubber restriction scheme, see Thompson, op. cit., pp. 479–83.

[28]Three kinds of sugar are produced in Thailand: coconut, palmyra and cane. Crude sugar from the palmyra palm accounted for one-quarter of total sugar production while coconut and palmyra sugar between them, important for the domestic economy, equalled cane in terms of production.

[29]The high value of salt per unit of weight made it an important article of trade in the nineteenth century and it still served as a medium of exchange on the Korat Plateau in the 1920s.

[30]British-American Tobacco was incorporated in the Straits Settlements and owed its rise to the successful ousting of local tobacco in favour of imported cigars and cigarettes.

[31]Lac was a well-known product of Thailand as much as it was of Burma, Cambodia or Vietnam and played an important role in the local economy. According to the Florentine traveller, Giovanni di Nicola, the industry was well established in the seventeenth century and was centred on Ayuthia and Tenasserim (then under Thai control). Lac lost a great deal of its commercial value with the introduction of aniline dyes by the Germans after the Great War, since it too had been used as a dye, but new uses for it were found in international commerce in the manufacture of gramophone records, sealing wax and insulating materials. However, although output doubled between 1911 and 1926, the Thai product was less favoured by foreign buyers than its Burmese or Indo-Chinese competitors because of its inferior quality and relative scarcity.

[32]C.A. Fisher, *South-East Asia: A Social, Economic and Political Geography*, Macmillan, London, 1964, p. 504.

[33]In trying to define 'Chinese' in the context of Thailand, great care has to be exercised. Interpreted ethnically or by ancestry, Chinese may refer to anyone who has at least one parent of Chinese blood; it may be restricted to Chinese born in China as opposed to those born in Thailand itself—the latter being considered Thai nationals—it may apply to Sino-Thais (*lukchin*). The task of ascertaining the number of Chinese in the country at any given period is not made lighter by the absence or unreliability of official statistics. There were three nation-wide censuses held between 1900 and 1941 (i.e. 1919, 1929 and 1937) but all were marred by inexperienced personnel, improper techniques and, as far as the Chinese community itself was concerned, a reluctance to be counted in the face of the growing strength of Thai nationalism. Official statistics of Chinese entering and leaving the country are also confusing since they fail to distinguish between immigrants and those in transit and also do not take into account illegal immigration. Prior to the 1880s when the bulk of immigrants started to arrive on the decks of Western steamers, one has to rely on the figures and estimates given by individual observers which are generally highly subjective and impressionistic. However Coughlin (*Double Identity: The Chinese in Modern Thailand*, Hong Kong University Press, 1960, pp. 13–14), Skinner (op. cit., pp. 58–9) and Ingram (op. cit., p. 7 and p. 211) have managed to put the figures into perspective.

[34]However, the credit-ticket system, so familiar in the Straits Settlements, also flourished in Thailand and gave rise to the usual abuses. For descriptions of the system in practice, see Skinner, op. cit., pp. 54–8. It continued to flourish, even after being officially prohibited in 1888 but the worst abuses associated with it mostly disappeared.

[35]See Skinner, op. cit., pp. 52–3 for more telling quotes about these conditions.

[36]Victor Purcell, *The Chinese in South-East Asia*, Oxford University Press, London, 1965, p. 131.

[37]This was clearly illustrated by the spread of Teochew and Hakka groups into areas of long-established Hokkien and Cantonese dominance following the railway lines and

the general imposition of the Bangkok pattern of Chinese speech-groups on the Chinese community in Thailand as a whole with the development of the railway system.

[38]Chinese tradition speaks of Lin Tao-ch'ien, 'one of the most notorious sea-pirates and bandits in Kwangtung and Fukien', fleeing his homeland and conquering Patani, which is partially corroborated by the Malay Patani Annals which named Lin as a Hokkien arsenal foreman who settled down in Patani and married a Malay. According to Dutch and English observers in the early seventeenth century, the Chinese at Patani outnumbered the local Malay population. There was also a flourishing Chinese colony at Nakhorn Sri Thammarat at this period.

[39]Landon, quoted by Purcell, op. cit., p. 128.

[40]For a discussion on this point, see Skinner, op. cit., pp. 97–8.

[41]The Chinese and Westerners were of course bitter rivals and often in direct competition with one another. The Chinese soon ousted the Westerners from rice-milling, quickly acquiring the necessary technical know-how to run modern mills and to run them at half the cost of a Western enterprise. But the unassailable position they had enjoyed in Thai society before Bowring's Treaty was radically altered after 1855, although they survived and continued to prosper. The first Western victory was in shipping; the steamship proved unbeatable and gave the Westerners their dominating stake in the import-export trade. But as at Singapore, Western merchants found the Chinese middleman indispensable in their efforts to gain access to the Thai domestic market, while the Chinese made full use of the expansion in trade and the contacts with the world market that the Westerners brought with them.

[42]Farms for gambling and alcohol had existed during the Ayuthia period but the system was truly developed during the reign of Rama III (Nang Klao, 1824–51), when a wide range of items, mostly goods for export, were included. In the early 1890s the opium and gambling farms realized two-fifths of the national revenue.

[43]Quoted by Skinner, op. cit., pp. 159–60.

[44]The king wrote articles in the Thai press under the pseudonym of 'Asavabahu' (Pegasus), which in 1914 were reprinted as a pamphlet entitled 'The Jews of the East'.

[45]The anti-Chinese argument, as summarized by Skinner, was that they were unassimilable, opportunistic, lacking in civil consciousness, materialistic and parasitical. Skinner also points out (op. cit., p. 244) that many of the most ardent anti-Chinese nationalists of the 1930s were themselves of part Chinese extraction, including the most radical of them all, Luang Pradit Manutham (Pridi Phanomyong) whose father was a Teochew. In fact, nearly half (21 out of 47) of the members of the Thai Senate in 1934 had Chinese blood.

[46]Modern Chinese nationalsim made its way into Thailand in the 1900s via Singapore, when Shen Liang-fang, one of Singapore's pioneer Chinese nationalists, opened a branch of his firm in Bangkok, partly with an eye on canvassing nationalist support. In 1906 the first Chinese nationalist newspaper appeared in Bangkok and the next year Sun Yat-sen sent one of his most trusted lieutenants there to organize a branch of the revolutionary anti-Manchu T'ung Meng Hui. In 1908 Sun himself arrived in Thailand but as a result of British pressure his stay was a short one. Between 1908 and 1911 nationalist cells were founded amongst the Chinese throughout the country and the first Chinese schools were opened in Bangkok.

[47]However, the most serious clash between the Chinese and the Thai authorities took place in Betong in the extreme south in 1933 over a misunderstanding between the local Chinese and the police which led to bloodshed. The general official attitude was further conditioned by Thailand's dependence on British and Japanese goodwill, both of whom demonstrated anti-Chinese poses, though for different reasons.

[48]The 1913 law proclaimed that 'every person born to a Thai father on Thai or foreign territory' was Thai, as well as all those born in Thailand. Naturalization was open to adult residents of at least 5 years, of good character and conduct.

[49]In fact these Acts probably made little difference to the inflow of migrants which was controlled primarily by economic factors. Although, for instance, the 1927–8 Act empowered the Minister to restrict immigration, no attempt to do so was made until

1947. Conditions regarding literacy, character, record or assets were either ineffective or not applied. The imposition of fees under the Immigration Amendment Act of 1931–2 had some impact, causing an increase in the pace of illegal immigration. Indeed Bangkok's basic motive may well have been to increase its sources of revenue than actually to discourage immigration, particularly in view of the fact that the liberal naturalization terms were kept in force.

[50] The *Ratha Niyon* or Fifth Cultural Mandate of the State was enunciated by Phibun Songgram and encouraged the people to eat Thai, buy Thai, dress Thai, support Thai enterprise and behave honestly in business.

[51] The resurgent secret societies, in particular, exploited the situation by engaging in smuggling, protection and extortion rackets and illegal money-making schemes.

[52] Broadly speaking, the hill peoples fell into two categories—primitive Mongoloid elements and later Tibeto-Burma hill tribes. There were also the Semang of the peninsular south, who had some links with some of the aborigines of the Malayan jungles, and the Katong Luang, an isolated folk living in small family groups in the mountains of the north-east, the south and the Korat Plateau.

[53] Apart from the Malays proper of the south, there were also other groups of Thai Muslims scattered around the country, notably at Chantabun, Ayuthia and Bangkok, probably descendants of Malay prisoners-of-war.

[54] The main Thai sub-groups, which today are rapidly losing their separate identities, were the Central Thai (the most numerous)—the Thai Lao or Yuan—the Thao Korat, and the Thai/Lao of the north-east. The Thao Korat were the descendants of the Thai soldiers who conquered the region from the Khmer in the fourteenth century. The Lao/Thai of the north-east were further subdivided into six dialect groups. Another rather obscure group were the Phu Thai in the eastern part of the north-east.

[55] Zimmerman's estimate was the highest. Andrews, in his 1934 Report, put it at 100 million baht, while the Thai newspaper *Sri Kung* estimated the total to be around 80 to 90 million baht.

[56] However, in the north there was a problem of land fragmentation, springing from a semi-feudal system of land tenure.

[57] In 1928, on the eve of the Great Depression, 33 per cent of the people on the Central Plain were landless, but many of them were merchants and shop-keepers as well as labourers.

[58] According to Andrews, the Chinese were more interested in business than in money-lending and that when they did lend, it was on a businesslike basis and below the official maxima. Thai moneylenders were more numerous and their demands higher.

[59] The proposed land reform involved the purchasing and redistribution of the land within the context of a planned economy which would be controlled by the state. This programme, with its communistic overtones, was too much for the far stronger rightist elements amongst the oligarchs who now ruled Thailand, and led to Pradit's downfall.

[60] Farming never yielded more than a 2 per cent return on capital invested, a consequence of poor techniques and inefficient and uneconomic organization. Zimmerman was able to show in his Report that expenditure on agricultural costs generally approximated cash incomes.

[61] Though this view is commonly held, it might be exaggerated. In the 1850s there was evidence of many talented craftsmen of high calibre to be found throughout the kingdom, of whom a fair proportion were Chinese.

[62] It has been suggested that the abolition of slavery was possible because of the rise in land values, but whether this was a motivating factor or not has yet to be proven.

[63] In the 1930s the labour shortage became acute as a result of the new restrictions on immigration, particularly in the south where, on occasion, rubber tapping was held up by the lack of ready labour available. In 1936 Chinese mineowners unsuccessfully petitioned for special permission to import 3,000 Chinese coolies who would be exempted from the normal immigration tax; an attempt to recruit Lao labour for the southern rubber holdings only met with partial success.

[64]The rising unemployment amongst the educated middle-classes, aggravated by King Prajadhipok's economies, was a major factor in the Revolution of 1932.

[65]The 1913 regulations required all rickshaw pullers to be licensed, for which they had to pay a small fee, be physically fit, aged between 18 and 40, and conversant with Thai.

[66]The new nationalist leaders of the 1930s were confronted by a conflict of interest between their socialist leanings and their commitment to Thai nationalism. The dilemma was brought into the forefront by the rise of Chinese-dominated trade unions demanding better working conditions. Ninety per cent of the labour force in the country was alien. Other indigenous but non-Thai groups tended to hold specialized occupations with their own labour peculiarities. In the north, for example, the Khamus formed the backbone of the traditional working force in the teak forests, etc., that is, usually seasonal labourers in liege to a foreman who negotiated their contracts to his enormous benefit and to the minimum advantage of the tribesmen themselves.

[67]See Thompson, op. cit., p. 698.

[68]Zimmerman was opposed by Ellis, the Director of the Medical School of Bangkok, who argued that the proposed scheme for 'junior doctors' was impracticable and undesirable since it would endanger existing standards. By way of implementing Zimmerman's scheme, a school of junior doctors was opened at Chiengmai in 1935, offering a six-month course. 'Graduates' of the course could later continue their training at Chulalongkorn University.

[69]However, even medicine was susceptible to international colonial rivalries, although this field eventually became recognized as a specifically American preserve, just as Law belonged to the French and Finance to the British.

[70]Dr. Anigstein was a League of Nations expert requested by the Thai government in 1930 to go into the mosquito problem. He recommended the resettlement of foothill villages in uncultivated areas on the plains, the reorganization of quinine distribution, the creation of a body of sanitary inspectors and the widespread use of mosquito nets.

[71]In 1917 opium yielded a quarter of the returns of the national revenues and though steadily decreasing after that date was still providing some 10 million baht a year in the late 1930s.

[72]Despite the Opium Act of 1934 with its much stricter provisions, there was little public co-operation and not a little corruption. Having revealed a scandal involving high government officials in this connexion in 1935, the British Financial Adviser, James Baxter, resigned in protest.

Books and articles for further reading

BOOKS

Blanchard, Wendell (ed.), *Thailand; its people, its society, its culture*, HRAF Press, New Haven, Conn., 1966.

Cady, John F., *Thailand, Burma, Laos and Cambodia*, Prentice-Hall Inc., New Jersey, 1966.

Coughlin, Richard J., *Double Identity: The Chinese in Modern Thailand*, Hong Kong University Press, 1960.

Fisher, C.A., *South-East Asia: A Social, Economic and Political Geography*, Methuen, London, 1964.

Ingram, James C., *Economic Change in Thailand, 1850–1970*, Oxford University Press, Kuala Lumpur, 1971.

Jacoby, Erich H., *Agrarian Unrest in South-East Asia*, Asia Publishing House, Bombay, 1961.

Purcell, Victor, *The Chinese in South-East Asia*, Oxford University Press, London, 1965.

Skinner, G. William, *Chinese Society in Thailand: An Analytical History*, Cornell University Press, New York, 1957.

Steinberg, David Joel (ed.), *In Search of South-East Asia: A Modern History*, Oxford University Press, Kuala Lumpur, 1971.

Thompson, Virginia, *Thailand: the New Siam*, Paragon Book Reprint Corp., New York, 1967.

ARTICLES

Evers, Hans-Dieters, 'Social Mobility amongst Thai Bureaucrats', *JSEAH*, VII, 2, 1966.

Hanks, Lucien M., 'Bang Chan and Bangkok', *JSEAH*, VIII, 2, 1967.

Jiang, Joseph P.L., 'The Chinese in Thailand', *JSEAH*, VII, 1, 1966.

Sternstein, Larry, 'Thai Centres of the Mid-nineteenth Century', *JSEAH*, VII, 1, 1966.

Wyatt, David K., 'Family Politics in 19th Century Thailand', *JSEAH*, XI, 2, 1968.

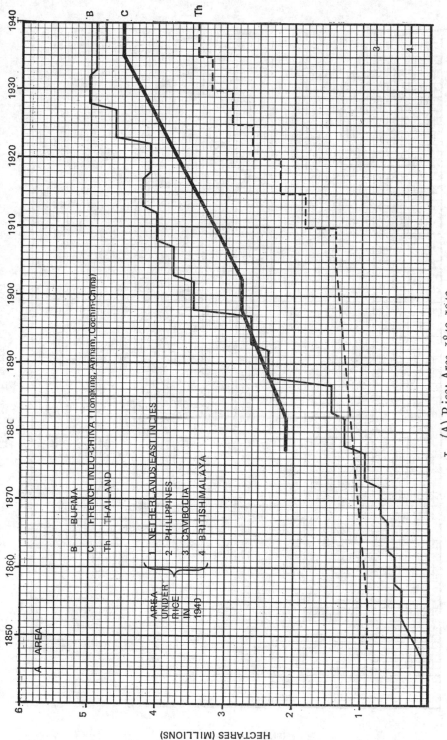

I. (A) Rice: Area, 1840–1940

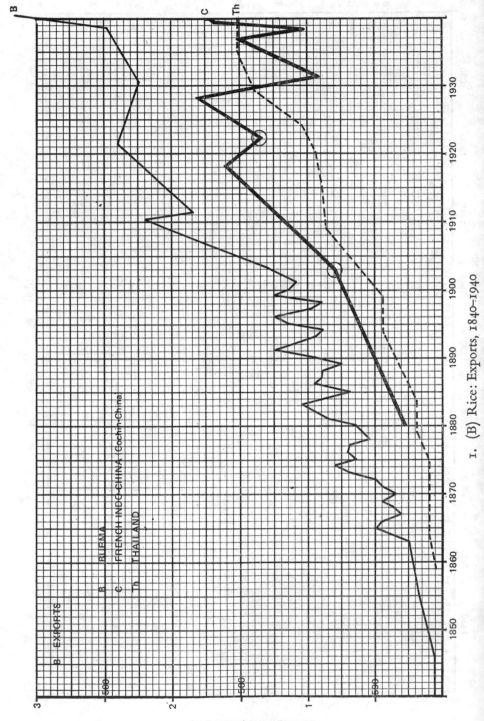

1. (B) Rice: Exports, 1840–1940

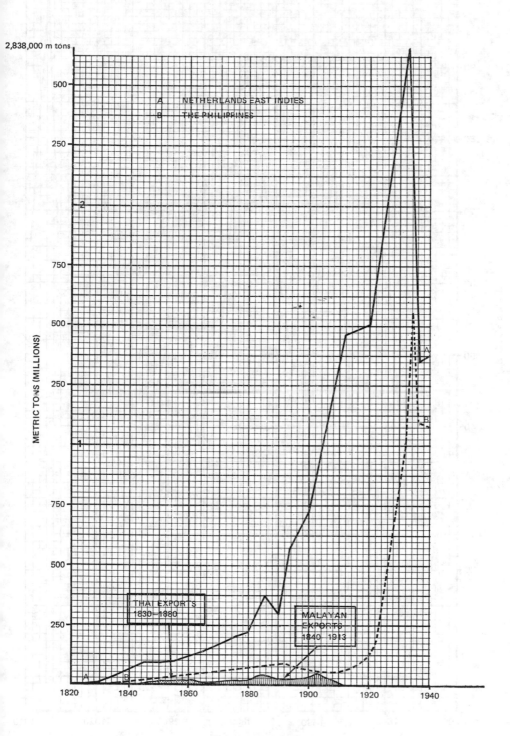

2. Sugar Exports, 1820–1940

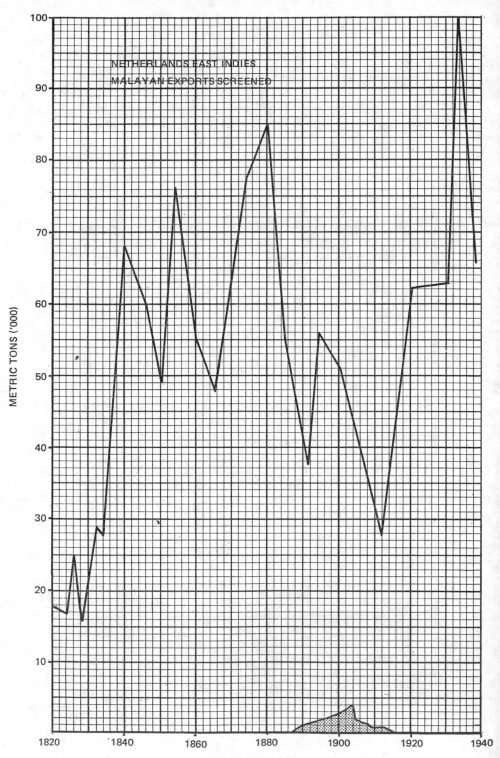

NETHERLANDS EAST INDIES
MALAYAN EXPORTS SCREENED

METRIC TONS ('000)

3.   Coffee Exports, 1820–1940

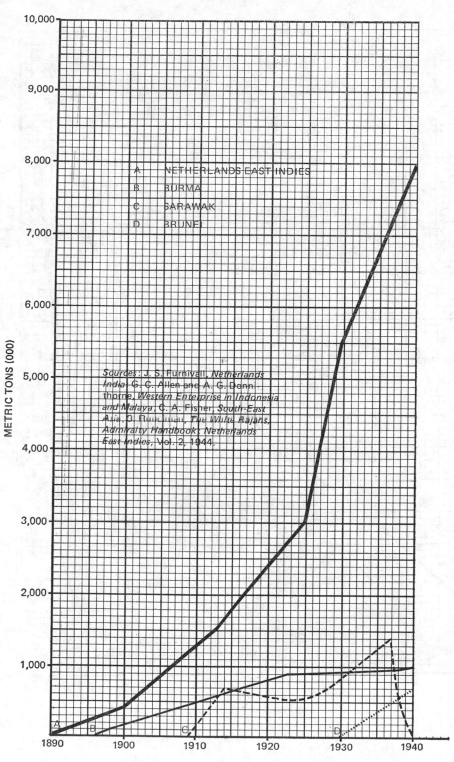

10,000

9,000

8,000

A   NETHERLANDS EAST INDIES
B   BURMA
C   SARAWAK
D   BRUNEI

7,000

6,000

METRIC TONS (000)

5,000

Sources: J. S. Furnivall, Netherlands India, G. C. Allen and A. G. Donnthorne, Western Enterprise in Indonesia and Malaya, C. A. Fisher, South-East Asia, S. Runciman, The White Rajahs, Admiralty Handbook: Netherlands East Indies, Vol. 2, 1944.

4,000

3,000

2,000

1,000

A   B   C   D

1890   1900   1910   1920   1930   1940

4. Oil (Petroleum) Production, 1890–1940

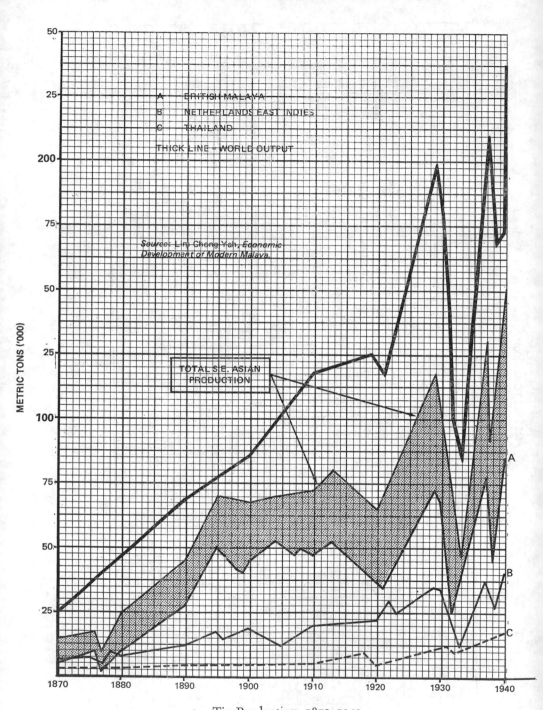

5. Tin Production, 1870–1940

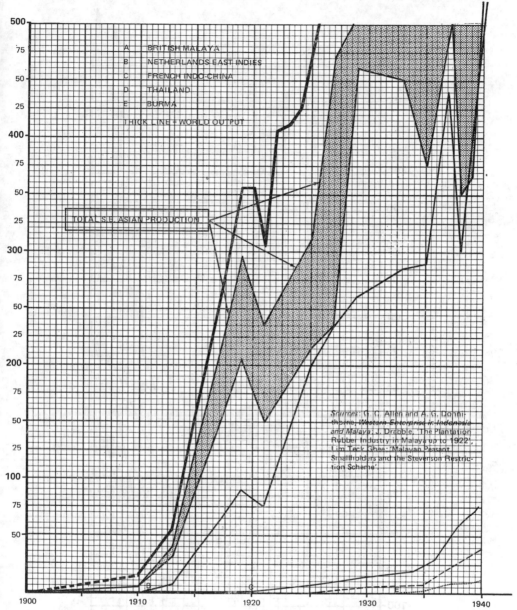

6. Rubber (Natural) Production, 1900–1940

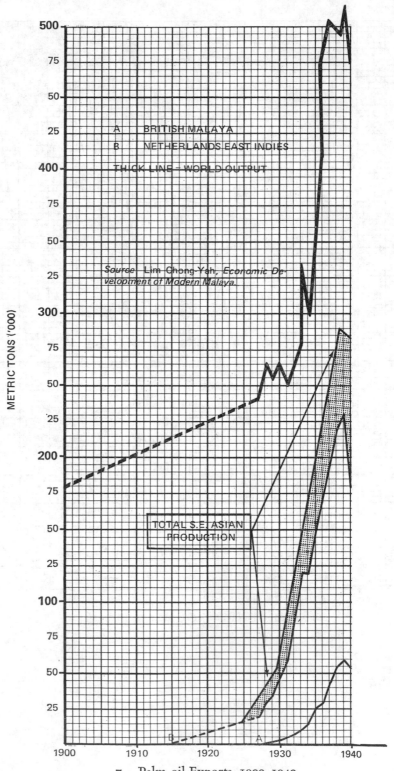

7. Palm-oil Exports, 1900–1940

Index